CONTEMPORARY BUSINESS MATHEMATICS

Ignacio Bello

Hillsborough Community College

W. B. SAUNDERS COMPANY

Philadelphia, London, Toronto

W. B. Saunders Company: West Washington Square
Philadelphia, PA 19105

1 St. Anne's Road
Eastbourne, East Sussex BN21 3UN, England

1 Goldthorne Avenue
Toronto, Ontario M8Z 5T9, Canada

Library of Congress Cataloging in Publication Data

Bello, Ignacio.

Contemporary business mathematics.

1. Business mathematics.   I. Title.

HF5691.B525 1975   513′.93   74–6679

ISBN 0–7216–1693–3

Contemporary Business Mathematics   ISBN 0-7216-1693-3

Last digit is the print number: 9   8   7   6   5   4   3   2

PREFACE

This book is intended as a first course in mathematics for the business student in an associate degree program in a junior college or university. The material can be covered in a course offered in either one or two semesters.

The primary objective of *Contemporary Business Mathematics* is to develop the mathematical and computational skills necessary for subsequent or concurrent courses in retailing, accounting, banking, investments, finance, insurance, probability, statistics, and related business subjects. The student with minimal or no algebra background will find the text suitable to his abilities.

Organization

The book is divided into five parts:

Part One contains a review of skills involving fundamental operations, fractions, and decimals, as well as the application of these skills to specific business problems. The student with a satisfactory background may omit Part One.

Part Two introduces the topics of ratio, proportion, and per cent, as well as the application of these ideas to problems in retailing, accounting, and related fields.

Part Three includes material on the calculation of simple and compound interest as well as the use of the Annual Percentage Rate tables required by the Federal Truth in Lending Act.

Part Four introduces the student to the mathematics used by investors in the areas of stocks, bonds, and insurance.

Part Five offers an introduction to the statistical and probabilistic tools used in business by persons in managerial positions. This part emphasizes decision making, employing probability and statistics as a guide for judgment and action.

Format

Each chapter is divided into sections. At the beginning of each section an actual application of the topic being treated, or a related cartoon, is given to arouse interest in the topic.

iii

The margin of the page is used for comments, notes, and remarks to aid the student in the learning process.

Many worked examples are given in each section, as well as progress tests, with answers provided at the bottom of the page, designed to allow the student practice in the types of problems presented in the examples. There is an exercise at the end of each section to provide more practice in handling the type of problem being studied. A typical examination is also provided at the end of each chapter.

Student Performance Objectives for each of the chapters are included at the beginning of the book. The objectives specify the skill to be developed by the student and can be modified by the instructor to achieve various performance levels.

Supportive Materials

Contemporary Business Mathematics is adequately supported by the Solutions Manual available to the instructor. The manual includes not only the answers but also detailed solutions to every problem in the text. Pretests for the various parts are available in the manual, as well as tests in Form A and Form B for each of the ten chapters.

Acknowledgments

I would like to express my appreciation to the following:

The able reviewers provided by W. B. Saunders Company—Professors Choo-Hua Jonah Eng, Delores Boecklen, Richard Howe, Betty Friesinger, William Michalka, and especially Calvin Lathan.

The businessmen who helped us prepare a text which is in line with current business practices—Allan Housend of Northside Bank of Tampa, Florida; Adolfo Perez of Merrill Lynch, Pierce, Fenner and Smith, Inc.; and Jack Taylor and Geneva Pepper of Taylor and O'Neal Insurance Company.

Our able typists, Aura Ferrell and Liz Raulerson.

Mr. John Snyder, the patient editor of W. B. Saunders Company who handled the details of securing permissions, cartoons, and illustrations, and coordinating production.

The staff of W. B. Saunders Company, especially Ms. Donna Musser of the Editorial Department, Mr. Tom O'Connor and Mr. Frank Polizzano of the Production Department, and Ms. Ivy Fleck Strickler of the Design Department.

And especially Professors Donald Clayton Rose II, Donna McMaster, and A. W. Goodman, who offered valuable suggestions for improving the text.

IGNACIO BELLO

STUDENT PERFORMANCE OBJECTIVES

Chapter One

After completion of Chapter 1, the student shall be able to:

1. Compute quickly and accurately using the four fundamental operations (addition, subtraction, multiplication, and division).

2. Apply the computational skills acquired in the chapter to solve business problems involving payrolls, income statements, invoices, and averages.

Chapter Two

After completion of Chapter 2, the student shall be able to:

1. Compute quickly and accurately with fractions and decimals.

2. Find the GCD and LCM of two or more numbers and apply these ideas to reduce fractions.

3. Apply the computational skills acquired in the chapter to solve business problems involving payrolls, mail orders, and time cards.

4. Convert decimals to fractions and vice versa.

Chapter Three

After completion of Chapter 3, the student shall be able to:

1. Reduce ratios of two numbers.

2. Understand and compute the important ratios used in business.

3. Use the idea of a proportion to find the index number.

4. Find the base, the rate, and the time.

5. Find the markup or the markdown of an article.

Chapter Four

After completion of Chapter 4, the student shall be able to:

1. Find the single trade discount or apply a series of trade discounts to an item.

2. Find the cash discount on an item using E.O.M., proximo, ordinary, R.O.G., or extra dating.

3. Find the commission on a sale or purchase.

4. Find the depreciation of an item, using the straight line, units of production, declining balance, or sum of the years' digits method.

5. Complete an income statement or balance sheet.

6. Find the excise, sales, or property tax on an item.

Chapter Five

After completion of Chapter 5, the student shall be able to:

1. Compute the simple interest on a transaction, using the formula $I = P \times r \times t$, or the 60-day, 6% method.

2. Find the exact and ordinary interest on a transaction.

3. Find the balance due on a transaction involving partial payments by using the Merchant's Rule or the U.S. Rule.

4. Find the bank discount on an interest or noninterest bearing note.

5. Find the present value and the interest rate equivalent to a specified bank discount rate on a given transaction.

Chapter Six

After completion of Chapter 6, the student shall be able to:

1. Compute the compound interest on a transaction, using tables.

2. Compute the effective rate, given the nominal rate.

3. Find the present value of an amount, using tables.

4. Find the finance charge and the APR on an item bought on the time plan.

5. Find the amount of refund due for early payments, using the Rule of 78.

Chapter Seven

After completion of Chapter 7, the student shall be able to:

1. Determine the price of a specified number of shares of stock by referring to the stock prices quoted in the newspaper.

2. Find the commission and tax on a stock transaction by referring to the appropriate tables.

3. Compute the annual yield, per cent of total gain, and capital gain on a transaction.

4. Determine the price of a specified number of bonds by referring to the bond prices quoted in the newspaper.

5. Find the commission and tax on a bond transaction by referring to the appropriate tables.

6. Find the current yield, the rate of yield to maturity, and the cost of a bond.

Chapter Eight

After completion of Chapter 8, the student shall be able to:

1. Compute the premium for a fire insurance or extended coverage policy, using the appropriate tables.

2. Find the proportion of losses paid by different insurance companies when a building is insured by multiple carriers.

3. Find the cost of a short term policy, or the amount of refund due when a policy is canceled.

4. Compute the premium for a collision, a comprehensive, or a liability insurance policy by using the appropriate table.

5. Compute the premium of a life insurance policy by using the appropriate table.

6. Find the net cost and the interest-adjusted net cost of an insurance policy.

Chapter Nine

After completion of Chapter 9, the student shall be able to:

1. Find the probability of an event, using the a priori, relative frequency, or subjective approach.

2. Compute the odds for a given event.

3. Compute the mathematical expectation of an event.

4. Apply the idea of the expected value of an event to determine the best course of action to follow under uncertainty.

5. Compute the probability of any compound event.

6. Determine if two events are independent.

Chapter Ten

After completion of Chapter 10, the student shall be able to:

1. Construct a frequency distribution, a histogram, and a frequency polygon.

2. Compute and interpret the mean, median, and mode.

3. Organize, display, and interpret data using bar graphs and pie charts.

4. Find the range and the standard deviation of a set of numbers.

CONTENTS

Chapter Ten

STATISTICS 451

APPENDICES

One

THE METRIC SYSTEM 481

Two

HAND CALCULATORS 489

Three

TABLES 493

part one

Essentials of Business
Mathematics

Operations with Counting Numbers and Integers

© 1965 United Feature Syndicate, Inc. Reprinted by permission.

1.1 SETS

In the cartoon above, Sally seems confused by the concepts involving **sets**. Actually, the concept of a **set** is one of the basic ideas in mathematics. In our normal day-to-day activities we may encounter **sets** of numbers (such as the set of counting numbers 1, 2, 3, and so on), a pen and pencil **set**, the **set** of accounts receivable of a particular company, and a **set** of golf clubs. Intuitively, we say that a set is a

The objects in a set are called the elements of the set.

30	THE WALL STREET JOURNAL, Friday, June 15, 1973					

Thursday's Volume
13,210,000 Shares; 189,600 Warrants

Volume since Jan. 1:	1973	1972	1971
Total shares	1,799,475,538	2,029,506,984	1,997,265,916
Total warrants ...	21,795,500	27,002,500	....

MOST ACTIVE STOCKS

		Open	High	Low	Close	Chg.	Volume
Marathn Oil	......	29¾	30¼	29⅛	29¼	− ¾	340,300
McDonald	......	64	64⅜	60	60¼	−5	215,100
Ill Power	......	28	28⅛	27½	27⅞	− ¼	143,500
Texasgulf	......	22⅝	23¼	22⅜	23	......	139,700
Am T&T wt	......	5⅞	5⅞	5¾	5⅞	......	120,100
Am Tel&Tel	......	50¾	51⅝	50¾	51	− ⅛	111,600
FedNat Mtg	......	15¾	16	15⅜	15⅜	− ⅝	109,400
NatCashR	......	35½	36¾	35	35⅜	−1⅛	103,100
Phillips Pet	......	54	54	52½	52½	− ¼	99,500
IntTelTel	......	32¼	32⅞	32	32¼	− ⅜	94,900

Average closing price of most active stocks: 33.27.

Figure 1–1   Reprinted by permission

collection (group, assemblage, aggregate) of objects called the **elements** or **members** of the set. The main characteristic of a set is that it is **well-defined.** That is, given any particular object we must be able to determine if the object is an element of the set or not. For example, if we consider the set of counting numbers 1, 2, 3, and so on, it is easy to determine if a given object is an element of the set. Thus, we agree

The set of counting numbers is well-defined.

that 5 and 6 are counting numbers but $\frac{1}{2}$ and $\sqrt{2}$ are not. We conclude that the set of counting numbers is **well-defined.** On the other hand, the set of "good" stocks in the American Stock Exchange or the set of "groovy" people in your class is not well defined, since there is no accepted criterion for deciding if a stock is "good" or a person "groovy." In Figure 1–1 we illustrate the set of the ten most active stocks in the New York Exchange for June 14, 1973.

Example 1

Which of the following descriptions define a set?
- (a) Weird people;
- (b) Counting numbers greater than 5;
- (c) Swinging teachers;
- (d) Students present in your class today;
- (e) Directors of the board of General Motors.

Solution

(b), (d), and (e) are the only descriptions that define a set. The sets in (b), (d), and (e) are **well defined.**

PROGRESS TEST 1*

1. In Mathematics a _____ is a collection of objects.

2. For a set to be well-defined we must be able to determine if any given _____ is a(n) _____ of the set.

3. The set of the three most active stocks in the New York Exchange for June 14, 1973, _____ well-defined.

---

*Answers to progress tests will always be given at the bottom of the page.
1. set   2. object, element   3. is

We use capital letters A,B,C,X,Y,Z, etc. to denote sets, and lower-case letters such as a,b,c,x,y,z to denote individual elements in these sets. Thus C might be the set of corporations with assets exceeding $2 million and c might stand for some particular corporation. In defining a set it is customary to list the elements within braces separated by commas. Thus, $A = \{5,8,9\}$ means that A is the set containing the elements 5, 8, and 9. To indicate the fact that "8 is an element of the set A" or "8 is in A," we write $8 \in A$ (read "8 is an element of the set A" or "8 is in A"). To denote that 3 is not in A, we write $3 \notin A$ (read "3 is not in A").

Example 2

Let $X = \{1,3,5,7\}$. Which of the following statements are true?
   (a) $3 \in X$ (b) $8 \notin X$ (c) $7 \notin X$

Solution

(a) and (b) are true statements.

There are two ways in which we can define a set: **Set notation**
   1. We can give a description of the set, for example, the set of counting numbers less than 5.
   2. We can list the elements in the set. For example, in the set mentioned in (1) above, the list is $\{1,2,3,4\}$.
   Here are some sets defined in the two ways mentioned above:

DESCRIPTION	LIST
The set of counting numbers	$\{1,2,3, \ldots\}$
The set of two most active stocks in the New York Exchange on June 14, 1973	{Marathon Oil, McDonald}
The counting numbers between 1 and 2	{ }

Note that the last set has no elements, since there is no counting number between 1 and 2. Such a set will be denoted by the Greek letter ϕ (phi, read "fee"). The set ϕ is called the **empty, null,** or **void** set. ϕ **is called the empty set.**

We finally remark that the order in which the elements of a set are listed is not important. Thus, $\{a,b\} = \{b,a\}$ and $\{1,2,3\} = \{3,2,1\}$. In general, two sets are **equal** if they have the same elements. Also, repeated listing does not affect membership, so $\{1,2,1\} = \{1,2\}$.   **Equality of sets**

PROGRESS TEST 2

1. Let X = {a,b}. Fill in the blanks with ∈ or ∉ so that the result is a true statement.
a _____ X, X _____ X, c _____ X.

2. Give a description for the set X given in 1.

3. Fill in the blanks with "=" or "≠" (not equal) so that the result is a true statement.
{1/2, 3} _____ {1, /, 2, 3}
{1/4, 5} _____ {5, 1/4}

EXERCISE 1.1

1. State whether or not each of the following descriptions defines a set.
   (a) Grumpy secretaries
   (b) Directors of U.S. Steel on June 13, 1967
   (c) States in the United States on July 4, 1950
   (d) Big cities in the United States
   (e) Accounts receivable of General Motors on April 30, 1970

2. The Howard Hues Paint Co. has three officers on its board of directors, Mr. Black, Mr. Brown, and Mr. White. We denote the set of directors of the company by D. Fill in the blanks with ∈ or ∉ so that the resulting statements are true.
   (a) Black _____ D   (b) D _____ D
   (c) White _____ D   (d) Purple _____ D

3. Referring to Problem 2, write the set D:
   (a) Using the description method
   (b) Using the listing method

4. Referring to Figure 1–1, write a description for each of the following sets:
   (a) {McDonald}
   (b) {Marathon Oil, McDonald}
   (c) {Int. Tel. Tel., Phillips Pet., Nat. Cash R.}

5. Referring to Figure 1–1, list the elements in the following sets:
   (a) Stocks whose volume of sale was larger than 143,000
   (b) Stocks whose volume of sale was larger than 500,000
   (c) Stocks whose volume of sale was larger than 90,000
   (d) Stocks whose volume of sale was larger than 109,400

---

1. ∈, ∉, ∉   2. The first two letters in the English alphabet   3. ≠, =

6. Let A = {2}, B = {t,w,o}, C = {t,o,w}, and D the set of letters in the word "papa". Find
   (a) the set that contains two elements.
   (b) a set that equals B.
   (c) the set containing the smallest even counting number.

7. List the elements in the following sets:
   (a) The set of counting numbers between 2 and 5 ("Between" means that 2 and 5 are not included.)
   (b) The set V, where V is the set of vowels in the English alphabet
   (c) The set of letters in the word "TALLAHASSEE"

8. In more advanced mathematics courses sets are written using **set builder** notation. In this notation the set of counting numbers less than 5 will be written as:

   $$\{x|x \text{ is a counting number less than } 5\}$$

   the set   of all   x   such that   x is a counting number less than 5.

   Using this notation, write the set S = {1,2,3}.

9. List the elements in {x|x is a counting number between 5 and 8}.

10 List the elements in {x|x is an odd counting number between 5 and 8}.

1.2 ADDITION OF COUNTING NUMBERS

In the cartoon above the man is **counting** the fish in the tank. The set of numbers used in this counting procedure is called the set of **counting numbers,** C = {1,2,3, . . .}. The set of counting numbers is an example of a **mathematical system.** A mathematical system consists of a **set of elements** (in our case C), **one or more operations** (such as addition, subtraction, multiplication, or division), **one or more relations** among the elements in the set (such as 3 + 2 = 5), and a **list of**

Mathematical Systems

Definition of Addition

rules (axioms, postulates) that the elements, operations and relations satisfy. In this section we shall study one of the operations defined in the set of counting numbers, the operation of **addition.** Addition is a process by which we can combine two or more numbers and arrive at a single total. The amounts to be added are called **addends** and the result of the addition is called the **sum** or **total.**

The sign to represent addition is "+" (read "plus"). Thus, $3 + 4 + 7$ is read as "3 plus 4 plus 7." There are many problems that require addition for their solution. For example, assume that Mr. Brown, a paint salesman, sells 18 gallons of paint now and 4 gallons later. The total number of gallons sold is $18 + 4 = 22$. In this case the **addends** (the numbers to be added) are 18 and 4 and the **sum** or **total** is 22. We usually write the operation described above in a vertical column. Thus, we write

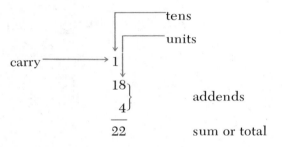

The Commutative Law

In the above example, when the 8 and 4 are added, the sum 12 is separated into 1 ten and 2 units. The 2 is written under the units column and the 1 is carried over to the tens column. Since $1 + 1 = 2$, we enter the 2 in the tens column. The resultant sum is 2 tens and 2 units, or 22. Note that if we had started our addition from the bottom of the column, that is, if we had added $4 + 18$, the result would still be 22. Similarly, $5 + 3 = 3 + 5$ and $172 + 92 = 92 + 172$. We can see that if "a" represents any counting number and "b" represents another one, when we add "a" and "b" (denoted $a + b$) we obtain the same answer as when we add "b" and "a" (denoted $b + a$); that is, $a + b = b + a$. This important rule of addition is called the **commutative law** and is summarized in Rule 1.1.

> **RULE 1.1**   If a and b are counting numbers,
>
> $$a + b = b + a$$
>
> Commutative Law (of addition)

The commutative law enables us to check the addition of two numbers by adding upward in each column after finding the sum in the ordinary way. Thus the addition

$$\begin{array}{r} 384 \\ +933 \\ \hline 1{,}317 \end{array}$$

is checked by adding

$$\begin{array}{r} 1,317 \\ 384\uparrow \\ +933 \end{array}$$

upward as shown.

PROGRESS TEST 1

1. A mathematical system consists of _____, _____, _____ and _____.
2. In the addition $3 + 9 = 12$, 3 and 9 are called the _____ and 12 is called the _____.
3. It is known that $4 + 7 = 7 + 4$. This fact is an illustration of the _____ law.

The Associative Law

We now return to our paint salesman, Mr. Brown, and assume that he has sold 9 more gallons of paint. The total number of gallons sold is $18 + 4 + 9$. This number can be added in two ways: by adding $18 + 4$ and then adding the total 22 to 9; or by adding 18 to the sum of 4 and 9. If we wish to add 18 and 4 first, we write $(18 + 4) + 9$. On the other hand, if we want to add $4 + 9$ first, we write $18 + (4 + 9)$. In either case, our answer is 31, so $(18 + 4) + 9 = 18 + (4 + 9)$. This fact illustrates another important property of addition, the associative law. We state this law in rule 1.2.

RULE 1.2 If a, b, and c are counting numbers,

$$a + (b + c) = (a + b) + c$$

Associative Law (of addition)

Reverse Addition

The application of Rules 1.1 and 1.2 to addition problems enables the student to verify the accuracy of the sum of two or more addends. The checking procedure consists in adding the addends in **reverse order,** that is, from bottom to top. Thus, the sum

$$\begin{array}{r} 123 \\ 181 \\ +728 \\ \hline 1,032 \end{array}$$

---

1. A set of elements, one or more operations, one or more relations, a set of rules
2. Addends, sum   3. Commutative

can be checked by adding thusly

$$\frac{1,032}{\begin{array}{l}123\\181\\728\end{array}}$$

The verification is complete if the sum obtained in both cases is identical.

Example 1

Add the numbers 187, 293, and 484. Verify your answer by adding in reverse order.

Solution

$$\begin{array}{ccc}\text{Add down} & 964 & \text{Add up to}\\ \text{to find} & \begin{array}{l}187\\293\\484\end{array} & \text{verify the}\\ \text{the sum.} & \overline{964} & \text{sum.}\end{array}$$

Casting out nines

A second method that can be employed to check the accuracy of addition problems is the **casting out 9's** method. This method depends on the concept of a **checking number**. The **checking number** of any counting number is the remainder obtained when the number is divided by 9 (hence the term "casting out nines"). For example, the checking number of 38 is 2, since 38 divided by 9 leaves a remainder of 2 as shown.

$$9)\overline{38} \quad \begin{array}{l}4\\36\\\textcircled{2}\end{array}$$

We can also find the checking number of 38 by adding the digits in the number (3 + 8), dividing this sum (11) by 9 and finding the remainder (2). Thus, the checking number of 38 is 2 since 3 + 8 = 11 and

$$9)\overline{11} \quad \begin{array}{l}1\\9\\\textcircled{2}\end{array}$$

that is, 11 divided by 9 leaves a remainder of 2.

We could also have found the checking number of 38 by adding the digits in the number $(3 + 8)$, obtaining 11, and then adding the digits in 11 $(1 + 1)$ to obtain ②.

Example 2

Find the checking number for 1,482.

Solution

We can do the problem three ways.

(a) We divide 1,482 by 9. Since the remainder is 6, the checking number is 6.

$$\begin{array}{r} 164 \\ 9\overline{)1,482} \\ \underline{9} \\ 58 \\ \underline{54} \\ 42 \\ \underline{36} \\ ⑥ \end{array}$$

(b) We add the digits in 1,482.
$1 + 4 + 8 + 2 = 15.$
Divide the result by 9. The remainder is 6, so the checking number is 6.

$$\begin{array}{r} 1 \\ 9\overline{)15} \\ \underline{9} \\ ⑥ \end{array}$$

(c) We add the digits in 1,482 and obtain 15. We then add the digits in 15 and obtain ⑥ the checking number.

In finding the checking number of larger quantities, it is advantageous to "cast out" any sums that add up to a multiple of 9 (or any multiples of 9 already present). For example, to find the checking number of 1,482, we find the sum of the digits $1 + 4 + 8 + 2$. We notice that $1 + 8 = 9$, so we "cast out" the $8 + 1$ leaving $4 + 2 = 6$ as the checking number. With this in mind, the checking number of 9,367 can be found as follows:

$$9,367 \longrightarrow \cancel{9} + 3 + 6 + 7 \longrightarrow ⑦$$
$$\text{"cast out"}$$

To check addition by casting out nines we proceed as follows:
1. Find the checking number of each of the addends.
2. Add the checking numbers of the addends (casting out nines if necessary).

The sum of the checking numbers of the addends should have the same checking number as that of the original sum. We illustrate this procedure in the following Example.

Example 3

Check the addition   4,953   by casting out nines.
                       7,813
                      12,766

Solution

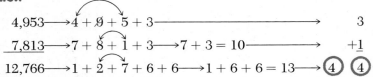

$$4,953 \longrightarrow 4 + \cancel{9} + 5 + 3 \longrightarrow \hspace{4cm} 3$$
$$\underline{7,813} \longrightarrow 7 + 8 + 1 + 3 \longrightarrow 7 + 3 = 10 \longrightarrow \hspace{1.5cm} \underline{+1}$$
$$12,766 \longrightarrow 1 + 2 + 7 + 6 + 6 \longrightarrow 1 + 6 + 6 = 13 \longrightarrow ④ \quad ④$$

Since the sum of the checking numbers of the addends $(3 + 1 = 4)$ is the same as the checking number of the original sum, we can be reasonably sure that the sum is correct.

Most of the work in the Example above can be done mentally, so we usually shall write

$$4,953 \longrightarrow 3$$
$$\underline{7,813} \longrightarrow 1$$
$$12,766 \longrightarrow ④ \quad ④$$

PROGRESS TEST 2

1. It is known that $3 + (4 + 8) = (3 + 4) + 8$. This illustrates the use of the _____.
2. Find the sum $1,231 + 849 + 348$ and check your answer by adding in reverse order.
3. The checking number for 3,847 is _____.

Horizontal Addition   Sometimes "horizontal" addition is utilized in totaling employees' hours or when daily and weekly tallies of sales in two or more departments are kept. Horizontal addition is performed by adding the units digits first, then the tens digits, etc. For example, to add 148, 392, and 457 horizontally we proceed as follows:

---

1. Associative law   2. The sum is 2428   3. 4

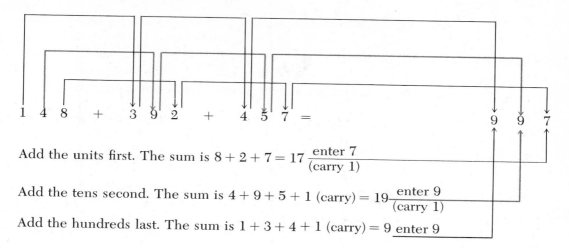

Add the units first. The sum is $8 + 2 + 7 = 17$ $\dfrac{\text{enter } 7}{\text{(carry 1)}}$

Add the tens second. The sum is $4 + 9 + 5 + 1$ (carry) $= 19$ $\dfrac{\text{enter } 9}{\text{(carry 1)}}$

Add the hundreds last. The sum is $1 + 3 + 4 + 1$ (carry) $= 9$ enter 9

We use this idea in the next two problems.

Example 4

A necessary procedure for a business is the determination of the pay-roll. If employees are paid biweekly, the hours worked each day are recorded and added to determine the total hours for the first week. The same procedure is repeated the second week. To obtain the number of hours worked during the two weeks, the hours worked the first week are added to the hours worked the second week. The hourly

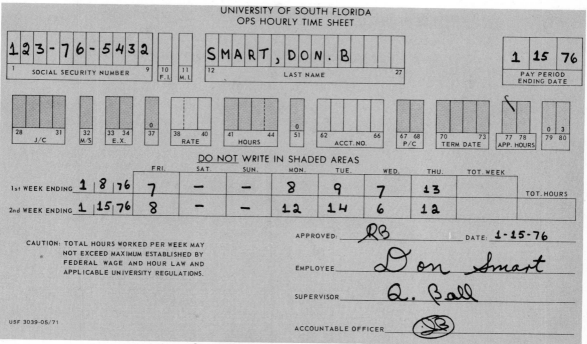

Courtesy of University of South Florida.

sheet for U.S.F. is shown on page 13. Add the hours for the first week horizontally, then add the hours for the second week in the same manner. Record the totals in the column labeled "Tot. Week" and add these two columns to obtain the "Tot. Hours" for both weeks.

Example 5

Dears Department Store keeps track of daily sales in three departments with daily and weekly sales for each as shown below. Add the weekly totals horizontally and enter them in the "totals" column. Now verify that the final answer is correct by adding the totals horizontally and vertically.

DEPARTMENT	MON	TUES	WED	THURS	FRI	TOTALS
Books	$238	$223	$197	$208	$346	
Shoe	$347	$408	$390	$297	$403	
Dress	$508	$506	$703	$849	$987	
Totals						[ ]
						Total Sales for week

EXERCISE 1.2

In problems 1 through 20, add the given column of figures.

1.	8	2.	7	3.	6	4.	3	5.	23
	9		8		8		9		54

6.	37	7.	198	8.	753	9.	1,453	10.	9,847
	53		354		986		2,859		3,972

11.	54	12.	83	13.	47	14.	98	15.	21
	43		46		68		94		38
	97		23		95		31		38

16.	312	17.	461	18.	345	19.	498	20.	345
	463		396		957		980		980
	837		496		451		958		749
	762		959		650		329		962

21. Which of the following statements can be justified by using the commutative property?
    (a) $3 + 7 = 7 + 3$
    (b) $3 + (7 + 8) = (3 + 7) + 8$
    (c) $3 + (7 + 8) = 3 + (8 + 7)$
    (d) $(3 + 9) + 15 = 12 + 15$

22. Which of the following statements can be justified by using the associative property?
    (a) $3 + (5 + 9) = (3 + 5) + 9$
    (b) $5 + (8 + 4) = 5 + 12$
    (c) $6 + (12 + 15) = 6 + (15 + 12)$
    (d) $3 + 47 = (3+7) + 40$

Short Cut Methods

Most competent accountants and arithmeticians do not add figures in a number-by-number fashion. Instead, they recognize combinations of 10 and add these combinations first. Thus, to add $6 + 9 + 4 + 1 + 3$ they proceed as follows: $6 + 4 = 10$, and $9 + 1 = 10$; thus the sum is $10 + 10 + 3 = 23$. Using this short cut method, add the following columns of figures.

23.		24.		25.		26.		27.	
	13		37		48		634		345
	24		98		54		258		237
	17		23		12		176		123
	+97		+78		+26		+732		+285

28. Find the checking number for:
    (a) 1,346   (b) 3,456   (c) 7,652   (d) 124,396

29. Find the checking number for:
    (a) 3,098   (b) 32,546   (c) 323,549   (d) 234,543

30. Verify the sums obtained in problems 11 and 12 by:
    (a) reverse addition   (b) casting out nines

31. Verify the results obtained in problems 6 and 7 by:
    (a) reverse addition   (b) casting out nines

Applications to Accounting

One of the basic equations in accounting states that the assets equal the sum of the liabilities and the Owner's Equity, that is,

$$\text{Assets} = \text{Liabilities} + \text{Owner Equity}$$

In problems 32 through 34, verify that the sum of the Assets equals the sum of the Liabilities and the Owner's Equity.

		Assets			Liability	Owner Equity
	Cash +	Supplies +	Equipment +	Automobile =	Office Supply Co. +	Thomas Doubting Equity
32.	$165	$65	$1700	$2100	$300	$3730
33.	$365	$65	$1250	$2100	$ 0	$3780
34.	$500	$65	$1250	$2100	$135	$3780

The most simple account form looks like the letter "T" and it is called a "T Account". On a T account the increases are placed on one side of the account and the decreases on the other. The increases and decreases in the Cash account of Pete Putter's Golf Shop appear as follows:

Increases	Cash	Decreases	
Investments	$5000	Payment of rent	$ 235
Sales	$ 834	Purchase of truck	$3000
Collection of bills	$ 57	Purchase of furniture	$1200
Down payments received	$ 149	Payment of telephone bill	$ 17

35.   Find the sum of the cash increases in Pete Putter's Golf Shop.

36.   Find the sum of the cash decreases in Pete Putter's Golf Shop.

37.   If the Investments, Sales, Collections, and Down payments for Pete Putter amounted to $4000, $945, $93, and $187, respectively, find the sum of the cash increases in Pete Putter's Golf Shop.

38.   If the rent, truck, furniture, and telephone cost Pete $245, $3098, $565, and $19, respectively, find the sum of the cash decreases in Pete Putter's Golf shop.

The income statement for the Bar Nothin' Ranch is shown below:

BAR NOTHIN' RANCH

Income Statement for Year Ended December 31, 19___

Revenue $34,895

Operating Expenses

Wages	$18,305
Supplies	905
Utilities	687
Depreciation	1,263

Total Operating Expenses   _____

Other Expenses

Gas, oil, repairs $ 678
Depreciation of farm equipment   1,978

Total Other Expenses   _____

Total Expenses   _____

39.   Find the sum of the Operating Expenses and of the Other Expenses for the Bar Nothin' Ranch.

40.   Find the Total Expenses for the Bar Nothin' Ranch.

Applications to Marketing

41.   The Inventory of Elder, Sew, and Sew revealed the following:
> 97 square yards of green cloth
> 198 square yards of red cloth
> 1404 square yards of white cloth
> 708 square yards of black cloth

Find the total number of square yards of cloth in stock.

42.   The manager of Quick Shop Supermarkets bought merchandise for the following amounts:

Bread and Pastries	$ 456
Canned Goods	1348
Milk and Dairy Products	564
Vegetables	96

How much money did the manager spend?

43.   If in the problem above, Bread and Pastries, Canned Goods, Milk and Dairy Products, and Vegetables are $567, $1342, $564, and $89, respectively, how much money did the manager spend?

Applications to Advertising

44.   The top T.V. network advertisers and their expenditures (approximated to the nearest million) for 1970 are shown on the next page. Find the total expenditures of the 15 companies.

45.   The leading foreign countries in advertising expenditures and their expenditures (approximated to the nearest million) for 1968 appear on the next page. Find the total expenditures.

46.   Follow the procedure of Example 4 in this section and find the total number of hours for the employee given on page 19.

Top 15 TV Network Advertisers, 1970
In millions of dollars

COMPANY	EXPENDITURES
1. Procter & Gamble Company	$128
2. Bristol-Myers Company	57
3. R. J. Reynolds Industries	52
4. Colgate-Palmolive Company	46
5. Warner-Lambert Pharmaceutical Company	46
6. General Foods Corp.	45
7. Sterling Drug, Inc.	41
8. American Home Products Corp.	40
9. Lever Bros.	38
10. Philip Morris, Inc.	37
11. General Motors Corporation	32
12. Ford Motor Company	31
13. Miles Laboratories, Inc.	29
14. S. C. Johnson & Son	29
15. American Brands, Inc.	28

Courtesy of Television Bureau of Advertising, Inc.

Leading Foreign Countries in Advertising Expenditures, 1968
In millions of dollars

COUNTRY	EXPENDITURES
West Germany	$2,152
Great Britain	1,705
Japan	1,478
Canada	902
France	890
Italy	550
Sweden	418
Switzerland	406
Australia	385
Netherlands	285
Spain	276

Adapted, by permission, from *Advertising Age*, September 22, 1969, p. 51.

HILLSBOROUGH COMMUNITY COLLEGE
NON-EXEMPT PERSONNEL   TIME RECORD

NAME: J. Clemente   SOC. SEC. # 123-45-6789   DEPT. 97   WORK LOC. YC.   WEEK OF 10/6/75

INSTRUCTIONS: TIME WORKED WILL BE SHOWN AS ACTUAL STARTING TIME, LUNCH TIME AND STOPPING TIME. ALL TIME IS TO BE RECORDED TO THE NEAREST 1/4 HOUR. ALL OVERTIME MUST BE APPROVED BY YOUR IMMEDIATE SUPERVISOR PRIOR TO BEING WORKED.

	MON TIME	HRS	TUE TIME	HRS	WED TIME	HRS	THUR TIME	HRS	FRI TIME	HRS	SAT TIME	HRS	SUN TIME	HRS
IN	8		9		9		8		9					
LUNCH	12	4	12	3	11	2	11	3	12	3				
	1		1		2		1		1					
OUT	5	4	6	5	5	3	6	5	4	3				
IN	6		7				7		6					
OUT	8	2	8	1			10	3	9	3				
TOTAL	10		9		5		11		9					

I CERTIFY THIS RECORD IS ACCURATE AND TRUE   TOTAL HOURS

SIGNATURE: _____

APPROVED: _____ IMMEDIATE SUPERVISOR

PLEASE HAVE TIME SHEETS APPROVED AND FORWARDED NO LATER THAN MONDAY TO THE PAYROLL OFFICE

SYMBOLS FOR ABSENTEEISM:

S - PERSONAL SICKNESS	H - HOLIDAY	UP - PERSONAL WITHOUT PAY
SF - SICKNESS IN FAMILY	M - MILITARY DUTY	F - FUNERAL
A - PERSONAL ACCIDENT	JD - JURY DUTY	D - DEATH IN FAMILY
AF - ACCIDENT IN FAMILY	C - ATTENDING COURT	E - EMERGENCY
V - VACATION		R - RELIGIOUS
		O - OTHER (MUST BE EXPLAINED)

FOR PAYROLL OFFICE USE ONLY

DUTY HOURS _____ O/T HOURS (REG) _____ O/T HOURS (PREM) _____

SICK LEAVE _____ VACATION LEAVE _____ HOLIDAY _____

TOTAL HOURS _____

Courtesy of Hillsborough Community College.

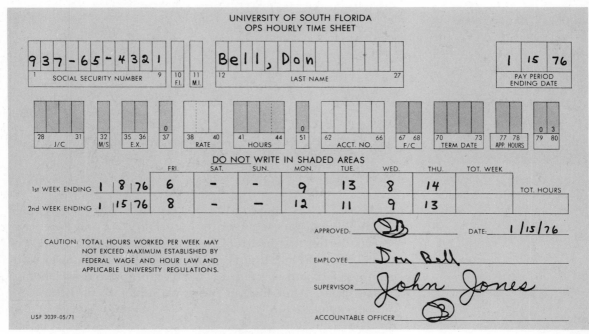

Courtesy of University of South Florida

47. The last row in the form at left shows the number of hours worked each day by an employee. Find the total number of hours worked by the employee.

48. Use horizontal addition to find
(a) the number of issues traded from Monday to Friday.
(b) the number of advances from Monday to Friday.

Reprinted, by permission, from *The Wall Street Journal*, October 29, 1973, p. 22

Volume, All Issues 5,937,600
SINCE JANUARY 1

	1973	1972	1971
Total sales	1,323,712,700	1,825,721,000	....

MARKET DIARY

	Fri	Thur	Wed	Tues	Mon
Issues traded	2,962	2,962	2,960	2,961	2,962
Advances	628	514	566	434	273
Declines	415	591	524	722	921
Unchanged	1,919	1,857	1,870	1,805	1,768

49. Use horizontal addition to find
(a) the number of issues traded from Friday to Thursday.
(b) the number of advances from Friday to Thursday.

Reprinted, by permission, from *The Wall Street Journal*, October 26, 1973, p. 28

MARKET DIARY

	Thur	Wed	Tues	Mon	Fri
Issues traded	2,962	2960	2,961	2,962	2,965
Advances	514	566	434	273	638
Declines	591	524	722	921	459
Unchanged	1,857	1,870	1,805	1,768	1,868

GENERAL MOTORS CORP.	June 1973	June 1972	% Chg.
Chevrolet Div.	237,114	223,418	+ 6.1
Pontiac Div.	63,161	65,652	− 3.8
Oldsmobile Div.	73,832	71,723	+ 2.9
Buick Div.	81,386	68,983	+18.0
Cadillac Div.	21,728	21,096	+ 3.0
Total cars			
FORD MOTOR CO.			
Ford Div.	204,322	209,626	− 2.5
Lincoln-Mercury Div.	45,230	45,784	− 1.2
Total cars			
CHRYSLER CORP.			
Chry-Plym Div.	89,203	87,371	+ 2.1
Dodge Div.	54,909	53,655	+ 2.3
Total cars			
AMERICAN MOTORS CORP.			
Total cars ...	37,600	28,818	+30.5
U.S. industry total			

Reprinted, by permission, from *The Wall Street Journal*, July 6, 1973, p. 4

50.   The number of cars sold by GM, Ford, Chrysler, and American Motors during the month of June in 1973 and 1972 is shown above. Find the total number of cars each manufacturer sold in June, 1972 and in June, 1973 and enter in the rows labeled "Total Cars". After finding the three subtotals, find the U.S. Industry total.

51.   The number of bond issues traded in the American Stock Exchange on July 2, 1973 is shown below. For Tuesday, the issues traded were 71 while the advanced, declined, and unchanged issues were 27, 29, and 15, respectively. Since 27 + 29 + 15 = 71, the figures for Tuesday are correct. However, the figures in one of the columns are NOT correct. Which column is it? What should be the correct entry in the Advances row?

	Fri	Thurs	Wed	Tues
Issues traded	66	80	73	71
Advances	29	2	22	27
Declines	21	33	32	29
Unchanged	16	21	19	15

Reprinted, by permission, from *The Wall Street Journal*, July 2, 1973

52.   It is a common practice in business to reimburse employees for the miles traveled during a business trip. For this reason an accurate record of the distance traveled should be kept. The following chart shows the distances between different points on the Florida Turnpike. Under the column labeled INTERCHANGE we can read the distances (in miles) between exits. For example, the distance between the Interstate 75 Interchange and Leesburg is 5 + 18 = 23 miles. Find the distance between

(a) Wildwood and Kissimmee-St. Cloud.

(b) Wildwood and Palm Beach.

(c) Yeehaw Junction and Hollywood.

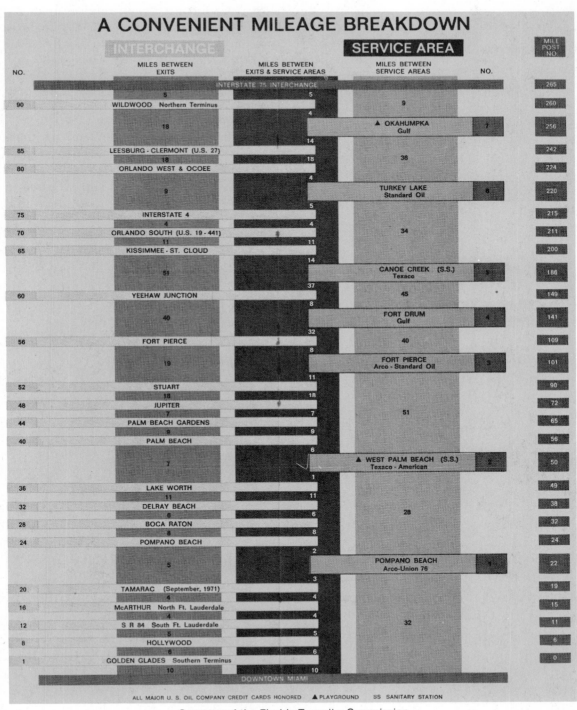

Courtesy of the Florida Turnpike Commission.

53. A procedure similar to the one used in the problem above can be used to determine the distance between Service Areas on the Florida Turnpike. The column labeled SERVICE AREAS contains the distances (in miles) between service areas. For example, the distance between the Okahumpka Service Area and the Canoe Creek Service Area is $36 + 34 = 70$ miles. Find the distance between the Okahumpka Service area and
(a) Fort Drum.
(b) West Palm Beach.
(c) Pompano Beach.

54. Many individuals and businesses carry on banking transactions. One of the most common transactions is to deposit money in a savings account.
The slip shown illustrates a savings deposit slip prepared by depositor B. Thrifty. Find the total amount to be deposited.

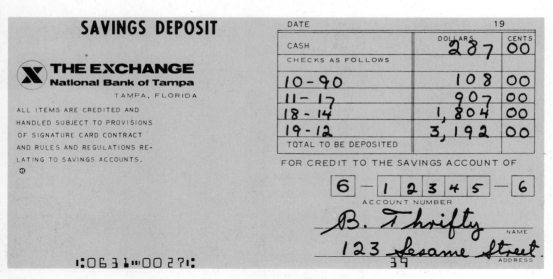

Courtesy of the Exchange National Bank of Tampa.

55. A **budget** is a plan which estimates how income is going to be spent (or saved). In the problem below, find the estimated monthly expenditures of Family A and Family B.

	Family A	Family B
Housing	$255	$243
Food	$240	$198
Clothing	$130	$125
Transportation	$197	$123
Recreation	$122	$108
Savings	$110	$155

*Filtrol Cuts Dividend
To 15 From 35 Cents,
Effective in 3rd Period*

1.3   SUBTRACTION OF COUNTING NUMBERS

In the headline above, the Filtrol Company has decreased its dividends from 35 cents a share to 15 cents a share. The decrease is an example of the operation of **subtraction.** If we wish to determine the amount by which the dividend decreased, we can think of the problem as follows: The dividends are now 15 cents; how many more cents do they have to increase to be 35 cents again? We could write the problem as $15 + ? = 35$. The answer is obviously 20 cents. Similarly, if a 40¢ item is bought and paid for with a dollar bill, the cashier usually makes change by saying $40 + 60$ (your change) $= \$1.00$. From these examples we can see that the operation of subtraction is closely related to addition, since every subtraction problem can be written as an addition question. In our case, instead of solving the problem $35 - 15 = ?$, we solved the problem $15 + ? = 35$. For this reason we say that subtraction is the **inverse** operation of addition. In general, if we substitute "a" for the number 35, "b" for 15 and "c" for the ? sign, we can write that $a - b = c$ if $b + c = a$. Based on this discussion we give the following definition.

> **DEFINITION 1.1**   If a, b, and c are counting numbers, the difference of a and b, denoted by $a - b$, is the unique counting number c, provided that $b + c = a$.

The **minus sign** (−) is used to designate the operation of subtraction. The expression $8 - 3$ is read "subtract 3 from 8" or simply "8 minus 3". When this problem is written in a column

$$\begin{array}{r} 8 \\ -3 \\ \hline 5 \end{array}$$

the number 8 is called the **minuend,** 3 is called the **subtrahend,** and 5 is called the **difference.** Note that, by Definition 1.1, $8 - 3 = 5$, *because* $3 + 5 = 8$. Similarly,

$$9 - 4 = 5 \text{ because } 4 + 5 = 9$$
$$15 - 8 = 7 \text{ because } 8 + 7 = 15, \text{ etc.}$$

But what about $5 - 7$? If we use Definition 1.1, we say that $5 - 7 = c$ if $7 + c = 5$. Can you find a counting number c that added to 7 gives

Subtraction is the
inverse of addition.

Definition of
Subtraction

you 5? The answer is obviously no. We can see from this example that the subtraction of counting numbers is possible only when the first number (the minuend) is greater than the second number (the subtrahend). In this section, we shall cover only problems in which the first number is greater than the second; however, in Section 1.6 we shall see that subtraction of a larger number from a smaller one is indeed possible.

PROGRESS TEST 1

1. By subtraction, 23 − 8 = _____ because _____.

2. In the subtraction problem

$$\begin{array}{r} 23 \\ -13 \\ \hline 10 \end{array}$$

23 is called the _____, 13 is called the _____, and 10 is called the _____.

3. 3 − 8 = _____.

4. In order to obtain a counting number as the difference of two counting numbers, we can only subtract a _____ number from a _____ one.

As you are probably aware, many of our subtraction problems require "borrowing". We illustrate this procedure in the Example below.

Example 1

Subtract 298 from 585.

Solution

We set up the problem in the usual way: $\begin{array}{r} 585 \\ -298 \end{array}$ Since we cannot subtract 8 units from 5 units we "borrow" 1 ten (10 units) from the column to the left (which is now reduced to 7) and add it to the amount in the units column, making it 15. Now 15 units minus 8 units is 7 units. We proceed to the middle column. We cannot subtract 9 tens from 7 tens, so we borrow 100 from the column to the left. Now 17

---

1. 15, 8 + 15 = 23   2. minuend, subtrahend, difference   3. no solution
for counting numbers   4. smaller, larger

tens $-$ 9 tens $=$ 8 tens. Finally, we subtract 2 hundreds from 4 hundreds. In effect, we have regrouped the number 585 from five 100's, 8 10's, and five 1's into four 100's, seventeen 10's, and fifteen 1's. Both groupings equal 585, as shown to the right of the computation.

				Original number	Regrouped number	
	(four 100's)					
	(seventeen 10's)					
	(fifteen 1's)					
4	17	15		500	400	(four 100's)
5̶	8̶	5̶		80	170	(seventeen 10's)
$-$ 2	9	8		5	15	(fifteen 1's)
2	8	7		585	585	

The problem in Example 1 can easily be checked by adding the difference (287) to the subtrahend (298) to obtain the minuend (585). The fact that this procedure works is a direct result of Definition 1.1. We illustrate this method of checking subtraction, as well as the method of casting out nines, in the following Example.

Checking Subtraction

Example 2

Subtract 298 from 585 and check the result (a) by adding the difference to the subtrahend and obtaining the minuend; (b) by the method of casting out nines.

Solution

(a)
$$\begin{array}{r} 585 \\ -298 \\ \hline 287 \\ \hline 585 \end{array}+$$

We add $298 + 287 = 585$; hence the answer is correct. Sometimes this procedure is performed in the problem itself as it is shown.

(b) To check subtraction by the method of casting out nines, we add the checking numbers of the subtrahend and the difference, casting out nines if necessary. The result should be identical to the checking number of the minuend.

$$\begin{array}{l} 585 \rightarrow 5+8+5 = 18 \text{ and } 18 = 8+1 = 9 \rightarrow ⓪ \\ -298 \rightarrow 2+9̶+8 = 2+8 = 10 \text{ and } 10 \longrightarrow 1 \\ 287 \rightarrow 2+8+7 = 17 \text{ and } 17 = 1+7 = 8 \rightarrow 8 \end{array} \left.\begin{array}{r} \\ + \\ \end{array}\right\} = 9 \rightarrow ⓪$$

Note that when we add the checking number of the difference (8), to that of the subtrahend (1), we obtain 9, whose checking number 0 is identical to the checking number of the minuend; thus we are reasonably sure that the subtraction is correct.

PROGRESS TEST 2

1. To check a subtraction problem you add the _____ and the _____ to obtain the _____.

2. To check subtraction by the method of casting out nines, find the checking number of the _____ and add it to the checking number of the _____ to obtain the checking number of the _____.

We remark that the operation of subtraction is neither commutative nor associative. For example, $5 - 3 \neq 3 - 5$ because $5 - 3 = 2$ and the result of $3 - 5$ is not a counting number. Also

$$(5 - 3) - 1 \neq 5 - (3 - 1)$$

because $(5 - 3) - 1 = 2 - 1 = 1$ but $5 - (3 - 1) = 5 - 2 = 3$. (Recall that parentheses indicate that you should perform the operations contained within them first.)

Income Statements

One of the most important documents in business is the income statement. This report enables the owners, stockholders, or executives to determine if there is a gain or loss in the business. Basically, to prepare an income statement it is only necessary to know how to add and subtract. We now give an Example that illustrates the computations involved in the preparation of income statements.

Example 3

John Swift opened a small gift shop. He imported 100 items from Japan at a cost of $280. When the items were delivered, he paid import duties of $28 and freight charges of $53. If the sales of the gifts brought him $576, how much did he make or lose on his investment?

Solution

INCOME		
Total Sales		$576
EXPENSES		
Purchase Price	$280	
Import Duties	28	
Freight	53	
Total Expenses		$361
Net INCOME (Sales − Expenses)		$215

---

1. difference, subtrahend, minuend   2. subtrahend, difference, minuend

In the Income Statement below find (for both years) the Total *PROBLEM 1* Operating Income, the Total Operating Expenses, and the Income before income taxes and securities transactions (the difference between Total Operating Income and Total Operating Expenses).

CONSOLIDATED STATEMENT OF INCOME
EXCHANGE BANCORPORATION, INC. AND SUBSIDIARIES

	Year Ended December 31	
	1972	1971
Operating income:		
Interest and fees on loans	$17,384,943	$14,126,602
Income on federal funds sold and securities purchased under agreements to resell	353,078	268,940
Interest and dividends on investment securities:		
U.S. Treasury securities	1,844,042	1,687,235
Securities of other U.S. Government agencies and corporations	759,254	673,230
Obligations of states and political subdivisions	2,797,402	2,309,293
Trust department income	763,665	652,771
Service charges on deposit accounts	940,688	816,297
Other operating income	1,557,445	1,029,445
TOTAL OPERATING INCOME		
Operating expenses:		
Salaries, wages and employee benefits	6,355,660	5,465,849
Interest on deposits	8,190,142	6,496,168
Expense of federal funds purchased and securities sold under agreements to repurchase	1,046,870	635,108
Interest on capital notes and debentures	416,915	25,144
Net occupancy expenses	646,724	597,306
Equipment expenses	1,045,857	883,403
Provision for possible loan losses	528,133	394,656
Other operating expenses	3,490,759	2,897,335
TOTAL OPERATING EXPENSES		
Income before income taxes and securities transactions		
Federal and state income taxes	986,227	870,840
Minority interests	209,680	204,884
INCOME BEFORE SECURITIES TRANSACTIONS	3,483,550	3,093,120
Net securities gains, less related income tax effect ($36,136 and $100,829) and minority interests ($2,438 and $8,805) in 1972 and 1971, respectively	29,039	122,625
NET INCOME	$ 3,512,589	$ 3,215,745
Earnings per share of Common Stock, assuming no dilution:		
Income before securities transactions	$1.37	$1.22
Net income	1.38	1.27
Earnings per share of Common Stock, assuming full dilution:		
Income before securities transactions	1.26	1.22
Net income	1.27	1.27

See notes to consolidated financial statements.

Courtesy of Exchange Bancorporation, Inc. and Subsidiaries.

EXERCISE 1.3

In Problems 1 and 2, compute the difference.

1. (a) 32   (b) 45   (c) 545   (d) 674   (e) 965
        −18   −39   −349   −435   −877

2. (a) 4567   (b) 9876   (c) 4538   (d) 1232   (e) 3452
        −3789   −3478   −3498   − 839   − 149

3. Check the problems in 1 by addition and by casting out nines.

4. Check the problems in 2 by addition and by casting out nines.

5. The rates for the Pier 66 Resort are given below. Find the price difference between a Marina Studio and an Ocean Studio on December 23.

DAILY RATE SCHEDULE		Marina Waterway View		Ocean Golf Course View		European Plan. Same rates for single or double occupancy Effective April 26, 1974	
	Floors	Studio	Twin or Double Beds	Studio	Twin or Double Beds	Executive Suite	Extra Person
April 26 thru December 9	1-5	$22.	$24.	$24.	$26.	$32.	
	6-10	24.	26.	26.	28.	34.	$4.
	11-15	26.	28.	28.	30.	36.	
December 10 thru April 25	1-5	$32.	$34.	$36.	$38.	$52.	
	6-10	36.	38.	40.	42.	54.	$6.
	11-15	38.	40.	42.	44.	56.	

6. Referring to the rates above, find the difference between a Marina room with double beds and an Ocean room with twin beds on April 23.

7. Referring to the rates above, find the difference between a Marina Studio in which an extra person will be staying and an Executive Suite (no extra person) on October 11.

8. Find the difference between the Original Price and the Sales Price for each item of merchandise shown in the form at left on the next page.

Furnishings Miscellaneous Code Card		
ITEM CODE AND/OR DESCRIPTION	ORIGINAL PRICE	SALES PRICE
Nylon Shirt	14.00	9.00
Sport Coat	49.00	36.00
Suit	119.00	63.00

Furnishings Miscellaneous Code Card		
ITEM CODE AND/OR DESCRIPTION	ORIGINAL PRICE	SALES PRICE
Dress	$69.00	$43.00
Coat	$189.00	$167.00
Shoes	$26.00	$19.00

9. Find the difference between the Original Price and the Sales Price of the merchandise shown in the form at right above.

10. If a calculator originally costing $379 is now selling for $195, find the amount of money you save by buying at the reduced price.

11. Find the amount of money you save by buying the chair advertised below.

VELVET ACCENT CHAIRS
Regularly 149.00 each
119.00

12. In the ad below, the advertiser claims that you will save $71. Is this claim true?

SAVE $71!
RCA XL100 100% SOLID STATE 25" DIAGONAL CONSOLE COLOR TV
Regularly 699.95
628.00

Courtesy of RCA

Short Cut Methods

Using Definition 1.1 it can be shown that if $a - b = c$ then $(a + m) - (b + m) = c$. In other words, if the same number is added to the minuend and subtrahend, the difference is unchanged. Thus, $53 - 18 = 55 - 20$. (Adding 2 to the minuend and subtrahend.) You can clearly see that it is easier to subtract 20 from 55 than it is to subtract 18 from 53. Using this procedure many subtraction problems can be transformed into easier ones. Use this procedure in solving problems 13 through 20 and check by doing the computation without using this principle.

13. $58 - 17$ 14. $47 - 18$ 15. $432 - 392$ 16. $683 - 491$

17. $573 - 289$ 18. $564 - 191$ 19. $453 - 187$ 20. $741 - 462$

Applications to Accounting

On a T-Account the Increases are placed on the left and the Decreases on the right. The increases and decreases in the Cash Account for Woody Harcore's Lumber are shown below:

Increases		Cash	Decreases	
Investments	$5000		Payment of rent	$ 235
Sales	3432		Purchase of lumber	1345
Collection of bills	198		Payment of telephone bill	17

21.   Find the difference between the increases and the decreases (the balance of cash remaining).

22.   If in problem 21 the investments were $3000, the sales $1765, the collection of bills $545, the rent $235, the lumber $1385, and the telephone $23, find the difference between increases and decreases.

23.   The Bar Nothin' Ranch had $34,789 of revenue and $24,987 of expenses. What was the difference between revenues and expenses?

24.   If in the preceding problem the revenues were $53,678 and the expenses $43,545, what would be the difference between the revenues and the expenses?

25.   The current book value of an item is the previous year's book value of the item minus the depreciation. A car had a book value of $3600 last year and its depreciation this year was $2400. What is its present book value?

26.   The following table shows the depreciation of a $10,000 truck. Fill in the rest of the table.

Annual depreciation	Remaining book value
$4000	$6000
2400	3600
1440	_____
864	_____
518	_____

27. The Spendmore Loan Co. had a cash balance of $345,989. They received $34,567 and loaned out $145,672. What was their new cash balance?

28. The Casino Bakery has a production budget of 30,000 loaves of bread per week. Their daily production (a certain week) was 3,234, 4,236, 4,567, 5,678, and 7,345. Determine the difference between the actual production and the planned production.

29. The Penthouse Apartments' gross monthly rent receipts total $2346. They have collected checks for $198, 235, 342, 349, 198, and 345. Calculate the amount of the outstanding rent.

30. Moo Dairy started the day with 18,657 gallons of milk. They sold 4,535 gallons to supermarkets, 6,845 gallons to vending machines, 3,469 gallons to hospitals, and 2,341 gallons to schools. How many gallons were left?

31. Follow the procedure in Example 3 and prepare an Income Statement for the following situation: Fifi La Rue, the owner of the B-U-T-Full Gift Shop bought 200 items from Mexico at a price of $342. She paid import duties of $35 and delivery charges of $75. If she sold the merchandise for $653, what was her profit (or loss) on the merchandise?

32. Referring to the preceding problem, if Fifi sold the merchandise for $450, what was her profit (or loss) on the merchandise?

33. In the Income Statement on the following page, find the Total Operating Income and the Total Operating Expenses for the year 1971. With this information, find the Income before Taxes for 1971. Now find the Income before Securities Gains or Losses.

34. In the above Income Statement, find the Total Operating Income and the Total Operating Expenses for the year 1972. With this information, find the Income before Taxes for 1972. Now find the Income before Securities Gains or Losses.

35. What is the difference in the Income before Taxes between 1971 and 1972?

36. What is the difference in the Income before Securities Gains or Losses between 1971 and 1972?

FIRST FLORIDA BANCORPORATION AND SUBSIDIARIES

| | Year Ended December 31, | |
	1972	1971
Operating Income		
Interest and fees on loans	$24,632,053	$19,795,864
Income on federal funds sold	1,058,626	904,321
Interest and dividends on:		
United States Treasury securities	3,560,570	3,767,581
Securities of other United States		
Government agencies	1,413,556	1,205,906
Obligations of states and political subdivisions	5,447,247	4,017,536
Other securities	103,242	23,559
Trust department income	583,748	525,205
Service charges on deposit accounts	2,170,934	2,002,980
Other service charges and fees	1,831,518	1,828,950
Other operating income	978,225	770,906
Total operating income		
Operating Expenses		
Salaries	8,583,428	7,553,884
Employee benefits	1,618,340	1,109,484
Interest on deposits	13,603,478	11,492,622
Expense of federal funds purchased	885,653	542,110
Interest on capital debentures and notes	101,071	54,507
Net occupancy expense	1,212,803	982,971
Equipment expenses	1,537,625	1,406,941
Provision for loan losses — Note F	1,026,517	1,216,483
Other operating expenses	5,691,974	5,059,958
Total operating expenses		
Income before income taxes, minority interest and securities gains or losses		
Less:		
Applicable income taxes — Note H	979,374	548,712
Minority interest	277,473	221,642
INCOME BEFORE SECURITIES GAINS OR LOSSES		
Gains (losses) on sale of securities, less applicable income tax effect: 1972 — $152,325; 1971 — $196,566..	(148,714)	254,724
Less minority interest	4,815	(13,430)
Securities gains (losses) after income taxes and minority interest	(143,899)	241,294
NET INCOME	$ 6,118,084	$ 4,894,788
Earnings per weighted average Common share outstanding (3,283,788 shares in each year):		
Income before securities gains or losses	$ 1.91	$ 1.42
Net income	$ 1.86	$ 1.49

Courtesy of Flagship Banks Inc. of Miami

37.   The chart below gives the number of employed people and the population figures for 1970 to 1973. For each of these years find the number of persons *not* employed.

People and Jobs

Year	Population	Employed
1970	204,879,000	78,627,000
1971	207,049,000	79,120,000
1972	208,837,000	81,702,000
1973	209,866,000	84,000,000

Reprinted, by permission, from *The Wall Street Journal*, July 2, 1973, p. 2

© 1967 United Feature Syndicate, Inc. Reprinted by permission.

1.4 MULTIPLICATION OF COUNTING NUMBERS

In the last two sections we discussed the addition and subtraction of counting numbers. In this section we shall discuss the multiplication of counting numbers. As you are probably aware, the multiplication of numbers can be interpreted as a process of repeated addition. For example, suppose we have 4 boxes, each containing 6 objects as indicated below

Multiplication is a process of repeated addition.

and we are asked to find the total number of objects in the boxes. We can count the objects and arrive at the correct answer, 24. However, the problem can be simplified by reasoning that since we have 4 boxes with 6 objects in each, the total number of objects is $4 \times 6 = 24$. From this discussion we can see that $6 + 6 + 6 + 6 = 24$. In general, the operation of multiplication can be defined as a process of repeated addition, as stated in Definition 1.2.

> **DEFINITION 1.2** If a and b are counting numbers, the product of a and b, denoted by a × b is defined by
> $$\underbrace{b + b + b \ldots + b}_{a \text{ times}}$$

Definition of Multiplication

$a \times b$ is called the **product** of a and b and may also be written as a · b, a(b), (a)(b), or (a)b or simply ab. The numbers a and b are called **factors,** of if we wish to make a distinction between factors we call a the **multiplier** and b the **multiplicand.** Thus, 3×4 can be thought of as $4 + 4 + 4 = 12$. 3 is called the multiplier, 4 is called the multiplicand and the result, 12, is called the **product.** We usually write multiplication problems in column form; thus, the problem 123×402 is written as:

$$
\begin{array}{rl}
402 & \leftarrow \text{multiplicand} \\
\underline{123} & \leftarrow \text{multiplier} \\
1206 & \leftarrow 3 \times 402 \\
8040 & \leftarrow 20 \times 402 \\
\underline{40200} & \leftarrow 100 \times 402 \\
49446 & \leftarrow \text{product}
\end{array}
$$

The multiplier 123 is composed of the numbers one hundred (100), twenty (20) and three (3).

Just as with addition, the order in which we multiply the factors does not affect the outcome. For example, $3 \times 4 = 4 \times 3$ and $5 \times 8 = 8 \times 5$. We express this fact in Rule 1.3.

> **RULE 1.3**   If a and b are counting numbers $a \times b = b \times a$
> Commutative Law (for multiplication)

The use of the commutative law enables us to check multiplication problems by interchanging the multiplicand and the multiplier. Thus, to check that the indicated multiplication problem 176 is correct,
$$\times 231$$
we could multiply 231. If the result obtained, the product, is
$$\times 176$$
identical in both cases, the multiplication is correct.

Like addition, multiplication is an associative operation. We state this in Rule 1.4.

> **RULE 1.4**   If a, b, and c are counting numbers
>
> $$a \times (b \times c) = (a \times b) \times c$$
>
> Associative Law (for multiplication)

The associative law enables us to transform some problems that are hard to compute into problems that can easily be determined mentally. For example, $18 \times 5 = (9 \times 2) \times 5 = 9 \times (2 \times 5) = 9 \times 10 = 90$. If we use both the commutative and the associative law, we can simplify certain types of computations. Thus to multiply 24×15, we go through the following steps:

$$24 \times 15 = (12 \times 2) \times (5 \times 3)$$
$$= 12 \times (2 \times 5) \times 3$$
$$= (2 \times 5) \times (12 \times 3)$$
$$= 10 \times (36) = 360$$

and

$$26 \times 45 = (13 \times 2) \times (5 \times 9)$$
$$= 13 \times (2 \times 5) \times 9$$
$$= (2 \times 5) \times (13 \times 9)$$
$$= 10 \times (117) = 1,170$$

PROGRESS TEST 1

1. In the problem $3 \times 5 = 15$, 3 is called the _____, 5 is called the _____, and 15 is called the _____.

2. It is known that $8 \times 3 = 3 \times 8$; this fact is an example of the _____.

3. The fact that $3 \times (4 \times 5) = (3 \times 4) \times 5$ is an illustration of the _____.

A study of multiplication of counting numbers (or a look at the "times" tables) reveals a useful property which is unique to the number 1, namely, that the product of any counting number "a" and 1 equals "a". We state this formally in Rule 1.5.

Identity Law for Multiplication

RULE 1.5   For any counting number a, $a \times 1 = 1 \times a = a$.

Identity Law (for multiplication)

1 is called the multiplicative identity.

We remark that 1 is called the identity element with respect to multiplication or simply the multiplicative identity.

Is there an identity with respect to addition? That is, is there a counting number "a" such that $a + x = x + a = a$? The answer is no. However, since it is convenient to have a number with the property mentioned above, we expand the set of counting numbers and form a new set of whole numbers $W = \{0, 1, 2, 3, \ldots\}$. The student should be aware that all the rules stated previously (Rules 1.1 through 1.5) are still valid for the set of whole numbers. In addition, we now give the following rule:

RULE 1.6   For any whole number a, $a + 0 = 0 + a = a$.

Identity Law (for addition)

Identity for Addition

Note that if Definition 1.2 is extended to cover the whole numbers, $a \times 0 = \underbrace{0 + 0 + 0 \ldots + 0}_{a \text{ times}}$. That is, for any whole number a

$$a \times 0 = 0 = 0 \times a$$

---

1. multiplier, multiplicand, product   2. Commutative Law for multiplication
3. Associative Law for multiplication

PROGRESS TEST 2

1. If we multiply 3,456 by 1 we obtain _____.
2. 4,356 + _____ = 4,356.
3. The set of whole numbers W = _____.
4. The only element of the set of whole numbers that is not a counting number is _____.

If a product involves numbers that are not too large, then it is likely that we have worked the problem earlier and memorized the results. These are the usual "times tables" that we are all supposed to know. For example, $7 \times 9 = 63$ and $8 \times 7 = 56$ because years ago we checked these results by repeated addition. If the product involves larger numbers, we need to break up the problem into simpler parts. The following rule will help us do it.

Distributive Law

> **RULE 1.7** If a, b, and c are whole numbers
>
> $$a \times (b + c) = a \times b + a \times c$$
>
> Distributive Law (of multiplication over addition)

With this rule in mind, the problem 9×19 can be solved as follows:

$$9 \times 19 = 9 \times (10 + 9) = 9 \times 10 + 9 \times 9 = 90 + 81 = 171.$$

We now show how this property is used in solving multiplication problems.

Example 1

Multiply 38 by 9.

Solution

Traditionally, we write the problem in column form:

$$\begin{array}{r} 38 \\ \times\ 9 \\ \hline \end{array}$$

We multiply 9 by 8 to obtain 72, write the 2 in the units place and carry the 7. We then multiply $9 \times 3 = 27$ and add the 7 we carried to obtain 34. Then we write the 4 in the tens place and the 3 in the hundreds place, yielding the product 342. Thus, to multiply 38 by 9, we have proceeded as follows:

$$9 \times 38 = 9 \times (30 + 8) = 9 \times 30 + 9 \times 8 = 270 + 72 = 342$$

---

1. 3,456   2. 0   3. {0,1,2,3 . . .}   4. 0 (zero)

We now mention two methods that can be used to check multiplication. One of the methods, which has already been mentioned, is most useful when the multiplicand and multiplier have the same number of digits. Thus, to check a problem such as

$$
\begin{array}{r}
345 \\
\times 748 \\
\end{array}
$$

we reverse the multiplicand and the multiplier, and solve the problem

$$
\begin{array}{r}
748 \\
\times 345 \\
\end{array}
$$

If the product is identical in both cases, the result is correct. The second procedure, which we will illustrate in the next example, is the "casting out of nines." To verify a multiplication problem by the method of casting out nines, we find the checking number of the multiplicand, and the checking number of the multiplier. We then multiply the two, casting out nines if necessary. If the multiplication has been done properly, the result must be identical to the checking number of the product.

Example 2

Multiply 342 by 46 and verify the result by the method of casting out nines.

Solution

$$
\begin{array}{r}
342 \rightarrow 3+4+2 \longrightarrow 0 \\
\times 46 \rightarrow 6+4 = 10 \longrightarrow \times 1 \\
\hline
2052 \qquad\qquad\qquad \textcircled{0} \\
1368 \\
\hline
15732 \rightarrow 1+5+7+3+2 \rightarrow \textcircled{0}
\end{array}
$$

PROGRESS TEST 3

   1. The distributive law of multiplication over addition states that _____

_____.

   2. To multiply 10 × 45 by using the distributive law we could write 10 × (_____).
   3. To verify that the product 340 × 803 is correct we could solve the problem _____.

---

1. For any whole numbers a, b, and c, a × (b + c) = a × b + a × c   2. (40 + 5)
3. 803 × 340

We finally consider several cases involving products in which at least one of the factors ends in zero. For example, when multiplying 674 by 100 we could proceed as follows:

$$
\begin{array}{r}
674 \\
\times 100 \\
\hline
000 \\
000 \\
674 \\
\hline
67400
\end{array}
$$

We could have obtained a similar result by adding to the multiplicand (674) as many zeros as there are in the multiplier (100). Thus, we add two zeros to 674, obtaining 67400 as a result. Similarly, $453 \times 1000 = 453000$ (adding to the multiplicand as many zeros as there are in the multiplier).

A similar technique is used when the multiplicand ends in zero. For example, to multiply 340 by 31 we normally proceed as follows:

$$
\begin{array}{r}
340 \\
\times 31 \\
\hline
340 \\
1020 \\
\hline
10540
\end{array}
$$

A similar result could have been obtained, as the following example illustrates, by dropping the zero from the multiplicand, computing the resulting multiplication problem, and adding the zero to the product obtained.

$$
\begin{array}{r}
340 \\
\times 31| \\
\hline
34| \\
102 \downarrow \\
\hline
10540
\end{array}
$$

If both factors end in zero, we can always multiply the factors without the zeros and add the zeros later. For example, to multiply 120 by 3600 we can proceed as follows:

$$
\begin{array}{r}
12 \\
\times 36 \\
\hline
72 \\
36 \\
\hline
432
\end{array}
$$

Adding the zero from 120 and the two zeros from 3,600 we obtain 432,000 as the product. Similarly, $3100 \times 90 = 279,000$ can be obtained by dropping the zeros, computing $31 \times 9 = 279$ and adding three zeros. Finally, we consider the case in which a zero appears within one of the factors. For example, to multiply 231×502 we could proceed as follows:

$$
\begin{array}{r}
231 \\
\times 502 \\
\hline
462 \\
000 \\
1155 \\
\hline
115962
\end{array}
$$

A similar result could have been obtained by skipping one extra space before writing the product of 5 × 231 as shown:

$$
\begin{array}{r}
231 \\
\times 502 \\
\hline
462 \\
1155 \\
\hline
115962
\end{array}
$$

PROGRESS TEST 4

1. The product 564 × 1000 equals _____.
2. The product 450 × 41 equals _____.
3. The product 1650 × 400 equals _____.
4. The product 405 × 82 equals _____.

Example 3

When goods are sold, an itemized statement of goods is prepared by the seller (vendor). The **invoice** is an itemized list of the merchandise being sent by the vendor. The Figure on the following page shows an invoice for a carpet distributor. Note that the unit price of each item (column 6) is multiplied by the quantity shipped (column 4), and the answer recorded in the amount column. The amount is thus found by multiplying the number in column 4 by the number in column 6. Complete the amount column and find the total sale price.

Invoices

EXERCISE 1.4

1. Compute the following products:

   (a) $\begin{array}{r} 342 \\ \times\ 45 \\ \hline \end{array}$ (b) $\begin{array}{r} 478 \\ \times\ 63 \\ \hline \end{array}$ (c) $\begin{array}{r} 629 \\ \times\ 39 \\ \hline \end{array}$ (d) $\begin{array}{r} 969 \\ \times\ 38 \\ \hline \end{array}$

2. Compute the following products:

   (a) $\begin{array}{r} 349 \\ \times\ 87 \\ \hline \end{array}$ (b) $\begin{array}{r} 439 \\ \times\ 48 \\ \hline \end{array}$ (c) $\begin{array}{r} 342 \\ \times 197 \\ \hline \end{array}$ (d) $\begin{array}{r} 965 \\ \times 987 \\ \hline \end{array}$

3. Check the products in Problem 1 by using the "casting out nines" method.

---

1. 564,000   2. 18,450   3. 660,000   4. 33,210

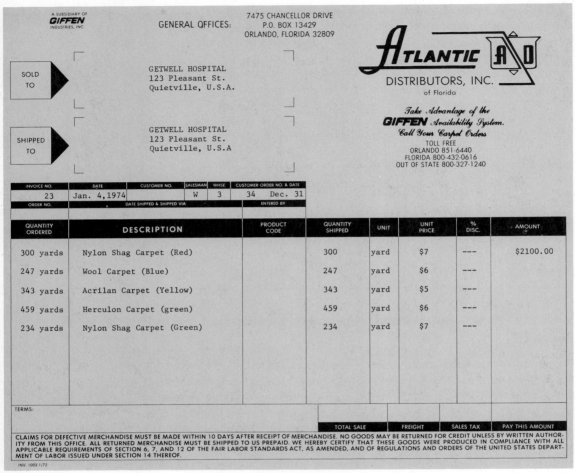

From Atlantic Distributors, Inc. of Florida

4. Check the products in Problem 2 by using the "casting out nines" method.

5. Find the missing numbers that will make the following statements true:
   (a) $18 \times (3 + 4) = 18 \times 3 + ? \times 4$
   (b) $13 \times (6 + 8) = 13 \times ? + 13 \times 8$
   (c) $32 \times (5 + 2) = 32 \times 5 + 32 \times ?$
   (d) $49 \times (3 + 2) = ? \times 3 + 49 \times 2$

6. Find the missing numbers (represented by the letter x) that will make the following statements true:
   (a) $34 \cdot 18 = (30 + x)18$ (b) $21 \cdot 19 = 21 \cdot (x + 9)$
   (c) $21 \cdot 17 = 20 \cdot 17 + x \cdot 17$ (d) $5 \cdot 13 = 5 \cdot 6 + x \cdot 7$

7. Use the Distributive Law of multiplication over addition (Rule 1.7) and compute each of the following mentally.

     (a) 18×21 (b) $19 \cdot 21$ (c) 14×32

     (d) $12 \cdot 22$ (e) $(6 \times 3) + (7 \times 3)$ (f) $(27 \cdot 51) + (3 \cdot 51)$

In addition to the distributive property of multiplication over addition, there is a distributive property of multiplication over subtraction which states that $a \times (b - c) = a \times b - a \times c$. With this property in mind, we can compute the product $31 \times 9 = 31 \times (10 - 1)$ $= 31 \times 10 - 31 \times 1 = 310 - 31 = 279$. Using this method, compute the products in Problems 8 and 9.

8.   (a) 6×29 (b) 4×39 (c) 8×98 (d) 5×49

9.   (a) 8×49 (b) 5×38 (c) 7×99 (d) 4×48

10.   Compute the following products:

     (a) 985×800 (b) 453×1000 (c) 432×200 (d) 324×3000

11.   Compute the following products:

     (a) 350×31 (b) 502×23 (c) $407 \cdot 12$ (d) $301 \cdot 51$

12.   Compute the following products:

     (a) 3400×120 (b) 230×900 (c) $4500 \cdot 1300$ (d) $6400 \cdot 120$

13.   Compute the following products:

     (a) 405×31 (b) 302×42 (c) $307 \cdot 22$ (d) $908 \cdot 120$

14.   The Cone Tracting Company has a subdivision consisting of 24 rows of 18 houses each. How many houses are there in this subdivision?

15.   If the cost of each of the houses in the problem above is $10,000, what is the total cost of the subdivision?

16.   Rip Cutwell worked 39 hours in a carpentry shop. If he is paid at the rate of $6 an hour, what will his salary be?

17.   If in the preceding problem Rip worked 42 hours, what will his salary be?

18.   It is a usual practice in business to pay overtime salary to employees working more than 40 hours per week. Bob Grabber, an employee of U.S. Steel, gets paid $4 an hour with double time for overtime. If Mr. Grabber worked a total of 47 hours last week, what will his salary be?

19.   If in the preceding problem Mr. Grabber worked for 52 hours, what will his salary be?

20.   A square lot 95 feet on each side is to be fenced. If a foot of fence is $2, what will be the cost of the fence?

21.   If in Example 3 of this section the amounts of carpet to be bought are 250, 300, 456, 439, and 230 yards, respectively, what will be the total amount of the sale?

HILLSBOROUGH COMMUNITY COLLEGE
REQUISITION FOR MATERIALS AND SERVICES

REQUISITION NO. 1-04023

DATE: __3/5/74__

DEPARTMENT	LOCATION	DATE REQUIRED	REQUISITIONED BY	APPROVED BY DEPT. HEAD
Math	Ybor City	2/3/74	I.B.	I.B.

ITEM NO.	QUANTITY	UNIT	DESCRIPTION	UNIT PRICE	TOTAL
1	1	1	IBM Selectric Typewriter	$750	$750
2	3	1	4 by 12 Blackboards	78	
3	2	1	Faculty Desks	178	
4	2	1	Matching Chairs	56	

Courtesy of Hillsborough Community College

22. Follow the procedure of Example 3 and find the total price for the purchase order shown above.

23. Follow the procedure of Example 3 and find the total price for the purchase order shown on the opposite page.

24. The table on page 43 gives the rates for placing a classified ad in a newspaper. For example, to run 5 words for 3 days, we find the rate for 3 days and multiply this rate × words × days, that is, $18 \times 5 \times 3 = 270$¢ = $2.70. Follow a similar procedure and find the rate for
(a) 8 words for 6 days.
(b) 6 words for 3 days.
(c) 9 words for 7 days.

25. Using the table given in Problem 24, find the rates for
(a) 15 words for 6 days.
(b) 10 words for 10 days.
(c) 17 words for 3 days.

HILLSBOROUGH COMMUNITY COLLEGE
REQUISITION FOR MATERIALS AND SERVICES

REQUISITION NO. 1-04022

DATE: 3/4/74

DEPARTMENT	LOCATION	DATE REQUIRED	REQUISITIONED BY	APPROVED BY
Physics	Ybor City	10/4/74	I.B.	DEPT. HEAD I.B.

ITEM NO.	QUANTITY	UNIT	DESCRIPTION	UNIT PRICE	TOTAL
1	2	1	IBM Selectric Typewriter	$817	
2	3	1	4 by 12 Blackboards	84	
3	3	1	Faculty Desks	194	
4	3	1	Matching Chairs	56	
5	3	1	Mahogany Bookcases	131	

Courtesy of Hillsborough Community College

Reprinted, by permission, from *The Tampa Times*, August 14, 1973, p. 11c

1.5   DIVISION OF COUNTING NUMBERS

In section 1.3 we mentioned that subtraction was closely related to addition, since every subtraction problem could be written as an addition question. A similar relationship exists between division and multiplication. Just as subtraction is the **inverse** operation of addition, division is the **inverse** operation of multiplication. For example, suppose an employer has $100 to be equally distributed among 5 employees. If we wish to find out each employee's share, we must divide 100 by 5. In symbols we write $100 \div 5 = $ ___?___ (Read "100 divided by 5 equals what?") Obviously, the answer is 20, as can be easily verified by multiplying 20×5. Thus, $100 \div 5 = 20$ because $5 \times 20 = 100$. In general, we have the following definition.

Definition of Division

> **DEFINITION 1.3**   For any counting numbers a and b, $a \div b = c$ provided that $a = b \times c$.*

When we are dividing a by b we are trying to find out how many times b is contained in a. The number a is the number being divided and it is called the **dividend**; the number b is the number by which the dividend is being divided and is called the **divisor**; c is the result of the division or **quotient** and it shows the number of times the divisor goes into the dividend. Thus, in the example

$$
\begin{array}{r}
15 \\
3\overline{)45} \\
\underline{3} \\
15 \\
\underline{15} \\
0
\end{array}
$$

45 is the **dividend**, 3 is the **divisor**, and 15 is the **quotient.**

There are different notations that can be used to indicate a division problem. For example, if we wish to divide 15 by 5 we can write $15 \div 5$, $\frac{15}{5}$, 15/5, or $5\overline{)15}$. It is fairly obvious that not all division problems have an exact or whole number as an answer. For example, if we have 5 books and we want to distribute them equally between

---

*In this section we will limit ourselves to cases in which a is greater than b.

2 friends each of the friends could receive two books but there would be one left (unless we decide to cut that one in half and give each of our friends half a book). The operation we have performed is usually written as follows:

$$
\begin{array}{r}
2 \leftarrow \text{quotient} \\
\text{divisor} \rightarrow 2\overline{)5} \leftarrow \text{dividend} \\
\underline{4} \\
1 \leftarrow \text{remainder}
\end{array}
$$

Thus, we say that 5 divided by 2 is 2, with a remainder of 1. Sometimes we write the answer as $2\frac{1}{2}$. A similar procedure is employed to perform division problems involving larger numbers. We illustrate the procedure in Example 1.

Example 1

Divide 496 by 6.

Solution

We set up the problem in the usual way and write

$$\text{divisor} \rightarrow 6\overline{)496} \leftarrow \text{dividend}$$

Since it is difficult to determine by inspection how many 6s there are in 496, we consider only part of the dividend and find a partial quotient. Since 8×6 does not exceed 49 but 9×6 does, we write

$$
\begin{array}{r}
8 \leftarrow \text{partial quotient} \\
6\overline{)496} \\
\underline{48} \\
16 \leftarrow \text{new dividend}
\end{array}
$$

We divide again using the remainder 16 as our new dividend. We have to find out how many 6s there are in 16. Since $(2 \times 6) + 4 = 16$ we write:

$$
\begin{array}{r}
82 \leftarrow \text{quotient} \\
\text{divisor} \rightarrow 6\overline{)496} \leftarrow \text{dividend} \\
\underline{48} \\
16 \\
\underline{12} \\
4 \leftarrow \text{remainder}
\end{array}
$$

Thus, we say that 496 divided by 6 equals 82 with a remainder of 4. We could also write the answer as $82\frac{4}{6}$.

The division problem of Example 1 (or any other division problem) can easily be checked by multiplying the quotient by the divisor and adding the remainder. The result must be equal to the dividend. Thus, we have to check if $(82 \times 6) + 4 = 496$. Since the equality is true, the problem is correct.

The procedure used in problems having more digits in the dividend or divisor is similar to the one employed in Example 1; however, partial quotients are determined differently in these cases. For example,

$$
\begin{array}{r}
84 \leftarrow \text{quotients} \\
\text{divisor} \rightarrow 583)\overline{49456} \\
4664 \\
\hline
2816 \\
2332 \\
\hline
484 \leftarrow \text{remainder}
\end{array}
$$

In order to divide 49,456 by 583 we would like to know the partial quotient found by dividing 4945 by 583. Since this result is not readily apparent, we revert to a technique of estimation. To obtain an estimate we round off 583 to the nearest hundred, 600, and the partial dividend to the nearest thousand, 5000, and consider the number of 6s in 50. Since the answer is 8, we enter the 8 as a partial quotient and then multiply $8 \times 583 = 4664$ and place this answer directly under the 4945. Subtract 4664 from 4945 to obtain 281. Since 583 does not go into 281, we bring down the 6 from the dividend and now have 2816. We round off the 2816 to 2800, the 583 to 600 and estimate that 6 goes into 28 four times. We place the 4 in the quotient, multiply 4 by 583 and place the product 2332 under the 2816. Now, 2332 subtracted from 2816 is 484. We have used each of the numbers in the dividend and have a quotient of 84 and a remainder of 484. We have hence determined that 583 is contained 84 times within 49456 (with a remainder of 484). As usual, we could write the answer as $84\frac{484}{583}$.

To check the accuracy of the computation we have just finished, we multiply 583×84 and add 484 to the product. Thus, we have $(583 \times 84) + 484 = 48972 + 484 = 49,456$. Since the result is equal to the dividend, the division is correct.

We now give a second method for checking division, the method of "casting out nines". The method is based on the relationship

$$\text{Divisor} \times \text{Quotient} + \text{Remainder} = \text{Dividend}$$

and is performed as follows: Find the checking number of the divisor and quotient, multiply them together and cast out nines if necessary. Add the checking number of the remainder. The result must be equal to the checking number of the dividend or we have made an error.

Thus, to check the problem above by casting out nines we proceed as indicated:

$$
\begin{array}{lll}
\text{divisor} & 583 \rightarrow & 7 \\
\text{quotient} & 84 \rightarrow & \times\ 3 \\
& & \overline{21\ \rightarrow\quad 3} \\
\text{remainder} & 484 \rightarrow & \rightarrow + 7 \\
& & \overline{10 \rightarrow \textcircled{1}}
\end{array}
$$

Since the checking number of the dividend is also 1, we assume our result is correct.

PROGRESS TEST 1

1. If it is known that a ÷ b = c, we call a the _____, b the _____, and c the _____.
2. In the division problem 46)2453 the quotient is _____ and the remainder is _____.
3. 1560 ÷ 100 equals _____.

In many business situations we use the concept of an **average.** The average is the result obtained by dividing the sum of two or more quantities by the number of quantities. For example, the average of 10 and 8 is $\dfrac{10+8}{2} = 9$, and that of 9, 7, 3, and 5 is $\dfrac{9+7+3+5}{4} = 6$. In business we use average prices, average profits, and average inventories.

Averages

Example 2

A survey revealed that a particular product sold for $18 at one store, $20 in another, and $16 in a third one. Find the average price of the product.

Solution

The average price is $\dfrac{18 + 20 + 16}{3} = \$18$.

---

1. dividend, divisor, quotient   2. 53, 15   3. 15 with a remainder of 60 or $15\dfrac{60}{100}$.

PROGRESS TEST 2

1. An average is the result obtained by _____ the _____ of two or more quantities by the _____ of quantities.

2. The average of 8, 3, 4, and 5 is _____.

3. A student has taken three tests and obtained 60, 70, and 83. His average for the three tests is _____.

EXERCISE 1.5

1. Compute:
   (a) $456 \div 134$ (b) $578 \div 234$ (c) $8456 \div 345$
   (d) $9300 \div 10$

2. Compute:
   (a) $8456 \div 1307$ (b) $12{,}345 \div 2345$ (c) $12{,}378 \div 345$

3. Check the results of problem 1 by using the relationship:

$$\text{Divisor} \times \text{Quotient} + \text{Remainder} = \text{Dividend}$$

4. Check the results of problem 2 by using the method of "casting out nines".

5. C. Angler works 35 hours per week in a fish-market. If his weekly salary amounts to $140, what is his hourly rate?

6. If Mr. Angler makes $175 per week and still works 35 hours per week, what is his hourly rate?

7. Gudget Manufacturing Company bought 347 gidgets and 243 gadgets. They paid $2429 for the gidgets and $2187 for the gadgets. Find the price of one gidget and the price of one gadget.

8. A bill of sale for Gudget Manufacturing totaled $4,616. If it is known that the invoice included the purchase of 243 gadgets at $9 each and the total number of items received was 590, how many gidgets did they buy? What was the price per gidget?

9. A student has the following grades: 68, 75, and 49. What is his average grade?

10. Mr. Don Bell has an annual salary of $3900. What is his monthly salary?

1. dividing, sum, number   2. 5   3. 71

11. If Mr. Bell's salary is increased to $3984 from $3900, how much more does he get each month?

12. In Problem 11, find Mr. Bell's new monthly salary.

13. Find the unit price (before taxes) of each of the four types of tires advertised.

14. Find the price per item in the accompanying ad when you buy 3.

3 Classic Style.					
Back Hook	Cup	State size	Shpg. wt. ea.	Each	3 for
18 T 54644F...	...Full-B.....	...34, 36, 38, 40, 42, 44.................	...5 ounces...	...$2.44...	...$6.00
18 T 54645F...	...Full-C.....	...32, 34, 36, 38, 40, 42, 44, 46.........	...5 ounces...	... 2.44...	... 6.00
18 T 54646F...	...Full-D....	...32, 34, 36, 38, 40, 42, 44, 46, 48, 50...	...5 ounces...	... 3.44...	... 9.00
18 T 54647F...	...Full-DD...	...34, 36, 38, 40, 42, 44, 46, 48.........	...5 ounces...	... 4.44...	...12.00
18 T 54648F...	...Full-F.....	...34, 36, 38, 40, 42, 44.................	...5 ounces...	... 4.44...	...12.00

15. Find the average of the following numbers:
    (a) 10, 15, 17
    (b) 8, 9, 4, 3
    (c) 50, 84, 16
    (d) 280, 290, 270

16. In the ad given find the price of:
    (a) 1 bottle of charm detergent
    (b) 1 roll of paper towels
    (c) 1 box of facial tissue
    (d) 1 pack of envelopes

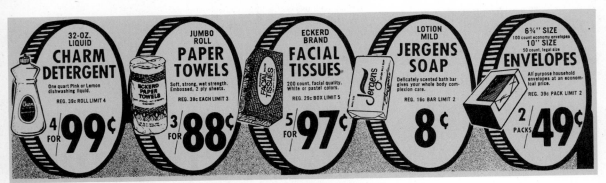

Courtesy of Jack Eckerd Corporation

17. Eggs can be packed in boxes of 12 or in cartons of 24. A farm has a total of 19,032 eggs,
   (a) how many boxes of 12 would they need to pack the eggs?
   (b) how many cartons of 24 would they need to pack the eggs?
   (c) If they decide to sell 800 dozen eggs in boxes of 12, how many cartons of 24 do they need to pack the rest of the eggs?

18. The table below shows the weekly sales (in hundreds of dollars) of 4 salespersons.

NAME	WEEK 1	WEEK 2	WEEK 3	WEEK 4
Bob	136	152	128	138
Carol	158	170	145	142
Ted	162	144	166	150
Alice	152	208	181	130
Avg. sales for week				

   (a) Find the average weekly sales for each salesperson.
   (b) Find the average sales for each week.

19. Referring to the table below, find the average number of transactions between 10 and 3 on Thursday.

20. Referring to the table in Problem 19, find the average number of transactions between 10 and 3 on Tuesday.

TOTAL STOCK TRANSACTIONS	Thursday	Tuesday	Monday
10:00 to 11:00	2,530,000	2,740,000	2,960,000
11:00 to 12:00	2,140,000	2,150,000	1,820,000
12:00 to 1:00	1,440,000	1,750,000	1,480,000
1:00 to 2:00	1,490,000	1,030,000	910,000
2:00 to 3:00	1,650,000	1,690,000	1,480,000
3:00 to 3:30	1,250,000	1,200,000	1,180,000
Total	10,500,000	10,560,000	9,830,000

© 1957 United Feature Syndicate, Inc. Reprinted by permission.

1.6 ADDITION AND SUBTRACTION OF INTEGERS

In the cartoon above Linus is trying to subtract six from four; that is, he is seeking a solution for the problem $4 - 6 = ?$ Using Definition 1.1 we know that $4 - 6 = c$, if $6 + c = 4$. However, it is impossible to find a **whole** number c that when added to 6 will give us 4. Similarly, if the temperature drops below 0° (zero degrees) there is no whole number that can be used to denote what the temperature is. For this reason we introduce a new system called the set of integers I = $\{. . . -3,-2,-1,0,1,2,3 . . .\}$. Now, if we wish to subtract 6 from 4 we can find an integer c such that $6 + c = 4$. Obviously, if we let $c = -2$ we have the solution to the problem. Thus we say that $4 - 6 = -2$. In the same manner, if the temperature is 5 degrees below 0, we can denote this temperature by $-5°$. We have now added an important concept to the idea of a number, the concept of direction. To help us to visualize this concept, we draw a straight line, choose a point on this line, and label it 0. (See Figure 1–2.) We then measure successive equal intervals to the right of 0 and label them with the positive integers in their order $1,2,3, ...$ Those to the left of 0 are labeled with the negative integers in their order $-1,-2,-3, ...$

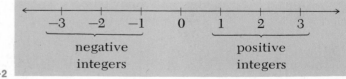

Figure 1–2

We can see that there are three kinds of integers:

The positive integers, $1,2,3 . . .$
The negative integers, $-1,-2,-3 . . .$
The integer 0

Note that for every positive integer, there is a negative integer. Thus, associated with the positive integer 3, we have the negative integer -3. We say that -3 is the **opposite** or the **additive inverse** of 3. Similarly, -5 is the opposite of 5. We make this idea precise in the next definition.

DEFINITION 1.4 Every integer a, has a unique additive inverse −a such that a + (−a) = 0 = (−a) + a.
Note that the additive inverse of −a is a, that is, −(−a) = a.

Using the definition we can see that the additive inverse of 7 is −7 and the additive inverse of −8 is 8. Note that any number and its inverse are equidistant from 0.

PROGRESS TEST 1

1. The set of integers is divided into 3 parts. The _____ integers, the _____ integers, and the _____ integer.
2. The additive inverse of 9 is _____.
3. The additive inverse of −5 is _____.

The number line given in Figure 1–2 can also be used to help us visualize the concept of addition of integers. To represent graphically the addition of integers, we start at 0, and move to the right if the number is positive and to the left if the number is negative. Thus, to add 3 + 2, we start at 0, move 3 units to the right, then 2 more units to the right and arrive at 5 (see Figure 1–3). Thus, 3 + 2 = 5.

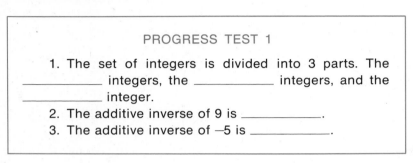

Figure 1–3

Now consider the sum of 5 + (−4). We begin at 0 and move 5 units to the right followed by 4 units to the left to obtain 1. Thus, 5 + (−4) = 1 (see Figure 1–4).

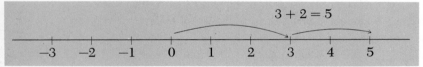

Figure 1–4

Finally, consider the sum (−3) + (−1). We begin at 0 and move 3 units to the left followed by 1 more unit to the left to arrive at −4. Thus, (−3) + (−1) = −4 (see Figure 1–5).

1. positive, negative, 0   2. −9   3. 5

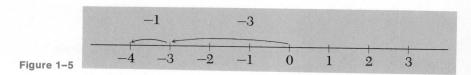

Figure 1–5

We summarize the types of additions illustrated above in Rules 1.8 and 1.9.

> **RULE 1.8** In adding integers with the same sign, add the numerical value and give the sum the common sign.

Addition of Integers

Thus, $3 + 5 = 8$, $9 + 1 = 10$ and $(-3) + (-5) = -8$, $(-6) + (-7) = -13$.

> **RULE 1.9** In adding two integers with different signs, subtract the smaller from the larger and give the difference the sign of the larger.

Thus, $8 + (-3) = 5$, $7 + (-4) = 3$ and $3 + (-8) = -5$, $4 + (-9) = -5$.

In case we are adding more than two integers, we can always add all the positive integers, and then all the negative integers. We then add the two sums. The procedure is illustrated in Example 1.

Example 1

Add $5 + (-2) + 6 + (-4) + 3 + (-9)$.

Solution

We add all the positive numbers first. $5 + 6 + 3 = 14$.
We then add all the negative numbers. $(-2) + (-4) + (-9) = -15$.
The sum is $14 + (-15) = -1$.

Subtraction of integers is defined in the same manner in which subtraction of whole numbers was defined. We now give the definition.

Subtraction of Integers

> **DEFINITION 1.5** If a, b, and c are integers,
>
> $$a - b = c \text{ if } a = b + c$$
>
> a is called the **minuend,** b the **subtrahend,** and c the **difference.**

Thus, $5 - 3 = 2$ because $5 = 3 + 2$
$3 - 5 = -2$ because $3 = 5 + (-2)$
$4 - (-3) = 7$ because $4 = (-3) + 7$

Example 2

Perform the given operations and illustrate the results on the number line.

(a) $8 - 2$ (b) $2 - 8$ (c) $(-3) - 5$ (d) $5 - (-3)$

Solution

(a) We begin at 0 and move 8 units to the right and 2 to the left; the result is 6. Thus, $8 - 2 = 6$ (see Figure 1–6).

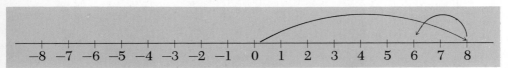

Figure 1–6

(b) We begin at 0 and move 2 units to the right and 8 to the left; the result is -6. Thus, $2 - 8 = -6$ (see Figure 1–7).

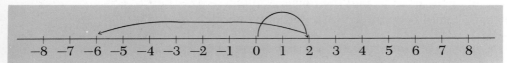

Figure 1–7

(c) We begin at 0 and move 3 units to the left followed by 5 more units to the left. The result is -8. Thus, $(-3) - 5 = -8$ (see Figure 1–8).

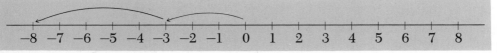

Figure 1–8

(d) We remark that when the subtrahend is a positive number, we move the corresponding number of units to the left. Hence, if the subtrahend is a negative number we shall move the corresponding number of units to the right. That is, $-(-3)$ means go 3 units to the right of 0, so $-(-3) = 3$. With this result we can see that to subtract (-3) from 5 we start at 0, go 5 units to the right and then 3 more units to the right. The result is 8. Thus, $5 - (-3) = 5 + 3 = 8$.

Figure 1–9

Example 3

Figure 1–10 below shows some non-farm civilian employment statistics (in thousands) for successive years. Verify that the change is as shown.

Recession	NON-FARM CIVILIAN EMPLOYMENT		
	Start	End	Change
1948–49	50,793	50,455	− 338
1953–54	55,130	53,766	−1,364
1957–58	58,139	57,029	−1,110
1960–61	60,700	60,116	− 584
1969–70	75,066	75,126	+ 60

Figure 1–10 Reprinted, by permission, from *The Wall Street Journal*, June 11, 1973.

Solution

(a) $50,455 - 50,793 = -338$ because $50,455 = 50,793 + (-338)$
(b) $53,766 - 55,130 = -1,364$ because $53,766 = 55,130 + (-1,364)$
(c) $57,029 - 58,139 = -1,110$ because $57,029 = 58,139 + (-1,110)$
(d) $60,116 - 60,700 = -584$ because $60,116 = 60,700 + (-584)$
(e) $75,126 - 75,066 = +60$ because $75,126 = 75,066 + 60$

PROGRESS TEST 2

1. $3 + 7 =$ _____.
2. $3 - 7 =$ _____.
3. $7 - 3 =$ _____.
4. $3 + (-7) =$ _____.

5. $(-7) - (-3) =$ _____.
6. $(-4) + (-5) =$ _____.
7. $(5) - (-6) =$ _____.

Example 4

In Figure 1–11 below, the supply of various types of grain (in thousands of bushels) is given for the week ended on June 15, 1973.

U.S. Visible Grain Supply

CHICAGO—U.S. visible grain supply, according to the Chicago Board of Trade (in bushels, 000 omitted):

	Wk Ended June 15, 1973	Chge From Wk. Ago	Yr. Ago
Wheat	103,892	+ 3,627	162,549
Corn	80,543	− 4,226	78,377
Oats	63,291	+ 1,036	77,517
Rye	10,175	− 778	15,547
Barley	15,667	+ 511	15,809
Soybeans	25,895	− 1,974	31,101
Grain sorghums	17,870	− 253	27,973

Figure 1–11 Reprinted, by permission, from *The Wall Street Journal*, June 19, 1973, p. 30.

---

1. 10   2. −4   3. 4   4. −4   5. −4   6. −9   7. 11

(a) The supply of wheat was 103,892 on June 15, 1973. This amount represents 3627 more than the supply a week before. What was the supply a week earlier?

(b) The supply of rye was 10,175 on June 15, 1973. This amount represents 778 less than a week before. What was the supply a week earlier?

Solution

(a) The supply a week earlier was $103,892 - 3,627 = 100,265$

(b) The supply a week earlier was $10,175 + 778 = 10,953$

PROGRESS TEST 3

1. Referring to Figure 1–11, the supply of corn a week earlier was _____.

2. Referring to Figure 1–11, the supply of oats a week earlier was _____.

3. The difference between the supply of rye on June 15, 1973 and a year earlier is _____.

EXERCISE 1.6

1. Find the additive inverse (opposite) of:
    (a) 18   (b) −14   (c) 9   (d) −8   (e) −(−4)

2. Find the additive inverse of:
    (a) −(3)   (b) (−4)   (c) 0   (d) −0

3. Find the additive inverse of:
    (a) 3   (b) −3   (c) −(−8)   (d) 10

4. Find the additive inverse of:
    (a) −10   (b) $5 - 2$ (c) $3 - 5$ (d) $5 - (-3)$

5. Find the following sums using the number line:
    (a) $2 + 3$ (b) $2 + (-3)$ (c) $-3 + 2$ (d) $-3 + (-4)$

6. Find the sums given in Problem 5 by using Rules 1.8 and 1.9.

7. Find the following sums using the number line:
    (a) $7 + (-4)$ (b) $3 + (4 + (-3))$ (c) $4 + (3 + (-7))$

8. Find the sums given in Problem 7 by using Rules 1.8 and 1.9.

9. Find the following differences using Definition 1.5.
    (a) $3 - 4$ (b) $8 - 6$ (c) $3 - (-4)$ (d) $8 - (-3)$

10. Find the differences in Problem 9 by using the number line.

---

1. 84,769   2. 62,255   3. −5,372

11. Find the following differences using Definition 1.5.
   (a) $8 - (-4)$ (b) $0 - (-3)$ (c) $-9 - (-8)$
   (d) $-(-3) - (-4)$

12. Find the difference given in Problem 11 by using the number line.

13. Referring to Figure 1–11, find the supply of barley a week earlier.

14. Referring to Figure 1–11, find the supply of soybeans a week earlier.

15. Referring to the given ad, find the savings when buying:
   (a) Sweet and Low   (d) Protein 21 Hair Spray
   (b) Efferdent Tablets   (e) Mennen Deodorant
   (c) Pampers   (f) April Showers Dusting Powder

16. Referring to the given ad, find the savings when buying:
   (a) The Drexel bedroom
   (b) The Oak veneer bedroom
   (c) The Florida Spanish bedroom
   (d) The Mediterranean bedroom

17. A company has the following incomes (in millions) for the years indicated:

1969	243	1972	−54
1970	−48	1973	−60
1971	93		

Find the total income (or loss) for the five year period.

18. If the incomes for the company of Problem 17 are −250, −30, 98, 140, and −80, find the total income (or loss) for the five year period.

19. Find the balance for Mr. B. Thrifty.

20. If in Problem 19 the deposits are +80, +43, +90, and +87 and the withdrawals are −56, −43, and −56, find the balance.

Commercial Marine Bank

NAME ___ **B. Thrifty** _____

A/C # ___ **12-2346-78** _____

REGISTER OF DEPOSITS AND WITHDRAWALS

THIS REGISTER IS PROVIDED FOR YOUR CONVENIENCE IF YOU WISH TO KEEP A RECORD OF DEPOSITS AND WITHDRAWALS DURING THE PERIOD UNTIL YOUR NEXT STATEMENT IS RECEIVED FROM THE BANK.

DATE	DEPOSITS / WITHDRAWALS	+/−	BALANCE
BALANCE FORWARDED →			180
1/5/76	+89		
1/6/76	+43		
1/15/76	−98		
1/30/76	−45		
2/3/76	+46		

•MEMBER FEDERAL DEPOSIT INSURANCE CORP.

(SEE RULES & REGULATIONS INSIDE)

Courtesy of Commercial Marine Bank of Tampa.

"Say, I think I see where we went off. Isn't eight times seven fifty-six?"

Drawing by Ed Fisher; Copr. 1954 The New Yorker Magazine, Inc. Reprinted by permission.

1.7 MULTIPLICATION AND DIVISION OF INTEGERS

In the cartoon above, the scientists have forgotten some of the basic facts about products of whole numbers. Products (and quotients) of integers can be found in the same way as products and quotients of whole numbers. Thus, if the multiplication and division of whole numbers (covered in sections 1.4 and 1.5) are understood, the only problem that remains is that of finding the sign of each product or quotient. We first consider the definition of multiplication of integers.

DEFINITION 1.6 For any non-negative integers m and n,

(a) $m \times n$ is the product of the whole numbers m and n

(b) $m \times (-n) = -(m \times n)$

(c) $(-m) \times n = -(m \times n)$

(d) $(-m) \times (-n) = m \times n$

Definition of Multiplication

Example 1

Find the following products using Definition 1.6.

(a) 3×4
(b) $3 \times (-4)$
(c) $(-3) \times 4$
(d) $(-3) \times (-4)$

Solution

(a) $3 \times 4 = 12$
(b) $3 \times (-4) = -(3 \times 4) = -12$
(c) $(-3) \times 4 = -(3 \times 4) \times -12$
(d) $(-3) \times (-4) = 3 \times 4 = 12$

Definition 1.6 can be summarized by the rule that follows:

> **RULE 1.10** The product of two nonzero integers with like signs is positive and the product of two nonzero integers with unlike signs is negative. If either factor is 0 (as illustrated in the cartoon below) the product is 0.

Parts (a), (b), and (c) of Definition 1.6 are easily accepted, but part (d) causes difficulties to some people. Let us take an example to illustrate all the cases. Suppose that a man makes the following offer: Here is a box. Put some money in it or take some money from it. Take some of my debts from the box and pay them or put some of your debts in the box and I shall pay them for you.

His first friend put 3 five dollar bills in the box. The man gained $(3) \times (5) = 15$ dollars. Thus, $(+) \times (+) = (+)$.

His second friend (who was very poor) put 2 of his unpaid

debts in the amount of $5 each in the box. Hence the man had a loss of $(2) \times (-5) = -10$ dollars. Thus, $(+) \times (-) = (-)$.

His third friend took away 2 five dollar bills from the box. The man lost $(-2) \times (5) = -10$ dollars. Thus, $(-) \times (+) = (-)$.

His last friend decided to take away 2 five dollar debts. The man gained $(-2) \times (-5) = 10$ dollars. Thus, $(-) \times (-) = (+)$.

PROGRESS TEST 1

1. The product of 6 and 7 equals _____.
2. The product of 6 and −7 equals _____.
3. The product of −6 and 7 equals _____.
4. The product of −6 and −7 equals _____.

We now define division.

DEFINITION 1.7   For any integers a, b, and c, (b ≠ 0), $a \div b = c$ if $a = b \times c$.

Definition of Division

We remark that since division is defined in terms of multiplication, the sign of a quotient is found in the same way as the sign of a product. That is, if a and b are non-negative we have:

RULE 1.11   (a) $a \div (-b) = -(a \div b)$
(b) $(-a) \div (b) = -(a \div b)$
(c) $(-a) \div (-b) = a \div b$

Thus, we can say that the quotient of two nonzero integers with like signs is positive and the quotient of two nonzero integers with unlike signs is negative.

Example 2

Find the following quotients:
   (a) $15 \div (-3)$ (b) $(-15) \div 3$ (c) $(-15) \div (-3)$

Solution

   (a) $15 \div (-3) = -5$ because $15 = (-3) \times (-5)$
   (b) $(-15) \div 3 = -5$ because $-15 = 3 \times (-5)$
   (c) $(-15) \div (-3) = 5$ because $-15 = (-3) \times 5$

---

1. 42   2. −42   3. −42   4. 42

PROGRESS TEST 2

1. The quotient of 35 and −7 equals _____.
2. The quotient of −35 and 7 equals _____.
3. The quotient of −35 and −7 equals _____.

We finally remark that more complicated division problems can be solved by using Definition 1.7 and the procedures learned in Section 1.5. For example, to divide 1,345 by −7, we just keep in mind that the answer is negative and then proceed as usual, as illustrated.

$$
\begin{array}{r}
-192 \\
-7\overline{)1{,}345} \\
7 \\
\hline
64 \\
63 \\
\hline
15 \\
14 \\
\hline
1
\end{array}
$$

Thus the answer is −192 with a remainder of 1, which can be written as $-192\frac{1}{7}$.

EXERCISE 1.7

1. Find the following products using definition 1.6.
   (a) 8×4 (b) -8×7 (c) 5×-9 (d) $-9 \times (-3)$

2. Find the following products:
   (a) $32 \times (-48)$ (b) 34×98 (c) -98×45 (d) $-43 \times (-42)$

3. Find the following products:
   (a) $-(-3) \times 4$ (b) $4 \times -(-8)$

4. Find the following quotients:
   (a) $\dfrac{8}{4}$ (b) $\dfrac{-72}{9}$ (c) $\dfrac{108}{-12}$ (d) $\dfrac{-345}{-3}$

5. Find the following quotients:
   (a) $\dfrac{972}{9}$ (b) $\dfrac{452}{-4}$ (c) $\dfrac{-972}{9}$ (d) $\dfrac{-339}{-3}$

6. The table below gives the Average Income of person with different years of school. This average is obtained by dividing the life income by the number of years the average person received an income (45). Thus, a person with 0–7 years of schooling has a life income of $283,950 and an average income of $283,950/45 = $6,310. Find the average income for the rest of the classifications given.

---

1. −5   2. −5   3. 5

Years of School	Aver. Income	Life (45-yr.) Income
0-7	$6,310 + +	$283,950
8		320,535
1-3 high school		402,525
4 high school		449,820
1-3 college		526,545
4 college		645,795

7.   The accompanying ad gives the monthly rate for leasing different cars.

     Find the yearly rate for each of the cars.

Olds Supr., Buick Regal . . . . $99 Mo.
Chevy Impala . . . . $94 Mo.
Buick Riviera or Electra . . . $131 Mo.
Cadillac Coupe de Ville . . . $159 Mo.
Pontiac Grand Prix . . . . $122 Mo.
Eldorado or Mark IV . . . . . $216 Mo.

Courtesy of Main Line Leasing Agency.

8.   Referring to the accompanying ad find the price of:

    (a) 3 cans of corn   (d) 2 cans of pork and beans

    (b) 4 cans of spinach   (e) 3 cans of beets

    (c) 4 cans of green beans   (f) 3 cans of beans

CANNED VEGTS.

☐ **CORN** Cream White . . . . 303 Can **28°**
☐ **PEAS** Garden . . . . 303 Can **28°**
☐ **SPINACH** . . . . 303 Can **24°**
☐ **GRN. BEANS** W/Bacon . . . . 16 Oz. **19°**
☐ **GRN. BEANS** . . . . 303 Can **19°**
☐ **PORK 'N BEANS** . . . . . . 52 Oz. **49°**
☐ **SALAD** MIXED BEAN . . . . 17 Oz. **39°**
☐ **MUSHROOMS** Sliced . . . 2½ Oz. **34°**
☐ **BEETS** Harvard . . . . 16 Oz. **32°**
☐ **BEANS** Kidney . . . . 300 Can **24°**

9. Hurts Rent-a-car decides to buy some new cars in 1973. The wholesale price for different models is given below:

    Chevrolet Impala $2,900
    Buick LeSabre $3,100
    Oldsmobile 98 $3,800

    If the company decides to buy 5 Chevrolets, 5 Buicks, and 7 Oldsmobiles, what will the total price (before taxes) be?

10. If in Problem 9 the company decides to buy 6 Chevrolets, 5 Buicks, and 8 Oldsmobiles, what will the total price (before taxes) be?

11. The net loss of a small company was −$7,700. If the company has 3,850 stock holders and the losses are distributed equally, how much money did each of the stockholders lose?

12. In a certain week the Dow Jones Industrials registered the following changes: Mon. −2, Tues, −3, Wed. −4, Thurs, −2, Fri. −4. What was the average change during the week?

13. If in Problem 12 the changes were −2, 3, −4, −1, and −1, what was the average change during the week?

14. A real estate salesman had annual earnings of $16,080. What was his average monthly salary?

15. Annual sales for the golf shop owned by Sam Swatter, Pete Putter, and Slim Slammer totaled $246,000 and expenses were $153,000. If the three partners share profits equally, how much will each receive?

16. The premiums (for 20 years) on an insurance policy are $3,300. If the cash value (the amount they pay you for the policy at the end of the 20 years) is $2,600, what is the cost per year of the policy?

17. Walt's Auto Supply bought 93 generators at a cost of $30 each and resold them at $49 each. What was Walt's total profit on the purchase?

18. A student at U.S.F. pays $16 per credit hour, a $10 parking fee, and $80 for books and supplies. If Stan Studious is taking 6 credit hours at U.S.F. what will his total cost be?

19. A rock concert promotor sold 7000 three dollar tickets, 5000 four dollars tickets, and 3000 five dollar tickets. If the performers charged him $50,000, what was his Gross Profit or Loss?

20. If in Problem 19 the performers charged $60,000, what was the Gross Profit or Loss?

SELF-TEST/CHAPTER 1

1.   List the elements in each of the following sets:
   _____ a.   The set of the first three letters in the English alphabet
   _____ b.   The set of counting numbers less than 5
   _____ c.   The set of letters in the word BUSINESS

2.   _____   Which of the following is an example of the commutative law of addition?
   a. $6 + (4 + 5) = (6 + 4) + 5$
   b. $3 + 0 = 3$
   c. $(2 + 4) + 5 = (4 + 2) + 5$
   d. $8 + (-8) = 0$
   e. none of these.

3.   _____   Which of the following is an example of the associative law of multiplication.
   a. $6 \times (3 \times 5) = (6 \times 3) \times 5$
   b. $6 \times (+ 8) = (6 \times 3) + (6 \times 8)$
   c. $4 \times (2 \times 8) = 4 \times (8 \times 2)$
   d. $6 \times 1 = 6$
   e. none of these.

4.   Find the checking number for each of the following numbers:
   _____ a.   1,389
   _____ b.   8,347
   _____ c.   4,988

5.   In the accompanying Market Diary find
   _____ a.   the total number of issues traded.
   _____ b.   the total number of advances.

Reprinted, by permission, from *The Wall Street Journal*, July 23, 1973, p. 20.

MARKET DIARY

	Fri	Thur	Wed	Tues	Mon
Issues traded	3,060	3,061	3,062	3,064	3,065
Advances	935	768	809	863	700
Declines	319	424	393	355	380
Unchanged	1,806	1,869	1,860	1,846	1,985

6.   The accompanying table gives the rates for placing ads in a newspaper. Find the charge for
   _____ a.   running 5 words for 3 days.
   _____ b.   running 8 words for 5 days.
   _____ c.   running 7 words for 2 days.

Reprinted, by permission, from *The Tampa Times*, August 14, 1973, p. 11c.

7. In the chart below find the total number of hours worked during the week by each employee. Then find the total wages earned by each employee.

EMPLOYEE	M	T	W	TH	F	TOTAL HOURS WORKED	RATE PER HOUR	TOTAL WAGES
Rex, T.	6	8	8	8	5	_____	$2.50	_____
Jones, J.	8	8	7	6	8	_____	$3.10	_____
Phillips, P.	5	5	8	7	8	_____	$2.80	_____

8. Compute each of the following:
_____ a. $-8 \times -(-2)$
_____ b. $3 - (-4)$
_____ c. $(-5) \times (-8)$

9. Give the additive inverse (opposite) of each of the following:
_____ a. -3
_____ b. -9×3
_____ c. $\frac{348}{(-3)}$

10. Find the sum illustrating the answer by use of the number line.
_____ a. $3-5$

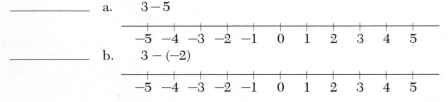

_____ b. $3 - (-2)$

11. Find the quotients:
_____ a. $\frac{8280}{23}$
_____ b. $\frac{62,361}{-123}$
_____ c. $\frac{-690}{-6}$

12. _____ A student obtained grades of 60, 70 and 86 on three tests. His average for these tests is __?__.

13.   In the accompanying income statement find
_____ a.   the Total Operating Expenses.
_____ b.   the Total Other Expenses.
_____ c.   the Total Expenses.

BAR NOTHIN' RANCH

Income statement for year Ended Dec. 31, 19__

Revenue		$34,895
Operating Expenses		
Wages	$10,500	
Supplies	638	
Utilities	960	
Depreciation	1,586	
Total Operating Expenses		_____
Other Expenses		
Gas, oil, repairs	$ 963	
Depreciation of farm equipment	1,298	
Total Other Expenses		_____
Total Expenses		_____

---

14.   _____ Which of the following is an example of the
distributive law of multiplication over addition?
a. $3 \times (4 + 5) = 3 \times (5 + 4)$
b. $3 \times (4 \times 5) = 3 \times (5 \times 4)$
c. $3 \times (4 + 5) = (3 \times 4) + (3 \times 5)$
d. $3 \times 1 = 3$
e. none of these

15.   In the accompanying chart find the savings between shipping
via Surface and Northwest from
_____ a.   New York to Seattle.
_____ b.   Washington to Los Angeles.
_____ c.   Tampa to Chicago.

FROM	TO	COMMODITY	WEIGHT	VIA SURFACE	NORTHWEST
New York	Seattle	Machine Parts	3200 lbs.	$302.00	$276.00
Philadelphia	Mpls./St. Paul	Machine Parts	3200 lbs.	$232.00	$130.00
Miami/ Ft. Lauderdale	Chicago	Citrus Products	3200 lbs.	$128.00	$108.00
Washington, D.C.	Los Angeles	Machine Parts	3200 lbs.	$430.00	$261.00
Tampa	Chicago	Machine Parts	3200 lbs.	$225.00	$119.00

Rates subject to change.
Reprinted, by permission, from *The Wall Street Journal,* September 19, 1973, p. 12.

two

Operations with Fractions and Decimals

2.1 FRACTIONS

In the cartoon above, the little girl is very upset with the concept of a **fraction.** The word fraction is derived from the Latin word "fracto", which means "to divide" or "to break". Thus, we can take one unit and "divide it" into two equal parts. Each of these parts is written as $\frac{1}{2}$ or 1/2 (read "one half"). the **fraction** $\frac{1}{2}$ consists of two numbers. The number above the line is called the **numerator** and indicates the number of equal parts of the whole being used. The number below the line is called the **denominator** and indicates the number of equal parts into which the whole has been divided. The line separating the 1 and the 2 is called a bar and means "divided by". In the fraction $\frac{3}{4}$ the **numerator** is 3, and the **denominator** is 4. The

fraction $\frac{3}{4}$ is used to represent 3 parts of a whole consisting of 4 parts. We can visualize this concept by using a diagram such as ,

, or  . The number $\frac{3}{4}$ can also be interpreted as a ratio. For example, stock market reports sometimes indicate that "the ratio of advancing issues to declining issues is 3 to 4"; that is, for every 7 stocks, 3 advanced and 4 declined (in price). For this reason, fractions are sometimes called rational numbers. We now give the definition of a rational number.

> The numerator of a fraction indicates the number of equal parts of the whole being used.

> The denominator of a fraction indicates the number of equal parts into which the whole has been divided.

Definition of rational number

DEFINITION 2.1 A rational number is a number which can be put in the form $\frac{a}{b}$, where a and b are integers and $b \neq 0$. The integer a is called the numerator and b is called the denominator.

In this chapter we shall call the rational number $\frac{a}{b}$ a fraction.

There are three different types of fractions:

Proper fractions. Fractions in which the numerator a is less than the denominator b (a and b positive). For example, $\frac{2}{3}$, $\frac{3}{5}$, and $\frac{4}{9}$.

Improper fractions. Fractions in which the numerator a is greater than or equal to the denominator b (a and b positive). For example, $\frac{3}{2}$, $\frac{9}{7}$, and $\frac{8}{8}$.

Mixed numbers. A number consisting of a whole number part and a fractional part. For example $3\frac{1}{4}$, $6\frac{6}{7}$, and $8\frac{3}{4}$.

Note that mixed numbers represent the addition of two numbers, a whole number and a fraction. Thus, $3\frac{1}{4}$ means $3 + \frac{1}{4}$ and $8\frac{3}{4}$ means $8 + \frac{3}{4}$. Mixed numbers can always be written as improper fractions by using the following procedure:

Changing mixed numbers to improper fractions

RULE 2.1 To change a mixed number to an improper fraction, multiply the whole number part by the denominator of the fractional part; add this product to the numerator of the fractional part to obtain the numerator of the improper fraction. The denominator of the improper fraction remains the same as the denominator of the fractional part of the mixed number.

Thus, $4\frac{3}{5}$ can be written as $\frac{(4 \times 5) + 3}{5} = \frac{23}{5}$

$3\frac{2}{9}$ can be written as $\frac{(3 \times 9) + 2}{9} = \frac{29}{9}$

and

$5\frac{7}{8}$ can be written as $\frac{(5 \times 8) + 7}{8} = \frac{47}{8}$.

Note that Rule 2.1 works because, for example, $4\frac{3}{5} = 4 + \frac{3}{5} = \frac{20}{5} + \frac{3}{5} = \frac{23}{5}$.

An alternate method for deducing the same result makes use of the following definition.

Equality of fractions

DEFINITION 2.2 $\frac{a}{b} = \frac{c}{d}$ provided that $a \times d = b \times c$.

Thus, $4 = \frac{4}{1} = \frac{20}{5}$ because $4 \times 5 = 1 \times 20$. Similarly, $\frac{-3}{5} = \frac{6}{-10}$ because

$(-3)(-10) = 5 \times 6$. Using Definition 2.2 we can also see that $\frac{1}{2}, \frac{2}{4}$, and $\frac{3}{6}$ are equal. We are now able to state the fundamental rule governing fractions.

Fundamental rule of fractions

> **RULE 2.2** If the numerator and denominator of a fraction are multiplied or divided by the same nonzero integer, the resulting fraction is equal to the original one.

Reduction of fractions

Thus, $\frac{9}{12}$ can be **reduced** to the equivalent fraction $\frac{3}{4}$ by dividing the numerator and denominator by 3. Since $\frac{3}{4}$ cannot be reduced any further (because 3 and 4 have no common divisor other than 1) we say that $\frac{3}{4}$ is in lowest terms. In general, a fraction is said to be reduced to **lowest terms** when there is no whole number greater than 1 which can be divided exactly (with no remainder) into both the numerator and the denominator. For example, the fraction $\frac{66}{99}$ can be reduced to $\frac{22}{33}$ by dividing the numerator and denominator by 3 (using Rule 2.2). However, $\frac{22}{33}$ is not reduced to lowest terms, since we can divide the numerator and denominator by 11 and obtain $\frac{2}{3}$. We usually write these steps in the form

$$
\begin{array}{c} 2 \\ \cancel{22} \\ \cancel{66} \\ \cancel{99} \\ \cancel{33} \\ 3 \end{array} \quad \text{or} \quad \frac{66}{99} = \frac{22}{33} = \frac{2}{3}
$$

Thus, $\frac{66}{99}$ reduced to lowest terms is $\frac{2}{3}$. The method that we have used will be referred to as the **trial and error method**.

Example 1

Reduce each of the following fractions to lowest terms.

(a) $\frac{66}{88}$ (b) $\frac{125}{175}$ (c) $\frac{226}{244}$

Solution

(a) We divide the numerator and denominator by 2 to obtain $\frac{66}{88} = \frac{33}{44}$. We then divide the numerator and denominator by 11, so that $\frac{66}{88} = \frac{33}{44} = \frac{3}{4}$. Thus, $\frac{66}{88}$ reduced to lowest terms is $\frac{3}{4}$.

(b) We divide the numerator and denominator by 5 to obtain $\frac{125}{175} = \frac{25}{35}$. We again divide the numerator and denominator by 5, so that $\frac{25}{35} = \frac{5}{7}$. Hence $\frac{125}{175} = \frac{25}{35} = \frac{5}{7}$. Thus, $\frac{125}{175}$ reduced to lowest terms is $\frac{5}{7}$.

(c) We divide the numerator and denominator by 2 to obtain $\frac{226}{244} = \frac{113}{122}$. But 113 and 122 have no common factors, thus $\frac{226}{244}$ reduced to lowest terms is $\frac{113}{122}$.

We finally remark that Rule 2.2 can also be used to change a fraction to an equivalent fraction with a given denominator. Thus, if we desire to change the fraction $\frac{2}{3}$ to a fraction with a denominator of 9, we can multiply the numerator and denominator of $\frac{2}{3}$ by 3 to obtain $\frac{2}{3} = \frac{2 \times 3}{3 \times 3} = \frac{6}{9}$.

Changing a fraction to an equivalent one with a given denominator

Example 2

Change the given fractions to an equivalent one with the given denominator.

(a) $\frac{2}{3}$ to a fraction with denominator 12

(b) $\frac{3}{4}$ to a fraction with denominator 16

(c) $\frac{9}{8}$ to a fraction with denominator 72

Solution

(a) We multiply the numerator and denominator by 4 to obtain $\frac{2}{3} = \frac{2 \times 4}{3 \times 4} = \frac{8}{12}$. Note that the number 4 was chosen because the original fraction had a denominator of 3 and we desired to obtain a denominator of 12 ($3 \times 4 = 12$).

(b) Since we want a denominator of 16, and we have 4 as a denominator, we multiply numerator and denominator by 4 to obtain $\frac{3}{4} = \frac{3 \times 4}{4 \times 4} = \frac{12}{16}$.

Remember, multiplying a number by $\frac{4}{4} = 1$ does not change the number.

(c) In this case, we wish to have a denominator of 72, so we multiply the numerator and denominator by 9 to obtain $\frac{9}{8} = \frac{9 \times 9}{8 \times 9} = \frac{81}{72}$.

PROGRESS TEST 1

1. In the fraction $\frac{3}{5}$, 3 is called the _____ and 5 is called the _____.

2. There are 3 kinds of fractions: _____, _____, and _____ numbers.

3. When reduced to lowest terms, the fraction $\frac{44}{36}$ equals _____.

4. When written as a fraction with a denominator of 12, the fraction $\frac{5}{6}$ equals _____.

EXERCISE 2.1

1. Classify each of the following fractions as proper, improper, or a mixed number.

    (a) $\frac{3}{4}$ (b) $\frac{5}{6}$ (c) $\frac{7}{3}$ (d) $3\frac{1}{8}$ (e) $\frac{5}{9}$ (f) $4\frac{1}{3}$

2. In Figure 2–1, the change (Chg.) for each of the most active stocks on Friday, May 25, 1973, is shown. Classify this change as a proper fraction, an improper fraction, or a mixed number. (Disregard the + or − sign.)

3. In Figure 2–1, the Opening Price (Open) for each of the most active stocks on Friday, May 25, 1973, is shown. Classify this fraction as proper, improper, or a mixed number.

---

1. numerator, denominator   2. proper, improper, mixed   3. $\frac{11}{9}$ 4. $\frac{10}{12}$

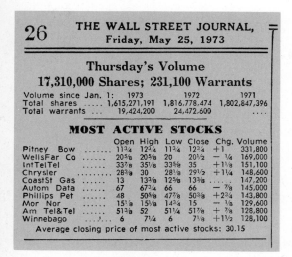

Figure 2–1   Reprinted by permission.

4. In Figure 2–1, the changes for Chrysler and Phillips Petroleum are $1\frac{1}{4}$ and $2\frac{3}{4}$, respectively. Change these two mixed numbers to improper fractions.

5. In Figure 2–1, the Open(ing) prices for Pitney Bow. and Wells Far. Co. are $11\frac{3}{4}$ and $20\frac{5}{8}$, respectively. Change these mixed numbers to improper fractions.

6. In the preceding chapter we remarked that $\frac{15}{6}$ equals 15 divided by 6 and wrote the following:

Converting improper fractions to mixed numbers.

$$\begin{array}{r} 2 \\ 6\overline{)15} \\ \underline{12} \\ 3 \end{array}$$

We then said that 15 divided by 6 equals 2 with a remainder of 3. This answer could also be written as $2\frac{3}{6}$. Thus, $\frac{15}{6} = 2\frac{3}{6}$. In general, to convert an improper fraction to a mixed number we divide the numerator by the denominator. The result is the whole part of the mixed number. The remainder over the denominator is the fractional part of the mixed number. For example, $\frac{7}{2} = 3\frac{1}{2}$ since 7 divided by 2 equals 3 with a remainder of 1. Using this procedure, convert the following improper fractions to mixed numbers:

(a) $\frac{11}{4}$ (b) $\frac{34}{7}$ (c) $\frac{99}{7}$ (d) $\frac{108}{11}$

7. Find the fraction that is equal to $\frac{13}{22}$:

(a) $\frac{52}{78}$ (b) $\frac{143}{2}$ (c) $\frac{52}{88}$ (d) $\frac{26}{12}$

8. Find the fraction that is equal to $\frac{7}{4}$:

(a) $\frac{36}{63}$ (b) $\frac{4}{7}$ (c) $1\frac{12}{16}$ (d) $2\frac{3}{2}$

9. Reduce to lowest terms:

(a) $\frac{125}{225}$ (b) $\frac{124}{155}$ (c) $\frac{81}{189}$ (d) $\frac{16}{140}$

10. Reduce to lowest terms:

(a) $\frac{66}{77}$ (b) $\frac{144}{240}$ (c) $\frac{38}{114}$ (d) $\frac{46}{184}$

11. Use Definition 2.2 to determine which of the following statements are true.

(a) $\dfrac{2}{5} = \dfrac{4}{10}$ (b) $\dfrac{-2}{-4} = \dfrac{1}{2}$ (c) $\dfrac{8}{13} = \dfrac{13}{21}$

(d) $\dfrac{-1}{3} = \dfrac{3}{-9}$ (e) $\dfrac{3}{-4} = \dfrac{-9}{12}$ (f) $\dfrac{13}{21} = \dfrac{21}{34}$

12. Use Rule 2.2 to find the missing number:

(a) $\dfrac{3}{4} = \dfrac{9}{?}$ (b) $\dfrac{16}{6} = \dfrac{8}{?}$ (c) $\dfrac{6}{15} = \dfrac{-24}{?}$ (e) $\dfrac{3}{-5} = \dfrac{-9}{?}$

13. Use Rule 2.2 to find the missing number:

(a) $\dfrac{3}{4} = \dfrac{?}{16}$ (b) $\dfrac{16}{6} = \dfrac{?}{36}$ (c) $\dfrac{6}{15} = \dfrac{?}{-90}$ (d) $\dfrac{3}{-5} = \dfrac{12}{?}$

14. In Figure 2-1, change all the fractions in the column labeled "Chg." to fractions with a denominator of 8.

15. In Figure 2-1, change all the fractions in the column labeled "Chg." to fractions with a denominator of 16.

2.2 THE GCD AND LCM OF TWO NUMBERS

The trial and error method of reducing fractions discussed in the preceding section is suitable when the fractions involved are not too large. For larger fractions the number of successive divisions may become too cumbersome. For example, to reduce $\dfrac{64}{256}$ we may divide numerator and denominator by 2 and obtain $\dfrac{32}{128}$. Dividing by 2 again we get $\dfrac{16}{64}$. Another division by 2 yields $\dfrac{8}{32}$, etc. Finally, after a total of 6 divisions by 2 we find that $\dfrac{64}{256} = \dfrac{1}{4}$. We could have simplified this problem if we had noticed that the highest number that divides 64 and 256 is 64. The integer 64 is called the greatest common factor (GCF) of 64 and 256.

Definition of GCD

In general, the **greatest common divisor** (GCD) of two integers is the largest integer that will divide both integers evenly (exactly). This number is sometimes called the greatest common factor (GCF).

Using the GCD to reduce fractions

To reduce a fraction to lowest terms with a single division, we should choose as divisors the largest number which will divide both the numerator and denominator of the fraction being reduced, that is, the GCD of the numerator and denominator. For example, to reduce $\frac{12}{18}$ to lowest terms, we could divide the numerator and denominator by 3 and obtain $\frac{4}{6}$, and then divide again the numerator and denominator of the new fraction $\frac{4}{6}$ by 2, obtaining $\frac{2}{3}$. However, instead of dividing by 3 and then again by 2, we could have divided by 6, the GCD of 12 and 18, and reduced $\frac{12}{18}$ to $\frac{2}{3}$ with a single division.

Example 1

Reduce $\frac{48}{60}$ to lowest terms.

Solution

The largest number that will divide both 48 and 60 (their GCD) is 12, so we divide the numerator and denominator by 12, obtaining $\frac{4}{5}$.

There is a procedure that can be used to find the GCD of any two numbers. To describe this procedure, which depends on the concept of a **prime** number, we need the following definition.

> **DEFINITION 2.3** A prime number is a whole number greater than 1 which is evenly (exactly) divisible by no positive whole number except itself and 1.

Definition of Prime Number

Thus, 4 is not a prime number since it is divisible by 2, but 3 is prime since 3 is only divisible by itself and 1. The first few prime numbers are 2, 3, 5, 7, 11, 13, 17, 19, etc. (One of the largest known primes appears at the beginning of this section. This number, discovered at the University of Illinois, is printed on letters mailed from the school.)

To find the greatest common divisor (GCD) of two numbers we use the following rule.

Finding the GCD of two numbers

> **RULE 2.3** (a) Write each number as a product of primes.
> (b) Select the factors **common** to both numbers.
> (c) The product of the factors selected in (b) is the GCD.
> (In case there are no common prime factors, the GCD is 1.)

For example, to find the GCD of 60 and 18 we write:

$$60 = 2 \times \boxed{2} \times \boxed{3} \times 5$$
$$18 = \boxed{2} \times \boxed{3} \times 3$$

The factors common to both numbers are 2 and 3; hence the GCD of 60 and 18 is $2 \times 3 = 6$.

To write 60 as a product of primes we could have used successive divisions by primes, that is, divide 60 by 2 to obtain 30, then divide 30 by 2 to obtain 15, then divide 15 by 3 to obtain 5 and finally divide 5 by 5 to obtain 1. We usually write this procedure as:

$$
\begin{array}{r|l}
60 & 2 \leftarrow \text{divide by 2} \\
30 & 2 \leftarrow \text{divide by 2} \\
15 & 3 \leftarrow \text{divide by 3} \\
5 & 5 \leftarrow \text{divide by 5} \\
1 &
\end{array}
\quad \text{so } 60 = 2 \times 2 \times 3 \times 5.
$$

Similarly,

$$
\begin{array}{r|l}
18 & 2 \leftarrow \text{divide by 2} \\
9 & 3 \leftarrow \text{divide by 3} \\
3 & 3 \leftarrow \text{divide by 3} \\
1 &
\end{array}
\quad \text{so } 18 = 2 \times 3 \times 3.
$$

5^4 exponent
↑
base

For convenience, we write 18 as 2×3^2. The number 3^2 means 3×3; the 2 is called the **exponent** and the 3 is the **base**. Similarly, $5^4 = 5 \times 5 \times 5 \times 5$. Here 4 is the exponent and 5 is the base.

Example 2

Find the GCD of 40 and 220.

Solution

$$
\begin{array}{r|l}
40 & 2 \\
20 & 2 \\
10 & 2 \\
5 & 5 \\
1 &
\end{array}
\qquad\qquad
\begin{array}{r|l}
220 & 2 \\
110 & 2 \\
55 & 5 \\
11 & 11 \\
1 &
\end{array}
$$

(a) $40 = 2 \times \boxed{2} \times \boxed{2} \times \boxed{5}$
$ 220 = \boxed{2} \times \boxed{2} \times \boxed{5} \times 11$

(b) The factors common to both numbers are 2, 2, and 5.
(c) The GCD of 40 and 220 is $2 \times 2 \times 5 = 20$ (the product of the numbers listed in (b)).

In a similar manner, the GCD of 60 and 126 is obtained as follows:

$$60 = 2 \times \boxed{2} \times \boxed{3} \times 5$$
$$126 = \boxed{2} \times \boxed{3} \times 3 \times 7$$

Thus the GCD of 60 and 126 is $2 \times 3 = 6$.

Example 3

Reduce the fractions $\dfrac{40}{220}$ and $\dfrac{60}{126}$.

Solution

Since the GCD of 40 and 220 is 20, we divide the numerator and denominator by 20 so, $\dfrac{40}{220} = \dfrac{40/20}{220/20} = \dfrac{2}{11}$. Similarly, since the GCD of 60 and 126 is 6 we divide the numerator and denominator by 6, so $\dfrac{60}{126} = \dfrac{60/6}{126/6} = \dfrac{10}{21}$.

PROGRESS TEST 1

1. The greatest common divisor of the two integers a and b is the largest integer c that will _____ into both a and b.

2. When written as a product of primes, 42 equals _____.

3. The GCD of 30 and 44 is _____.

4. To reduce the fraction $\dfrac{44}{66}$ we first find the _____ which is _____.

Another useful concept which depends upon the prime factorization of a number (the expression of the number as a product of primes) is that of the **lowest common denominator** (LCD) of two or more fractions. We use the lowest common denominator of two or more fractions when we add or subtract these fractions. For example, when adding $\dfrac{3}{4}$, $\dfrac{5}{6}$, and $\dfrac{1}{3}$ we must find a common denominator for the given fractions. For ease of computation we look for the LCD of the fractions. The LCD is the **smallest** number which all the denominators of the given fractions will divide evenly. This number is also called the LCM (least common multiple) of the denominators. In the case of the fractions $\dfrac{3}{4}$, $\dfrac{5}{6}$, and $\dfrac{1}{3}$, the LCD is 12, since it is the smallest number which all three denominators (4, 3 and 6) will divide evenly. To add these fractions, replace them by equivalent ones with denominators of 12 and then add, using the general rule for fractions with like denominators. Hence

$$\frac{3}{4} + \frac{5}{6} + \frac{1}{3} = \frac{9}{12} + \frac{10}{12} + \frac{4}{12} = \frac{23}{12}.$$

Finding the LCD of two or more fractions

---

1. divide evenly   2. $2 \times 3 \times 7$ 3. 2   4. GCD of 44 and 66, 22

In this example, we found by inspection that 12 was the LCD of $\frac{3}{4}$, $\frac{5}{6}$, and $\frac{1}{3}$. However, when working with more complicated fractions, it would be convenient to have a systematic procedure for finding the lowest common denominator. For example, if we wish to find the sum of $\frac{3}{4}$ and $\frac{7}{18}$, we first find the LCD of $\frac{3}{4}$ and $\frac{7}{18}$, or equivalently, the least common multiple (LCM) of 4 and 18. We first note that $4 = 2 \times 2 = 2^2$ and $18 = 2 \times 3 \times 3 = 2 \times 3^2$. We compare the powers of the primes present in all of the numbers and then select each such prime factor raised to the highest power to which it occurs (in this case the 2^2 and 3^2). Thus the LCM of 4 and 18 is $2^2 \times 3^2 = 4 \times 9 = 36$. Hence the LCD of $\frac{3}{4}$ and $\frac{7}{18}$ is 36. To find their sum we simply replace $\frac{3}{4}$ and $\frac{7}{18}$ by the equivalent fractions $\frac{27}{36}$ and $\frac{14}{36}$, respectively, and add as indicated:

$$\frac{3}{4} + \frac{7}{18} = \frac{27}{36} + \frac{14}{36} = \frac{27 + 14}{36} = \frac{41}{36}$$

Finding the LCM of two or more numbers

In general, we can find the LCM of two numbers using the following rule:

> **RULE 2.4** (a) Write each number as a product of primes (using exponents).
> (b) Compare the powers of the primes present in all of the numbers and select each such prime factor, raised to the **highest** power to which it occurs.
> (c) The product of the factors obtained in (b) is the LCM of the numbers.

Example 4

Find the LCM of 30 and 132.

Solution

$$
\begin{array}{r|l} 30 & 2 \\ 15 & 3 \\ 5 & 5 \\ 1 & \end{array}
\qquad\qquad
\begin{array}{r|l} 132 & 2 \\ 66 & 2 \\ 33 & 3 \\ 11 & 11 \\ 1 & \end{array}
$$

so $30 = 2 \times 3 \times 5$ and $132 = 2^2 \times 3 \times 11$

We select $2^2, 3, 5,$ and 11; hence the LCM is $2^2 \times 3 \times 5 \times 11 = 660$.

PROGRESS TEST 2

1. $\frac{3}{5} + \frac{1}{5}$ equals _____

2. The LCD of two or more fractions is the _____ number which all the denominators of the given fraction will divide evenly. This number is sometimes called the

_____.

3. The GCD of 60 and 264 is _____.

Finally we remark that the LCM or GCD of three or more numbers can be found by using a technique similar to the one used for two numbers. For example, to find the GCD of 15, 20, and 30 we proceed as follows:

$$
\begin{array}{c|c}
15 & 3 \\
5 & 5 \\
1 &
\end{array}
\qquad
\begin{array}{c|c}
20 & 2 \\
10 & 2 \\
5 & 5 \\
1 &
\end{array}
\qquad
\begin{array}{c|c}
30 & 2 \\
15 & 3 \\
5 & 5 \\
1 &
\end{array}
$$

Thus,

$$15 = 3 \times \boxed{5}$$
$$20 = 2 \times 2 \times \boxed{5}$$
$$30 = 2 \times 3 \times \boxed{5}$$

We now select the factor common to all numbers. The GCD is 5. (Note that 3 was not included in the GCD since 3 is not a factor of 20.) Similarly, to obtain the LCM of 15, 20 and 30 we write:

$$15 = 3 \times 5 = 3 \times 5$$
$$20 = 2 \times 2 \times 5 = 2^2 \times 5$$
$$30 = 2 \times 3 \times 5 = 2 \times 3 \times 5$$

For each prime we select the prime factors raised to the highest power to which they occur, in this case 2^2, 3 and 5. The LCM of 15, 20, and 30 is $2^2 \times 3 \times 5 = 60$.

This method can be shortened by following the following procedure:

(1) Write the numbers in a horizontal row and then divide by a prime factor common to **two or more** of the numbers.

(2) Continue this process until there are no two quotients that are divisible by any prime number.

The product of the prime numbers and the final quotients will equal the LCM. For example, the LCM of 18, 12 and 20 can be found by following steps (1) and (2).

$$
\begin{array}{r|ccc}
2 & 18 & 12 & 20 \\
2 & 9 & 6 & 10 \\
3 & 9 & 3 & 5 \\
  & 3 & 1 & 5
\end{array}
$$

1. $\frac{4}{5}$ 2. smallest, least common multiple (LCM)   3. 12

The LCM is $2 \times 2 \times 3 \times 3 \times 1 \times 5 = 180.$* We proceed similarly to find the LCM of 10, 18 and 25.

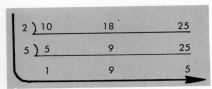

The LCM is $2 \times 5 \times 9 \times 5 = 450$. Note that in this case, the LCM is **not** expressed as a product of primes. If we wish to express the LCM as a product of primes, we proceed as follows:

2)10	18	25
3) 5	9	25
3) 5	3	25
5) 5	1	25
5)1	1	5
1	1	1

The LCM is $2 \times 3 \times 3 \times 5 \times 5 = 450$. In this case we divided by successive primes and the LCM is expressed as a **product of primes.**

EXERCISE 2.2

1. Reduce the following fractions to lowest terms by finding the GCD of the numerator and denominator.
   (a) $\dfrac{12}{16}$ (b) $\dfrac{63}{70}$ (c) $\dfrac{39}{52}$ (d) $\dfrac{48}{72}$ (e) $\dfrac{0}{10}$

2. Reduce the following fractions to lowest terms by finding the GCD of the numerator and denominator.
   (a) $\dfrac{15}{35}$ (b) $\dfrac{27}{81}$ (c) $\dfrac{42}{49}$ (d) $\dfrac{63}{147}$

3. Write each of the following numbers as a product of primes
   (a) 324   (b) 180   (c) 1200   (d) 252   (e) 7350

4. Find the GCD of:
   (a) 5 and 10   (b) 18 and 27   (c) 42 and 35

5. Find the GCD of:
   (a) 3 and 7   (b) 15 and 25   (c) 90 and 27

6. Find the LCM of:
   (a) 5 and 10   (b) 18 and 27   (c) 42 and 35

7. Find the LCM of:
   (a) 3 and 7   (b) 15 and 25   (c) 90 and 27

---

*Instead of writing $2 \times 2 \times 3 \times 3 \times 1 \times 5$ we shall henceforth omit the 1 and write $2 \times 2 \times 3 \times 3 \times 5$.

8. Find the LCD for the following fractions:

    (a) $\dfrac{11}{15}, \dfrac{3}{5}$ (b) $\dfrac{2}{5}, \dfrac{6}{7}$ (c) $\dfrac{1}{14}, \dfrac{1}{35}$

9. Find the LCD for the following fractions:

    (a) $\dfrac{1}{15}$ and $\dfrac{1}{25}$ (b) $\dfrac{1}{18}$ and $\dfrac{1}{27}$ (c) $\dfrac{1}{90}$ and $\dfrac{1}{27}$

10. Find the LCM of:
    (a) 3, 6 and 21   (b) 12, 15 and 30   (c) 15, 45 and 90

11. Find the LCM of:
    (a) 3, 15 and 2   (b) 12, 6 and 15   (c) 12, 18 and 24

12. Find the GCD of:
    (a) 3, 6 and 21   (b) 12, 15 and 30   (c) 15, 45 and 90

13. Find the GCD of:
    (a) 3, 15 and 2   (b) 12, 6 and 15   (c) 12, 18 and 24

14. Using the results obtained in Problem 10, add the following fractions:

    (a) $\dfrac{1}{3} + \dfrac{1}{6} + \dfrac{1}{21}$ (b) $\dfrac{1}{12} + \dfrac{1}{15} + \dfrac{1}{30}$

    (c) $\dfrac{1}{15} + \dfrac{1}{45} + \dfrac{1}{90}$

15. Using the results obtained in Problem 11, add the following fractions:

    (a) $\dfrac{1}{3} + \dfrac{1}{15} + \dfrac{1}{2}$ (b) $\dfrac{1}{12} + \dfrac{1}{6} + \dfrac{1}{15}$

    (c) $\dfrac{1}{12} + \dfrac{1}{18} + \dfrac{1}{24}$

2.3 ADDITION AND SUBTRACTION OF FRACTIONS

In the headline on the preceding page left, The First of Chicago Bank has **increased** the Prime Rate by $\frac{1}{4}$%. This is an example of the operation of **addition**. On the other hand, the headline on the right states that The Chase Manhattan Bank has **cut** the Prime Rate (by $\frac{1}{4}$%). This is an example of the operation of **subtraction**.

Addition of fractions with like denominators

In the preceding section we mentioned that two fractions with "like" denominators could be added by simply adding the numerators and placing the result over the same denominator. Thus, $\frac{3}{7}+\frac{2}{7}=\frac{5}{7}$, $\frac{1}{9}+\frac{4}{9}=\frac{5}{9}$ and $\frac{3}{11}+\frac{7}{11}=\frac{10}{11}$. In general, we have:

DEFINITION 2.4 $\dfrac{a}{b}+\dfrac{c}{b}=\dfrac{a+c}{b}$

If more than two fractions are involved, we use a similar procedure. Thus, to add $\frac{1}{7}+\frac{2}{7}+\frac{3}{7}$, we proceed similarly and obtain $\frac{1+2+3}{7}=\frac{6}{7}$.

Addition of fractions with different denominators

To add two fractions with different denominators we give the following definition:

DEFINITION 2.5 $\dfrac{a}{b}+\dfrac{c}{d}=\dfrac{ad}{bd}+\dfrac{bc}{bd}=\dfrac{ad+bc}{bd}$

Example 1

Using Definition 2.5, find the sum of $\frac{2}{3}+\frac{3}{8}$.

Solution

$\frac{2}{3}+\frac{3}{8}=\frac{a}{b}+\frac{c}{d}=\frac{ad+bc}{bd}$. Thus, a = 2, b = 3, c = 3, d = 8, so ad + bc = $(2\times8)+(3\times3)$ and bd = $3\times8=24$. Hence, $\frac{2}{3}+\frac{3}{8}=\frac{(2\times8)+(3\times3)}{3\times8}$ $=\frac{16+9}{24}=\frac{25}{24}$.

We usually skip the intermediate steps and simply write

$$\frac{2}{3}+\frac{3}{8}=\frac{16+9}{24}=\frac{25}{24}.$$

The procedure given in Definition 2.5 sometimes produces a denominator that is larger than needed. For example, in adding $\frac{2}{3} + \frac{1}{6}$ using Definition 2.5 we would use 3×6 as our denominator and obtain $\frac{12+3}{18} = \frac{15}{18} = \frac{5}{6}$. If we had observed that the LCM of 3 and 6 is 6, we would have used 6 as our **lowest** common denominator and obtained $\frac{4}{6} + \frac{1}{6} = \frac{4+1}{6} = \frac{5}{6}$. Thus, an alternate procedure for adding two or more fractions is given below.

> **RULE 2.5**   To add two or more fractions:
> (1) Find the LCD of the fractions (using Rule 2.4).
> (2) Express each fraction as an equivalent fraction having the LCD as denominator (using Rule 2.2).
> (3) Add the resulting fractions (using Definition 2.4).
> (4) Reduce to lowest terms if necessary (using Rule 2.2).

Example 2

Using the LCD to add fractions

$$\frac{1}{2} + \frac{5}{16} + \frac{5}{12}.$$

Solution

(1) The LCD of 2, 16, and 12 is 48.

(2) $\frac{1}{2} = \frac{24}{48}$

$\frac{5}{16} = \frac{15}{48}$

$\frac{5}{12} = \frac{20}{48}$

(3) $\frac{1}{2} + \frac{5}{16} + \frac{5}{12} = \frac{24}{48} + \frac{15}{48} + \frac{20}{48} = \frac{59}{48}$

PROGRESS TEST 1

1. The sum of $\frac{3}{7}$ and $\frac{2}{7}$ equals _____.

2. If we use Definition 2.5 to add $\frac{3}{4}$ and $\frac{5}{6}$, the denominator of the new fraction will be _____.

3. The LCD of $\frac{3}{4}$ and $\frac{5}{6}$ is _____.

4. $\frac{3}{4} + \frac{5}{6}$ equals _____.

---

1. $\frac{5}{7}$ 2. 24   3. 12   4. $\frac{19}{12}$

The procedure outlined in Rule 2.5 can be modified to subtract fractions. Thus, to subtract $\frac{3}{4}$ from $\frac{5}{6}$, that is, to find $\frac{5}{6} - \frac{3}{4}$, we follow a procedure similar to the one in Rule 2.5.

(1) The LCD is 12

(2) $\frac{5}{6} = \frac{10}{12}$ $\frac{3}{4} = \frac{9}{12}$

(3) $\frac{5}{6} - \frac{3}{4} = \frac{10-9}{12} = \frac{1}{12}$

Example 3

Subtract $\frac{5}{9}$ from $\frac{5}{6}$.

Solution

Following Rule 2.5 we have

(1) the LCD of $\frac{5}{9}$ and $\frac{5}{6}$ is 18

(2) $\frac{5}{6} = \frac{15}{18}$ $\frac{5}{9} = \frac{10}{18}$

(3) $\frac{5}{6} - \frac{5}{9} = \frac{15-10}{18} = \frac{5}{18}$

Addition and subtraction of mixed numbers

When mixed numbers are to be added (or subtracted), the whole numbers and fractions may be added (or subtracted) separately and then the results combined. For example, $3\frac{3}{4}$ and $5\frac{2}{5}$ can be added as follows:

(1) The LCD of 4 and 5 is 20

(2) $3\frac{3}{4} = 3\frac{15}{20}$

$5\frac{2}{5} = 5\frac{8}{20}$

The sum is $8\frac{23}{20} = 9\frac{3}{20}$.

Alternately, we could have proceeded as follows:

$$3\frac{3}{4} = \frac{15}{4} \text{ and } 5\frac{2}{5} = \frac{27}{5}$$

so

$$3\frac{3}{4} + 5\frac{2}{5} = \frac{15}{4} + \frac{27}{5}$$

Using Rule 2.5 we have

(1) The LCD of $\dfrac{15}{4}$ and $\dfrac{27}{5}$ is 20

(2) $\dfrac{15}{4} = \dfrac{75}{20}$ and $\dfrac{27}{5} = \dfrac{108}{20}$

(3) $\dfrac{15}{4} + \dfrac{27}{5} = \dfrac{75}{20} + \dfrac{108}{20} = \dfrac{183}{20} = 9\dfrac{3}{20}$

Example 4

Find the sum of $3\dfrac{5}{18} + 5\dfrac{7}{40}$.

Solution

We first find the LCM of 18 and 40 by using Rule 2.4.

$$
\begin{array}{c|c}
18 & 2 \\
9 & 3 \\
3 & 3 \\
1 &
\end{array}
\qquad\qquad
\begin{array}{c|c}
40 & 2 \\
20 & 2 \\
10 & 2 \\
5 & 5 \\
1 &
\end{array}
$$

So

$$18 = 2 \times 3 \times 3 = 2 \times 3^2$$
$$40 = 2 \times 2 \times 2 \times 5 = 2^3 \times 5$$

We select 2^3, 3^2, and 5, hence the LCM is $2^3 \times 3^2 \times 5 = 360$. Next we add the whole numbers and fractions separately.

$$3\dfrac{5}{18} = 3\dfrac{100}{360}$$
$$+\,5\dfrac{7}{40} = 5\dfrac{63}{360}$$
$$\overline{\qquad\qquad 8\dfrac{163}{360}}$$

Thus, $3\dfrac{5}{18} + 5\dfrac{7}{40} = 8\dfrac{163}{360}$. Similarly, to compute $3\dfrac{5}{18} - 1\dfrac{7}{40}$ we proceed as follows:

$$3\dfrac{5}{18} = 3\dfrac{100}{360}$$
$$-\,1\dfrac{7}{40} = 1\dfrac{63}{360}$$
$$\overline{\qquad\qquad 2\dfrac{37}{360}}$$

In case the fractional part of the number to be subtracted is larger than the fractional part from which we are subtracting, it is advantageous to first convert the mixed numbers to improper fractions and then perform the subtraction in the usual manner. For example, to compute $5\frac{7}{40} - 3\frac{5}{18}$ we might try to proceed as in the problem above. However, we notice that $\frac{100}{360}$ is larger than $\frac{63}{360}$, so we convert $5\frac{7}{40}$ to $\frac{207}{40}$ and $3\frac{5}{18}$ to $\frac{59}{18}$. Then,

$$5\frac{7}{40} - 3\frac{5}{18} = \frac{207}{40} - \frac{59}{18}$$

The LCM of 40 and 18 is 360 so we rewrite $\frac{207}{40}$ as $\frac{1863}{360}$ and $\frac{59}{18}$ as $\frac{1180}{360}$. Thus,

$$5\frac{7}{40} - 3\frac{5}{18} = \frac{207}{40} - \frac{59}{18} = \frac{1863}{360} - \frac{1180}{360} = \frac{683}{360} = 1\frac{323}{360}$$

PROGRESS TEST 2

1. $\frac{7}{8} - \frac{5}{12}$ equals _____.

2. $2\frac{1}{4} + 5\frac{3}{9}$ equals _____.

3. $3\frac{8}{9} + 7\frac{1}{12} - 2\frac{3}{18}$ equals _____.

Many problems in business require a knowledge of addition and subtraction of fractions. We now present a few of these problems.

Example 5

A necessary procedure for a business is the determination of the payroll. The hourly sheet for USF is shown below. Add the hours for the first week, and then for the second week. Find the "Tot. Hours" for both weeks.

Solution

The hours for the first week are:

$$5\frac{3}{4} + 8\frac{1}{4} + 8 + 7\frac{1}{2} + 8\frac{3}{4}$$

---

1. $\frac{11}{24}$ 2. $7\frac{7}{12}$ 3. $8\frac{29}{36}$

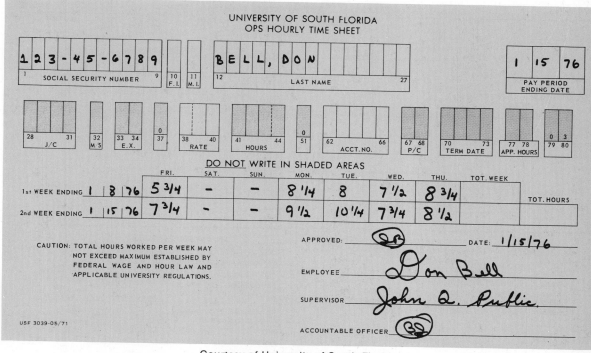

Courtesy of University of South Florida

We add the whole parts and the fractions separately, obtaining:

$$(5 + 8 + 8 + 7 + 8) + \left(\frac{3}{4} + \frac{1}{4} + \frac{1}{2} + \frac{3}{4}\right)$$

$$= 36 + \left(\frac{3}{4} + \frac{1}{4} + \frac{2}{4} + \frac{3}{4}\right)$$

$$= 36 + \frac{9}{4} = 36 + 2\frac{1}{4} = 38\frac{1}{4}$$

Similarly, the hours for the second week are

$$(7 + 9 + 10 + 7 + 8) + \left(\frac{3}{4} + \frac{1}{2} + \frac{1}{4} + \frac{3}{4} + \frac{1}{2}\right)$$

$$= 41 + \left(\frac{3}{4} + \frac{2}{4} + \frac{1}{4} + \frac{3}{4} + \frac{2}{4}\right) = 41 + \frac{11}{4} = 41 + 2\frac{3}{4} = 43\frac{3}{4}$$

Therefore, the total hours are

$$38\frac{1}{4} + 43\frac{3}{4} = 81 + \frac{1}{4} + \frac{3}{4} = 82$$

Example 6

(An Application). When ordering merchandise through the mail, it is very important to know the weight of the merchandise. In the following form, add the weight of the individual items and find the total weight.

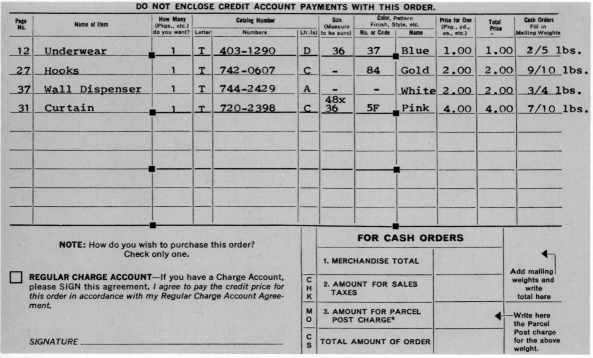

Page No.	Name of Item	How Many (Pkgs., etc.) do you want?	Catalog Number		Size (Measure to be sure)	Color, Pattern Finish, Style, etc.		Price for One (Pkg., yd., ea., etc.)	Total Price	Cash Orders Fill in Mailing Weights
			Letter	Numbers	Ltr.(s)	No. or Code	Name			
12	Underwear	1	T	403-1290	D	36	37	Blue	1.00	1.00	2/5 lbs.
27	Hooks	1	T	742-0607	C	-	84	Gold	2.00	2.00	9/10 lbs.
37	Wall Dispenser	1	T	744-2429	A	-	-	White	2.00	2.00	3/4 lbs.
31	Curtain	1	T	720-2398	C	48x 36	5F	Pink	4.00	4.00	7/10 lbs.

DO NOT ENCLOSE CREDIT ACCOUNT PAYMENTS WITH THIS ORDER.

NOTE: How do you wish to purchase this order?
Check only one.

☐ **REGULAR CHARGE ACCOUNT**—If you have a Charge Account, please SIGN this agreement. *I agree to pay the credit price for this order in accordance with my Regular Charge Account Agreement.*

SIGNATURE _____

FOR CASH ORDERS

C H K M O C S	1. MERCHANDISE TOTAL	
	2. AMOUNT FOR SALES TAXES	
	3. AMOUNT FOR PARCEL POST CHARGE*	
	TOTAL AMOUNT OF ORDER	

Add mailing weights and write total here

Write here the Parcel Post charge for the above weight.

Courtesy of J. C. Penney Company, Inc.

Solution

To find the total weight we have to add $\dfrac{2}{5} + \dfrac{9}{10} + \dfrac{3}{4} + \dfrac{7}{10}$. The LCD is 20. Writing each fraction with 20 as denominator we have

$$\frac{2}{5} = \frac{8}{20}, \quad \frac{9}{10} = \frac{18}{20}, \quad \frac{3}{4} = \frac{15}{20}, \quad \frac{7}{10} = \frac{14}{20}.$$

Hence $\dfrac{2}{5} + \dfrac{9}{10} + \dfrac{3}{4} + \dfrac{7}{10} = \dfrac{8}{20} + \dfrac{18}{20} + \dfrac{15}{20} + \dfrac{14}{20} = \dfrac{55}{20} = 2\dfrac{15}{20}.$

Thus, the total weight is $2\dfrac{15}{20} = 2\dfrac{3}{4}$ lbs.

EXERCISE 2.3

1. Find the indicated sums:

   (a) $\dfrac{3}{8} + \dfrac{2}{8}$ (b) $\dfrac{3}{17} + \dfrac{4}{17}$ (c) $\dfrac{18}{94} + \dfrac{32}{94}$

2. Find the indicated sums:

   (a) $\dfrac{14}{77} + \dfrac{3}{77} + \dfrac{48}{77}$ (b) $\dfrac{4}{187} + \dfrac{3}{187} + \dfrac{169}{187}$

3. Find the indicated differences:

   (a) $\dfrac{7}{8} - \dfrac{3}{8}$ (b) $\dfrac{4}{7} - \dfrac{2}{7}$ (c) $\dfrac{3}{19} - \dfrac{1}{19}$

4. Find the indicated differences:

   (a) $\dfrac{144}{177} - \dfrac{107}{177}$ (b) $\dfrac{345}{979} - \dfrac{279}{979}$

5. Use Definition 2.5 to find the sums:

   (a) $\dfrac{3}{4} + \dfrac{2}{3}$ (b) $\dfrac{3}{7} + \dfrac{3}{8}$ (c) $\dfrac{8}{13} + \dfrac{4}{5}$

6. Use Rule 2.5 to find the sums:

   (a) $\dfrac{1}{12} + \dfrac{7}{8}$ (b) $\dfrac{3}{14} + \dfrac{5}{21}$ (c) $\dfrac{9}{14} + \dfrac{7}{8}$

7. Add the following fractions:

   (a) $\dfrac{3}{4} + \dfrac{7}{12}$ (b) $\dfrac{5}{9} + \dfrac{17}{18}$ (c) $\dfrac{7}{8} + \dfrac{19}{36}$

8. Add the following fractions:

   (a) $\dfrac{7}{10} + \dfrac{7}{15} + \dfrac{3}{5}$ (b) $\dfrac{3}{4} + \dfrac{7}{15} + \dfrac{7}{12}$

9. Find the LCM of 16 and 40; then add $\dfrac{1}{16} + \dfrac{1}{40}$.

10. Find the LCM of 14 and 6; then add $\dfrac{1}{14} + \dfrac{1}{6}$.

11. Find the LCM of 42 and 12; then subtract $\dfrac{1}{12} - \dfrac{1}{42}$.

12. Find the LCM of 18 and 30; then subtract $\dfrac{1}{18} - \dfrac{1}{30}$.

13. Perform the following operations:

   (a) $\dfrac{1}{4} + \dfrac{1}{3} + \dfrac{7}{8} - \dfrac{1}{6}$

   (b) $\dfrac{3}{4} - \dfrac{1}{14} + \dfrac{3}{8} - \dfrac{1}{7} - \dfrac{1}{2}$

14. Perform the following operations:

   (a) $\dfrac{3}{5} + \dfrac{4}{9} + \dfrac{1}{18} - \dfrac{5}{18}$

   (b) $\dfrac{1}{5} + \dfrac{2}{15} + \dfrac{7}{6} - \dfrac{3}{4}$

15. Add the following mixed numbers:

   (a) $3\dfrac{3}{4} + 5\dfrac{7}{8}$ (b) $7\dfrac{6}{7} + 11\dfrac{1}{12}$ (c) $8\dfrac{7}{8} + 13\dfrac{7}{12}$

16. Add the following mixed numbers:

   (a) $3\dfrac{8}{9} + 11\dfrac{2}{7} + 3\dfrac{4}{7}$

   (b) $4\dfrac{3}{7} + 3\dfrac{1}{12} + 4\dfrac{5}{6}$

17. Subtract the following mixed numbers:

(a) $9\frac{3}{8} - 7\frac{1}{5}$

(b) $3\frac{5}{8} - 1\frac{2}{7}$

18. Subtract the following mixed numbers:

(a) $6\frac{1}{4} - 2\frac{3}{8}$

(b) $7\frac{1}{2} - 2\frac{7}{8}$

19. If in Example 5 of this section the employee worked $6\frac{3}{4}$, $5\frac{1}{2}$, $3\frac{1}{4}$, $7\frac{3}{4}$, and $8\frac{1}{2}$ hours each day, respectively, what was the total number of hours for the week?

20. If the hours worked were $10\frac{1}{8}$, $7\frac{3}{4}$, $9\frac{1}{2}$, $8\frac{3}{8}$, and $11\frac{2}{5}$ each day, respectively, what was the total number of hours worked for the week?

21. If in Example 6 of this section the weight of the items was $\frac{4}{5}$, $\frac{3}{7}$, $\frac{1}{2}$ and $\frac{7}{10}$ lb., respectively, what was the total weight?

22. If a man needed $36\frac{1}{4}$ feet of baseboard for his living room and $45\frac{3}{8}$ feet for his kitchen, what was the total amount of baseboard he needed?

23. If the man of Problem 22 needed $28\frac{3}{5}$, $17\frac{2}{3}$, and $16\frac{1}{6}$ feet each for three other rooms, what was the additional amount of baseboard he needed?

24. A square room $12\frac{3}{8}$ feet on each side needed a baseboard installed on each of the four walls. Rip Cutwell, the carpenter in charge of the installation, noticed that the door opening (which did not take any baseboard) was $3\frac{1}{12}$ feet. How much baseboard was needed for the room?

25. If in Problem 24 the room was $11\frac{2}{5}$ feet on each side, how much baseboard was needed?

26. Ms. Sue Ann Sew needed $7\frac{3}{4}$ yards of material for her curtains. If she had only $6\frac{7}{12}$ yards, how much more material did she need?

27.   If the curtains of Problem 26 required $7\frac{1}{8}$ yards, how much more material would be needed?

28.   A mail order house mailed 3 packages weighing $20\frac{1}{8}$, $3\frac{3}{4}$, and $7\frac{1}{12}$ lb., respectively. What was the total weight of the three packages?

29.   If in Problem 28, the weights were $5\frac{1}{8}$, $6\frac{3}{4}$, and $8\frac{7}{12}$ lb., what was the total weight of the three packages?

30.   A component manufactured by Heavy Brothers weighs $57\frac{3}{4}$ lb. If a similar component manufactured by Light Brothers weighs $28\frac{7}{8}$ lb., what is the difference in weight between the two components?

31.   A recipe for French dressing calls for the following ingredients:

$\frac{1}{4}$ cup of oil $\frac{1}{16}$ cup of paprika

$\frac{3}{4}$ cup of mayonnaise $\frac{1}{16}$ cup of mustard

$\frac{1}{4}$ cup of vinegar $\frac{1}{32}$ cup of salt

$\frac{1}{8}$ cup of sugar

If you combine all these ingredients, how many cups of French dressing will you have? (Assume there is no volume loss in the mixture.)

32.   The Good Taste Restaurant uses the following ingredients to make medium gravy:
1 cup of meat broth

$\frac{1}{4}$ cup of cold water

$\frac{1}{8}$ cup of flour

How much medium gravy can we make with these ingredients? (Assume there is no volume loss in the mixture.)

33.   A door is $3\frac{7}{16}$ feet wide. If the door opening is $3\frac{1}{8}$ feet, how much must we cut from the edge of the door to fit it into the opening?

34.   U-Tackle Shop has a piece of rope 100 feet long. During the day they sold three pieces measuring $8\frac{3}{4}$, $25\frac{1}{2}$, and $17\frac{7}{16}$ feet, respectively. How much more must they sell to be at the end of their rope?

2.4 MULTIPLICATION AND DIVISION OF FRACTIONS

In the ad above we can see that each package of peas weighs $1\frac{1}{2} = \frac{3}{2}$ lbs. If we buy 3 packages how many pounds of peas are we buying? To obtain the answer to this problem we would have to multiply 3 times $\frac{3}{2}$. In Chapter 1 we defined the operation of multiplication as a process of repeated addition; extending this idea to fractions we can deduce that $3 \times \frac{3}{2} = \frac{3}{2} + \frac{3}{2} + \frac{3}{2} = \frac{9}{2}$. We define the multiplication of fractions precisely in this manner.

Multiplication of fractions

> **DEFINITION 2.6** The product of $\frac{a}{b}$ and $\frac{c}{d}$ denoted by $\frac{a}{b} \times \frac{c}{d}$ is defined by
>
> $$\frac{a}{b} \times \frac{c}{d} = \frac{a \times c}{b \times d} = \frac{ac}{bd}$$

Thus, the solution of the problem stated at the beginning of this section is $\frac{3 \times 3}{1 \times 2} = \frac{9}{2} = 4\frac{1}{2}$ pounds. Note that any integer can be written as a fraction with a denominator of 1. Thus, $4 = \frac{4}{1}$, $-3 = \frac{-3}{1}$, and $0 = \frac{0}{1}$. This means that every integer is a rational number, since every integer a can be written in the form $\frac{a}{b}$ where $b = 1$.

Example 1

Compute the following products.

    (a) $\frac{3}{8} \times \frac{3}{7}$ (b) $\frac{2}{15} \times \frac{3}{7}$ (c) $\frac{7}{11} \times \frac{3}{4}$

Solution

(a) $\dfrac{3}{8} \times \dfrac{3}{7} = \dfrac{3 \times 3}{8 \times 7} = \dfrac{9}{56}$

(b) $\dfrac{2}{15} \times \dfrac{3}{7} = \dfrac{2 \times 3}{15 \times 7} = \dfrac{6}{105} = \dfrac{2}{35}$

(c) $\dfrac{7}{11} \times \dfrac{3}{4} = \dfrac{7 \times 3}{11 \times 4} = \dfrac{21}{44}$

In many instances, it is possible to simplify multiplication problems by the use of Rule 2.2. For example, to solve the problem $\dfrac{3}{8} \times \dfrac{4}{5}$ we use Definition 2.6 and obtain $\dfrac{3}{8} \times \dfrac{4}{5} = \dfrac{3 \times 4}{8 \times 5} = \dfrac{12}{40} = \dfrac{3}{10}$.

However, since the value of a fraction does not change if the numerator and denominator are divided by the same number (Rule 2.2), we could have proceeded as follows:

$$\dfrac{3}{8} \times \dfrac{4}{5} = \dfrac{3}{\overset{}{\underset{2}{8}}} \times \dfrac{\overset{1}{4}}{5} = \dfrac{3}{10}$$

(dividing the numerator and denominator by 4 as indicated).
For computational speed we generally write

$$\dfrac{3}{\overset{}{\underset{2}{8}}} \times \dfrac{\overset{1}{4}}{5} = \dfrac{3}{10}$$

Similarly, to multiply $\dfrac{5}{7}$ times $\dfrac{14}{15}$ we write

$$\dfrac{\overset{1}{5}}{\underset{1}{7}} \times \dfrac{\overset{2}{14}}{\underset{3}{15}} = \dfrac{2}{3}$$

(dividing out common factors of 5 and 7 in the numerator and denominator of the indicated product).

Example 2

Perform the indicated multiplication.

(a) $\dfrac{14}{15} \times \dfrac{3}{7}$

(b) $8 \times \dfrac{3}{16}$

Solution

$$\text{(a)} \quad \frac{\overset{2}{\cancel{14}}}{\underset{5}{\cancel{15}}} \times \frac{\overset{1}{\cancel{3}}}{\underset{1}{\cancel{7}}} = \frac{2}{5}$$

$$\text{(b)} \quad 8 \times \frac{3}{16} = \frac{8}{1} \times \frac{3}{\underset{2}{\cancel{16}}}^{1} = \frac{3}{2} = 1\frac{1}{2}$$

Mixed numbers can be multiplied by converting them to improper fractions and proceeding as illustrated in Example 2.

Multiplication of mixed numbers

Example 3

Multiply $2\frac{2}{3}$ and $2\frac{3}{8}$.

Solution

$$2\frac{2}{3} = \frac{8}{3} \text{ and } 2\frac{3}{8} = \frac{19}{8}$$

so

$$2\frac{2}{3} \times 2\frac{3}{8} = \frac{\overset{1}{\cancel{8}}}{3} \times \frac{19}{\underset{1}{\cancel{8}}} = \frac{19}{3} = 6\frac{1}{3}$$

Example 4

On Monday, July 2, 1973, the cost of one share of American Motors stock was \$$7\frac{1}{8}$. If an investor decided to buy 16 shares, what was the cost to the investor (not including commission and tax)?

Solution

The cost was $16 \times 7\frac{1}{8} = \frac{\overset{2}{\cancel{16}}}{1} \times \frac{57}{\cancel{8}} = 114$

PROGRESS TEST 1

1. $\frac{3}{8} \times \frac{1}{5}$ equals _____.

2. $\frac{3}{20} \times \frac{5}{9}$ equals _____.

3. $2\frac{1}{7} \times 4\frac{2}{3}$ equals _____.

4. If the investor of Example 4 buys 20 stocks, his cost is _____.

In Chapter 1 we defined division in terms of multiplication. For example, $10 \div 5 = 2$ because $10 = 5 \times 2$. Similarly, we define division of fractions in terms of multiplication of fractions.

Divisions of fractions

DEFINITION 2.7 $\quad \frac{a}{b} \div \frac{c}{d} = \frac{a}{b} \times \frac{d}{c}$

According to Definition 2.7, to divide $\frac{a}{b}$ by $\frac{c}{d}$ we **invert** the fraction $\frac{c}{d}$, obtaining $\frac{d}{c}$, and then multiply $\frac{a}{b}$ by $\frac{d}{c}$. For this reason it is often said that to divide $\frac{a}{b}$ by $\frac{c}{d}$ we "invert and multiply." Mathematically, we are actually multiplying $\frac{a}{b}$ by the reciprocal (inverse) of $\frac{c}{d}$. For example,

$$\frac{3}{4} \div \frac{1}{7} = \frac{3}{4} \times \frac{7}{1} = \frac{21}{4} = 5\frac{1}{4} \text{ and } \frac{7}{8} \div \frac{9}{16} = \frac{7}{\cancel{8}} \times \frac{\cancel{16}^{2}}{9} = \frac{14}{9} = 1\frac{5}{9}$$

When mixed numbers are involved, we first convert the mixed numbers to improper fractions and then use Definition 2.7 as illustrated in Example 5 (b).

Division of mixed numbers

Example 5

Divide (a) $\quad \frac{3}{5}$ by $\frac{9}{5}$ $\qquad$ (b) $\quad 2\frac{5}{8}$ by $1\frac{3}{4}$

---

1. $\frac{3}{40}$ $\qquad$ 2. $\frac{1}{12}$ $\qquad$ 3. 10 $\qquad$ 4. $\$142\frac{1}{2}$

Solution

(a) $\dfrac{3}{5} \div \dfrac{9}{5} = \dfrac{\cancel{3}}{\cancel{5}} \times \dfrac{\cancel{5}}{\cancel{9}} = \dfrac{1}{3}$

(b) $2\dfrac{5}{8} = \dfrac{21}{8}$ and $1\dfrac{3}{4} = \dfrac{7}{4}$

so

$$2\dfrac{5}{8} \div 1\dfrac{3}{4} = \dfrac{21}{8} \div \dfrac{7}{4} = \dfrac{\cancel{21}}{\cancel{8}} \times \dfrac{\cancel{4}}{\cancel{7}} = \dfrac{3}{2} = 1\dfrac{1}{2}$$

Example 6

On July 2, 1973, the price of one share of Xerox Corporation stock was $156\dfrac{5}{8}$. If 3 partners agreed to buy one share and split the cost equally, what did each of the partners have to pay?

Solution

Each had to pay $156\dfrac{5}{8} \div 3 = \dfrac{1253}{8} \div \dfrac{3}{1} = \dfrac{1253}{8} \times \dfrac{1}{3} = \dfrac{1253}{24} = \$52\dfrac{5}{24}$

PROGRESS TEST 2

1. $\dfrac{3}{4} \div \dfrac{9}{4}$ equals _____.

2. The reciprocal of $\dfrac{3}{7}$ is _____.

3. $1\dfrac{5}{7} \div 3\dfrac{3}{7}$ equals _____.

4. If in Example 6, 7 persons decided to buy one share, the cost per person would be _____.

Time cards

One of the most important applications of multiplication of fractions in business occurs in the determination of an employee's earnings. Most employees are paid weekly, based on an hourly rate, with one and one-half times the normal rate for any hours worked over 8 hours in one day, or over 40 hours in one week. Figure 2–2 shows a

1. $\dfrac{1}{3}$ 2. $\dfrac{7}{3}$ 3. $\dfrac{1}{2}$ 4. $\$22\dfrac{3}{8}$

WEEKLY TIME CARD						
EMPLOYEE NAME _John Jones_			**EMPLOYEE NUMBER** _0123_			
HOURLY RATE _$4_			**WEEK ENDING** _1/2/76_			
	Hours			Pay		
	Regular	Overtime	Total	Regular	Overtime	Total
Monday	8	1	9	$32	$6	$38
Tuesday	8	0	8	$32	0	$32
Wednesday	8	2	10	$32	$12	$44
Thursday	8	1	9	$32	$6	$38
Friday	8	0	8	$32	0	$32
Saturday	0	4	4	0	$24	$24
Total	40	8	48	$160	$48	$208

Figure 2–2

typical weekly time card for John Jones. The hourly rate for Jones is $4, with time and a half for overtime.

Mr. Jones's earnings were determined as follows:

1. Eight hours daily, Monday through Friday, at $4 per hour yields $40 \times \$4 = \$160$ regular earnings.

2. The overtime rate is $1\frac{1}{2} \times \$4 = \frac{3}{\overset{2}{\cancel{2}}} \times \overset{2}{\cancel{4}} = \$6$ per hour.

3. 8 hours of overtime at $6 per hour yields $8 \times \$6 = \$48$ overtime earnings.

4. Total earnings is $\$160 + 48 = \$208$.

EXERCISE 2.4

1. Find the products:

   (a) $\dfrac{3}{4} \times \dfrac{2}{5}$ (b) $\dfrac{9}{10} \times \dfrac{2}{3}$ (c) $\dfrac{7}{8} \times \dfrac{4}{5}$

2. Find the products:

   (a) $\dfrac{9}{4} \times \dfrac{2}{18}$ (b) $\dfrac{7}{10} \times \dfrac{5}{14}$ (c) $\dfrac{3}{5} \times \dfrac{14}{15} \times \dfrac{5}{7}$

3. Find the following products:

   (a) $2\dfrac{2}{3} \times \dfrac{3}{8}$ (b) $5\dfrac{5}{6} \times 3\dfrac{2}{3}$ (c) $7\dfrac{1}{3} \times 8\dfrac{2}{5}$

4. Find the following products:

   (a) $5\dfrac{1}{6} \times 3\dfrac{2}{3}$ (b) $5\dfrac{1}{10} \times 4\dfrac{2}{5}$ (c) $1\dfrac{7}{8} \times \dfrac{8}{15} \times 3\dfrac{3}{4}$

5. Perform the following divisions:

   (a) $\dfrac{7}{8} \div \dfrac{3}{4}$ (b) $\dfrac{7}{25} \div \dfrac{18}{75}$ (c) $3\dfrac{1}{2} \div \dfrac{7}{8}$

6.   (a) $\dfrac{5}{7} \div \dfrac{2}{3}$ (b) $\dfrac{15}{16} \div \dfrac{3}{8}$ (c) $5\dfrac{3}{5} \div 15\dfrac{3}{4}$

7.   Perform the indicated operations:

    (a) $\left(3\dfrac{1}{2} \times \dfrac{2}{8}\right) \div \dfrac{7}{8}$ (b) $\left(\dfrac{4}{15} \times 1\dfrac{1}{2}\right) \div \dfrac{2}{3}$ (c) $\left(3\dfrac{1}{2} \times 5\dfrac{2}{5}\right) \div \dfrac{3}{19}$

8.   (a) $\left(\dfrac{3}{8} \times 12\right) \div \dfrac{6}{23}$ (b) $\left(\dfrac{3}{4} \times 1\dfrac{1}{5} \times 2\dfrac{1}{2}\right) \div \left(\dfrac{1}{4} \div 1\dfrac{9}{16}\right)$

9.   Figure 2–3 shows the bid price and the asked price (in dollars) of certain stocks. Assume that the actual cost of one share is the bid price. For example, the cost of one share of Reliable Life Ins. is $\$15\dfrac{1}{4}$ and that of Residex Corp. is \$2. Find

    (a) the price of ten shares of Reliable Invest. stock.
    (b) the price of seven shares of Rex Precis. Prod. stock.
    (c) the price of fifteen shares of Rexco Indust. Inc. stock.

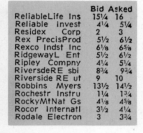

	Bid	Asked
ReliableLife Ins	15¼	16
Reliable invest	4¼	5¼
Residex Corp	2	3
Rex PrecisProd	5½	6½
Rexco Indst Inc	6⅛	6⅝
RidgewayL Ent	5½	6½
Ripley Compny	4¼	5¼
RiversdeRE sbi	8¾	9¾
Riverside RE ut	9	10
Robbins Myers	13½	14½
Rochestr Instru	1¼	1¾
RockyMtNat Gs	4⅛	4⅝
Rocor Internatl	3½	4¼
Rodale Electron	3	3¾

Figure 2–3   Reprinted, by permission, from *The Wall Street Journal*, December 20, 1973, p. 30.

10.   Referring to Figure 2–3 (Problem 9) assume that the actual price of one share is the asked price; for example, the price of one share of Residex Corp. stock is \$3. If three partners were to split the cost evenly, find each partner's portion when buying one share of
    (a) Reliable Life Ins.
    (b) Reliable Invest.
    (c) Robbins Myers

11.   Repeat Problem 10, assuming that the actual price of one share of stock is the bid price.

12.   A recipe for French dressing calls for $\dfrac{3}{4}$ cup of mayonnaise and yields enough dressing for four persons. How many cups of mayonnaise should the manager of a restaurant order to make French dressing for
    (a) 16 persons
    (b) 40 persons
    (c) 50 persons

13.   The recipe of Problem 12 also calls for $\dfrac{1}{4}$ cup of corn oil (which still yields enough dressing for four persons). How

many cups of oil should the manager of a restaurant order to make French dressing for
(a) 16 persons
(b) 40 persons
(c) 50 persons

14. How many quarts of oil should the manager of Problem 13 order when preparing French dressing for 16, 40, and 50 persons, respectively. (Hint: 1 quart = 4 cups.)

15. If you were the cashier at the store using the accompanying ad, how much would you reduce the price of a bathing suit listed for: (Give answer as a whole or mixed number.)
(a) $8   (b) $15   (c) $19

16. If the store of Problem 15 decides to reduce their merchandise by $\frac{1}{4}$ instead of $\frac{1}{3}$, how much reduction in price is there on merchandise listed for: (Answer as a whole or mixed number.)
(a) $8   (b) $15   (c) $19

17. On July 2, 1973, the price of one share of General Foods stock was $25\frac{1}{4}$. If a man decided to buy 15 shares, what would his price be?

18. Repeat Problem 17 for 15 shares of Heinz stock, whose price was $40\frac{7}{8}$.

19. Bob, Carol, Ted, and Alice form a partnership whereby Bob gets $\frac{3}{10}$ of the profits, Carol $\frac{2}{10}$, Ted $\frac{1}{10}$, and Alice the rest. If there is a $7500 profit, how much does each get?

20. Repeat Problem 19 assuming there is a $540 profit.

21. A garage has 16,200 square feet of parking space. Allowing each car $40\frac{1}{2}$ square feet of parking space, how many cars can be parked in this garage at one time?

22. If the garage of Problem 21 had 324,000 square feet of parking space, how many cars could be parked in this garage at one time?

23. A worker in an assembly line produces $13\frac{2}{5}$ pieces per hour. If he has produced a batch of $33\frac{1}{2}$ pieces, how long has he worked?

24. An automobile gets $17\frac{2}{10}$ miles per gallon of gasoline costing $41\frac{2}{5}$¢ per gallon. How far can this car go on a gasoline purchase of $2.07 (207¢)?

Jobless Rate Rose 0.2 Point to 4.9% During December

Reprinted, by permission, from *The Wall Street Journal*, January 7, 1974, p. 3.

2.5 FRACTION-DECIMAL CONVERSION

The headline above states that the jobless rate rose 0.2 (read "two tenths") of a point. The **decimal** 0.2 can also be expressed as the proper fraction $\frac{2}{10}$. In Section 2.1 we mentioned that proper fractions represent values less than 1 or quantities less than a whole unit. In this case the fraction $\frac{2}{10}$ represents two parts of a whole which has been equally divided into ten parts. Thus, the headline above indicates that the jobless rate rose two tenths of one point. The fraction $\frac{2}{10}$ is an example of a decimal fraction. A **decimal fraction** is a fraction whose denominator is a "power" of 10. (10,100,1000,10,000, etc., are "powers" of 10.) For example, $\frac{3}{10}$, $\frac{7}{100}$, $\frac{83}{1000}$, and $\frac{97}{10,000}$ are decimal fractions. **Decimal fractions** can be written as **decimals** by writing the numerator to the right of a dot called the decimal point.

The number of digits appearing to the right of the decimal point is the same as the number of zeros in the denominator of the decimal fraction. For example,

one zero	$\dfrac{3}{10}$	= .3	(read "three tenths")

one digit to the right of the decimal

two zeros	$\dfrac{7}{100}$	= .07	(read "seven hundredths")

two digits to the right of the decimal

three zeros	$\dfrac{83}{1000}$	= .083	(read "eighty three one-thousandths")

three digits to the right of the decimal

four zeros	$\dfrac{97}{10,000}$	= .0097	(read "ninety seven ten-thousandths")

four digits to the right of the decimal

Note that zeros to the right of the last significant digit, or zeros to the left of the decimal point, do not affect the value of the fraction. Thus, .07 = .070 = .0700, and .07 = 0.07 = 00.07.

Example 1

Write the following decimal fractions as decimals:

(a) $\dfrac{9}{10}$ (b) $\dfrac{3}{100}$ (c) $\dfrac{47}{1000}$ (d) $\dfrac{49}{10,000}$

Solution

(a) $\dfrac{9}{10}$ = .9   (one digit after the decimal point, since the denominator has one zero)

(b) $\dfrac{3}{100}$ = .03   (two digits after the decimal point, since the denominator has two zeros)

(c) $\dfrac{47}{1000}$ = .047   (three digits after the decimal point, since the denominator has three zeros)

(d) $\dfrac{49}{10,000}$ = .0049 (four digits after the decimal point, since the denominator has four zeros)

PROGRESS TEST 1

1. A decimal fraction is a fraction whose denominator is a _____ of 10.

2. The denominator of a decimal fraction indicates the number of _____ appearing to the _____ of the decimal point.

3. When written as a decimal, the decimal fraction $\frac{32}{1,000}$ equals _____.

The decimal system

The student is no doubt aware that the system used to write decimal fractions is called the **decimal system.** The decimal system is a place value system based on 10. When we express a whole number in the decimal system, the unit's place has a value of 1, and each place to the left has a value ten times that of the place to its right. Conversely, each place to the right of the unit's place has a value which is $\frac{1}{10}$ of that to its left. Thus, the number 428 means 4 hundreds, 2 tens, and 8 units. This number can be written in **expanded notation** as

$$428 = (4 \times 100) + (2 \times 10) + 8$$

place value 100
place value 10
place value   1

Exponents

Sometimes it is convenient to use **exponents** when writing numbers in expanded notation. An exponent is a (whole) number that tells how many times another number, called the base, is a factor in a product. Thus, in the expression 10^3 (read "ten cubed"), 3 is the exponent, 10 is the base, and $10 \times 10 \times 10 = 10^3$. Note also that $10 \times 10 = 10^2$ (read "ten squared"), $10^1 = 10$, and $10^0 = 1.$* With this

Any nonzero number raised to the 0 power equals 1

notation, 428 can be written in expanded notation as $428 = (4 \times 10^2) + (2 \times 10^1) + (8 \times 10^0)$. In case the number to be expressed in expanded notation has a decimal part, for example, 23.98, we have to introduce the idea of **negative exponents.** Thus, we define $10^{-1} = \frac{1}{10}$, $10^{-2} = \frac{1}{10^2}$, $10^{-3} = \frac{1}{10^3}$, etc. With this convention $23.98 = (2 \times 10^1) + (3 \times 10^0) + (9 \times 10^{-1}) + (8 \times 10^{-2})$. Note that the powers of 10 decrease by 1 as you move from left to right.

---

1. power   2. digits, right   3. .032
*We define $k^0 = 1$ for any nonzero number k.

Example 2

Write in expanded notation:
(a) 1,387.94   (b) 204.967

Solution

(a) $1,387.94 = (1 \times 10^3) + (3 \times 10^2) + (8 \times 10^1) + (7 \times 10^0) + (9 \times 10^{-1})$
$+ (4 \times 10^{-2})$

(b) $204.967 = (2 \times 10^2) + (4 \times 10^0) + (9 \times 10^{-1}) + (6 \times 10^{-2}) + (7 \times 10^{-3})$

Note that in (b) there is no term containing 10^1 since a 0 (zero) occupies the ten's place and $0 \times 10^1 = 0$.

Remember, 0 times any number equals 0.

The idea of expanded notation is widely used in business, since all business transactions are performed with decimal units of money; thus, $183.92 may be considered as representing one $100 bill, eight $10 bills, three $1 bills, nine dimes, and two pennies.

Applications of expanded notation

PROGRESS TEST 2

1. When written in expanded notation, 245 = _____
_____.

2. When written in expanded notation, 38.407 =
_____.

3. When expressed in expanded notation $173.56 can be thought of as _____
_____.

Since both fractions and decimals represent parts of a whole unit, fractions can be changed to decimals and vice versa. In many cases, such a conversion may simplify the computations in a problem. For instance, if we wish to multiply $33\frac{1}{2}$ by 457, we can change the $33\frac{1}{2}$ to the improper fraction $\frac{67}{2}$ and then multiply by 457. Another way, however, would be to think of $33\frac{1}{2}$ as 33.5 and then multiply by 457. We now give the rules used to convert fractions to decimals and vice versa.

Changing fractions to decimals and vice versa

---

1. $(2 \times 10^2) + (4 \times 10^1) + (5 \times 10^0)$ 2. $(3 \times 10^1) + (8 \times 10^0) + (4 \times 10^{-1})$
$+ (7 \times 10^{-3})$ 3. One $100 bill, seven $10 bills, three $1 bills, five dimes, and six pennies.

> **RULE 2.6** To convert a decimal fraction to a decimal:
> (1) Write the numerator of the fraction with a decimal
>   point directly over the last digit.
> (2) Move the decimal point as many places to the left
>   (filling in the vacant places with 0's if necessary) as
>   there are zeros in the denominator.

Thus,

$$\frac{31}{100} = .31. = .31 \qquad \text{and} \qquad \frac{387}{10000} = .0387. = .0387$$

$$2 \text{ zeros} \qquad 2 \text{ places} \qquad 4 \text{ zeros} \qquad 4 \text{ places}$$

Since a common fraction is an implied division problem, to convert a fraction to a decimal we merely divide the numerator by the denominator. This idea is stated in the following rule.

> **RULE 2.7** To convert a fraction to a decimal, divide
> the numerator by the denominator.

Thus,

$$\frac{3}{5} = .6 \text{ because } 5\overline{)3.0} \quad \text{and} \quad \frac{13}{200} = .065 \text{ because } 200\overline{)13.00}$$

$$\begin{array}{r} .6 \\ 5\overline{)3.0} \\ \underline{3\ 0} \\ 0 \end{array} \qquad \begin{array}{r} .065 \\ 200\overline{)13.00} \\ \underline{12\ 00} \\ 1\ 000 \\ \underline{1\ 000} \\ 0 \end{array}$$

In these examples we add to the dividend (3 and 13) as many zeros as necessary to complete the division process. Fortunately in these two cases, the division stops at an early stage (the remainder is zero). Whenever this occurs, we say that the decimal representation is **terminating.** In some cases we may not be so fortunate. For example, if we try to express $\frac{1}{3}$ as a decimal fraction we obtain

$$\begin{array}{r} .333... \\ 3\overline{)1.000} \\ \underline{9} \\ 10 \\ \underline{9} \\ 10 \\ \underline{9} \\ \text{etc.} \end{array}$$

and there is always a remainder of 1 (1 appears as a remainder). We then say that the fraction $\frac{1}{3}$ does not have a terminating decimal representation and write $\frac{1}{3} = .333\ldots$ or simply $\frac{1}{3} = .\overline{3}.$

To determine if a fraction has a terminating decimal representation, reduce the fraction and express the denominator as a product of primes. If the *only* primes present are 2s or 5s, the fraction will be terminating. Thus, $\frac{1}{2}$ has a terminating decimal representation ($\frac{1}{2} = .50$), $\frac{1}{5}$ has a terminating decimal representation ($\frac{1}{5} = .20$), and $\frac{13}{50}$ has a terminating decimal representation, since $50 = 2 \times 5 \times 5$ $\left(\frac{13}{50} = .26\right)$.

If the fraction does not have a terminating decimal representation, the recommended procedure is to divide to the hundredths place (two decimal places) and express the remainder as a fraction. Thus,

$$\frac{3}{7} = 7\overline{)3}^{.42\frac{6}{7}} = .42\frac{6}{7}, \text{ and } \frac{7}{9} = 9\overline{)7}^{.77\frac{7}{9}} = .77\frac{7}{9}$$

Example 3

Convert to a decimal: (a) $\frac{37}{100}$ (b) $\frac{7}{8}$ (c) $\frac{4}{7}$

Solution

(a) By Rule 2.6, we see that $\frac{37}{100} = .37$.

(b) We note that $\frac{7}{8}$ has a denominator of $8 = 2 \times 2 \times 2$. Since the denominator has only 2s as factors, the fraction is terminating.

$$
\begin{array}{r}
.875 \\
8\overline{)7.000} \\
\underline{64} \\
60 \\
\underline{56} \\
40 \\
\underline{40} \\
0
\end{array}
$$

(c) Since $\frac{4}{7}$ has a denominator of 7 (and thus is not a 2 or a 5), the fraction does not have a terminating decimal representation:

$$\frac{4}{7} = 7\overline{)4.0}^{.57\frac{1}{7}} = .57\frac{1}{7}$$

(verify this).

To convert a mixed number to a decimal, we convert it to an improper fraction first and then use Rule 2.7. For example,

$$3\frac{1}{2} = \frac{7}{2} = 3.5 \text{ and } 4\frac{1}{8} = \frac{33}{8} = 4.125.$$

PROGRESS TEST 3

1. When written as a decimal, $\frac{497}{10,000}$ equals _____.

2. When written as a decimal, $\frac{4}{5}$ equals _____.

3. The fraction $\frac{3}{8}$ _____ a terminating decimal representation.

4. When written as a decimal, $\frac{6}{7}$ equals _____.

5. When written as a decimal, $3\frac{2}{5}$ equals _____.

Converting decimals to fractions

We finally give the rule used to convert a (terminating) decimal to a fraction.

> **RULE 2.8** To convert a (terminating) decimal to a fraction:
> (1) Delete the decimal and use the resulting integer as the numerator.
> (2) Count the number of places the decimal point would have to be moved in the given decimal to get it just to the right of the units digit in the numerator. (For example, in 31.410 it will be 3 places.)
> (3) The denominator will be a 1 followed by as many zeros as places counted in step 2.

For example, to convert .313 to a fraction we proceed as follows:
1. We use 313 as the numerator.
2. The number of places the decimal point has to be moved to be to the right of the units place is 3.
3. $.313 = \frac{313}{1000}$

Similarly, $41.21 = \frac{4121}{100}$.

---

1. 0.0497   2. 0.8   3. has   4. $.85\frac{5}{7}$ 5. 3.4

Example 3

Convert to a fraction:
  (a) .3184   (b) 384.321

Solution

$$\text{(a) } .3184 = \frac{3184}{10,000} \text{ (by Rule 2.8)}$$

$$\text{(b) } 384.321 = \frac{384,321}{1,000} \text{ (by Rule 2.8)}$$

PROGRESS TEST 4

1. When written as a fraction, .38 equals _____.
2. When written as a fraction, 21.73 equals _____.

In Figure 2–4 we give a table of equivalent decimals and fractions. The numbers in the top row represent the numerator of the fraction, while the numbers in the first column to the left represent the denominators. To find the decimal equivalent of $\frac{6}{11}$, for example, we go to the first row, locate the 6 and go down in that same column until we find the row marked 11; the equivalent decimal is $0.54\frac{6}{11}$.

EXERCISE 2.5

1. Write the following decimal fractions as decimals:
     (a) $\frac{7}{10}$ (b) $\frac{17}{100}$ (c) $\frac{378}{10,000}$ (d) $\frac{30}{1,000}$

2. Write the following decimal fractions as decimals:
     (a) $\frac{11}{1,000}$ (b) $\frac{987}{10,000}$ (c) $\frac{4}{10,000}$ (d) $\frac{71}{100,000}$

3. Write the following numbers in expanded notation:
     (a) 42   (b) 387   (c) 4,073   (d) 40,308

4. Write the following numbers in expanded notation:
     (a) 807   (b) 38.4   (c) 307.703   (d) 1,308.7034

5. Write the following numbers in base 10 (usual) notation:
     (a) $(3 \times 10^2) + (8 \times 10^1) + (7 \times 10^0)$
     (b) $(8 \times 10^3) + (7 \times 10^2) + (2 \times 10^1) + (2 \times 10^0)$

---

1. $\frac{38}{100} = \frac{19}{50}$ 2. $\frac{2173}{100}$

NUMERATOR OF COMMON FRACTION

Denominator of common fraction	1	2	3	4	5	6	7	8	9	10	11	12	13	14	15
2	$.50$														
	50%														
3	$.33\frac{1}{3}$	$.66\frac{2}{3}$													
	$33\frac{1}{3}\%$	$66\frac{2}{3}\%$													
4	$.25$	$.50$	$.75$												
	25%	50%	75%												
5	$.20$	$.40$	$.60$	$.80$											
	20%	40%	60%	80%											
6	$.16\frac{2}{3}$	$.33\frac{1}{3}$	$.50$	$.66\frac{2}{3}$	$.83\frac{1}{3}$										
	$16\frac{2}{3}\%$	$33\frac{1}{3}\%$	50%	$66\frac{2}{3}\%$	$83\frac{1}{3}\%$										
7	$.14\frac{2}{7}$	$.28\frac{4}{7}$	$.42\frac{6}{7}$	$.57\frac{1}{7}$	$.71\frac{3}{7}$	$.85\frac{5}{7}$									
	$14\frac{2}{7}\%$	$28\frac{4}{7}\%$	$42\frac{6}{7}\%$	$57\frac{1}{7}\%$	$71\frac{3}{7}\%$	$85\frac{5}{7}\%$									
8	$.12\frac{1}{2}$	$.25$	$.37\frac{1}{2}$	$.50$	$.62\frac{1}{2}$	$.75$	$.87\frac{1}{2}$								
	$12\frac{1}{2}\%$	25%	$37\frac{1}{2}\%$	50%	$62\frac{1}{2}$	75%	$87\frac{1}{2}\%$								
9	$.11\frac{1}{9}$	$.22\frac{2}{9}$	$.33\frac{1}{3}$	$.44\frac{4}{9}$	$.55\frac{5}{9}$	$.66\frac{2}{3}$	$.77\frac{7}{9}$	$.88\frac{8}{9}$							
	$11\frac{1}{9}\%$	$22\frac{2}{9}\%$	$33\frac{1}{3}\%$	$44\frac{4}{9}\%$	$55\frac{5}{9}\%$	$66\frac{2}{3}\%$	$77\frac{7}{9}\%$	$88\frac{8}{9}\%$							
10	$.10$	$.20$	$.30$	$.40$	$.50$	$.60$	$.70$	$.80$	$.90$						
	10%	20%	30%	40%	50%	60%	70%	80%	90%						
11	$.09\frac{1}{11}$	$.18\frac{2}{11}$	$.27\frac{3}{11}$	$.36\frac{4}{11}$	$.45\frac{5}{11}$	$.54\frac{6}{11}$	$.63\frac{7}{11}$	$.72\frac{8}{11}$	$.81\frac{9}{11}$	$.90\frac{10}{11}$					
	$9\frac{1}{11}\%$	$18\frac{2}{11}\%$	$27\frac{3}{11}\%$	$36\frac{4}{11}\%$	$45\frac{5}{11}\%$	$54\frac{6}{11}\%$	$63\frac{7}{11}\%$	$72\frac{8}{11}\%$	$81\frac{9}{11}\%$	$90\frac{10}{11}\%$					
12	$.08\frac{1}{3}$	$.16\frac{2}{3}$	$.25$	$.33\frac{1}{3}$	$.41\frac{2}{3}$	$.50$	$.58\frac{1}{3}$	$.66\frac{2}{3}$	$.75$	$.83\frac{1}{3}$	$.91\frac{2}{3}$				
	$8\frac{1}{3}\%$	$16\frac{2}{3}\%$	25%	$33\frac{1}{3}\%$	$41\frac{2}{3}\%$	50%	$58\frac{1}{3}\%$	$66\frac{2}{3}\%$	75%	$83\frac{1}{3}\%$	$91\frac{2}{3}\%$				
13	$.07\frac{9}{13}$	$.15\frac{5}{13}$	$.23\frac{1}{13}$	$.30\frac{10}{13}$	$.38\frac{6}{13}$	$.46\frac{2}{13}$	$.53\frac{11}{13}$	$.61\frac{7}{13}$	$.69\frac{3}{13}$	$.76\frac{12}{13}$	$.84\frac{3}{13}$	$.92\frac{4}{13}$			
	$7\frac{9}{13}\%$	$15\frac{5}{13}\%$	$23\frac{1}{13}\%$	$30\frac{10}{13}\%$	$38\frac{6}{13}\%$	$46\frac{2}{13}\%$	$53\frac{11}{13}\%$	$61\frac{7}{13}\%$	$69\frac{3}{13}\%$	$76\frac{12}{13}\%$	$84\frac{3}{13}\%$	$92\frac{4}{13}\%$			
14	$.07\frac{1}{7}$	$.14\frac{2}{7}$	$.21\frac{3}{7}$	$.28\frac{4}{7}$	$.35\frac{5}{7}$	$.42\frac{6}{7}$	$.50$	$.57\frac{1}{7}$	$.64\frac{2}{7}$	$.71\frac{3}{7}$	$.78\frac{4}{7}$	$.85\frac{5}{7}$	$.92\frac{6}{7}$		
	$7\frac{1}{7}\%$	$14\frac{2}{7}\%$	$21\frac{3}{7}\%$	$28\frac{4}{7}\%$	$35\frac{5}{7}\%$	$42\frac{6}{7}\%$	50%	$57\frac{1}{7}\%$	$64\frac{2}{7}\%$	$71\frac{3}{7}\%$	$78\frac{4}{7}\%$	$85\frac{5}{7}\%$	$92\frac{6}{7}\%$		
15	$.06\frac{2}{3}$	$.13\frac{1}{3}$	$.20$	$.26\frac{2}{3}$	$.33\frac{1}{3}$	$.40$	$.46\frac{2}{3}$	$.53\frac{1}{3}$	$.60$	$.66\frac{2}{3}$	$.73\frac{1}{3}$	$.80$	$.86\frac{2}{3}$	$.93\frac{1}{3}$	
	$6\frac{2}{3}\%$	$13\frac{1}{3}\%$	20%	$26\frac{2}{3}\%$	$33\frac{1}{3}\%$	40%	$46\frac{2}{3}\%$	$53\frac{1}{3}\%$	60%	$66\frac{2}{3}\%$	$73\frac{1}{3}\%$	80%	$86\frac{2}{3}\%$	$93\frac{1}{3}\%$	
16	$.06\frac{1}{4}$	$.12\frac{1}{2}$	$.18\frac{3}{4}$	$.25$	$.31\frac{1}{4}$	$.37\frac{1}{2}$	$.43\frac{3}{4}$	$.50$	$.56\frac{1}{4}$	$.62\frac{1}{2}$	$.68\frac{3}{4}$	$.75$	$.81\frac{1}{4}$	$.87\frac{1}{2}$	$.93\frac{3}{4}$
	$6\frac{1}{4}\%$	$12\frac{1}{2}\%$	$18\frac{3}{4}\%$	25%	$31\frac{1}{4}\%$	$37\frac{1}{2}\%$	$43\frac{3}{4}\%$	50%	$56\frac{1}{4}\%$	$62\frac{1}{2}\%$	$68\frac{3}{4}\%$	75%	$81\frac{1}{4}\%$	$87\frac{1}{2}\%$	$93\frac{3}{4}\%$

Figure 2–4

(c) $(4 \times 10^3) + (7 \times 10^2) + (3 \times 10^0)$

(d) $(4 \times 10^5) + (2 \times 10^3) + (1 \times 10^2) + (3 \times 10^0)$

6.   Write the following numbers in base 10 (usual) notation:

(a) $(3 \times 10^2) + (2 \times 10^1) + (7 \times 10^0) + (3 \times 10^{-1})$

(b) $(3 \times 10^0) + (7 \times 10^{-1}) + (3 \times 10^{-2})$

(c) $(2 \times 10^0) + (9 \times 10^{-1}) + (8 \times 10^{-2}) + (3 \times 10^{-3})$

(d) $(4 \times 10^{-2}) + (3 \times 10^{-4}) + (5 \times 10^{-5})$

7. Convert the following fractions to decimals:

    (a) $\frac{37}{100}$　　　(b) $\frac{393}{1,000}$　　　(c) $\frac{21}{10,000}$　　　(d) $\frac{893}{100}$

8. Convert the following fractions to decimals:

    (a) $\frac{31}{1000}$　　　(b) $\frac{84}{2000}$　　　(c) $\frac{92}{2000}$　　　(d) $\frac{42}{500}$

    (Hint: First convert to an equivalent fraction whose denominator is 1000.)

9. Determine which of the following fractions have a terminating decimal expansion:

    (a) $\frac{3}{8}$　　　(b) $\frac{2}{3}$　　　(c) $\frac{1}{7}$　　　(d) $\frac{1}{5}$　　　(e) $\frac{3}{2}$

10. Determine which of the following fractions have a terminating decimal expansion:

    (a) $\frac{3}{25}$　　(b) $\frac{5}{11}$　　(c) $\frac{3}{15}$　　(d) $\frac{21}{42}$　　(e) $\frac{8}{5}$　　(f) $\frac{73}{146}$

11. Convert the fractions of Problem 9 to decimals.

12. Convert the fractions of Problem 10 to decimals.

13. Convert the following decimals to fractions:
    (a) .33　　　(b) 3.28　　　(c) 221.374

14. Convert the following decimals to fractions:
    (a) 3.21　　　(b) .0037　　　(c) .0712

15. Using the table given in Figure 2–4, find the decimal expression for:

    (a) $\frac{1}{3}$　　　(b) $\frac{1}{5}$　　　(c) $\frac{3}{7}$　　　(d) $\frac{4}{9}$

16. Using the table given in Figure 2–4, find the decimal expression for:

    (a) $\frac{5}{12}$　　　(b) $\frac{3}{14}$　　　(c) $\frac{10}{13}$　　　(d) $\frac{11}{16}$

17. Using the table given in Figure 2–4, find the fractional representation for:

    (a) $.08\frac{1}{3}$　　　(b) $.23\frac{1}{13}$　　　(c) .30　　　(d) $.12\frac{1}{2}$

18. Do the same as in Problem 17 for the following numbers:

    (a) $.06\frac{1}{4}$　　　(b) $.18\frac{3}{4}$　　　(c) $.31\frac{1}{4}$　　　(d) $.37\frac{1}{2}$

19. The price of one share of stock is quoted using fractions. For example, the price of one share of General Foods stock on July 2, 1973 was $\$25\frac{1}{4}$. When expressed in decimal notation this price is $25.25. Using the accompanying table write the open, high, low, and close prices of the first three Most Active Stocks in decimal notation.

20 THE WALL STREET JOURNAL, Friday, December 28, 1973

Thursday's Volume

22,720,000 Shares; 196,400 Warrants

Volume since Jan. 1:	1973	1972	1971
Total warrants	42,950,900	52,854,000	....
Total shares	4,008,421,631	4,110,632,916	3,877,269,211

MOST ACTIVE STOCKS

	Open	High	Low	Close	Chg.	Volume
Gulf Oil	21¾	21⅞	21½	21⅞	+ ⅝	182,500
Gen Motors	48⅛	48¾	48⅛	48¾	+ ¾	170,800
Nat Can	7⅞	7⅞	7⅜	7½	− ⅜	155,000
StdOil Cal	32⅜	34	32⅜	34	+1⅜	138,900
CBS pf	17½	17¾	17½	17¾	− ¾	135,100
US Steel	37½	38¼	37½	37⅞	+ ⅝	131,300
Occiden Pet	8½	9¼	8½	9⅛	+ ¾	128,200
IntTelTel	27¾	27⅞	27⅜	27¾	+ ½	126,100
Westgh El	26⅝	26⅞	26⅜	26½	+ ⅛	124,900
Melv Shoe	10¾	11⅛	10⅝	10⅞	− ¼	123,300

Average closing price of most active stocks: 24.20.

Reprinted by permission.

20. Do the same as in Problem 19 for the last three Most Active Stocks.

21. The accompanying table gives the N.A. (net asset) value of a fund share as a decimal. For example, the value of one share of Adm. Exp. is $14.64 = 14\frac{64}{100} = 14\frac{16}{25}$. Write the N.A. values of the first five Funds as fractions.

Closed-End Funds

Friday, April 6, 1973

Following is a weekly listing of unaudited net asset values of closed-end investment fund shares, reported by the companies as of Friday's close. Also shown is the closing listed market price or a dealer-to-dealer askea price of each fund's shares, with the percentage of difference.

	N.A. Value	Stk Price	% Diff
AdmExp	14.64	12⅝	−13.8
Advance	13.46	14¾	+ 9.6
aAmGnBd	24.83	27⅜	+10.2
AmGenCv	20.69	19⅞	− 3.9
Am-SoAf	65.42	62⅞	− 3.9
Bancroft	20.89	16⅛	−22.8
BayrckUt	14.39	11½	−20.1
Carriers	18.90	15½	−17.9
CentSec	9.13	5⅝	−38.4
ChaseCvB	11.64	10⅞	− 6.7
aClConv	21.68	18	−17.0
CLIC	16.92	17⅜	+ 2.7
Diebold	9.71	4	−58.8
Dominick	10.63	8¼	−22.4
DrexelBd	22.80	21⅞	− 4.1
DrexelUt	22.50	22½	.. ...
GenAInv	24.78	24¼	− 2.1
IndSqIS	22.80	23⅜	+ 2.5
IntlHold	17.41	14⅞	−14.6
Japan	16.05	14¼	−11.2
J Hancock	24.31	26¼	+ 7.9

	N.A. Value	Stk Price	% Diff
JH Sec v	20.29	22⅜	+10.3
KeysnOTC	9.94	8	−19.5
Lehman	18.73	16¾	−10.6
Madison	13.26	12⅛	− 8.6
MMIncInv	13.76	14½	+ 5.4
MntgStInc	23.21	24⅝	+ 6.1
MuOmaha	18.27	18	− 1.5
NatlAvia	22.98	18⅝	−18.9
NiagraSh	18.36	16⅝	− 9.4
O'seasSec	5.10	5¼	+ 3.0
PetroCp	22.50	22¼	− 1.1
REIT C	9.97	11	+10.3
SourceCap	18.90	9⅛	−51.7
StdSh	31.10	25½	−18.0
SurvFnd	26.60	20⅜	−23.4
Tri-Contl	34.64	30⅛	−13.0
United	12.38	9	−27.3
US&For	29.00	29	.. ...
USLIFE	13.35	14	+ 6.1
VILnDvCp	7.70	3½	−54.5

a-Ex-dividend.

Reprinted, by permission, from *The Wall Street Journal.*

22. Do the same as in Problem 21 for the first five Funds (starting with JH Sec v) in the right hand column.

23. In the Closed-end Funds table, the stock price of each share is given as a fraction. Write the stock price of the first five shares as a decimal. (Hint: Change the fractional part to a decimal first. For example $12\frac{5}{8} = 12.625$ since $\frac{5}{8} = .625$.)

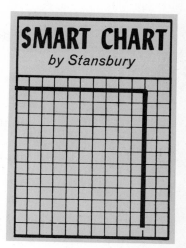

"The computer modified our cash position. It moved the decimal two places to the right on all dividend checks." Reproduced by permission of Herbert Stansbury.

2.6 ADDITION AND SUBTRACTION OF DECIMALS; BANKING RECORDS

In the chart above, the computer has misplaced the decimal point. Actually, when adding or subtracting decimals, it is easy to determine the location of the decimal point. The decimal point of the numbers to be added (or subtracted) must be placed in a vertical column before performing the addition (or subtraction). For example, to add 0.6, 2.35, 30.495, and 0.05, we first write the numbers in a column:

When adding or subtracting decimals, the decimal points are written in a vertical column.

$$
\begin{array}{r}
0.6 \\
2.35 \\
30.495 \\
\underline{0.05}
\end{array}
\quad \text{or as} \quad
\begin{array}{r}
.600 \\
2.350 \\
30.495 \\
\underline{0.050}
\end{array}
$$

Note that all the decimal points are written in a vertical column and that in the right column zeros were added for better visual alignment of the numbers. After the vertical alignment of the decimal point, we perform the addition in the usual manner, placing the decimal point in the answer in line with the decimal points of the problem. In our example, the sum is 33.495. (Verify this.) The subtraction of decimals is performed in a similar manner. The decimal point must be in a vertical column and, moreover, each of the amounts must have the same number of decimal places, so it may be necessary to add zeros before performing the subtraction. Thus, to subtract 2.9 from 3.871 we add two zeros at the end of the 2.9, obtaining 2.900, so that both amounts have the same number of decimal places. We then write

$$
\begin{array}{r}
3.871 \\
\underline{-2.900}
\end{array}
$$

and proceed in the usual manner, placing the decimal point in the answer beneath the decimal points in the problem. In our example, the difference is 0.971. (Verify this.)

Example 1

Subtract 238.9 from 7,170.87.

Solution

When we write the problem, we make sure that the decimal points are in a vertical column.

$$7{,}170.87$$
$$\underline{\phantom{7{,}1}238.90} \leftarrow \text{(adding one zero so that both amounts have}$$
the same number of decimals)

We then proceed as in a usual subtraction problem, obtaining 6931.97 as the answer. (Verify this result by adding the difference to the subtrahend and comparing the sum to the minuend.)

PROGRESS TEST 1

1. The addition of 45.6, 3.91, and 23.567 equals _____.
2. A man paid $2.60 for a book, $3.45 for supplies, and $.63 for two light bulbs. The amount the man spent is

_____.

3. The difference of 8.45 and .9756 is _____.

Deposit slips, checks and check stubs

One of the most important applications of addition and subtraction of decimals occurs in our dealings with a bank. We can deposit

---

1. 73.077   2. $6.68   3. 7.4744

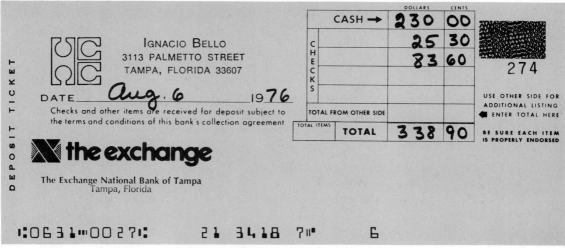

Figure 2–5   Courtesy of the Exchange National Bank of Tampa.

cash, currency, and checks into a checking account and then write
checks against the balance on deposit. The forms most commonly
used in our transactions with a bank are the **deposit slip,** the **check
and check stub,** the **bank statement,** and the **reconciliation form.**
Whenever a customer deposits money in the bank, he makes out a
deposit slip indicating the items deposited. Figure 2–5 shows a deposit slip prepared by depositor Ignacio Bello. It contains the name
of the bank, the name and address of the depositor, his account number, the date of the deposit, and the amount of cash and checks
being deposited.

On the other hand, when a customer wishes to use his money to
pay some obligations, he withdraws the money by writing **checks**
against his bank balance. A **check** is a written order from a depositor
to his bank to pay to a designated party a specified amount from funds
on deposit. To help customers keep a record of the transactions of
their checking account, either **checkbooks** are provided with a page
(called a **check register**) used to record checks and deposits or the
checks are attached to a **check stub.** The **check stub** is permanently
attached to the checkbook and separated from the check by a per-
forated line so that the check may be torn out. The check stub contains a record of the checks written, the name of the person to whom
the check was written and for what purpose, the date and amount of
any deposits made, and the account balance before and after writing
the check. Figure 2–6 shows a check and its stub written by I. Bello.
The check itself contains the date the check was written, the name
of the person to whom the check is payable (the payee), the amount
to be paid (written in both figures and words), and the signature of
the account holder.

At the beginning (or at the end) of each month, the bank will
send to its depositors a bank statement. A **bank statement** is a docu-

Bank statements

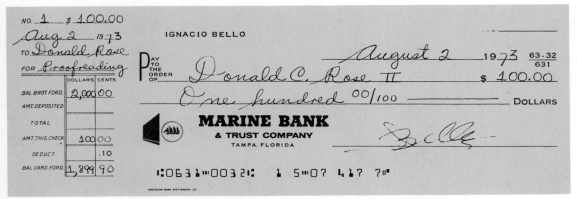

NO. 1 $ 100.00
Aug. 2   1973
TO Donald Rose
FOR Proofreading

	DOLLARS	CENTS
BAL. BROT. FORD.	2,000	00
AMT. DEPOSITED		
TOTAL		
AMT. THIS CHECK	100	00
DEDUCT		.10
BAL. CARD. FORD.	1,899	90

IGNACIO BELLO

August 2   1973   63-32/631

PAY TO THE ORDER OF   Donald C. Rose II $ 100.00

One hundred 00/100 ——————————— DOLLARS

MARINE BANK & TRUST COMPANY
TAMPA, FLORIDA

⑆0631⑆0032⑆ 1 5⑉07 417 7⑈

Figure 2–6   Courtesy of Marine Bank and Trust Company.

ment that shows the transactions in the checking account. This statement shows the amounts deposited, the amounts charged for checks written and for other services, and the balance at the end of the month. Figure 2–7 shows a bank statement sent to Mr. B. Thrifty.

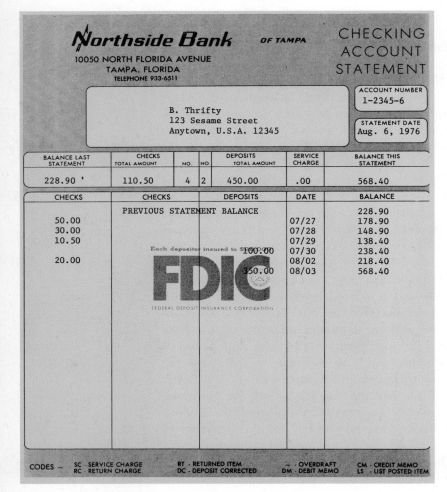

Northside Bank OF TAMPA

10050 NORTH FLORIDA AVENUE
TAMPA, FLORIDA
TELEPHONE 933-6511

CHECKING ACCOUNT STATEMENT

ACCOUNT NUMBER
1-2345-6

B. Thrifty
123 Sesame Street
Anytown, U.S.A. 12345

STATEMENT DATE
Aug. 6, 1976

BALANCE LAST STATEMENT	CHECKS TOTAL AMOUNT	NO.	NO.	DEPOSITS TOTAL AMOUNT	SERVICE CHARGE	BALANCE THIS STATEMENT
228.90	110.50	4	2	450.00	.00	568.40

CHECKS	CHECKS	DEPOSITS	DATE	BALANCE
	PREVIOUS STATEMENT BALANCE			228.90
50.00			07/27	178.90
30.00			07/28	148.90
10.50			07/29	138.40
		100.00	07/30	238.40
20.00			08/02	218.40
		350.00	08/03	568.40

Each depositor insured to $100,000

FDIC
FEDERAL DEPOSIT INSURANCE CORPORATION

CODES —	SC - SERVICE CHARGE	RT - RETURNED ITEM	— - OVERDRAFT	CM - CREDIT MEMO
	RC - RETURN CHARGE	DC - DEPOSIT CORRECTED	DM - DEBIT MEMO	LS - LIST POSTED ITEM

Figure 2–7   Courtesy of Northside Bank of Tampa.

Unfortunately, the balance shown on the bank statement may differ from the balance appearing on the depositor's check register or stub. The difference in balances may be due to checks written that have not yet cleared the bank but are charged to the depositor's account, deposits made during the last days of the month or while the statement was being prepared (and thus have not been recorded by the bank) and other charges made by the bank which have not been deducted by the depositor. On the reverse side of the bank statement there is a **reconciliation form** which may be used by the depositor to reconcile his balance with that of the bank. Figure 2–8 shows a reconciliation form prepared by Mr. B. Thrifty after receiving his bank statement. Note that on the reconciliation form Mr. Thrifty added to this account two deposits (for $90.00 and $60.30) that had not been credited to his account and subtracted 3 checks, #307, #311, and #313 (for $27.50, $50.00, and $10.00) that had not been charged against his account. This was necessary in order to account for the apparent difference of $62.80 between Mr. Thrifty's check stub balance of $631.20 and the bank statement balance of $568.40.

Reconciliation form

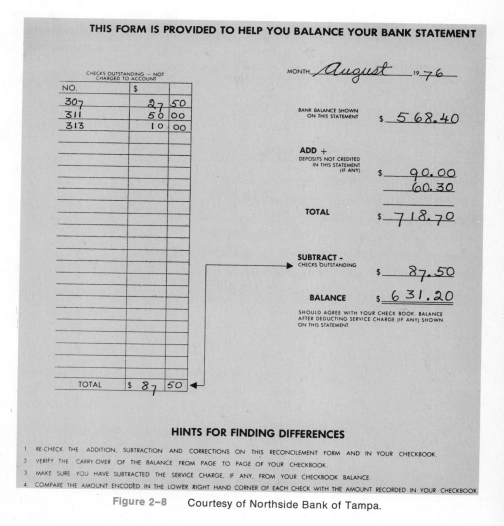

THIS FORM IS PROVIDED TO HELP YOU BALANCE YOUR BANK STATEMENT

CHECKS OUTSTANDING — NOT CHARGED TO ACCOUNT		
NO.	$	
307	27	50
311	50	00
313	10	00
TOTAL	$ 87	50

MONTH *August* 19 76

BANK BALANCE SHOWN ON THIS STATEMENT $ 568.40

ADD +
DEPOSITS NOT CREDITED IN THIS STATEMENT (IF ANY) $ 90.00
60.30

TOTAL $ 718.70

SUBTRACT -
CHECKS OUTSTANDING $ 87.50

BALANCE $ 631.20

SHOULD AGREE WITH YOUR CHECK BOOK. BALANCE AFTER DEDUCTING SERVICE CHARGE (IF ANY) SHOWN ON THIS STATEMENT

HINTS FOR FINDING DIFFERENCES

1. RE-CHECK THE ADDITION, SUBTRACTION AND CORRECTIONS ON THIS RECONCILEMENT FORM AND IN YOUR CHECKBOOK.
2. VERIFY THE CARRY-OVER OF THE BALANCE FROM PAGE TO PAGE OF YOUR CHECKBOOK.
3. MAKE SURE YOU HAVE SUBTRACTED THE SERVICE CHARGE, IF ANY, FROM YOUR CHECKBOOK BALANCE.
4. COMPARE THE AMOUNT ENCODED IN THE LOWER RIGHT HAND CORNER OF EACH CHECK WITH THE AMOUNT RECORDED IN YOUR CHECKBOOK.

Figure 2–8   Courtesy of Northside Bank of Tampa.

EXERCISE 2.6

In Problems 1 through 8, perform the indicated addition problems.

1. $3.05 + 12.07$ 2. $8.32 + .38 + 201.3$

3. $40.08 + 19.34 + .005$ 4. $17.05 + 3.07 + .003$

5. $.26 + 8.21 + 3.008$ 6. $380 + 3.04 + 71.053$

7. $.003 + .02 + .0032$ 8. $384.3 + .047 + 3.01$

In Problems 9 through 16, perform the indicated subtraction problems.

9. $71.31 - 2.82$ 10. $7.08 - .003$

11. $50.04 - .68$ 12. $.0987 - .094$

13. $29.03 - .384$ 14. $784 - .078$

15. $87.07 - 20.008$ 16. $25,234.507 - 16,344.78$

17. Use the accompanying ad to find the amount of money saved when buying:
    (a) the first item listed   (b) the 2nd item listed
    (c) the 3rd item listed   (d) the 4th item listed
    (e) the 5th item listed   (f) the 6th item listed
    (g) the 7th item listed

18. Complete the total and balances on the following check stubs, proceeding in numerical order and carrying each balance to the next check stub. (See figure on following page.)

19. Using the accompanying bank reconciliation form, reconcile Mr. B. Thrifty's account, which showed a bank statement balance of $730.48, a checkbook balance of $582.37, outstanding checks of $40.54, $30.15, and $80.92, and a service charge of $3.50.

NO. _1_ $ 20.00		
Aug 3 ___ 19 __		
TO Walt's Auto		
FOR Parts		
	DOLLARS	CENTS
BAL. BROT. FORD.	380	57
AMT. DEPOSITED	120	00
TOTAL		
AMT. THIS CHECK	20	00
DEDUCT		.10
BAL. CARD. FORD.		

NO. _2_ $ 152.10		
Aug 4 ___ 19 __		
TO Acme Mortgage		
FOR House Payment		
	DOLLARS	CENTS
BAL. BROT. FORD.		
AMT. DEPOSITED		
TOTAL		
AMT. THIS CHECK	152	10
DEDUCT		.10
BAL. CARD. FORD.		

NO. _3_ $ 12.50		
Aug 6 ___ 19 __		
TO Gen. Tel.		
FOR Phone Bill		
	DOLLARS	CENTS
BAL. BROT. FORD.		
AMT. DEPOSITED		
TOTAL		
AMT. THIS CHECK	12	50
DEDUCT		.10
BAL. CARD. FORD.		

NO. _4_ $ 58.10		
Aug 8 ___ 19 __		
TO T. E. Co.		
FOR Electric Bill		
	DOLLARS	CENTS
BAL. BROT. FORD.		
AMT. DEPOSITED	60	00
TOTAL		
AMT. THIS CHECK	58	10
DEDUCT		.10
BAL. CARD. FORD.		

NO. _5_ $ 112.80		
Aug 9 ___ 19 __		
TO Four States Ins.		
FOR Insurance Premium		
	DOLLARS	CENTS
BAL. BROT. FORD.		
AMT. DEPOSITED		
TOTAL		
AMT. THIS CHECK	112	80
DEDUCT		.10
BAL. CARD. FORD.		

NO. _6_ $ 40.59		
Aug 10 ___ 19 __		
TO U-Save Market		
FOR Food		
	DOLLARS	CENTS
BAL. BROT. FORD.		
AMT. DEPOSITED		
TOTAL		
AMT. THIS CHECK	40	59
DEDUCT		.10
BAL. CARD. FORD.		

20. Using a reconciliation form similar to the one given in Problem 19, reconcile the following account: The checkbook balance was $314.30 and the bank statement balance was $703.92. Outstanding checks were in the amounts of $50.84, $20.98, $120.50, and $300.00. A service charge of $2.70 had been deducted, and a $100 deposit was not included in the statement.

Bank Balance	$		Checkbook balance	$
Add: Outstanding Deposit	$_____			
Total	$			
Less: Outstanding Checks	$		Less: Bank charges	$
Adjusted balance	$_____		Adjusted balance	$_____

21. Using a reconciliation form similar to the one given in Problem 19, reconcile the following account: The bank statement balance was $609.35, and the checkbook balance was $736.95. Outstanding checks were in the amounts of $50.90, $30.40, and $8.75. The monthly service charge was $2.50, new checks cost $1.75, and a check of $10.00 that was deposited was returned for insufficient funds (hence the bank charges it against the account). A deposit of $203.40 was omitted from the bank statement.

22. Use the accompanying reconciliation form to reconcile an account with a bank balance of $393.50, a checkbook balance of $348.29, deposits of $50.93 and $40.98 not credited, and outstanding checks #30–68 for $113.40 and #30–69 for $43.97. A returned check amounted to $15, a service charge was $2.50, and a check printing charge was $2.75.

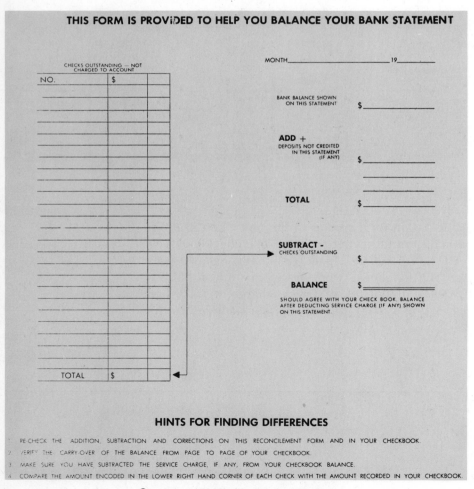

Courtesy of Northside Bank of Tampa.

2.7 MULTIPLICATION AND DIVISION OF DECIMALS

In the ad above, the price of one pound of sirloin steak is $1.49. If we wish to buy 2 pounds of sirloin, the price will be 2 × $1.49. In order to obtain the answer to the problem 2 × $1.49, we must know how to multiply decimals. Decimals are actually multiplied in the same manner as whole numbers. The only difference is that the decimal point must be placed correctly in the answer. In order to do this we count the number of digits to the right of the decimal points in the multiplicand and multiplier; we then count the same number of places from right to left in the product and insert the decimal point. Thus, if we wish to buy 3.5 pounds of meat at $1.49 per pound the cost would be

$$
\begin{array}{rl}
\$1.49 & \text{2 decimal places} \\
\times\, 3.5 & \text{1 decimal place} \\
\hline
745 & \\
447 & \\
\hline
\$5.215 & \text{2 + 1 = 3 decimal places}
\end{array}
$$

If we were buying 21 pounds the cost would be

$$
\begin{array}{rl}
\$1.49 & \text{2 decimal places} \\
\times\, 21 & \\
\hline
149 & \\
298 & \\
\hline
\$31.29 & \text{2 decimal places}
\end{array}
$$

Finally, if we were buying .5 (1/2) pound the cost would be

$$
\begin{array}{rl}
\$1.49 & \text{2 decimal places} \\
\times\, .5 & \text{1 decimal place} \\
\hline
\$.745 & \text{2 + 1 = 3 decimal places}
\end{array}
$$

In some cases it is necessary to add zeros in the product to obtain the required number of decimal places. We illustrate such an occurrence in the following Example.

Example 1

Multiply .00051 × 3.24

Solution

$$
\begin{array}{r}
3.24 \\
\times\ .00051 \\
\hline
324 \\
1620 \\
\hline
.0016524
\end{array}
$$

3.24   2 decimal places
× .00051   5 decimal places
.0016524   5 + 2 = 7 decimal places

└─Zeros inserted here to obtain 7 decimal places.

Multiplication involving powers of 10

    If the multiplication involves powers of 10, the decimal point in the multiplicand must be moved as many places to the right as there are zeros in the multiplier. Thus,

$10 \times 3.21 = 32.1$ (moving the decimal point one place to the right)

$100 \times 3.21 = 321$ (moving the decimal point two places to the right)

$10,000 \times .321 = 3,210$ (moving the decimal point four places to the right)

PROGRESS TEST 1

1. The product of 3.2 and 4.11 equals _____.
2. The product of .35 and .15 equals _____.
3. The product of .01 and 1.5 equals _____.
4. $100 \times 3.456 =$ _____.
5. $10 \times .0056 =$ _____.

Inventory Summary Sheets

    The ideas used in multiplication of decimals can be applied in the preparation of the Inventory Summary Sheet. The Inventory Summary Sheet includes the amount, price, description, and actual cost of all goods owned by the business and held for sale. It is common practice to price inventory items at cost or market value, *whichever is lower.* The Inventory Summary Sheet given in Figure 2–9 was received by the accounting department of the Might-T-Fine Company. To complete the sheet we must multiply the number of units of each product by the corresponding price. Complete the In-

---

1. 13.152   2. .0525   3. .015   4. 345.6   5. .056

INVENTORY SUMMARY SHEET

Item	Quantity on Hand	Date Purchased	Sales Price	Cost Price	Market Price	Inventory Value
White shirts	4	11–13	4 50	3 50	4 00	
Brown slacks	3	11–18	7 50	6 00	7 00	
Men's socks	4	12–12	1 50	1 00	1 25	
Men's belts	5	12–15	2 00	1 50	1 25	

Figure 2–9

ventory Sheet of Figure 2–9 by finding the Inventory Value of each of the items listed. (Recall that the unit price of every item equals the cost or the market value, *whichever is lowest.*)

When dividing decimals, it is easier to change the divisor to a whole number. This is accomplished by moving the decimal point in the divisor to the right until the divisor becomes a whole number. The decimal point in the dividend is then moved the same number of places and the decimal point in the quotient is placed directly above the new decimal point in the dividend. We illustrate several cases in the following Examples.

Division of decimals

Example 2

Divide 24.28 by 1.2.

Solution

We move the decimal point one place to the right so that the divisor is a whole number and obtain $24.2.8 \div 1.2.$

$$
\begin{array}{r}
2\,0.23 \\
1.2\,\overline{)24.2.800} \\
24 \\
\hline
0\,2\,8 \\
2\,4 \\
\hline
40 \\
36 \\
\hline
40
\end{array}
$$

Example 3

Divide 8.5 by .012.

Solution

We move the decimal point three places to the right so that the divisor is a whole number and obtain $8.500. \div .012$.

$$
\begin{array}{r}
708.33 \\
.012.\overline{)8.500.00} \\
84 \\
\overline{100} \\
96 \\
\overline{40} \\
36 \\
\overline{40} \\
36 \\
\overline{4}
\end{array}
$$

Example 4

Divide 198 by 38.

Solution

Since the divisor is a whole number, we proceed in the usual manner.

$$
\begin{array}{r}
5.21 \\
38\overline{)198.00} \\
190 \\
\overline{8\,0} \\
7\,6 \\
\overline{40} \\
38 \\
\overline{2}
\end{array}
$$

Example 5

Divide 80 by .14.

Solution

We move the decimal point two places to the right so that the divisor is a whole number and obtain $80.00. \div .14$.

$$
\begin{array}{r}
5\,71.42 \\
.14.\overline{)80.00.00} \\
70 \\
\overline{100} \\
98 \\
\overline{20} \\
14 \\
\overline{60} \\
56 \\
\overline{40} \\
28 \\
\overline{12}
\end{array}
$$

The fact that the method used in Examples 2 through 5 works is a direct consequence of the following properties:

1. Any number divided by itself equals 1.
2. 1 multiplied by any number equals the number.

Consider the problem of Example 2, $24.28 \div 1.2$.

$$\text{By (1)} \ \frac{10}{10} = 1. \ \text{By (2)} \ \frac{10}{10} \times \frac{24.28}{1.2} = \frac{24.2{,}8}{1.2{,}}.$$

But

$$\frac{24.28}{1.2} = \frac{10}{10} \times \frac{24.28}{1.2} = \frac{10 \times 24.28}{10 \times 1.2} = \frac{242.8}{12}.$$

equivalent problems

We remark that in certain cases it is required to **round off** an answer (approximate) to a specified number of decimal places. To round off a given number to a desired number of decimal places, the general rule is as follows: If the portion to be dropped begins with 5 (or a larger number) we add 1 to the last digit retained; if the portion to be dropped is less than 5, discard it. The answers to Examples 2 through 5, when rounded off to one decimal place, are 20.2, 708.3, 5.2, and 571.4, respectively. On the other hand, 34.56 rounded to one decimal place equals 34.6, and $0.197 = 0.20$ when rounded to two decimal places.

Rounding off numbers

PROGRESS TEST 2

In problems 1 through 4, work out answers to three decimal places and round off to two.
1. $36.38 \div 1.4$ equals _____.
2. $9.3 \div .014$ equals _____.
3. $734 \div 34$ equals _____.
4. $95 \div 15$ equals _____.
5. The number 3.05, when rounded to one decimal place, equals _____.

When the divisor is a power of 10 we move the decimal point of the dividend as many places to the left as there are zeros in the divisor. For example,

Division involving powers of 10

$47.43 \div 10 \quad = 4.743 \quad$ (The decimal point is moved one place to the left.)

---

1. 25.99   2. 664.29   3. 21.59   4. 6.33   5. 3.1

$4,045 \div 100 \quad = 40.45$ (The decimal point is moved two places to the left.)

$59.4 \div 1,000 = .0594$ (The decimal point is moved three places to the left.)

Divisions by powers of 10 is of particular importance to wholesale firms since prices are quoted by the hundred or by the thousand. Thus, to find the unit price of an item, we have to divide by 100 or 1000. For example, if the price of 100 items is $567.40 the unit price is $567.40 \div 100 = \$5.6740$ or $5.67 (rounded off to the nearest cent).

EXERCISE 2.7

1.   Find the following products:
   (a) 73×5.2 (b) 8.9×2.4 (c) $.003 \times 50.2$
   (d) $.01 \times 8.3$ (e) $731 \times .0006$ (f) $.009 \times 8,341.2$

2.   Using the prices given in the accompanying ad, find the cost of:
   (a) 7 pounds of cubed steaks
   (b) 8 pounds of Delmonico steaks
   (c) 6 pounds of English cut roast

U.S.D.A. Choice Heavy Western Beef
Beef Cubed Steak . per lb. $1⁵⁹

U.S.D.A. Choice Heavy Western Beef
Delmonico Steaks . per lb. $2²⁹

U.S.D.A. Choice Heavy Western Beef Boneless
English Cut Roast . . per lb. $1³⁹

3.   Using the prices in the ad of Problem 2, find the cost of:
   (a) 12 pounds of cubed steaks
   (b) 18 pounds of Delmonico steaks
   (c) 13 pounds of English cut roast

4.   The manager of the Good Taste Restaurant decides to buy 100 lb. of beef cubed steak, 100 lb. of Delmonico steaks, and 100 lb. of English cut roast. Using the prices given in Problem 2, find the total cost of the beef.

5.   Using the prices given in the accompanying ad, find the cost of:
   (a) 5 pounds of wieners
   (b) 7 packages of ham
   (c) 3 pounds of lamb

Regular Flavorful or All Beef
Oscar Mayer Wieners . .
1-lb. pkg. $1 29

Plumrose Imported Sliced
Cooked Ham . . . .
4-oz. pkg. 89 ¢

Quick Frozen New Zealand
Leg O' Lamb . . . .
per lb. $1 29

Courtesy of Oscar Mayer & Co.

6. If a company wishes to have 7 pages of black-and-white advertisements appearing in 8,000 issues of "Homelife", what will the cost of the ad be? (Hint: The cost is $2.05 × (number of pages) × (number of thousands).)

— And for all these Homelife "firsts," advertisers pay only $2.05 per thousand, for a black-and-white page. And only $2.75 per thousand for a 4-color page.

Reprinted by permission, from *The Wall Street Journal*, July 26, 1973, p. 11.

7. Using the ad in Problem 6, find the cost of 3 pages of 4-color advertisements appearing in 4,000 issues.

8. Using the accompanying ad, find the total amount paid on a loan of $3,000 borrowed for a period of:
   (a) 3 years (36 months)
   (b) 5 years (60 months)
   (c) 7 years (84 months)

Secondary financing for any worthwhile purpose: Home Improvements, debt consolidation, business, educational expenses or assume an existing mortgage.

Amount Financed	3 Years		5 Years		7 Years	
	Monthly Pmt.	Total of Pmts.	Monthly Pmt.	Total of Pmts.	Monthly Pmt	Total of Pmts.
3,000.00	96.81		63.75		49.81	
5,000.00	161.34		106.24		83.01	
7,000.00	225.88		148.73		116.21	

all loans are 10% ANNUAL PERCENTAGE RATE
The above includes all closing costs except recording. Mortgage cancellation insurance available.
Loans From $1,000.00 — Terms To 10 Years

9. Do the same as in Problem 8 for a loan of $5,000.

10. Do the same as in Problem 8 for a loan of $7,000.

11. There are many situations in which we have to convert cents to dollars. For example, if an article costs 57¢ and we buy 2, the cost is $57 \times 2 = 114$¢ or $1.14. To convert cents to dollars we move the decimal two places to the left. Using this idea find the price of:
    (a) 15 lb. of bananas   (b) 18 lb. of cabbage

Tropical Taste Treat
Golden Bananas . . . . per lb. **12ᶜ**
Perfect for Slaw, Hard
Green Cabbage . . . . per lb. **12ᶜ**
Delicate Flavored Tender
Zucchini Squash . . . . per lb. **29ᶜ**

12. The manager of the Gardenview Restaurant decided to buy 100 lb. of bananas and 100 lb. of zucchini. What would be the cost of the purchase?

13. In the accompanying advertisement the price of one tire is obtained by adding the sale price and the F.E. tax. Find the cost of 4 tires if the size is:
    (a) A78–13
    (b) B78–13
    (c) C78–13
    (d) C78–14

SIZE	SALE PRICE	PLUS F.E. TAX
A78-13	16.44	1.86
B78-13	16.66	1.81
C78-13	17.76	1.95
C78-14	17.89	2.08
E78-14	19.07	2.24
F78-14	20.05	2.39
G78-14	21.42	2.56
H78-14	22.44	2.75
G78-15	21.09	2.63
H78-15	22.57	2.81
J78-15	23.79	3.01
L78-15	24.29	3.16

14.   The Fleet-Service Company wishes to buy 100 size L78–15 tires. What will be the cost of the purchase?

15.   Find the cost (including tax) of 4 tires of each of the following sizes:
  (a) E78–14
  (b) F78–14
  (c) G78–14
  (d) H78–14

16.   In the ad below, multiply the cost of each item by the quantity to obtain the "Total". Then add the column labeled "Total" to obtain the price of the order.

Send me the items marked below. I enclose check, money order or charge card information.

Item	Size	Qty.	Cost ea.	Total
A. Men's roll-up hat. Washable cotton. Sizes S, M, L.	7¼	3	$2 50	
B. Budweiser tote bag. 100% cotton with plastic lining.	—	2	2.95	
C. "Bud Man" tank top. Cotton waffle weave knit. Sizes S, M, L.	∟	4	2.95	
D. Lady's floppy sun hat. Sizes S, M, L, XL.	XL	2	3.95	
E. "Budvisor" sun cap. One size fits all.	—	3	1.50	
F. Budweiser surfer cap. Hefty construction, reversible.	7¼	3	2.50	

Price includes mailing.   TOTAL $

NAME ___Fred   Boozer___

ADDRESS ___123 Busch Boulevard___

CITY ___Tampa___ STATE ___Fla___ ZIP __33621__

$_____ enclosed by ☐ Check ☐ Money Order

☐ BankAmericard #_____ ☐ Master Charge #_____

SIGNATURE ___Fred Boozer___

No proof of purchase necessary. Allow 30 days for delivery. Void where prohibited by law.

MAIL TO: BUSCH GARDENS GIFT SHOP, P. O. BOX 9158, TAMPA, FLORIDA 33604.
TV1-6

Courtesy of Busch Gardens Gift Shop.

17.   Follow the procedure outlined in Figure 2–9 of this section and find the Inventory Value of each of the items given in the figure on page 128, then find the total Inventory Value.

18.   Find the following quotients (approximate your answers to the nearest hundredths):
  (a) $8.36 \div 42$ (b) $32.64 \div 19$ (c) $844.39 \div 98$

19.   Find the following quotients (approximate your answers to the nearest hundredths):
  (a) $3.1 \div 4.3$ (b) $14.289 \div .191$ (c) $14.06 \div .006$

20.   Find the following quotients (approximate your answers to the nearest hundredths):
  (a) $6.3214 \div .071$ (b) $17.3 \div .05$ (c) $3.92 \div .029$

Item	Quantity on Hand	Date Purchased	Sales Price		Cost Price		Market Price		Inventory Value	
INVENTORY SUMMARY SHEET										
Hammers	6	6–15	1	50	1	00	1	35		
Screw Drivers	8	6–18	1	25		75	1	00		
Hand Saws	4	6–20	5	50	4	00	4	50		

21.   In the ad below, the price per acre of the first tract of land is $19,500 ÷ 2.188. Find the price per acre of the
(a) first tract.
(b) second tract.
(c) third tract.
(d) fourth tract.

ACREAGE	PRICE
2.188	$19,500
2.403	21,900
3.463	26,400
2.328	11,000
2.798	12,500
2.464	10,500
3.615	15,900
3.806	13,800

LaMonte-Shimberg Corporation   **Quail Hollow**

Reprinted, by permission, from *The Tampa Times,* August 17, 1973, p. 7c.

22.   Do the same as in Problem 21 for the following:
(a) fifth tract
(b) sixth tract
(c) seventh tract
(d) eighth tract

23.   The accompanying chart gives the five-year operating cost of different brands of air conditioners. The yearly operating cost is obtained by dividing the five-year operating cost by 5. For

example, the average yearly operating cost for a Friedrich is $309.60 ÷ 5 = $61.92. Find the average yearly operating cost of:

(a) an Airtemp
(b) an Amana
(c) a Coldspot
(d) an Emerson QuietKool
(e) a Fedders

BRAND	MODEL	AHAM VOLTS	AHAM BTU/HR	AHAM WATTS	AHAM AMPS	ENERGY EFFICIENCY RATIO BTU/WATT	5-YEAR OPERATING COST*	% SAVED WITH FRIEDRICH
FRIEDRICH	SM 10310A	115	10300	860	7.5	12.0	$309.60	—
Airtemp	S10-20GT	115	10000	1375	12.0	7.3	509.90	39%
Amana	11-2J	115	10000	1380	12.0	7.2	511.70	40%
Coldspot	106.73280	115	11000	1380	12.0	8.0	465.20	33%
Emerson QuietKool	10BH1D	115	10000	1350	12.0	7.4	500.60	38%
Fedders	ACT10F2E	115	10000	1360	12.0	7.4	504.30	39%
Frigidaire	AE3-10MU	115	10000	1360	12.0	7.4	504.30	39%
General Elec.	AGCE811AA	115	10500	1375	12.0	7.6	485.60	36%
Hotpoint	AHCQ810AA	115	10000	1350	12.0	7.4	500.60	38%
Penncrest	865-3210-30-080	115	10000	1350	12.0	7.4	500.60	38%
Signature	UFO-5173	115	10000	1360	12.0	7.4	504.30	39%
Westinghouse	AH107P1	115	10000	1375	12.0	7.3	509.90	39%
Whirlpool	AXC-100-21	115	10000	1380	12.0	7.2	511.70	40%
York	RD 100-2A	115	10000	1370	12.0	7.3	508.00	39%

*BASIS OF COMPARISON: Operating cost based on 2.5¢/KWH average. Wattage adjusted for equal BTU/Hr. in each category. 5-year period based on 14,400 hours of operation...average 12 hr/day, 30 days/mo, 8 mo/yr.

SOURCE OF COMPARISON: 1973 Directory of Certified Room Air Conditioners (1) published by the Association of Home Appliance Manufacturers.

Courtesy of Friedrich Refrigerators Incorporated.

24. Do the same as in Problem 23 for:
(a) a Frigidaire
(b) a General Electric
(c) a Hotpoint
(d) a Penncrest
(e) a Signature

25. A **unit processing cost** is determined by dividing costs by the number of units processed. For example, if a department is charged with $1,000 worth of materials during a certain period and it produces 500 units in this period, the cost per unit of the materials is $1,000 ÷ 500 units = $2 per unit. Find the material cost per unit (to the nearest cent) of Gudget Manufacturing, a factory that uses $2,700 of materials and produces
(a) 500 units   (b) 350 units   (c) 800 units

26. The idea of unit processing cost can be extended to cover everyday problems. For example, if a can of Brand X beans contains 12 ounces and costs 80 cents, while Brand Y contains 8 ounces and costs 50 cents, the cost per ounce of Brand X is 80 ÷ 12 = 6.67¢ and that of Brand Y is 50 ÷ 8 = 6.25¢. Ob-

viously, all other factors being equal, Brand Y is a better buy. Use this idea to find which is a better buy in the following problems.

Brand X	Brand Y
(a) Real Roast Chunky Peanut Butter ($1.12 for 38 ounces)	Real Roast Creamy Peanut Butter (52¢ for 18 ounces)
(b) Shedd's Smooth Peanut Butter (81¢ for 24 ounces)	Nu Made Extra Smooth Creamy Peanut Butter (56¢ for 18 ounces)

SELF-TEST/CHAPTER 2

1. In the figure below, the close price for each of the ten most active stocks on April 11, 1973, is shown. The close prices of the last three stocks, when written as improper fractions, are: _____, _____ and _____.

2. Find:
_____ a.   The GCF of 60 and 36
_____ b.   The LCM of 60 and 36

MOST ACTIVE STOCKS

	Volume	Close	Chgs.
Champ Ho	138,100	6¾	— ½
N Kinny Cp	137,900	7½	— ⅛
Coit Intl	120,800	6¾	— ⅞
Richton Int	111,400	2½	— ⅝
TWA wt	91,400	22⅞	+ ½
Bowmar Ins	51,700	30⅞	—1⅝
Telepromp	51,500	23¼	—1⅛
Bartons Cdy	50,300	3½	....
Syntex	43,200	55⅞	— ⅛
LCA Cp wt	41,100	3¾	— ¼

List includes most active stocks selling at over $1.

Reprinted, by permission, from *The Wall Street Journal*, April 11, 1973, p. 28.

3. Perform the following operations:

_____ a. $\dfrac{11}{60} + \dfrac{1}{36}$

_____ b. $12 - 2\dfrac{5}{6}$

_____ c. $2\dfrac{1}{2} \times 4\dfrac{2}{5}$

_____ d. $8 \div \dfrac{2}{3}$

Bank Balance	$		Checkbook balance	$
Add: Outstanding Deposit	$_____			
Total	$			
Less: Outstanding Checks	$		Less: Bank Charges	$
Adjusted Balance	$_____		Adjusted balance	$_____

4. In the figure given in Problem 1 above, find:
    _____ a.   the difference between the close price of one
                    share of Telepromp and one share of TWA.
    _____ b.   the close price of 3 shares of Champ Ho.

5. Referring to the figure in Problem 1 above, find the total
    close price paid by an investor who bought:
    _____ a.   One share of Champ Ho, one share of Richton
                    Int., and one share of TWA.
    _____ b.   One third of a share of Syntex.

6. Perform the following operations:
    _____ a. $1.4 + 8 + .07 + 12.125$
    _____ b. 0.332×8.12
    _____ c. $0.823 \div 0.71$ (Round off answer to two decimal
                    places.)

7. Using the accompanying reconciliation form, reconcile Mr.
    B. Timid's account, which showed a bank statement balance
    of $840.50, a checkbook balance of $1,062.17, outstanding
    checks of $40.90 and $50.42, an outstanding deposit of $310.49,
    and a service charge of $2.50.

8. Convert the following to fractions in lowest terms:
    _____ a.   0.312
    _____ b. $0.81\frac{1}{2}$
    _____ c.   0.333 . . .

9. Convert the following fractions to decimals:
    _____ a. $\dfrac{9}{100}$
    _____ b. $\dfrac{5}{8}$
    _____ c. $\dfrac{3}{7}$

10. Referring to the ad below, find

_____ a. the difference in acreage between the first and the last tract.

_____ b. the price per acre of the first tract.

_____ c. the total acreage you will have if you buy the first three tracts.

CLOSE-OUT: BIG VALUES ON BIG GOLF COURSE HOMESITES!

Some right on the fairways, others very near. Developed and ready for construction or investment opportunity for individuals or groups. Minutes from Tampa via I-75. Wooded tracts from two to over three acres. Phone 879-1950, 8 - 5 weekdays. Sales office open noon - 5 weekends, phone 949-2118.

ACREAGE	PRICE
2.188	$19,500
2.403	21,900
3.463	26,400
2.328	11,000
2.798	12,500
2.464	10,500
3.615	15,900
3.806	13,800

LaMonte-Shimberg Corporation

Quail Hollow

part two

The Neighbors   By George Clark

CHECK OUT

"There's been a mistake, madam. You can't use this 18c off
coupon on this product . . . it only costs 16c!"

The Mathematics of
Retailing and Accounting

three

Ratio, Proportion, Per Cent, Markups, and Markdowns

TV service technicians say yes. Again.

Nationwide survey names Zenith, by more than 2 to 1 over the next best brand, as the color TV needing fewest repairs.

Courtesy of Zenith.

3.1 RATIOS

We are often confronted with situations in which two quantities are compared. For example, the ad above states that in a nationwide survey of T.V. service technicians, it was found that for every two technicians who named Zenith as the color T.V. needing fewer repairs, there was another who named the next best brand. Mathematically we say that "the *ratio* of technicians naming Zenith over the next best brand is 2 to 1." A *ratio* is a way of comparing two or more numbers. The ratio 2 to 1 may also be written as 2:1, or $\frac{2}{1}$. In general, the ratio of a number **a** to another number **b** may be written in any of three ways: (1) a to b   (2) a:b   (3) $\frac{a}{b}$

Definition of ratio

Example 1

Write the ratios 4:3, 3:1, and 3 to 7 as fractions.

Solution

4:3 is written as $\frac{4}{3}$, 3:1 is written as $\frac{3}{1}$, and 3 to 7 is written as $\frac{3}{7}$.

135

PROGRESS TEST 1

1. A ratio is a way of _____ two or more numbers.

2. The ratio 5 to 2 can be written as _____ and also as _____.

3. When written as a fraction, the ratio 5:2 equals _____.

Reduction of ratios.

In business, ratios are used to compare two or more quantities. For example, if there are 10 women and 20 men working in an office, we can say that the ratio of women to men is 10 to 20. This ratio can be **reduced** by expressing the ratio 10 to 20 as $\frac{10}{20}$ and reducing the

To reduce a ratio, express it as a fraction and reduce the fraction.

fraction $\frac{10}{20}$ to $\frac{1}{2}$. Thus, the reduced ratio is 1:2. To **reduce** a ratio, we express it as a fraction and reduce the fraction.

Example 2

There are 50 administrators and 150 teachers at State College.
(a) Find the ratio of administrators to teachers.
(b) Reduce the ratio obtained in (a).

Solution

(a) The ratio is 50:150.
(b) Since $\frac{50}{150} = \frac{1}{3}$, the reduced ratio is 1:3 $\left(\text{or } \frac{1}{3}\right)$.

Comparison-to-one ratio

Another common ratio is the **comparison-to-one ratio.** When we say that a car gives 18 miles to the gallon, we are expressing the fact that the car can go 18 miles for each (one) gallon of gasoline. Thus, if we go 60 miles and use 4 gallons of gas, the car gives $\frac{60}{4} = 15$ miles

To express a ratio as a comparison-to-one ratio, divide the numerator by the denominator. The quotient is the ratio to one.

per gallon. We have thus expressed the ratio 60:4 as a **comparison-to-one ratio** (15:1). To express a ratio as a comparison-to-one ratio, express the ratio as a fraction, and divide the numerator by the denominator. The quotient will be the ratio to one. For example, to express the ratio 3:6 as a comparison-to-one ratio, we write 3:6 as $\frac{3}{6} = 0.5$ and write the ratio as 0.5:1 (or simply 0.5).

---

1. comparing   2. 5:2, $\frac{5}{2}$ 3. $\frac{5}{2}$

Example 3

Write the ratios 4:7 and 6:4 as comparison-to-one ratio.

Solution

4:7 is $\frac{4}{7} \simeq .57^*$; hence the comparison-to-one ratio is 0.57:1, or 0.57.†

6:4 is $\frac{6}{4} = 1.5$; hence the comparison-to-one ratio is 1.5:1, or 1.5.

Example 4

The Gross Profit for Clankem Manufacturing amounted to $5,000 while its Sales were $40,000.
    (a) Find the reduced ratio of Gross Profits to Sales.
    (b) Express the reduced ratio as a comparison-to-one ratio.

Solution

(a) The ratio of Gross Profits to Sales, $5,000:$40,000 is $\frac{5,000}{40,000} = \frac{1}{8}$.

(b) Dividing 1 by 8, we obtain 0.125; hence the comparison-to-one ratio is 0.125:1, or 0.125.

PROGRESS TEST 2

    1. A company has 10 administrators and 50 employees. The ratio of administrators to employees, when reduced, is _____.

    2. When written as a comparison-to-one ratio, 12:8 equals _____.

    3. If the Gross Profit of Clankem Manufacturing amounted to $7,500, while its Sales were $60,000, the reduced ratio of Gross Profits to Sales would be _____.

We illustrate the use of ratios in the next three examples.

---

  *"$\simeq$" means "approximately equal to".

  †Recall that $\frac{4}{7} = \overline{0.571428}$; approximating $\frac{4}{7} \simeq 0.57$.

1. $\frac{1}{5}$ 2. 1.5 to 1 or simply 1.5   3. $\frac{1}{8}$

Example 5

The B. Fair Company wants to maintain their ratio of secretaries to department managers as 2:1. If they are planning to hire 300 persons, how many managers and how many secretaries should be hired?

Solution

(Method 1) The ratio 2:1 indicates that for every 2 secretaries hired, one manager should also be hired. We divide the workers to be hired into $2 + 1 = 3$ parts. 2 of the parts should be secretaries, and one part managers, so they should hire $\frac{2}{3}$ of $300 = 200$ secretaries, and $\frac{1}{3}$ of $300 = 100$ managers.

(Method 2) We divide the workers into $2 + 1 = 3$ parts. Then we have:

$$\text{number of secretaries} + \text{number of managers} = \text{total}$$
$$2 \text{ parts} + \qquad\qquad 1 \text{ part} = 300$$
$$3 \text{ parts} = 300, \text{ hence}$$
$$(\text{dividing by 3}) \quad 1 \text{ part} = 100$$

So they should hire 200 secretaries and 100 managers.

Example 6

A man divided his estate among his wife and two children in the ratio of 5:3:3. If his estate is valued at $22,000, how much will each receive?

Solution

(Method 1) The ratio 5:3:3 indicates that for every $5 the wife gets, each child should get $3. We first divide the estate into $5 + 3 + 3 = 11$ shares. The wife receives $\frac{5}{11}$ of $22,000 = \$10,000$ and each child receives $\frac{3}{11}$ of $22,000 = \$6,000$.

(Method 2) We divide the estate into $5 + 3 + 3 = 11$. Then

$$\text{wife's} + \text{first child's} + \text{second child's} = \text{total estate}$$
$$\text{part} \qquad\quad \text{part} \qquad\qquad \text{part}$$
$$5 \text{ shares} + 3 \text{ shares} + \qquad 3 \text{ shares} = \$22,000$$
$$11 \text{ shares} = \$22,000$$

Hence,

$$(\text{dividing by 11}) \quad 1 \text{ share} = \$2,000$$

So the wife gets $5 \times (\$2,000) = \$10,000$, and each child receives $3 \times (\$2,000) = \$6,000$.

Example 7

An employee is paid at the rate of $130 per week (5 working days). How much will he earn in 12 working days?

Solution

If the employee earns $130 in 5 days, his earning ratio is $\dfrac{\$130}{5} = \$26$ for one day's work; hence he will earn $12 \times 26 = \$312$ for 12 days' work.

PROGRESS TEST 3

1. If the secretary to manager ratio in the B. Fair Company is 3:2, and they plan to hire 300 employees (and maintain the same ratio) they should hire _____ secretaries and _____ managers.

2. $50 is to be divided among 3 persons in the ratio 5:2:3. The first person should receive _____, the second person should receive _____, the third should receive _____ .

3. A man earns $44 per day (8 hours of work). If he worked 3 hours on a certain day, his salary for that day would be _____.

EXERCISE 3.1

1. Write the following ratios as fractions:
   (a) 3:5   (b) 8 to 7
   (c) 4:9   (d) 55 to 25

2. Reduce the following ratios and express them in each of the three ratio forms:
   (a) 3 to 6   (b) 19 to 57
   (c) $600 to $2000   (d) 55 to 35
   (e) $24,000 to $5,000   (f) $690 to $1300

3. A company employs 3200 women and 4000 men. What is the reduced ratio of women to men in this company?

4. In a recent math test, 20 students failed and 95 passed. What is the reduced ratio of failures to passes for this test?

5. In the spring of 1972 the University of Delaware had 700 persons on their teaching staff, and they enrolled 10,600 students.

---

1. 180, 120   2. $25, $10, $15   3. $16.50

What is the reduced teacher to student ratio at the University of Delaware?

6. In the 1968 Presidential election the number of votes received by Hubert Humphrey in Wirt County, West Virginia was 820. If George Wallace obtained 140 votes in this county, what is the reduced ratio of Humphrey to Wallace votes?

7. In 1971, the number of employed persons in the U.S. was approximately 80 million persons, while the number of unemployed persons totaled approximately 5 million. What is the ratio of employed persons to unemployed persons in the U.S. for the year 1971?

8. A dozen pencils cost 80¢. How much will 18 pencils cost?

9. How much will 3 pounds of sugar cost if 5 pounds cost 50¢?

10. $27 is to be divided among three persons in the ratio of 2:3:4. What amount will each of these persons get?

11. Two automobile salesmen sold cars in the ratio of 5:4. If at the end of the year the company offered a $2700 bonus to be divided between them based on their sales, how much should each salesman get?

12. Three companies are sharing their computer costs according to the number of hours each company is using the computer. How much of the $75,000 bill should each company pay if they use the computer 3, 7 and 5 hours daily?

Applications to Finance and Accounting

13. A company pays $3.60 per share of stock every quarter (120 days). What would be the amount of dividends per share collected after 480 days?

14. Two partners, Al and Bob, agree to divide the profits of a business in a 3 to 2 ratio. If the net income is $15,000, what is each one's share?

15. Bob invested $15,000 in a business, while Al contributed $10,000. They agree to divide the profits in the same ratio as each partner's capital investment. If the business shows a net profit of $30,000, what is each partner's share of the profits?

Applications to Economics

The Malthusian Theory of Economics states that the productivity of agriculture (food) can be increased arithmetically, but population will increase geometrically. In the chart below, the increase in population is compared with the increase in food over a period of 6 years.

	I	II	III	IV	V	VI
Population	1	2	4	8	16	32
Food	1	2	3	4	5	6

16. Give the ratios of food to population for years I, II, III, IV, V, and VI.

17. The price-earning (P/E) ratio of a stock is defined to be the market price of the stock divided by its actual or indicated annual earning per share. In the table below, some stocks and their P/E ratios are shown. Fill in the missing P/E ratios in the table.

STOCK	RECENT PRICE	YEARLY DIVIDEND	EARNINGS (1971)	P/E RATIO
Coca-Cola	$101	$1.58	$2.80	36
Eastman Corp.	$ 77	$1.32	$2.60	30
Xerox Corp.	$113	$0.80	$2.70	
Polaroid Corp.	$102	$0.32	$2.20	

18. The Dividend Yield (D.Y.) is defined to be the current annual dividend divided by the current market price. For example, the D.Y. for the Coca-Cola Company (see the table in Problem 17) is $\frac{1.58}{101} = 0.014$. Find the dividend yield for Eastman Corporation.

19. Find the dividend yield for Xerox Corporation.

20. Find the dividend yield for Polaroid Corporation.

Index Up at 21.5% Annual Rate for First Quarter of Year— Farm Costs Key Factor

3.2 IMPORTANT RATIOS IN BUSINESS

The preparation of **Index Numbers** requires the use of ratios. The best known index is the Consumer Price Index which is prepared by the Federal Government. The **Consumer Price Index** measures average change in prices of goods and services purchased

Index Numbers and the Consumer Price Index

by urban wage-earners, clerical workers' families, and single workers living alone. We now give an example to show how the Index Numbers are calculated. In Example 1 we assign a value of 100 to the base period, the year 1967.

Example 1

Item	Average Cost (1967)	Index Number (1967)	Average Cost (1971)	Index Number (1971)
Food	$2100	100	$2478	118
Housing	$1600	100	$1984	124
Apparel	$ 620	100	$ 744	120

Solution

The index number is the ratio of the cost in the year to be compared to the cost in the base year multiplied by 100.

The Index Number in the last column is calculated by finding the ratio of the year to be compared (1971) to the base year (1967) and multiplying by 100. Thus we have the following Index Numbers:

For food: $\dfrac{\$2478}{\$2100} \times 100 = 1.18 \times 100 = 118$

For housing: $\dfrac{\$1984}{\$1600} \times 100 = 1.24 \times 100 = 124$

For apparel: $\dfrac{\$\ ?}{\$\ ?} \times 100 = 1.20 \times 100 = 120$ (Fill in the blanks.)

The earning power of a company and the comparison of a company's profit margins to those of other firms are of great importance in economics. Here we present four ratios that are commonly used to evaluate a firm's profitability.

Business ratios

1. **The Operating Profit Ratio** (O.P.R.). This is the ratio of the firm's operating profit (O.P.) to net sales (N.S.). The ratio indicates how well the company is performing in its selling operation. The ratio is defined as follows: $\text{O.P.R.} = \dfrac{\text{O.P.}}{\text{N.S.}}$

2. **The Net Profit Ratio** (N.P.R.). This is the ratio of net profits after taxes (N.P.A.T.) to net sales. The ratio gives a general view of the performance of the company in a given year. The ratio is defined as follows: $\text{N.P.R.} = \dfrac{\text{N.P.A.T.}}{\text{N.S.}}$

3. **The Return on Total Assets Ratio** (R.T.A.R.). This is the ratio of net profits after taxes to total Assets (T.A.). The ratio measures the rate of return on the total asset investment in the firm and indicates how much the total assets are producing. The ratio is defined as follows: $\text{R.T.A.R.} = \dfrac{\text{N.P.A.T.}}{\text{T.A.}}$

4. **The Return on Net Worth Ratio** (R.N.W.R.). This is the ratio of net profits after taxes to net worth (N.W.). The ratio measures the rate of return on the stockholders' investment and indicates how well the stockholders' funds are being utilized. The ratio is defined as follows: $R.N.W.R. = \dfrac{N.P.A.T.}{N.W.}$

Finally we present a ratio that is sometimes used by management to measure the solvency of a business. This ratio, called the Current Ratio (C.R.), is defined to be the ratio of Current Assets (C.A.) to Current Liabilities (C.L.); that is, $C.R. = \dfrac{C.A.}{C.L.}$. The ratio indicates the company's ability to pay all current liabilities if all current assets were converted into cash. As a general rule, this ratio should be 2 to 1. In recent years the Current Ratio for U.S. corporations has averaged about 1.85 to 1.

Definition of Current Ratio

Example 2

The Gadget Manufacturing Company reports the following information:

Net Sales	$22,000		Current Assets	$22,180
			Total Assets	$33,920
Operating Profits		$1,980	Current Liabilities	$ 3,680
Estimated Taxes		$ 660	Net Worth	$30,240
Net Profit After Taxes		$1,320	Total: Liabilities and	
			Net Worth	$33,920

Find: (a) The O.P.R.   (b) The N.P.R.   (c) The R.T.A.R.
(d) The R.N.W.R.   (e) The C.R.

Solution

(a) $O.P.R. = \dfrac{O.P.}{N.S.} = \dfrac{\$\ 1,980}{\$22,000} = 0.09$

(b) $N.P.R. = \dfrac{N.P.A.T.}{N.S.} = \dfrac{\$\ 1,320}{\$22,000} = 0.06$

(c) $R.T.A.R. = \dfrac{N.P.A.T.}{T.A.} = \dfrac{\$\ 1,320}{\$33,920} = 0.04$

(d) $R.N.W.R. = \dfrac{N.P.A.T.}{N.W.} = \dfrac{\$\ 1,320}{\$30,240} = 0.04$

(e) $C.R. = \dfrac{C.A.}{C.L.} = \dfrac{\$22,180}{\$\ 3,680} = 6.03$

PROGRESS TEST 1

The AAA Company, with total assets of $10,000 and a net worth of $1,250, has $5,000 in operating profits and estimates a $2,500 tax. If their net sales amounted to $50,000,

1. their O.P.R. equals_____.
2. their N.P.R. equals_____.
3. their R.T.A.R. equals_____.
4. their R.N.W.R. equals_____.

EXERCISE 3.2

The following table will be used in Problems 1 through 3.

Item	Average Cost (1967)	Index Number (1967)	Average Cost (1971)	Index Number (1971)
Transportation	$ 570	100	$ 741	(a)
Health	312	100	434	(b)
Other	1000	100	1350	(c)

1.   Find the Index Number that belongs in (a) above.

2.   Find the Index Number that belongs in (b) above.

3.   Find the Index Number that belongs in (c) above.

The following information will be used in Problems 4 through 7.

CLANKEM MANUFACTURING

INCOME STATEMENT

Net Sales	$6500
Cost of Goods and Expenses	5400
Operating Profits	$1100
Dividends	100
TOTAL INCOME	$1200
Interest Paid	100
Profits before Taxes	1100
Estimated Taxes	540
Net Profit After Taxes	$ 560

BALANCE SHEET

Current Assets	$6000
Non-current Assets	300
Fixed Assets	3200
Other Assets	200
TOTAL ASSETS	$9700
Liabilities and Net Worth	
Current Liability	2720
Payable Bonds	2700
TOTAL LIABILITIES	$5420
Total Net Worth	4280
TOTAL LIABILITY AND NET WORTH	$9700

1. .1   2. .05   3. .25   4. 2

4. Based on the information above, find the O.P.R. for the Clankem Manufacturing Company.

5. Based on the information above, find the N.P.R. for the Clankem Manufacturing Company.

6. Based on the information above, find the R.T.A.R. for the Clankem Manufacturing Company.

7. Based on the information above, find the R.N.W.R. for the Clankem Manufacturing Company.

8. The Income Statement for the Hustle-Bustle Company shows $4000 in current assets, while liabilities amount to $1600. What is the Current Ratio of the Hustle-Bustle Company? For every dollar of current liabilities, how much is available in current assets?

9. If in the problem above the current assets are $15,000 and the current liabilities are $4000, what is the Current Ratio for the Hustle-Bustle Company?

10. To estimate accurately the Gross National Product (G.N.P.), the yearly output (measured in **current** dollars) is expressed in **constant** dollars of another year. In the table below, the production of the Gadget Manufacturing Company is given. Column (4) expresses the price listed in column (3) in the form of **Index Numbers**. Fill in the missing ratios in the table below.

(1) Year	(2) No. of Gadgets	(3) Price of Gadgets	(4) Price index: ratio of current price to price in year 1	(5) Output in current dollars of each year (2) × (3)	(6) Price of output in current dollars of year 1
1	2	$2	2 to 2 = 1	$ 4	4 to 1 = $4
2	3	$4	4 to 2 = 2	_____	_____
3	5	$5	_____	_____	_____
4	8	$6	_____	$48	48 to 3 = $16

914:610:914 = 36:24:36

Reprinted by permission of the Construction Industry Training Board, London, England.

3.3 PROPORTIONS

The picture above, used by the Construction Industry Training Board to prepare citizens for the shift from British units to metric units, illustrates the fact that the ratios 914:610:914 (measured in millimeters) and 36:24:36 (measured in inches) represent the same ratios; that is, they are **proportional.**[*]

Definition of proportion

A proportion is a statement of equality between ratios. Thus, $\frac{2}{5} = \frac{4}{10}$ and 2:5 = 4:10 are examples of proportions. In general, the quantities a, b, c, and d are said to be **in proportion** if the ratio of a to b equals the ratio of c to d. The proportion is written in either of 2 ways:

a and d are the extremes; b and c are the means.

(1) a/b = c/d (Read "a is to b as c is to d".)

(2) a:b = c:d (read "the ratio of a to b is equal to the ratio of c to d".

The first term, a, and the last or fourth term, d, are called the **extremes** of the proportion. The second term, b, and the third term,

---

[*]We first consider proportions involving four numbers.

c, are called the **means.** Thus, in the proportion 3:2 = 6:4, 3 and 4 are the extremes, while 2 and 6 are the means.

Since a proportion is a statement of equality of two ratios, any operation which may be performed on an equation may be performed on a proportion as well. Thus, in the proportion a/b = c/d, we can multiply both sides of the equation by bd (the common denominator) and obtain

$$\frac{a}{b}(bd) = \frac{c}{d}(bd) \text{ or } ad = bc.$$

This equation gives rise to the following rule:

> **RULE 3.1** The product of the extremes (a and d) equals the product of the means (b and c).

This result indicates that if we cross multiply the terms in the proportion a/b = c/d, the products are equal. Thus, given any three terms in a proportion, the missing term can be found by using Rule 3.1 or by **cross multiplication.** The following examples illustrate the uses of proportions in solving different types of problems.

Example 1

Find x if 11:3 = 33:x.

3 and 33 are the means;
11 and x are the extremes.

Solution

(Method 1) Since the product of the extremes equals the product of the means (Rule 3.1) we have 11x = 99. Dividing by 11 we obtain

$$\frac{\cancel{11}x}{\cancel{11}} = \frac{\overset{9}{\cancel{99}}}{\cancel{11}} = 9$$

(Method 2) We write the proportion as an equality of ratios; that is, $\frac{11}{3} = \frac{33}{x}$. The fraction on the right has a numerator of 33. This numerator can be obtained by multiplying the fraction on the left by $\frac{3}{3}$. Thus, $\frac{3}{3} \times \frac{11}{3} = \frac{33}{x}$. Since the numerators and denominators of these two fractions should be equal, x = 9.

We remark here that Method 1 can also be used in solving the next 3 examples. The ambitious student may check the solutions to these examples by solving them using Method 1.

Example 2

A manufactured article sold for $15 and its production cost was $12. If the company producing this article has total sales of $45,000, what is the total production cost?

Solution

The sales to cost ratio is $\frac{15}{12}$. The total sales to total cost ratio is $\frac{45,000}{x}$,

where x is the total production cost. Since the two ratios are propor-

tional, we have $\frac{15}{12} = \frac{45,000}{x}$. The fraction on the right has a numerator

of 45,000. This numerator can be obtained by multiplying the fraction

on the left by $\frac{3,000}{3,000}$. Thus, $\frac{3,000}{3,000} \times \frac{15}{12} = \frac{45,000}{x}$. Since the numerators

and denominators of these two fractions should be equal, we see that
x = 3,000 × 12 = $36,000.

12 and 45 are the means;
15 and x are the extremes.

Example 3

1 and A are the means;
2 and 30,000 are the
extremes.

The recommended (or desired) Current Ratio for U.S. corporations is 2:1. If a company has $30,000 in Current Liabilities, what should the Current Assets of the company be to have the recommended (or de-

sired) Current Ratio? Hint: Recall that the C.R. $= \dfrac{\text{Current Assets}}{\text{Current Liabilities}}$.

Solution

The desired ratio is $\frac{2}{1}$. The company has a ratio of $\frac{A}{30,000}$, where A

denotes the amount of Current Assets. Since these two ratios are

proportional, we have $\frac{2}{1} = \frac{A}{30,000}$. The fraction on the right has a

denominator of 30,000. This denominator can be obtained by multi-

plying the fraction on the left by $\frac{30,000}{30,000}$. Thus, $\frac{30,000}{30,000} \times \frac{2}{1} = \frac{A}{30,000}$.

Since the numerators and denominators of these two fractions should
be equal, A = 30,000 × 2 = $60,000.

PROGRESS TEST 1

1. If 3:4 = 12:x, x equals _____.
2. If 2/x = 4/4, x equals _____.
3. If x:9 = 2:6, x equals _____.
4. The current ratio for U.S. corporations is 2:1. A company has $8,000 in current liabilities. Their current assets, to maintain the current ratio, should be _____.

Example 4

The Index Numbers mentioned in Section 3.2, Example 1, can be calculated by using proportions.

ITEM	AVERAGE COST (1967)	INDEX NUMBER (1967)	AVERAGE COST (1971)	INDEX NUMBER (1971)
Food	$2100	100	$2478	x
Housing	1600	100	1984	y
Apparel	620	100	744	z

Solution

In the table above, we calculate the Index Numbers in the last column as follows:

For Food: The ratio of cost in 1971 to the Index in 1971 is $\dfrac{2478}{x}$.

The ratio of cost in 1967 to the Index in 1967 is $\dfrac{2100}{100}$. Since these

ratios are proportional, we have $\dfrac{2478}{x} = \dfrac{2100}{100} = \dfrac{21}{1}$. Hence $\dfrac{2478}{x} = \dfrac{21}{1}$.

The fraction on the left has a numerator of 2,478. This numerator can

be obtained by multiplying the fraction on the right by $\dfrac{118}{118}$. Thus

$\dfrac{2478}{x} = \dfrac{118}{118} \times \dfrac{21}{1}$, and x = $118.

x and 21,000 are the means; 2478 and 100 are the extremes.

For Housing: The ratio of cost in 1971 to the Index in 1971 is

$\dfrac{\$1984}{y}$. The ratio of cost in 1967 to the Index in 1967 is $\dfrac{\$1600}{100}$. Since

these ratios are proportional, we have $\dfrac{1984}{y} = \dfrac{1600}{100} = \dfrac{16}{1}$. Hence

$\dfrac{1984}{y} = \dfrac{16}{1}$. The fraction on the left has a numerator of 1984. This

numerator can be obtained by multiplying the fraction on the right by

$\dfrac{124}{124}$. Thus, $\dfrac{1984}{y} = \dfrac{124}{124} \times \dfrac{16}{1}$, and y = $124.

y and 16,000 are the means; 1984 and 100 are the extremes.

---

1. 16   2. 2   3. 3   4. $16,000

PROGRESS TEST 2

1. In Example 4 above, the ratio of cost for apparel in 1971 to the Index in 1971 is _____.

2. The ratio of cost for apparel in 1967 to the Index in 1967 is _____.

3. The Index number z for the year 1971 is _____.

EXERCISE 3.3

In each of the following proportions, find the missing number.

1.	$?/9 = 2/3$	2.	$x/6 = 7/2$	3.	$6/x = 2/7$
4.	$52/? = 2/3$	5.	$3/4 = x/48$	6.	$2/3 = ?/48$
7.	$5/6 = 30/x$	8.	$3/4 = 12/x$	9.	$3:2 = ?:4$
10.	$2:7 = ?:21$	11.	$7:x = 14:56$	12.	$2:x = 8:32$
13.	$x:7 = 9:3$				

14. In a certain map, $\frac{5}{16}$ of an inch equals 100 miles. What distance is represented by 10 inches?

15. In the problem above, what distance is represented by 15 inches?

16. The Environmental Protection Agency (E.P.A.) recommends a maximum safe ratio of $\frac{1}{100}$ micrograms of PCB (polychlorinated biphenyls) per liter of water in rivers and lakes. A company has a small lake containing 10,000 liters of water. How many micrograms of PCB can the company discharge into the lake before reaching the E.P.A.'s maximum safe ratio?

17. If in the problem above, the lake contains 250,000 liters of water, how many micrograms of PCB can the company discharge into the lake before reaching the E.P.A.'s maximum safe ratio?

The following table will be used in Problems 18 through 20.

ITEM	AVERAGE COST (1967)	ITEM NUMBER (1967)	AVERAGE COST (1971)	INDEX NUMBER (1971)
Transportation	$ 570	100	$ 741	(a)
Health	$ 312	100	$ 434	(b)
Other	$1000	100	$1350	(c)

---

1. 744:z   2. 620:100   3. 120

18. Using proportions, find the Index Number that belongs in (a) above.

19. Using proportions, find the Index Number that belongs in (b) above.

20. Using proportions, find the Index Number that belongs in (c) above.

21. A car goes 46 miles on 4 gallons of gas. How far will it go on 6 gallons?

22. 60 yards of cloth cost $25. How much will 24 yards cost?

Applications to Insurance

23. The death rate in motor vehicle accidents is approximately 25 per 1,000 persons. A town has a population of 80,000 persons. If an insurance company is established in this town, how many deaths due to motor vehicle accidents should the company expect?

24. If in the problem above, the company is established in a town with 160,000 inhabitants, how many deaths due to motor vehicle accidents should the company expect?

25. Most insurance policies contain an exclusion clause to withhold payment in case of suicide. The suicide rate is approximately 11 per 1,000 persons. In a town of 97,000, how many suicides should an insurance company expect?

26. If the company above operates in a town of 44,500 inhabitants, how many suicides should the company expect?

Applications to Accounting

A **proportional** tax is a tax in which the same rate applies to all, regardless of the assessed valuation. For example, a property tax rate of $10 for every $1,000 assessed valuation, regardless of how much property is owned, is a **proportional** tax.

27. The property tax in a certain state is $9 for every $1,000 assessed valuation. A firm owns property assessed at $47,500. How much should the accountant of the firm estimate for property taxes?

28. If the property of the firm above is assessed at $59,200, how much should the accountant of the firm estimate for property taxes?

29. Do Problem 27 assuming that the state levies a tax of $7.50 for every $1,000 of assessed property.

30. Do Problem 28 assuming that the state levies a tax of $6.75 for every $1,000 of assessed property.

3.4 PER CENT

"Per cent" means "by the hundred". "%" is used to denote "per cent".

The term **per cent** is derived from the Latin words "per" and "centum" meaning "by the hundred". Thus, per cent is another way to express hundredths. The symbol "%" is used to denote per cent. The ad above states "just 5% down", which means that for every 100 dollars the Condominium costs, the buyer will have to pay 5 dollars down.

In previous chapters we learned two other ways in which hundredths can be expressed, namely as fractions or as decimals. For example,

$$40\% = \frac{40}{100} = \frac{2}{5} \qquad\qquad 125\% = \frac{125}{100} = \frac{5}{4}$$

$$75\% = \frac{75}{100} = \frac{3}{4} \qquad\qquad 2.3\% = \frac{2.3}{100} = \frac{23}{1000}$$

$$67\% = \frac{67}{100} \qquad\qquad\qquad 2\% = \frac{2}{100} = \frac{1}{50}$$

Changing per cents to fractions

Thus, we have the following rule:

RULE 3.2 To change a per cent to a fraction, drop the per cent sign, place the number over 100, and reduce the fraction to lowest terms. If the numerator results in a decimal, multiply numerator and denominator by an appropriate power of 10 to clear the decimal.

Example 1

Change the following per cents to fractions.

(a) 5%   (b) 15%   (c) 31%   (d) 5.5%

Solution

We drop the per cent sign, place the number over 100, and reduce the fraction. Thus,

(a) $5\% = \dfrac{5}{100} = \dfrac{1}{20}$ (b) $15\% = \dfrac{15}{100} = \dfrac{3}{20}$

(c) $31\% = \dfrac{31}{100}$ (d) $5.5\% = \dfrac{5.5}{100} = \dfrac{55}{1000} = \dfrac{11}{200}$

Note that in (d) we multiply $\dfrac{5.5}{100}$ by $\dfrac{10}{10}$ to clear the decimal.

A procedure opposite to the one used in Example 1 can usually be applied to change a fraction to a per cent; that is, we write the fraction with a denominator of 100, drop the denominator, and add the per cent sign to the numerator. Thus,

Changing fractions to per cents

$$\frac{1}{20} = \frac{5}{100} = 5\%, \quad \frac{3}{20} = \frac{15}{100} = 15\%, \quad \frac{31}{100} = 31\%,$$

$$\frac{1}{5} = \frac{20}{100} = 20\%, \quad 27 = \frac{27}{1} = \frac{2700}{100} = 2700\%$$

Some fractions, however, can not readily be expressed as a fraction whose denominator is 100. To change such fractions to per cents, convert the fraction to a decimal and then to a per cent. Thus, $\frac{4}{9} \approx .4444 = 44.44\%$ and $\frac{6}{7} \approx .8571 = 85.71\%$

Warning: some fractions can not be easily expressed as a fraction with a denominator of 100.

As we mentioned above, a per cent can also be expressed as a decimal. Thus,

$$40\% = \frac{40}{100} = .40 \quad \text{hence } 40\% = .40$$

$$75\% = \frac{75}{100} = .75 \quad \text{hence } 75\% = .75$$

$$67\% = \frac{67}{100} = .67 \quad \text{hence } 67\% = .67$$

$$2\% = \frac{2}{100} = .02 \quad \text{hence } 2\% = .02$$

From the examples above, we deduce the following rule:

RULE 3.3   To change a per cent to a decimal, move the decimal point two places to the left and drop the per cent sign.

Changing per cents to decimals

Example 2

Change the following per cents to decimals:

(a) 12%   (b) 3%   (c) 42%

Solution

We move the decimal point two places to the left and drop the per cent sign.

(a) 12% = .12% = .12
(b)   3% = .03% = .03
(c) 42% = .42% = .42

Changing decimals to per cents

A procedure opposite to the one used in Example 2 can be applied to change a decimal to a per cent; that is, we move the decimal point two places to the right and add the per cent sign. Thus,

(a) .12 = 12.% = 12%   (b) .03 = 03.% = 3%
(c) .42 = 42.% = 42%   (d) 3.5 = 350.% = 350%

PROGRESS TEST 1

1. When expressed as a reduced fraction, 18% is _____.

2. When expressed as a fraction, 2.5% is _____.
3. When expressed as a per cent, 7/20 is _____.
4. When expressed as a per cent, 5/9 is _____.
5. When expressed as a per cent, .04 is _____.
6. When expressed as a per cent, 3.8 is _____.

We have already seen that a fraction can be expressed as a per cent. Thus, a per cent is another way of expressing the ratio between two numbers. The ad at the beginning of this section states that the buyer of the condominium should give 5% of the total price as a down payment. That is, for every $100 of the total cost, $5 must be given as a down payment. If the cost of the condominium is $12,000, how much should the buyer give as a down payment? To solve this problem we consider $12,000 as the whole (base) price and 5% as the rate. We want 5% of $12,000. Written in mathematical symbols, we have

The percentage equals the rate times the base.

$\frac{5}{100} \times \$12,000 = \$600$. The problem above suggests

FORMULA 1
$$P = R \cdot B$$

where P is the percentage, R is the rate (number of hundredths of the total) and B is the base (number or quantity taken as a whole).

---

1. $\frac{9}{50}$ 2. $\frac{1}{40}$ 3. 35%   4. 55.56%   5. 4%   6. 380%

Courtesy of Schulstad & Huffman, Inc.

Given any two of the three quantities in Formula 1, the other two can be found. We illustrate this procedure in the next three examples.

Example 3

In the ad above, the price of the house (base) is $68,000 and the rate is 29%. Find the percentage (P) that has to be paid down.

Finding the percentage given the base and the rate

Solution

Using Formula 1, $P = R \cdot B$, where $R = 29\%$ and $B = \$68,000$. Substituting, $P = \dfrac{29}{100} \times \$68,000 = \$19,720$; hence P, the percentage, is $19,720.

Example 4

In the ad below, the price of the house (base) is $31,500, and the down payment (the percentage) is $3,150. Find the rate.

Finding the rate given the base and the percentage

Solution

The problem can be restated by asking "$3,150 is what per cent of $31,500?" By Formula 1, $P = R \cdot B$. Thus, solving for R in Formula 1, we obtain

If $P = R \cdot B$, we can divide both sides of the equation by B and obtain $\dfrac{P}{B} = \dfrac{R \cdot B}{B}$.

Hence, $R = \dfrac{P}{B}$: the rate equals the percentage divided by the base.

FORMULA 2
$$R = P/B$$

In this case, $P = \$3,150$ and $B = \$31,500$. Hence $R = \dfrac{3150}{31,500} = \dfrac{1}{10} = 10\%$.

Finding the base given the percentage and the rate

Note that we converted the fraction $\frac{1}{10}$ to a per cent, since the rate is usually given as a per cent.

Example 5

In the ad above the percentage after discount ($225) and the rate (50%) are given. How much was the copier originally?

Solution

The problem can be restated by asking "$225 is 50% of what number?" By Formula 1, $P = R \cdot B$. Thus, solving for B we have

If $P = R \cdot B$, we can divide both sides of the equation by R and obtain $\frac{P}{R} = \frac{\cancel{R}B}{\cancel{R}}$: the base equals the percentage divided by the rate.

FORMULA 3
$$B = \frac{P}{R}$$

In our case $P = \$225$ and $R = 50/100$. Hence,

$$B = \frac{225}{50/100} = 225 \times \frac{100}{50} = \$450$$

Finally, we give a problem illustrating the use of Formulas 1, 2, and 3.

Example 6

   (a) Find 12% of 25.
   (b) 20 is what per cent of 80?
   (c) 80 is 20% of what number?

Solution

(a) In this problem R (the rate) is $\frac{12}{100}$ and B (the base) is 25. We want to find P (the percentage). Using Formula 1, we have:

$$P = R \cdot B = \frac{12}{100} \cdot 25 = \frac{300}{100} = 3.$$

(b) In this problem P (the percentage) is 20, and B (the base) is 80. We want to find R (the rate). Using Formula 2, we find that:

$$R = \frac{P}{B} = \frac{20}{80} = \frac{1}{4} = 25\%.$$

(c) In this problem P (the percentage) is 80 and R (the rate) is 20%. We want to find B (the base). Using Formula 3, we find that:

$$B = \frac{P}{R} = \frac{80}{20/100} = 80 \cdot \frac{100}{20} = 400.$$

We finally state Formulas 1, 2, and 3 (so they can be easily referred to) in

> **RULE 3.4** Formula 1: $P = RB$
>
> Formula 2: $R = \dfrac{P}{B}$
>
> Formula 3: $B = \dfrac{P}{R}$

PROGRESS TEST 2

1. The price of a house is $15,000. If the owner requires 8% as a down payment, the down payment on this house is _____.

2. An article is on sale for $2.40. If its original price was $6.00, the article has been discounted _____ per cent.

3. 30 is _____ per cent of 120.

4. An article was sold for $2.73. If the buyer received a 9% discount, the original (list) price of the article was

_____.

5. 30 is 25% of _____.

EXERCISE 3.4

Express each of the following as a fraction in lowest terms.

1.   22%   2.   34%   3.   150%

---

1. $1,200   2. 60%   3. 25%   4. $3.00   5. 120

4. 225%   5. 3.5%   6. 7.5%

7. .2%   8. .45%

Express each of the following as a per cent.

9. $\frac{1}{4}$ 10. $\frac{1}{5}$ 11. $\frac{4}{5}$

12. $\frac{3}{4}$ 13. $\frac{5}{7}$ 14. $\frac{7}{9}$

15. $\frac{3}{7}$ 16. $\frac{4}{7}$ 17. .22

18. .37   19. 3.7   20. 4.3

21. 21.3   22. .0043   23. 0.33

24. $\frac{4.5}{8.25}$ 25. $\frac{1.44}{1.20}$ 26. $68\frac{2}{3}$

27. $20\frac{1}{4}$

28. Find:

(a) 42% of 640   (b) 30% of 340   (c) 4.5% of 700

29. Find:

(a) 58% of 900   (b) 40% of 780   (c) 3.5% of 300

30. 40 is what per cent of:

(a) 120   (b) 180   (c) 200

31. 60 is what per cent of:

(a) 120   (b) 180   (c) 300

32. 40 is:

(a) 25% of what number   (b) 20% of what number
(c) 60% of what number

33. 60 is:

(a) 25% of what number   (b) 20% of what number
(c) 60% of what number

34. A house is selling for $15,500. If the owner requires a 12% down payment, how much will the down payment on this house be?

35. If in the problem above, the owner requires a 15% down payment, how much will the down payment on this house be?

36. A down payment on a house amounts to $4500. If the price of the house is $15,000, what per cent of the total price is being paid as the down payment?

37. If in the problem above, the down payment is $3500, what per cent of the total price is being paid as the down payment?

38.   A house is on sale for $12,500. The owner claims that this price represents a 5% discount on the original price of the house. What was the original price of the house?

39.   If in the problem above, the owner claims that the new price represents a 15% discount on the original price of the house, what was the original price of the house?

40.   An article was bought for $24.50 and sold for $32. What per cent of the cost is the profit?

41.   In the problem above, what per cent of the selling price is the profit?

42.   A waitress found $2.25 in tips at her table. If the tip represents 15% of the total bill, what was the total bill?

43.   A man sold an automobile for 80% of the original cost. (a) What per cent did the man lose? (b) If the car cost him $4,000, how much did he sell it for?

44.   A stock paid $1.25 in dividends per share. If this amount represents 5% of the original investment per share, what was the original investment per share?

"Surveys show that 98.9% of all marriages are happy. It's only after the ceremony that the percentage drops off!"

"Strictly Business" by Dale McFeatters. Courtesy of Publishers-Hall Syndicate.

45.   A cloth will shrink 2% after washing. If 156.8 inches are needed, how long should the cloth be before washing?

46.   The accompanying cartoon states that 98.6% of all marriages are happy. If the number of marriages is 240, how many of them are happy?

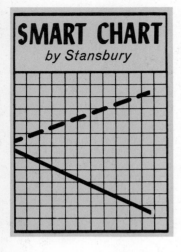

"This is our Market Analyst Doll. Wind him up, he estimates a 50% increase, then falls on his face." Reproduced by permission of Herbert Stansbury.

47.   If in Problem 46, the number of marriages is 390, how many of them are happy?

48.   If in Problem 46, the number of marriages is 445, how many of them are happy?

49.   If a company produces 17,328 units and the Market Analyst Doll (see cartoon) predicts a 50% increase,
      (a) how many more units will the Market Analyst Doll predict?
      (b) what will be the total estimated production?

50.   Do the same as in Problem 49, assuming the company produces 129,340 units.

3.5   MARKUPS

In our American economy, where production is not for self consumption but for sale to others, merchants offer their goods for sale with the intention of making a profit.

Markup

In pricing goods retailers work on the basis of a **markup** (profit, gross profit, or margin). The markup on an item is the difference between the selling price and the cost of the item. Thus, in the ad above, the markup is $100. The relationship between cost (C), selling price (S), and markup (M) can be expressed by means of

> **FORMULA 4**
> $$S = C + M \quad \text{or} \quad M = S - C \quad \text{or} \quad C = S - M$$

Note that these three
equations are equivalent.

Usually the retailer knows from past experience the markup that has to be maintained in order to derive profits from his business. In the next two examples we illustrate the manner in which the per cent of markup is used in determining the selling price and cost of an article.

Example 1

An article costs $15 and the markup is 10% of the cost. What is the selling price of this article?

Finding the selling price
given the cost and
the markup

Solution

By using Formula 4, $S = M + C$, $M = \dfrac{10}{100}$ of $15 = \$1.50$. Hence, $S = \$1.50 + \$15 = \$16.50$.

"Strictly Business" by Dale McFeatters. Courtesy of Publishers-Hall Syndicate.

"We're more than happy to take it back! The price has gone up 20 per cent since you bought it!"

Example 2

In the cartoon above, the (selling) price of the article has gone up 20%. If the (selling) price of the article was $80, what is the new selling price?

Solution

The new selling price is $\$80 + (\dfrac{20}{100} \times 80) = \$80 + \$16 = \$96$.

Example 3

The cost of an item is $120 and the markup is 40% of the selling price. What should the selling price be?

Solution

(Method 1) Since the markup is 40% of the selling price, the cost is 60% (100% − 40%) of the selling price. We have P (the percentage) = $120 and R (the rate) = 60%.

Let S = B (the base), where S is selling price. By Formula 3,

Remember, $B = \frac{P}{R}$.

$$S = B = \frac{P}{R} = \frac{120}{60/100} = \frac{120 \times 100}{60} = \$200.$$

(Method 2) Let S be the selling price. $S = M + C = \left(\frac{40}{100} \cdot S\right) + \$120.$

Subtracting $\frac{40}{100} \cdot S$ from both sides of the equation, we have $\frac{60}{100} \cdot S$

= $120. Multiplying both sides by $\frac{100}{60}$ we obtain $S = \frac{120 \times 100}{60} = \$200.$

Example 4

Finding the cost given the selling price and the markup

The selling price of an article is $30 and the markup is 20% of the cost. Find the cost of the article.

Solution

(Method 1) Since the markup is 20% of the cost, the selling price is 120% (100% + 20%) of the cost. We have P (the percentage) = $30 and R (the rate) = 120%. Let C = B (the base), where C is the cost.

By Formula 3, $C = B = \frac{P}{R} = \frac{30}{120/100} = \frac{30 \times 100}{120} = \$25.$

(Method 2) Let C be the cost. $S = C + \left(\frac{20}{100} \cdot C\right) = \frac{120}{100} \cdot C.$ Since

$S = \$30$, we have $30 = \frac{120}{100} \cdot C.$ Hence, multiplying by $\frac{100}{120}$ we obtain

$C = \frac{30 \times 100}{120} = \$25.$

PROGRESS TEST 1

1. If in Example 1, the markup is 15% of the cost, the selling price of the article is _____.
2. If in Example 3, the cost is $30, the selling price is _____.
3. If in Example 4, the selling price is $24, the cost is _____.

---

1. $17.25   2. $50   3. $20

In the examples above, we have seen that the per cent of markup can be computed with respect to either cost or selling price. In the next examples, we learn how to find the per cent of markup on cost and on selling price and to understand the relationship between the two.

Finding the per cent of markup on cost and on selling price

Example 5

An article costs $20 and is sold for $25. Find
    (a) the markup.
    (b) the per cent of markup on cost.
    (c) the per cent of markup on selling price.

Solution

(a) By Formula 4, $M = S - C = \$25 - \$20 = \$5$.
(b) To find the per cent of markup on **cost**, we wish to find what per cent 5 is of 20. In this case P (the percentage) is 5 and B (the base) is 20. Using Formula 2 of Section 3.4, we have $R = \dfrac{P}{B} = \dfrac{5}{20} = \dfrac{1}{4} = 25\%$.
Thus, the per cent of markup on cost is 25%.
(c) Here P = 5 and B = 25. Hence, using Formula 2 of Section 3.4, $R = \dfrac{P}{B} = \dfrac{5}{25} = \dfrac{1}{5} = 20\%$. Thus, the per cent of markup on selling price is 20%.

From the discussion above we can derive the following:
The per cent of markup on cost is given by

FORMULA 5 $\dfrac{M}{C} \times 100 = \left(\dfrac{S - C}{C}\right) \times 100$

The per cent of markup on selling price is given by

FORMULA 6 $\dfrac{M}{S} \times 100 = \left(\dfrac{S - C}{S}\right) \times 100$

Retail concerns and manufacturers usually base their per cent of markup on cost, whereas large retail concerns base their per cent of markup on selling price. For this reason retailers use Table 3–1 below to convert per cent of markup based on selling price to per cent of markup on cost.

TABLE 3-1   Merchandise Markup Table

Per cent of Markup Based on Selling Price		Per cent of Markup Based on Cost Price
10		11.1
11	If you want to make a gross	12.4
12	profit of	13.6
13	←	15.0
14		16.3
15		17.7
20	Add to the cost price	25.0
25	→	33.3
30		42.9
33		49.1
35		53.8
40		66.7
50		100.0

We now illustrate by example how the numbers in the table are related.

Example 6

A 20% markup on selling price is equivalent to what per cent of markup on cost?

Solution

(Method 1)   The selling price is 100%. The markup is 20%. Hence, the cost is 80%. We have to find what per cent 20% is of 80%. We have $\frac{20\%}{80\%} = \frac{.20}{.80} = \frac{1}{4} = 25\%$. Thus, a 20% markup on selling price is equivalent to a 25% markup on cost (see Table 3–1).

(Method 2)   Let S be the selling price and C the cost. $S - \left(\frac{20}{100} \times S\right) = C.$ We now find what per cent the markup on selling price $\left(\frac{20}{100} \times S\right)$ is of the cost $\left(S - \left(\frac{20}{100} \times S\right) = \frac{80}{100} \times S\right)$. We have

$$\frac{\frac{20}{100} \times \$}{\frac{80}{100} \times \$} = \frac{1}{4} = 25\%$$

Verify this in Table 3–1.   Thus a 20% markup on selling price is equivalent to a 25% markup on cost.

Example 7

A 15% markup on cost is equivalent to what per cent of markup on selling price?

Solution

(Method 1)   The cost is 100%. The markup on cost is 15%. Hence, the selling price is 115%. We now find what per cent 15% is of 115%. We have $\frac{15\%}{115\%} = \frac{0.15}{1.15} \approx 13\%$. Thus, a 15% markup on cost is equivalent to a 13% markup on selling price.

(Method 2)   Let C be the cost and S the selling price. $C + \left(\frac{15}{100} \times C\right) = S$.

We now find what per cent the markup on cost $\left(\frac{15}{100} \times C\right)$ is of the selling price $\left(C + \left(\frac{15}{100} \times C\right) = \frac{115}{100} \times C\right)$. We have

Verify this in Table 3–1.

$$\frac{\frac{15}{100} \times \cancel{C}}{\frac{115}{100} \times \cancel{C}} = \frac{15}{115} \approx 13\%$$

PROGRESS TEST 2

1. An article costs $40 and is sold for $50. The per cent of markup on cost for this article is _____.

2. In the problem above, the per cent of markup on the selling price for the article is _____.

3. A 40% markup on selling price is equivalent to a _____ markup on cost.

4. A 100% markup on cost is equivalent to a _____ markup on selling price.

EXERCISE 3.5

In Problems 1 through 6, find the selling price.

	Cost	Per cent of markup (on cost)
1.	$40	10%
2.	$7.50	12%
3.	$26.50	6%

	Cost	Per cent of markup (on selling price)
4.	$27	10%

---

1. 25%   2. 20%   3. 66.7%   4. 50%

| 5. | $35.20 | 20% |
| 6. | $31.15 | 11% |

In Problems 7 through 12, find the cost.

	Selling price	Per cent of markup (on cost)
7.	$39.76	42%
8.	$13.86	13%
9.	$578.68	36%

	Selling price	Per cent of markup (on cost)
10.	$36	40%
11.	$19.30	19%
12.	$40	50%

13. The gross profit (markup) of a jewelry store is 35% of cost. Find (a) the gross profit (markup) and (b) the selling price of a ring that costs $36.

14. The cost of an article is $44. The operating expenses are 20% of the cost and the net profit is 5% of the cost. What should the selling price of the article be?

15. If in the problem above, the cost of the article is $50, what should the selling price of the article be?

16. The gross profit (markup) of the Crash and Carry Supermarket is 35% of the selling price. What are (a) the selling price and (b) the gross profit (markup) of an article that costs $1.30?

17. The cost of a dozen appliances is $1800, and the operating expenses are 18% of the selling price. If it is desired to have a 7% net profit on the selling price, what should be the price of each of the appliances?

18. A builder wants to sell a house for $9600. He knows that his operating expenses are 35% of the selling price. If he wants to have a 20% net profit on the house, what is the highest price he can pay the contractor for building this house?

19. If in the problem above, the builder wishes to sell the house for $28,800, what is the highest price he can pay the contractor for building the house?

20. Dear's Dress Shop sells a dozen dresses for $300. If his operating expenses are 16% of the selling price and he wishes to have a 16% net profit on the selling price, what was the cost of each dress to the shop owner?

In Problems 21 through 26, find (a) the markup, (b) the per cent of markup on selling price, and (c) the per cent of markup on cost.

	Selling price	Cost			Selling price	Cost
21.	$120	$90	24.		$16.50	$12
22.	$41	$30	25.		$257	$172.40
23.	$25	$21	26.		$37.50	$34.98

In Problems 27 through 30, fill in the missing entries.

	Per cent of markup (on cost)	Per cent of markup (on selling price)
27.	10%	_____
28.	_____	30%
29.	_____	35%
30.	50%	_____

Reprinted by permission of the Chicago Tribune-New York News Syndicate, Inc.

"There's been a mistake, madam. You can't use this 18c off coupon on this product . . . it only costs 16c!"

3.6 MARKDOWNS

Unfortunately for the retailer, but fortunately for the consumer, it is sometimes necessary to mark merchandise down, that is, to lower its price. A markdown is simply a reduction in the original price. Thus, in the ad above, the merchandise has been reduced (marked

Definition of markdown

down) from its original price of $4.99 to $3.88. In this case the mark-down is $4.99 − $3.88 = $1.11, and the **per cent of markdown** is $\frac{1.11}{4.99} = 22\%$ (to the nearest per cent).

We illustrate this idea further in the following examples:

Example 1

An article is marked down from its original price of $60 to a discount price of $48. Find (a) the markdown, and (b) the per cent of markdown.

Solution

(a) The markdown is $60 − $48 = $12.

(b) The per cent of markdown is $\frac{\$12}{\$60} = \frac{1}{5} = 20\%$.

Example 2

The Hap-E-Kiddie store anticipated sales of $20,000 during the month of December. One week before Christmas, sales had totaled $15,000. The sales manager decided to mark down the remaining $5,000 of merchandise by 20%. (a) What was the total markdown? (b) What was the selling price of the marked-down merchandise?

Solution

(a) The total markdown was $\frac{20}{100} \times 5,000 = \$1,000$.

(b) The new selling price is the original selling price minus the markdown; that is, $5,000 − $1,000 = $4,000.

Example 3

If in Example 2, the markup on the merchandise was 40% of the selling price,

   (a) what was the overall markup after the price reduction?
   (b) what was the overall per cent of markup on the selling price?

Solution

The selling price of all merchandise (including merchandise marked down) was $15,000 + $4,000 = $19,000. The cost of all merchandise (including merchandise marked down) was 60% of the selling price, or $\frac{60}{100} \times 20,000 = \$12,000$. (a) Using the formula, $M = S − C$, we find that the overall markup after the price reduction amounts to $19,000 − $12,000 = $7,000.

(b) The per cent of markup on selling price is $\frac{7,000}{19,000} = 36.84\%$.

A common practice in retailing (when the inventory is very low) is to mark down the remaining merchandise to cost. We illustrate such an occurrence in the following example:

Example 4

If in Example 2 the remaining $5,000 in merchandise is marked down to cost and the markup is 40% of the selling price, what is the overall per cent of markup?

Solution

The markup on the $15,000 is $\frac{40}{100} \times 15,000 = \$6,000$. The cost of the remaining $5,000 is $\$5,000 - \left(\frac{40}{100} \times 5,000\right) = \$5,000 - \$2,000 = \$3,000$. The total sales price is $\$15,000 + \$3,000 = \$18,000$. Thus, the markup is $\frac{6,000}{18,000} = \frac{1}{3} = 33\frac{1}{3}\%$.

PROGRESS TEST 1

1. An article is marked down from its original price of $100 to a discount price of $75. The markdown price on selling is _____.

2. In the problem above, the per cent of markdown is _____.

3. Merchandise in a store has a 20% markup on selling price and a $10,000 retail value. After selling $8,000 of merchandise, the remaining $2,000 is reduced to cost. The overall markup is _____.

EXERCISE 3.6

In Problems 1 through 12, find (a) the markdown, and (b) the per cent of markdown (approximate to the nearest per cent).
(Use the prices listed in the ad on following page for Problems 2 through 12.)

Original price, $120
Discount price, $96

---

1. $25   2. 25%   3. $1,600

Courtesy of Sears, Roebuck and Co.

13. In Problems 2 through 12, which article has the lowest per cent of markdown (approximated to the nearest per cent)?

14. In Problems 2 through 12, which article has the highest per cent of markdown (approximated to the nearest per cent)?

15. After obtaining answers to Problems 13 and 14, can you justify the claim at the top of the ad that you will save 10% to 25%? Explain.

16. A store anticipated sales of $30,000 during the month of April. Two days before Easter, sales had totaled $20,000. The sales manager decided to mark down the remaining $10,000 of merchandise by 10%. What was (a) the total markdown and (b) the selling price of the marked-down merchandise?

17. Do Problem 16, assuming that the anticipated sales amounted to $40,000.

18. If in Problem 16 the markup on the merchandise was 20% of the selling price, find (a) the overall markup after the re-

duction and (b) the overall per cent of markup on the selling price.

19. If in Problem 16 the remaining $10,000 of merchandise is marked down to **cost**, what is (a) the overall markup and (b) the overall per cent of markup? (Assume the markup is 20% of selling Price.)

20. The Casino Bakery makes 100 loaves of Cuban bread at a cost of 25¢ a loaf. About 10% of these will be marked down as "old bread" and sold for 10¢ a loaf. Find the selling price of a loaf so that the bakery may make 48% on cost.

SELF-TEST/CHAPTER 3

1. _____ a. In a certain office there are 50 secretaries and 10 supervisors. Find the reduced ratio of secretaries to supervisors.

    _____ b. If the company decided to employ 30 more persons and maintain the same ratio as in part (a), how many secretaries and how many supervisors should be hired?

2. . _____ In a certain Profit Sharing plan the stocks were divided among executives, managers, and employees in the ratio of 4:3:3. If the number of stocks to be divided is 2,000, find the number of stocks received by the executives, the managers, and the employees.

3. _____ Al invested $5,000 in a certain business while his partner Bob contributed $10,000. If they agree to divide the profits in the same ratio as each partner's capital investment, and the business shows a net profit of $30,000, what is each partner's share of the profits?

4. _____ The Grow-Kwik Fertilizer Company has current assets of $10,000 and current liabilities of $2,000. The current ratio of the Grow-Kwik Company is?

5. Solve for the missing number:
  _____ a. $6:8 = 24:?$
  _____ b. $2:? = 8:4$
  _____ c. $?:18 = 4:12$
  _____ d. $16:8 = ?:32$

6. Find
  _____ a. 25% of 160
  _____ b. 3.5% of 140

7. _____ a. 30 is what per cent of 90?
  _____ b. 90 is 20% of what number?

8. _____ An article costs $40 and the markup is 20% of the cost. Find the selling price of this article.

9. _____ The cost of an item is $160 and the markup is 20% of the selling price. Find the selling price of this item.

10. _____ The selling price of an article is $60 and the markup is 20% of the cost. Find the cost of the article.

11. An article costs $180 and is sold for $200. Find
   _____ a. the markup.
   _____ b. the per cent of markup on cost.
   _____ c. the per cent of markup on selling price.

12. _____ a. A 20% markup on selling price is equivalent to what per cent of markup on cost?
    _____ b. A 15% markup on cost is equivalent to what per cent of markup on selling price?

13. An article is marked down from $50 to $40. Find
   _____ a. the markdown
   _____ b. the per cent of markdown.

14. _____ A store anticipated sales of $40,000. When sales had totaled $20,000 the manager marked down the rest of the merchandise by 25%. Find the markdown and the sales price of the marked down merchandise.

four

Discounts, Commissions, Depreciation, and Taxes

"NO STRINGS" DISCOUNT COUPON

FOR THE EXCLUSIVE USE OF

I   BELLO

The Amount Of   TEN PER CENT   Discount

Order as many items as you wish—there's no limit! As long as your order totals $3.95 or more, you are authorized to take the discount specified above from the total. Just sign your name on the back of this Discount Coupon and enclose it with the envelope order form in the center fold. **Not Transferable!**

Not Valid After   SEPTEMBER 30, 1973

4.1 TRADE DISCOUNTS

Many manufacturers and wholesalers issue catalogs containing pictures, descriptions, and prices of the items sold by their companies. The prices of items contained in these catalogs (usually called **catalog** or **list prices**) are subject to frequent change. To avoid costly republication of catalogs when the prices change, **trade discounts** are commonly used by manufacturers and wholesalers. A **trade discount** is a deduction from a list or catalog price and is used in determining the actual price of goods.

Single trade discounts

Trade discounts may be stated either as a single per cent or as a chain or series of per cents. We illustrate the use of a single trade discount in the following example.

Example 1

The list price of an article is $1,000. If the wholesaler offers a single trade discount of 25%, find the discount and the net price of the article.

Solution

(Method 1) 25% of $1,000 = $\dfrac{25}{100}$ × 1,000 = $250, the discount. $1,000 − $250 = $750, the net price.

(Method 2a) The net price of the item is 75% (100% − 25%) of $1,000 = $\dfrac{75}{100}$ × 1,000 = $750. Since the list price is $1,000, the discount is $1,000 − $750 = $250.

(Method 2b) The net price of the item is 75% of $1,000. From Figure 2–4, page 108, we can see that 75% = $\dfrac{3}{4}$. Thus, 75% of $1,000 = $\dfrac{3}{4}$ × $1,000 = $750, the net price. The discount is $1,000 − $750 = $250.

As mentioned earlier, a trade discount may be stated as a chain or series of per cents. For example, when new car models appear on the market, a wholesaler might issue a discount sheet announcing to buyers that in addition to their usual 20% discount, they will receive a 5% discount on last year's models. We illustrate the use of a chain or series of trade discounts in the following example.

Chain or series of trade discounts

Example 2

Find the discount and the net price of a car that lists for $3,500, subject to trade discounts of 20% and 5%.

Solution

We can use the same two solution methods illustrated in Example 1. (Method 1)

$3,500   (list price)

− 700   (20%, or $\dfrac{1}{5}$ of $3,500, first discount)

$2,800

− 140   (5%, or $\dfrac{1}{20}$ of $2,800, second discount)

2,660   (net price)

The discount is computed as the difference between the list price and the net price.

$3,500

−2,660

$ 840, total discount.

(Method 2) The price of the item after the first discount is 80%
$(100\% - 20\%)$ of $\$3,500 = \dfrac{80}{100} \times \$3,500 = \$2,800$. The price of the
item after the second discount is 95% $(100\% - 5\%)$ of $\$2,800 = \dfrac{95}{100} \times$
$\$2,800 = \$2,660$ (the net price). Hence, the total discount is $\$3,500 -$
$\$2,660 = \$840$.

In the solution to Example 2 (Method 2) we first computed 80%
$(100\% - 20\%)$ of $\$3,500$ and then found 95% $(100\% - 5\%)$ of this
quantity; that is, we found 95% of [80% of $\$3,500$].

Since the order in which we multiply these factors makes no
difference, we could have obtained the same answer by computing
80% of [95% of $\$3,500$]. From Figure 2–4, page 108, $80\% = \dfrac{4}{5}$ and
$95\% = \dfrac{19}{20}$; hence,

$$80\% \text{ of } 95\% \text{ of } \$3,500 = \frac{4}{5} \times \frac{19}{20} \times \$3,500 = \frac{4 \times 19 \times \$3,500}{5 \times 20} = \$2,660$$

This discussion suggests the following rule:

> **RULE 4.1** To find the net price of an item subject to
> a series of trade discounts, we proceed as follows:
>   1. Subtract each discount from 100% and express
> as a fraction in lowest terms. (Use Figure 2–4.)
>   2. Multiply the fractions obtained in Step 1 by the
> list price. The result is the net price.

Thus, using Rule 4.1, the solution to Example 2 would be found
as follows:

1. Subtracting each discount rate from 100% and expressing
as a fraction in lowest terms, we have $100\% - 20\% = 80\% = \dfrac{4}{5}$, and
$100\% - 5\% = 95\% = \dfrac{19}{20}$.

2. The net price is $\dfrac{4}{5} \times \dfrac{19}{20} \times 3,500 = \dfrac{4 \times 19 \times 3,500}{100} = \$2,660$.

Example 3

An appliance dealer is allowed discounts of $16\frac{2}{3}\%$ and 10% on all
appliances obtained from Colonel Electric, a manufacturer of major
appliances. If the dealer bought an appliance listed in the catalog
for $\$180$, what amount of trade discount did he receive, and what
was the net price?

Solution

Using Rule 4.1 we have the following procedure:

1. $100\% - 16\frac{2}{3}\% = 83\frac{1}{3}\% = \frac{5}{6}$ and $100\% - 10\% = 90\% = \frac{9}{10}$.

2. The net price is $\frac{5}{6} \times \frac{9}{10} \times \$180 = \frac{5 \times 9 \times \$\overset{3}{\cancel{180}}}{\cancel{60}} = \$135$. Thus, the discount is $\$180 - \$135 = \$45$.

> ### PROGRESS TEST 1
>
>   1. The list price of a pair of Runaround Shoes is $35. If the manufacturer offers a single trade discount of 15%, the net price of one pair of shoes is _____.
>   2. The list price of a 1973 Lincoln Continental is $8,000. If the dealer offers 20% and 5% discounts, the net price of the car will be _____.

In many cases the same series of discounts is used for a number of items in a catalog. In such instances, it is more convenient (and quicker) to use a single discount rate which is equivalent to the series of discounts. We illustrate in the following example the procedure to be followed to convert a series of discounts to an equivalent single discount.

Single discounts that are equivalent to a series of discounts

---

Example 4

Find the single-discount equivalent of 40%, $16\frac{2}{3}\%$, and 10%.

Solution

(Method 1)

$$
\begin{array}{rl}
100\% & \text{is the list price} \\
\underline{-40\%} & (40\% \text{ or } \frac{2}{5} \text{ of } 100\%) \\
60\% & \\
\underline{-10\%} & (16\frac{2}{3}\% \text{ or } \frac{1}{6} \text{ of } 60\%) \\
50\% & \\
\underline{-\ 5\%} & (10\% \text{ or } \frac{1}{10} \text{ of } 50\%) \\
45\% & \text{of the list price is the net price.}
\end{array}
$$

Since the remaining percentage of the list price is the discount, the single-discount equivalent is $100\% - 45\% = 55\%$.

---

1. $29.75   2. $6,080

(Method 2)

$$100\% - 40\% = 60\% = \frac{3}{5}$$

$$100\% - 16\frac{2}{3}\% = 83\frac{1}{3}\% = \frac{5}{6}$$

$$100\% - 10\% = 90\% = \frac{9}{10}$$

Thus, the percentage of the list price which represents the net price is $100\% \times \frac{3}{5} \times \frac{5}{6} \times \frac{9}{10} = 45\%$. Hence, the single-discount equivalent is $100\% - 45\% = 55\%$.

Thus, if an article lists for $300 and the trade discounts are 40%, $16\frac{2}{3}\%$, and 10%, the net price of the article can be found by applying the series of discounts or, equivalently, by using the equivalent single-discount of 55%. In either case, the net price of the item will be $300 - $165 = $135.

PROGRESS TEST 2

1. The single-discount equivalent of the series of discounts, 20%, 10%, and $11\frac{1}{9}\%$ is _____.

2. If an article lists for $700 and the discounts are as given in 1, the net price will be _____.

EXERCISE 4.1

Find the discount and net price of each of the following purchases:

1. $700 less 25%   2. $850 less 20%

3. $673 less $33\frac{1}{3}\%$ 4. $600 less $16\frac{2}{3}\%$

In Problems 5 through 10, find the net price and the equivalent single discount rate.

	LIST PRICE	RATES OF TRADE DISCOUNTS
5.	$50	12%, 15%
6.	$4,700	25%, 5%
7.	$5,680	10%, 5%
8.	$1,500	$33\frac{1}{3}\%, 37\frac{1}{2}\%, 88\frac{8}{9}\%$

---

1. 36%   2. $448

Her Majesty, The Queen
One day back in 1847 these two stamps sold in the Post Office at Port Louis on the island of Mauritius in the south Indian Ocean for two pennies. We bought these same stamps at a New York auction on October 21, 1968, for $380,000.00.

WEILL OF NEW ORLEANS
The most important stock of Rare Stamps in the hands of any Professional.

Reprinted by permission of Weill of New Orleans.

9. $2,480 $33\frac{1}{3}\%, 25\%, 10\%$

10. $868 $66\frac{2}{3}\%, 28\frac{4}{7}\%, 75\%$

11. Getwell Hospital purchased 50 chairs from E-Z Manufacturing at a list price of $20 each. If the trade discount was 35%, find (a) the net price of each chair, (b) the amount of discount of each chair, and (c) the net price of the invoice.

12. Repeat Problem 11 for a purchase of 75 chairs at a 20% discount.

13. If Weill decides to sell the stamps shown above for $500,000 less a 10% and a 5% discount, what will be the net price? Will Weill have a profit or a loss (and how much) on the sale?

14. If in the ad below the retailer offers 25% and 20% discounts, find the net price of each of the items. (Hint: Find the single-discount equivalent first.)

LIMITED QUANTITIES SPECIALS

7 only UNDER COUNTER **DISHWASHER**	**$198**
2 only 2-SPEED AUTOMATIC **WASHER**	**$179**
8 only 30" ELECTRIC **RANGE**	**$158**
4 only 17 cu. ft. Frost-Free, Avocado only **REFRIGERATOR**	**$288**
6 only CHEST 8 cu. ft. **FREEZER**	**$178**
3 only Frost-Free 19 cu. ft. **REFRIGERATOR**	**$348**

15. If in Problem 14 the discounts are 25%, 10%, and $33\frac{1}{3}$%, find the net price of each of the items.

In Problems 16 through 21, find the single-discount equivalent for each of the discount series.

16. 20% and 10%

17. $16\frac{2}{3}$% and 10%

18. 20%, $12\frac{1}{2}$%, and 10%

19. 20%, 10%, and 5%

20. $12\frac{1}{2}$%, $72\frac{8}{11}$%, and $91\frac{2}{3}$%

21. 20%, $57\frac{1}{7}$%, and $12\frac{1}{2}$%

22. a. A furniture dealer can buy a chair from E-Z Manufacturing for $40, less discounts of 10% and 15%, or from Hardy Chair Company for $50, less discounts of 20%, 15%, and 5%. Which manufacturer has the lower net price?
   b. If the discounts for E-Z chairs are 5% and 20%, which manufacturer has the lower price (after discounts)?

23. A retailer can cover his expenses and make a fair profit if he sells his televisions for $400. What should be the list price in his catalog so that he can allow a series of discounts of 25% and $33\frac{1}{3}$%?

24. Repeat Problem 23, assuming the retailer can sell the televisions (and still make a fair profit) for as low as $200.

25. The best price of an X-Press-O coffee pot is $9.30, less discounts of 15% and 12%. Owing to inflation, the company changed the 12% discount to 10%. What is the change in the net price?

DISCOUNT TABLE:

Up to $25.00, net 30 days
$ 25.01 to $ 75.00, 2% 15 days, net 30 days
$ 75.01 to $100.00, 4% 15 days, net 30 days
$100.01 to $200.00, 5% 15 days, net 30 days
$200.01 to $300.00, 7% 15 days, net 30 days
$300.01 to $400.00, 8% 15 days, net 30 days
$400.01 to $500.00, 10% 15 days, net 30 days
$500.01 to $600.00, 12% 15 days, net 30 days
$600.01 to $700.00, 15% 15 days, net 30 days
$700.01 to $800.00, 16% 15 days, net 30 days
$800.01 to $900.00, 17% 15 days, net 30 days
$900.01 to $1000.00, 18% 15 days, net 30 days
$1000.01 and up,   20% 15 days, net 30 days

Courtesy of Filers of Yucaipa, California.

4.2 CASH DISCOUNTS

In some instances creditors grant discounts, called **cash discounts**, as incentive for early payment. For example, in the discount table given (taken from an actual catalog), a 2% discount is offered on purchases costing more than $25 and up to $75 if payment is received within 15 days of the date on the invoice. On the other hand, if payment is not made within the discount period, the customer must pay the full (net) amount.

The terms of payment appear on an invoice and are very explicit so that there will be no disagreement as to the amount and time of payment. These terms usually depend upon the custom of the trade. In some trades it is customary for the net amount of an invoice to become due and payable within 10 days after the end of the month in which the invoice is dated. The notation used to indicate this on the invoice is "n/10, E.O.M." or "n/10, prox." The abbreviation "prox." stands for the word *proximo*, which means "in the next month" and the n stands for *net*. In case the creditor decides to allow a 2% discount for payment within the first 10 days after the end of the month in which the invoice is dated, the notation used on the invoice is "2/10, E.O.M." or "2/10, prox."

E.O.M. and proximo dating

If an invoice is dated on or after the twenty-sixth of the month on E.O.M. or prox. terms, the customer is usually allowed a one month extension of the discount period. Thus, a customer receiving an invoice dated June 29, terms 5/10, E.O.M. or prox., would normally be granted a 5% cash discount for payment of the account on or before August 10. When the discount period expires, E.O.M. or prox. dated invoices must be paid in full within 20 days. After this time the account is considered overdue and is subject to an interest charge.

Invoices dated after the twenty-sixth of the month on E.O.M. terms receive a one-month extension.

Example 1

An invoice, with a net amount of $288, dated June 4, is subject to terms of 5/10, E.O.M. How much is due if the invoice amount is paid in full on July 7?

Solution

Since payment is made within 10 days after the end of the month in which the invoice is dated (June), the customer is entitled to the 5% discount.

$$5\% \text{ of } \$288 = \$14.40 \text{ (the cash discount)}$$
$$\$288 - \$14.40 = \$273.60 \text{ (the amount due)}$$

Example 2

The terms of an invoice with a net amount of $345, dated June 28, are 3/10 prox. Find the amount due if the invoice is paid in full (a) on August 10; (b) on August 11.

Solution

a. Since the invoice is dated after the twenty-sixth of the month, a one month extension of the discount period is granted to the customer. The payment was made within this extension, so the customer is entitled to a 3% discount.

$$3\% \text{ of } \$345 \quad = \$10.35 \text{ (the cash discount)}$$
$$\$345 - \$10.35 = \$334.65 \text{ (the amount due)}$$

b. Since the invoice was paid after the discount period had expired, the amount due is $345, the net amount of the invoice.

PROGRESS TEST 1

1. The terms of an invoice with a net amount of $340, dated June 7, are 2/10, E.O.M. The amount due if the invoice is paid in full on July 10 is _____.
2. The terms of an invoice with a net amount of $260, dated July 29, are 3/10, prox. The amount due if the invoice is paid in full on August 11 is _____.

Ordinary dating

A second method for expressing the terms of a sale on an invoice is called **ordinary dating.** The terms "2/10, n/30" (read "two ten, net thirty") mean that a 2% discount may be taken if payment is made within ten days after the invoice date and the net amount is due within thirty days after the date of the invoice if payment is not made within the discount period. If payment is not made within thirty days of the date of the invoice, the account is considered overdue and is subject to an interest charge.

Thirty days after the invoice date, interest is charged on overdue accounts.

Example 3

The terms of an invoice with a net amount of $230, dated June 8, are 2/10, n/30. Find the amount due if the invoice was received by the customer on June 9 and paid in full on June 18.

Solution

Since the invoice was *dated* June 8, the customer is entitled to the discount if payment is made on or before June 18.

$$2\% \text{ of } \$230 = \$4.60 \text{ (the cash discount)}$$
$$\$230 - \$4.60 = \$225.40 \text{ (the amount due)}$$

---

1. $333.20   2. $252.20.

A third way to specify the discount period (used when the time required for the delivery of merchandise is not known because of the distance involved or other factors) is based on the date of the **receipt of goods (R.O.G.).** An ordinary-dated invoice bearing the initials **R.O.G.** entitles the customer to a cash discount if payment is made within a specified number of days following the receipt of the merchandise. For example, an invoice bearing terms 5/10, n/30, R.O.G., accompanying goods received by the customer on January 5, would entitle the customer to a 5% discount if the amount due was paid on or before January 15. Otherwise, the net amount would have to be paid by February 4 to avoid an interest charge. If the net period is not stated, a 20-day period following the last day of the discount period is customarily allowed. After this time, the account is considered overdue and is subject to an interest charge.

Example 4

The terms of an invoice having a net amount of $300 and dated June 8 are 2/10, n/30, R.O.G. The customer receives the merchandise on August 13 and sends full payment for the entire shipment on August 23. Find the amount of the payment.

Solution

Since the goods were *received* on August 13, the customer is entitled to the discount if payment is made on or before August 23.

$$2\% \text{ of } \$300 = \$6.00 \text{ (the cash discount)}$$
$$\$300 - \$6 = \$294 \text{ (the amount of payment)}$$

Finally, we consider a fourth method of specifying the discount period, known as **extra dating.** The method is used primarily to induce customers to buy goods out of season (for example, air conditioners during the winter or snow tires during the summer), thereby relieving the manufacturer of the burden of storage. The terms on an **extra-dated** invoice might be shown as "3/10–90x", "3/10–90 extra", or "3/10–90ex", where the term "3/10–90x" means that a 3% cash discount may be taken if payment is made any time within 100 days (10 days plus 90 extra days) after the date on the invoice.

Example 5

The terms of an invoice with a net amount of $563, dated July 30, are 5/10–90x.
  a. What is the last day on which the customer can pay the amount due and obtain a discount?
  b. How much is due if the invoice amount is paid in full within the discount period?

Solution

a. The last day on which the customer can pay the invoice amount and obtain a discount is 100 days after July 30, that is, November 7.

b. 5% of $563 = $28.15 (the cash discount)
$563 − $28.15 = $534.85 (the amount due)

PROGRESS TEST 2

1. Merchandise valued at $500 was purchased on July 7 and received on December 2. The terms shown on the invoice are 4/10, n/30, R.O.G. The minimum amount needed on December 12 to pay for the merchandise is_____.

2. An invoice having a net amount of $315, bearing terms 3/10–60x, is dated June 15. The minimum amount needed to pay this debt on August 20 is _____.

EXERCISE 4.2

In Problems 1 through 10, find (a) the amount of the cash discount; (b) the amount paid.

	INVOICE AMOUNT	INVOICE DATE	TERMS	PAYMENT DATE
1.	$29.00	August 23	2/10, E.O.M.	September 9
2.	$33.40	September 28	3/10, prox.	November 5
3.	$45.50	January 8	4/10, E.O.M.	February 10
4.	$60.30	January 11	2/10, prox.	February 10
5.	$40.50	June 18	2/10, n/30	June 28
6.	$50.40	July 29	3/10, n/30	August 9
7.	$29.80	September 29	2/10, n/30	October 9
8.	$53.00	October 19	2/10–30x	November 28
9.	$83.00	December 24	2/10–30x	February 3
10.	$54.47	December 28	2/10–30x	February 7

1. $480   2. $305.55

In Problems 11 through 14, find (a) the amount of cash discount; (b) the amount paid.

	INVOICE AMOUNT	INVOICE DATE	GOODS RECEIVED	TERMS	PAYMENT DATE
11.	$40.80	August 15	September 8	2/10, R.O.G.	September 18
12.	$50.30	August 8	September 3	3/10, R.O.G.	September 14
13.	$20.44	August 9	December 3	3/10, R.O.G.	December 13
14.	$30.98	August 3	November 4	2/10, R.O.G.	December 4

15. A check dated January 28 was sent as payment in full of an invoice with a net amount of $240.50, dated January 18. The terms on the invoice are 2/10, n/30. Find the amount of the check.

16. An invoice dated February 18 and amounting to $460 is paid March 10. The terms on the invoice are 3/10, E.O.M. Find the cash discount and the amount due.

17. Repeat Problem 16, assuming the terms on the invoice are 2/10, prox.

18. On August 4, Brimstone Tire receives a shipment of tires. The invoice dated June 30 shows a net amount of $1,348 and the terms are 3/10, n/30, R.O.G. (a) What is the final day on which Brimstone Tire can make payment and still take advantage of the discount? (b) Find the amount to be paid if payment is sent within the discount period.

19. Repeat Problem 15, assuming, in addition, that the seller gives trade discounts of 5% and 10%. (Calculate the trade discounts first in order to determine the net amount of the invoice.)

20. Repeat Problem 16, assuming, in addition, that the seller gives trade discounts of 5% and 10%.

21. Repeat Problem 17, assuming, in addition, that the seller gives trade discounts of 5% and 10%.

22. Repeat Problem 18, assuming, in addition, that the seller gives trade discounts of 5% and 10%.

23. An incomplete invoice is shown on the following page. Complete the invoice by filling in the correct amount in the "Total Price" column. Add the freight charges and find the invoice total. Then find (a) the amount due if the invoice is paid on January 15. (Hint: Deduct the freight charges from the total amount of the invoice before calculating the cash discount.) (b) the final date on which the total shown on the invoice is due.

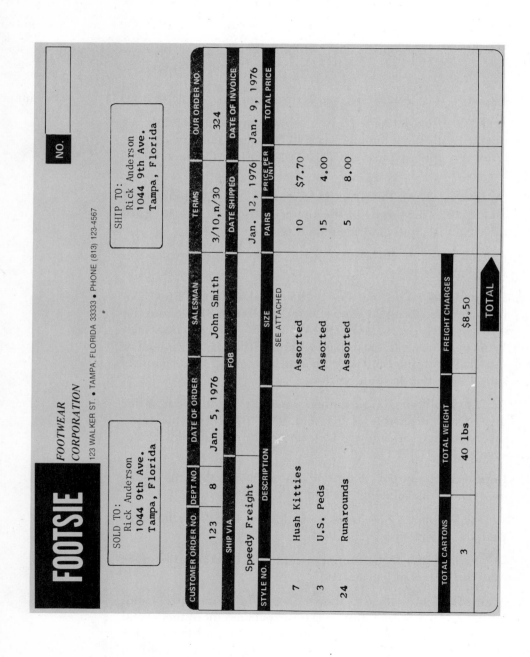

24.   Repeat problem 23, assuming Footsie offers trade discounts of 3% and 5%.

25.   Repeat Problem 23, assuming the terms are 3/10, 2/20, n/30 and the invoice amount is paid on January 23.

4.3 COMMISSIONS

In the preceding sections we have made reference to two types of merchants, called wholesalers and retailers. These merchants take title to goods and carry them in stock, assuming the risks involved in owning these goods and extending credit. However, there are other types of merchants that do not take title to the goods themselves; rather they act as middlemen in purchasing or selling merchandise for other persons, called **principals.** These middlemen (agents) are compensated by receiving a **commission** or fee which represents a certain percentage of the buying or selling price. For example, the ad above calls for a salesman who believes he is capable of making enough sales to earn for himself $20,000 in **commissions.** If a salesman's earnings are based solely on a percentage of sales, then the salesman is said to work on a **straight commission basis.** To compute the salary (or commission) of a salesman on straight commission, we use Rule 4.2.

Commission sales

RULE 4.2

Commission (for selling) = Commission Rate $\times$ Selling Price

Thus, if B. Smoothy, a salesman being paid on a straight commission basis, sells a house for $18,500 and his rate of commission is 5%, his commission is $\frac{5}{100} \times \$18,500 = \$925$. If, however, in addition to his commission, Mr. Smoothy receives a $50 weekly salary, his wages for the week would be $925 + $50 = $975.

As we previously mentioned, there are merchants representing buyers who are compensated by receiving a commission. Their commissions (or fees) are based on a percentage of the **prime cost** (the purchase price). The prime cost includes the price paid to the seller but not other expenses incurred for incidentals such as freight, packaging, etc. To find the commission of a merchant representing a buyer (sometimes called a **purchasing agent**), we use Rule 4.3.

Commission purchases

> **RULE 4.3**
> Commission (for buying) = Commission Rate × Prime Cost

Thus, if a purchasing agent buys $700 worth of merchandise and charges 3% commission for his services, the commission is $\frac{3}{100} \times \$700 = \$21$. Goods returned or orders canceled are deducted so that commissions are paid only on actual purchases.

Example 1

In 1969 Cartier's of New York acquired a 69.42 carat diamond for $1,050,000. The next day, October 24, this ring was bought for Elizabeth Taylor by her husband Richard Burton at a price of $1,200,000. If the salesman for Cartier's received $3\frac{1}{2}\%$ of the selling price as his commission on the sale, what was his commission?

Solution

By Rule 4.2, Commission = Commission Rate × Selling Price.

$$\frac{3.5}{100} \times \$1,200,000 = \$42,000$$

Example 2

Mr. U. Gogetti, a purchasing agent for Land Developers, Inc., bought 3 lots for $6,200 each. If his commission rate is 4%, find his commission.

Solution

By Rule 4.3, Commission = Commission Rate × Prime Cost.

$$\frac{4}{100} \times (3 \times \$6,200) = \$744$$

PROGRESS TEST 1

1. The purchase price is also called the _____
_____.

2. If in Example 1, the salesman received a commission based on gross profit, his commission would be
_____.

3. If in Example 2, the price of each lot is $7,300, then the salesman's commission is _____.

Sometimes producers entrust their goods to commission merchants to be sold at the best available market price. Such shipments are said to be **on consignment**. The producer, or person sending the shipment, is called the **consignor** and the agent to whom the shipment is sent is called the **consignee**. The commission earned by the agent, together with other expenses incurred when making a sale (such as transportation, advertising, packaging, insurance, etc.), comprises **the charges.** When the charges are deducted from the selling price (gross proceeds), the result is the **net proceeds.** The net proceeds are the amount received by the principal from his agent. This discussion is summarized in the following rule.

RULE 4.4
Selling Price (gross proceeds) — Charges = Net Proceeds

On the other hand, commission merchants sometimes act as purchasing agents. In such cases the gross cost (the price that the principal pays) of the merchandise is obtained by adding the prime cost and the charges. Thus we have the following rule:

RULE 4.5 Gross Cost = Prime Cost + Charges.

In the following example we illustrate the use of Rule 4.4 by means of a statement, called an account sales, issued to the principal by the agent.

Example 3

J. B. Elbmin of Plant City, Florida, shipped 60 bags of oranges and 52 crates of strawberries to Jack B. Quick, a commission merchant of Tampa, Florida. On January 18, Quick sold the oranges for 30 cents per bag and the strawberries for $6.50 per crate. If Quick's commis-

---

1. Prime cost   2. $5,250   3. $876

sion rate was 3% and he paid $17 in freight charges and $7.50 for storage, what was the amount of net proceeds sent to the producer, Mr. Elbmin?

Solution

The account sales for the transaction appears in Figure 4–1.

ACCOUNT SALES
JACK B. QUICK Commission Merchant Tampa, Fla.

Sold for Account of:

J. B. Elbmin
41 Main Street
Plant City, Florida

19__				
Jan	18	60 bags of oranges @ $ .30	$ 18.00	
		52 crates of strawberries @ $6.50	338.00	
		Gross Proceeds		$356.00
		Charges:		
		Freight	17.00	
		Commission, 3% of $356.00	10.68	
		Storage	7.50	
				35.18
		Net Proceeds		$320.82

Figure 4–1

In the following example we illustrate the use of Rule 4.5 by means of a statement, called an account purchase, issued to the principal by the agent.

Example 4

Swift and Brothers, commission merchants of Tampa, Florida, bought on the order of Cuban Industries, Inc., of Miami, Florida, 380 pounds of coffee at 58 cents per pound and 250 pounds of sugar at 8 cents per pound. If the charges were $32.40 for storage, 4% commission, and $27.80 for freight, find the gross cost.

Solution

The account purchase for the transaction appears in Figure 4–2.

ACCOUNT PURCHASE

SWIFT AND BROS.
Commission Merchants
Tampa, Fla.

Bought for the account of:

Cuban Industries, Inc.
123 Flagler Street
Miami, Fla.

19___						
July	14	380 lb coffee @ $ .58	$220	40		
		250 lb sugar @ .08	20	00		
		Prime Cost			$240	40
		Charges: Storage	32	40		
		Commission, 4% of $240.40	9	62		
		Freight	27	80		
					69	82
		Gross Cost			$310	22

Figure 4–2

EXERCISE 4.3

1. Complete the following table:

	RATE	NET SALES	COMMISSION
a.	3%	$4,700	
b.	4%	$6,200	
c.	$3\frac{1}{4}\%$	$8,200	

2. Complete the following table:

	RATE	NET SALES	COMMISSION	SALARY	TOTAL WAGES
a.	2%	$3,500		$50	
b.	$3\frac{1}{2}\%$	$2,100		$45	
c.	$4\frac{1}{4}\%$	$3,800		$75	

3. A salesman at Speedy Auto Supermarket sold 2 Chevys, 1 custom coupe, 1 LTD, and 2 Pinto wagons at the prices quoted in the accompanying ad. If his commission rate was 2%, what was his commission?

Nice selection of fresh rentals, '73's & '72's in Stock Now, All with Factory Air, Power assist.

'73 Chevy
4 Dr **$3299**

'73 Custom
Coupe **$3499**

'73 LTD
2 Dr **$3499**

'73 LTD
4 dr's **$3499**

'73 Pinto
Wag **$2799**

4. Repeat Problem 3, assuming his commission rate was 1.5%.

5. A furniture salesperson made sales totaling $14,318 with sales returns and allowances of $118. If the salesperson receives a 4% commission on net sales, how much are her wages?

6. The B. Tough Collection Agency charged as its fee $12\frac{1}{2}\%$ of the total amount collected on an unpaid account. If it collected $673 of a delinquent account, what was its fee?

7. I. M. Rich, a salesman for Land Developers, Inc., is paid on the following basis:

    2% of the first $10,000 of sales
    3% of the next $10,000 of sales
    4.5% on all additional sales

    If his sales amounted to $223,500, what was his commission?

8. If Mr. Rich sold 3 lots for $6,000 each, 2 lots for $7,500 each, and 1 lot for $10,000, what was his commission?

9. Hueblein's consigned to Christie's of San Francisco one bottle of Chateau Lafitte Rothschild 1846. Michael Broadbent of Christie's sold this bottle for $5,000 (thus making it the most expensive bottle of wine per fluid ounce). If Mr. Broadbent incurred expenses totaling $192 and charged a 1.5% rate of commission, what was his total fee?

10. Phyllis Phillips, a salesclerk for Afton Cosmetics, receives a weekly salary of $30 plus a $3\frac{1}{2}\%$ commission on all sales *exceeding* $500. If her sales last week totaled $1,875 and returns and allowances amounted to $85, what were her wages for the week?

11. If in Problem 10, Phyllis's net sales were $2,450, what were her wages for the week?

12. Complete the following payroll:

Payroll for Week Ending June 9, 19___

NAME	M	T	SALES W	T	F	S	TOTAL SALES	COMMISSION RATE	COMMIS-SION
Bell, Don	$320	$180		$190	$250	$410		3%	
Lariz, Desi		$200	$210	$180	$300	$450		5%	
Tryon, Tricia	$120	$200	$210	$160	$400	$320		4%	

13. Repeat Problem 12, assuming the rates are 3.5%, 4.5%, and 3%, respectively.

14. Complete the following account sales:

```
                        ACCOUNT SALES

                      IDAHO GROWERS ASSN.
                       Commission Merchants
                          Boise, Idaho

        Sold for account of:

            Pocatello Farms
            Pocatello, Idaho
```

19__						
July	17	3,850 lb. potatoes @ $ .07				
	17	1,550 lb. white rice @ $ .09				
	18	1,300 lb. brown rice @ $ .14				
	19	2,500 lb. potatoes @ $ .08				
		Gross Proceeds				
		Charges:				
		Freight				
		Commission, 5%	$108	50		
		Net Proceeds				

15.   Complete the following account purchase:

```
                     ACCOUNT PURCHASE
                     CONNOISSEUR FOODS

        Bought for account of:

            The Good Taste Restaurant
            847 14th Street
            Tampa, Florida
```

19__						
July	13	65 lb. meat @ $1.80				
	13	40 lb. rice @ $ .16				
	14	90 lb. blackbeans @ $ .24				
		Prime Cost				
		Charges:				
		Commission, 3%				
		Freight	$30	50		
		Gross Cost				

In Problems 16 to 18, prepare an account sales (similar to the one given in Example 3) showing the details of each sale and the charges.

16. A Plant City fruit grower shipped 148 bags of oranges to an agent in Tampa, Florida, to be sold on a $3\frac{1}{2}\%$ commission. The oranges were sold at 36 cents per bag. The freight amounted to $19.60 and the storage was $18.50. Find the net proceeds.

17. Mongo Rodriquez, a commission merchant, received a shipment of 310 cases of lettuce from Coswell Riper. He stored the shipment for two days at a cost of 3 cents a case per day. He then sold the entire lot for $1.75 per case. If Mr. Rodriquez charged 5% of the selling price as his commission, how much did Coswell Riper receive?

18. A commission merchant received a shipment of 4,000 bushels of corn sent to him by a corn dealer. The charges were as follows: freight, $3\frac{1}{4}$ cents per bushel; insurance, $34.50; storage and handling, 2 cents per bushel; and commission, 3%. The corn was sold at $1.90 per bushel. Find the net proceeds.

19. A commission merchant purchased 3,500 bushels of corn at $1.80 per bushel. The freight amounted to $35.90, and the commission was $3\frac{1}{2}\%$. Prepare an account purchase similar to the one in Example 4 and find the gross cost of the corn.

20. A principal received an account purchase showing the following items:

> 10 cartons of eggs, 6 dozen to a carton at 65 cents per dozen
> 125 bushels of corn, at $1.70 per bushel
> 250 bushels of apples, 50 pounds to a bushel, at 10 cents per pound

The charges for freight were $94.50, the commission rate was 3%, and the purchaser had miscellaneous expenses totaling $23.00. Find the total amount charged to the principal's account.

UNITED STATES

STATUTES AT LARGE

CONTAINING THE

Internal Revenue Code
of 1954

4.4 DEPRECIATION

A fixed asset is an asset having a productive or service life that
is longer than a year (or a single accounting period). The fixed assets
of a business are its buildings, machinery, equipment, and similar
properties. These assets are usually regarded as a capital expenditure,
which means that the money paid for these items may not be deducted
as a business expense in the year of purchase. However, the Internal
Revenue Service allows a loss in the value of the article because of
physical deterioration (as in the case of a typewriter) or obsolescence
(as in the case of computers). This decline in the useful value of an
article is called **depreciation.** Since depreciation is tax-deductible on
business income tax returns, the Internal Revenue Service regulates
the different methods used to compute depreciation. These regulations appear in the *Internal Revenue Code of 1954.*

In this section we will consider four different methods of computing depreciation: the straight line method, the units of production
method, the declining balance (or fixed rate) method, and the sum of
the years' digits method. In these methods the depreciation is computed by multiplying a base times a rate. We now illustrate the use
of these four methods.

The straight line method is probably the most common method of
computing depreciation. This method is based on the assumption that
the cost of an item will be spread equally over its useful life. The
formulas for finding the **annual depreciation** and the **annual rate of
depreciation** are given in the following rule:

Definition of fixed asset

Definition of depreciation

Straight line method

RULE 4.6a

$$\text{Annual Depreciation} = \frac{\text{Cost} - \text{Salvage Value}}{\text{Estimated Years of Life}}$$

4.6b

$$\text{Annual Rate of Depreciation} = \frac{\text{Annual Depreciation}}{\text{Total Depreciation}}$$

Example 1

The V-Con End Dump Truck (see Figure 4–4) has an advertised price of $700,000. If it is assumed that the truck will have an estimated useful life of five years and that at the end of five years it will have a salvage value (trade-in or scrap value) of $100,000, find the annual depreciation and the annual rate of depreciation.

Solution

$$\text{Annual Depreciation} = \frac{\text{Cost} - \text{Salvage Value}}{\text{Estimated Years of Life}}$$

$$= \frac{\$700,000 - \$100,000}{5} = \$120,000$$

$$\text{Annual Rate of Depreciation} = \frac{\text{Annual Depreciation}}{\text{Total Depreciation}}$$

$$= \frac{\$120,000}{\$600,000} = 20\%$$

The information obtained in this problem is usually summarized in a document called a **depreciation schedule.** This schedule shows the annual depreciation, the accumulated depreciation, and the book value (cost − accumulated depreciation) of the asset. The depreciation schedule for the V-Con End Dump Truck is shown in Figure 4–3.

DEPRECIATION SCHEDULE (Straight line method)			
(1)	(2)	(3)	(4)
END OF YEAR	ANNUAL DEPRECIATION	ACCUMULATED DEPRECIATION	BOOK VALUE $700,000 − (3)
0	—	—	$700,000
1	$120,000	$120,000	$580,000
2	$120,000	$240,000	$460,000
3	$120,000	$360,000	$340,000
4	$120,000	$480,000	$220,000
5	$120,000	$600,000	$100,000

Figure 4–3

Figure 4–4   The V-Con End Dump Truck, the world's largest truck, manu-factured by the Vehicle Constructors Division of Marion Power Shovel Company, has an advertised price of $700,000. (Courtesy of Vehicle Constructors Division of Marion Power Shovel Company, Inc., Dallas, Texas.)

Units of production method

In some businesses the use of assets varies greatly from year to year. For example, a company may use a particular piece of machinery for a month and then not use it again for many months. For such an asset, the straight line method may not be fair. In such cases another method, called the **units of production method,** is used.

When the units of production method is used, the cost of an asset minus its salvage value is divided by the estimated number of units it will produce during its estimated service life. This **quotient** is the **depreciation per unit of production.** The amount the asset depreciates each period is determined by multiplying the number of units produced during the period by the depreciation per unit. We summarize this procedure in Rule 4.7.

Rule 4.7

Depreciation per

$$\text{Unit of Production} = \frac{\text{Cost} - \text{Salvage Value}}{\text{Estimated Units of Production}}$$

Example 2

A Green Cab costing $4,900 is estimated to have a $900 salvage value. The Green Cab Company estimates that the cab's service life is 50,000 miles. Find the depreciation per unit of production and the depreciation for the first and second years if the cab is driven 15,000 miles the first year and 10,000 the second.

Solution

$$\text{Depreciation per Unit of Production} = \frac{\text{Cost} - \text{Salvage Value}}{\text{Estimated Units of Production}}$$

$$= \frac{\$4,900 - \$900}{50,000 \text{ miles}} = \$.08 \text{ per mile}$$

The depreciation for the first year is $15,000 \times \$0.08 = \$1,200$.
The depreciation for the second year is $10,000 \times \$0.08 = \$800$.

PROGRESS TEST 1

1. A delivery truck costing $5,400 has a $1,400 salvage value. Its useful life was estimated at five years and the useful mileage was estimated to be 40,000 miles. During its first year the truck traveled 15,000 miles. The depreciation for the first year using the straight line method is _____.

2. The depreciation for the first year using the units of production method is _____.

Declining balance method

Most assets decrease in value very rapidly during the first year of their service life. Recognizing this rapid early depreciation, the *Internal Revenue Code of 1954* authorized depreciation methods which result in higher depreciation charges during the early years of an asset's life. One of these methods is the **declining balance method** (sometimes called the **fixed rate method**). Under the declining balance method, a rate of depreciation not to exceed twice the straight line annual rate may be applied each year to the declining book value of a new fixed asset having an estimated life of three years or more. We now give a method that can be used to find the annual depreciation rate of an asset using the declining balance method.

---

1. $800   2. $1,500

RULE 4.8 To find the maximum annual depreciation of an asset, using the declining balance method:
1. Find the annual straight line depreciation rate. This rate always equals the reciprocal* of the estimated life of the asset.
2. Double the rate obtained in 1.
3. The maximum annual depreciation is obtained by multiplying the book value of the item by the rate obtained in 2.

Note that the scrap or salvage value is not deducted from the cost of the item prior to the rate application.

Example 3

Using the declining balance method, find the book value at the end of three years for a $20,000 new asset with an estimated five year life and a $500 salvage value.

Solution

1. The annual straight line depreciation **rate** is $\frac{1}{5} = 20\%$, the reciprocal of the estimated number of years of the asset (years of useful life).
2. We double this rate, obtaining 40%.
3. Annual depreciation charges are calculated as shown in Figure 4–5.

YEAR	ANNUAL DEPRECIATION	REMAINING BOOK VALUE
0	0	$20,000
1	40% of $20,000 = $8,000	$12,000
2	40% of $12,000 = $4,800	$ 7,200
3	40% of $7,200 = $2,880	$ 4,320

Figure 4–5

The book value at the end of three years is seen to be $4,320.
Note that under the declining balance method, the book value of an asset never reaches zero. Thus, if an asset has a salvage value, we must be careful not to depreciate the asset beyond this salvage value.
Another method that provides a higher depreciation in the early years is the **sum of the years' digits method.** When this method is used, the years in an asset's estimated life are added and their sum becomes the denominator of a series of fractions used to determine the

Sum of the years' digits method

---

*The reciprocal of a number a is $\frac{1}{a}$; for example, the reciprocal of 5 is $\frac{1}{5}$ and the reciprocal of 10 is $\frac{1}{10}$.

depreciation of the asset. The numerator of these fractions is the years left in the asset's life, used in reverse order. Thus, if the estimated life of an asset is four years, the denominator of the fraction will be the sum $4+3+2+1=10$. The sum of the years' digits may be found by using the formula $\frac{n(n+1)}{2}$, where n is the estimated number of years of service life of the asset. Thus, for $n=4$ the sum of the years' digits is $\frac{4(4+1)}{2}=\frac{4\times5}{2}=10$, and for $n=6$ the sum of the years' digits is $\frac{6(6+1)}{2}=\frac{6\times7}{2}=21$. The numerator of the fraction is the number of years of service life remaining at the beginning of the year for which depreciation is being computed. Thus, for an asset with an estimated life of four years, the depreciation the first year will be $\frac{4}{10}$ of the cost less the salvage value, the depreciation the second year will be $\frac{3}{10}$ of the cost less the salvage value, and for the succeeding years $\frac{2}{10}$ and $\frac{1}{10}$.

Example 4

The V-Con End Dump Truck of Example 1 is priced at $700,000 and has an estimated life of five years and a salvage value of $100,000. Prepare a Depreciation Schedule similar to the one given in Figure 4–3, using the sum of the years' digits method.

Solution

The sum of the years' digits is $5+4+3+2+1=\frac{5\times6}{2}=15$. The depreciations will be $\frac{5}{15}$ of $600,000, then $\frac{4}{15}$ of $600,000, etc.

DEPRECIATION SCHEDULE (Sum of the years' digits method)			
(1)	(2)	(3)	(4)
END OF YEAR	ANNUAL DEPRECIATION	ACCUMULATED DEPRECIATION	BOOK VALUE $700,000 − (3)
0	—	—	$700,000
1	5/15 of $600,000 = $200,000	$200,000	$500,000
2	4/15 of $600,000 = $160,000	$360,000	$340,000
3	3/15 of $600,000 = $120,000	$480,000	$220,000
4	2/15 of $600,000 = $ 80,000	$560,000	$140,000
5	1/15 of $600,000 = $ 40,000	$600,000	$100,000

Figure 4–6

PROGRESS TEST 2

1. A tractor that costs $9,800 will have a salvage value of $800 at the end of its estimated life of five years. The book value of this tractor at the end of the second year, using the declining balance method, is _____.

2. The book value of the tractor after two years, using the sum of the years' digits method, is _____.

EXERCISE 4.4

1. The longest vehicle in the world, measuring 572 feet in length, was constructed for the U.S. Army in 1961 at a cost of $3,755,000. In 1971 the vehicle was sold for $47,900. Find the straight line depreciation of this vehicle over the ten years.

2. The vehicle described in Problem 1 had a top speed of 20 m.p.h. If it is assumed that the estimated service life of this vehicle is 10,000 miles and that the vehicle traveled 1,000 miles during its first year of operation, what is the depreciation of the vehicle according to the units of production method?

3. Using the declining balance method, find the first year's depreciation of the vehicle described in Problem 1.

4. Using the sum of the years' digits method, find the first year's depreciation of the vehicle described in Problem 1.

5. Prepare a Depreciation Schedule similar to the one given in Figure 4–5 to show the annual depreciation of the vehicle of Problem 1 when the declining balance method is used. From this schedule, find the difference between the book value at the end of ten years, and the scrap value of the vehicle.

6. Prepare a Depreciation Schedule similar to the one given in Figure 4–6 to show the annual depreciation of the vehicle in Problem 1 when the sum of the years' digits method is used.

Compute the annual depreciation and prepare a Depreciation Schedule for each of the following items, using the data and methods indicated on the following page.

1. $3,528   2. $4,400

	COST	SALVAGE VALUE	ESTIMATED LIFE	DEPRECIATION METHOD
7.	$4,600	$1,000	5 years	Straight line
8.	$4,600	$1,000	5 years	Declining balance
9.	$4,600	$1,000	5 years	Sum of the years' digits
10.	$4,800	$ 800	50,000 miles	Units of production

In each of the following problems, compute the annual straight line depreciation of the given item.

	COST	ESTIMATED LIFE	SALVAGE VALUE
11.	$4,800	5 years	$ 800
12.	$18,400	5 years	$1,400
13.	$27,200	20 years	$3,200

14. The Drilling Press Company bought a drill press at a cost of $3,800 with an estimated life of seven years. Find the annual straight line depreciation of the press.

15. A Quicke adding machine that cost $245 has a trade-in value of $85 at the end of five years. Find the annual straight line depreciation for this machine. Find the monthly straight line depreciation for this machine.

16. A Speedy Delivery truck that cost $5,400 will have a trade-in value of $750 in five years. If the truck is being depreciated using the straight line method, find the accumulated depreciation at the end of three years.

17. The Cone-Tracting Company bought a tractor for $7,500. Company accountants estimated that the life of the tractor would be six years, at which time it would have a trade-in value of $1,500. After the tractor was depreciated for five years on the straight line method, it had to be junked for $175. How much difference was there between the book value and the junk value of the tractor?

18. The Green Cab Company bought a car for $4,200 and after using it for 60,000 miles traded it in for a new car. The trade-in allowance was $600. Find the per-mile depreciation for this car.

19. The Howard Hues Paint Company bought a machine for $5,400. The machine is expected to have a trade-in value of $300 after it has been used to produce 50,000 units. If this machine produced 8,500 units during the first year, find the depreciation charges for the year, using the units of production method.

20. Intercontinental Airlines bought an airplane engine at a cost of $29,200 and estimated that after 30,000 hours of operation

the engine would have a salvage value of $2,200. If this engine is operated 5,840 hours during one year, find the depreciation for the year, using the units of production method.

21. Gadget Manufacturing bought a machine for $10,600. The useful life of the machine was estimated to be 400,000 units, after which time the machine was estimated to have a $1,000 trade-in value. The production schedule for this machine was as follows:

	FIRST YEAR	SECOND YEAR	THIRD YEAR	FOURTH YEAR	FIFTH YEAR
Units	76,000	92,000	72,000	96,000	64,000

Use the units of production method to compute the depreciation charges for each year.

22. The Gutemberg Press bought a printing machine for $48,000. The machine was estimated to last for six years, after which time it would have a salvage value of $1,500. Find the maximum depreciation of this machine for each of the first two years by using the declining balance method.

23. A machine with an estimated life of eight years costs $6,000 and has a trade-in value of $100. Find the maximum depreciation of this machine during the third year, using the declining balance method.

24. The Blue Cab Company purchased a car for $4,000. It is estimated that the car will have a useful life of four years and that at the end of this time it will have salvage value of $100. Find the maximum depreciation for each of the first two years, using the declining balance method.

25. Prepare a Depreciation Schedule similar to the one in Figure 4–5 for the car in Problem 24.

26. If in Problem 24 the salvage value had been $400, what would be the maximum depreciation for the fourth year, using the declining balance method?

27. The Kata-Kola Bottling Company bought a machine that costs $11,200 and has an estimated life of four years. If this machine has a scrap value of $200, find the depreciation charges for the second year, using the sum of the years' digits method.

28. Prepare a Depreciation Schedule similar to the one in Figure 4–6 to show the yearly depreciation (over the four years) of the machine in Problem 27.

29. Willie Highman, a traveling salesman, bought a new car for $3,500. He estimates that he can use the car for five years, at which time it will have a trade-in value of $500. Find the

amount of depreciation during the second year, using the sum of the years' digits method.

30. Prepare a Depreciation Schedule similar to the one in Figure 4–6 to show the yearly depreciation of the car in Problem 29. ~

31. The Robin Good Company, manufacturer of bows and arrows, bought a machine with an estimated life of four years at a cost of $3,400 and a salvage value of $400. Prepare a Depreciation Schedule similar to the one in Figure 4–6 to show the yearly depreciation of this machine.

Tax Information on Depreciation

1974 Edition

For use in preparing 1973 Returns

Department of the Treasury
Internal Revenue Service

Publication 534

4.5 INTERNAL REVENUE SERVICE REGULATIONS

Maximum allowable rates

As we mentioned in the previous section, the *Internal Revenue Code of 1954* authorized depreciation methods which result in higher depreciation charges during the early years of an asset's life. One of the provisions of the code states that under the declining balance method, the maximum rate (per cent) allowable for a new fixed asset having an estimated life of three or more years shall not exceed twice the straight line rate. Thus, if the straight line method is used to depreciate an asset with an expected life of ten years, the depreciation will be $\frac{1}{10} = 10\%$ of the cost. The maximum declining balance rate on the same item is twice 10%, or 20%.

Note: You can not claim the additional 20% depreciation unless the item has an estimated life of at least six years.

Another Internal Revenue Service regulation contained in Publication 534, *Tax Information on Depreciation*, allows businesses an additional 20% first-year depreciation over and above the depreciation claimed by any of the methods discussed in the previous section. This additional depreciation is only applicable to machinery and equipment (not to buildings) with an estimated life of **at least six years**. We illustrate the use of this additional depreciation in the following example.

Example 1

The Dew Drop Inn paid $7,000 for a microwave oven with an estimated life of eight years and a trade-in value of $1,600. Find the additional 20% first-year depreciation and the maximum depreciation for the first year using the (a) straight line method, (b) sum of the years' digits method, and (c) declining balance method.

Solution

The 20% additional depreciation is 20% of $7,000 = $1,400.

    a.

Cost	$7,000
Additional Depreciation	− 1,400
	$5,600
Salvage Value	− 1,600
Remaining Value	$4,000

The remaining value distributed over eight years gives $\dfrac{\$4,000}{8}$ = $500.* Thus, depreciation by the straight line method will amount to $500 each year after the first year. During the first year the total straight line depreciation will be:

$500 (ordinary depreciation) + $1,400 (additional) = $1,900

    b. The additional first-year depreciation and the salvage value have to be deducted from the cost. Thus, the remaining value is identical to the one obtained in (a), $4,000. The sum of the years' digits is $\dfrac{(8 \times 9)}{2}$ = 36. Thus, the total depreciation for the first year will be $\dfrac{8}{36}$ of $4,000 (ordinary depreciation) + $1,400 (additional) = $2,288.89.

    c. The maximum rate is twice the straight line rate; that is, 2 × $\dfrac{1}{8}$ = 25%. The balance to be depreciated the first year is $7,000 − $1,400 = $5,600. Thus, the ordinary first year depreciation will be 25% of $5,600 = $1,400, and the total depreciation for the first year will be $1,400 (ordinary depreciation) + $1,400 (additional) = $2,800.

Finally, we give an example that compares the straight line, sum of the years' digits, and declining balance methods of computing the depreciation of an asset.

---

*Note that the straight line rate of depreciation during the eight years will be $\dfrac{500}{4000} = \dfrac{1}{8}$, the reciprocal of the number of years. This is always so. Thus, the straight line rate for an asset with an estimated life of nine years will be $\dfrac{1}{9}$ and the rate for an asset with an estimated life of ten years will be $\dfrac{1}{10}$.

Example 2

Find the annual depreciation of an asset costing $5,400 that has an estimated life of six years and a trade-in value of $600, if it is decided to claim the additional 20% first year allowance and to depreciate the machine using (a) the straight line method; (b) the sum of the years' digits method; (c) the declining balance method.

Solution

The 20% first year additional allowance is 20% of $5,400 = $1,080.

	(a) Straight line	(b) Sum of the years' digits	(c) Declining balance
Cost	$5,400	$5,400	$5,400
First year allowance	− 1,080	− 1,080	− 1,080
	4,320	4,320	4,320
Salvage value	600	600	–
Remaining value	$3,720	$3,720	$4,320

The rates of depreciation for each year are as follows: (a) The straight line rate is the reciprocal of the estimated number of years of useful life; that is, $\frac{1}{6} = 16\frac{2}{3}\%$. (b) The sum of the years' digits is $\frac{6 \times 7}{2} = 21$. (c) The maximum declining balance rate is twice the straight line rate; that is, $2 \times \frac{1}{6} = \frac{1}{3} = 33\frac{1}{3}\%$.

Thus, we have the following tabulation:

TABLE 4–1   **Comparison of Methods of Computing Depreciation**

YEAR	STRAIGHT LINE		SUM OF THE YEARS' DIGITS		DECLINING BALANCE METHOD	
	Annual Dep.	Book Value	Annual Dep.	Book Value	Annual Dep.	Book Value
(1) Additional	$1,080.00		$1,080.00		$1,080.00	
Ordinary	620.00		1,062.86		1,440.00	
Total 1st year	$1,700.00	$3,700.00	$2,142.86	$3,257.14	$2,520.00	$2,880.00
(2)	620.00	3,080.00	885.71	2,371.43	960.00	1,920.00
(3)	620.00	2,460.00	708.57	1,662.86	640.00	1,280.00
(4)	620.00	1,840.00	531.43	1,131.43	426.67	853.33
(5)	620.00	1,220.00	354.29	777.14	253.33	600.00
(6)	620.00	600.00	177.14	600.00	0.00	600.00

PROGRESS TEST 1

1. According to the *Internal Revenue Code of 1954,* certain new assets can be depreciated using a maximum rate not exceeding _____ the annual straight line rate.

2. An additional _____ depreciation of the original cost can be claimed the _____ year of the life of an asset.

EXERCISE 4.5

1. The Good Taste Restaurant paid $4,200 for an electronic oven with an estimated life of six years and a trade-in value of $600. Find (a) the additional 20% first year depreciation allowance; (b) the total (ordinary + additional) first year depreciation, using the straight line method.

2. Repeat Problem 1, using the declining balance method.

3. Repeat Problem 1, using the sum of the years' digits method.

4. The Blue Cab Company paid $4,875 for a car with an estimated life of ten years and a trade-in value of $800. Find the annual depreciation for each of the first three years if the company decides to claim the 20% additional first-year allowance and to depreciate the car using the straight line method.

5. The Fuller Fashions Dress Shop bought an air conditioner with an estimated life of ten years at a cost of $6,000. Find the book value of the air conditioner at the end of three years if the owner decides to claim the 20% additional first-year allowance and depreciate the air conditioner using the declining balance method.

6. Play-Tell Toys paid $10,000 for a stamping machine with an estimated life of eight years and a salvage value of $1,600. Find the annual depreciation schedule for each of the first three years if the company decides to claim the 20% additional first year allowance and to depreciate the machine using the sum of the years' digits method.

7. Intercontinental Airlines bought an airplane engine for $10,000. After six years of use the engine's value will be $2,000. Construct a depreciation schedule for this engine using the straight line method and including the 20% additional first-year depreciation.

1. twice   2. 20%, first

8. Play-Pal Magazine bought a quick set machine with an estimated life of six years at a cost of $6,000. Prepare a Depreciation Schedule for this machine using the declining balance method, the maximum rate, and the additional first-year allowance.

9. Gadget Manufacturing paid $8,000 for a machine with an estimated life of seven years and a salvage value of $800. Prepare a Depreciation Schedule for this machine using the sum of the years' digits method and taking the 20% additional first-year allowance.

10. A machine costing $9,100 has an estimated life of six years and a scrap value of $1,200. Prepare a Depreciation Schedule similar to the one given in Table 4–1, showing the annual depreciation at the end of each of the six years if the depreciation is computed by the declining balance method (using the maximum rate allowable) and by the sum of the years' digits method. Assume that the 20% additional first-year allowance is applied to each method.

A practical way to report 6 month earnings.

	Six Months Ended June 30,		
	1973	1972	1971
Net Sales and Service Revenues	$609,106,000	$524,905,000	$532,522,000
Income Before Federal and Foreign Income Taxes	20,549,000	15,740,000	14,506,000
Income Before Extraordinary Gain ..	11,917,000	9,457,000	7,993,000
Extraordinary Gain		399,000	
Net Income	11,917,000	9,856,000	7,993,000
Earnings Per Common Share:			
Income before extraordinary gain	$1.07	$.77	$.64
Extraordinary gain		.04	
Net income	$1.07	$.81	$.64
Earnings Per Common Share— Assuming Full Dilution:			
Income before extraordinary gain	$1.00	$.76	$.64
Extraordinary gain		.03	
Net income	$1.00	$.79	$.64

Want to know more?
For Ogden Corporation's Semi-Annual Report, write us at
161 East 42nd Street, New York, New York 10017.

OGDEN

Courtesy of Ogden Corporation.

4.6 INCOME STATEMENTS AND BALANCE SHEETS

In the document above, the Ogden Company claims to have a "practical way to report 6 month earnings". Actually, at the end of each accounting period (usually a year), financial reports are prepared to determine the financial condition of the business. These reports invariably include an **income statement** and a **balance sheet**. The **income statement** shows the gain or loss incurred by the business during the year and is based on the following calculations:

RULE 4.9

```
          Net Sales
 — Cost of Goods Sold
       Gross Profit
 — Operating Expenses
         Net Income
```

Since in most businesses the primary source of revenue is derived from sales, it is customary to convert the dollar amounts to **per cents** of the total net sales. For example, the per cent of Total Operating Expenses to Net Sales in the Shoe Biz Income Statement (see Fig. 4–7) is computed as follows:

$$\frac{(13,000) \text{ Total Operating Expenses}}{(25,000) \text{ Net Sales}} = 52\%$$

Example 1

SHOE BIZ, INC. Income Statement For Month Ended December 31, 19___			PER CENTS	
Income:				
Sales..		$25,750		103.0
Less sales returns and allowances..............		750		3.0
Net sales..		$25,000		100.0
Less cost of goods sold:				
Inventory, December 1, 19___........................	$ 4,500		18.0	
Purchases..	9,750		39.0	
Goods available for sale...........................	$14,250		57.0	
Less inventory, December 31, 19___..............	5,500		22.0	
Cost of goods sold..................................		8,750		35.0
Gross profit on sales...............................		$16,250		65.0
Operating expenses:				
Selling expenses.....................................	$ 6,000		24.0	
Delivery expenses....................................	3,000		12.0	
Office expenses.......................................	1,500		6.0	
Miscellaneous expenses............................	2,500		10.0	
Total operating expenses.........................		$13,000		52.0
Net income...		$ 3,250		13.0

Figure 4–7   Income Statement for Shoe Biz, Inc.

The per cents indicated in the right hand column answer three questions of interest to managers and investors: (1) What per cent of sales was the cost of goods? (35%) (2) What per cent of sales was the gross profit? (65%) (3) What per cent of sales was the operating expenses? (52%)

Of course, the most important and probably most frequently asked question about an income statement is (4) What per cent of sales was the net income? (13%)

Horizontal and vertical analysis

All of these per cents represent **vertical analysis;** that is, each item is represented as a per cent of the total during a *single* time period.

To analyze the progress of a business during a particular period of time, recent figures should be compared with corresponding figures from the previous periods. This type of comparison is called a **horizontal analysis.** Example 2, Figure 4–8, illustrates horizontal analysis. In this comparative statement, the amount of increase or decrease of an item is found and entered in the third column. The per cent of increase or decrease of the item is then calculated by dividing the increase or decrease of the item by the amount shown for the item in the base year. The figure obtained is entered in the fourth column. For example, in the comparative income statement for Maw's Brothers, net sales increased from $100,000 in 1976 to $120,000 in 1977. This is an increase of $20,000, which represents an increase of $\frac{20,000}{100,000} = 20\%$.

Example 2

MAW'S BROTHERS Comparative Income Statement For Years Ended December 31, 1977 and 1976				
	1977	1976	INCREASE OR DECREASE DURING 1977	
			Amount	*Per Cent*
Sales..	$124,000	$103,000	$21,000	20.4
Less sales returns and allowances.................	4,000	3,000	1,000	33.3
Net sales..	$120,000	$100,000	$20,000	20.0
Less cost of goods sold:				
Merchandise inventory, January 1..................	$ 60,000	$ 50,000	$10,000	20.0
Purchases..	60,000	48,000	$12,000	25.0
Goods available for sale...............................	$120,000	$ 98,000	$22,000	22.4
Less inventory, December 31........................	$ 33,600	$ 32,000	$ 1,600	10.0
Cost of goods sold.................................	$ 86,400	$ 66,000	$20,400	30.9
Gross profit...	$ 33,600	$ 34,000	400*	1.2*
Operating expenses:				
Selling expenses...	$ 13,200	$ 12,000	$ 1,200	10.0
General expenses.......................................	10,000	8,000	2,000	25.0
Total operating expenses........................	$ 23,200	$ 20,000	$ 3,200	16.0
Net income..	$ 10,400	$ 14,000	$ 3,600*	25.7*

*Represents a decrease.   Figure 4–8

The second type of financial statement that we shall consider in this section is the **balance sheet.** The balance sheet gives the financial position of a business by presenting the nature and value of the assets, liabilities, and owner equity. (The **assets** of the business are its possessions and the money owed to it; the **liabilities** are the debts of the business.) When the liabilities are subtracted from the

The balance sheet

Definition of assets and liabilities

assets, the balance remaining is called the **owner equity**; assets, liabilities, and owner equity are related by the following equation:

RULE 4.10   Assets = Liabilities + Owner Equity.

In Figure 4–9 we give an example of a balance sheet that illustrates vertical analysis; that is, each asset (as well as each liability and the owner equity) is represented as a per cent of the total assets.

Example 3

PEP-O DRUG COMPANY Balance Sheet December 31, 19___			PER CENTS	
ASSETS				
Current assets:				
Cash	$ 1,200		2.0	
Notes receivable	3,000		5.0	
Accounts receivable	3,600		6.0	
Merchandise inventory	6,000		10.0	
Total current assets		$13,800		23.0
Fixed assets:				
Equipment (office and store)	$15,000		25.0	
Building	22,800		38.0	
Land	8,400		14.0	
Total fixed assets		$46,200		77.0
Total assets		$60,000		100.0
LIABILITIES				
Current liabilities:				
Notes payable	$ 2,400		4.0	
Accounts payable	5,400		9.0	
Total current liabilities		$ 7,800		13.0
Long-term liabilities:				
Mortgage payable		$10,800		18.0
Total liabilities		$18,600		31.0
OWNER EQUITY				
J. Strong, equity		$41,400		69.0
Total liabilities and owner equity		$60,000		100.0

Figure 4–9

In order to analyze the relationship between an individual or group total in the current balance sheet and the corresponding item or total in a preceding balance sheet, we use a Comparative Balance Sheet which shows the value of the assets, the liabilities, and the owner equity on two or more specified dates. In Figure 4–10 we give an example of a Comparative Balance Sheet prepared for Denny's Department Store.

Example 4

DENNY'S DEPARTMENT STORE Comparative Balance Sheet June 30, 1977 and 1976				
			INCREASE OR DECREASE*	
ASSETS	1977	1976	*Amount*	*Per Cents*
Current assets..	$21,000	$20,000	$ 1,000	5.0
Investments..	30,000	25,000	5,000	20.0
Fixed assets (net)...................................	40,000	44,000	4,000*	9.1*
Total assets..	$91,000	$89,000	$ 2,000	2.2
LIABILITIES				
Current liabilities....................................	$20,000	$25,000	$ 5,000*	20.0*
Long-term liabilities...............................	10,000	15,000	5,000*	33.3*
Total liabilities.......................................	$30,000	$40,000	$10,000*	25.0*
STOCKHOLDERS' EQUITY				
Preferred stock (6%, $100 par)................	$13,000	$12,000	$ 1,000	8.3
Common stock ($10 par)..........................	25,000	20,000	5,000	25.0
Retained earnings...................................	23,000	17,000	6,000	35.3
Total stockholders' equity.......................	$61,000	$49,000	$12,000	24.5
Total liabilities & stockholders' equity.....	$91,000	$89,000	$ 2,000	2.2

Figure 4–10

PROGRESS TEST 1

1. The income statement shows the _____ or
_____ in the business.
2. Gross Profit — Operating Expenses = _____
_____.

3. When the liabilities are subtracted from the assets,
the result is _____.

EXERCISE 4.6

1. Woody's Hardware had net sales of $25,000. If the mer-
chandise cost Woody $18,600, what is his gross profit? (Hint:
See Rule 4.9.)

1. gains, losses   2. Net Income   3. owner equity

2.   Dear's Department Store had net sales of $30,000 on merchandise costing $23,800. If the operating expenses amounted to $2,500, what was the Net Income for Dear's? (Hint: See Rule 4.9.)

3.   Using the information contained in Problem 2, complete the following Income Statement:

DEAR'S DEPARTMENT STORE
Income Statement
For the Month Ending June 30, 1976

Net Sales

Cost of Goods Sold

    Gross Profit

Operating Expenses

    Net Income

---

4.   The assets of Intercontinental Airlines total $347,000. If the liabilities amount to $97,800, what is the owner equity for the airline?

5.   From the income statement below find the indicated per cent based on net sales. (Round off to nearest .1%.)

6.   From the income statement (opposite top) find the indicated per cent based on net sales. (Round off to nearest .1%.)

BRIMSTONE TIRE COMPANY
Income Statement
For Month Ended December 31, 19___

			PER CENTS	
Income:				
Sales..		$51,000		
Less sales returns and allowances..............		1,000		
Net sales...		$50,000		
Less cost of goods sold:				
Inventory, December 1, 19___............................	$ 5,000			
Purchases...	30,000			
Goods available for sale......................	$35,000			
Less inventory, December 31, 19___........................	5,500			
Cost of goods sold.................................		$29,500		
Gross profit on sales...		$20,500		
Operating expenses:				
Selling expenses..	$12,500			
Delivery expenses..	2,000			
Office expenses..	3,000			
Miscellaneous expenses.....................................	1,000			
Total operating expenses.........................		$18,500		
Net income...		$ 2,000		

HOWARD HUES PAINT Income Statement For Month Ended December 31, 19__			PER CENTS
Income:			
Sales..		$45,900	
Less sales returns and allowances..............		900	
Net sales......................................		$45,000	
Less cost of goods sold:			
Inventory December 1, 19__....................	$ 4,500		
Purchases.....................................	20,250		
Goods available for sale......................	$24,750		
Less inventory, December 31, 19__............	5,400		
Cost of goods sold............................		$19,350	
Gross profit on sales...........................		$25,650	
Operating expenses:			
Selling expenses..............................	$ 9,000		
Delivery expenses.............................	7,200		
Office expenses...............................	2,250		
Miscellaneous expenses.......................	3,600		
Total operating expenses...................		$22,050	
Net income....................................		$ 3,600	

7. In the following Comparative Income Statement, find the amount and the per cent of change of each item (using 1976 as the base year). (Round off to the nearest .1%.)

Comparative Income Statement For Years Ended December 31, 1977 and 1976			INCREASE OR DECREASE* DURING 1977	
	1977	1976	Amount	Per Cent
Sales..	$112,000	$111,000		
Less sales returns and allowances.................	2,000	11,000		
Net sales....................................	110,000	100,000		
Less cost of goods sold:				
Merchandise inventory, January 1..................	$ 60,000	$ 50,000		
Purchases....................................	50,000	40,000		
Goods available for sale.......................	$110,000	$ 90,000		
Less inventory, December 31...................	33,600	32,000		
Cost of goods sold...........................	76,400	58,000		
Gross profit.................................	$ 33,600	$ 42,000		
Operating expenses:				
Selling expenses.............................	$ 12,000	$ 10,000		
General expenses.............................	12,000	8,000		
Total operating expenses....................	$ 24,000	$ 18,000		
Net income..................................	$ 9,600	$ 24,000	*	*

8. Supply the information needed in the Comparative Income Statement for the Avid Reader Bookstore. (Round off to nearest .1%; indicate decreases by *.)

AVID READER BOOK STORE
Comparative Income Statement
For Years Ended December 31, 1977 and 1976

	1977		1976		INCREASE/DECREASE* DURING 1977	
	Amount	Per Cent	Amount	Per Cent	Amount	Per Cent
Net sales.............................	$300,000		$250,000			
Cost of goods sold..................	204,000					
Gross profit...........................			$ 82,000			
Operating expenses:						
Salary expense...............	$ 38,400		37,500			
Advertising.....................	1,000		800			
Supplies........................	6,000		5,000			
Depreciation						
Delivery.........................	3,000		4,200			
Miscellaneous expenses...	11,000		10,000			
Total operating expenses...............	$ 59,400		$ 57,500			
Net income.........................						

9. In the accompanying Comparative Balance Sheet, find the amount and per cent of change of each item from 1976 to 1977. (Round off to the nearest .1%; indicate decreases by *.)

HOWARD HUES PAINT COMPANY
Comparative Balance Sheet
June 30, 1977 and 1976

	1977	1976	INCREASE OR DECREASE*	
			Amount	Per Cents
ASSETS				
Current assets...	$ 32,000	$ 30,000		
Investments..	57,000	50,000		
Fixed assets (net)...	65,000	60,000		
Total assets..	$154,000	$140,000		
LIABILITIES				
Current liabilities...	$ 42,000	$ 35,000		
Long-term liabilities...	45,000	50,000		
Total liabilities..	$ 87,000	$ 85,000		
STOCKHOLDERS' EQUITY				
Preferred stock (6%, $100 par)...........................	$ 20,000	$ 12,000		
Common stock ($10 par).....................................	40,000	32,000		
Retained earnings..	7,000	11,000		
Total stockholders' equity....................................	$ 67,000	$ 55,000		
Total liabilities & stockholders' equity..................	$154,000	$140,000		

10. In the accompanying Balance Sheet, find what per cent each asset is of the total assets.

KATA-KOLA Balance Sheet December 31, 19__				PER CENTS
ASSETS				
Current assets:				
Cash	$ 4,000			
Notes receivable	6,000			
Accounts receivable	10,000			
Merchandise inventory	5,600			
Total current assets		$25,600		
Fixed assets:				
Equipment	$20,000			
Building	30,000			
Land	4,400			
Total fixed assets		$54,400		
Total assets		$80,000		100
LIABILITIES				
Current liabilities:				
Notes payable	$ 3,400			
Accounts payable	6,400			
Total current liabilities		$ 9,800		
Long-term liabilities:				
Mortgage payable		$20,000		
Total liabilities		$29,800		___
OWNER EQUITY				
Joe Kata, owner equity		$50,200		
Total liabilities and owner equity		$80,000		100

Drawing by Piet Hein; Copr. 1951.
The New Yorker Magazine, Inc.

4.7 EXCISE, SALES, AND PROPERTY TAXES

Sales taxes

In the cartoon above, the man has been ruined by taxes. A **tax** is an amount of money levied by the government upon persons or property. A tax levied on the sale of goods and services is called a **sales tax.** Usually sales taxes are collected by the seller. We now give a rule that can be used to calculate the amount of sales tax.

RULE 4.11　Sales Tax = Sales × Sales Tax Rate.

TABLE 4–2　　Sales Taxes

3% SALES TAX RATE		4% SALES TAX RATE		5% SALES TAX RATE	
Transaction	*Tax*	*Transaction*	*Tax*	*Transaction*	*Tax*
1¢ to 14¢	none	1¢ to 14¢	none	1¢ to 10¢	none
15¢ to 42¢	1¢	15¢ to 28¢	1¢	11¢ to 27¢	1¢
43¢ to 73¢	2¢	29¢ to 54¢	2¢	28¢ to 47¢	2¢
74¢ to $1	3¢	55¢ to 80¢	3¢	48¢ to 68¢	3¢
		81¢ to $1	4¢	69¢ to 89¢	4¢
				90¢ to $1	5¢
Plus 3% on each additional dollar in the transaction.		Plus 4% on each additional dollar in the transaction.		Plus 5% on each additional dollar in the transaction.	

Thus, if an article costs $3.00 and the tax rate is 3%, Sales Tax = $3.00 × 0.03 = $0.09 or 9 cents. To avoid charges of fractional cents when the sale is for less than one dollar, the sales tax is based on a table that shows the tax on various fractional parts of a dollar. Table 4–2 shows a Sales Tax Table based on sales tax rates of 3%, 4%, and 5%. The tax intervals used are arbitrarily fixed and may vary from state to state. Check the correct intervals and rates for your area.

Example 1

Using Table 4–2 and assuming that the Sales Tax Rate is 4%, find the sales tax on each of the following sales:
(a) 64¢   (b) 32¢   (c) $30.40

Solution

    a. Tax on 64¢ is 3¢ (see Table 4–2, 55¢ to 80¢ tax).
    b. Tax on 32¢ is 2¢ (see Table 4–2, 29¢ to 54¢ tax).
    c. (Method 1) Using Rule 4.1 we have Sales Tax = Sales × Sales Tax Rate = $30.40 × .04 = $1.2160 ≈ $1.22.
        (Method 2) Tax on $30 is $30 × .04 = $1.20. Tax on .40 is .02 (see Table 4–2). Tax on $30.40 is $1.22.

Many companies do not keep a separate record of the sales tax on each sale. In such cases the total amount (including the sales tax) is recorded for each sale. At the end of each accounting period (usually a month or a quarter) the sales tax liability is computed and paid to the government. The following example illustrates the computations used.

Example 2

The King Bee Store collected $2,912, which includes sales and sales taxes. If the sales tax rate is 4%, find (a) the amount of the sales, and (b) the amount of the sales tax.

Solution

    a. Sales are 100%. Tax is 4% of sales. Total of sales and taxes is 104% = $2,912. Thus, the amount of sales is $\frac{\$2,912}{1.04}$ = $2,800.

    b. The amount of Sales Tax is: Sales × Sales Tax Rate = $2,800 × .04 = $112.

```
PROGRESS TEST 1

1. Sales Tax = _____.
2. If an article sells for $45 and the tax rate is 3%, the
tax on this article is _____.
3. If an article sells for 83¢ and the tax rate is 5%,
the sales tax on this article, according to Table 4–2, is

_____.

4. If the King Bee Store of Example 2 collected
$3,328, the amount of sales is _____.
```

Excise tax

An **excise tax** is a tax levied on the manufacture, sale, or consumption of a commodity, or on any of various privileges such as licenses, or permission to practice or to conduct certain sports, trades, or occupations. Among the excise taxes today are those on theatre tickets, gasoline, tires, and jewelry. These taxes are calculated in a manner similar to that of determining sales tax; that is,

$$\text{Excise Tax} = \text{Selling Price} \times \text{Excise Tax Rate}$$

We now give a table that shows the Excise Tax Rate for various articles:

TABLE 4–3   **Excise Taxes Based on Manufacturer's Selling Price**

ARTICLE	TAX RATE
Trucks, trailers, buses..	10%
Passenger automobiles..	7%
Fishing equipment...	10%
Pistols and revolvers..	10%
Shells and cartridges on firearms..	11%
Tires (highway vehicle type)..(per pound)	10¢
Gasoline..(per gallon)	4¢

Example 3

The most expensive car ever built was the Presidential 1969 Lincoln Continental Executive with an approximate cost of $500,000. Using Table 4–3, find the excise tax that must be paid on this car if the selling price is $505,000.

Solution

$$\text{Excise Tax} = \text{Selling Price} \times \text{Tax Rate} = \$505{,}000 \times .07 = \$35{,}350.$$

1. Sales × Sales Tax Rate   2. $1.35   3. 4¢   4. $3,200

Finally, we consider a third type of tax that is levied on real and personal property, the **property tax.** To determine the property tax for each person, the total amount of taxes that must be raised is divided among all property owners in accordance with the value of the property they own. For example, if a town must raise $10,000 in taxes and the total value of the property in this town is $200,000, then for each dollar value of property, the town must raise 5¢. This means that the tax rate for this town is 5¢ per dollar. The **tax rate** for an area might be expressed as cents per dollar, dollars per $100,

dollars per $1,000, or **mills,** a **mill** being $\frac{1}{10}$ of a cent. Thus, expressing a tax rate in mills is another way of expressing it as a rate of dollars per $1,000.

Property tax is usually paid on the **assessed value** rather than on the actual market value of the property. The **assessed value** is determined by the **tax assessor,** usually by taking a certain per cent of the estimated market value of the property. Thus, if the market value of a home is $20,000 and the home is assessed at 40% of the market value, the assessed value of this house will be $8,000 (40% of $20,000). From the preceding discussion we can see that to find the **tax rate** we can apply the following rule:

RULE 4.12 Tax rate = $\dfrac{\text{Amount of Taxes Needed}}{\text{Total Assessed Valuation}}$

Example 4

The city of Spendmore has an annual budget of $2,000,000. The assessed value of the property in Spendmore is $25,000,000. (a) Find the tax rate. (b) Express the tax rate as an amount per $1,000. (c) Express the tax rate in mills.

Solution

a. Tax rate = $\dfrac{\text{Amount of Taxes Needed}}{\text{Total Assessed Valuation}} = \dfrac{\$2,000,000}{\$25,000,000} = .08 = 8\%$

b. If the tax rate is 8%, the owners are paying $8 per $100 of assessed valuation, and hence they will pay $80 per $1,000.

c. The rate in mills is 80 mills (since expressing a rate in mills is another way of expressing it as a rate of dollars per $1,000).

In the event that the tax rate must be rounded off, we always go up to the next highest digit. Thus, if the tax rate is .08756, the amount per $100 is $8.76.

We now give a formula that can be used to compute the property tax.

RULE 4.13 Tax = Tax Rate × Assessed Valuation.

Example 5

A house is assessed at 60% of its market value of $20,000. Find the tax that must be paid if the tax rate is (a) $3 per hundred; (b) $8 per $1,000; (c) 7 mills.

Solution

a. The rate is $3 per $100 or $\frac{3}{100}$, and the assessed valuation is $12,000 (60% of $20,000). Using Rule 4.13, we have

$$\text{Tax} = \text{Tax Rate} \times \text{Assessed Valuation} = \frac{3}{100} \times \$12,000 = \$360$$

b. The tax rate is $8 per $1,000 or $\frac{8}{1,000}$; hence, the tax is $\frac{8}{1,000} \times \$12,000 = \$96$.

c. The rate of 7 mills means $7 per $1,000 or $\frac{7}{1,000}$; hence, the tax is $\frac{7}{1,000} \times \$12,000 = \$84$.

EXERCISE 4.7

1. Use Table 4–2 to find the sales tax at a 3% rate on the following transactions: (a) 31¢   (b) 78¢   (c) 42¢   (d) $4.12

2. Repeat Problem 1, assuming that the tax rate is 4%.

3. Repeat Problem 1, assuming that the tax rate is 5%.

4. Fattie's Store operating in Florida (4% sales tax) collected $3,120 that included sales and sales taxes. Find (a) the amount of the sales; (b) the amount of the sales tax.

5. If Fattie's was operating in a state with a 3% sales tax and collected $3,296 that included sales and sales taxes, find (a) the amount of sales; (b) the amount of the sales tax.

6. Using Table 4–3, find the amount of excise tax on each of the following articles:
   a. Fishing equipment selling for $42
   b. A Colonel Motors car selling for $4,200
   c. A Modern Mover trailer selling for $8,300

7. Using Table 4–3, find the amount of excise tax on each of the following articles:
   a. A pistol selling for $98.99

b. A Brimstone tire weighing $24\frac{1}{2}$ pounds

c. $18\frac{3}{4}$ gallons of gasoline

8. Find the property tax rate per $100 of assessed valuation for each of the following:

	ASSESSED VALUATION	AMOUNT OF TAXES NEEDED
a.	$5,295,000	$111,195
b.	$15,300,000	$459,000
c.	$29,300,000	$1,904,500

9. Find the property tax rate per $1,000 of assessed valuation for each of the properties in Problem 8.

10. Change each of the tax rates below to an equivalent one using the new base indicated:

TAX RATE	NEW RATE
a. $.0892 per $1 =	_____ per $100
b. $.0892 per $1 =	_____ per $1,000
c. $5.35 per $100 =	_____ per $1,000
d. 80 mills =	_____ per $100

11. A man is paying personal property tax at the rate of 20 mills. Find the tax rate in dollars per $100.

12. The real property tax rate in Town A was $8.29 per $100 and that of Town B was 6 cents per $1. Which town had the greater tax rate?

13. If in Problem 12 we desire to have a tax rate in Town A equivalent to the one being used in Town B and expressed in dollars per hundred, what will this rate be?

14. Find the property tax on each of the following:

	ASSESSED VALUATION	TAX RATE
a.	$10,200	$3.28 per $100
b.	$20,500	8 mills
c.	$18,300	$7 per $1,000

15. Find the property tax on each of the following:

	MARKET VALUE	RATE ASSESSED	TAX RATE
a.	$12,000	60%	$2.45 per $100
b.	$18,500	70%	9 mills

16. Property in Muskegee is assessed at 70% of its market value. Find the tax on a house that can be sold for $17,500, if the tax rate is $3.50 per $100.

17. A certain town turns over 25% of its property tax to the county government. If a piece of property was assessed for $15,000 and the tax rate is $2.80 per $1,000, how much of the tax was given to the county?

18. Donald Scrooge owns two buildings assessed at 70% of their value and having market values of $32,400 and $39,000, respectively. If the tax rate is $4.53 per $100, how much property tax does Mr. Scrooge have to pay?

19. In Quietville, houses are assessed at 45% of their market value and the tax rate is 25 mills. Mr. Seymour bought a house for $30,000. (a) Find his yearly property tax. (b) If 46% of the property taxes are spent on education, how much of Mr. Seymour's taxes will go toward the education of his children? (c) If Mr. Seymour has three children, how much will the education of each child cost Mr. Seymour this year?

20. The property in a certain city was assessed at $31,750,000 and the tax rate was $9.52 per $100. Find the amount of taxes this city expects to collect. (Hint: Use Rule 4.12.)

SELF-TEST/CHAPTER 4

1. The list price of an article is $2500. If the wholesaler offers a single trade discount of 15%, find:
    _____ a. the discount.
    _____ b. the net price of the article.

2. An article lists for $5,000, subject to trade discount of 10 and 15%. Find
    _____ a. the single trade discount equivalent to the 10 and 15% discounts.
    _____ b. the total discount after the 10 and 15% discounts.
    _____ c. the net price of the item.

3. The terms of an invoice with a net amount of $400 dated June 29 are 3/10, E.O.M. Find the amount due if the invoice is paid in full on
    _____ a. July 10.
    _____ b. August 10.

4. Find the amount due in the invoice of Problem 3 if the terms are
    _____ a. 2/10, n/30 and the invoice is paid in full on July 9.
    _____ b. 5/10–30x and the invoice is paid in full on August 8.

5. John Seller shipped 60 bags of grapefruit and 50 sacks of beans to B. A. Goodman, a commission merchant. Mr. Goodman sold the grapefruit at 50¢ per bag and the beans at $22 per sack. If Goodman's commission rate was 5% and he paid $20 in freight charges and $8.50 for storage, find
    _____ a. the charges.
    _____ b. the net proceeds sent to Mr. Seller.

6. Shipley Brothers, commission merchants of Dallas, Texas, bought on the orders of the Good Taste Restaurant 400 pounds of meat at $1.50 per pound and 100 pounds of rice at 16 cents per pound. If the charges were $30 for storage, 5% commission, and $43.50 for freight, find
    _____ a. the prime cost.
    _____ b. the charges.
    _____ c. the gross cost.

7. An automobile costs $8,000 and has an estimated life of six years. At the end of this period the salvage value of this automobile is $1,000. Find the depreciation of this automobile the first year, using
    _____ a. the sum of the years' digits method.
    _____ b. the straight line method.
    _____ c. the declining balance method.

8.   If in the problem above, the additional 20% first year depreciation is claimed, find the total first year depreciation, using

_____ a.   the sum of the years' digits method.

_____ b.   the straight line method.

_____ c.   the declining balance method.

9.   a.   From the following Income Statement, find the indicated per cent based on net sales. (Round off to the nearest .1%.)

HOWARD HUES PAINT Income Statement For Month Ended December 31, 19___			PER CENTS	
Income:				
Sales.....		$91,800		
Less sales returns and allowances..........		1,800		
Net sales.....		$90,000		
Less cost of goods sold:				
Inventory, December 1, 19___.....	$ 9,000			
Purchases.....	40,500			
Goods available for sale.....	$49,500			
Less inventory, December 31, 19___.....	10,800			
Cost of goods sold.....		$38,700		
Gross profit on sales.....		$51,300		
Operating expenses:				
Selling expenses.....	$18,000			
Delivery expenses.....	14,400			
Office expenses.....	4,500			
Miscellaneous expenses.....	7,200			
Total operating expenses.....		$44,100		
Net income.....		$ 7,200		

9.   b.   In the Comparative Income Statement on opposite page find the amount and the per cent of change of each item, using 1976 as the base year. (Round off to the nearest .1%.)

10.   A house is selling for $30,000. Find

_____ a.   the sales tax, if the tax rate is 4%.

_____ b.   the assessed value of the house, if houses are assessed at 80% of the market value.

_____ c.   the tax on the house, if the tax rate is 8 mills.

Comparative Income Statement For Years Ended December 31, 1977 and 1976			INCREASE OR DECREASE* DURING 1977	
	1977	1976	Amount	Per Cent
Sales..	$224,000	$222,000		
Less sales returns and allowances................	4,000	22,000	*	*
Net sales...	220,000	200,000		
Less cost of goods sold:				
Merchandise inventory, January 1.................	$120,000	$100,000		
Purchases..	100,000	80,000		
Goods available for sale...............................	$220,000	$180,000		
Less inventory, December 31........................	67,200	64,000		
Cost of goods sold...............................	152,800	116,000		
Gross profit...	$ 67,200	$ 84,000	*	*
Operating expenses:				
Selling expenses..	$ 24,000	$ 20,000		
General expenses.......................................	24,000	16,000		
Total operating expenses......................	$ 48,000	$ 36,000		
Net income...	$ 19,200	$ 48,000	*	*

part three

The Mathematics
of Banking

five

Simple Interest

NOW EARN THE HIGHEST INTEREST ON THE LOWEST DEPOSITS IN TOWN.
7½ PERCENT.

Reprinted, by permission, from *The Tampa Tribune*, November 16, 1973, p. 5E.

5.1 SIMPLE INTEREST

In the ad above, a bank is claiming to pay the highest interest on the lowest deposits in town. **Interest** is the price paid for the use of borrowed money. In this case, the bank "borrowing" the money will pay its depositors $7\frac{1}{2}\%$. If we assume the interest is paid annually, this means that the depositor receives as interest $7\frac{1}{2}$ cents for each dollar left in the bank for a period of one year. As you can see, the amount of interest paid depends on three factors:

Definition of interest

1. **The Principal:** the amount of money borrowed in an interest transaction.
2. **The Interest Rate:** that portion of the principal which is charged for the use of the principal (usually expressed as a per cent).
3. **The Time (or Term):** the period during which the borrwoer has the use of all or part of the borrowed money.

Simple interest (I) is defined as the product of the principal (P), rate (r), and time (t). This is computed by the following simple interest formula:

Finding the interest

FORMULA 5.1 $I = P \times r \times t$

Thus, if a person opens an account with a deposit of $300 with the bank (whose rate is $7\frac{1}{2}\%$) publishing the ad at the beginning of this section, the interest the person will receive in two years will be

$$I = 300 \times 7\frac{1}{2}\% \times 2 = 300 \times \frac{7.5}{100} \times 2 = \$45$$

Example 1

A bank pays simple interest at a rate of 5% on savings accounts. A person opens an account with a deposit of $450. How much interest will this person receive in two years?

Solution

Here $P = \$450$, $r = 5\%$, and $t = 2$ years. By Formula 5.1, the person will receive in two years $I = \$450 \times 5\% \times 2 = \$45$.

Note that up to now we have tacitly assumed that the rate r and the time t are both in years. In general, r and t must be consistently stated; that is, if the rate is given in years, the time must also be stated in years. It is the usual practice to state a simple interest transaction on an annual (per annum) basis. In this text, rates are **annual** rates unless otherwise specified.

Example 2

A man borrowed $6,000 from a bank for a period of six months. If the simple interest rate is 6%,
  a. how much interest did he pay?
  b. what is the total amount he paid back to the bank?

Solution

  a. Since the rate is given in years, the time (six months) must be expressed in years. Thus, $P = \$6,000$, $r = 6\%$, $t = \frac{6}{12} = \frac{1}{2}$ year, and $I = 6,000 \times 6\% \times \frac{1}{2} = \$180$.

  b. The total amount paid back to the bank is the amount of money originally borrowed ($6,000) plus the interest ($180), that is, $6,180.

Finding the amount or sum

As you can see from the preceding example, the amount is the sum of the principal and the interest. If we denote this quantity by S, we obtain the following formula:

$$S = P + I$$

or

$$S = P + (P \times r \times t)$$

Factoring, we obtain

> **FORMULA 5.2** $S = P \times (1 + (r \times t))$

Example 3

A man borrows $400 for eight weeks at 13%.
  a. What amount must he repay?
  b. What interest must he pay?

Solution

a. Since the rate is an annual rate, the time (eight weeks) must be expressed in years. Thus, $P = \$400$, $r = 13\%$, and $t = \dfrac{8}{52} = \dfrac{2}{13}$ year.

Substituting in Formula 5.2, we have

$$S = 400 \times \left(1 + \left(\frac{13}{100} \times \frac{2}{13}\right)\right) = 400 \times (1.02) = \$408$$

b. Since the amount is $408 and the principal is $400, the interest is $I = \$408 - \$400 = \$8$.

PROGRESS TEST 1

1. A bank pays 6% simple interest on savings accounts. A person opens an account with a deposit of $500. The interest this person will receive at the end of two years is _____.

2. A person borrowed $500 for a period of six weeks. If the interest rate is 6.5%, the amount this person paid was _____.

3. The interest paid by the person in the preceding problem was _____.

Example 4

A person desires to buy the house advertised in the ad on the following page. If the person borrowed $20,000 at $7\frac{1}{2}\%$ for 360 months, find the interest the person paid *the first month* and the amount of house purchased with the first payment of $140.45.

Solution

$P = \$20,000$, $r = 7\frac{1}{2}\%$, and $t = \dfrac{1}{12}$. Substituting in Formula 5.1,

$I = 20,000 \times 7\frac{1}{2}\% \times \dfrac{1}{12} = \$125$. Since the payment is $140.45, the

---

1. $60   2. $503.75   3. $3.75

person is purchasing $140.45 − $125 = $15.45 worth of house with his first payment. The $15.45 is applied to the reduction of this debt and is called the reduction of his principal. Thus, in the next month he owes only $20,000 − $15.45 = $19,984.55. Interest is then charged for the loan on this slightly smaller amount.

3 bedrooms, 1 bath, $140.45 a month*

Reprinted, by permission, from *The Tampa Tribune*, January 13, 1974, p. 7F.

EXERCISE 5.1

In Problems 1 through 10, find the simple interest.

	PRINCIPAL	RATE	TIME
1.	$700	4%	3 years
2.	$950	6%	2 years
3.	$325	4%	6 months
4.	$1,275	7%	4 months
5.	$800	5%	18 months
6.	$250	8%	15 months
7.	$1,200	5%	1 year, 8 months
8.	$2,400	6%	2 years, 6 months
9.	$5,200	5%	10 weeks
10.	$2,600	6%	10 weeks

In Problems 11 through 16, find the amount.

	PRINCIPAL	RATE	TIME
11.	$240	5%	2 years
12.	$350	8%	5 years
13.	$600	12%	7 months
14.	$700	6%	8 months
15.	$900	13%	16 weeks
16.	$2,500	6.5%	8 weeks

17. A couple get a $20,000 loan for buying a house. If their monthly payments are $140, and the interest rate is 8%, how much interest do they pay the first month and what is the amount of house purchased with the first payment?

18. If the couple of Problem 17 get a $30,000 loan, how much interest do they pay the first month and what amount of house do they purchase with their first payment of $210.00?

19. A woman borrows $20,000 to buy a house. If the interest rate is 6% and the monthly payment is $128.50, how much of the first payment is applied to the interest and how much to the principal?

20. The Friendly Credit Union advertises a rate of 8% paid semiannually. Deposits made by the tenth of the month earn dividends (interest) for the entire month. Deposits made after the tenth earn dividends from the first of the following month. A depositor had a balance of $1,250 on June 30, 1976. He deposited $350 on September 6, 1976. If dividends are credited on June 30 and December 31, how much will he have in his account on December 31, 1976?

21. Repeat Problem 20 with a $350 deposit made on October 12, 1976.

22. Fred Frederick had $1,250 in his savings account, which earns $5\frac{1}{2}\%$ interest. If interest is credited quarterly, how much interest did he receive three months later if he made no additions (deposits) or withdrawals during this time?

23. James Bond owns five bonds with a face value of $1,000 each. How much interest does he receive quarterly (every three months) if the interest rate is $5\frac{1}{4}\%$?

24. A man invested $4,600 at 14% for a period of 48 months. How much interest did he earn? If the interest was divided into 48 parts which were paid to him every month, what was his monthly payment?

The following ad will be used in Problems 25 through 30.

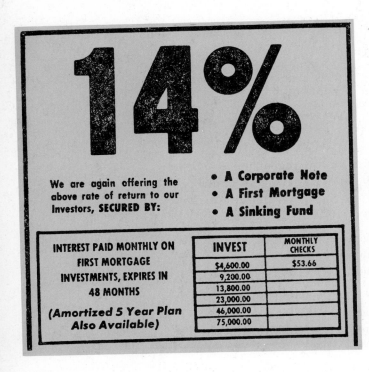

Reprinted, by permission, from *The Tampa Tribune*, January 13, 1974, p. 7E.

25. In the ad above, an investor invests $4,600 at 14% for 48 months (four years). The interest earned will be I = $4,600 × 14% × 4 = $2,576. If this amount is divided into 48 equal monthly payments, each payment will amount to $53.66 (see the column labeled "Monthly Checks" in the ad). Find the amount of the monthly checks when an investor invests $9,200.

26. Do the same as in Problem 25 for an investment of $13,800.

27. Do the same as in Problem 25 for an investment of $23,000.

28. Do the same as in Problem 25 for an investment of $46,000.

29. Do the same as in Problem 25 for an investment of $50,000.

30. Do the same as in Problem 25 for an investment of $75,000.

Reprinted, by permission, from *The Tampa Times*, January 14, 1974, p. 4.

5.2 EXACT AND ORDINARY INTEREST

As you can see from the preceding ad, time is very important in the computation of interest. In this section we shall consider the cases in which the time in the simple interest formula is given in days. In these cases, there are two ways in which the interest can be computed.

1. **Exact Interest:** The interest is computed under the assumption that the year has 365 (or 366 in the case of leap year) days.

2. **Ordinary Interest:** The interest is computed under the assumption that the year has 360 days.

We compare these two methods of computing interest in the following example.

Example 1

Find the exact and the ordinary interest on a 60-day loan of $730 if the rate of interest is 6%.

Solution

$$\text{Exact Interest} = 730 \times 6\% \times \frac{60}{365} = \$7.20$$

$$\text{Ordinary Interest} = 730 \times 6\% \times \frac{60}{360} = \$7.30$$

Note that the ordinary interest is greater than the exact interest.

There are also two methods of calculating the number of days between two calendar dates.

1. **Exact Time:** This method includes all days except the first.

2. **Approximate Time:** This method assumes that all months of the year contain 30 days.

A simple way to calculate the exact number of days between two calendar dates is by the use of Table 5–1. (page 239)

To determine the number of days between May 4 and July 14, for example, we find in the table that May 4 is the 124th day of the year and July 14 the 195th day. Thus, the exact time between May 4 and July 14 is $195 - 124 = 71$ days.

If a table is not available we can proceed as follows:

May 4 to May 31	$31 - 4 = 27$ days
June	30 days
July	14 days
Total	71 days

From the preceding discussion we can clearly see that it is important to remember the number of days in each month. The following scheme, in which each knuckle (starting with the index finger of your right hand) and each space between knuckles represents a month, can be used to facilitate this memorization.

TABLE 5–1

THE NUMBER OF EACH DAY OF THE YEAR

Day of Month	Jan.	Feb.	Mar.	Apr.	May	June	July	Aug.	Sept.	Oct.	Nov.	Dec.	Day of Month
1	1	32	60	91	121	152	182	213	244	274	305	335	1
2	2	33	61	92	122	153	183	214	245	275	306	336	2
3	3	34	62	93	123	154	184	215	246	276	307	337	3
4	4	35	63	94	124	155	185	216	247	277	308	338	4
5	5	36	64	95	125	156	186	217	248	278	309	339	5
6	6	37	65	96	126	157	187	218	249	279	310	340	6
7	7	38	66	97	127	158	188	219	250	280	311	341	7
8	8	39	67	98	128	159	189	220	251	281	312	342	8
9	9	40	68	99	129	160	190	221	252	282	313	343	9
10	10	41	69	100	130	161	191	222	253	283	314	344	10
11	11	42	70	101	131	162	192	223	254	284	315	345	11
12	12	43	71	102	132	163	193	224	255	285	316	346	12
13	13	44	72	103	133	164	194	225	256	286	317	347	13
14	14	45	73	104	134	165	195	226	257	287	318	348	14
15	15	46	74	105	135	166	196	227	258	288	319	349	15
16	16	47	75	106	136	167	197	228	259	289	320	350	16
17	17	48	76	107	137	168	198	229	260	290	321	351	17
18	18	49	77	108	138	169	199	230	261	291	322	352	18
19	19	50	78	109	139	170	200	231	262	292	323	353	19
20	20	51	79	110	140	171	201	232	263	293	324	354	20
21	21	52	80	111	141	172	202	233	264	294	325	355	21
22	22	53	81	112	142	173	203	234	265	295	326	356	22
23	23	54	82	113	143	174	204	235	266	296	327	357	23
24	24	55	83	114	144	175	205	236	267	297	328	358	24
25	25	56	84	115	145	176	206	237	268	298	329	359	25
26	26	57	85	116	146	177	207	238	269	299	330	360	26
27	27	58	86	117	147	178	208	239	270	300	331	361	27
28	28	59	87	118	148	179	209	240	271	301	332	362	28
29	29	*	88	119	149	180	210	241	272	302	333	363	29
30	30		89	120	150	181	211	242	273	303	334	364	30
31	31		90		151		212	243		304		365	31

*For leap years, February has 29 days, and the number of each day from March 1 is one greater than the number given in the table.

Reprinted, by permission, from Stephen P. Shao, ed., *Mathematics for Management and Finance,* 2nd ed., South-Western Publishing Co., 1969, Appendix p. 1.

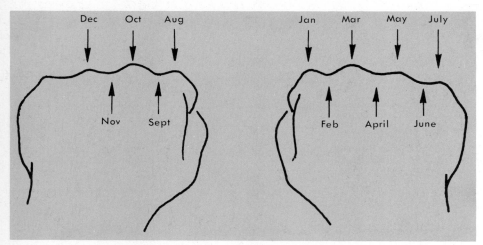

Figure 5–1

As you can see from the figure, each knuckle represents a month with 31 days and each space between knuckles represents a month with 30 days (except February).

Example 2

Find the number of days between June 15, 1975, and September 18, 1975, using (a) exact time; (b) approximate time.

Solution

a.
June 15 to June 30	$30 - 15 =$ 15 days
July	31 days
August	31 days
September	18 days
Total	95 days

Or, we can find in Table 5–1 that June 15 is the 166th day of the year and September 18 is the 261st day. Thus, the exact time between June 15 and September 18 is $261 - 166 = 95$ days.

    b. We write the given dates, placing the number of the months to the left and of the days to the right, and then subtract.

Month	Day
Sept (9)	18
June (6)	15

3 months + 3 days = 93 days

PROGRESS TEST 1

1. The exact and ordinary interest on a 60-day loan of $1,095 at a 6% interest rate are, respectively, _____ and _____.

2. The exact and approximate times in days between January 19, 1976, and March 19, 1976 (a leap year), are _____ and _____ days, respectively.

From the preceding discussion we can see that there are four ways to compute simple interest:

1. Ordinary interest using exact time (**Banker's Rule**)
2. Ordinary interest using approximate time
3. Exact interest using exact time
4. Exact interest using approximate time

We present an example comparing these four methods.

Example 3

On March 13, Phyllis Phillips borrowed $1,460 at 6%. The loan was repaid on June 11 of the same year. Find the interest paid by Phyllis, using each of the four methods mentioned in this section.

Solution

EXACT TIME	APPROXIMATE TIME

EXACT TIME

March 13 is the 72nd day.
June 11 is the 162nd day.
Thus, the number of days
is $162 - 72 = 90$.

APPROXIMATE TIME

March 13 to March 30 = 17 days
April   30 days
May   30 days
June   11 days
Total   88 days

Ordinary interest; exact time: $I = 1{,}460 \times 6\% \times \dfrac{90}{360} = \$21.90$

Ordinary interest; approximate time: $I = 1{,}460 \times 6\% \times \dfrac{88}{360} = \$21.41$

Exact interest; exact time: $I = 1{,}460 \times 6\% \times \dfrac{90}{365} = \$21.60$

Exact interest; approximate time: $I = 1{,}460 \times 6\% \times \dfrac{88}{365} = \$21.12$

---

1. $10.80, $10.95   2. 60 days, 60 days

As you can see from Example 3, the method combining ordinary interest and exact time (known as the Banker's Rule) yields the highest interest. This method is used by banks, installment houses, and merchants. In this book, unless otherwise specified, we shall use ordinary interest and exact time (Banker's Rule).

PROGRESS TEST 2

1. On July 14, 1975, Tom Thomas borrowed $2,920 at 6%. The loan was repaid on Oct. 12 of the same year. The interest paid by Thomas, using the Banker's Rule, was _____.

2. The ordinary interest Thomas would have paid based on the approximate time is _____.

3. The exact interest Thomas would have paid based on the exact time is _____.

4. The exact interest Thomas would have paid based on the approximate time is _____.

EXERCISE 5.2

1. Find the exact and the ordinary interest on a 90-day loan of $1,095 if the rate of interest is 6%.

2. Repeat Problem 1 for the rate of interest of 5%.

3. Find the exact number of days between July 3, 1974, and December 12, 1974.

4. Find the approximate number of days between July 3, 1974, and December 12, 1974.

5. On January 4, 1972 (a leap year), Simon Simple borrowed $3,650 at 6%. The loan was repaid on May 3, 1972. Find the interest Mr. Simple would have paid using:
   a. ordinary interest and exact time (Banker's Rule).
   b. ordinary interest and approximate time.
   c. exact interest and exact time.
   d. exact interest and approximate time.

6. Repeat Problem 5 for the rate of interest of 5%.

---

1. $43.80   2. $42.83   3. $43.20   4. $42.24

7. If $P = \$5,000$ and $r = 5\frac{3}{4}\%$, find the ordinary and exact interest for a 90-day loan.

8. Using exact time, find the ordinary and exact interest on a $600 loan at 10% obtained on December 20, 1972, and repaid on August 17, 1973.

In Problems 9 through 13, use Banker's Rule.

9. A man borrows $4,000 on July 18, 1977. He repays the debt on October 16 of the same year with interest of 8%. Find the interest due and the amount paid.

10. Don Doer borrowed $600 on June 1 and promised to pay back the money in 120 days at 6% interest. What amount does Mr. Doer have to pay when the loan is due?

11. A woman borrowed $518 on January 11, 1972. If the rate of interest was 9%, what was the amount she had to repay on February 20, 1972?

12. Find the interest on a $2,500 loan at 8% obtained on June 13 and repaid on July 13 of the same year.

13. The Second Local Bank borrows $1,500,000 from the First Local Bank for a period of five days at 8%. How much is the interest?

14. A construction loan is a special type of loan in which funds are advanced gradually as construction progresses. These loans must be repaid in a lump sum shortly after completion of the project. The builder of an apartment obtained one of these loans for $50,000 at an annual rate of 10%. The money was advanced as follows:

June 1	$20,000
July 1	$10,000
August 1	$20,000

The building was completed on September 1 and the loan repaid on January 1. Find (a) the total interest paid, using ordinary interest and approximate time; (b) the amount the builder paid back.

15. On December 31, a man has $2,000 in a savings account earning 5% interest if left on deposit until June 30, the next interest date. On April 1 the man needs $1,000. Instead of withdrawing the money from his account, he obtains a loan for this amount. If the rate of the loan is 6% and he pays it on June 30, how much money does the man save? (Assume the interest on the loan is computed using Banker's Rule.)

© 1974 King Features Syndicate, Inc. Reprinted by permission.

5.3 ORDINARY INTEREST SHORT CUTS

As you can see from the cartoon, in many cases it is necessary to make calculations that require special methods. For example, persons calculating ordinary interest use a shortcut method called the **60-day, 6% method.** Here is how this method works:

The 60-day 6% method of calculating ordinary interest

Let us assume that you wish to find the ordinary interest on $130 for 60 days at 6%. By Formula 5.1 for interest, we have

$$I = 130 \times \frac{\overset{1}{\cancel{6}}}{\underset{\underset{1}{\cancel{6}}}{100}} \times \frac{\overset{1}{\cancel{60}}}{360} = \$1.30$$

As you can see, since 60 days $= \frac{60}{360} = \frac{1}{6}$ year and $\frac{6}{100} \times \frac{1}{6} = \frac{1}{100}$, to find the ordinary interest on any principal for 60 days at 6% we move the decimal point in the principal two places to the left, as stated in the following rule.

> **RULE 5.1** To find the ordinary interest on any principal for 60 days at 6%, move the decimal point in the principal two places to the left. *

Thus, the ordinary interest on $340 for 60 days at 6% is $3.40 and that on $649 is $6.49.

Example 1

Find the ordinary interest on $280 at 6% for 60 days.

---

*A similar procedure can be used to find the ordinary interest at 4% for 90 days, at 3% for 120 days, at 12% for 30 days, or any other combination whose product is 360.

Solution

We use Rule 5.1 and move the decimal point of the principal two places to the left as shown: $2.80. Thus, the interest is $2.80.

The 60-day, 6% method can also be used to compute the interest for periods of time other than 60 days. For example, to find the ordinary interest on a $300 loan at 6% for 120 days, we find the interest on $300 at 6% for 60 days, and double this interest. The procedure can be expressed in tabular form as follows:

Interest on $300 at 6% for 60 days.................$3.00
Interest on $300 at 6% for 60 days.................$3.00
Interest on $300 at 6% for 120 days..............$6.00

Using the 60-day, 6% method to compute interest for periods of time other than 60 days

Example 2

Find the ordinary interest on $450 at 6% for 66 days.

Solution

Interest on $450 at 6% for 60 days.................$4.50
Interest on $450 at 6% for 6 days.................$0.45
Interest on $450 at 6% for 66 days.................$4.95

PROGRESS TEST 1

1. The ordinary interest on a loan of $313 at 6% for 60 days is _____.

2. The ordinary interest on $600 at 6% for 70 days is _____.

3. The ordinary interest on $1,000 at 6% for 93 days is _____.

Ordinary interest can also be determined by using Table 5–2. For example, to find the interest on $500 for 17 days at 7% we proceed as follows:

1. Find the column headed by the specified rate of interest (7%) in the rate row at the top of the table.

2. Use the time column at the left of the table to find the row beginning with the desired number of days (17), and then move to

1. $3.13   2. $7.00   3. $10 + $5 + $0.50 = $15.50

TABLE 5-2   Simple-Interest Table ($100 on a 360-Day-Year Basis)

TIME	2½%	3%	3½%	4%	4½%	5%	5½%	6%	6½%	7%
1 day	.0069	.0083	.0097	.0111	.0125	.0139	.0153	.0167	.0181	.0194
2 days	.0139	.0167	.0194	.0222	.0250	.0278	.0306	.0333	.0361	.0389
3 days	.0208	.0250	.0292	.0333	.0375	.0417	.0458	.0500	.0542	.0583
4 days	.0278	.0333	.0389	.0444	.0500	.0556	.0611	.0667	.0722	.0778
5 days	.0347	.0417	.0486	.0556	.0625	.0694	.0764	.0833	.0903	.0972
6 days	0417	.0500	.0583	.0667	.0750	.0833	.0917	.1000	.1083	.1167
7 days	.0486	.0583	.0681	.0778	.0875	.0972	.1069	.1167	.1264	.1361
8 days	.0556	.0667	.0778	.0889	.1000	.1111	.1222	.1333	.1444	.1556
9 days	.0625	.0750	.0875	.1000	.1125	.1250	.1375	.1500	.1625	.1750
10 days	.0694	.0833	.0972	.1111	.1250	.1389	.1528	.1667	.1806	.1944
11 days	.0764	.0917	.1069	.1222	.1375	.1528	.1681	.1833	.1986	.2139
12 days	.0833	.1000	.1167	.1333	.1500	.1667	.1833	.2000	.2167	.2333
13 days	.0903	.1083	.1264	.1444	.1625	.1806	.1986	.2167	.2347	.2528
14 days	.0972	.1167	.1361	.1556	.1750	.1944	.2139	.2333	.2528	.2722
15 days	.1042	.1250	.1458	.1667	.1875	.2083	.2292	.2500	.2708	.2917
16 days	.1111	.1333	.1556	.1778	.2000	.2222	.2444	.2667	.2889	.3111
17 days	.1181	.1417	.1653	.1889	.2125	.2361	.2597	.2833	.3069	.3306
18 days	.1250	.1500	.1750	.2000	.2250	.2500	.2750	.3000	.3250	.3500
19 days	.1319	.1583	.1847	.2111	.2375	.2639	.2903	.3167	.3431	.3694
20 days	.1389	.1667	.1944	.2222	.2500	.2778	.3056	.3333	.3611	.3889
21 days	.1458	.1750	.2042	.2333	.2625	.2917	.3208	.3500	.3792	.4083
22 days	.1528	.1833	.2139	.2444	.2750	.3056	.3361	.3667	.3972	.4278
23 days	.1597	.1917	.2236	.2556	.2875	.3194	.3514	.3833	.4153	.4472
24 days	.1667	.2000	.2333	.2667	.3000	.3333	.3667	.4000	.4333	.4667
25 days	.1736	.2083	.2431	.2778	.3125	.3472	.3819	.4167	.4514	.4861
26 days	.1806	.2167	.2528	.2889	.3250	.3611	.3972	.4333	.4694	.5056
27 days	.1875	.2250	.2625	.3000	.3375	.3750	.4125	.4500	.4875	.5250
28 days	.1944	.2333	.2722	.3111	.3500	.3889	.4278	.4667	.5056	.5444
29 days	.2014	.2417	.2819	.3222	.3625	.4028	.4431	.4833	.5236	.5639
1 month	.2083	.2500	.2917	.3333	.3750	.4167	.4583	.5000	.5417	.5833
2 months	.4167	.5000	.5833	.6667	.7500	.8333	.9167	1.0000	1.0833	1.1667
3 months	.6230	.7500	.8750	1.0000	1.1250	1.2500	1.3750	1.5000	1.6250	1.7500
4 months	.8333	1.0000	1.1667	1.3333	1.5000	1.6667	1.8333	2.0000	2.1667	2.3333
5 months	1.0417	1.2500	1.4583	1.6667	1.8750	2.0833	2.2917	2.5000	2.7083	2.9160
6 months	1.2500	1.5000	1.7500	2.0000	2.2500	2.5000	2.7500	3.0000	3.2500	3.5000

the right until you reach the "7%" column. The amount shown (.3306) represents the interest on $100 at the given rate and time.

3. Divide this interest by 100 (by moving the decimal point two places to the left) to find the interest on $1 (0.003306).

4. Multiply the interest on $1 by the given principal ($500). The result ($500 × 0.003306 = $1.65) is the desired interest.

Example 2

Find the ordinary interest on a $630 loan for 95 days at 6%.

Solution

Since the number of days (95) is not in the table, we first find the interest for 90 days (3 months) and add to this amount the interest for 5 days.

Interest on $100 for 90 days at 6%......$1.50
Interest on $100 for 5 days at 6%......$0.08333
Interest on $100 for 95 days at 6%......$1.58333

Interest on $1 for 95 days at 6%...........$1.58333 ÷ 100 = $0.0158333

Interest on $630 for 95 days at 6%......$630 × 0.0158333 = $9.97

PROGRESS TEST 2

1. The ordinary interest on $100 at $4\frac{1}{2}$% for 60 days
is _____.

2. The ordinary interest on $100 at $4\frac{1}{2}$% for 7 days
is _____.

3. The ordinary interest on $100 at $4\frac{1}{2}$% for 67 days
is _____.

4. The ordinary interest on $900 at $4\frac{1}{2}$% for 67 days
is _____.

EXERCISE 5.3

In Problems 1 through 15, find the ordinary interest, using the 60-day, 6% method.

	PRINCIPAL	RATE	TIME
1.	$360	6%	60 days
2.	$720	6%	70 days
3.	$360	6%	76 days
4.	$600	8%	60 days
5.	$600	9%	60 days
6.	$480	4%	60 days
7.	$480	4%	66 days
8.	$1,292	$7\frac{1}{2}$%	60 days

---

1. $0.75   2. $0.0875 ≈ $0.09   3. $0.75 + $0.0875 = $0.8375 ≈ $0.84
4. 9 × $0.8375 = $7.5375 = $7.54

9.	$1,292	$7\frac{1}{2}\%$	90 days
10.	$1,008	5%	30 days
11.	$216	6%	37 days
12.	$193.68	9%	76 days
13.	$1,440	$5\frac{1}{2}\%$	40 days
14.	$360	2%	149 days
15.	$216	8%	37 days

In Problems 16 through 20, find the ordinary interest, using Table 5–2.

	PRINCIPAL	RATE	TIME
16.	$360	6%	3 months
17.	$500	6%	120 days
18.	$1,200	$4\frac{1}{2}\%$	27 days
19.	$41.74	7%	120 days
20.	$41.74	7%	117 days

In Problems 21 through 25, find the ordinary interest at exact time, using Table 5–2.

	PRINCIPAL	RATE	TIME
21.	$300	6%	March 4 to May 8
22.	$175	5%	February 24 to July 24
23.	$2,472.60	$4\frac{1}{2}\%$	March 26 to July 23
24.	$214	4%	November 23, 1971, to April 21, 1972
25.	$1,872.52	$4\frac{1}{2}\%$	December 14, 1973 to August 4, 1974

26. A loan for $2,025 at $5\frac{1}{2}\%$ is due in two months. Find the ordinary interest that has to be paid on this loan and the amount to be repaid.

27. A bill for $1,500 was due on March 1 but was not paid until May 18. If the interest on overdue bills is 18 per cent ordinary interest computed at exact time, find the amount necessary to pay this bill.

28. A piece of property owned by Landis Lord is assessed at $7,500. Taxes of 8.5% of the assessed value are due in two

equal payments, the first due on December 15 and the second one on April 15. Overdue payments are charged 6% ordinary interest at exact time. If Mr. Lord made his first payment on January 3 and his second payment on July 14, find his total payment for the tax year.

29. Mr. I. Makeim, a building contractor, obtained an $80,000 construction loan at $4\frac{1}{2}$%. The money was advanced as follows:

March 15	$30,000
June 15	$20,000
September 15	$20,000
December 15	$10,000

The loan was repaid on March 15 of the following year. Find the total amount paid, using ordinary interest and approximate time.

Reprinted, by permission, from *The Tampa Tribune*, January 27, 1974, p. 8E.

5.4 FINDING THE PRINCIPAL, RATE, AND TIME

The ad above suggests that you can obtain up to a 7.50% interest rate of return (tax free) on your investment. Lending institutions as well as investors, brokers, and executives in large corporations ask questions such as the following: What will be the rate of an investment when the principal, interest, and time are given? How much principal will be required to produce a given amount of interest income (or yield) when the interest rate and the time are known? How much time will it take for an amount of money (principal) to produce a given yield when the interest rate is known? In this section we will answer these and similar questions.

There are three different types of problems that involve finding the principal:

1. When the interest, the rate, and the time are given:

$$P = \frac{I}{r \times t}$$

2. When the amount and the interest are given:

$$P = S - I$$

3. When the amount, the rate, and the time are given:

$$P = \frac{S}{(1 + (r \times t))}$$

We shall illustrate the use of these formulas in the following examples.

Example 1

A savings account yielded $22.50 interest in a period of one year. If the interest rate on this account was $7\frac{1}{2}\%$, what was the amount of money (principal) in the account?

Solution

Here $I = \$22.50$, $r = 7\frac{1}{2}\%$, and, by Formula 5.1, $I = P \times r \times t$. Dividing both sides by rt, we have

FORMULA 5.3 $P = \dfrac{I}{r \times t}$

Substituting in Formula 5.3,

$$P = \frac{22.50}{7.5\% \times 1} = 22.50 \times \frac{100}{7.5} = \$300$$

Example 2

Mr. B. Thrifty deposited a certain amount of money in a savings account. At the end of one year his balance was $294.25 and he had earned $19.25 in interest. How much money had he deposited a year ago?

Solution

Here I = \$19.25, S = \$294.25, and by the definition of S, S = P + I. Subtracting I from both sides of the equation, we have

FORMULA 5.4 $P = S - I$

Substituting in Formula 5.4, P = \$294.25 − \$19.25 = \$275.

Example 3

A man paid a 6%, 60-day loan with a check for \$505. How much money had he borrowed?

Solution

Here S = \$505, r = 6%, $t = \frac{60}{360} = \frac{1}{6}$ year, and by Formula 5.2, S = P × (1 + (r × t)). Dividing both sides by (1 + (r × t)), we have

FORMULA 5.5 $P = \dfrac{S}{1 + (r \times t)}$

Substituting in Formula 5.5,

$$P = \frac{505}{1 + (6\% \times 1/6)} = \frac{505}{1 + (6/100 \times 1/6)} = \frac{505}{101/100} = \frac{505 \times 100}{101} = \$500$$

PROGRESS TEST 1

1. If I = \$5.62, r = 9%, and t = 3 months, then P = _____.

2. A man deposited a certain amount of money in a savings account. At the end of one year his balance was \$265 and it included \$15 in interest. His original deposit was for _____.

3. A man paid a 4-month loan with a check for \$512.50. If the interest rate was $7\frac{1}{2}$%, the loan was for _____.

In many cases it is desirable to compare two investments to determine which one yields the higher rate of return. For example, an in-

---

1. \$249.78   2. \$250   3. \$500

vestment company might offer $45 interest for investing $600 for a period of one year, while another one offers a return of $32 for investing $400 for one year. To find the rate of interest the first company is using, we recall that $I = P \times r \times t$; dividing both sides of this equation by $P \times t$, we obtain

FORMULA 5.6 $r = \dfrac{I}{P \times t}$

Substituting in Formula 5.6, $r = \dfrac{45}{600 \times 1} = 7.5\%$. For the second company, $r = \dfrac{32}{400 \times 1} = 8\%$. Thus, it would be better to invest $400 in the second company than $600 in the first.

Example 4

The interest paid on a loan of $3,200 for six months was $96. What was the interest rate?

Solution

Here $I = \$96$, $P = \$3,200$, and $t = \dfrac{6}{12} = \dfrac{1}{2}$ year. Substituting in Formula 5.6, we have

$$r = \frac{96}{3,200 \times 1/2} = \frac{96}{1,600} = 6\%$$

Example 5

How long will it take $300 to earn $36 interest at 6%?

Solution

Here $I = \$36$, $P = \$300$, $r = 6\%$, and by Formula 5.1, $I = P \times r \times t$. Dividing both sides by $P \times r$, we have

FORMULA 5.7 $t = \dfrac{I}{P \times r}$

Substituting in Formula 5.7,

$$t = \frac{36}{300 \times 6/100} = 2 \text{ years}$$

PROGRESS TEST 2

1. The interest paid on a $600 loan for three months was $12. The interest rate on this loan was _____.

2. An $800 investment earned $20 at an interest rate of 6%. The amount of time the money was invested was _____.

For your convenience, we now list the formulas we have used. This summary will be helpful when working the exercises.

FORMULA 5.1 $I = P \times r \times t$

FORMULA 5.2 $S = P \times (1 + (r \times t))$

FORMULA 5.3 $P = \dfrac{I}{r \times t}$

FORMULA 5.4 $P = S - I$

FORMULA 5.5 $P = \dfrac{S}{1 + (r \times t)}$

FORMULA 5.6 $r = \dfrac{I}{P \times t}$

FORMULA 5.7 $t = \dfrac{I}{P \times r}$

Here P, the principal, is sometimes called the **present value.**

EXERCISE 5.4

In Problems 1 through 14, find the unknown values indicated by the symbols P, S, r, and t.

	PRINCIPAL	ANNUAL INTEREST RATE	TIME	INTEREST	AMOUNT
1.	P	8%	30 days	$0.80	S
2.	P	5%	90 days	$37.50	S
3.	P	6%	300 days	$225	S
4.	P	—	—	$60	$240
5.	P	—	—	$79.60	$438.38

1. 8%   2. $\dfrac{5}{12}$ year = 5 months

6.	P	8%	30 days	—	$241.60
7.	P	5%	90 days	—	$3,037.50
8.	P	8%	3 months	—	$6,630
9.	$380	r	6 months	$13.60	—
10.	$616	r	2 months	I	$622.16
11.	$462.60	r	8 months	I	$487.28
12.	$961	8%	t	$38.44	—
13.	$134.40	5%	t	$10.08	—
14.	$780	5%	t	$48.75	—

15. Find the principal necessary to yield $96 in two years at 4%.

16. Find the principal necessary to yield $180 in 90 days at $7\frac{1}{2}\%$.

17. Find the principal necessary to yield $316 in 50 days at 6%.

18. Find the interest rate necessary to produce $13 on an investment of $650 for a period of three months.

19. Find the interest rate necessary to produce $168.75 on an investment of $1,125 for a period of two and one-half years.

20. A man invested his life savings of $85,000 in stocks. At the end of 90 days he received a dividend check of $1,487.50. What is the annual interest rate of his investment?

21. A man borrowed $1,500 and paid back $1,535 four months later. What was the interest rate charged for the debt?

22. At what interest rate will a $900 investment note yield $18 in three months?

23. A carpenter borrowed $250 from Sharkley's Loan Company. At the end of one month he paid the company $257.50. What annual rate of interest did he pay?

24. A loan shark made a loan of $96 to be paid the following month in the amount of $100. What was the annual interest rate?

25. How many months are required for $860 to yield $34.40 in interest at 6%?

26. How many days are required for $1,440 to yield $8.80 in interest at 5.5%?

27. If a person loans $3,000 at 5%, how long will it take him to get $3,018.75?

28. Find the time necessary for $12,500 to produce $337.50 at 6% interest.

29. A businessman borrowed $2,000 at 9% interest. At a later date,

he was unable to make a payment on the principal, but he did pay $198, the interest due at that time. Find the time that had elapsed between the day he borrowed the money and the day he paid the interest.

30. Repeat the problem above with the amount paid in interest of $220.

HAZEL

"How much down and how many months to pay?"

5.5   PARTIAL PAYMENTS

As you can see from the cartoon, in many cases it is necessary to make payments on a debt. A **partial payment** (or payment on account) is the payment of any part of a debt or similar obligation. When partial payments are made before the due date, it is desirable to reach an agreement with the creditor (or borrower) to reduce the amount of interest paid. There are two methods to receive interest credit on payments made before the due date: the Merchant's Rule and the United States Rule.

Under the Merchant's Rule, the principal, as well as each partial payment, draws interest from the date the debt is contracted to the date of final settlement. The balance due on the settlement date is the difference between the amount of the debt and the sum of the amounts (payment + interest) of the payments.

The Merchant's Rule

Example 1

On June 1, 1970, Mr. Tiny Banks borrowed $3000 at 6%. He paid $1,000 on July 1 and $600 on August 30. Find the balance due on September 29 using the Merchant's Rule.

Solution

We give the computations below.

Original debt...$3,000.00
Add: Interest on $3,000 for 120 days
   (June 1 to Sept. 29)...   60.00
                                                                          3,060.00

First Payment (July 1).....................$1,000
Interest on $1,000 for 90 days
   (July 1 to Sept. 29).......................   15

                                               $1,015

Second Payment (August 30)............   600
Interest on $600 for 30 days
   (August 30 to Sept. 29).................   3

                                          603

Sum of Partial Payments and Interest.............................   1,618.00

Balance Due on September 29.......................................$1,442.00

PROGRESS TEST 1

1. If in Example 1, the second payment was $500, the sum of the partial payments would be _____.
2. If in Example 1, the second payment was $500, the balance due on September 29 would be _____.

The United States Rule

The second method of receiving interest credit on payments made before the due date is mainly used to settle debts with the government and, for this reason, is called the United States Rule (U.S. Rule). The method is based on a decision made by the U.S. Supreme Court which stated, in part:

The rule for casting interest when partial payments have been made is to apply the payment, in the first place, to the discharge of the interest then due.

---

1. $1,517.50   2. $1,542.50

If the payment exceeds the interest, the surplus goes toward discharging the principal, and the subsequent interest is to be computed on the balance of the principal remaining due.

If the payment is less than the interest, the surplus of interest must not be taken to augment the principal, but the interest continues on the former principal until the period when the payments, taken together, exceed the interest due, and then the surplus is applied toward discharging the principal, and the interest is to be computed on the balance as aforesaid.

The procedure used to deduct partial payments using the U.S. Rule can be summarized as follows:

1. Find the interest on the principal from the date of borrowing to the date of the first partial payment.
2. Deduct this interest from the first payment.
3. Subtract the amount found in step 2 from the principal.
4. Continue this procedure for any subsequent partial payments, using as principal the amount obtained in 3 and the time between payments.

Example 2

Solve Example 1 by using the U.S. Rule.

Solution

We give the computations below.

Original Debt (June 1)...$3,000.00
First Payment (July 1)..............................$1,000.00
Less: Interest on $3,000 from June 1 to July 1____15.00

    Remainder applied to principal............................ 985.00
Balance owed on July 1... 2,015.00
Second Payment (August 30)....................... 600.00
Less: Interest on $2,015 from July 1 to
    August 30.. 20.15

    Remainder applied to principal............................ 579.85
Balance owed on August 30... 1,435.15
Interest on $1,435.15 from August 30 to September 29........ 7.18
Balance owed on September 29....................................$1,442.33

As you can see from Examples 1 and 2, the balance on September 29 is slightly higher when using the U.S. Rule. Hence it is better for a debtor to use the Merchant's Rule in reducing a debt by partial payments.

Finally, we give an example that shows how to handle a payment that is smaller than the interest.

Example 3

On June 1, 1970, Janie Jones borrowed $3,000 at 6%. She paid $1,000 on July 1, $20 on August 30, and $600 on September 29. Find the balance due on October 29 by using the U.S. Rule.

Solution

We give the computations below.

Original Debt (June 1)..		$3,000.00
First Payment (July 1)................................	$1,000.00	
Less: Interest on $3,000 from June 1 to July 1	15.00	
Remainder applied to principal............................		985.00
Balance owed on July 1..		2,015.00
Second Payment (August 30)........................	20.00*	
Third Payment (September 29).....................	600.00	
Total Payment as of September 29...............	620.00	
Less: Interest on $2,015 from July 1 to Sept. 29..	30.23	
Remainder applied to principal............................		589.77
Balance owed on September 29.......................................		1,425.23
Interest on $1,425.23 from Sept. 29 to Oct. 29.....................		7.13
Balance owed on October 29...		$1,432.36

EXERCISE 5.5

In Problems 1 through 11, find the unpaid balance on the indicated date, using (a) the Merchant's Rule; (b) the U.S. Rule.

Use Table 5–1 to find the exact number of days between dates.

	DATE OF LOAN	PRINCIPAL	INTEREST RATE	FIRST PAYMENT DATE	AMOUNT	SECOND PAYMENT DATE	AMOUNT	UNPAID BALANCE ON:
1.	March 1	$1,000	8%	March 16	$300	April 15	$500	April 30
2.	April 1	$280	9%	April 21	$100	—	—	May 31
3.	March 15	$6,000	8%	May 14	$2,000	June 13	$2,000	Dec. 13
4.	April 5	$2,100	10%	May 5	$1,500	—	—	May 15
5.	June 4	$5,000	5%	Aug. 3	$2,000	Oct. 2	$2,000	Dec. 1
6.	April 1	$7,000	4%	May 31	$1,500	July 30	$2,000	Sept. 28
7.	Aug. 1	$1,200	8%	Sept. 1	$400	Oct. 1	$300	Nov. 30

*The interest on $2,015 at 6% for 60 days is $20.15 and exceeds the $20 payment. Thus, the payment is held and included in the next payment.

8.	March 1	$4,000		6%	May 30	$500	Nov. 26	$20		Dec. 26
9.	April 1	$6,000		6%	May 31	$50	Sept. 28	$1,000		Nov. 27
10.	July 1	$4,500		7%	July 31	$800	Sept. 29	$1,500		Dec. 28

11. Mr. Bill Board borrowed $1,800 at 6% and promised to pay the money in six months. He paid $600 toward his debt one month later and $800 three months after. What will he owe on the maturity date?

12. Mr. James Farmer borrowed $2,000 at 8% on March 15. He made payments of $600, $800 and $600 on the fifteenth of each successive month. If he discharged his obligation on September 15, find the amount he paid, using (a) the Merchant's Rule; (b) the U.S. Rule. (Use approximate time.)

Reprinted, by permission, from *The Wall Street Journal*, January 24, 1974, p. 25.

5.6 BANK DISCOUNT

In the ad above, a lending company offers loans from $2,600 to $15,000. If a businessman needs cash to meet his current obligations, he may borrow the money from this lending institution or a bank, and give the institution or bank a **promissory note**. A **promissory note** (sometimes called a **note receivable** or **note payable**) is a written promise to pay a certain amount of money at a definite time in the future. These notes can be of two classes:

Promissory notes

1. **An Interest Bearing Note** is a note carrying the amount of interest expressed as a per cent. Thus in Figure 5–2, William Jones has given the bank a promissory note for $1,000 with interest at 6% and due in 30 days. On August 30, the amount due is $1,000 + $5 = $1,005. Here Jones pays $5 **interest** after using the money for 30 days.

| $ 1,000.00 | Tampa, July 31 | 19 |

Thirty days **after date** I **promise to pay to**

the order of The Third National Bank

- - - - - - - - - - one thousand no/100 - - - - - - - - - - - - **Dollars**

AT THE OFFICE OF The Third National Bank   FOR VALUE RECEIVED

WITH INTEREST FROM July 31 AT THE RATE OF 6 PER CENT PER ANNUM UNTIL PAID.

NOW, SHOULD IT BECOME NECESSARY TO COLLECT THIS NOTE THROUGH AN ATTORNEY, EITHER OF US, WHETHER MAKER, SE-CURITY OR ENDORSER ON THIS NOTE, HEREBY AGREES TO PAY ALL COSTS OF SUCH COLLECTION INCLUDING A REASONABLE ATTORNEY'S FEE. THE DRAWERS AND ENDORSERS SEVERALLY WAIVE PRESENTMENT FOR PAYMENT, PROTEST AND NOTICE OF PRO-TEST AND NON-PAYMENT OF THIS NOTE.

No. 35   *William Jones* (SEAL)

Due August 30   (SEAL)

Figure 5–2

2. **A Non-Interesting Bearing Note** is a note that does not carry interest.

A non-interest bearing note can be sold to a bank. Selling a note to a bank is referred to as **discounting the note.** Thus, if the note of Figure 5–3 is discounted by Mr. Jones on July 31 at 6%, he will receive $1,000 − $5 = $995. In this case Mr. Jones has paid $5 **in advance** for using the $995. The $5 paid on the discounted note is called the **bank discount*** or **discount.** The money which the borrower received ($995 in this case) is called the **bank proceeds** or **proceeds,** and the per cent used in computing the discount (6% in this example) is called the **bank discount rate** or **discount rate.** The discussion above leads to the following formula:

Discounts and proceeds

---

*You can think of the bank discount as interest paid in advance.

| $ 1,000.00 | Tampa, July 31 | 19 |

Thirty days **after date** I **promise to pay to**

the order of The Third National Bank

- - - - - - - - - - one thousand no/100 - - - - - - - - - - - - **Dollars**

AT THE OFFICE OF The Third National Bank   FOR VALUE RECEIVED

WITH INTEREST FROM - - - - - AT THE RATE OF - - - PER CENT PER ANNUM UNTIL PAID.

NOW, SHOULD IT BECOME NECESSARY TO COLLECT THIS NOTE THROUGH AN ATTORNEY, EITHER OF US, WHETHER MAKER, SE-CURITY OR ENDORSER ON THIS NOTE, HEREBY AGREES TO PAY ALL COSTS OF SUCH COLLECTION INCLUDING A REASONABLE ATTORNEY'S FEE. THE DRAWERS AND ENDORSERS SEVERALLY WAIVE PRESENTMENT FOR PAYMENT, PROTEST AND NOTICE OF PRO-TEST AND NON-PAYMENT OF THIS NOTE.

No. 28   *William Jones* (SEAL)

Due August 30   (SEAL)

Figure 5–3

FORMULA 5.8 $D = S \times d \times t$

where D is the bank discount (in dollars), S is the amount or maturity value, d is the discount rate, and t is the time.

To find the discount on a non-interest bearing note, we find the number of days between the date the note is discounted and the maturity date, and then use Formula 5.8.

Example 1

A man wishes to borrow $200 for two years from a bank which uses a discount rate of 6%. Find (a) the discount; (b) the proceeds, the amount the borrower receives after the bank deducts the discount.

Solution

a. By Formula 5.8, $D = S \times d \times t$. Here $S = \$200$, $d = 6\%$, and $t = 2$. Thus, $D = 200 \times 6\% \times 2 = \$24$.
b. The proceeds are the amount the borrower receives; that is $\$200 - \$24 = \$176$.

Example 2

Speedy bought a motorcycle from Johnny and gave him a $500 non-interest bearing note. The note is due on November 15. However, Johnny needed money sooner, so on July 18 he sold the note to his bank. The bank discounted the note at 8%. Find (a) the bank discount; (b) the proceeds (the amount Johnny received).

Solution

a. From Table 5–1 we can see that the number of days between the date the note was discounted (July 18) and the maturity date (November 15) is $319 - 199 = 120$. Therefore,

$$D = S \times d \times t = 500 \times 8\% \times \frac{120}{360} = \$13.33$$

b. The proceeds are $\$500 - \$13.33 = \$486.67$.

PROGRESS TEST 1

1. A man borrowed $750 for a year from a bank which uses a 5% rate of discount. The bank discount is _____. The proceeds from this transaction are _____.
2. A $700 3-month non-interest bearing note dated May 8 was discounted on July 7 at 4%. The bank discount and the proceeds are, respectively, _____ and _____.

Maturity value

Interest bearing notes can also be discounted by using a procedure similar to the one given in Examples 1 and 2. However, before we find the discount on an interest bearing note, we have to find the **maturity value** of the note. The maturity value is the sum of the interest and the principal. We then find the discount on the maturity value rather than on the principal.

Example 3

The note of Figure 5–2 is to be discounted on August 15 at 8%. Find (a) the maturity value of the note; (b) the discount; (c) the proceeds.

Solution

a. The maturity value of the note is the sum of the interest $(1,000 \times \frac{6}{100} \times \frac{30}{360} = \$5)$ and the principal; that is, $\$1,000 + \$5 = \$1,005$.

b. The discount is $1,005 \times \frac{8}{100} \times \frac{15}{360} = \$3.35$. (The time is 15 days, from August 15 to August 30.)

c. The proceeds are $\$1,005 - \$3.35 = \$1,001.65$.

PROGRESS TEST 2

1. A $1,000.00, 180-day, 6% interest bearing note dated July 1 is discounted on October 1 at 5%. The interest on this note is _____.
2. The maturity value of the note above is _____.
3. The time that has to be used to discount this note is _____ days.
4. The discount on this note is _____.
5. The proceeds on this note are _____.

1. $37.50; $712.50   2. $2.33; $697.67
1. $30   2. $1,030   3. 88   4. $12.59   5. $1,017.41

EXERCISE 5.6

In Problems 1 through 6, find the discount and the proceeds.

	LOAN	DISCOUNT RATE	TIME
1.	$1,000	6%	3 months
2.	$3,000	4%	90 days
3.	$1,500	8%	2 years
4.	$6,200	7%	2 months
5.	$380	4.5%	75 days
6.	$550	7.5%	3 years

In Problems 7 through 12, find the proceeds of the given non-interest bearing notes. (Use approximate time in Problems 7 through 9, exact time in Problems 10 through 12, and assume a 360-day year.)

	AMOUNT OF NOTE	MATURITY DATE	DISCOUNT DATE	DISCOUNT RATE
7.	$600	July 1	March 1	6%
8.	$1,300	August 15	May 15	5%
9.	$2,200	March 3	January 3	7%
10.	$1,500	October 7	January 15	5%
11.	$4,100	September 7	July 9	4.5%
12.	$840	August 4	June 5	7%

In Problems 13 through 20, find the proceeds for the discounted interest bearing notes. (Use approximate time in Problems 13 through 17, exact time in Problems 18 through 20, and assume a 360-day year.)

	NOTE	INTEREST RATE	TIME	MATURITY DATE	DISCOUNT DATE	DISCOUNT RATE
13.	$500	6%	1 year	June 20	March 20	8%
14.	$950	5%	90 days	December 4	October 4	6%
15.	$295	10%	6 months	November 2	September 2	12%
16.	$780	4.5%	10 months	December 11	June 11	6%
17.	$330	8%	90 days	May 5	March 5	10%
18.	$900	7%	90 days	June 30	May 5	9%
19.	$500	8%	1 year	May 20	January 10	8.5%
20.	$593	8.5%	1 year	April 3	January 2	9%

21. On September 4, Mr. Carl Carpenter discounts a 6%, $750 note dated July 6 and due October 4. If the bank charges a discount rate of 8%, find the proceeds.

22. Repeat Problem 21, assuming the note is for $800.

23. On February 1, Mr. Bob Brown discounts a 5%, $800 note dated January 15 and due March 1. If the bank charges a discount rate of 6% how much will Mr. Brown get?

24. On March 5, Mr. John Smith discounts a 6%, $1,000 note dated February 3 and due April 4. If the bank charges a discount rate of 10%, how much will Mr. Smith get?

25. There exists a U. S. Treasury note for $500,000,000 bearing interest at $6\frac{1}{4}$% for 14 years. If this note is discounted at 5% ten years before its maturity date, what will the proceeds be?

5.7 PRESENT VALUE AND INTEREST RATE EQUIVALENT TO A BANK DISCOUNT RATE

As you can see in the ad, a finance company is offering loans by mail up to $10,000. Let us assume that you need $100 today. Since the loan company will discount the loan, it will be necessary for you to ask for an amount exceeding $100. How can we find this amount? We first recall that the proceeds (sometimes called the **present value**) of a loan can be obtained by subtracting the discount D from the amount or maturity value S of the loan, that is,

$$P = S - D$$

Since $D = S \times d \times t$, we have

$$P = S - (S \times d \times t)$$

By the distributive law,

$$P = S \times (1 - (d \times t))$$

Dividing by $(1 - (d \times t))$, we arrive at the following formula:

FORMULA 5.9 $S = \dfrac{P}{1 - (d \times t)}$

Thus, if we wish to obtain $100 cash on a loan to be paid in one year at a 6% discount rate, we need to borrow

$$S = \frac{100}{1 - (6\% \times 1)} = \frac{100}{.94} = \$106.38$$

Example 1

Tim Jones wants to get $1,000 in cash from a loan to be repaid in six months. If he borrows the money from a finance company that charges a 5% discount rate, how much money should he ask for?

Solution

Here $P = \$1,000$, $d = 5\%$, and $t = \frac{1}{2}$ year. Using Formula 5.9, we have

$$S = \frac{1,000}{1 - (5\% \times 1/2)} = \frac{1,000}{1 - 5/200} = \frac{1,000}{195/200} = \$1,025.64$$

That is, Mr. Jones would have to ask for a loan of $1,025.64. Note that the proceeds on such a loan at 5% for six months are

$$\$1,025.64 - \left(1,025.64 \times 5\% \times \frac{1}{2}\right) = 1,025.64 - 25.64 = \$1,000$$

As we have mentioned before, bank discount is sometimes referred to as interest paid in advance because the interest is **discounted** before the borrower takes possession of the money. For this reason, a given bank discount rate results in a larger money return to the lender than the same simple interest rate. We compare the two methods in the next example.

Example 2

Find the present value of $1,000 due in one year at a simple interest rate of 6% and at a bank discount rate of 6%.

Solution

By Formula 5.5, the present value is

$$P = \frac{\$1,000}{1 + (6\% \times 1)} = \frac{1,000}{106/100} = \$943.40$$

To find the discount, we use Formula 5.8 and obtain

$$D = 1,000 \times 6\% \times 1 = \$60$$

The proceeds or present value is $1,000 - \$60 = \$940$. Note that the present value at 6% discount is $3.40 less than the corresponding present value at simple interest.

PROGRESS TEST 1

1. The present value of $100 due in one year at 6% simple interest is _____.

2. The present value of $100 at 6% discount interest is _____.

3. The difference between the present value of $100 at 6% simple interest and at a bank discount rate of 6% is _____.

Converting discount rates to simple interest rates

If we wish to compare the rates given in Example 2, we can convert the 6% discount rate to an equivalent simple interest rate. since the proceeds were $940 and the discount was $60, the equivalent simple interest rate is $\frac{60}{940} = 6.38\%$. From this illustration, we can see that the bank discount rate of 6% is equivalent to a simple interest rate of 6.38%. In general, the relationship between a simple interest rate and a discount rate may be expressed by the following formulas:

FORMULA 5.10 $r = \dfrac{d}{1 - (d \times t)}$

FORMULA 5.11 $d = \dfrac{r}{1 + (r \times t)}$

where r is the simple interest rate, d is the discount rate, and t is the time.

By applying Formula 5.10, find that the 6% discount rate of Example 2 is equivalent to a simple interest rate of

$$r = \frac{6\%}{1 - (6\% \times 1)} = \frac{6/100}{94/100} = 6.38\%$$

Example 3

A bank discounts a 60-day note at 5%. What is the equivalent simple interest rate earned by the bank?

Solution

Here $d = 5\%$ and $t = \frac{1}{6}$ year. Substituting in Formula 5.10, we have

$$r = \frac{5\%}{1 - (5\% \times 1/6)} = \frac{5\%}{1 - 5/600} = \frac{5/100}{595/600} = 5.04\%$$

---

1. $94.34   2. $94   3. $0.34

Example 4

According to the *Guinness Book of World Records*, the highest legal interest in 1972 was Brazil's at 20%.[*] If this rate represents a simple interest rate per annum, at what rate should a Brazilian Bank discount a year's note if the bank is to earn the equivalent of the 20% simple interest rate?

Solution

Here $r = 20\%$ and $t = 1$ year. Substituting in Formula 5.11, we have

$$d = \frac{20\%}{1 + 20\%} = \frac{20/100}{120/100} = 16.67\%$$

PROGRESS TEST 2

1. A bank discounts a 90-day note at 6%. The equivalent simple interest earned by the bank is _____.
2. According to the Guinness Book of Records, the lowest interest rate in 1971 was Morocco's at $3\frac{1}{2}\%$. If this rate represents a simple interest rate per annum, the equivalent bank discount rate is _____.

EXERCISE 5.7

In Problems 1 through 5, find the amount of the notes that give the indicated proceeds in one year.

	PROCEEDS	DISCOUNT RATE
1.	$384	4%
2.	$658	6%
3.	$279	7%
4.	$378	5.5%
5.	$1,000	9.5%

6. A bank charges 6% for discounting loans. If a man wishes to get $500 in cash to be repaid in six months, how much money should he request?

7. Repeat Problem 6, assuming the bank charges 8% for discounting loans.

---

[*]From the *Guinness Book of World Records*, © 1974 by Sterling Publishing Co., Inc., N.Y. 10016.

1. 6.09%   2. 3.38%

8. Phyllis Phillips wants a loan of $2,000 for three months. What size loan should she request if the bank charges a discount of 6%?

9. Bob Brown wants $1,000 for nine months. What size loan should he request if the bank charges a discount rate of 4%?

10. Freddie Borrows needs $8,000 on July 5. He expects to repay the money on September 3. What size loan should Freddie request if the discount rate is 6%?

11. A $900 obligation is due on December 15. What is the present value of this obligation on November 15 if the discount rate is 8%?

12. Find the present value of $2,000 due in one year at a simple interest rate of 6% and at a bank discount rate of 6%.

13. Find the present value of $500 due in six months at a simple interest rate of 8% and at a bank discount rate of 8%.

14. The maturity value of a 6% interest bearing note a year from today is $1,000. Find (a) the present value of this note; (b) the proceeds if the note is discounted in three months at a 6% rate.

15. The maturity value of a 10% interest bearing note in one year is $500. Find (a) the present value of this note; (b) the proceeds if the note is discounted in six months at a 12% rate.

In Problems 16 through 23, find the unknown rates, indicated by d or r.

	DISCOUNT PERIOD	DISCOUNT RATE	SIMPLE INTEREST RATE
16.	1 month	d	8%
17.	45 days	d	10%
18.	60 days	d	12%
19.	1 year	d	4%
20.	4 months	8%	r
21.	45 days	10%	r
22.	60 days	12%	r
23.	1 year	4%	r

24. A sum of money is due in 180 days. What is the interest rate equivalent to a discount of (a) 8%? (b) 6%?

25. Friendly Financial Services wants to get a 4% interest rate on loans made for a period of one year. What discount rate should they use?

SELF-TEST/CHAPTER 5

1. A man borrowed $10,000 from a bank for a period of six months. If the simple interest rate is 8%, find

_____ a. how much interest he paid.
_____ b. the total amount paid to the bank.

2. A contractor borrowed $131,400 at 6% for 90 days. Find the interest paid on this loan using

_____ a. the Banker's Rule.
_____ b. exact interest.

3. Find

_____ a. the ordinary interest on $864 at 6% for 60 days.
_____ b. the ordinary interest on $864 at 6% for 90 days.

4. A savings account yielded $100 interest in a period of two years. If the interest rate on the account was $6\frac{1}{4}\%$,

_____ a. what was the principal in the account?
_____ b. what was the sum received at the end of the two years?

5. A lady paid a 6%, 60-day loan with a check for $454.50.
_____ a. How much did she borrow?
_____ b. What was the interest paid on the loan?

6. A man borrowed $1,000 at 6% on June 1. He paid $100 on July 31 and $500 on August 30. Find the balance on September 29, using

_____ a. the Merchant's Rule.
_____ b. the U.S. Rule.

7. A man wishes to borrow $1,000 from a bank that charges a discount rate of 6%. If the money is to be repaid in one year, find

_____ a. the discount.
_____ b. the proceeds.

8. John Jones wants to get $2,000 in cash from a loan to be repaid in six months. If the finance company charges Mr. Jones a 6% discount rate,

_____ a. how much money should he ask for?
_____ b. how much is the discount?

9. _____ Find the simple interest rate equivalent to a 5% bank discount on a 90-day loan.

10. _____ Find the bank discount equivalent to a 5% simple interest 90-day loan.

six

Compound Interest

6.1 COMPOUND INTEREST

In the cartoon above, Nancy is waiting for her interest to **compound.** If you have a savings account, the money you have deposited in the account earns interest. This interest is usually computed at regular intervals during the year. If the interest earned is left in the account, this interest is added to the principal and in the next interest period you receive interest on it too. The process of collecting interest on the earned interest is called **compounding** the interest. Note that compound interest is nothing more than simple interest applied over and over to a sum increased by the simple interest earned in each time period.

The ad opposite states that you can earn up to $8\frac{3}{4}\%$ simple interest on your money, or more when the interest is compounded quarterly and paid at maturity. For example, let us assume that we invest $100 for a period of one year. According to the ad, we should get 7% interest compounded quarterly. Let us see how this works.

At the end of the first quarter ($\frac{1}{4}$ of a year), the interest will be $100 × 7% $\times \frac{1}{4}$ = $1.75, and the new balance will be $100 + $1.75 = $101.75.

At the end of the second quarter, the interest will be $101.75 × 7% × $\frac{1}{4}$ = $1.78, and the new balance will be $101.75 + $1.78 = $103.53.

At the end of the third quarter, the interest will be $103.53 × 7% × $\frac{1}{4}$ = $1.81, and the new balance will be $103.53 + $1.81 = $105.34.

270

This announcement is neither an offer to sell, nor a solicitation of an offer to buy these securities. The offer is made only by the Prospectus.

New issue. Earn up to 8¾%

on your money— even more when compounded quarterly

with 10-Year Associates Investment Notes.

Invest as little as $100 and earn from 7% to 8¾% annual interest, payable quarterly (or monthly on notes of $5,000 or more). Earn even more when interest is compounded quarterly and paid at maturity.

Maturities	Annual Interest Rate Interest Paid Quarterly Or Monthly	Effective Annual Yield Interest Compounded Quarterly And Paid At Maturity
1 Year	7 %	7.18%
3 Years	7½%	7.71%
5 Years	8¼%	8.51%
10 Years	8¾%	9.04%

Reprinted, by permission, from *The Tampa Tribune*, February 5, 1974.

At the end of the fourth quarter, the interest will be $105.34 \times 7\% \times \frac{1}{4}$ = $1.84, and the new balance will be $105.34 + $1.84 = $107.18.

Thus, the amount paid at maturity (compound amount) will be $107.18, and the **compound interest** will be $107.18 − $100 = $7.18. If the $100 had been invested at 7% **simple interest** for one year, the simple interest would have been $7, so you can see the advantage of compounding the interest.

If the time in the problem above were extended to cover a period of ten or more years, with the interest compounded quarterly, we would need a shorter and easier method for computing the compound amount and the compound interest.

The formula to find the amount S is given by

$$S = P \times (1 + i)^n$$

where S is the compound amount, P is the principal, i is the rate per conversion period, and n is the number of conversion periods.

Conversion periods are the intervals at which interest is compounded.

In practical business usage, compound interest tables have been calculated to help with the computation of compound interest. Table A–1, page 494, shows the compound amount of $1 at selected rates for different conversion periods. Portions of this table are shown in Table 6–1.

TABLE 6-1   **Compound Interest Rates***

n	3½%	4%	5%	6%	7%	8%
1	1.0350 0000	1.0400 0000	1.0500 0000	1.0600 0000	1.0700 0000	1.0800 0000
2	1.0712 2500	1.0816 0000	1.1025 0000	1.1236 0000	1.1449 0000	1.1664 0000
3	1.1087 1798	1.1248 6400	1.1576 2500	1.1910 1600	1.2250 4300	1.2597 1200
4	1.1475 2300	1.1698 5856	1.2155 0625	1.2624 7696	1.3107 9601	1.3604 8896
5	1.1876 8631	1.2166 5290	1.2762 8156	1.3382 2558	1.4025 5173	1.4693 2808
6	1.2292 5533	1.2653 1902	1.3400 9564	1.4185 1911	1.5007 3035	1.5868 7432
7	1.2722 7926	1.3159 3178	1.4071 0042	1.5036 3026	1.6057 8148	1.7138 2427
8	1.3168 0904	1.3685 6905	1.4774 5544	1.5938 4807	1.7181 8618	1.8509 3021
9	1.3628 9735	1.4233 1181	1.5513 2822	1.6894 7896	1.8384 5921	1.9990 0463
10	1.4105 9876	1.4802 4428	1.6288 9463	1.7908 4770	1.9671 5136	2.1589 2500
11	1.4599 6972	1.5394 5406	1.7103 3936	1.8982 9856	2.1048 5195	2.3316 3900
12	1.5110 6866	1.6010 3222	1.7958 5633	2.0121 9647	2.2521 9159	2.5181 7012
13	1.5639 5606	1.6650 7351	1.8856 4914	2.1329 2826	2.4098 4300	2.7196 2373
14	1.6186 9452	1.7316 7645	1.9799 3160	2.2609 0396	2.5785 3415	2.9371 9362
15	1.6653 4883	1.8009 4351	2.0789 2818	2.3965 5819	2.7590 3154	3.1721 6911
16	1.7339 8604	1.8729 8125	2.1828 7459	2.5403 5168	2.9521 6375	3.4259 4264
17	1.7946 7555	1.9479 0050	2.2920 1832	2.6927 7279	3.1588 1521	3.7000 1805
18	1.8574 8920	2.0258 1652	2.4066 1923	2.8543 3915	3.3799 3228	3.9960 1950
19	1.9225 0132	2.1068 4918	2.5269 5020	3.0255 9950	3.6165 2754	4.3157 0106
20	1.9897 8886	2.1911 2314	2.6532 9771	3.2071 3547	3.8696 8446	4.6609 5714
21	2.0594 3147	2.2787 6807	2.7859 6259	3.3995 6360	4.1405 6237	5.0338 3372
22	2.1315 1158	2.3699 1879	2.9252 6072	3.6035 3742	4.4304 0174	5.4365 4041
23	2.2061 1448	2.4647 1554	3.0715 2376	3.8197 4966	4.7405 2986	5.8714 6365
24	2.2833 2849	2.5633 0416	3.2250 9994	4.0489 3464	5.0723 6695	6.3411 8074
25	2.3632 4498	2.6658 3633	3.3863 5494	4.2918 7072	5.4274 3264	6.8484 7520
26	2.4459 5856	2.7724 6978	3.5556 7269	4.5493 8296	5.8073 5292	7.3963 5321
27	2.5315 6711	2.8833 6858	3.7334 5632	4.8223 4594	6.2138 6763	7.9880 6147
28	2.6201 7196	2.9987 0332	3.9201 2914	5.1116 8670	6.6488 3836	8.6271 0639
29	2.7118 7798	3.1186 5145	4.1161 3560	5.4183 8790	7.1142 5750	9.3172 7490
30	2.8067 9370	3.2433 9751	4.3219 4238	5.7434 9117	7.6122 5504	10.0626 5689
31	2.9050 3148	3.3731 3341	4.5380 3949	6.0881 0064	8.1451 1290	10.8676 6944
32	3.0067 0759	3.5080 5875	4.7649 4147	6.4533 8668	8.7152 7080	11.7370 8300
33	3.1119 4235	3.6483 8110	5.0031 8854	6.8405 8988	9.3253 3975	12.6760 4964
34	3.2208 6033	3.7943 1634	5.2533 4797	7.2510 2528	9.9781 1354	13.6901 3361
35	3.3335 9045	3.9460 8899	5.5160 1537	7.6860 8679	10.6765 8148	14.7853 4429
36	3.4502 6611	4.1039 3255	5.7918 1614	8.1472 5200	11.4239 4219	15.9681 7184
37	3.5710 2543	4.2680 8986	6.0814 0694	8.6360 8712	12.2236 1814	17.2456 2558
38	3.6960 1132	4.4388 1345	6.3854 7729	9.1542 5235	13.0792 7141	18.6252 7563
39	3.8253 7171	4.6163 6599	6.7047 5115	9.7035 0749	13.9948 2041	20.1152 9768
40	3.9592 5972	4.8010 2063	7.0399 8871	10.2857 1794	14.9744 5784	21.7245 2150
41	4.0978 3381	4.9930 6145	7.3919 8815	10.9028 6101	16.0226 6989	23.4624 8322
42	4.2414 5799	5.1927 8391	7.7615 8756	11.5570 3267	17.1442 5678	25.3394 8187
43	4.3897 0202	5.4004 9527	8.1496 6693	12.2504 5463	18.3443 5475	27.3666 4042
44	4.5433 4100	5.6165 1508	8.5571 5028	12.9854 8191	19.6284 5959	29.5559 7166
45	4.7023 5855	5.8411 7568	8.9850 0779	13.7646 1083	21.0024 5176	31.9204 4939
46	4.8669 4110	6.0748 2271	9.4342 5818	14.5904 8748	22.4726 2338	34.4740 8534
47	5.0372 8404	6.3178 1562	9.9059 7109	15.4659 1673	24.0457 0702	37.2320 1217
48	5.2135 8898	6.5705 2824	10.4012 6965	16.3938 7173	25.7289 0651	40.2105 7314
49	5.3960 6459	6.8333 4937	10.9213 3313	17.3775 0403	27.5299 2997	43.4274 1899
50	5.5849 2686	7.1066 8335	11.4673 9979	18.4201 5428	29.4570 2506	46.9016 1251

*Compiled, by permission, from Stephen P. Shao, ed., *Mathematics for Management and Finance,* 2nd ed., South-Western Publishing Co., 1969, Appendix pp. 39–43. Adapted from Charles H. Gushee, *Financial Compound Interest and Annuity Tables,* Financial Publishing Company, Boston, 1958, and James W. Glover, *Compound Interest and Insurance Tables,* Wahr's University Bookstore, Ann Arbor, 1957.

From Table 6–1 you can see that if $1 is compounded for one conversion period (for example, one year) at $3\frac{1}{2}\%$, the compound amount will be $1.03500000 (the number in the $3\frac{1}{2}\%$ column opposite one period). To find the compound amount of any principal for the same rate and time, ($3\frac{1}{2}\%$ for one year) we simply multiply the principal by the value in the table (1.03500000) and round off the result to two decimal places. For example, the compound amount of $10 at $3\frac{1}{2}\%$ for one year is $10 \times 1.03500000 = $10.35 and that of $15.50 is $15.50 \times 1.03500000 = $16.04.

Before using the table, we have to find the rate of interest per conversion period and the number of conversion periods. For example, to find the compound amount of $10 at 14% interest compound quarterly for five years, we proceed as follows:

1. Since the interest is compounded quarterly, the interest rate per conversion period is $(\frac{14}{4}\%) = 3\frac{1}{2}\%$.

2. The number of conversion periods (quarters) in five years is $4 \times 5 = 20$.

3. We find the number under $3\frac{1}{2}\%$ and opposite 20 periods (1.98978886) and multiply this number by $10. The compound amount is $10 \times 1.98978886 = $19.90.

Example 1

Find the compound amount of $20 at 8% interest compounded semiannually for ten years.

Solution

We proceed in three steps;

1. The interest rate per conversion period is $\dfrac{8\%}{2} = 4\%$.
2. The number of conversion periods is $2 \times 10 = 20$.
3. The number under 4% and opposite 20 periods is 2.19112314. Thus, the compound amount is $20 \times 2.19112314 = $43.82.

PROGRESS TEST 1

1. If $90.50 is compounded at 7% semiannually for ten years, the interest rate per conversion period will be

_____ .

2. The number of conversion periods will be _____

_____ .

3. The compound amount will be _____ .

1. $3\frac{1}{2}\%$ 2. 20   3. $90.50 \times 1.98978886 = $180.08

Daily compounding

As we have seen in the examples above, the periods used to compound interest may vary. However, the nominal (quoted or published) rates that banks may pay on time and savings deposits are regulated by the Board of Governors of the Federal Reserve Board in member banks, the Federal Deposit Insurance Corporation in insured nonmember banks, and the Federal Home Loan Bank Board in federally insured savings and loan associations. Because of this, banks and loan associations try to attract depositors by increasing the frequency of compounding. In order to obtain the compound amount of $1, the Financial Publishing Company has published daily growth factor tables for common interest rates. Table 6–2 shows the compound amount of $1 when compounded daily at 5% on a 360-day basis. For example, $1 compounded at 5% daily for a period of 180 days will yield $1.0253133406. Thus, $1,000 invested at 5% compounded daily for 180 days will yield $1,000 × 1.0253133406 = $1,025.31.

Example 2

The Third National Bank advertises a 5% interest rate compounded daily from the date of deposit to the date of withdrawal. A man deposits $1,000 on July 13 and withdraws the money on November 10. Find the interest accrued and the compounded amount.

Solution

There are 120 days from July 13 to November 10 (see Table 5–1). The compound amount of $1 at 5% for 120 days is $1.0168051536. Thus the compound amount for $1,000 is $1,000 × 1.0168051536 = $1,016.81 and the compound interest earned is $1,016.81 − $1,000 = $16.81.

Continuous compounding

To be ahead of the daily compounders, some institutions have gone to continuous (or instantaneous) compounding. This means that the interest is accumulating continuously. Table 6–3 shows the compound amount of $1 when compounded continuously at 5% on a 360-day basis.

For example, $1 compounded continuously for 60 days will yield $1.0083681522. Thus, $1,000 invested at 5% interest compounded continuously for 60 days will yield $1,000 × 1.0083681522 = $1,008.37.

Example 3

Here are the rates paid by two savings institutions:
    Institution A: 5% compounded daily

TABLE 6–2   5% Compounded Daily, 360-Day Basis*

Period	Amount of 1	Period	Amount of 1	Period	Amount of 1
1	1.000 138 8889	61	1.008 507 6198	121	1.016 946 3766
2	1.000 277 7971	62	1.008 647 6903	122	1.017 087 6191
3	1.000 416 7245	63	1.008 787 7802	123	1.017 228 8813
4	1.000 555 6713	64	1.008 927 8896	124	1.017 370 1631
5	1.000 694 6374	65	1.009 068 0185	125	1.017 511 4645
6	1.000 833 6227	66	1.009 208 1668	126	1.017 652 7855
7	1.000 972 6274	67	1.009 348 3347	127	1.017 794 1262
8	1.001 111 6514	68	1.009 488 5219	128	1.017 935 4865
9	1.001 250 6947	69	1.009 628 7287	129	1.018 076 8664
10	1.001 389 7573	70	1.009 768 9549	130	1.018 218 2660
11	1.001 528 8392	71	1.009 909 2006	131	1.018 359 6852
12	1.001 667 9404	72	1.010 049 4657	132	1.018 501 1240
13	1.001 807 0610	73	1.010 189 7504	133	1.018 642 5825
14	1.001 946 2008	74	1.010 330 0545	134	1.018 784 0607
15	1.002 085 3600	75	1.010 470 3781	135	1.018 925 5584
16	1.002 224 5385	76	1.010 610 7212	136	1.019 067 0759
17	1.002 363 7364	77	1.010 751 0838	137	1.019 208 6130
18	1.002 502 9536	78	1.010 891 4659	138	1.019 350 1697
19	1.002 642 1901	79	1.011 031 8675	139	1.019 491 7461
20	1.002 781 4460	80	1.011 172 2886	140	1.019 633 3422
21	1.002 920 7212	81	1.011 312 7292	141	1.019 774 9580
22	1.003 060 0157	82	1.011 453 1893	142	1.019 916 5934
23	1.003 199 3296	83	1.011 593 6689	143	1.020 058 2485
24	1.003 338 6628	84	1.011 734 1680	144	1.020 190 9232
25	1.003 478 0154	85	1.011 874 6867	145	1.020 341 6176
26	1.003 617 3874	86	1.012 015 2248	146	1.020 483 3318
27	1.003 756 7787	87	1.012 155 7825	147	1.020 625 0656
28	1.003 896 1893	88	1.012 296 3597	148	1.020 766 8190
29	1.004 035 6194	89	1.012 436 9564	149	1.020 908 5922
30	1.004 175 0688	90	1.012 577 5726	150	1.021 050 3851
31	1.004 314 5375	91	1.012 718 2084	151	1.021 192 1976
32	1.004 454 0256	92	1.012 858 8637	152	1.021 334 0299
33	1.004 593 5332	93	1.012 999 5386	153	1.021 475 8818
34	1.004 733 0600	94	1.013 140 2330	154	1.021 617 7535
35	1.004 872 6063	95	1.013 280 9469	155	1.021 759 6448
36	1.005 012 1719	96	1.013 421 6803	156	1.021 901 5559
37	1.005 151 7570	97	1.013 562 4333	157	1.022 043 4867
38	1.005 291 3614	98	1.013 703 2059	158	1.022 185 4371
39	1.005 430 9852	99	1.013 843 9980	159	1.022 327 4073
40	1.005 570 6284	100	1.013 984 8097	160	1.022 469 3973
41	1.005 710 2909	101	1.014 125 6409	161	1.022 611 4069
42	1.005 849 9729	102	1.014 266 4917	162	1.022 753 4363
43	1.005 989 6743	103	1.014 407 3620	163	1.022 895 4853
44	1.006 129 3951	104	1.014 548 2520	164	1.023 037 5542
45	1.006 269 1353	105	1.014 689 1614	165	1.023 179 6427
46	1.006 408 8949	106	1.014 830 0905	166	1.023 321 7510
47	1.006 548 6739	107	1.014 971 0391	167	1.023 463 8790
48	1.006 688 4723	108	1.015 112 0073	168	1.023 606 0268
49	1.006 828 2902	109	1.015 252 9951	169	1.023 748 1943
50	1.006 968 1274	110	1.015 394 0024	170	1.023 890 3815
51	1.007 107 9841	111	1.015 535 0294	171	1.024 032 5885
52	1.007 247 8602	112	1.015 676 0759	172	1.024 174 8153
53	1.007 387 7558	113	1.015 817 1420	173	1.024 317 0618
54	1.007 527 6707	114	1.015 958 2278	174	1.024 459 3280
55	1.007 667 6051	115	1.016 099 3331	175	1.024 601 6161
56	1.007 807 5590	116	1.016 240 4580	176	1.024 743 9198
57	1.007 947 5322	117	1.016 381 6025	177	1.024 886 2454
58	1.008 087 5250	118	1.016 522 7666	178	1.025 028 5907
59	1.008 227 5371	119	1.016 663 9503	179	1.025 170 9558
60	1.008 367 5687	120	1.016 805 1536	180	1.025 313 3406

*Courtesy of the Financial Publishing Company of Boston.

TABLE 6–3   **5% Compounded Continuously, 360-Day Basis***

PERIOD	AMOUNT OF 1	PERIOD	AMOUNT OF 1	PERIOD	AMOUNT OF 1
1	1.000 138 8985	61	1.008 508 2131	121	1.016 947 5633
2	1.000 277 8164	62	1.008 648 2934	122	1.017 088 8158
3	1.000 416 7535	63	1.008 788 3931	123	1.017 230 0880
4	1.000 555 7099	64	1.008 928 5124	124	1.017 371 3797
5	1.000 694 6856	65	1.009 068 6511	125	1.017 512 6911
6	1.000 833 6807	66	1.009 208 8092	126	1.017 654 0222
7	1.000 972 6950	67	1.009 348 9869	127	1.017 795 3728
8	1.001 111 7286	68	1.009 489 1839	128	1.017 936 7431
9	1.001 250 7816	69	1.009 629 4005	129	1.018 078 1330
10	1.001 389 8538	70	1.009 769 6366	130	1.018 219 5426
11	1.001 528 9454	71	1.009 909 8921	131	1.018 360 9718
12	1.001 668 0563	72	1.010 050 1671	132	1.018 502 4206
13	1.001 807 1866	73	1.010 190 4616	133	1.018 643 8891
14	1.001 946 3361	74	1.010 330 7755	134	1.018 785 3773
15	1.002 085 5050	75	1.010 471 1090	135	1.018 926 8851
16	1.002 224 6932	76	1.010 611 4620	136	1.019 068 4125
17	1.002 363 9007	77	1.010 751 8344	137	1.019 209 9596
18	1.002 503 1276	78	1.010 892 2264	138	1.019 351 5264
19	1.002 642 3738	79	1.011 032 6378	139	1.019 493 1128
20	1.002 781 6394	80	1.011 173 0688	140	1.019 634 7189
21	1.002 920 9243	81	1.011 313 5192	141	1.019 776 3447
22	1.003 060 2285	82	1.011 453 9892	142	1.019 917 9901
23	1.003 199 5521	83	1.011 594 4787	143	1.020 059 6552
24	1.003 338 8951	84	1.011 734 9877	144	1.020 201 3400
25	1.003 478 2574	85	1.011 875 5162	145	1.020 343 0445
26	1.003 617 6390	86	1.012 016 0642	146	1.020 484 7687
27	1.003 757 0400	87	1.012 156 6317	147	1.020 626 5125
28	1.003 896 4604	88	1.012 297 2188	148	1.020 768 2760
29	1.004 035 9002	89	1.012 437 8254	149	1.020 910 0592
30	1.004 175 3593	90	1.012 578 4515	150	1.021 051 8621
31	1.004 314 8378	91	1.012 719 0972	151	1.021 193 6848
32	1.004 454 3356	92	1.012 859 7624	152	1.021 335 5271
33	1.004 593 8529	93	1.012 000 4471	153	1.021 477 3891
34	1.004 733 3895	94	1.013 141 1514	154	1.021 619 2708
35	1.004 872 9455	95	1.013 281 8752	155	1.021 761 1722
36	1.005 012 5209	96	1.013 422 6186	156	1.021 903 0933
37	1.005 152 1156	97	1.013 563 3815	157	1.022 045 0342
38	1.005 291 7298	98	1.013 704 1640	158	1.022 186 9947
39	1.005 431 3633	99	1.013 844 9660	159	1.022 328 9750
40	1.005 571 0163	100	1.013 985 7876	160	1.022 470 9750
41	1.005 710 6886	101	1.014 126 6287	161	1.022 612 9947
42	1.005 850 3804	102	1.014 267 4894	162	1.022 755 0342
43	1.005 990 0915	103	1.014 408 3697	163	1.022 897 0933
44	1.006 129 8220	104	1.014 549 2695	164	1.023 039 1722
45	1.006 269 5720	105	1.014 690 1889	165	1.023 181 2709
46	1.006 409 3414	106	1.014 831 1279	166	1.023 323 3893
47	1.006 549 1302	107	1.014 972 0865	167	1.023 465 5274
48	1.006 688 9384	108	1.015 113 0646	168	1.023 607 6852
49	1.006 828 7660	109	1.015 254 0623	169	1.023 749 8629
50	1.006 968 6130	110	1.015 395 0796	170	1.023 892 0602
51	1.007 108 4795	111	1.015 536 1165	171	1.024 034 2773
52	1.007 248 3654	112	1.015 677 1730	172	1.024 176 5142
53	1.007 388 2707	113	1.015 818 2491	173	1.024 318 7708
54	1.007 528 1954	114	1.015 959 3447	174	1.024 461 0472
55	1.007 668 1396	115	1.016 100 4600	175	1.024 603 3433
56	1.007 808 1033	116	1.016 241 5949	176	1.024 745 6592
57	1.007 948 0863	117	1.016 382 7493	177	1.024 887 9949
58	1.008 088 0888	118	1.016 523 9234	178	1.025 030 3503
59	1.008 228 1108	119	1.016 665 1171	179	1.025 172 7255
60	1.008 368 1522	120	1.016 806 3304	180	1.025 315 1205

*Courtesy of the Financial Publishing Company of Boston.

Institution B: 5% compounded continuously

If a man invests $1,000 for 180 days $\left(\frac{1}{2} \text{ year}\right)$ in each of these institutions, what is the compound amount in each case?

Solution

INSTITUTION	AMOUNT OF $1	AMOUNT OF $1,000	COMPOUND INTEREST
A	1.0253133406	$1,025.31	$25.31
B	1.0253151205	$1,025.32	$25.32

From this example you can see that the difference in the interest when $1,000 earns interest at 5% compounded daily as opposed to continuously for 180 days is 1 cent!

PROGRESS TEST 1

1. The rates paid by two saving institutions are as follows:
   A. 5% compounded quarterly
   B. 5% compounded daily
If a man invests $1,000 for 180 days in each of these institutions, the compound amount received from Institution A will be _____.

2. The *difference* in interest paid between A and B at the end of the 180 days will be _____.

EXERCISE 6.1

In Problems 1 through 10, find (a) the interest rate per conversion period; (b) the number of conversion periods; (c) the compound amount.

PRINCIPAL	RATE AND FREQUENCY OF COMPOUNDING	TIME
1. $1	7% compounded annually	10 years
2. $1	5% compounded annually	12 years
3. $1	8% compounded semiannually	6 years
4. $1	6% compounded semiannually	5 years

1. $1,025.16   2. 15 ¢

5.	$300	14% compounded quarterly	5 years
6.	$600	7% compounded semiannually	2 years
7.	$1,000	8% compounded semiannually	5 years
8.	$3,000	7% compounded semiannually	10 years
9.	$1,000	7% compounded semiannually	$4\frac{1}{2}$ years
10.	$2,000	14% compounded quarterly	$3\frac{1}{2}$ years

In Problems 10 through 14, find the compound amount.

PRINCIPAL	RATE AND FREQUENCY OF COMPOUNDING	TIME
11.	$5,000	5% compounded daily	180 days
12.	$5,000	5% compounded continuously	180 days
13.	$8,000	5% compounded daily	90 days
14.	$8,000	5% compounded continuously	90 days

15.   Find the difference in compound interest between $5,000 invested at 5% interest compounded daily for 180 days and another $5,000 invested at 5% interest compounded continuously for 180 days.

16.   Find the compound amount and the compound interest earned on $500 invested at 2% interest compounded annually for five years.

17.   Find the compound amount and the compound interest earned if $1,000 is borrowed at 5% compounded quarterly for a period of five years.

18.   How much money will have to be repaid on March 15, 1976, on a loan of $5,000 at a rate of 6% interest compounded semiannually if the loan was obtained on March 15, 1971?

19.   When Desiree was born, her parents placed $100 in a savings account paying 4% interest compounded semiannually. How much money will be in Desiree's account when she becomes 18 years of age?

20.   A man deposited $2,000 in the Teacher's Credit Union, which pays 6% compounded quarterly. At the end of two years, he had to withdraw $1,000. What was the amount of money in the account at the end of five years (if the man made no further withdrawals)?

21.   What would be the answer to Problem 20 if the withdrawal were made at the end of three years?

22.   Here are the rates paid by three savings institutions:

INSTITUTION   RATE AND FREQUENCY OF COMPOUNDING

A   5% compounded quarterly
B   5% compounded daily
C   5% compounded continuously

If a man invests $10,000 in each of these institutions, find the compound amount in each case at the end of $\frac{1}{2}$ year.

23.   In Problem 22, find the difference between the interest earned in Institution B and the interest earned in Institution C.

24.   On July 6, 1973, St. Petersburg Federal Savings and Loan Association published the following statement in the St. Petersburg Times:

How much interest would you earn, in 10 years, on a $20,000 CD (Certificate of Deposit) paying 6% per annum? If your answer is $12,000, you're wrong. At SFS&L, you'd get a whopping _____ _____.*

What number should be inserted in the blank if the interest on CD's is 6% compounded quarterly? (Check your answer by looking at the ad at the beginning of the next section.)

*St. Petersburg Times, July 16, 1973, p. 9-B.

Courtesy of St. Petersburg Federal Savings and Loan Association, St. Petersburg, Florida.

6.2   NOMINAL AND EFFECTIVE INTEREST RATES

As you can see from the ad above, the **nominal** (quoted or published) interest rates and the actual **effective annual yield** are not the same. To be able to compare different rates and different frequencies of conversion (periods) we determine the **effective annual yield**. The **effective annual yield** is the rate which, compounded annually, will produce the same amount of interest as the nominal rate compounded

Definition of effective annual yield

n times per year (n is the number of times the interest is computed in one year). Thus, according to the ad, 6% compounded daily is equivalent to 6.14% compounded annually. This is because each $1 of principal compounded quarterly at 6% $\left(\frac{6}{4}\% = 1\frac{1}{2}\% \text{ per quarter, 4 periods}\right)$ will yield $1.06136355. This means the annual interest earned is $1.06136355 − 1 = 0.06136355, which is equivalent to an effective annual yield of 6.14%. If we are given any nominal rate, we can follow the procedure above and find the effective annual yield with the aid of Table A–1, page 494.

Example 1

Find the effective annual yield equivalent to 8% compounded quarterly.

Solution

We proceed in three steps:

1. The compound amount of $1 at $\frac{8}{4}\% = 2\%$ for 4 periods is $1.08243216.
2. The compound interest earned is $1.08243216−1=0.08243216.
3. The effective annual yield is 8.24%.

Example 2

Find the effective annual yield equivalent to 10% compounded semiannually.

Solution

1. The compound amount of $1 at $\frac{10}{2}\% = 5\%$ for 2 periods is $1.1025000.
2. The compound interest earned is $1.10250000−1=0.10250000.
3. The effective annual yield is 10.25%.

PROGRESS TEST 1

1. The effective annual yield equivalent to 6% compounded semiannually is _____.
2. The effective annual yield equivalent to 8% compounded semiannually is _____.

The effective annual yield is of special interest to investors and borrowers. By comparing the effective annual yields from differ-

1. 6.09%   2. 8.16%

ent sources, investors may decide which investment will yield the highest return. On the other hand, borrowers may compare the effective annual interest rates to select the lending institution with the lowest rate.

Example 3

A woman could invest her money at 6% compounded quarterly or save it in the bank at 6% effective annual yield. Which is the better investment?

Solution

An investment at 6% compounded quarterly has an effective annual yield of 6.14%. (See the ad at the beginning of this section or compute it using Table A–1, page 494.) Since this interest is greater than 6%, it is better to invest the money at 6% compounded quarterly.

Example 4

A man wishes to borrow some money. Bank A charges 5% interest compounded daily, while Bank B charges $5\frac{1}{4}$% interest compounded every four months. Which of the two banks should the man select? (Hint: The effective annual rate of interest equivalent to 5% compounded daily can be found in the ad at the beginning of this section.)

Solution

From the ad, the effective annual interest rate equivalent to 5% compounded daily is 5.13%. The effective annual interest rate equivalent to $5\frac{1}{4}$% compounded every four months $\left(5\frac{1}{4}\% \div 3 = 1\frac{3}{4}\%\right.$ for three periods) is 5.34%. Thus, it is better to borrow from Bank A.

PROGRESS TEST 2

1. A bank offers loans at 9% compounded quarterly while another bank offers loans at 9% compounded semi-annually. The effective annual interest rate offered by the first bank is _____.

2. The effective annual interest rate offered by the second bank is _____.

3. Based on the answers to Questions 2 and 3, which bank would you borrow money from? _____
_____.

---

1. 9.31%   2. 9.20%   3. The second bank

EXERCISE 6.2

In Problems 1 through 10, find the effective annual yield for the given nominal rates. (Round answers to the nearest hundredth of a per cent.)

	NOMINAL RATE	COMPOUNDING PERIOD
1.	6%	Semiannually
2.	5%	Semiannually
3.	8%	Semiannually
4.	7%	Semiannually
5.	10%	Semiannually
6.	12%	Semiannually
7.	5%	Quarterly
8.	6%	Quarterly
9.	7%	Quarterly
10.	10%	Quarterly

11. Which gives a higher effective annual yield, 8% compounded quarterly or 10% compounded semiannually?

12. Which gives a higher effective annual yield, $7\frac{1}{8}$% compounded annually or 7% compounded quarterly?

13. SFS&L is paying $5\frac{1}{4}$% compounded daily on passbook accounts. According to the ad, this is equivalent to 5.39% effective annual yield. An investor in New York has his money in a passbook account paying 5% compounded quarterly. If the New Yorker transfers $100 to the SFS&L, how much additional interest will he be getting per year?

14. Which yields more interest, 15% compounded monthly or 16.07% compounded annually?

15. On Wednesday, October 24, 1973, Public Federal Savings and Loan Association advertised in the *Wall Street Journal* one-year certificates with a nominal interest rate of 8% compounded daily (8.45% effective annual yield). Is this better or worse than investing the money at $8\frac{1}{2}$% compounded semiannually? (Hint: The rate per period is 1.08680625.)

Courtesy of the United States Department of the Treasury

6.3 PRESENT VALUE AT COMPOUND INTEREST

In many business transactions it is necessary to find the **present value** of an amount of money that is due in the future. For example, the U. S. Savings Bond shown in the illustration will be worth $50 in five years and ten months. The Federal Reserve Bank or your local bank will sell one of these bonds for $37.50. Thus, the **present value** of a $50 bond due in five years and ten months is $37.50.

Definition of present value

The **present value** is defined as the principal that will amount to a given sum in a given period of time. The difference between the future amount and the present value is called the **compound discount.** The present value can be found by solving the compound interest formula for P, obtaining:

$$P = \frac{S}{(1 + i)^n}$$

P is the principal or present value, S is the amount due in the future, i is the rate per conversion period, and n is the number of conversion periods.

In practical business usage, present value tables have been calculated to help with the computations of present values. Table A–2, page 506, shows the present value of $1 at selected rates for various conversion periods. Portions of this table are given in Table 6–4.

TABLE 6-4   **Present Value Rates***

n	3½%	4%	5%	6%	7%	8%
1	0.9661 8357	0.9615 3846	0.9523 8095	0.9433 9623	0.9345 7944	0.9259 2593
2	0.9335 1070	0.9245 5621	0.9070 2948	0.8899 9644	0.8734 3873	0.8573 3882
3	0.9019 4271	0.8889 9636	0.8638 3760	0.8396 1928	0.8162 9788	0.7938 3224
4	0.8714 4223	0.8548 0419	0.8227 0247	0.7920 9366	0.7628 9521	0.7350 2985
5	0.8419 7317	0.8219 2711	0.7835 2617	0.7472 5817	0.7129 8618	0.6805 8320
6	0.8135 0064	0.7903 1453	0.7462 1540	0.7049 6054	0.6663 4222	0.6301 6963
7	0.7659 9096	0.7599 1781	0.7106 8133	0.6650 5711	0.6227 4974	0.5834 9040
8	0.7594 1156	0.7306 9020	0.6768 3936	0.6274 1237	0.5820 0910	0.5402 6888
9	0.7337 3097	0.7025 8674	0.6446 0892	0.5918 9846	0.5439 3374	0.5002 4897
10	0.7089 1881	0.6755 6417	0.6139 1325	0.5583 9478	0.5083 4929	0.4631 9349
11	0.6849 4571	0.6495 8093	0.5846 7929	0.5267 8753	0.4750 9280	0.4288 8286
12	0.6617 8330	0.6245 9705	0.5568 3742	0.4969 6936	0.4440 1196	0.3971 1376
13	0.6394 0415	0.6005 7409	0.5303 2135	0.4688 3902	0.4149 6445	0.3676 9792
14	0.6177 8179	0.5774 7508	0.5050 6795	0.4423 0096	0.3878 1724	0.3404 6104
15	0.5968 9062	0.5552 6450	0.4810 1710	0.4172 6506	0.3624 4602	0.3152 4170
16	0.5767 0591	0.5339 0818	0.4581 1152	0.3936 4628	0.3387 3460	0.2918 9047
17	0.5572 0378	0.5133 7325	0.4362 9669	0.3713 6442	0.3165 7439	0.2720 6895
18	0.5383 6114	0.4936 2812	0.4155 2065	0.3503 4379	0.2958 6392	0.2502 4903
19	0.5201 5569	0.4746 4242	0.3957 3396	0.3305 1301	0.2765 0833	0.2317 1206
20	0.5025 6588	0.4563 8695	0.3768 8948	0.3118 0473	0.2584 1900	0.2145 4821
21	0.4855 7090	0.4388 3360	0.3589 4236	0.2941 5540	0.2415 1309	0.1986 5575
22	0.4691 5063	0.4219 5539	0.3418 4987	0.2775 0510	0.2257 1317	0.1839 4051
23	0.4532 8563	0.4057 2633	0.3255 7131	0.2617 9726	0.2109 4688	0.1703 1528
24	0.4379 5713	0.3901 2147	0.3100 6791	0.2469 7855	0.1971 4662	0.1576 9934
25	0.4231 4699	0.3751 1680	0.2953 0277	0.2329 9863	0.1842 4918	0.1460 1790
26	0.4088 3767	0.3606 8923	0.2812 4074	0.2198 1003	0.1721 9549	0.1352 0176
27	0.3950 1224	0.3468 1657	0.2678 4832	0.2073 6795	0.1609 3037	0.1251 8682
28	0.3816 5434	0.3334 7747	0.2550 9364	0.1956 3014	0.1504 0221	0.1159 1372
29	0.3687 4816	0.3206 5141	0.2429 4632	0.1845 5674	0.1405 6282	0.1073 2752
30	0.3562 7841	0.3083 1867	0.2313 7745	0.1741 1013	0.1313 6712	0.0993 7733
31	0.3442 3035	0.2964 6026	0.2203 5947	0.1642 5484	0.1227 7301	0.0920 1605
32	0.3325 8971	0.2850 5794	0.2098 6617	0.1549 5740	0.1147 4113	0.0852 0005
33	0.3213 4271	0.2740 9417	0.1998 7254	0.1461 8622	0.1072 3470	0.0788 8893
34	0.3104 7605	0.2635 5209	0.1903 5480	0.1379 1153	0.1002 1934	0.0730 4531
35	0.2999 7686	0.2534 1547	0.1812 9029	0.1301 0522	0.0936 6294	0.0676 3454
36	0.2898 3272	0.2436 6872	0.1726 5741	0.1227 4077	0.0875 3546	0.0626 2458
37	0.2800 3161	0.2342 9685	0.1644 3563	0.1157 9318	0.0818 0884	0.0579 8572
38	0.2705 6194	0.2252 8543	0.1566 0536	0.1099 3885	0.0764 5686	0.0536 9048
39	0.2614 1250	0.2166 2061	0.1491 4794	0.1030 5552	0.0714 5501	0.0497 1341
40	0.2525 7247	0.2082 8904	0.1420 4568	0.0972 2219	0.0667 8038	0.0460 3093
41	0.2440 3137	0.2002 7793	0.1352 8160	0.0917 1904	0.0624 1157	0.0426 2123
42	0.2357 7910	0.1925 7493	0.1288 3962	0.0865 2740	0.0583 2857	0.0394 6411
43	0.2278 0590	0.1851 6820	0.1227 0440	0.0816 2962	0.0545 1268	0.0365 4084
44	0.2201 0231	0.1780 4635	0.1168 6133	0.0770 0908	0.0509 4643	0.0338 3411
45	0.2126 5924	0.1711 9841	0.1112 9651	0.0726 5007	0.0476 1349	0.0313 2788
46	0.2054 6787	0.1646 1386	0.1059 9668	0.0685 3781	0.0444 9859	0.0290 0730
47	0.1985 1968	0.1582 8256	0.1009 4921	0.0646 5831	0.0415 8746	0.0268 5861
48	0.1918 0645	0.1521 9476	0.0961 4211	0.0609 9840	0.0388 6679	0.0248 6908
49	0.1853 2024	0.1463 4112	0.0915 6391	0.0575 4566	0.0363 2410	0.0230 2693
50	0.1790 5337	0.1407 1262	0.0872 0373	0.0542 8836	0.0339 4776	0.0213 2123

*Compiled, by permission, from Stephen P. Shao, ed., Mathematics for Management and Finance, 2nd ed., South-Western Publishing Co., 1969, Appendix pp. 62–66. Adapted from Charles H. Gushee, Financial Compound Interest and Annuity Tables, Financial Publishing Company, Boston, 1958, and James W. Glover, Compound Interest and Insurance Tables, Wahr's University Bookstore, Ann Arbor, 1957.

From Table 6–4 you can see that the present value of $1 due in one year (one conversion period) at $3\frac{1}{2}\%$ is $0.96618357 (the number under the $3\frac{1}{2}\%$ column, opposite one period).

Example 1

Find the present value of $1,000 due in five years at 8% compounded semiannually.

Solution

We proceed in three steps:

1. The interest rate per conversion period is $\frac{8}{2}\% = 4\%$.
2. The number of conversion periods is $2 \times 5 = 10$.
3. The value in the 4% column opposite 10 is 0.67556417. Thus, the present value of $1,000 due in five years at 8% compounded semi-annually is $1,000 \times 0.67556417 = $675.56.

This means that if $675.56 is deposited in a bank at 8% interest compounded semiannually, in five years the compound amount will be $1,000.

PROGRESS TEST 1

1. To find the present value of $500 due in five years at 7% compounded semiannually, we first find that the interest rate per conversion period is _____.
2. The number of conversion periods is _____.
3. The present value of $500 due in five years at 7% compounded semiannually is _____.

The present value of an amount is of special interest to investors who must make decisions based on various alternative courses of action. We illustrate this in the following example.

Example 2

Land Developers, Inc. can buy some land for $8,000 cash or for $4,000 down and $5,000 in five years. If the company is earning 4% interest compounded semiannually on its money, which is the better deal, and by how much?

---

1. $\frac{7}{2}\% = 3\frac{1}{2}\%$ 2. $2 \times 5 = 10$ 3. $500 \times 0.70891881 = $354.46

Solution

The present value of $5,000 due in five years at 4% compounded semiannually is $5,000 × 0.82034830 = $4,101.74. Adding the down payment of $4,000, the present value of the time deal is $8,101.74. Thus, it is better to pay $8,000 cash and save $101.74.

Example 3

A man can buy a piece of land from Land Developers, Inc. for $4,700 cash. A salesman from Land Developers told the man that in one year the same property would be selling for $5,000. If money is worth 8% compounded quarterly, should the man buy the land now or in a year?

Solution

The present value of $5,000 at 8% quarterly, due one year from now is $5,000 × 0.92384543 = $4,619.23. This is less than the amount the land is worth now, so by waiting a year the man will be saving $4,700 − $4,619.23 = $80.77.

PROGRESS TEST 2

1. If in Example 3 the money were worth 6% compounded annually, then the present value of the $5,000 due in one year would be _____.
2. If money were worth 6% compounded annually, the man would be wise to _____.
3. The amount saved by buying the land now with cash when money is worth 6% compounded annually is _____.

EXERCISE 6.3

In Problems 1 through 10, find the present value.

	PRINCIPAL	RATE AND FREQUENCY OF COMPOUNDING	DUE
1.	$1	7% compounded annually	1 year
2.	$1	8% compounded annually	5 years

---

1. $5,000 × 0.94339623 = $4,716.98   2. Buy now with cash.   3. $16.98

3.	$1	7% compounded semiannually	6 years
4.	$1	8% compounded semiannually	8 years
5.	$300	14% compounded quarterly	5 years
6.	$600	7% compounded quarterly	10 years
7.	$1,000	8% compounded semiannually	10 years
8.	$3,000	7% compounded semiannually	20 years
9.	$1,000	5% compounded quarterly	5 years
10.	$2,000	10% compounded quarterly	5 years

11. How much money must be deposited now in a savings account paying 9% interest compounded semiannually so that at the end of eight years the balance of the account will be $6,000?

12. Repeat Problem 11, assuming the amount desired at the end of eight years is $10,000.

13. Find the present value of $1,000 due in three years if money is worth 5% compounded semiannually.

14. A woman can buy some land for $4,700 cash, or for $2,000 down and $3,000 in two years. If money is worth 5% compounded semiannually, which is a better deal, and by how much?

15. If in Problem 14, money is worth 5% compounded quarterly, which is a better deal, and by how much?

16. A man can buy a lot for $9,200 cash. A salesman told him that in a year the lot would be selling for $10,000. If money is worth 8% compounded quarterly, should the man buy the lot now or in a year?

17. If in Problem 16 the price of the lot was $9,300, should the man buy the lot now or in a year?

18. A man owns a note for $1,000 due in five years. What should a buyer pay for this note if money is worth 8% compounded quarterly?

19. On December 20, Mr. Pete Putter buys some golf equipment from the Whack-It Corporation. He signs a note promising to pay the $1,000 plus 6% interest compounded quarterly in two years.
a. How much does he owe two years hence?
b. If the Whack-It Corporation sells the note to a finance company that charges 8% interest compounded quarterly for discounting the note, how much does the Whack-It Corporation get for the note?

20.   A $3,000 note is due in five years. If it is sold four years be-
fore maturity at a price that will yield the buyer 6% simple
interest, how much is paid for the note?

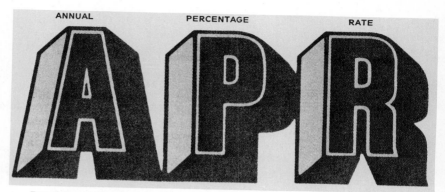

6.4   PERIODIC PAYMENT PLANS

Until several years ago, it was not possible for the consumer to
compare readily the cost of credit offered by one institution to that of
another. These costs were expressed in various percentages, such as
6% simple interest, 6% discount, 6% add-on, $6 per hundred, and
$\frac{1}{2}$% per month.

The Congress of the United States, recognizing this difficulty,
enacted what is known as the Federal Truth-in-Lending Act on July 1,
1969. In conjunction with this law, the Board of Governors of the
Federal Reserve System have issued Regulation Z, requiring all
lenders who make consumer loans to disclose certain information
regarding the cost of consumer credit.

Contained in the Federal Truth-in-Lending Act are two terms
of crucial importance to consumers:

1. **The Finance Charge:** The total of all costs which the customer
must pay, directly or indirectly, for obtaining credit.

2. **The Annual Percentage Rate (APR):** The effective or true
annual interest rate computed on an actuarial basis (that is, compounded).

For example, in the Pinto ad, the cash price of the car is $2,442.
If one buys the car using the suggested credit plan, he gives $442
dollars as a down payment and pays $66.50 per month for 36 months.
In this case, the amount to be financed is $2,442 − $442 = $2,000, and
the finance charge is (36 × $66.50) − $2,000 = $2,394 − $2,000 = $394.

Build Your Own '74 Pinto 2-Door $66⁵⁰ PER MONTH

From Only $2442

CUSTOM EQUIPPED TO SUIT YOUR DRIVING NEEDS

Payments Based on Financing $2000 for 36 months, with $442 Down, Cash or Trade, Plus Tax Tag & Title, Total of Payments $2394 APR 11.95

Reprinted, by permission, from *The Tampa Tribune*, February 15, 1974, p. 20E.

Example 1

A car sells for $2,895 cash. An available credit purchase plan requires a down payment of $295 and monthly payments of $85.22 for 36 months. Find the finance charge.

Solution

1. The amount to be financed is $2,895 − $295 = $2,600.
2. The amount paid in 36 months is $36 \times \$85.22 = \$3,067.92$.
3. The finance charge is $3,067.92 − $2,600 = $467.92.

Example 2

Mrs. A. Ford bought an automobile on a credit purchase plan. The price included the following: invoice price, $2,500; sales tax, $100; registration fee, $50; fire, theft, and casualty insurance, $150 (required); credit life insurance, $130 (optional); credit investigation fee, $10; interest, $450. Find the finance charge.

Solution

The finance charge consists of the following:

Fire, theft, and casualty insurance	$150
Credit investigation fee	10
Interest	450
Total Finance Charge	$610

Note that the sales tax, registration fee, and credit life insurance are not included in the finance charge since they are not necessary for the extension of credit.

PROGRESS TEST 1

1. A car sells for $3,199 cash. It can also be bought on credit by giving a down payment of $399 and paying $83.15 for 42 months. The amount to be financed is _____.

2. The amount paid in 42 months is _____.

3. The finance charge is _____.

In the ad given in connection with Example 1, the dealer quoted the APR (Annual Percentage Rate) for the suggested credit plan. The APR is calculated by the compound interest (actuarial) method. In practical business usage, tables have been prepared to find the APR. The tables given in the following pages are used as follows:

Finding the APR using a table

1. Find the finance charge per $100 of the amount financed. This can be done by multiplying the finance charge by $100 and dividing by the amount financed. (That is, express the finance charge as a percentage of the amount financed.)

2. Find the number of payments in the extreme left hand column of the proper (monthly or weekly) schedule and, reading across, locate the value that is nearest to the amount found in step 1. The rate listed at the top of that column is the appropriate APR, accurate to within $\frac{1}{4}$ of 1% of the true effective rate.

3. In case more accuracy is desired, one can interpolate* from the APR table on the following pages.

Example 3

Here is the ad for the car mentioned in Example 1.
Find the APR for the suggested credit purchase plan.

Reprinted, by permission, from *The Tampa Tribune*, February 15, 1974, p. 21E.

---

1. $2,800   2. 42 × $83.15 = $3,492.30   3. $3,492.30 − $2,800 = $692.30
*See page 299 for explanation of how to interpolate.

(Text continued on page 299.)

FRB-102-M

NUMBER OF PAYMENTS	ANNUAL PERCENTAGE RATE															
	6.00%	6.25%	6.50%	6.75%	7.00%	7.25%	7.50%	7.75%	8.00%	8.25%	8.50%	8.75%	9.00%	9.25%	9.50%	9.75%
	(FINANCE CHARGE PER $100 OF AMOUNT FINANCED)															
1	0.50	0.52	0.54	0.56	0.58	0.60	0.62	0.65	0.67	0.69	0.71	0.73	0.75	0.77	0.79	0.81
2	0.75	0.78	0.81	0.84	0.88	0.91	0.94	0.97	1.00	1.03	1.06	1.10	1.13	1.16	1.19	1.22
3	1.00	1.04	1.09	1.13	1.17	1.21	1.25	1.29	1.34	1.38	1.42	1.46	1.50	1.55	1.59	1.63
4	1.25	1.31	1.36	1.41	1.46	1.51	1.57	1.62	1.67	1.72	1.78	1.83	1.88	1.93	1.99	2.04
5	1.50	1.57	1.63	1.69	1.76	1.82	1.88	1.95	2.01	2.07	2.13	2.20	2.26	2.32	2.39	2.45
6	1.76	1.83	1.90	1.98	2.05	2.13	2.20	2.27	2.35	2.42	2.49	2.57	2.64	2.72	2.79	2.86
7	2.01	2.09	2.18	2.26	2.35	2.43	2.52	2.60	2.68	2.77	2.85	2.94	3.02	3.11	3.19	3.28
8	2.26	2.36	2.45	2.55	2.64	2.74	2.83	2.93	3.02	3.12	3.21	3.31	3.40	3.50	3.60	3.69
9	2.52	2.62	2.73	2.83	2.94	3.05	3.15	3.26	3.36	3.47	3.57	3.68	3.79	3.89	4.00	4.11
10	2.77	2.89	3.00	3.12	3.24	3.35	3.47	3.59	3.70	3.82	3.94	4.05	4.17	4.29	4.41	4.52
11	3.02	3.15	3.28	3.41	3.53	3.66	3.79	3.92	4.04	4.17	4.30	4.43	4.56	4.68	4.81	4.94
12	3.28	3.42	3.56	3.69	3.83	3.97	4.11	4.25	4.39	4.52	4.66	4.80	4.94	5.08	5.22	5.36
13	3.53	3.68	3.83	3.98	4.13	4.28	4.43	4.58	4.73	4.88	5.03	5.18	5.33	5.48	5.63	5.78
14	3.79	3.95	4.11	4.27	4.43	4.59	4.75	4.91	5.07	5.23	5.39	5.55	5.72	5.88	6.04	6.20
15	4.05	4.22	4.39	4.56	4.73	4.90	5.07	5.24	5.42	5.59	5.76	5.93	6.10	6.28	6.45	6.62
16	4.30	4.48	4.67	4.85	5.03	5.21	5.40	5.58	5.76	5.94	6.13	6.31	6.49	6.68	6.86	7.05
17	4.56	4.75	4.95	5.14	5.33	5.52	5.72	5.91	6.11	6.30	6.49	6.69	6.88	7.08	7.27	7.47
18	4.82	5.02	5.22	5.43	5.63	5.84	6.04	6.25	6.45	6.66	6.86	7.07	7.28	7.48	7.69	7.90
19	5.07	5.29	5.50	5.72	5.94	6.15	6.37	6.58	6.80	7.02	7.23	7.45	7.67	7.89	8.10	8.32
20	5.33	5.56	5.78	6.01	6.24	6.46	6.69	6.92	7.15	7.38	7.60	7.83	8.06	8.29	8.52	8.75
21	5.59	5.83	6.07	6.30	6.54	6.78	7.02	7.26	7.50	7.74	7.97	8.21	8.46	8.70	8.94	9.18
22	5.85	6.10	6.35	6.60	6.84	7.09	7.34	7.59	7.84	8.10	8.35	8.60	8.85	9.10	9.36	9.61
23	6.11	6.37	6.63	6.89	7.15	7.41	7.67	7.93	8.19	8.46	8.72	8.98	9.25	9.51	9.77	10.04
24	6.37	6.64	6.91	7.18	7.45	7.73	8.00	8.27	8.55	8.82	9.09	9.37	9.64	9.92	10.19	10.47
25	6.63	6.91	7.19	7.48	7.76	8.04	8.33	8.61	8.90	9.18	9.47	9.75	10.04	10.33	10.62	10.90
26	6.89	7.18	7.48	7.77	8.07	8.36	8.66	8.95	9.25	9.55	9.84	10.14	10.44	10.74	11.04	11.34
27	7.15	7.46	7.76	8.07	8.37	8.68	8.99	9.29	9.60	9.91	10.22	10.53	10.84	11.15	11.46	11.77
28	7.41	7.73	8.05	8.36	8.68	9.00	9.32	9.64	9.96	10.28	10.60	10.92	11.24	11.56	11.89	12.21
29	7.67	8.00	8.33	8.66	8.99	9.32	9.65	9.98	10.31	10.64	10.97	11.31	11.64	11.98	12.31	12.65
30	7.94	8.28	8.61	8.96	9.30	9.64	9.98	10.32	10.66	11.01	11.35	11.70	12.04	12.39	12.74	13.09
31	8.20	8.55	8.90	9.25	9.60	9.96	10.31	10.67	11.02	11.38	11.73	12.09	12.45	12.81	13.17	13.53
32	8.46	8.82	9.19	9.55	9.91	10.28	10.64	11.01	11.38	11.74	12.11	12.48	12.85	13.22	13.59	13.97
33	8.73	9.10	9.47	9.85	10.22	10.60	10.98	11.36	11.73	12.11	12.49	12.88	13.26	13.64	14.02	14.41
34	8.99	9.37	9.76	10.15	10.53	10.92	11.31	11.70	12.09	12.48	12.88	13.27	13.66	14.06	14.45	14.85
35	9.25	9.65	10.05	10.45	10.85	11.25	11.65	12.05	12.45	12.85	13.26	13.66	14.07	14.48	14.89	15.29
36	9.52	9.93	10.34	10.75	11.16	11.57	11.98	12.40	12.81	13.23	13.64	14.06	14.48	14.90	15.32	15.74
37	9.78	10.20	10.63	11.05	11.47	11.89	12.32	12.74	13.17	13.60	14.03	14.46	14.89	15.32	15.75	16.19
38	10.05	10.48	10.91	11.35	11.78	12.22	12.66	13.09	13.53	13.97	14.41	14.85	15.30	15.74	16.19	16.63
39	10.32	10.76	11.20	11.65	12.10	12.54	12.99	13.44	13.89	14.35	14.80	15.25	15.71	16.17	16.62	17.08
40	10.58	11.04	11.49	11.95	12.41	12.87	13.33	13.79	14.26	14.72	15.19	15.65	16.12	16.59	17.06	17.53
41	10.85	11.32	11.78	12.25	12.72	13.20	13.67	14.14	14.62	15.10	15.57	16.05	16.53	17.01	17.50	17.98
42	11.12	11.60	12.08	12.56	13.04	13.52	14.01	14.50	14.98	15.47	15.96	16.45	16.95	17.44	17.94	18.43
43	11.38	11.87	12.37	12.86	13.36	13.85	14.35	14.85	15.35	15.85	16.35	16.86	17.36	17.87	18.38	18.89
44	11.65	12.15	12.66	13.16	13.67	14.18	14.69	15.20	15.71	16.23	16.74	17.26	17.78	18.30	18.82	19.34
45	11.92	12.44	12.95	13.47	13.99	14.51	15.03	15.55	16.08	16.61	17.13	17.66	18.19	18.73	19.26	19.79
46	12.19	12.72	13.24	13.77	14.31	14.84	15.37	15.91	16.45	16.99	17.53	18.07	18.61	19.16	19.70	20.25
47	12.46	13.00	13.54	14.08	14.62	15.17	15.72	16.26	16.81	17.37	17.92	18.47	19.03	19.59	20.15	20.71
48	12.73	13.28	13.83	14.39	14.94	15.50	16.06	16.62	17.18	17.75	18.31	18.88	19.45	20.02	20.59	21.16
49	13.00	13.56	14.13	14.69	15.26	15.83	16.40	16.98	17.55	18.13	18.71	19.29	19.87	20.45	21.04	21.62
50	13.27	13.84	14.42	15.00	15.58	16.16	16.75	17.33	17.92	18.51	19.10	19.69	20.29	20.89	21.48	22.08
51	13.54	14.13	14.72	15.31	15.90	16.50	17.09	17.69	18.29	18.89	19.50	20.10	20.71	21.32	21.93	22.55
52	13.81	14.41	15.01	15.62	16.22	16.83	17.44	18.05	18.66	19.28	19.89	20.51	21.13	21.76	22.38	23.01
53	14.08	14.69	15.31	15.92	16.54	17.16	17.78	18.41	19.03	19.66	20.29	20.92	21.56	22.19	22.83	23.47
54	14.36	14.98	15.61	16.23	16.86	17.50	18.13	18.77	19.41	20.05	20.69	21.34	21.98	22.63	23.28	23.94
55	14.63	15.26	15.90	16.54	17.19	17.83	18.48	19.13	19.78	20.43	21.09	21.75	22.41	23.07	23.73	24.40
56	14.90	15.55	16.20	16.85	17.51	18.17	18.83	19.49	20.15	20.82	21.49	22.16	22.83	23.51	24.19	24.87
57	15.17	15.84	16.50	17.17	17.83	18.50	19.18	19.85	20.53	21.21	21.89	22.58	23.27	23.95	24.64	25.34
58	15.45	16.12	16.80	17.48	18.16	18.84	19.53	20.21	20.91	21.60	22.29	22.99	23.69	24.39	25.10	25.80
59	15.72	16.41	17.10	17.79	18.48	19.18	19.88	20.58	21.28	21.99	22.70	23.41	24.12	24.84	25.55	26.27
60	16.00	16.70	17.40	18.10	18.81	19.52	20.23	20.94	21.66	22.38	23.10	23.82	24.55	25.28	26.01	26.75

(From *Truth in Lending, Regulation Z: Annual Percentage Rate Tables.* Washington, D.C.: Board of Govenors of the Federal Reserve System.)

FRB-103-M

ANNUAL PERCENTAGE RATE

(FINANCE CHARGE PER $100 OF AMOUNT FINANCED)

NUMBER OF PAYMENTS	10.00%	10.25%	10.50%	10.75%	11.00%	11.25%	11.50%	11.75%	12.00%	12.25%	12.50%	12.75%	13.00%	13.25%	13.50%	13.75%
1	0.83	0.85	0.87	0.90	0.92	0.94	0.96	0.98	1.00	1.02	1.04	1.06	1.08	1.10	1.12	1.15
2	1.25	1.28	1.31	1.35	1.38	1.41	1.44	1.47	1.50	1.53	1.57	1.60	1.63	1.66	1.69	1.72
3	1.67	1.71	1.76	1.80	1.84	1.88	1.92	1.96	2.01	2.05	2.09	2.13	2.17	2.22	2.26	2.30
4	2.09	2.14	2.20	2.25	2.30	2.35	2.41	2.46	2.51	2.57	2.62	2.67	2.72	2.78	2.83	2.88
5	2.51	2.58	2.64	2.70	2.77	2.83	2.89	2.96	3.02	3.08	3.15	3.21	3.27	3.34	3.40	3.46
6	2.94	3.01	3.08	3.16	3.23	3.31	3.38	3.45	3.53	3.60	3.68	3.75	3.83	3.90	3.97	4.05
7	3.36	3.45	3.53	3.62	3.70	3.78	3.87	3.95	4.04	4.12	4.21	4.29	4.38	4.47	4.55	4.64
8	3.79	3.88	3.98	4.07	4.17	4.26	4.36	4.46	4.55	4.65	4.74	4.84	4.94	5.03	5.13	5.22
9	4.21	4.32	4.43	4.53	4.64	4.75	4.85	4.96	5.07	5.17	5.28	5.39	5.49	5.60	5.71	5.82
10	4.64	4.76	4.88	4.99	5.11	5.23	5.35	5.46	5.58	5.70	5.82	5.94	6.05	6.17	6.29	6.41
11	5.07	5.20	5.33	5.45	5.58	5.71	5.84	5.97	6.10	6.23	6.36	6.49	6.62	6.75	6.88	7.01
12	5.50	5.64	5.78	5.92	6.06	6.20	6.34	6.48	6.62	6.76	6.90	7.04	7.18	7.32	7.46	7.60
13	5.93	6.08	6.23	6.38	6.53	6.68	6.84	6.99	7.14	7.29	7.44	7.59	7.75	7.90	8.05	8.20
14	6.36	6.52	6.69	6.85	7.01	7.17	7.34	7.50	7.66	7.82	7.99	8.15	8.31	8.48	8.64	8.81
15	6.80	6.97	7.14	7.32	7.49	7.66	7.84	8.01	8.19	8.36	8.53	8.71	8.88	9.06	9.23	9.41
16	7.23	7.41	7.60	7.78	7.97	8.15	8.34	8.53	8.71	8.90	9.08	9.27	9.46	9.64	9.83	10.02
17	7.67	7.86	8.06	8.25	8.45	8.65	8.84	9.04	9.24	9.44	9.63	9.83	10.03	10.23	10.43	10.63
18	8.10	8.31	8.52	8.73	8.93	9.14	9.35	9.56	9.77	9.98	10.19	10.40	10.61	10.82	11.03	11.24
19	8.54	8.76	8.98	9.20	9.42	9.64	9.86	10.08	10.30	10.52	10.74	10.96	11.18	11.41	11.63	11.85
20	8.98	9.21	9.44	9.67	9.90	10.13	10.37	10.60	10.83	11.06	11.30	11.53	11.76	12.00	12.23	12.46
21	9.42	9.66	9.90	10.15	10.39	10.63	10.88	11.12	11.36	11.61	11.85	12.10	12.34	12.59	12.84	13.08
22	9.86	10.12	10.37	10.62	10.88	11.13	11.39	11.64	11.90	12.16	12.41	12.67	12.93	13.19	13.44	13.70
23	10.30	10.57	10.84	11.10	11.37	11.63	11.90	12.17	12.44	12.71	12.97	13.24	13.51	13.78	14.05	14.32
24	10.75	11.02	11.30	11.58	11.86	12.14	12.42	12.70	12.98	13.26	13.54	13.82	14.10	14.38	14.66	14.95
25	11.19	11.48	11.77	12.06	12.35	12.64	12.93	13.22	13.52	13.81	14.10	14.40	14.69	14.98	15.28	15.57
26	11.64	11.94	12.24	12.54	12.85	13.15	13.45	13.75	14.06	14.36	14.67	14.97	15.28	15.59	15.89	16.20
27	12.09	12.40	12.71	13.03	13.34	13.66	13.97	14.29	14.60	14.92	15.24	15.56	15.87	16.19	16.51	16.83
28	12.53	12.86	13.18	13.51	13.84	14.16	14.49	14.82	15.15	15.48	15.81	16.14	16.47	16.80	17.13	17.46
29	12.98	13.32	13.66	14.00	14.33	14.67	15.01	15.35	15.70	16.04	16.38	16.72	17.07	17.41	17.75	18.10
30	13.43	13.78	14.13	14.48	14.83	15.19	15.54	15.89	16.24	16.60	16.95	17.31	17.66	18.02	18.38	18.74
31	13.89	14.25	14.61	14.97	15.33	15.70	16.06	16.43	16.79	17.16	17.53	17.90	18.27	18.63	19.00	19.38
32	14.34	14.71	15.09	15.46	15.84	16.21	16.59	16.97	17.35	17.73	18.11	18.49	18.87	19.25	19.63	20.02
33	14.79	15.18	15.57	15.95	16.34	16.73	17.12	17.51	17.90	18.29	18.69	19.08	19.47	19.87	20.26	20.66
34	15.25	15.65	16.05	16.44	16.85	17.25	17.65	18.05	18.46	18.86	19.27	19.67	20.08	20.49	20.90	21.31
35	15.70	16.11	16.53	16.94	17.35	17.77	18.18	18.60	19.01	19.43	19.85	20.27	20.69	21.11	21.53	21.95
36	16.16	16.58	17.01	17.43	17.86	18.29	18.71	19.14	19.57	20.00	20.43	20.87	21.30	21.73	22.17	22.60
37	16.62	17.06	17.49	17.93	18.37	18.81	19.25	19.69	20.13	20.58	21.02	21.46	21.91	22.36	22.81	23.25
38	17.08	17.53	17.98	18.43	18.88	19.33	19.78	20.24	20.69	21.15	21.61	22.07	22.52	22.99	23.45	23.91
39	17.54	18.00	18.46	18.93	19.39	19.86	20.32	20.79	21.26	21.73	22.20	22.67	23.14	23.61	24.09	24.56
40	18.00	18.48	18.95	19.43	19.90	20.38	20.86	21.34	21.82	22.30	22.79	23.27	23.76	24.25	24.73	25.22
41	18.47	18.95	19.44	19.93	20.42	20.91	21.40	21.89	22.39	22.88	23.38	23.88	24.38	24.88	25.38	25.88
42	18.93	19.43	19.93	20.43	20.93	21.44	21.94	22.45	22.96	23.47	23.98	24.49	25.00	25.51	26.03	26.55
43	19.40	19.91	20.42	20.94	21.45	21.97	22.49	23.01	23.53	24.05	24.57	25.10	25.62	26.15	26.68	27.21
44	19.86	20.39	20.91	21.44	21.97	22.50	23.03	23.57	24.10	24.64	25.17	25.71	26.25	26.79	27.33	27.88
45	20.33	20.87	21.41	21.95	22.49	23.03	23.58	24.12	24.67	25.22	25.77	26.32	26.88	27.43	27.99	28.55
46	20.80	21.35	21.90	22.46	23.01	23.57	24.13	24.69	25.25	25.81	26.37	26.94	27.51	28.08	28.65	29.22
47	21.27	21.83	22.40	22.97	23.53	24.10	24.68	25.25	25.82	26.40	26.98	27.56	28.14	28.72	29.31	29.89
48	21.74	22.32	22.90	23.48	24.06	24.64	25.23	25.81	26.40	26.99	27.58	28.18	28.77	29.37	29.97	30.57
49	22.21	22.80	23.39	23.99	24.58	25.18	25.78	26.38	26.98	27.59	28.19	28.80	29.41	30.02	30.63	31.24
50	22.69	23.29	23.89	24.50	25.11	25.72	26.33	26.95	27.56	28.18	28.80	29.42	30.04	30.67	31.29	31.92
51	23.16	23.78	24.40	25.02	25.64	26.26	26.89	27.52	28.15	28.78	29.41	30.05	30.68	31.32	31.96	32.60
52	23.64	24.27	24.90	25.53	26.17	26.81	27.45	28.09	28.73	29.38	30.02	30.67	31.32	31.98	32.63	33.29
53	24.11	24.76	25.40	26.05	26.70	27.35	28.00	28.66	29.32	29.98	30.64	31.30	31.97	32.63	33.30	33.97
54	24.59	25.25	25.91	26.57	27.23	27.90	28.56	29.23	29.91	30.58	31.25	31.93	32.61	33.29	33.98	34.66
55	25.07	25.74	26.41	27.09	27.77	28.44	29.13	29.81	30.50	31.18	31.87	32.56	33.26	33.95	34.65	35.35
56	25.55	26.23	26.92	27.61	28.30	28.99	29.69	30.39	31.09	31.79	32.49	33.20	33.91	34.62	35.33	36.04
57	26.03	26.73	27.43	28.13	28.84	29.54	30.25	30.97	31.68	32.39	33.11	33.83	34.56	35.28	36.01	36.74
58	26.51	27.23	27.94	28.66	29.37	30.10	30.82	31.55	32.27	33.00	33.74	34.47	35.21	35.95	36.69	37.43
59	27.00	27.72	28.45	29.18	29.91	30.65	31.39	32.13	32.87	33.61	34.36	35.11	35.86	36.62	37.37	38.13
60	27.48	28.22	28.96	29.71	30.45	31.20	31.96	32.71	33.47	34.23	34.99	35.75	36.52	37.29	38.06	38.83

FRB-104-M

NUMBER OF PAYMENTS	ANNUAL PERCENTAGE RATE															
	14.00%	14.25%	14.50%	14.75%	15.00%	15.25%	15.50%	15.75%	16.00%	16.25%	16.50%	16.75%	17.00%	17.25%	17.50%	17.75%
	(FINANCE CHARGE PER $100 OF AMOUNT FINANCED)															
1	1.17	1.19	1.21	1.23	1.25	1.27	1.29	1.31	1.33	1.35	1.37	1.40	1.42	1.44	1.46	1.48
2	1.75	1.78	1.82	1.85	1.88	1.91	1.94	1.97	2.00	2.04	2.07	2.10	2.13	2.16	2.19	2.22
3	2.34	2.38	2.43	2.47	2.51	2.55	2.59	2.64	2.68	2.72	2.76	2.80	2.85	2.89	2.93	2.97
4	2.93	2.99	3.04	3.09	3.14	3.20	3.25	3.30	3.36	3.41	3.46	3.51	3.57	3.62	3.67	3.73
5	3.53	3.59	3.65	3.72	3.78	3.84	3.91	3.97	4.04	4.10	4.16	4.23	4.29	4.35	4.42	4.48
6	4.12	4.20	4.27	4.35	4.42	4.49	4.57	4.64	4.72	4.79	4.87	4.94	5.02	5.09	5.17	5.24
7	4.72	4.81	4.89	4.98	5.06	5.15	5.23	5.32	5.40	5.49	5.58	5.66	5.75	5.83	5.92	6.00
8	5.32	5.42	5.51	5.61	5.71	5.80	5.90	6.00	6.09	6.19	6.29	6.38	6.48	6.58	6.67	6.77
9	5.92	6.03	6.14	6.25	6.35	6.46	6.57	6.68	6.78	6.89	7.00	7.11	7.22	7.32	7.43	7.54
10	6.53	6.65	6.77	6.88	7.00	7.12	7.24	7.36	7.48	7.60	7.72	7.84	7.96	8.08	8.19	8.31
11	7.14	7.27	7.40	7.53	7.66	7.79	7.92	8.05	8.18	8.31	8.44	8.57	8.70	8.83	8.96	9.09
12	7.74	7.89	8.03	8.17	8.31	8.45	8.59	8.74	8.88	9.02	9.16	9.30	9.45	9.59	9.73	9.87
13	8.36	8.51	8.66	8.81	8.97	9.12	9.27	9.43	9.58	9.73	9.89	10.04	10.20	10.35	10.50	10.66
14	8.97	9.13	9.30	9.46	9.63	9.79	9.96	10.12	10.29	10.45	10.62	10.78	10.95	11.11	11.28	11.45
15	9.59	9.76	9.94	10.11	10.29	10.47	10.64	10.82	11.00	11.17	11.35	11.53	11.71	11.88	12.06	12.24
16	10.20	10.39	10.58	10.77	10.95	11.14	11.33	11.52	11.71	11.90	12.09	12.28	12.46	12.65	12.84	13.03
17	10.82	11.02	11.22	11.42	11.62	11.82	12.02	12.22	12.42	12.62	12.83	13.03	13.23	13.43	13.63	13.83
18	11.45	11.66	11.87	12.08	12.29	12.50	12.72	12.93	13.14	13.35	13.57	13.78	13.99	14.21	14.42	14.64
19	12.07	12.30	12.52	12.74	12.97	13.19	13.41	13.64	13.86	14.09	14.31	14.54	14.76	14.99	15.22	15.44
20	12.70	12.93	13.17	13.41	13.64	13.88	14.11	14.35	14.59	14.82	15.06	15.30	15.54	15.77	16.01	16.25
21	13.33	13.58	13.82	14.07	14.32	14.57	14.82	15.06	15.31	15.56	15.81	16.06	16.31	16.56	16.81	17.07
22	13.96	14.22	14.48	14.74	15.00	15.26	15.52	15.78	16.04	16.30	16.57	16.83	17.09	17.36	17.62	17.88
23	14.59	14.87	15.14	15.41	15.68	15.96	16.23	16.50	16.78	17.05	17.32	17.60	17.88	18.15	18.43	18.70
24	15.23	15.51	15.80	16.08	16.37	16.65	16.94	17.22	17.51	17.80	18.09	18.37	18.66	18.95	19.24	19.53
25	15.87	16.17	16.46	16.76	17.06	17.35	17.65	17.95	18.25	18.55	18.85	19.15	19.45	19.75	20.05	20.36
26	16.51	16.82	17.13	17.44	17.75	18.06	18.37	18.68	18.99	19.30	19.62	19.93	20.24	20.56	20.87	21.19
27	17.15	17.47	17.80	18.12	18.44	18.76	19.09	19.41	19.74	20.06	20.39	20.71	21.04	21.37	21.69	22.02
28	17.80	18.13	18.47	18.80	19.14	19.47	19.81	20.15	20.48	20.82	21.16	21.50	21.84	22.18	22.52	22.86
29	18.45	18.79	19.14	19.49	19.83	20.18	20.53	20.89	21.23	21.58	21.94	22.29	22.64	22.99	23.35	23.70
30	19.10	19.45	19.81	20.17	20.54	20.90	21.26	21.62	21.99	22.35	22.72	23.08	23.45	23.81	24.18	24.55
31	19.75	20.12	20.49	20.87	21.24	21.61	21.99	22.37	22.74	23.12	23.50	23.88	24.26	24.64	25.02	25.40
32	20.40	20.79	21.17	21.56	21.95	22.33	22.72	23.11	23.50	23.89	24.28	24.68	25.07	25.46	25.86	26.25
33	21.06	21.46	21.85	22.25	22.65	23.06	23.46	23.86	24.26	24.67	25.07	25.48	25.88	26.29	26.70	27.11
34	21.72	22.13	22.54	22.95	23.37	23.78	24.19	24.61	25.03	25.44	25.86	26.28	26.70	27.12	27.54	27.97
35	22.38	22.80	23.23	23.65	24.08	24.51	24.94	25.36	25.79	26.23	26.66	27.09	27.52	27.96	28.39	28.83
36	23.04	23.48	23.92	24.35	24.80	25.24	25.68	26.12	26.57	27.01	27.46	27.90	28.35	28.80	29.25	29.70
37	23.70	24.16	24.61	25.06	25.51	25.97	26.42	26.88	27.34	27.80	28.26	28.72	29.18	29.64	30.10	30.57
38	24.37	24.84	25.30	25.77	26.24	26.70	27.17	27.64	28.11	28.59	29.06	29.53	30.01	30.49	30.96	31.44
39	25.04	25.52	26.00	26.48	26.96	27.44	27.92	28.41	28.89	29.38	29.87	30.36	30.85	31.34	31.83	32.32
40	25.71	26.20	26.70	27.19	27.69	28.18	28.68	29.18	29.68	30.18	30.68	31.19	31.68	32.19	32.69	33.20
41	26.39	26.89	27.40	27.91	28.41	28.92	29.44	29.95	30.46	30.97	31.49	32.01	32.52	33.04	33.56	34.08
42	27.06	27.58	28.10	28.62	29.15	29.67	30.19	30.72	31.25	31.78	32.31	32.84	33.37	33.90	34.44	34.97
43	27.74	28.27	28.81	29.34	29.88	30.42	30.96	31.50	32.04	32.58	33.13	33.67	34.22	34.76	35.31	35.86
44	28.42	28.97	29.52	30.07	30.62	31.17	31.72	32.28	32.83	33.39	33.95	34.51	35.07	35.63	36.19	36.76
45	29.11	29.67	30.23	30.79	31.36	31.92	32.49	33.06	33.63	34.20	34.77	35.35	35.92	36.50	37.08	37.66
46	29.79	30.36	30.94	31.52	32.10	32.68	33.26	33.84	34.43	35.01	35.60	36.19	36.78	37.37	37.96	38.56
47	30.48	31.07	31.66	32.25	32.84	33.44	34.03	34.63	35.23	35.83	36.43	37.04	37.64	38.25	38.86	39.46
48	31.17	31.77	32.37	32.98	33.59	34.20	34.81	35.42	36.03	36.65	37.27	37.88	38.50	39.13	39.75	40.37
49	31.86	32.48	33.09	33.71	34.34	34.96	35.59	36.21	36.84	37.47	38.10	38.74	39.37	40.01	40.65	41.29
50	32.55	33.18	33.82	34.45	35.09	35.73	36.37	37.01	37.65	38.30	38.94	39.59	40.24	40.89	41.55	42.20
51	33.25	33.89	34.54	35.19	35.84	36.49	37.15	37.81	38.46	39.12	39.79	40.45	41.11	41.78	42.45	43.12
52	33.95	34.61	35.27	35.93	36.60	37.27	37.94	38.61	39.28	39.96	40.63	41.31	41.99	42.67	43.36	44.04
53	34.65	35.32	36.00	36.68	37.36	38.04	38.72	39.41	40.10	40.79	41.48	42.17	42.87	43.57	44.27	44.97
54	35.35	36.04	36.73	37.42	38.12	38.82	39.52	40.22	40.92	41.63	42.33	43.04	43.75	44.47	45.18	45.90
55	36.05	36.76	37.46	38.17	38.88	39.60	40.31	41.03	41.74	42.47	43.19	43.91	44.64	45.37	46.10	46.83
56	36.76	37.48	38.20	38.92	39.65	40.38	41.11	41.84	42.57	43.31	44.05	44.79	45.53	46.27	47.02	47.77
57	37.47	38.20	38.94	39.68	40.42	41.16	41.91	42.65	43.40	44.15	44.91	45.66	46.42	47.18	47.94	48.71
58	38.18	38.93	39.68	40.43	41.19	41.95	42.71	43.47	44.23	45.00	45.77	46.54	47.32	48.09	48.87	49.65
59	38.89	39.66	40.42	41.19	41.96	42.74	43.51	44.29	45.07	45.85	46.64	47.42	48.21	49.01	49.80	50.60
60	39.61	40.39	41.17	41.95	42.74	43.53	44.32	45.11	45.91	46.71	47.51	48.31	49.12	49.92	50.73	51.55

NUMBER OF PAYMENTS	ANNUAL PERCENTAGE RATE FRB-105-M															
	18.00%	18.25%	18.50%	18.75%	19.00%	19.25%	19.50%	19.75%	20.00%	20.25%	20.50%	20.75%	21.00%	21.25%	21.50%	21.75%
	(FINANCE CHARGE PER $100 OF AMOUNT FINANCED)															
1	1.50	1.52	1.54	1.56	1.58	1.60	1.62	1.65	1.67	1.69	1.71	1.73	1.75	1.77	1.79	1.81
2	2.26	2.29	2.32	2.35	2.38	2.41	2.44	2.48	2.51	2.54	2.57	2.60	2.63	2.66	2.70	2.73
3	3.01	3.06	3.10	3.14	3.18	3.23	3.27	3.31	3.35	3.39	3.44	3.48	3.52	3.56	3.60	3.65
4	3.78	3.83	3.88	3.94	3.99	4.04	4.10	4.15	4.20	4.25	4.31	4.36	4.41	4.47	4.52	4.57
5	4.54	4.61	4.67	4.74	4.80	4.86	4.93	4.99	5.06	5.12	5.18	5.25	5.31	5.37	5.44	5.50
6	5.32	5.39	5.46	5.54	5.61	5.69	5.76	5.84	5.91	5.99	6.06	6.14	6.21	6.29	6.36	6.44
7	6.09	6.18	6.26	6.35	6.43	6.52	6.60	6.69	6.78	6.86	6.95	7.04	7.12	7.21	7.29	7.38
8	6.87	6.96	7.06	7.16	7.26	7.35	7.45	7.55	7.64	7.74	7.84	7.94	8.03	8.13	8.23	8.33
9	7.65	7.76	7.87	7.97	8.08	8.19	8.30	8.41	8.52	8.63	8.73	8.84	8.95	9.06	9.17	9.28
10	8.43	8.55	8.67	8.79	8.91	9.03	9.15	9.27	9.39	9.51	9.63	9.75	9.88	10.00	10.12	10.24
11	9.22	9.35	9.49	9.62	9.75	9.88	10.01	10.14	10.28	10.41	10.54	10.67	10.80	10.94	11.07	11.20
12	10.02	10.16	10.30	10.44	10.59	10.73	10.87	11.02	11.16	11.31	11.45	11.59	11.74	11.88	12.02	12.17
13	10.81	10.97	11.12	11.28	11.43	11.59	11.74	11.90	12.05	12.21	12.36	12.52	12.67	12.83	12.99	13.14
14	11.61	11.78	11.95	12.11	12.28	12.45	12.61	12.78	12.95	13.11	13.28	13.45	13.62	13.79	13.95	14.12
15	12.42	12.59	12.77	12.95	13.13	13.31	13.49	13.67	13.85	14.03	14.21	14.39	14.57	14.75	14.93	15.11
16	13.22	13.41	13.60	13.80	13.99	14.18	14.37	14.56	14.75	14.94	15.13	15.33	15.52	15.71	15.90	16.10
17	14.04	14.24	14.44	14.64	14.85	15.05	15.25	15.46	15.66	15.86	16.07	16.27	16.48	16.68	16.89	17.09
18	14.85	15.07	15.28	15.49	15.71	15.93	16.14	16.36	16.57	16.79	17.01	17.22	17.44	17.66	17.88	18.09
19	15.67	15.90	16.12	16.35	16.58	16.81	17.03	17.26	17.49	17.72	17.95	18.18	18.41	18.64	18.87	19.10
20	16.49	16.73	16.97	17.21	17.45	17.69	17.93	18.17	18.41	18.66	18.90	19.14	19.38	19.63	19.87	20.11
21	17.32	17.57	17.82	18.07	18.33	18.58	18.83	19.09	19.34	19.60	19.85	20.11	20.36	20.62	20.87	21.13
22	18.15	18.41	18.68	18.94	19.21	19.47	19.74	20.01	20.27	20.54	20.81	21.08	21.34	21.61	21.88	22.15
23	18.98	19.26	19.54	19.81	20.09	20.37	20.65	20.93	21.21	21.49	21.77	22.05	22.33	22.61	22.90	23.18
24	19.82	20.11	20.40	20.69	20.98	21.27	21.56	21.86	22.15	22.44	22.74	23.03	23.33	23.62	23.92	24.21
25	20.66	20.96	21.27	21.57	21.87	22.18	22.48	22.79	23.10	23.40	23.71	24.02	24.32	24.63	24.94	25.25
26	21.50	21.82	22.14	22.45	22.77	23.09	23.41	23.73	24.04	24.36	24.68	25.01	25.33	25.65	25.97	26.29
27	22.35	22.68	23.01	23.34	23.67	24.00	24.33	24.67	25.00	25.33	25.67	26.00	26.34	26.67	27.01	27.34
28	23.20	23.55	23.89	24.23	24.58	24.92	25.27	25.61	25.96	26.30	26.65	27.00	27.35	27.70	28.05	28.40
29	24.06	24.41	24.77	25.13	25.49	25.84	26.20	26.56	26.92	27.28	27.64	28.00	28.37	28.73	29.09	29.46
30	24.92	25.29	25.66	26.03	26.40	26.77	27.14	27.52	27.89	28.26	28.64	29.01	29.39	29.77	30.14	30.52
31	25.78	26.16	26.55	26.93	27.32	27.70	28.09	28.47	28.86	29.25	29.64	30.03	30.42	30.81	31.20	31.59
32	26.65	27.04	27.44	27.84	28.24	28.64	29.04	29.44	29.84	30.24	30.64	31.05	31.45	31.85	32.26	32.67
33	27.52	27.93	28.34	28.75	29.16	29.57	29.99	30.40	30.82	31.23	31.65	32.07	32.49	32.91	33.33	33.75
34	28.39	28.81	29.24	29.66	30.09	30.52	30.95	31.37	31.80	32.23	32.67	33.10	33.53	33.96	34.40	34.83
35	29.27	29.71	30.14	30.58	31.02	31.47	31.91	32.35	32.79	33.24	33.68	34.13	34.58	35.03	35.47	35.92
36	30.15	30.60	31.05	31.51	31.96	32.42	32.87	33.33	33.79	34.25	34.71	35.17	35.63	36.09	36.56	37.02
37	31.03	31.50	31.97	32.43	32.90	33.37	33.84	34.32	34.79	35.26	35.74	36.21	36.69	37.16	37.64	38.12
38	31.92	32.40	32.88	33.37	33.85	34.33	34.82	35.30	35.79	36.28	36.77	37.26	37.75	38.24	38.73	39.23
39	32.81	33.31	33.80	34.30	34.80	35.30	35.80	36.30	36.80	37.30	37.81	38.31	38.82	39.32	39.83	40.34
40	33.71	34.22	34.73	35.24	35.75	36.26	36.78	37.29	37.81	38.33	38.85	39.37	39.89	40.41	40.93	41.46
41	34.61	35.13	35.66	36.18	36.71	37.24	37.77	38.30	38.83	39.36	39.89	40.43	40.96	41.50	42.04	42.58
42	35.51	36.05	36.59	37.13	37.67	38.21	38.76	39.30	39.85	40.40	40.95	41.50	42.05	42.60	43.15	43.71
43	36.42	36.97	37.52	38.08	38.63	39.19	39.75	40.31	40.87	41.44	42.00	42.57	43.13	43.70	44.27	44.84
44	37.33	37.89	38.46	39.03	39.60	40.18	40.75	41.33	41.90	42.48	43.06	43.64	44.22	44.81	45.39	45.98
45	38.24	38.82	39.41	39.99	40.58	41.17	41.75	42.35	42.94	43.53	44.13	44.72	45.32	45.92	46.52	47.12
46	39.16	39.75	40.35	40.95	41.55	42.16	42.76	43.37	43.98	44.58	45.20	45.81	46.42	47.03	47.65	48.27
47	40.08	40.69	41.30	41.92	42.54	43.15	43.77	44.40	45.02	45.64	46.27	46.90	47.53	48.16	48.79	49.42
48	41.00	41.63	42.26	42.89	43.52	44.15	44.79	45.43	46.07	46.71	47.35	47.99	48.64	49.28	49.93	50.58
49	41.93	42.57	43.22	43.86	44.51	45.16	45.81	46.46	47.12	47.77	48.43	49.09	49.75	50.41	51.08	51.74
50	42.86	43.52	44.18	44.84	45.50	46.17	46.83	47.50	48.17	48.84	49.52	50.19	50.87	51.55	52.23	52.91
51	43.79	44.47	45.14	45.82	46.50	47.18	47.86	48.55	49.23	49.92	50.61	51.30	51.99	52.69	53.38	54.08
52	44.73	45.42	46.11	46.80	47.50	48.20	48.89	49.59	50.30	51.00	51.71	52.41	53.12	53.83	54.55	55.26
53	45.67	46.38	47.08	47.79	48.50	49.22	49.93	50.65	51.37	52.09	52.81	53.53	54.26	54.98	55.71	56.44
54	46.62	47.34	48.06	48.79	49.51	50.24	50.97	51.70	52.44	53.17	53.91	54.65	55.39	56.14	56.88	57.63
55	47.57	48.30	49.04	49.78	50.52	51.27	52.02	52.76	53.52	54.27	55.02	55.78	56.54	57.30	58.06	58.82
56	48.52	49.27	50.03	50.78	51.54	52.30	53.06	53.83	54.60	55.37	56.14	56.91	57.68	58.46	59.24	60.02
57	49.47	50.24	51.01	51.79	52.56	53.34	54.12	54.90	55.68	56.47	57.25	58.04	58.84	59.63	60.43	61.22
58	50.43	51.22	52.00	52.79	53.58	54.38	55.17	55.97	56.77	57.57	58.38	59.18	59.99	60.80	61.62	62.43
59	51.39	52.20	53.00	53.80	54.61	55.42	56.23	57.05	57.87	58.68	59.51	60.33	61.15	61.98	62.81	63.64
60	52.36	53.18	54.00	54.82	55.64	56.47	57.30	58.13	58.96	59.80	60.64	61.48	62.32	63.17	64.01	64.86

SIX/COMPOUND INTEREST

FRB-106-M

NUMBER OF PAYMENTS	ANNUAL PERCENTAGE RATE															
	22.00%	22.25%	22.50%	22.75%	23.00%	23.25%	23.50%	23.75%	24.00%	24.25%	24.50%	24.75%	25.00%	25.25%	25.50%	25.75%
	(FINANCE CHARGE PER $100 OF AMOUNT FINANCED)															
1	1.83	1.85	1.87	1.90	1.92	1.94	1.96	1.98	2.00	2.02	2.04	2.06	2.08	2.10	2.12	2.15
2	2.76	2.79	2.82	2.85	2.88	2.92	2.95	2.98	3.01	3.04	3.07	3.10	3.14	3.17	3.20	3.23
3	3.69	3.73	3.77	3.82	3.86	3.90	3.94	3.98	4.03	4.07	4.11	4.15	4.20	4.24	4.28	4.32
4	4.62	4.68	4.73	4.78	4.84	4.89	4.94	5.00	5.05	5.10	5.16	5.21	5.26	5.32	5.37	5.42
5	5.57	5.63	5.69	5.76	5.82	5.89	5.95	6.02	6.08	6.14	6.21	6.27	6.34	6.40	6.46	6.53
6	6.51	6.59	6.66	6.74	6.81	6.89	6.96	7.04	7.12	7.19	7.27	7.34	7.42	7.49	7.57	7.64
7	7.47	7.55	7.64	7.73	7.81	7.90	7.99	8.07	8.16	8.24	8.33	8.42	8.51	8.59	8.68	8.77
8	8.42	8.52	8.62	8.72	8.82	8.91	9.01	9.11	9.21	9.31	9.40	9.50	9.60	9.70	9.80	9.90
9	9.39	9.50	9.61	9.72	9.83	9.94	10.04	10.15	10.26	10.37	10.48	10.59	10.70	10.81	10.92	11.03
10	10.36	10.48	10.60	10.72	10.84	10.96	11.08	11.21	11.33	11.45	11.57	11.69	11.81	11.93	12.06	12.18
11	11.33	11.47	11.60	11.73	11.86	12.00	12.13	12.26	12.40	12.53	12.66	12.80	12.93	13.06	13.20	13.33
12	12.31	12.46	12.60	12.75	12.89	13.04	13.18	13.33	13.47	13.62	13.76	13.91	14.05	14.20	14.34	14.49
13	13.30	13.46	13.61	13.77	13.93	14.08	14.24	14.40	14.55	14.71	14.87	15.03	15.18	15.34	15.50	15.66
14	14.29	14.46	14.63	14.80	14.97	15.13	15.30	15.47	15.64	15.81	15.98	16.15	16.32	16.49	16.66	16.83
15	15.29	15.47	15.65	15.83	16.01	16.19	16.37	16.56	16.74	16.92	17.10	17.28	17.47	17.65	17.83	18.02
16	16.29	16.48	16.68	16.87	17.06	17.26	17.45	17.65	17.84	18.03	18.23	18.42	18.62	18.81	19.01	19.21
17	17.30	17.50	17.71	17.92	18.12	18.33	18.53	18.74	18.95	19.16	19.36	19.57	19.78	19.99	20.20	20.40
18	18.31	18.53	18.75	18.97	19.19	19.41	19.62	19.84	20.06	20.28	20.50	20.72	20.95	21.17	21.39	21.61
19	19.33	19.56	19.79	20.02	20.26	20.49	20.72	20.95	21.19	21.42	21.65	21.89	22.12	22.35	22.59	22.82
20	20.35	20.60	20.84	21.09	21.33	21.58	21.82	22.07	22.31	22.56	22.81	23.05	23.30	23.55	23.79	24.04
21	21.38	21.64	21.90	22.16	22.41	22.67	22.93	23.19	23.45	23.71	23.97	24.23	24.49	24.75	25.01	25.27
22	22.42	22.69	22.96	23.23	23.50	23.77	24.04	24.32	24.59	24.86	25.13	25.41	25.68	25.96	26.23	26.50
23	23.46	23.74	24.03	24.31	24.60	24.88	25.17	25.45	25.74	26.02	26.31	26.60	26.88	27.17	27.46	27.75
24	24.51	24.80	25.10	25.40	25.70	25.99	26.29	26.59	26.89	27.19	27.49	27.79	28.09	28.39	28.69	29.00
25	25.56	25.87	26.18	26.49	26.80	27.11	27.43	27.74	28.05	28.36	28.68	28.99	29.31	29.62	29.94	30.25
26	26.62	26.94	27.26	27.59	27.91	28.24	28.56	28.89	29.22	29.55	29.87	30.20	30.53	30.86	31.19	31.52
27	27.68	28.02	28.35	28.69	29.03	29.37	29.71	30.05	30.39	30.73	31.07	31.42	31.76	32.10	32.45	32.79
28	28.75	29.10	29.45	29.80	30.15	30.51	30.86	31.22	31.57	31.93	32.28	32.64	33.00	33.35	33.71	34.07
29	29.82	30.19	30.55	30.92	31.28	31.65	32.02	32.39	32.76	33.13	33.50	33.87	34.24	34.61	34.98	35.36
30	30.90	31.28	31.66	32.04	32.42	32.80	33.18	33.57	33.95	34.33	34.72	35.10	35.49	35.88	36.26	36.65
31	31.98	32.38	32.77	33.17	33.56	33.96	34.35	34.75	35.15	35.55	35.95	36.35	36.75	37.15	37.55	37.95
32	33.07	33.48	33.89	34.30	34.71	35.12	35.53	35.94	36.35	36.77	37.18	37.60	38.01	38.43	38.84	39.26
33	34.17	34.59	35.01	35.44	35.86	36.29	36.71	37.14	37.57	37.99	38.42	38.85	39.28	39.71	40.14	40.58
34	35.27	35.71	36.14	36.58	37.02	37.46	37.90	38.34	38.78	39.23	39.67	40.11	40.56	41.01	41.45	41.90
35	36.37	36.83	37.28	37.73	38.18	38.64	39.09	39.55	40.01	40.47	40.92	41.38	41.84	42.31	42.77	43.23
36	37.49	37.95	38.42	38.89	39.35	39.82	40.29	40.77	41.24	41.71	42.19	42.66	43.14	43.61	44.09	44.57
37	38.60	39.08	39.56	40.05	40.53	41.02	41.50	41.99	42.48	42.96	43.45	43.94	44.43	44.93	45.42	45.91
38	39.72	40.22	40.72	41.21	41.71	42.21	42.71	43.22	43.72	44.22	44.73	45.23	45.74	46.25	46.75	47.26
39	40.85	41.36	41.87	42.39	42.90	43.42	43.93	44.45	44.97	45.49	46.01	46.53	47.05	47.57	48.10	48.62
40	41.98	42.51	43.04	43.56	44.09	44.62	45.16	45.69	46.22	46.76	47.29	47.83	48.37	48.91	49.45	49.99
41	43.12	43.66	44.20	44.75	45.29	45.84	46.39	46.94	47.48	48.04	48.59	49.14	49.69	50.25	50.80	51.36
42	44.26	44.82	45.38	45.94	46.50	47.06	47.62	48.19	48.75	49.32	49.89	50.46	51.03	51.60	52.17	52.74
43	45.41	45.98	46.56	47.13	47.71	48.29	48.87	49.45	50.03	50.61	51.19	51.78	52.36	52.95	53.54	54.13
44	46.56	47.15	47.74	48.33	48.93	49.52	50.11	50.71	51.31	51.91	52.51	53.11	53.71	54.31	54.92	55.52
45	47.72	48.33	48.93	49.54	50.15	50.76	51.37	51.98	52.59	53.21	53.82	54.44	55.06	55.68	56.30	56.92
46	48.89	49.51	50.13	50.75	51.37	52.00	52.63	53.26	53.89	54.52	55.15	55.78	56.42	57.05	57.69	58.33
47	50.06	50.69	51.33	51.97	52.61	53.25	53.89	54.54	55.18	55.83	56.48	57.13	57.78	58.44	59.09	59.75
48	51.23	51.88	52.54	53.19	53.85	54.51	55.16	55.83	56.49	57.15	57.82	58.49	59.15	59.82	60.50	61.17
49	52.41	53.08	53.75	54.42	55.09	55.77	56.44	57.12	57.80	58.48	59.16	59.85	60.53	61.22	61.91	62.60
50	53.59	54.28	54.96	55.65	56.34	57.03	57.73	58.42	59.12	59.81	60.51	61.21	61.92	62.62	63.33	64.03
51	54.78	55.48	56.19	56.89	57.60	58.30	59.01	59.73	60.44	61.15	61.87	62.59	63.31	64.03	64.75	65.47
52	55.98	56.69	57.41	58.13	58.86	59.58	60.31	61.04	61.77	62.50	63.23	63.97	64.70	65.44	66.18	66.92
53	57.18	57.91	58.65	59.38	60.12	60.87	61.61	62.35	63.10	63.85	64.60	65.35	66.11	66.86	67.62	68.38
54	58.38	59.13	59.88	60.64	61.40	62.16	62.92	63.68	64.44	65.21	65.98	66.75	67.52	68.29	69.07	69.84
55	59.59	60.36	61.13	61.90	62.67	63.45	64.23	65.01	65.79	66.57	67.36	68.14	68.93	69.72	70.52	71.31
56	60.80	61.59	62.38	63.17	63.96	64.75	65.54	66.34	67.14	67.94	68.74	69.55	70.36	71.16	71.97	72.79
57	62.02	62.83	63.63	64.44	65.25	66.06	66.87	67.68	68.50	69.32	70.14	70.96	71.78	72.61	73.44	74.27
58	63.25	64.07	64.89	65.71	66.54	67.37	68.20	69.03	69.86	70.70	71.54	72.38	73.22	74.06	74.91	75.76
59	64.48	65.32	66.15	67.00	67.84	68.68	69.53	70.38	71.23	72.09	72.94	73.80	74.66	75.52	76.39	77.25
60	65.71	66.57	67.42	68.28	69.14	70.01	70.87	71.74	72.61	73.48	74.35	75.23	76.11	76.99	77.87	78.76

FRB-107-M

NUMBER OF PAYMENTS	ANNUAL PERCENTAGE RATE															
	26.00%	26.25%	26.50%	26.75%	27.00%	27.25%	27.50%	27.75%	28.00%	28.25%	28.50%	28.75%	29.00%	29.25%	29.50%	29.75%
	(FINANCE CHARGE PER $100 OF AMOUNT FINANCED)															
1	2.17	2.19	2.21	2.23	2.25	2.27	2.29	2.31	2.33	2.35	2.37	2.40	2.42	2.44	2.46	2.48
2	3.26	3.29	3.32	3.36	3.39	3.42	3.45	3.48	3.51	3.54	3.58	3.61	3.64	3.67	3.70	3.73
3	4.36	4.41	4.45	4.49	4.53	4.58	4.62	4.66	4.70	4.74	4.79	4.83	4.87	4.91	4.96	5.00
4	5.47	5.53	5.58	5.63	5.69	5.74	5.79	5.85	5.90	5.95	6.01	6.06	6.11	6.17	6.22	6.27
5	6.59	6.66	6.72	6.79	6.85	6.91	6.98	7.04	7.11	7.17	7.24	7.30	7.37	7.43	7.49	7.56
6	7.72	7.79	7.87	7.95	8.02	8.10	8.17	8.25	8.32	8.40	8.48	8.55	8.63	8.70	8.78	8.85
7	8.85	8.94	9.03	9.11	9.20	9.29	9.37	9.46	9.55	9.64	9.72	9.81	9.90	9.98	10.07	10.16
8	9.99	10.09	10.19	10.29	10.39	10.49	10.58	10.68	10.78	10.88	10.98	11.08	11.18	11.28	11.38	11.47
9	11.14	11.25	11.36	11.47	11.58	11.69	11.80	11.91	12.03	12.14	12.25	12.36	12.47	12.58	12.69	12.80
10	12.30	12.42	12.54	12.67	12.79	12.91	13.03	13.15	13.28	13.40	13.52	13.64	13.77	13.89	14.01	14.14
11	13.46	13.60	13.73	13.87	14.00	14.13	14.27	14.40	14.54	14.67	14.81	14.94	15.08	15.21	15.35	15.48
12	14.64	14.78	14.93	15.07	15.22	15.37	15.51	15.66	15.81	15.95	16.10	16.25	16.40	16.54	16.69	16.84
13	15.82	15.97	16.13	16.29	16.45	16.61	16.77	16.93	17.09	17.24	17.40	17.56	17.72	17.88	18.04	18.20
14	17.00	17.17	17.35	17.52	17.69	17.86	18.03	18.20	18.37	18.54	18.72	18.89	19.06	19.23	19.41	19.58
15	18.20	18.38	18.57	18.75	18.93	19.12	19.30	19.48	19.67	19.85	20.04	20.22	20.41	20.59	20.78	20.96
16	19.40	19.60	19.79	19.99	20.19	20.38	20.58	20.78	20.97	21.17	21.37	21.57	21.76	21.96	22.16	22.36
17	20.61	20.82	21.03	21.24	21.45	21.66	21.87	22.08	22.29	22.50	22.71	22.92	23.13	23.34	23.55	23.77
18	21.83	22.05	22.27	22.50	22.72	22.94	23.16	23.39	23.61	23.83	24.06	24.28	24.51	24.73	24.96	25.18
19	23.06	23.29	23.53	23.76	24.00	24.23	24.47	24.71	24.94	25.18	25.42	25.65	25.89	26.13	26.37	26.61
20	24.29	24.54	24.79	25.04	25.28	25.53	25.78	26.03	26.28	26.53	26.78	27.04	27.29	27.54	27.79	28.04
21	25.53	25.79	26.05	26.32	26.58	26.84	27.11	27.37	27.63	27.90	28.16	28.43	28.69	28.96	29.22	29.49
22	26.78	27.05	27.33	27.61	27.88	28.16	28.44	28.71	28.99	29.27	29.55	29.82	30.10	30.38	30.66	30.94
23	28.04	28.32	28.61	28.90	29.19	29.48	29.77	30.07	30.36	30.65	30.94	31.23	31.53	31.82	32.11	32.41
24	29.30	29.60	29.90	30.21	30.51	30.82	31.12	31.43	31.73	32.04	32.34	32.65	32.96	33.27	33.57	33.88
25	30.57	30.89	31.20	31.52	31.84	32.16	32.48	32.80	33.12	33.44	33.76	34.08	34.40	34.72	35.04	35.37
26	31.85	32.18	32.51	32.84	33.18	33.51	33.84	34.18	34.51	34.84	35.18	35.51	35.85	36.19	36.52	36.86
27	33.14	33.48	33.83	34.17	34.52	34.87	35.21	35.56	35.91	36.26	36.61	36.96	37.31	37.66	38.01	38.36
28	34.43	34.79	35.15	35.51	35.87	36.23	36.59	36.96	37.32	37.68	38.05	38.41	38.78	39.15	39.51	39.88
29	35.73	36.10	36.48	36.85	37.23	37.61	37.98	38.36	38.74	39.12	39.50	39.88	40.26	40.64	41.02	41.40
30	37.04	37.43	37.82	38.21	38.60	38.99	39.38	39.77	40.17	40.56	40.95	41.35	41.75	42.14	42.54	42.94
31	38.35	38.76	39.16	39.57	39.97	40.38	40.79	41.19	41.60	42.01	42.42	42.83	43.24	43.65	44.06	44.48
32	39.68	40.10	40.52	40.94	41.36	41.78	42.20	42.62	43.05	43.47	43.90	44.32	44.75	45.17	45.60	46.03
33	41.01	41.44	41.88	42.31	42.75	43.19	43.62	44.06	44.50	44.94	45.38	45.82	46.26	46.70	47.15	47.59
34	42.35	42.80	43.25	43.70	44.15	44.60	45.05	45.51	45.96	46.42	46.87	47.33	47.79	48.24	48.70	49.16
35	43.69	44.16	44.62	45.09	45.56	46.02	46.49	46.96	47.43	47.90	48.37	48.85	49.32	49.79	50.27	50.74
36	45.05	45.53	46.01	46.49	46.97	47.45	47.94	48.42	48.91	49.40	49.88	50.37	50.86	51.35	51.84	52.33
37	46.41	46.90	47.40	47.90	48.39	48.89	49.39	49.89	50.40	50.90	51.40	51.91	52.41	52.92	53.42	53.93
38	47.77	48.29	48.80	49.31	49.82	50.34	50.86	51.37	51.89	52.41	52.93	53.45	53.97	54.49	55.02	55.54
39	49.15	49.68	50.20	50.73	51.26	51.79	52.33	52.86	53.39	53.93	54.46	55.00	55.54	56.08	56.62	57.16
40	50.53	51.07	51.62	52.16	52.71	53.26	53.81	54.35	54.90	55.46	56.01	56.56	57.12	57.67	58.23	58.79
41	51.92	52.48	53.04	53.60	54.16	54.73	55.29	55.86	56.42	56.99	57.56	58.13	58.70	59.28	59.85	60.42
42	53.32	53.89	54.47	55.05	55.63	56.21	56.79	57.37	57.95	58.54	59.12	59.71	60.30	60.89	61.48	62.07
43	54.72	55.31	55.90	56.50	57.09	57.69	58.29	58.89	59.49	60.09	60.69	61.30	61.90	62.51	63.11	63.72
44	56.13	56.74	57.35	57.96	58.57	59.19	59.80	60.42	61.03	61.65	62.27	62.89	63.51	64.14	64.76	65.39
45	57.55	58.17	58.80	59.43	60.06	60.69	61.32	61.95	62.59	63.22	63.86	64.50	65.13	65.77	66.42	67.06
46	58.97	59.61	60.26	60.90	61.55	62.20	62.84	63.49	64.15	64.80	65.45	66.11	66.76	67.42	68.08	68.74
47	60.40	61.06	61.72	62.38	63.05	63.71	64.38	65.05	65.71	66.38	67.06	67.73	68.40	69.08	69.75	70.43
48	61.84	62.52	63.20	63.87	64.56	65.24	65.92	66.60	67.29	67.98	68.67	69.36	70.05	70.74	71.44	72.13
49	63.29	63.98	64.68	65.37	66.07	66.77	67.47	68.17	68.87	69.58	70.29	70.99	71.70	72.41	73.13	73.84
50	64.74	65.45	66.16	66.88	67.59	68.31	69.03	69.75	70.47	71.19	71.91	72.64	73.37	74.10	74.83	75.56
51	66.20	66.93	67.66	68.39	69.12	69.86	70.59	71.33	72.07	72.81	73.55	74.29	75.04	75.78	76.53	77.28
52	67.67	68.41	69.16	69.91	70.66	71.41	72.16	72.92	73.67	74.43	75.19	75.95	76.72	77.48	78.25	79.02
53	69.14	69.90	70.67	71.43	72.20	72.97	73.74	74.52	75.29	76.07	76.85	77.62	78.41	79.19	79.97	80.76
54	70.62	71.40	72.18	72.97	73.75	74.54	75.33	76.12	76.91	77.71	78.50	79.30	80.10	80.90	81.71	82.51
55	72.11	72.91	73.71	74.51	75.31	76.12	76.92	77.73	78.55	79.36	80.17	80.99	81.81	82.63	83.45	84.27
56	73.60	74.42	75.24	76.06	76.88	77.70	78.53	79.35	80.18	81.02	81.85	82.68	83.52	84.36	85.20	86.04
57	75.10	75.94	76.77	77.61	78.45	79.29	80.14	80.98	81.83	82.68	83.53	84.39	85.24	86.10	86.96	87.82
58	76.61	77.46	78.32	79.17	80.03	80.89	81.75	82.62	83.48	84.35	85.22	86.10	86.97	87.85	88.72	89.60
59	78.12	78.99	79.87	80.74	81.62	82.50	83.38	84.26	85.15	86.03	86.92	87.81	88.71	89.60	90.50	91.40
60	79.64	80.53	81.42	82.32	83.21	84.11	85.01	85.91	86.81	87.72	88.63	89.54	90.45	91.37	92.28	93.20

FRB-108-M

NUMBER OF PAYMENTS	ANNUAL PERCENTAGE RATE															
	30.00%	30.25%	30.50%	30.75%	31.00%	31.25%	31.50%	31.75%	32.00%	32.25%	32.50%	32.75%	33.00%	33.25%	33.50%	33.75%
	(FINANCE CHARGE PER $100 OF AMOUNT FINANCED)															
1	2.50	2.52	2.54	2.56	2.58	2.60	2.62	2.65	2.67	2.69	2.71	2.73	2.75	2.77	2.79	2.81
2	3.77	3.80	3.83	3.86	3.89	3.92	3.95	3.99	4.02	4.05	4.08	4.11	4.14	4.18	4.21	4.24
3	5.04	5.08	5.13	5.17	5.21	5.25	5.30	5.34	5.38	5.42	5.46	5.51	5.55	5.59	5.63	5.68
4	6.33	6.38	6.43	6.49	6.54	6.59	6.65	6.70	6.75	6.81	6.86	6.91	6.97	7.02	7.08	7.13
5	7.62	7.69	7.75	7.82	7.88	7.95	8.01	8.08	8.14	8.20	8.27	8.33	8.40	8.46	8.53	8.59
6	8.93	9.01	9.08	9.16	9.23	9.31	9.39	9.46	9.54	9.61	9.69	9.77	9.84	9.92	9.99	10.07
7	10.25	10.33	10.42	10.51	10.60	10.68	10.77	10.86	10.95	11.03	11.12	11.21	11.30	11.39	11.47	11.56
8	11.57	11.67	11.77	11.87	11.97	12.07	12.17	12.27	12.37	12.47	12.57	12.67	12.77	12.87	12.97	13.07
9	12.91	13.02	13.13	13.24	13.36	13.47	13.58	13.69	13.80	13.91	14.02	14.14	14.25	14.36	14.47	14.58
10	14.26	14.38	14.50	14.63	14.75	14.87	15.00	15.12	15.24	15.37	15.49	15.62	15.74	15.86	15.99	16.11
11	15.62	15.75	15.89	16.02	16.16	16.29	16.43	16.56	16.70	16.84	16.97	17.11	17.24	17.38	17.52	17.65
12	16.98	17.13	17.28	17.43	17.58	17.72	17.87	18.02	18.17	18.32	18.47	18.61	18.76	18.91	19.06	19.21
13	18.36	18.52	18.68	18.84	19.00	19.16	19.33	19.49	19.65	19.81	19.97	20.13	20.29	20.45	20.62	20.78
14	19.75	19.92	20.10	20.27	20.44	20.62	20.79	20.96	21.14	21.31	21.49	21.66	21.83	22.01	22.18	22.36
15	21.15	21.34	21.52	21.71	21.89	22.08	22.27	22.45	22.64	22.83	23.01	23.20	23.39	23.58	23.76	23.95
16	22.56	22.76	22.96	23.16	23.35	23.55	23.75	23.95	24.15	24.35	24.55	24.75	24.96	25.16	25.36	25.56
17	23.98	24.19	24.40	24.61	24.83	25.04	25.25	25.47	25.68	25.89	26.11	26.32	26.53	26.75	26.96	27.18
18	25.41	25.63	25.86	26.08	26.31	26.54	26.76	26.99	27.22	27.44	27.67	27.90	28.13	28.35	28.58	28.81
19	26.85	27.08	27.32	27.56	27.80	28.04	28.28	28.52	28.76	29.00	29.25	29.49	29.73	29.97	30.21	30.45
20	28.29	28.55	28.80	29.05	29.31	29.56	29.81	30.07	30.32	30.58	30.83	31.09	31.34	31.60	31.86	32.11
21	29.75	30.02	30.29	30.55	30.82	31.09	31.36	31.62	31.89	32.16	32.43	32.70	32.97	33.24	33.51	33.78
22	31.22	31.50	31.78	32.06	32.35	32.63	32.91	33.19	33.48	33.76	34.04	34.33	34.61	34.89	35.18	35.46
23	32.70	33.00	33.29	33.59	33.88	34.18	34.48	34.77	35.07	35.37	35.66	35.96	36.26	36.56	36.86	37.16
24	34.19	34.50	34.81	35.12	35.43	35.74	36.05	36.36	36.67	36.99	37.30	37.61	37.92	38.24	38.55	38.87
25	35.69	36.01	36.34	36.66	36.99	37.31	37.64	37.96	38.29	38.62	38.94	39.27	39.60	39.93	40.26	40.59
26	37.20	37.54	37.88	38.21	38.55	38.89	39.23	39.58	39.92	40.26	40.60	40.94	41.29	41.63	41.97	42.32
27	38.72	39.07	39.42	39.78	40.13	40.49	40.84	41.20	41.56	41.91	42.27	42.63	42.99	43.34	43.70	44.06
28	40.25	40.61	40.98	41.35	41.72	42.09	42.46	42.83	43.20	43.58	43.95	44.32	44.70	45.07	45.45	45.82
29	41.78	42.17	42.55	42.94	43.32	43.71	44.09	44.48	44.87	45.25	45.64	46.03	46.42	46.81	47.20	47.59
30	43.33	43.73	44.13	44.53	44.93	45.33	45.73	46.13	46.54	46.94	47.34	47.75	48.15	48.56	48.96	49.37
31	44.89	45.30	45.72	46.13	46.55	46.97	47.38	47.80	48.22	48.64	49.06	49.48	49.90	50.32	50.74	51.17
32	46.46	46.89	47.32	47.75	48.18	48.61	49.05	49.48	49.91	50.35	50.78	51.22	51.66	52.09	52.53	52.97
33	48.04	48.48	48.93	49.37	49.82	50.27	50.72	51.17	51.62	52.07	52.52	52.97	53.43	53.88	54.33	54.79
34	49.62	50.08	50.55	51.01	51.47	51.94	52.40	52.87	53.33	53.80	54.27	54.74	55.21	55.68	56.15	56.62
35	51.22	51.70	52.17	52.65	53.13	53.61	54.09	54.58	55.06	55.54	56.03	56.51	57.00	57.48	57.97	58.46
36	52.83	53.32	53.81	54.31	54.80	55.30	55.80	56.30	56.80	57.30	57.80	58.30	58.80	59.30	59.81	60.31
37	54.44	54.95	55.46	55.97	56.49	57.00	57.51	58.03	58.54	59.06	59.58	60.10	60.62	61.14	61.66	62.18
38	56.07	56.59	57.12	57.65	58.18	58.71	59.24	59.77	60.30	60.84	61.37	61.90	62.44	62.98	63.52	64.06
39	57.70	58.24	58.79	59.33	59.88	60.42	60.97	61.52	62.07	62.62	63.17	63.72	64.28	64.83	65.39	65.94
40	59.34	59.90	60.47	61.03	61.59	62.15	62.72	63.28	63.85	64.42	64.99	65.56	66.13	66.70	67.27	67.84
41	61.00	61.57	62.15	62.73	63.31	63.89	64.47	65.06	65.64	66.22	66.81	67.40	67.99	68.57	69.16	69.76
42	62.66	63.25	63.85	64.44	65.04	65.64	66.24	66.84	67.44	68.04	68.65	69.25	69.86	70.46	71.07	71.68
43	64.33	64.94	65.56	66.17	66.78	67.40	68.01	68.63	69.25	69.87	70.49	71.11	71.74	72.36	72.99	73.61
44	66.01	66.64	67.27	67.90	68.53	69.17	69.80	70.43	71.07	71.71	72.35	72.99	73.63	74.27	74.91	75.56
45	67.70	68.35	69.00	69.64	70.29	70.94	71.60	72.25	72.90	73.56	74.21	74.87	75.53	76.19	76.85	77.52
46	69.40	70.07	70.73	71.40	72.06	72.73	73.40	74.07	74.74	75.42	76.09	76.77	77.44	78.12	78.80	79.48
47	71.11	71.79	72.47	73.16	73.84	74.53	75.22	75.90	76.60	77.29	77.98	78.67	79.37	80.07	80.76	81.46
48	72.83	73.53	74.23	74.93	75.63	76.34	77.04	77.75	78.46	79.17	79.88	80.59	81.30	82.02	82.74	83.45
49	74.55	75.27	75.99	76.71	77.43	78.15	78.88	79.60	80.33	81.06	81.79	82.52	83.25	83.98	84.72	85.45
50	76.29	77.02	77.76	78.50	79.24	79.98	80.72	81.46	82.21	82.96	83.70	84.45	85.20	85.96	86.71	87.47
51	78.03	78.79	79.54	80.30	81.06	81.81	82.58	83.34	84.10	84.87	85.63	86.40	87.17	87.94	88.71	89.49
52	79.79	80.56	81.33	82.11	82.88	83.66	84.44	85.22	86.00	86.79	87.57	88.36	89.15	89.94	90.73	91.52
53	81.55	82.34	83.13	83.92	84.72	85.51	86.31	87.11	87.91	88.72	89.52	90.33	91.13	91.94	92.75	93.57
54	83.32	84.13	84.94	85.75	86.56	87.38	88.19	89.01	89.83	90.66	91.48	92.30	93.13	93.96	94.79	95.62
55	85.10	85.93	86.75	87.58	88.42	89.25	90.09	90.92	91.76	92.60	93.45	94.29	95.14	95.99	96.83	97.69
56	86.89	87.73	88.58	89.43	90.28	91.13	91.99	92.84	93.70	94.56	95.43	96.29	97.15	98.02	98.89	99.76
57	88.68	89.55	90.41	91.28	92.15	93.02	93.90	94.77	95.65	96.53	97.41	98.30	99.18	100.07	100.96	101.85
58	90.49	91.37	92.26	93.14	94.03	94.92	95.82	96.71	97.61	98.51	99.41	100.31	101.22	102.12	103.03	103.94
59	92.30	93.20	94.11	95.01	95.92	96.83	97.75	98.66	99.58	100.50	101.42	102.34	103.26	104.19	105.12	106.05
60	94.12	95.04	95.97	96.89	97.82	98.75	99.68	100.62	101.56	102.49	103.43	104.38	105.32	106.27	107.21	108.16

Solution

From Example 1, we know that the finance charge is $467.92.

  1. The finance charge per hundred is

$$\frac{467.92 \times 100}{2,600} = \$18.00$$

  2. We find the number of payments (36) in the extreme left hand column of the APR (monthly payment) table and read across until we find the value that is nearest to 18.00.

APR	11%	11.25%
Line 36	17.86	18.29

Since 18.00 is nearest to 17.86, the APR is 11.00%.

Procedure for interpolation

  Note that in the ad above, the APR is listed as 11.08%. This rate can be determined by interpolation. Since $18.00 falls between the columns headed 11.00% and 11.25%, the desired APR is the same fraction of the way from 11.00 to 11.25 as $18.00 is of the way from $17.86 to $18.29. The relationship is represented in the following diagram.

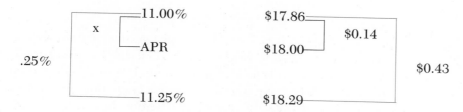

  From the above diagram, we can construct a proportion and solve for x.

  Thus, .14/.43 = x/.25; that is, x = 0.08, and the APR quoted to the nearest hundredth of a per cent is 11.00% + 0.08% = 11.08%. For the purpose of complying with Regulation Z, however, quoting an APR of 11% is sufficient.

PROGRESS TEST 2

  1. Referring to the ad following, the finance charge is _____ .

  2. The finance charge per hundred is _____ .
  3. The APR is _____ .
  4. The APR quoted in the ad is 11.90%. Does this figure agree with your answer?_____ .

---

1. $597.04   2. $22.96   3. 12%   4. No

Reprinted, by permission, from *The Tampa Tribune*, February 15, 1974, p. 21E.

In the preceding examples, we have verified the APR for different situations. Let us now consider the reverse of this procedure; that is, given a desired APR let us find the equal monthly payments needed to reduce an obligation and the associated finance charge for a given transaction. We illustrate the situation in the following example.

Example 4

The owner of Zyppy Used Cars wishes to run an ad in the newspaper featuring a car that he wants to sell for $2,800, with $200 down and the rest to be paid in 24 equal monthly payments. Let us assume that he desires to have an APR of 12%. Regulation Z requires that he also print in the ad the finance charge and the amount of each of the equal monthly payments. Find these two amounts.

Solution

Since the APR is 12% and the number of payments is 24, we look on the 24th line of the APR table, under the 12% column and find the finance charge per hundred. This amount is $12.98. Since the amount to be financed is $2,600 ($2,800 − $200), the number of hundred dollars to be financed is $\frac{2,600}{100} = 26$, and the total finance charge is

$26 \times 12.98 = \$337.48$. Thus, the total amount to be paid is $\$2,600 + 337.48$, and the monthly payments amount to

$$\frac{\$2,600 + 337.48}{24} = \$122.40$$

PROGRESS TEST 3

1. A man wishes to sell a car for $2,000, $250 down and the rest to be paid in 30 equal monthly payments. If he wishes to have a 12.75 APR, the finance charge per hundred is _____.
2. The total finance charge is _____.
3. The monthly payments are _____.

EXERCISE 6.4

In Problems 1 through 5, find the finance charges.

	DOWN PAYMENT	MONTHLY PAYMENT	NUMBER OF MONTHS	CASH SELLING PRICE
1.	$50	$ 6.50	12	$120.00
2.	$100	$ 7.00	24	$250.00
3.	$75	$30.00	12	$400.00
4.	$25	$10.65	18	$199.95
5.	$30	$11.22	30	$299.95

6. Find the APR (to the nearest $\frac{1}{4}$ of 1%) for the item in Problem 1.

7. Find the APR (to the nearest $\frac{1}{4}$ of 1%) for the item in Problem 2.

8. Find the APR (to the nearest $\frac{1}{4}$ of 1%) for the item in Problem 3.

9. Find the APR (to the nearest $\frac{1}{4}$ of 1%) for the item in Problem 4.

10. Find the APR (to the nearest $\frac{1}{4}$ of 1%) for the item in Problem 5.

1. $17.31   2. $302.93   3. $68.43

For Problems 11 through 15, refer to the ad below.

Reprinted, by permission, from *The Tampa Tribune,* February 15, 1974, p. 20E.

11.   Find the finance charge for the suggested credit purchase plan.

12.   Referring to Problem 11, find the finance charge per hundred.

13.   Referring to Problem 12, find the APR (to the nearest $\frac{1}{4}$ of 1%).

14.   By using interpolation, find the APR to the nearest hundredth of a per cent.

15.   Is the answer to Problem 14 consistent with the APR given in the ad?

For Problems 16 through 20, refer to the ad below.

Reprinted, by permission, from *The Tampa Tribune,* February 17, 1974, p. 31F.

16.   Find the finance charge for the suggested credit purchase plan.

17.   Referring to Problem 16, find the finance charge per hundred.

18.   Referring to Problem 17, find the APR (to the nearest $\frac{1}{4}$ of 1%).

19.   Using interpolation, find the APR to the nearest hundredth of a per cent.

20.   Is the answer to Problem 19 consistent with the APR quoted in the ad?

21.   A man wants to sell a car for $2,800. He asks for $300 down and $2,500 to be paid on the time plan. If he wishes to charge an APR of 12% and finance the car for 24 months, find the finance charge and the amount of the monthly payments.

22.   A dealer is selling a Pinto for $2,442, $442 down and the rest to be paid in 36 equal monthly payments. If the APR is 12%, find the finance charge and the amount of the monthly payments.

23.   Mickey's Auto Sales is selling a Mustang for $2,895, $295 down and the rest to be paid in 36 equal monthly payments. If the APR is 11%, find the finance charge and the amount of the monthly payments.

24.   A customer has the option of purchasing a car selling for $2,600, $200 down and the rest to be paid in 36 equal payments, with an APR of 11.25%, or another car selling for $2,900, $200 down and the rest to be paid in 30 equal monthly payments with an APR of 13%. If the customer wishes to select the car with the lowest monthly payment, regardless of APR, which car should she select?

25.   Referring to Problem 24, assume that the customer has the option of buying the $2,600 car mentioned or another car selling for $3,400, $500 down and the rest to be paid in 40 equal monthly payments with an APR of 11%. If the customer wishes to select the car with the lowest monthly payment, regardless of APR, which car should she select?

Courtesy of the Cameron Brown Company.

6.5   PERSONAL AND CREDIT UNION LOANS

As you can see from the ad above, loan companies also charge interest on loans. The repayment of these loans is usually accomplished by using a periodic payment plan which utilizes the ideas presented in the preceding section. In order to apply these ideas to more general loan transactions, one can think of a loan as buying money with no down payment. Thus, the amount borrowed can be regarded as the cash selling price and the sum of the repayments as the time selling price.

Let us assume that Mr. I. Spendmore decides to obtain a 2-year, $600 loan. Mr. Spendmore visits a financial service company on February 18, 1974, and notifies them of his intentions. The officer in charge interviews Mr. Spendmore and gives him the accompanying form.

From the form opposite you can see that Mr. Spendmore did not wish to have any insurance. (If he had obtained credit life insurance, for instance, the loan would have been paid off automatically in case of his death.) He immediately noticed that the loan was *not* for $600, but for $600.24. The officer explained that this was customarily done in order to have payments corresponding to whole amounts ($33 in this case). Since Mr. Spendmore was making 24 payments of $33 dollars each, his finance charge amounted to (24 × $33) − $600.24 = $792 − $600.24 = $191.76. From this, we can find the APR using the methods of the preceding section:

1. The finance charge per hundred is

$$\frac{191.76 \times 100}{600.24} = 31.95$$

2. We read across line 24 in the APR table until we find the value nearest the 31.95. This value is 32.04.

3. Since the value at the top of the column where the 32.04 appears is 28.25%, the APR is approximately this per cent. Note that the finance company used interpolation to obtain 28.18% as their APR.

The APR for the loan just discussed can also be approximated (however, not within the 1/4 of 1% accuracy required by Regulation Z) by using the following formula:

Approximating the APR

> **FORMULA 6.1** $\text{APR} = \dfrac{2 \times m \times I}{P \times (n + 1)}$
>
> m is the number of payment periods per year,
> I is the interest (or finance charge),
> P is the cash unpaid balance, and
> n is the number of periodic payments to be made.

Thus, using this formula, the approximate APR for the loan is

$$\frac{2 \times 12 \times 191.76}{600.24 \times (24 + 1)} = .3067 = 30.67\%$$

PROGRESS TEST 1

1. A man borrowed $2,000 for 60 months. If his monthly payments amounted to $41.52 each, then the corresponding APR, according to the table, is _____.
2. His APR, using Formula 6.1, is _____.

Credit unions

Another possible source from which one can obtain a loan is a credit union. To be eligible for membership in a credit union, one must share some common bond that defines the field of membership. To join, one makes a minimum payment, usually $5, and pays an entrance fee (typically, 25¢).

Let us assume that Mr. I. Spendless decides to compare loan options with Mr. I. Spendmore. To do this, he visits his credit union and informs them that he needs a 2-year, $600.24 loan. The loan officer has a table for 24-month transactions similar to the one given in Table 6–5.

From the table, one can see that there are no entries for $600.24 loans. However, the loan officer can determine the payments, finance charge, and interest by taking the average of the figures entered for $500 loans and those for $700 loans. For example, to obtain the payment for a $600.24 loan, the loan officer would add the payment for a $500 loan to that of a $700 loan and take the average obtaining $\frac{23.31 + 32.63}{2} = 27.97$.

A loan of $600 would be paid off by paying $27.97 for 24 months. Thus, the loan officer would add one cent to each payment (a total of 24 cents for 2 years) to repay a loan of $600.24. The calculations would look like this:

1. 9%   2. $\frac{2 \times 12 \times 491.20}{2,000 \times (60 + 1)} = .0966 = 9.66\%$

TABLE 6–5   **Monthly Payments and Finance Charges for 24-Month Loans***

AMOUNT OF LOAN	MONTHLY PAYMENTS	FINANCE CHARGE	TOTAL OF PAYMENTS
500	23.31	59.44	559.44
700	32.63	83.12	783.12
1,000	46.61	118.64	1,118.64
1,500	69.92	178.08	1,678.08
2,000	93.22	237.28	2,237.28
2,500	116.52	293.48	2,796.48
3,000	139.83	355.92	3,355.92
3,500	163.13	415.12	3,915.12

*From The Credit Union Courier. Published by Hillsborough County Teachers Credit Union, Tampa, Florida.

AMOUNT OF LOAN	MONTHLY PAYMENTS	FINANCE CHARGE	TOTAL OF PAYMENTS
$600.24	$27.98	$71.28	$671.52

The officer informed Mr. Spendless that insurance protection was included in the loan free of charge.

To finish the comparison of the two loans, we first compute the APR for Mr. Spendless's loan.

1. The finance charge per hundred is

$$\frac{71.28 \times 100}{600.24} = 11.88$$

2. We read across line 24 in the APR table until we find the value nearest to 11.88. This value is 11.86.

3. Since the value at the top of the column where the 11.86 appears is 11%, the APR is approximately 11%.

We compare the two loans in the table below:

	AMOUNT OF LOAN	MONTHLY PAYMENTS	FINANCE CHARGE	TOTAL OF PAYMENTS	APR
Finance Company	$600.24	$33.00	$191.76	$792.00	28.18%
Credit	$600.24	$27.98	$ 71.28	$671.52	11%

Note that, in addition, Mr. Spendless has credit life insurance included in the cost of the loan at no extra expense to him. This insurance on a $600 loan usually costs $59.40.

EXERCISE 6.5

In Problems 1 through 10, find (a) the total amount of all the payments; (b) the finance charge; (c) the approximate APR (from the tables).

	AMOUNT OF LOAN	MONTHLY PAYMENTS	NUMBER OF PAYMENTS
1.	$ 100	$ 8.84	12
2.	$1,000	$ 45.69	24
3.	$1,000	$ 32.27	36
4.	$2,000	$ 41.52	60
5.	$2,000	$ 94.15	24
6.	$4,000	$188.30	24

7.	$3,500	$ 72.66	60
8.	$5,000	$166.08	36
9.	$3,500	$114.59	36
10.	$5,000	$103.80	60

In Problems 11 through 16, fill in the blanks to obtain a cost comparison of 24-month loans from a finance company and a credit union.

	AMOUNT OF LOAN	MONTHLY PAYMENTS	FINANCE CHARGE	TOTAL OF PAYMENTS	APR	SOURCE
11.	$1,030.70	$ 55	(a)	(b)	(c)	Finance Company
12.	$1,030.70	$ 48.04	(a)	(b)	(c)	Credit Union
13.	$1,513.62	$ 70.55	(a)	(b)	(c)	Credit Union
14.	$1,513.62	$ 79	(a)	(b)	(c)	Finance Company
15.	$2,000.18	$103	(a)	(b)	(c)	Finance Company
16.	$2,000.18	$ 93.23	(a)	(b)	(c)	Credit Union

In Problem 17 through 20, find the approximate APR, using Formula 6.1.

	AMOUNT OF LOAN	MONTHLY PAYMENTS	NUMBER OF PAYMENTS
17.	$ 100	$ 8.84	12
18.	$1,000	$ 45.69	24
19.	$1,000	$ 32.27	36
20.	$2,000	$ 41.52	60

Reprinted, by permission, from *Changing Times,* the Kiplinger Magazine. Copyright September, 1973.

6.6 CREDIT CARDS AND REVOLVING CHARGE ACCOUNTS

One of the most popular periodic payment plans is used in connection with credit cards and revolving charge accounts. These accounts permit one to buy on credit and pay later, after receiving a monthly bill. If the bill is paid within a certain time (usually 25 days), there is no finance charge. However, if more time is desired, the rates below are usually applied:

UNPAID BALANCE	MONTHLY RATE	APR
$500 and under	$1\frac{1}{2}\%$	18% ($1\frac{1}{2}\% \times 12$ months)
Over $500	1%	12% ($1\% \times 12$ months)

A big attraction of these cards is that one does not have to repay all the money at once. The only requirement is that a minimum payment be made amounting to a fraction of the unpaid balance. For example, let us assume that a national credit card holder wishes to

use his credit card at a restaurant. Instead of paying cash, the cashier will place his card in a stamping machine which will print the card number, his name, the date, the expiration date of his card (all this information appears on his card), and the name of the restaurant on a receipt. The cashier will then write the amount of this purchase on the receipt and add the applicable tax. The customer then signs the receipt and keeps a copy for his own records (see Figure 6–1).

At the end of the month a statement is sent to the credit card holder. In Florida, if the balance is paid in full within 25 days, there is no finance charge. If the balance due is $10 or less, the account must be paid in full. Otherwise, it is only required that the card holder make a minimum payment of 5% of the balance due or ten dollars ($10), whichever is greater. These terms may vary from bank to bank.

Example 1

The customer signing the receipt in Figure 6–1 received a statement at the end of the month. The new balance was listed as $25.80. Find

a. the minimum payment that is due.

b. The finance charge that will be due next month if the minimum payment is made.

Solution:

a. Since the new balance is $25.80 and 5% of $25.80 is $1.29, the minimum payment is $10 (5% of the new balance or $10, whichever is greater).

b. Since the minimum payment is $10, the new balance will be $25.80 − $10.00 = $15.80. The finance charge is 1.5% per month; that is, 1.5% of $15.80 = 24¢. The balance for the next month will be $15.80 + $0.24 = $16.04.

c. In this case, the APR can be found by multiplying the monthly rate (1.5%) by 12, obtaining 18%.

Many large department stores prefer to handle their own credit business and therefore do not accept bank credit cards. There are two main advantages to following this procedure:

1. National credit cards charge the stores a 3% commission on the amount of the sale for their services.

2. The interest collected from the customers is a welcomed source of revenue to the department store.

Most charge accounts at department stores are called Revolving Charge Accounts. Even though the operational procedure of Revolving Charge Accounts is similar to that employed by national credit cards, there are several differences between them.

1. The interest for revolving charge accounts is $1\frac{1}{2}$% of the unpaid balance per month for balances under $500. If the balance is over $500, revolving charge accounts sometimes charge only 1% interest per month on the amount over $500.

2. The minimum monthly payment may be established by the department store, or may be similar to that of the national credit cards. Some stores require a minimum of $10 per month on balances up to $200, and 5% of the new balance on balances over $200.

Example 2

Ms. Lewis received her statement from the department store where she has a revolving charge account. Her previous balance was $225.59 and she charged an additional $18.72 to her account. Find (a) the finance charge for the month. (Sears charges interest on the average daily balance, see the form on page 312); (b) the new balance; (c) the minimum monthly payment.

Solution

a. Since the average daily balance amounted to $222.99, the finance charge is $1\frac{1}{2}$% (18% APR) of the $222.99.

$$1\frac{1}{2}\% = 0.015$$

$$0.015 \times \$222.99 = \$3.34$$

b. The new balance is calculated as follows:

Previous balance	$225.59
Finance charge	3.34
New purchases	18.72
New Balance	$247.65

Sears	REVOLVING CHARGE ACCOUNT

SEARS, ROEBUCK AND CO.

Please return this portion with your payment. You may pay at any Sears Store, or by mail. **Please allow 5 days to assure processing by the Billing Date.**

Please mention this number when ordering or writing.

Amount Due

97 11234 56789 7

MS MARY LEWIS
1234 MAIN ST
ANYWHERE IL 60606

INSTAL.PMT.   NONE DUE

NEW BALANCE

$_____
AMOUNT PAID

PLEASE DIRECT INQUIRIES TO YOUR NEAREST SEARS STORE AND REFER TO THIS STATEMENT WHEN MAKING AN INQUIRY.

DATE Mo. Day	Reference Number	TRANSACTION DESCRIPTION See reverse side for a more detailed description of the department numbers indicated below.	CHARGES	PAYMENTS AND CREDITS
		FINANCE CHARGE ON AVG DAILY BAL OF $222.99	3.34	
0608	TPBT	MENS WORK & SPORTSWEAR 41	18.72	

ACCOUNT NUMBER	BILLING DATE	PREVIOUS BALANCE	NEW BALANCE	MINIMUM PAYMENT
97 11234 56789 7	JULY 06 1975	$ 225.59	$	$

If the *FINANCE CHARGE* exceeds 50¢, the *ANNUAL PERCENTAGE RATE* is 18% of the AVERAGE DAILY BALANCE excluding any purchases added during the monthly billing period and excluding any unpaid Finance Charge.

To avoid a Finance Charge next month, pay this amount within 30 days from Billing Date.

If you prefer to pay in installments, pay this amount or more within 30 days from Billing Date. The sooner you pay and the more you pay, the smaller your Finance Charge.

NOTICE: See reverse side for important information.

14351-610 Rev. 7/74

Thank You for Shopping at Sears

Courtesy of Sears, Roebuck and Co.

c. The minimum monthly payment is found by using the table shown below, which appears on the reverse of the statement. Since the new balance is between $200.01 and $250, the minimum payment is $15.

On a Sears Revolving Charge Account your monthly payments decrease as your account balance decreases . . . and, likewise your monthly payments increase as your account balance increases. Payments are flexible with your balance, as shown on the table below.

New Balance	Minimum Payment
$ .01 to $ 10.00	Balance
10.01 to 200.00	$10.00
200.01 to 250.00	15.00
250.01 to 300.00	20.00
300.01 to 350.00	25.00
350.01 to 400.00	30.00
400.01 to 450.00	35.00
450.01 to 500.00	40.00
Over $500.00	1/10 of New Bal.

Courtesy of Sears, Roebuck and Co.

PROGRESS TEST 2

1. If in Example 2 the average daily balance amounted to $300, the finance charge would be _____ .
2. If in Example 2 the average daily balance amounted to $300, and new purchases of $20 and $55 were made, the new balance would be _____, and the minimum monthly payment would be _____.

EXERCISE 6.6

In problems 1 through 5, find the new balance, assuming that the bank charges $1\frac{1}{2}\%$ interest per month on the unpaid balance.

	PREVIOUS BALANCE	PAYMENT	NEW PURCHASES
1.	$100	$ 10	$ 50
2.	$300	$190	$ 25
3.	$134.39	$ 25	$ 73.98
4.	$145.96	$ 55	$ 44.97
5.	$378.93	$ 75	$248.99

In Problems 6 through 15, find (a) the finance charge for the month; (b) the new balance; (c) the minimum monthly payment. Use the following rates and payment tables.

MONTHLY RATE	UNPAID BALANCE	NEW BALANCE	MINIMUM PAYMENT
$1\frac{1}{2}\%$	Up to $500	Under $200	$10
1%	Over $500	Over $200	5% of new balance

	PREVIOUS BALANCE	NEW PURCHASES		PREVIOUS BALANCE	NEW PURCHASES
6.	$ 50.40	$173	8.	$154	$ 75
7.	$ 85	$150	9.	$344	$ 60

1. $4.50   2. $305.09; $25

10.	$666.80	$53.49	13.	$ 55.90	$35.99
11.	$ 80.45	$98.73	14.	$ 98.56	$45.01
12.	$ 34.97	$ 50	15.	$ 34.76	$87.53

16. Phyllis Phillips has a revolving charge account which charges a finance charge on the unpaid balance using the following schedule:

$1\frac{1}{2}\%$ per month on that portion of the balance up to $300

1% per month on that portion of the balance over $300
If the previous month's balance was $685, find (a) the finance charge; (b) the APR (use the formula $APR = \dfrac{I}{p \times t}$).

17. Daisy Rose has a credit card which charges a finance charge on the previous balance using the following schedule:

2% per month on balances up to $100

$1\frac{1}{2}\%$ per month on balances between $100 and $200

1% per month on balances of $200 or over
If the previous month's balance was $190, find (a) the finance charge; (b) the APR.

18. Mr. Dan Dapper received a statement from his clothing store indicating a finance charge of $1.50 on a previous balance of $100. Find (a) the monthly finance charge rate; (b) the APR.

19. Peter Peters received a statement from ABC Department Store indicating a previous balance of $90. If the ABC Store finance charges on the previous balance are equivalent to an 18% APR, find the finance charge for the month.

20. If in the problem above, the APR was equivalent to a 15% APR, find the finance charge for the month.

CREDIT COST TABLE

Here is a summary of the current costs of various types of credit generally available, together with our recommendations concerning each.

TYPE OF CREDIT	USUAL COST RATE PER ANNUM	RECOMMENDATION
College education loans	7%	OK for good students.
First mortgage home loans, open-end monthly payment plan	9¼ to 9½%	Good for most families with permanent, stable employment. Will clear the home from debt in 20 years or less, for rent money.
Unsecured home improvement loans from S. & L. assn's and banks	10 to 13%	Better than first mortgage refinancing for major improvements to homes with old, low-rate mortgage that will not secure advances. Otherwise not recommended except in cases of extreme need.
Credit union loans	9 to 12%	Cheapest and most satisfactory form of small credit and auto financing.
Revolving-credit plans of retail stores, including bank charge-card plans	18%	OK, if you *must*. But use it sparingly.
30-day retail credit, any plan, including charge-cards	None if paid in 30 days	OK for convenience, if the price of the goods is right and you *know* you can pay the bill when it comes. But check prices against cash stores.
Automobile loans	9% and UP!	Beware the high cost of required insurance. Better drive old car till you save enough money to trade up with cash.
Appliance loans	18% up	Cash will usually buy it for 20 to 30% less. Save and shop!
Personal loans—confidential— no questions asked	30% up	Not recommended.
Loans from friends, relatives or employers	?	Not for self-respecting people.
Loan sharks, unlicensed	The sky's the limit	No!!!

6.7 HOW TO SELECT YOUR CREDIT PLAN

The table above is a summary of the costs of various credit plans and recommendations concerning each. In any case, if one needs to borrow money, his selection of a credit plan should include a comparison of the following items:

1. the APR
2. the amount of the monthly payment
3. penalty clauses for early payment

In the case of credit cards, there is no penalty for early payment. Thus, if the full amount is paid within 25 days, no finance charge is assessed.

The accompanying chart compares five of the major credit cards and can be used to decide which one to select.

The five major credit cards

	MASTER CHARGE	BANKAMERICARD	DINERS CLUB	AMERICAN EXPRESS	CARTE BLANCHE
issued by	5,800 U.S. banks with 15,000 U.S. offices	4,500 U.S. banks with 12,000 U.S. offices	Diners Club Ten Columbus Circle New York, N.Y. 10019	American Express 770 Broadway New York, N.Y. 10006	Carte Blanche 3460 Wilshire Blvd. Los Angeles, Cal. 90054
approximate number of retail outlets	1,018,200 U.S.; 300,000 foreign	913,400 U.S.; 371,600 foreign	200,000 U.S.; 150,000 foreign	300,000 U.S. and foreign	250,000 U.S.; 50,000 foreign
annual fee	none	one bank charges $10 for each card; others have no charge	$15 for first ; $7.50 for additional cards	$15 for first; $10 for each additional card	$15 for first card; for additional card $10 if family, $7 if business
typical credit limit	ranges from $400 to $700	ranges from $450 to $650	no predetermined limit	no predetermined limit	no predetermined limit
extended payment on purchases	yes, for all goods and services	yes, for all goods and services	airline tickets only	airline tickets; package tours; certain items sold through direct mail	airline tickets and certain items sold through direct mail
interest rate on extended-payment purchases	typically 1% to 1½% a month (12%-18% APR)	typically 1% to 1½% a month (12%-18% APR)	1% a month (12% APR); you elect payment schedule at time of purchase—3, 6, 9, 12 months	1% month (12% APR); you elect payment schedule at time of purchase—3, 6, 9, 12 months	1½% a month (18% APR); you elect payment schedule at time of purchase—3, 6, 9, 12 months
cash advance	at all U.S. participating banks and their offices and most offices overseas	at most participating banks in U.S. and overseas—27,600 offices total	no	only with special Executive Card, available from about 560 banks; can use regular card with personal check to get $50 cash and $250 in traveler's checks in U.S., $50 and $450 in traveler's checks overseas	maximum $500 cash loan available at 1,400 Avco Financial Services offices in U.S. and Canada
interest rate on cash advance	typically at daily rate equal to 1% a month (12% APR); some banks assess a flat charge at time of advance	typically at daily rate equal to 1% a month (12% APR); some banks assess a flat charge at time of advance	doesn't apply	set by bank	subject to state loan statutes
minimum income required to get card	decided bank by bank	decided bank by bank	$10,000	$8,500	$10,000

Reprinted, by permission, from *Changing Times*, the Kiplinger Magazine, Copyright September, 1973.

Referring to item 3 above, Regulation Z requires creditors to disclose the method of determining the amount of finance charges and the method used in refunding finance charges which have been unearned because of early payoff. The most common method used to calculate these refunds is the "Rule of 78". The principle behind this method lies in the fact that the unearned finance charge is the same proportion of the total finance charge as the sum of the number of the remaining payments is to the sum of the number of total payments. We illustrate the use of this rule in the following example.

Example 1

A 12-month loan yielding a finance charge of $234 is paid in full with four payments remaining. Find the unearned portion of the finance charge by using the Rule of 78.

Solution

The sum of the number of the remaining payments is $4 + 3 + 2 + 1$ $= \dfrac{4 \times (4 + 1)}{2} = 10$. (Recall from Chapter 4, Section 4.4, that the sum of the first n consecutive integers is $\dfrac{n \times (n + 1)}{2}$.) The sum of the number of total payments is $1 + 2 + 3 + 4 + 5 + 6 + 7 + 8 + 9 + 10 + 11 + 12$ $= \dfrac{12 \times (12 + 1)}{2} = 78$. Thus, the unearned portion of the finance charge is $\dfrac{10}{78} \times \$234 = \$30$. Note that for any loan to be paid off in 12 monthly payments, the sum of the number of payments is 78. Thus, if the loan is to be paid off when five payments are left, the unearned part of the finance charge will be $\dfrac{15}{78}$ of the finance charge; if six payments are left, the unearned part of the finance charge will be $\dfrac{21}{78}$ of the finance charge; etc.

Example 2

B. Saunders is repaying a loan in 12 equal monthly payments of $20. With five payments remaining, he decides to pay the loan in full. How much is needed to pay the loan if the total finance charge amounted to $50.

Solution

The sum of the number of the remaining payments is $5 + 4 + 3 + 2 + 1$ $= \dfrac{5 \times (5 + 1)}{2} = 15$. The sum of the number of total payments is 78.

Thus, the unearned portion of the finance charge is $\dfrac{15}{78} \times 50 = \$9.62$.

Amount left to pay: 5 × $20	$100.00
Unearned finance charge	9.62
Balance	$ 90.38

PROGRESS TEST 1

1. Ms. Rose Wood is repaying a loan in 18 monthly payments of $30. With nine payments remaining, she decides to pay the loan in full. If the total finance charge amounted to $85.50, the unearned finance charge is _____ .

2. The amount needed to pay the loan off is _____ .

EXERCISE 6.7

In Problems 1 through 5, find (a) the unearned finance charge; (b) the amount needed to pay off the loan.

	FINANCE CHARGE	NUMBER OF PAYMENTS	FRE-QUENCY	AMOUNT	NUMBER OF PAYMENTS REMAINING
1.	$15.60	12	Monthly	$25	4
2.	$23.40	12	Monthly	$35	5
3.	$31.20	12	Monthly	$45	6
4.	$52.00	18	Weekly	$10	9
5.	$58.50	20	Weekly	$10	5

---

1. The sum of the number of remaining payments is $\dfrac{9 \times (9+1)}{2} = 45$, and the sum of the number of total payments is $\dfrac{18 \times (18+1)}{2} = 171$. The unearned finance charge is $\dfrac{45}{171} \times \$85.50 = \$22.50$.   2. $270.00 - $22.50 = $247.50.

SELF-TEST/CHAPTER 6

1. A man borrows $2,000 at 6% interest compounded quarterly for a period of five years.
   - ———— a. Find the interest paid.
   - ———— b. Find the amount the man paid the bank at the end of the five years.

2. A man can invest his money in a bank paying $8\frac{1}{4}$% interest compounded annually or in a second bank which pays 8% compounded quarterly.
   - ———— a. Find the effective annual yield of the 8% compounded quarterly.
   - ———— b. Which of the two banks offers a better return on his money?

3. A man wishes to have $2,000 in the bank five years from now. If his bank pays 8% interest compounded semiannually, find
   - ———— a. the present value of the $2,000 in five years at 8% compounded semiannually.
   - ———— b. the amount of money the man has to deposit in the bank in order to have the $2,000 in five years.

4. A car sells for $3,500 cash. An available credit purchase plan requires a down payment of $500, and 36 monthly payments of $100. Find
   - ———— a. the total amount paid after giving the $500 down.
   - ———— b. the finance charge.

5. ———— Find the APR $\left(\text{to the nearest } \frac{1}{4} \text{ of } 1\%\right)$ for the car of Problem 4.

6. A man wishes to sell a car for $3,500 with $500 down and the rest to be paid in 36 equal monthly payments. If he wishes to have an APR of 12%, find
   - ———— a. the total finance charge.
   - ———— b. the amount of the monthly payments.

7. A man can obtain a $1,030.70 loan from a finance company or from a credit union. The finance company charges him $55 a month for 24 months, while the credit union requires $48.04 a month for the same period. Find
   - ———— a. The finance charge on the finance company loan.
   - ———— b. the finance charge on the credit union loan.
   - ———— c. the savings if the man obtains the credit union loan.

8.   A national credit card charges $1\frac{1}{2}\%$ interest per month on the unpaid balance. If the previous balance amounted to $300, the person made payments totaling $50, and added new purchases of $100, find

_____ a.   the finance charge.

_____ b.   the new balance.

9.   A 12-month loan yielding a finance charge of $156 is paid in full with five payments remaining. If the payments amount to $30 per month, find

_____ a.   the unearned portion of the finance charge.

_____ b.   the amount needed to pay off the loan.

10.   A man can buy some land for $8,200 cash or for $4,000 down and $5,000 in five years. If the man can earn 4% interest compounded semiannually, find

_____ a.   the present value of the time deal.

_____ b.   the amount of money the man can save by buying the land on the time plan.

part four

The Mathematics
of Investments

seven

Stocks and Bonds

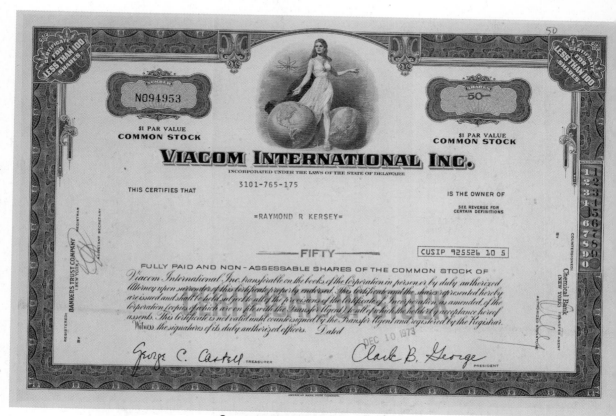

Courtesy of Viacom International Inc.

7.1 STOCK PRICES AND QUOTATIONS

If you have some surplus money, that is, more money than is needed to cover your expenses, there are two things that you can do with it: (1) you can buy something with it, or (2) you can lend it. In either case, you can become one of the millions of Americans that have put aside extra cash to become investors. There are several ways in which you can go about investing your money: you can put your money in a savings account and earn interest on the principal, you can buy life insurance and collect some money from your policy upon retirement, you can invest in real estate (land, houses, etc.), or you can buy stocks and bonds.

When you buy a **stock** you receive a certificate, called a **share**,

The par value of a stock is the value assigned to the stock when it is issued.

similar to the one shown at the beginning of this section. If you own a share of stock in a company, you own part of that company. The price of the share (**par value**) is set by the company when the stock is first sold, but once the original stock has been sold to the public, its price is determined by what the buyer is willing to pay and the seller is willing to accept. This value is called the **market value** and is published daily on the financial pages of most metropolitan newspapers. Here are some of the stock quotations taken from the *Wall Street Journal*.

As you can see from Table 7–1, the records for the first company listed appear like this:

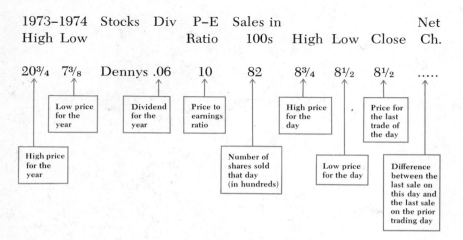

TABLE 7–1

New York Stock Exchange Transactions

Wednesday, January 2, 1974

–1973-74– High	Low	Stocks	Div	P-E Ratio	Sales in 100s	High	Low	Close	Net Chg.	–1973-74– High	Low	Stocks	Div	P-E Ratio	Sales in 100s	High	Low	Close	Net Chg.
20¼	7⅜	Dennys	.06	10	82	8¾	8½	8½	.....	19⅜	8½	GtWnUnt pf		...	9	11⅝	11¼	11½+	⅝
27¾	16¼	Dentsply	.76	15	24	22⅜	22	22⅛–	⅛	4⅞	1½	GrtWsh Inv		...	1	1⅝	1⅝	1⅝	.....
16¼	8	DeSotoIn	.60	5	48	9¾	9⅜	9⅝–	⅛	26⅞	17¼	GrenGiant	1	8	4	20⅛	19⅞	19⅞	.....
21¼	15⅞	DetEdis	1.45	9	69	16⅞	16⅜	16⅞+	½	18⅞	13¼	Greyhd	1.04	8	140	14½	14	14½+	½
120	106½	Det E pf9.32		...	220	108	108	108	.....	5	2½	Greyhnd wt		...	58	2⅞	2¾	2⅞+	¼
102½	87	Det E pf7.45		...	z50	87	87	87	– 1	15⅞	4¾	Grolier	.50	4	41	6⅛	5⅞	5⅞+	⅛
83	62¼	Det E pf5.50		...	1	64¼	64¼	64¼+	¼	12¼	8	Grumm	.15e		15	8⅝	8¼	8⅜	.....
24⅜	15⅜	Dial Finl	.54	13	42	22¾	22⅜	22⅜–	⅛	35⅜	12¼	Guardian In		9	1	14½	14¼	14½+	¼
36½	23⅝	Diamint	2	8	32	28¾	28⅜	28¾+	⅝	46⅞	22	GuarM 4.17e		5	41	26⅝	25⅛	26⅜+	1⅝
28⅞	16⅞	DiamSh	1.10	10	50	26¾	25¾	26	– ½	57⅛	25⅛	GlfLfH .10h		6	68	32⅛	30½	32⅛+	2⅛
18⅛	14½	Dia pf D1.20		..	9	15½	15¼	15½	....	10⅛	9⅜	GlfLfHld wi			20	10¾	10¼	10¾+	⅝
24¾	11	DickAB	.44	9	25	15⅞	14⅜	15⅞+	1⅛	28⅞	20	GulfOil 1.50		7	1221	24½	23⅝	24½+	⅞
14¾	7⅝	Dictaph	.48a	7	9	9¼	8¾	9	– ¼	12½	6½	Gulf Resrce		11	728	13⅜	12	13¼+	1⅜
57½	35¼	Diebold	.40b	15	170	34¾	33⅞	34¼–	1¼	17	9	GfR pfA.10k		...	16	18¼	17	18⅛+	1⅜
13⅜	7	DiGiorg	.66	5	25	7½	7¼	7⅜	.....	17½	12¾	GfR pfB.65k		...	47	19	17¾	18⅜+	⅞
119¼	73¼	Digital Eqpt		40	121	101½	96½	97¾–	4⅛	22⅜	13	GifStUt 1.12		8	244	14¾	14⅛	14¾+	⅜
10¾	5⅛	Dillingm	.40	7	28	5⅝	5⅜	5⅝+	½	35¾	21⅜	GulfWn	.72	4	42	24	23¾	23⅞+	⅛
39⅜	25¼	DillonCo	1b	13	4	28	27¾	28	.....	11¼	3¼	GlfWInd wt			62	6	5¾	5⅞+	⅛
123⅞	40½	Disney	.12b	27	324	47⅜	45	45⅝–	1⅝	146	88½	GlfW pf 3.50		...	1	99⅛	99⅛	99⅛	–⅞
22¾	10¼	Disston	.12	7	13	12½	12	12¼+	¼	67½	47½	GlfW pf 3.87		...	2	48	48	48	.....
49¼	37¼	DistSeag	.80	19	13	43	42½	42½+	⅜	77½	69½	GlfW pf5.75		...	1	70¾	70¾	70¾+	½
3⅜	1⅛	Diversfd In		15	117	2	1⅞	1⅞	.....	9	3	Gulton Ind		6	22	3⅜	3¼	3¼	.....
29⅜	13¼	DivMt	2.86e	5	252	15¾	15⅛	15¾+	½	38½	32	HckWat 2.36		7	2	32¾	32¾	32¾+	¼
30	18¾	DrPeppr	.24	45	48	22¼	21⅞	22¼+	¼	13¾	12⅛	HallFB	.36	12	13	12½	12¼	12½+	⅛

Reprinted, by permission, from *The Wall Street Journal*, January 3, 1974.

The prices are quoted in **points,** where

1/8 point = $1/8 = $.125	1/2 point =$1/2 = $.50
1/4 point = $1/4 = $.25	5/8 point = $5/8 = $.625
3/8 point = $3/8 = $.375	7/8 point = $7/8 = $.875

You can see that Dennys is currently paying dividends at the rate of $.06 per year for each share of stock owned. Thus, if you owned 50 shares of Dennys stock, the dividend would be $50 \times \$.06 = \$3.00$ per year. Note that the column labeled "Sales in 100s" shows the number of shares traded (bought and sold) that day. On the New York Stock Exchange, shares are usually traded in groups of 100 shares, called **round lots.** Thus, you can see that 82 round lot ($82 \times 100 = 8,200$) shares of Dennys stock were traded.

100 shares of stock is called a round lot.

Example 1

Referring to Table 7–1, find
   a. the total dividend paid last year to an investor owning five round lots of Desoto In. stock.
   b. the price of two round lots of Dial Fin. I. purchased at the closing price.
   c. the price of ten round lots of Dictaph purchased at the low price for the day.

Solution

   a. The dividend per share of DeSoto In. is $.60; thus the total dividend is $(5 \times 100) \times \$.60 = \$300$.

   b. The closing price of one share of Dial Fin. I. is $\$22\frac{3}{8} = \$22.375$. Thus, two round lots would be $(2 \times 100) \times 22.375 = \$4,475$,

Note: Buyers and sellers must pay a *commission* *stockbroker* for handling orders. Commission fees will be discussed in Section 7.2.

   c. The low price of a share of Dictaph. is $\$8\frac{3}{4} = \$8.75$. Thus, the low price of ten round lots would be $(10 \times 100) \times \$8.75 = \$8,750$.

PROGRESS TEST 1

   1. The total dividend paid to an investor owning six round lots of DetEdis last year was _____.
   2. The price of two round lots of DiamInt purchased at the high price for the day would be _____.
   3. The price of three round lots of Diebold purchased at the closing price would be _____.

---

   1. $(6 \times 100) \times \$1.45 = \$870$ 2. $(2 \times 100) \times \$28.75 = \$5,750$ 3. $(3 \times 100) \times \$34.25 = \$10,275$

GtWnUnt is the
abbreviation for
Great Western United.

Let us now look at the first entry in the right hand column of Table 7–1. The name of the stock (GtWnUnt) is followed by the abbreviation "pf". This means that GtWnUnt is a **preferred** stock. Basically, there are two kinds of stocks: **common** and **preferred.** Preferred stocks are usually issued with a par value of $100, but in recent times preferred stocks with a par value of $50 or $25 have become increasingly popular. Generally, the dividend on a preferred stock is fixed when the stock is issued. For example, a share of 7%, $100 par value preferred stock would pay a $7 dividend each year. The name preferred is used for two reasons: (1) no dividends can be paid to common stock holders until the preferred stock holders have been paid. (2) If the company goes bankrupt, the net assets are divided among the preferred stockholders before the common stockholders get anything.

Example 2

Typical Manufacturing has issued 1,000 shares of $100 par value common stock and 100 shares of 7%, $100 par value preferred stock. The company declared a $5,000 dividend for the year. What dividend will be paid on each class of stock?

Solution

The dividend on the preferred stock (which is computed first) is 7% of $100 = $7. The amount required to pay the 100 preferred stockholders is $100 \times \$7 = \$700$.

Total Dividend	$5,000
Dividend on the Preferred Stock	−700
Dividend for the Common stockholders	$4,300

$$\frac{\text{Total common Stock Dividend}}{\text{Number of Common Shares}} = \frac{\$4,300}{1,000} = \$4.30$$

The dividend per share of common stock is $4.30.

PROGRESS TEST 2

1. If in Example 2, the total dividend for the company was $10,000, the dividend per share of preferred stock would be _____.

2. The dividend per share of common stock would be _____.

---

1. $7   2. $9.30

In many cases, the board of directors may not think it advisable to declare a dividend even though a net profit exists. Thus, the owners may not receive a dividend during some years. To deal with this eventuality some companies issue **cumulative preferred stock** which, as the name implies, accumulates dividends from year to year. We now illustrate how these dividends are paid.

Cumulative preferred stocks accumulate unpaid dividends.

Example 3

Major Motors has issued 2,000 of $50 par value common stock and 500 shares of 6%, $50 par value cumulative preferred stock. If the company declared no dividend during last year, but approved a $5,000 dividend this year, what will be the dividend for each category of stock?

Solution

Since no dividends were paid last year to the stockholders, dividends for two years are now due on the cumulative preferred stock.

6% of $50 = $3.00 Yearly dividend for each cumulative preferred stock

$$\frac{\times 2 \text{ years}}{\$6.00}$$ Dividend per share on each cumulative preferred stock

500 × $6 = $3,000 Total payable to preferred stockholders

Total dividend	$5,000
Dividend on Preferred stock	−3,000
Dividend on common stock	$2,000
Dividend per share of common stock	$\frac{\$2,000}{2,000} = \$1$

PROGRESS TEST 3

1. If in Example 2, the dividends amounted to $10,000, the dividends on each preferred stock would be _____.
2. The dividend on each common stock would be _____.

1. $6.00   2. $3.50

EXERCISE 7.1

In Problems 1 through 5, find the total dividends. (Refer to Table 7–1.)

	STOCKS	NUMBER OF SHARES
1.	GrenGiant	100
2.	Greyhd	140
3.	GuarM	170
4.	GulfOil	200
5.	HallFb	240

In Problems 6 through 10, find the total price for the amount of stock shown at the indicated price.

	STOCK	ROUND LOTS	PRICE QUOTED
6.	GtWnUnt pf	3	Low
7.	GrenGiant	5	High
8.	Greyhd	6	Close
9.	Guardian In	7	Low
10.	Grolier	8	High

In Problems 11 through 15, find the dividend that should be paid on each share.

	NUMBER OF SHARES	TYPE OF STOCK	DIVIDEND DECLARED
11.	10,000	Common	$ 75,250
12.	30,000	Common	$105,000
	10,000	6%, $100 par value pf	
13.	40,000	Common	$ 30,000
	2,000	5%, $50 par value pf	
14.	20,000	Common	$120,000
	4,000	7%, $25 par value pf	
15.	50,000	Common	$100,000
	5,000	6%, $100 par value pf	

16. The Board of Directors of Sunshine Enterprises declared a $155,000 dividend. The company has issued 30,000 shares of common stock. What will be the dividend on each share?

17. The Board of Directors of Kata-Cola, Inc. declared a $95,000 dividend. If the company has issued 10,000 shares of 6% $100 par value preferred stock and 20,000 shares of common stock, what is the amount to be paid on each share?

18. Iota Motors declared no dividend during the past year. This year a dividend of $88,000 was approved by the board. The company has issued 30,000 shares of common stock and 2,000 shares of 7%, $50 par value cumulative preferred stock. Compute the earning for each share of stock.

19. The board of Round Tire Enterprises has not declared a dividend during the past two years. This year, however, a $300,000 dividend has been approved. If 50,000 shares of common stock, and 5,000 shares of 6%, $50 par value cumulative preferred stock have been issued, what dividend per share will be paid?

20. A supply shortage resulted in no dividends being declared in the last two years of operation of Noah's Boat Mart. This year, however, a $50,000 dividend has been approved. What dividend per share will be paid on each category of stock if 10,000 shares of common stock and 1,000 shares of 5%, $50 cumulative preferred stock have been issued?

Reprinted by permission of *The Chicago Tribune*. Copyright 1974. World Rights Reserved.

7.2 BUYING AND SELLING STOCK

The purchase and sale of stocks are usually made in organized stock exchanges and "over-the-counter" markets. The largest organized exchange is the New York Stock Exchange, which in the last

TABLE 7-2   Commission Rates of New York and American Stock Exchange Members*

SINGLE ROUND LOT ORDERS		MULTIPLE ROUND LOT ORDERS	
Money Value	Commission	Money Value	Commission
$100 but under $800 $800 but under $2,500 $2,500 add above	2.0% plus $6.40 1.3% plus $12.00 0.9% plus $22.00	$100 but under $2,500 $2,500 but under $20,000 $20,000 but under $30,000 $30,000 to $300,000	1.3% plus $12.00 0.9% plus $22.00 0.6 plus $82.00 0.4% plus $142.00
		PLUS: First to tenth round lot Eleventh round lot and over	 $6 per round lot $4 per round lot
Plus 10% of the commission on orders not exceeding $5,000 and 15% on orders involving amounts exceeding $5,000.			

*From *Standard and Poor's Stock Guide* (New York: Standard and Poor's Corporation, Publisher, 1974), p. 254.

quarter of 1968 handled an average of 15 million shares (purchases and sales) daily. When an individual stockholder wishes to sell his shares, he usually does not know who wants to buy. The stock exchange serve as a marketplace where people buy or sell stock. (It should be pointed out that the exchange does not own, sell, or buy any of the stocks.) **Stockbrokers** are agents helping buyers and sellers of securities (stocks and bonds). These agents charge a commission for performing their services. The commission on stocks selling at $1 per share and above is computed on the basis of the amount of money involved in an order. Table 7–2 shows the commission rates charged by member firms of the New York Stock Exchange. The amounts shown on the left represent the commission charged for a round lot of 100 shares. For transactions involving more than one round lot, the right hand side of the table is used. This commission schedule was made effective on September 25, 1973.*

Definition of
stockbroker

Example 1

The largest "share wise" transaction on record was made on March 14, 1972, for 5,245,000 shares of American Motors stock at $7\frac{1}{4}$ each. If a man bought 500 of these shares at $7\frac{1}{2}$, what commission did he pay?

Solution

The money value of the transaction is $500 \times \$7.50 = \$3,750$. Since the

*As of April 1974, the Securities and Exchange Commission has allowed brokers to charge flexible commissions on trades of $2,000 or less. Check your local broker for his fee schedule.

money value is more than $2,500 but under $20,000, the commission is:

The commission is found on the right hand side of Table 7–2.

0.9% of 3,750	$33.75
plus $22	22.00
plus $6 per round lot	30.00
	$85.75
plus 10% commission	8.58
Total Commission	$94.33

Definition of odd lot.

As you recall from the preceding section, a round lot consists of 100 shares. An **odd lot** is any number of shares less than 100. If a buyer wishes to obtain less than 100 shares, he may do so through an "odd lot broker". An odd lot broker buys shares in round lots and breaks them up into odd lots to be sold to small investors. The charge for this service is $\frac{1}{4}$ of a point per share if the price per share is $55 or more, or $\frac{1}{8}$ of a point if the price per share is less than $55. The commission on such transactions is $2 less than the amount charged using the rate for a single round lot order.

Example 2

Find the commission on the purchase of 250 shares of Harris International at $49\frac{7}{8}$.

Solution

Recall that the commission on odd lots is $2 less than the amount charged using the rate for a single round lot order.

The total commission is the sum of the commission for two round lots plus the commission for the odd lot excess. The price of 200 shares of Harris International is $200 \times 49\frac{7}{8} = \$9,975$. The commission on this amount is:

0.9% of 9,975 + $22	$111.78
plus $6 per round lot	12.00
	$123.78
plus 15% of the comm.	18.57
Commission on the 200	$142.35

The price per share is $49\frac{7}{8}$, which is less than $55. Thus, the odd lot broker charges 1/8 point per share. The odd lot price per share is

$49\frac{7}{8}+\frac{1}{8}=\$50.$ The price of 50 shares is $50\times\$50=\$2,500.$ The commission on the 50 shares is:

0.9% of $2,500 + $22	$44.50
less $2	2.00
	$42.50
plus 10% of the comm.	4.25
Odd Lot Commission	$46.75

The total commission is $142.35 + $46.75 = $189.10.

When stock is sold in odd lots, the seller must also pay an odd lot fee. This fee is identical to the one charged for buying stocks in odd lots and is deducted from the proceeds of the sale.

Example 3

Find the commission and the proceeds (selling price − commission) for selling an odd lot of 20 shares of Disney stock selling at $100\frac{1}{4}$.

Solution

The price per share is $100\frac{1}{4}$, which is more than $55. Thus, the odd lot fee is $\frac{1}{4}$ point per share. The odd lot proceeds per share are $100\frac{1}{4}-\frac{1}{4}$ = $100. The proceeds from 20 shares is $2,000. The commission on $2,000 is:

1.3% of 2,000 + $12.00	$38.00
less $2	2.00
	$36.00
plus 10% of the comm.	3.60
	$39.60

The proceeds are $2,000 − $39.60 = $1960.40.

PROGRESS TEST 1

1. The commission on the purchase of 50 shares of Heinz at $39\frac{7}{8}$ is _____.

2. The commission on the sale of 50 shares of Digital Equipment at $20\frac{1}{8}$ is _____.

---

1. The price per share is $40; thus, the commission is $39.60.   2. The proceeds per share is $20; thus, the commission is $25.30.

Taxes on sales of stocks

In addition to paying a commission on every transaction, a person must pay certain taxes and fees when selling stock. These taxes are:

1. The Federal Securities and Exchange Commission Tax. A fee of 1¢ on every $500 or fraction thereof of the money involved.

2. The New York State Tax (Transfer Tax).

NEW YORK STATE

A tax imposed by the state when a security is sold or transferred from one person to another. The tax is paid by the seller. Sales by out-of-state residents not employed in New York are taxed at reduced rates as indicated in second table below.

Shares selling at	TAX Per Sh.	SALES BY NON RESIDENTS TAX Per Sh.
Less than $5	1¼ ¢	0.625
$5 but less than $10	2½ ¢	1.25
$10 but less than $20	3¾ ¢	1.875
$20 or more	5¢	2.5

MAXIMUM tax on a 'single Taxable sale' is $350.

The rate on transfers not involving a sale is 2½ ¢ a share.

New York State does not impose a transfer tax on sales or transfers of rights to subscribe or warrants.

From *Standard and Poor's Stock Guide* (New York: Standard and Poor's Corporation, Publisher, 1974), p. 255.

---

3. State taxes. South Carolina, Florida, Texas, and some other states levy taxes against all stock sales made on registered exchanges in those states.

Example 4

Find (a) the SEC Tax, and (b) the New York State Non-Resident Tax on sales of a $3 stock totaling $201, $501, and $2,532 (excluding commission and taxes).

Solution

a. The SEC Tax on $201 is $0.01 × 1 = 1¢
   The SEC Tax on $501 is $0.01 × 2 = 2¢
   The SEC Tax on $2,532 is $0.01 × 6 = 6¢

b. The number of shares involved in each of the three transactions is:

$$\frac{201}{3} = 67, \frac{501}{3} = 167 \text{ and } \frac{2,532}{3} = 844$$

The New York State Non-Resident Tax on 67 shares costing less than $5 per share is $67 \times 0.625¢ = 42¢$.

The New York State Non-Resident Tax on 167 shares costing less than $5 per share is $167 \times 0.625¢ = \$1.04$.

The New York State Non-Resident Tax on 844 shares costing less than $5 per share is $844 \times 0.625¢ = \$5.28$.

PROGRESS TEST 2

1. The SEC Tax on sales totaling $804 is _____.
2. 500 shares of stock valued at $25 each are sold in the New York Stock Exchange. The New York State Resident Tax on this transaction is _____.
3. The New York State Non-Resident Tax on this transaction is _____.

EXERCISE 7.2

In Problems 1 through 5, find the commission on the following transactions.

	SHARES	STOCK	PRICE	TRANSACTION
1.	200	Ralston Purina	$40\frac{3}{4}$	Sale
2.	300	Disney World	$100\frac{1}{2}$	Purchase
3.	250	Standard Oil (O)	$150\frac{1}{4}$	Sale
4.	150	Uniroyal	$8\frac{7}{8}$	Purchase
5.	50	Xerox	$125\frac{1}{4}$	Sale

In Problems 6 through 10, find the commission and the proceeds (selling price − commission) for the following sales.

	SHARES	STOCK	PRICE
6.	175	American Air.	$10\frac{1}{8}$
7.	230	American Motors	$9\frac{1}{8}$
8.	310	Quaker State Oil	$25\frac{1}{2}$
9.	205	CBS	$27\frac{1}{4}$
10.	350	Delta Airline	$35\frac{5}{8}$

In Problems 10 through 15, find (a) the SEC Tax; (b) the New York Non-Resident Tax.

	SHARES	STOCK	PRICE	TRANSACTION
11.	200	Disney World	100	Sale

1. $0.01 × 2 = 2¢   2. 500 × 5¢ = $25   3. 500 × 2.5¢ = $12.50

12.	150	American Air.	$10\frac{1}{8}$	Sale
13.	350	CBS	25	Sale
14.	100	Delta Airlines	$35\frac{1}{4}$	Sale
15.	275	Uniroyal	8	Sale

In Problems 16 through 20, find the proceeds (selling price − commission − taxes) for the transactions in Problems 6 through 10. Assume that the seller is not a New York resident.

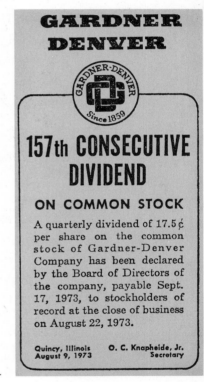

Courtesy of the Gardner-Denver Company.

7.3 RETURN ON STOCK INVESTMENT

As we previously mentioned, when you buy stock in a company you are part owner of that company. As such, you have the right to share any earnings the company may have. Most companies distribute from 40% to 70% of their earnings each year as **dividends.** The rest of the earnings are used for research, development, and working capital.

As you can see from the ad at the beginning of this section, Gardner-Denver is paying a quarterly dividend of 17.5¢ per share. The annual dividend is the return on the investment. If the dividend paid each quarter is 17.5¢, the annual dividend will be 4 × 17.5¢ = 70¢.

The ratio of the annual dividend to the price per share of stock is called the **annual yield.** The annual yield can be computed by using the following formula:

Definitions of
annual yield

FORMULA 7.1   Annual Yield $= \dfrac{\text{Annual Dividend}}{\text{Cost of the Stock}}$

Thus, if one share of Gardner-Denver costs $17\frac{1}{2}$, the rate of yield is

$$\frac{70¢}{\$17.50} = \frac{70}{1{,}750} = 4\%$$

Example 1

Find the rate of annual yield on Quaker State Oil common stock if the annual dividend is 50¢ and the price paid per share is $25.

Solution

By Formula 7.1, the annual yield is

$$\frac{50¢}{\$25} = \frac{50}{2500} = 2\%$$

Example 2

Find the rate of annual yield on RCA common stock if the dividend for each quarter is 87.5¢ and the cost per share was $50.

Solution

The annual dividend is $4 \times 87.5 = \$3.50$. By Formula 7.1, the annual yield is

$$\frac{\$3.50}{\$50} = \frac{350}{5{,}000} = 7\%$$

PROGRESS TEST 1

1. The rate of annual yield of a stock which sold for $23 per share and pays an annual dividend of 80.5¢ is _____.
2. The rate of annual yield of a stock selling for $46 per share and paying a quarterly dividend of 23¢ is _____.

---

1. 3.5%   2. 2%

In many cases investors make decisions regarding their stock (to sell or to buy more) on the basis of the estimated **total gain** obtained during a particular period of time. The total gain of a stock is the sum of the total dividends obtained during the time the stock was held and the capital gain (net proceeds − total cost). That is,

Definition of
total gain

$$\text{Total Gain} = \text{Dividends} + \text{Capital Gain}$$

We can also find the per cent of total gain relative to cost by using the following formula.

FORMULA 7.2   Per Cent of Total Gain $= \dfrac{\text{Total Gain}}{\text{Cost}} \times 100$

Definition of per cent
of total gain relative to cost

Example 3

J. Britton bought a block of common stock at $28 a share. His quarterly dividend amounted to 50¢ a share. After holding the stock for a period of $3\frac{1}{2}$ years, he sold all of it at $42 per share. If the buying and selling prices include all commissions and taxes, find the per cent of gain on cost.

Solution

Gain from dividends (14 quarters at 50¢)   7.00

Capital Gain ($42 − $28)................................$14.00

Total gain per share $21.00

$$\text{Per cent of total Gain} = \frac{\$21}{\$28} \times 100 = 75\%$$

Thus, the total gain represents 75% of the cost.

PROGRESS TEST 2

1. A man bought a block of stock at $20 a share. He received quarterly dividends of 75¢ for a period of two years, after which he sold all of his stock at $22 per share. Assuming that the prices includes all commission and taxes, his dividends per share for the two years were _____.

2. The per cent of gain on cost is _____.

1. $6.00   2. $\frac{8}{20} \times 100 = 40\%$

Example 4

D. Rose of Los Angeles, California, bought 200 shares of American Telephone and Telegraph at $45 per share, excluding commission. After holding the stock for two years, he sold all his shares at $50 per share, excluding commissions and taxes. If the dividend for AT and T amounted to 50¢ per quarter, find (a) the capital gain; (b) the total gain; (c) the per cent of total gain (relative to cost).

Solution

a. The capital gain is the net proceeds minus the total cost.

Money value of 200 shares at $50		$10,000.00
Commission on 200 shares at $50		
0.9% of $10,000	$90	
plus $22	22	
	112	
plus $6 per round lot	12	
	124	
plus 15%	18.60	
		142.60
SEC Tax, 1¢ per $500 of money involved		.20
New York Non-Resident Tax, 2.5¢ per share		5.00
Taxes and Commission		147.80
Net Proceeds		$ 9,852.20
Money value of 200 shares at $45	$ 9,000	
Commission on 200 shares at $45		
0.9% of $9,000	$81.00	
plus $22	22.00	
	103.00	
plus $6 per round lot	12.00	
	115.00	

plus 15%   17.25

132.25

Total Cost   9,132.25
Capital Gain $ 719.95

b. The dividend per share was 50¢ × 8 = $4. Thus, the total dividend is 200 × $4 = $800. Total Gain = Dividends + Capital Gains = $800 + $719.95 = $1,519.95.

c. The per cent of total gain is

$$\frac{\$1,519.95}{\$9,132.25} \times 100 = 16.6\%$$

EXERCISE 7.3

In Problems 1 through 10, use the accompanying list and find the rate of annual yield to the nearest tenth of a per cent. Assume the cost of the stock is the closing cost listed.

New York Stock Exchange Transactions
Friday, November 30, 1973

—1973— High	Low	Stocks. Div	P-E Ratio	Sales in 100s	High	Low	Close	Net Chg.	—1973— High	Low	Stocks Div	P-E Ratio	Sales in 100s	High	Low	Close	Net Chg.
38⅜	19⅛	DennMfg .90	5	11	20	19¼	19¼	— 1	30⅜	19⅞	Grace 1.50	8	110	23	22⅛	22¼	— ⅝
28	16¾	DennMf pf 1	...	6	18	18	18	— ¾	16⅞	9½	GrandUn .80	12	202	16⅛	15¾	15⅞	— ⅛
20¾	7⅜	Dennys .06	9	74	8⅜	8	8¼	— ¼	25⅞	19⅛	Granit 1.20a	4	7	19⅛	19	19	— ¼
27¾	16¼	Dentsply .76	15	35	23⅜	22⅝	22⅝	— ⅜	44⅜	12½	GrantW 1.50	6	254	12¾	12½	12½	— ⅜
16¼	9⅛	DeSotoIn .60	6	17	9⅞	9⅞	9⅞	......	28¼	7⅛	GrayDrg 1e	8	16	7¼	7⅛	7⅛	— ⅛
21¼	16¾	DetEdis 1.45	9	107	17¼	17	17⅛	......	40⅜	28½	GtAMt 3.33e	8	58	31¼	29⅝	29⅝	— 1⅝
120	111	Det E pf9.32	...	z120	111	110	110	— 1	19	9¼	Grt AtlPac	...	176	9⅞	9½	9⅝	— ¼
98¾	90½	Det E pf7.36	...	4	92	92	92	— ¼	31¾	16⅝	GtLkDr 1.20	...	3	16½	16½	16½	— ⅜
22⅝	12¾	Dexter .28	11	2	13⅜	13⅜	13⅜+	¼	12⅝	10	GtNoIr 1.10e	11	22	10⅛	10	10⅛+	⅛
24⅜	15⅜	Dial Finl .54	11	12	19¼	18⅞	19⅛+	½	59½	40	GtNNek 1.60	10	22	45⅜	44¾	44¾	— ¾
36½	26⅛	DiamInt 2	7	74	26⅝	25⅜	25½	— 1½	25	20½	GtNN pf1.60	...	1	22	22	22 +	½
28⅞	16⅞	DiamSh 1.10	9	130	24	23⅜	23⅝	— ⅝	34¾	14⅝	GtWnFin .40	6	81	17¼	16¾	17¼	— ¼
37¼	25½	Dia Sh pfC 2	...	10	30½	30⅛	30½+	⅜	8¼	3⅛	Gt Wn Unit	...	6	3⅛	3	3	— ⅛
18⅛	14½	Dia pf D1.20	...	10	15	14¾	15 +	⅛	19⅝	10	GtWnUnt pf	...	21	11	9¾	11 +	1
24¾	15⅛	DickAB .44	9	3	16⅛	16⅛	16⅛	— ⅛	4⅞	2⅜	GrtWsh Inv	...	4	2⅜	2⅜	2⅜	......
14¾	7⅝	Dictaph .48a	7	62	9⅝	9	9⅛	— ¼	26⅞	17⅝	GrenGiant T	7	17	18½	17⅞	18	— ¾

Reprinted, by permission, from *The Wall Street Journal*, December 3, 1973.

1. DennMfg
2. Dennys
3. DeSotoInt
4. Dexter
5. DialFinI
6. Grace
7. GrandUn
8. GrantW
9. GtLkDr
10. GtNNek

In Problems 11 through 15, find the annual yield to the nearest tenth of a per cent.

	STOCK	PRICE	QUARTERLY DIVIDEND
11.	Dow Chemical	$64.82	$0.30
12.	General Electric	$68.19	$0.50
13.	General Foods	$63.75	$0.55
14.	Sears, Roebuck	$32.50	$0.275
15.	Goodyear Tire	$96.88	$0.60

In Problems 16 through 20, follow the procedure of Example 4 in this section and find (a) the capital gain (or loss); (b) the total gain (or loss); (c) the per cent of total gain (relative to cost).

	STOCK	SHARES	PURCHASE PRICE	SALE PRICE	YEARLY DIVIDEND	TIME
16.	DennMfg	100	$20	$35	$0.90	1 year
17.	DialFin	100	$15	$25	$0.50	1 year
18.	DeSotoIn	100	$10	$15	$0.50	2 years
19.	Grace	200	$20	$30	$1.50	2 years
20.	GrandUn	200	$10	$15	$1.00	3 years

2192011/

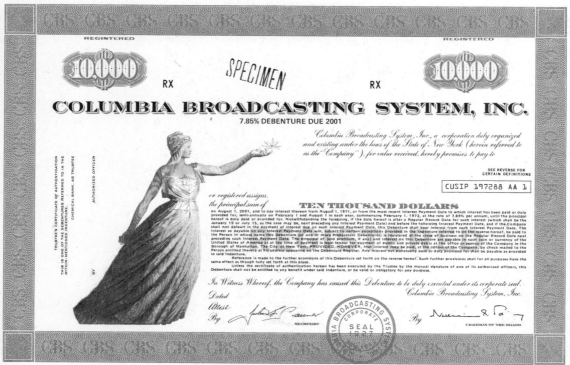

Courtesy of Columbia Broadcasting System, Inc.

7.4 BUYING AND SELLING BONDS

At the beginning of this chapter we listed two ways in which surplus money could be used: buying something with it or lending it. Let us examine more closely the possibilities of lending money. When you lend any considerable amount of money, you usually obtain an IOU (promissory note) from the borrower. Similarly, if you lend money to a corporation, a local government agency, or the federal government, you get an IOU in the form of a **bond.**

Definition of a bond

A bond is a promise to repay a specific amount of borrowed money in a specified time, and to pay a set rate of interest for the use of the money in the meantime. The **principal amount** that the issuer promises to pay per bond on the maturity date is printed on the bond itself and is called the **face value** or the **par value** of the bond. The face value of a bond is usually some simple figure such as $100, $500, or $1,000. The interest is usually payable every six months, or every year, on the dates specified on the bond certificate. As with stocks, bonds are bought and sold in stock exchanges and "over-the-counter" markets. The current value of bonds is published daily on the financial pages of most metropolitan newspapers. Here are some of the bond quotations taken from the *Wall Street Journal.*

As you can see from Table 7–3, the entries for the first bond listed appears like this:

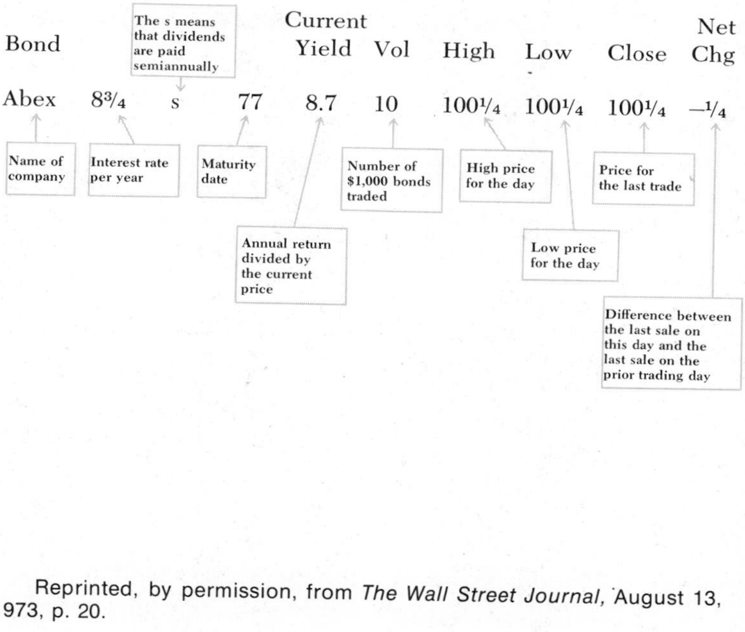
The s means that dividends are paid semiannually
Bond
Current Yield
Vol
High
Low
Close
Net Chg
Abex
8¾
s
77
8.7
10
100¼
100¼
100¼
–¼
Name of company
Interest rate per year
Maturity date
Annual return divided by the current price
Number of $1,000 bonds traded
High price for the day
Low price for the day
Price for the last trade
Difference between the last sale on this day and the last sale on the prior trading day

TABLE 7–3 Bond Quotations

CORPORATION BONDS
Volume, $15,860,000
A–B

Bonds	Cur Yld	Vol	High	Low	Close	Net Chg
Abex 8¾s77	8.7	10	100¼	100¼	100¼	– ¼
AddM 9⅜95	9.3	16	102⅜	100⅛	100⅛	+ ⅛
AlaP 9s2000	8.9	28	101	100½	101	–1
Alexn 5½96	cv	2	49⅞	49⅞	49⅞	.....
Alison 8¾79	8.8	1	98⅜	98⅜	98⅜	– ⅝
AllnGp 6s87	cv	2	70	70	70	.....
AldSu 5¾87	cv	35	57	56½	56½	– ½
Alcoa 5¼s91	cv	159	92	89⅜	89⅜	–2⅓
Amerce 5s92	cv	4	73½	73½	73½	+ ½
A Hes 6¾96	8.0	4	84	84	84	.....
AAirFil 6s90	cv	16	89½	89½	89½	.....
AAirln 11s88	10.	88	104	103½	103½	– ¾
AAirl 4¼s92	cv	50	54¼	53	53	–1
ABrnd 8⅞75	8.7	37	101¾	100½	101¾	+1¼
ABrnd 5⅞92	7.2	5	81⅛	81⅛	81⅛	+ ⅛
ACyan 7⅜01	7.9	4	92⅜	92⅜	92⅜	–7⅛
AExp 5¼93f	cv	68	10	9¼	10	+ ¼
AForP 5s30	10.	13	49½	49½	49½	.....
AFoP 4.8s87	8.5	26	56	55	56	.....
AInvt 9½s76	9.4	6	101	100⅛	100⅛	– ⅛
AInvt 8¾s89	8.9	1	98	98	98	– ¾
AMF 4¼s81	cv	18	78	77	77	–2½
AMedcp 5s97	cv	49	46	45½	45½	.....
AMeCI 7½78	7.8	10	96⅛	96	96	.....
AmMot 6s88	cv	17	79	78¼	79	+1⅜
ASug 5.3s93	7.7	1	68½	68½	68½	.....
ATT 8¾2000	8.3	626	104⅜	103¾	104¼	+ ⅜
ATT 8.7s02	8.4	265	103	102¾	103	+ ⅛
ATT 7.75s77	7.8	73	99	98¼	98¼	– ⅝
ATT 7⅛s03	8.0	57	89	88½	89	+ ⅝
ATT 7s01	8.0	45	88	87½	87½	+ ⅛
ATT 6½s79	7.0	26	92⅜	92	92⅜	.....
ATT 4⅜s85	6.1	9	71⅛	71⅛	71⅛	+ ⅛
ATT 3⅞s90	6.2	1	62¼	62¼	62¼	+ ¾
ATT 3⅜s73	3.4	52	98 1-32	98	98	–1-32
ATT 2¾s75	3.0	11	91	90¼	90¼	– ¼
ATT 2¾s80	3.8	34	72⅛	71⅝	71⅝	– ⅜
ATT 2¾s82	4.1	51	67	66	66⅝	+ ⅛
ATT 2⅝s86	4.5	10	57¾	57½	57½	– ¼
Amfac 5¼94	cv	97	63	62	62	–1¼
Ampx 5½94	cv	48	44	43½	44	.....
ApcoO 5s88	cv	55	62	60¼	60¼	–1¾

Reprinted, by permission, from *The Wall Street Journal,* August 13, 1973, p. 20.

The entry $8\frac{3}{4}$ s means that the bond pays $8\frac{3}{4}\%$ intrest per year, payable in semiannual installments. The 77 means that the **maturity date,** the date on which the bond principal becomes due and payable in full to the bondholder, is 1977. The 19 is omitted to save space.

The current yield (8.7%) can be obtained by dividing the annual return by the current price of the bond.

The column labeled "Vol" shows the number of $1,000 bonds traded (bought and sold) that day. The 10 means that ten $1,000 bonds were traded.

The prices of bonds (high, low, and close) are quoted in points that represent percentage points on the face value of the bond. In our case, the Abex bond was selling, at the close of the day, for $100\frac{1}{4}\%$ of $1,000, that is, $1,002.50. Similarly, a par value $1,000 bond quoted at 95 will be selling for 95% of $1,000, that is, $950.

Example 1

Referring to Table 7–3, find (a) the closing price of one ACyan bond; (b) the closing price of 5 AlaP bonds.

Solution

a. The quoted closing price in percentage points is $92\frac{3}{8}$. Thus, the closing price is 92.375% of $1,000 = $923.75.

b. The quoted closing price in percentage points (for one bond) is 101. Thus, the closing price for one bond is 101% of $1,000 = $1,010, and the closing price of 5 AlaP bonds is $5 \times \$1,010 = \$5,050$.

PROGRESS TEST 1

1. Referring to Table 7–3, the high price of one Alexn bond is _____.

2. Referring to Table 7–3, the closing price of one Alnvt $9\frac{1}{2}$ s 76 is _____.

As we mentioned before, the dates on which the interest on a bond is to be paid each year are printed on the bond certificate. When investors sell bonds on the interest payment date, they are entitled to the interest earned for the preceding interest period. In such cases, the cost or investment on a bond is the sum of the market value of the bond and the commission on the purchase. This commission is usually a flat fee of $5 per bond. However, if a bond is traded between interest payment dates, the seller is entitled to the accrued interest.

---

1. $49\frac{7}{8}\%$ of $1,000 = $498.75   2. $100\frac{1}{8}\%$ of $1,000 = $1,001.25.

In such cases the buyer pays for the market value of the bond plus all the interest that has accumulated from the date of the last interest payment to the settlement date. (The settlement date is ordinarily the fourth business day following the date on which the buyer and seller reach an agreement regarding the price.) Bonds earn simple interest computed on the basis of a 360-day year. To find the cost or total expenditure on bonds bought between interest payment dates, we proceed as follows:

How to find the cost on bonds bought between interest dates

  1. Find the market value of the bonds. This is done by multiplying the market value of one bond by the number of bonds being purchased.
  2. Find the accrued interest on the bonds.
  3. Find the commission charge per bond and multiply by the number of bonds to find the total commission charge.
  4. Add the market value, the accrued interest, and the total commission charges to find the cost or investment.

Example 2

Find the cost or investment on 5 AHes bonds quoted at 84 each, with 8% interest payable January 1 and July 1, if the settlement date on the bonds was April 1, and the commission is $5 per bond.

Solution

We proceed in steps.

  1. The market value of each bond is 84% of $1,000 = $840. Thus the total market value is 5 × $840 = $4,200.
  2. The accrued interest on each bond is the interest due from January 1 to April 1, that is, 90 days. This interest amounts to

$$\$1,000 \times \frac{8}{100} \times \frac{90}{360} = \$20 \text{ per bond}$$

and

$$5 \times \$20 = \$100 \text{ for all five bonds}$$

  3. The commission is $5 per bond or 5 × $5 = $25 for the five bonds.
  4. The cost or investment is

$$\$4,200 + \$100 + \$25 = \$4,325$$

PROGRESS TEST 2

1. The quoted price of a 6% bond whose interest is paid January 1, 1977, and July 1, 1977, is 90. If the settlement date to buy one of these bonds is April 1 and the commission is $5 per bond, the accrued interest on the bond is _____.

2. The cost or investment of this bond is _____.

---

1. $\$1,000 \times \frac{6}{100} \times \frac{100}{360} = \$16.67$ 2. $\$900 + \$16.67 + \$5 = \$921.67$

The broker's commission and accrued interest, if any, are computed in a similar manner for bond sales. However, it must be remembered that in selling bonds, the broker **deducts** the commission from the sales price. In addition, the SEC Tax must be paid on such sales. If bonds are sold between interest dates, the seller is entitled to the interest accrued from the preceding interest date to and including the day before the settlement date. From this discussion, we can see that the net proceeds from a sale can be obtained by using the following formula:

FORMULA 7.2

Net Proceeds = Market Value + Accrued Interest − Commission
− SEC Tax

Example 3

Find the net proceeds from the sale of ten General Electric bonds quoted at 95 each with 8% interest payable January 1, 1977, and July 1, 1977. The settlement date is April 1 and the commission is $5 per bond.

Solution

The market value of the ten bonds is $10 \times \$950 = \$9,500$. The interest from January 1 to April 1 is $\$1,000 \times \dfrac{8}{100} \times \dfrac{90}{360} = \$20$ per bond. Thus, the total accrued interest is $10 \times \$20 = \$200$. The commission is $\$5 \times 10 = \$50$. The SEC Tax is 1¢ per $500 of money involved. Since the market value of the bonds is $9,500, the SEC Tax is $0.19. Using Formula 7.3, we have:

Net Proceeds = Market Value + Accrued Interest − Commission
− SEC Tax = $\$9,500 + \$200 - \$50 - \$0.19 = \$9,649.81$.

PROGRESS TEST 3

1. The accrued interest on ten Sears, Roebuck Bonds quoted at 90 each with 8% interest payable January 1 and July 1, if the settlement date was April 1, is _____.
2. If the commission is $5 per bond, the net proceeds from the bonds in question 1 are _____.

---

1. $200   2. $\$9,000 + \$200 - \$50 - \$.18 = \$9,149.82$

EXERCISE 7.4

In Problems 1 through 5, use the accompanying table to find the required bond prices.

CORPORATION BONDS
Volume $18,530,000
A–B

Bonds	Cur Yld	Vol	High	Low	Close	Net Chg
Abex 8¾s77	8.7	7	102½	100½	100½	−2
Acme 9⅞90	9.2	10	107¼	107¼	107¼	+2¼
AirRe 3⅞87	cv	5	64⅛	64	64⅛	+ ⅛
AlaP 9s2000	8.5	3	105½	105½	105½	− ⅝
Alaska 6s96	cv	16	117½	116½	117½	+ ½
Alison 8¾79	8.7	14	100	99	100	+ ¼
AlldPd 7s84	8.7	1	80	80	80	.....
AlldSt 4½81	cv	3	85⅛	85⅛	85⅛	.....
AlldSt 4½92	cv	5	64	63½	63½	− ½
AldSu 5¾87	cv	8	53	53	53	.....
Alcoa 9s9	58.2	20	109	109	109	+ ⅞
Alcoa 6s92	7.0	5	85⅜	85⅜	85⅜	+ ⅛
Alcoa 5¼s91	cv	48	88	87¼	87¼	....
Amerce 5s92	cv	3	73	73	73	+ ¾
A Hes 6¾96	7.7	25	87	87	87	.....
AAirFil 6s90	cv	12	89	89	89	.....
AAirln 11s88	10.	10	106	106	106	−1⅜
AAirl 10⅞88	10.	15	107⅛	105⅝	105⅝	− ⅛
AAirl 4¼s92	cv	33	50¾	49½	50¾	+1¼
ABrnd 8⅞75	8.6	5	102¾	102¼	102¾	+ ¾
ACan 6s97	7.2	10	83	83	83	.....
ACeM 6¾91	cv	27	68	68	68	−2
AExp 5¼93f	cv	3	10¾	10¾	10¾	− ¼

Reprinted, by permission, from The Wall Street Journal, July 11, 1973, p. 30.

	BONDS	AMOUNT	PRICE QUOTED
1.	Abex	$1,000	Close
2.	Acme	$1,000	High
3.	AirRe	$1,000	Low
4.	AlaP	$5,000	Close
5.	Alaska	$5,000	High

In Problems 6 through 10, use the table above to find the cost plus the accrued interest for these $1,000 bonds. In each case, the price quoted is the closing price.

	BOND	INTEREST DATE	SETTLEMENT DATE
6.	AlaP	January 1	April 1
7.	AlldPd	April 1	June 30
8.	Alaska	June 2	August 1
9.	Amerce	January 1	March 2
10.	Abex	April 1	June 20

In Problems 11 through 15, refer to the table above and find

a. the total market value
b. the accrued interest.

c. the total commission, if the commission per bond is $2.50.
d. the total cost.
In each case, the price quoted is the closing price.

	BOND	NUMBER PURCHASED	INTEREST DATE	SETTLEMENT DATE
11.	AlaP	5	January 1	April 1
12.	AlldPd	5	April 1	June 30
13.	Alaska	10	June 2	August 1
14.	Amerce	10	January 1	March 2
15.	Abex	10	April 1	June 20

In Problems 16 through 20, refer to the table above and find
a. the total market value.
b. the total commission, if the commission per bond is $5.
c. the SEC Tax.

In each case the price quoted is the closing price.

	BOND	NUMBER SOLD	INTEREST DATE	SETTLEMENT DATE
16.	AlaP	10	January 1	April 1
17.	AlldPd	10	April 1	June 30
18.	Alaska	20	June 2	August 1
19.	Amerce	20	January 1	March 2
20.	Abex	20	April 1	June 20

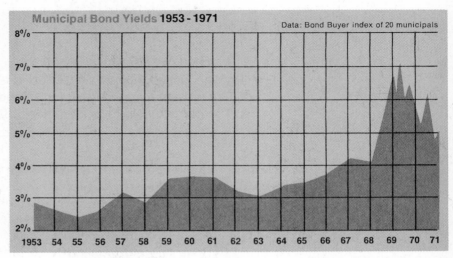

Chart courtesy Merrill Lynch, Pierce, Fenner & Smith, Inc.

7.5 RETURN ON BOND INVESTMENT

There are two widely accepted methods of measuring the rate of return on an investment in bonds:

1. The **current yield** is the term used to express the ratio of the annual return to the present market value.

Finding the current yield

2. The **rate of yield to maturity** is the term used to express the average annual return on an investment based on the amount paid, the interest rate, and the length of time to maturity.

To find the current yield on a bond, we divide the annual return by the market value of the bond; that is,

$$\text{Current Yield} = \frac{\text{Interest}}{\text{Market Value}}$$

For example, if a \$1,000 bond yielding 6% interest is quoted at 90, the current yield for this bond is $\frac{60}{900} = 6.67\%$.

Example 1

Find the current yield of Alcoa bonds quoted at 80 and yielding 8% interest.

Solution

$$\text{Current Yield} = \frac{\text{Interest}}{\text{Market Value}} = \frac{80}{800} = 10\%$$

PROGRESS TEST 1

1. A $1,000 Alaska bond is quoted at 120 and yields 6% interest. The annual interest on this bond is _____.
2. The present market value of this bond is _____.
3. The current yield of this bond is _____.

The second method used to find the rate of return on an investment usually requires the use of tables of bond yields. Since in many cases these tables are not available, we give a method called the Bond Salesman's Method for approximating within a few tenths of one per cent the rate of yield to maturity of a bond.

A premium bond is a bond purchased at more than 100% of its par value.

To find the rate of yield to maturity on **premium bonds** (bonds purchased at more than 100% of their par value), we proceed as follows:

1. Subtract the par value from the cost of the bond to obtain the **premium.**

Finding the rate of yield to maturity.

2. Divide the premium by the number of years to maturity to obtain the approximate annual premium amortization.*

3. Subtract the annual premium amortization from the annual yield to obtain the approximate effective annual yield.

4. Find the average investment of the bond by adding the cost and the par value and dividing the sum by 2.

5. Divide the number obtained in step 3, the approximate effective annual yield, by the number obtained in 4, the average investment on the bond.

Example 2

Find the rate of yield to maturity of a $1,000 bond bought at 110% of par value ten years before maturity if the bond pays 5% interest.

Solution

We proceed by steps.

1. The cost of the bond is $1,100; thus, the premium is

$$\$1,100 - \$1,000 = \$100$$

---

1. $60   2. $1,200   3. $\frac{60}{1,200} = 5\%$

*Amortization is the process of deducting from the annual yield of a bond a part of the premium proportional to the number of years between purchase and maturity in order to determine the effective (true) annual yield. For example, if a 10-year bond has cost $50 above par value, the premium is $50 ÷ 10 years = $5 per year. This $5 must be subtracted from the annual yield to arrive at the actual annual profit made on the bond.

2. The approximate annual premium amortization is

$$\$100 \div 10 = \$10$$

3. The annual yield of the bond is $50; thus, the approximate effective annual yield is

$$\$50 - \$10 = \$40$$

4. The average investment for the bond is

$$\frac{\$1,100 + \$1,000}{2} = \$1,050$$

5. The rate of yield to maturity is

$$\frac{\$40}{\$1,050} = 3.8\%$$

PROGRESS TEST 2

1. The rate of yield to maturity of a $1,000 bond bought at $103\frac{1}{2}\%$ of par value ten years before maturity, if the bond pays 5% interest, is _____.

To find the rate of yield to maturity on **discount bonds** (bonds purchased at less than 100% of their value), we proceed as follows:

A discount bond is a bond purchased at less than 100% of its par value.

1. Subtract the cost from the par value to obtain the **discount.**
2. Divide the discount by the number of years to maturity to obtain the approximate annual discount amortization, or accumulation.
3. Add the annual discount amortization to the annual yield to obtain the approximate effective annual yield.
4. Find the average investment of the bond by adding the cost and the par value and dividing the sum by 2.
5. Divide the number obtained in step 3, the approximate effective annual yield, by the number obtained in 4, the average investment on the bond.

Example 3

Find the rate of yield to maturity on a $1,000 bond bought at 90% of par value ten years before maturity, if the bond pays 5% interest.

---

1. 4.6%

Solution

We proceed by steps.

1. The cost of the bond is $900; thus, the discount is

$$\$1{,}000 - \$900 = \$100$$

2. The approximate annual discount amortization is

$$\$100 \div 10 = \$10$$

3. The annual yield of the bond is $50; thus, the approximate effective annual yield is

$$\$10 + \$50 = \$60$$

4. The average investment for the bond is

$$\frac{\$900 + \$1{,}000}{2} = \$950$$

5. The rate of yield to maturity is

$$\frac{\$60}{\$950} = 6.3\%$$

PROGRESS TEST 3

1. The rate of yield to maturity of a $1,000 bond bought at 94% of par value 15 years before maturity, if the bond pays 4% interest, is _____.

EXERCISE 7.5

In Problems 1 through 10, find (a) the annual interest, (b) the present market value of the bond, and (c) the current yield of the bond.

	NAME OF COMPANY	QUOTED PRICE	RATE OF ANNUAL INTEREST
1.	Abex	100	8%
2.	American	104	10%
3.	AT and T	105	$8\frac{1}{2}\%$
4.	Ford	99	$8\frac{1}{4}\%$

1. 4.5%

5.	Exxon	87	6%
6.	El Paso	$74\frac{3}{4}$	5%
7.	GAC	31	$5\frac{7}{8}\%$
8.	NY Tel.	101	8%
9.	Gen. El.	92	$6\frac{3}{4}\%$
10.	Xerox	$164\frac{1}{2}$	6%

In Problems 11 through 15, find the rate of yield to maturity for the given $1,000 bonds.

	QUOTED PRICE	RATE OF ANNUAL INTEREST	TIME OF PURCHASE
11.	110	6%	10 years before maturity
12.	120	5%	10 years before maturity
13.	110	5%	5 years before maturity
14.	120	10%	20 years before maturity
15.	110	8%	5 years before maturity

In Problems 16 through 20, find the rate of yield to maturity for the given $1,000 bonds.

	QUOTED PRICE	RATE OF ANNUAL INTEREST	TIME OF PURCHASE
16.	90	10%	10 years before maturity
17.	95	5%	10 years before maturity
18.	90	8%	20 years before maturity
19.	98	6%	5 years before maturity
20.	94	7%	15 years before maturity

Courtesy of American Telephone and Telegraph Company

7.6   WARRANTS

Warrants represent one of the most sophisticated gambling devices that man has invented. They are traded just as stocks are: by purchase or sale on the New York Stock Exchange, American Stock Exchange, one of the less prominent exchanges or OTC (over-the-counter). But a warrant differs from a share of stock in one fundamental way. When one buys a share of stock in a company, he is actually purchasing a partial ownership (no matter how small) in the company. For example, if a person buys 100 shares of Delta Air Lines at $40 a share (total cost $4000), he may imagine that he owns a block of seats on one of the Delta airplanes. If he buys 100 shares of Sears, Roebuck at $60 a share (total cost $6000), he may amuse himself with the thought that he now owns the washroom on the 6th floor of the Sears, Roebuck Building in Chicago.

On the other hand, if he buys 100 warrants in Trans World Airlines, he has no share at all in the company itself. Instead he has purchased a right to purchase shares of Trans World Airlines, and this right may be very valuable or it may be worthless, depending on the terms of the warrant and the price of the stock. To understand how warrants came into existence, and why people would buy them, let us look at a typical example. We will follow the fortunes of the TWA-warrants "from their birth to their death".

On June 1, 1961, Trans World Airlines offered for sale to the public 100 million dollars in bonds. These bonds paid interest at $6\frac{1}{2}\%$ and came due in 1978. The money raised by the sale of these bonds was used by the company to replace obsolete aircraft with new ones, to expand the size of its fleet, and to expand some of its facilities.

At that time the banks were paying about 5% interest on deposits and so these bonds formed an attractive investment. However, many potential investors might prefer to leave their money in the bank because (a) the bonds might decline in price, (b) the company might actually fail before 1978, or (c) the investor might hope that he could find a better place for his money later. The increase in interest income ($6.5\% - 5\% = 1.5\%$) might not outweigh the disadvantage of having the money invested in bonds.

To make the bond issue more attractive, the company occasionally "sweetens the issue" by attaching warrants to the bonds. The terms of the warrants may be anything that the company decides, as long as they do not violate the various corporate laws that have been enacted to protect both the stockholders and the public. In the case in question, Trans World Airlines attached one warrant for each $100 value of the bond. Each warrant permitted the holder to buy one share of TWA common stock at a price of $22.00. The privilege of making this purchase terminated on December 1, 1973. After that date the warrant was utterly worthless. Thus the TWA warrants were "born on June 1, 1961, and died on December 1, 1973".

Of course the company may issue new warrants with other provisions at any time it chooses.

PROGRESS TEST 1

1. On June 1, 1961, Sam Smart bought a $5000 TWA bond, $6\frac{1}{2}\%$, 78. How many warrants did he receive with this bond? _____.

2. With these warrants, how many shares of TWA stock could he buy on July 1, 1965? _____.

3. Ignoring commissions, how much would these shares cost? _____.

4. If Sam Smart decided to buy shares of Pan American World Airways instead, how many shares do the TWA warrants entitle him to purchase? _____

5. Sam Smart held his warrants until July 4, 1974. How much were they worth at that time? _____

We continue our study of these TWA warrants.

During the year 1960 the highest price paid for a share of TWA

---

1. 50   2. 50   3. $1,100   4. None   5. $0

stock was 19 and the lowest price was $11\frac{1}{8}$. For the year 1961 these high and low figures were $20\frac{3}{8}$ and $11\frac{7}{8}$. For the year 1962, the figures were $14\frac{1}{4}$ and $7\frac{1}{2}$. Consequently, when the company agreed (on June 1, 1961) to create more stock and offer it for sale to warrant holders at $22, per share, the company was not really giving away anthing of great value (at the time of the issue). To see why Mr. Smart would buy a $5000 bond and hold onto the warrants, let us look at the situation $2\frac{1}{2}$ years later.

On December 31, 1963, TWA stock was selling for $31 a share. At that time, if Sam Smart still held his 50 warrants, he could exercise the privilege granted by the warrants. He could (through his broker) buy 50 shares of TWA at $22, sell them the next day at $31 (the price might go up or down a little) and (ignoring the commission on the two sales) he would make in one day $50 \times (31 - 22) = \$450$. Further, Mr. Smart would still have the $5000 bond paying $6\frac{1}{2}\%$ interest.

To summarize, the true value of the warrant lies in the fact that the stock may increase in price beyond the exercise price* of the warrant. Those who expect the stock to go up will therefore pay a premium for the warrant. Those who hold the warrants and expect the stock to drop in price will be delighted to sell the warrants at a premium.

Would Mr. Smart really exercise his privilege and buy 50 shares of TWA on December 31, 1963? At first glance, it seems that he should, because it gives him a profit† of $450. But wait a minute. There were some investors who believed that TWA stock would go still higher, and they were willing to buy Smart's warrants from him. Indeed, on that same day the warrants were selling at $15\frac{1}{8}$. Thus, if Mr. Smart sold the warrants on December 31, 1963 (instead of exercising his rights), he would receive $\$50 \times 15\frac{1}{8} = \$756.25$. Clearly, this gives Mr. Smart a greater profit than the $450 he would make by exercising his rights to purchase the stock.

It would be interesting to follow the fluctuations in the price of these warrants through every trading day of their 12-year, 6-month life, but this would occupy too much space. Instead we use the price of the last sale on the last trading day of each year. In Table 7–4 we give this data for the years 1961 through 1967.

Some features of this table are worth examining.

When the stock was selling for $12 (first line), no intelligent

---

*The exercise price is the price at which stock may be purchased, as stated on the warrant.

†Throughout the rest of this section we will ignore the fact that commission and taxes are charged on each transaction. This will simplify the computation.

TABLE 7-4   Closing Prices for TWA Stocks and Warrants, 1961-1967

Date	Price of TWA Stock NYSE	Price TWA Warrant ASE
Dec. 29, 1961	12	5
Dec. 31, 1962	10 1/2	4 1/2
Dec. 31, 1963	31	15 1/8
Dec. 31, 1964	47 3/4	29 3/8
Dec. 31, 1965	63 1/2	44 1/4
Dec. 30, 1966	74 1/2	52 1/2
Dec. 29, 1967	50 5/8	36

person would exercise the warrant privilege and buy shares at $22. But some investors were willing to pay $5 apiece for the warrants. To understand this, we imagine that on that day Lester Little had $1200 to invest, and decided that TWA stock would probably go up. Mr. Little did not wish to participate in the initial TWA bond offering, but he could purchase the warrants on the American Stock Exchange. Should he buy the stock or warrants? It is clear that in either case he would lose money if he sold after one year. Let us suppose that he waited two years before selling. Using the data in Table 7-4, the computations can be arranged thus:

A. He buys stock December 29, 1961.

He receives $\frac{\$1200}{\$12} = 100$ shares of stock.

He sells stock December 31, 1963.
He receives $100 \times 31 = \$3,100$.
Net profit is $\$3,100 - \$1,200 = \$1,900$.

B. He buys warrants December 29, 1961.

He receives $\frac{\$1200}{\$5} = 240$ warrants.

He sells warrants December 31, 1963.

He receives $240 \times 15\frac{1}{8} = \$3,630$.

Net profit is $\$3,630 - \$1,200 = \$2,430$.

Clearly, Lester Little will make more money if he buys and sells the warrants.

Example 1

Suppose that Mr. Little holds his stock (or warrants) purchased on December 29, 1961, until December 30, 1966 (5 years). Compute his profit in each case.

Solution

A. He buys stock, and sells it on December 30, 1966.

He receives $100 \times 74\frac{1}{2} = \$7,450$.

Net profit is $\$7,450 - 1,200 = \$6,250$.

TABLE 7–5   Gains (Losses) in TWA Stock for the Years 1961–1973

Year	Gain (Loss) Per Share	Year	Gain (Loss) Per Share
1961	d 2.21	1968	1.78
1962	d 0.85	1969	1.63
1963	2.95	1970	d 6.43
1964	5.47	1971	0.11
1965	5.74	1972	3.01
1966	3.49	1973	3.25
1967	3.97		

B. He buys warrants, and sells them on December 30, 1966.

He receives $240 \times 52\frac{1}{2} = \$12,600$.

Net profit is $\$12,600 - 1,200 = \$11,400$.

Clearly, he should buy the warrants because if the stock is going up, the warrants may be expected to go up at a greater rate. Of course if the stock goes down, the warrants may be expected to go down even faster.

To understand why the price of a stock would go up or down, we must realize that a company may make a profit in some years and operate at a loss in other years. To evaluate the effect of such gains or losses, the investor is not concerned with the total gain or loss but rather with the gain or loss per share:

$$\text{Gain (loss) per Share} = \frac{\text{Total Profit (Loss)}}{\text{Number of Shares Outstanding}}$$

For Trans World Airlines these figures are given in Table 7–5. Note that the letter d means deficit or loss.

Looking at these figures, we can see that the stock did well during the years 1963 to 1967, and that one would expect both the stock and the warrants to fall during the years 1968 to 1972. This data is given in Table 7–6 (using the price of the last sale on the last trading day of each year).

TABLE 7–6   Closing Prices of TWA Stocks and Warrants

Date	Price of TWA Stock NYSE	Price of TWA Warrant ASE
Dec. 31, 1968	42 7/8	29 7/8
Dec. 31, 1969	23 3/8	12 7/8
Dec. 31, 1970	13 3/4	6 1/8
Dec. 31, 1971	41	25
Dec. 29, 1972	42 1/8	25 5/8

Example 2

Mr. Kautius heard that Mr. Little had made a profit of $11,400 by investing only $1,200 in TWA warrants (see Example 1). He withdrew $5,000 from the bank and invested it in Trans World Airlines on December 31, 1968. The decline in value frightened him, so he sold his holdings on December 31, 1970. How much did he lose (a) if he bought the stock and (b) if he bought the warrants?

Solution

As before, we ignore the commissions on each transaction, but the investor should observe that these commissions always *decrease his profit*, but they *increase his loss*. Further we do not buy fractions of shares, but round off to the nearest share. Using the data in Table 7–6, we arrange the computations thus:

A. Mr. Kautius bought the stock. With $5,000 he can buy 116 shares of TWA, spending $116 \times 42\frac{7}{8} = \$4,973.50$. The sale price on December 31, 1970, is $13\frac{3}{4}$. He receives $116 \times 13\frac{3}{4} = \$1,595.00$. His net loss is $\$4,973.50 - \$1,595.00 = \$3,378.50$.

B. Mr. Kautius bought the warrants. With $5,000 he can buy 167 warrants, spending $167 \times 29\frac{7}{8} = \$4,989.13$. The sale price on December 31, 1970, is $6\frac{1}{8}$. He receives $167 \times 6\frac{1}{8} = \$1,022.88$. His net loss is $\$4,989.13 - 1,022.88 = \$3,966.25$.

By picking very bad dates to enter and leave the market in TWA securities, Mr. Kautius lost the major part of his $5,000 investment. Comparing the losses in cases A and B, we find $\$3,966.25 - \$3,378.50 = \$587.75$. Thus, if Mr. Kautius selected the warrants he lost $587.75 more than if he selected the stock.

Let us examine the price of the warrant during the last year of its life. Here we can observe the devastating effect on the price of the warrant as the price of the stock falls below the exercise price specified in the warrant. The difference is usually called the tangible value of the warrant. Thus,

Tangible Value = Stock Prices (S.P.) − Exercise Price (E.P.)

If the difference is negative, it is customary to record zero, but in Table 7–7 we give the difference even when it is negative.

TABLE 7-7   **Tangible Values of TWA Warrants for the Period Dec. 29, 1972 to November 30, 1973**

Date	Price of TWA Stock NYSE	Price of TWA Warrant ASE	Tangible Value (S.P.–E.P.)
December 29, 1972	42 1/8	25 5/8	20 1/8
February 28, 1973	34 1/4	18 1/8	12 1/4
March 30, 1973	39 1/4	20 3/4	17 1/4
April 30, 1973	34 3/8	18	12 3/8
May 31, 1973	26 1/2	10 3/8	4 1/2
June 29, 1973	20 3/8	5 3/8	−1 5/8
July 31, 1973	21 3/4	6 1/2	−1/4
August 31,1973	20 3/4	5 3/8	−1 1/4
September 28, 1973	22 1/2	4 3/4	+1/2
October 31, 1973	22 1/8	3 3/8	+1/8
November 5, 1973	20	2 1/2	−2
November 9, 1973	20 1/8	2 1/8	−1 7/8
November 15, 1973	18	5/8	−4
November 20, 1973	16 3/4	1/4	−5 1/4
November 26, 1973	16 5/8	1/32	−5 3/8
November 29, 1973	15 3/8	No Sale	−6 5/8
November 30, 1973	14 3/4	No Sale	−7 1/4

It is easy to understand why the price of the warrants fell to zero as the expiration date of December 1, 1973, approached. In fact, on the last two days of their "life" there was no sale, because nobody wanted the warrants at any price.

In the analysis of any warrant, careful attention must be given to the specific provisions of the warrant. In some cases, one warrant may permit the purchase of more than one share of stock. For example, one Braniff Airways warrant (expires 1986) permits the holder to purchase three shares of Braniff Airways stock at $24.33 per share. Thus, in deciding whether or not to purchase Braniff Airways warrants, one might divide the cost by three, and compare that result with the cost of one share of the stock.

Some companies permit the use of their own bonds instead of cash to purchase stock when the warrant rights are exercised. If the bonds are selling at par or above, the feature is of no use. But if the bond is selling at below par, this feature is worth observing, and should be used when computing the tangible value of the warrant.

Example 3

The TWA warrants permitted the use of their $6\frac{1}{2}$, '78 bonds in place of cash for the purchase of the stock. If Sam Sadd held 500 TWA warrants on November 5, 1973, and the bonds were quoted at 75, should he sell his warrants or exercise his right to purchase the stock?

Partial Solution

A. If he sold the warrants on November 5, 1973, he would receive $500 \times 2\frac{1}{2} = \$1,250$.

B. If he bought one $10,000 bond and added $1,000 in cash, he could buy 500 shares of TWA from the company at $22 a share and sell them immediately on the market. Here is why.

Cost of $10,000 bond at 75	$7,500
Cash	1,000
Total Cost	$8,500

The bond at face value plus $1,000 in cash totaled $11,000 and, together with the 500 warrants, permitted Mr. Sadd to obtain 500 shares of TWA. On the sale of these shares he would receive $500 \times \$20 = \$10,000$. His net proceeds would be $\$10,000 - \$8,500 = \$1,500$.

If we ignore commissions, Mr. Sadd should follow Route B. However, we must remember that the commissions on the amounts in B will be greater than the commissions involved in A. In any case Mr. Sadd would have to act fast because ten days later the stock was down to 18 and the warrants were down to $\frac{5}{8}$. Twenty-five days later the stock had dropped to $14\frac{3}{4}$ and the warrants were worthless.

EXERCISE 7.6

In all of the problems of this set, ignore the fact that a commission is paid on each transaction.

1. With $2,000 dollars, how many shares of TWA could be purchased on the last trading day of 1962? How many warrants could be bought on that day?

2. If the investor from Problem 1 delayed his purchase until December 31, 1964, how many shares could he buy? How many warrants could he buy?

3. If the investor in Problem 1 sold his shares of stock on December 31, 1965, what would be his profit? Find his profit if he had invested in warrants.

4. Do Problem 3 for the investor described in Problem 2.

5. The investor from Problem 3 used $10,000 of his profits to purchase warrants on the last trading day of 1966. He held the warrants four years and then sold them. What was the result of this transaction?

6. Suppose the investor in Problem 5 bought and sold stock in TWA rather than the warrants. What would be the result?

SELF-TEST/CHAPTER 7

New York Stock Exchange Transactions

Wednesday, January 2, 1974

—1973-74— High	Low	Stocks	Div	P-E Ratio	Sales in 100s	High	Low	Close	Net Chg.	—1973-74— High	Low	Stocks	Div	P-E Ratio	Sales in 100s	High	Low	Close	Net Chg.
20¼	7⅜	Dennys	.06	10	82	8¾	8½	8½	....	19⅝	8½	GtWnUnt pf	...		9	11⅝	11¼	11½+	⅝
27¾	16¼	Dentsply	.76	15	24	22⅝	22	22⅛—	⅛	4⅞	1½	GrtWsh Inv	...		1	1⅝	1⅜	1⅝	....
16¼	8	DeSotoIn	.60	5	48	9¾	9⅝	9⅝—	⅛	26⅞	17¼	GrenGiant	1	8	4	20⅛	19⅞	19⅞	....
21¼	15⅞	DetEdis	1.45	9	69	16⅞	16⅜	16⅞+	½	18⅞	13¼	Greyhd	1.04	8	140	14½	14	14½+	½
120	106½	Det E pf9.32		...	z20	108	108	108	....	5	2½	Greyhnd wt	...		58	2⅞	2¾	2⅞+	¼
102½	87	Det E pf7.45		...	z50	87	87	87	— 1	15⅞	4¾	Grolier	.50	4	41	6⅛	5⅞	5⅞+	⅛
83	62¼	Det E pf5.50		...	1	64¼	64¼	64¼+	¼	12¼	8	Grumm	.15e	...	15	8⅝	8¼	8⅜	....
24⅜	15⅜	Dial Finl	.54	13	42	22¾	22⅜	22⅜—	⅛	35⅜	12¼	Guardian In		9	1	14½	14½	14½+	¼
36½	23⅝	Diamint	2	8	32	28¾	28⅜	28¾+	⅝	46⅞	22	GuarM	4.17e	5	41	26⅝	25⅛	26⅝+	1⅝
28⅞	16⅞	DiamSh	1.10	10	50	26¾	25¾	26	— ½	57⅛	25⅛	GlfLfH	.10h	6	68	32⅛	30½	32⅛+	2⅛
18⅛	14½	Dia pf D1.20		..	9	15½	15¼	15½	....	10⅛	9⅜	GlfLfHld wi	...		20	10¾	10¼	10¾+	⅝
24¾	11	DickAB	.44	9	25	15⅞	14⅜	15⅞+	1⅛	28⅞	20	GulfOil	1.50	7	1221	24½	23⅝	24½+	⅞
14¾	7⅝	Dictaph	.48a	7	9	9¼	8¾	9	— ¼	12½	6½	Gulf Resrce		11	728	13⅜	12	13¼+	1⅜
57½	35¼	Diebold	.40b	15	170	34¾	33⅞	34¼—	1¼	17	9	GfR pfA.10k	...		16	18¼	17	18⅛+	1⅜
13⅜	7	DiGiorg	.66	5	25	7½	7¼	7⅜	....	17½	12¾	GfR pfB.65k	...		47	19	17¾	18⅜+	⅞
119¼	73¼	Digital Eqpt		40	121	101½	96½	97¾—	4⅛	22⅜	13	GlfStUt	1.12	8	244	14¾	14⅛	14¾+	⅜
10¾	5⅛	Dillingm	.40	7	28	5⅝	5⅜	5⅝+	½	35¾	21⅜	GulfWn	.72	4	42	24	23¾	23⅞+	⅛
39⅜	25¼	DillonCo	1b	13	4	28	27¾	28	....	11¼	3¼	GlfWInd wt	...		62	6	5¾	5⅞+	⅛
123⅞	40½	Disney	.12b	27	324	47⅜	45	45⅝—	1⅝	146	88½	GlfW pf	3.50	...	1	99⅛	99⅛	99⅛	—⅞
22¾	10¼	Disston	.12	7	13	12½	12	12¼+	¼	67½	47½	GlfW pf	3.87	...	2	48	48	48	....
49¼	37¼	DistSeag	.80	19	13	43	42½	42½+	⅜	77½	69½	GlfW pf5.75		...	1	70¾	70¾	70¾+	½
3⅜	1⅛	Diversfd In		15	117	2	1⅞	1⅞	....	9	3	Gulton Ind		6	22	3⅜	3¼	3¼	....
29⅜	13¼	DivMt	2.86e	5	252	15¾	15⅛	15¾+	½	38½	32	HckWat	2.36	7	2	32¾	32¾	32¾+	¼
30	18¾	DrPeppr	.24	45	48	22¼	21⅞	22¼+	¼	13¾	12½	HallFB	.36	12	13	12½	12¼	12½+	⅛

1. Referring to the table above, find

    _____ a. the total dividend paid last year to an investor owning ten round lots of DeSotoInt.

    _____ b. the price of ten round lots of Greyhnd wt purchased at the low price for the day.

2. American Manufacturing has issued 1,000 shares of $100 par value common stock and 500 shares of 5%, $100 par value preferred stock. The company declared a $10,000 dividend for the year. Find

    _____ a. the dividend per share of preferred stock.

    _____ b. the dividend per share of common stock.

3. Continental Manufacturing has issued 1,000 shares of $100 par value common stock and 100 shares of 5%, $100 par value cumulative preferred stock. If the company declared no dividend during last year, but approved a $10,000 dividend this year, find

    _____ a. the dividend per share on each cumulative preferred stock.

    _____ b. the dividend per share on each common stock.

4. A man bought 350 shares of Disney stock at $49\frac{7}{8}$. Refer to the table opposite and find

    _____ a. the commission on the first 300 shares.

Commission Rates of New York and American Stock Exchange Members*

SINGLE ROUND LOT ORDERS		MULTIPLE ROUND LOT ORDERS	
Money Value	*Commission*	*Money Value*	*Commission*
$100 but under $800 $800 but under $2,500 $2,500 add above	2.0% plus $6.40 1.3% plus $12.00 0.9% plus $22.00	$100 but under $2,500 $2,500 but under $20,000 $20,000 but under $30,000 $30,000 to $300,000	1.3% plus $12.00 0.9% plus $22.00 0.6 plus $82.00 0.4% plus $142.00
		PLUS: First to tenth round lot Eleventh round lot and over	 $6 per round lot $4 per round lot
Plus 10% of the commission on orders not exceeding $5,000 and 15% on orders involving amounts exceeding $5,000.			

*From *Standard and Poor's Stock Guide* (New York: Standard and Poor's Corporation, Publisher, 1974), p. 254.

_____ b. the commission on the other 50 shares.

_____ c. the total commission for the purchase.

5. Sales of a stock selling for $3 a share totaled $5,064 (excluding commission and taxes). Find

_____ a. the SEC Tax on the transaction. (Recall that the S.E.C. tax is 1¢ for every $500 or fraction thereof of the money involved.)

_____ b. the New York State Resident Tax on the transaction.

See tax table on page 333.

6. The annual dividend on a stock selling for $46 per share (including commission and taxes) is $1.61. Find

_____ a. the annual yield.

_____ b. the per cent of total gain obtained after holding the stock for ten years and selling it then for $49.90 per share.

7. Referring to the table on following page, find

_____ a. the closing price of ten Alexn bonds.

_____ b. the accrued interest if interest is paid January 1, and the bond is bought January 31.

8. Find the current yield of

_____ a. an Alcoa bond quoted at 90 and yielding 9% interest.

_____ b. an AT and T bond quoted at 105 and yielding 6% interest.

9. TWA attached one warrant for each $100 value of the bond.

	CORPORATION BONDS					
	Volume, $15,860,000					
	A—B					
Bonds	Cur Yld	Vol	High	Low	Close	Net Chg
Abex 8¾s77	8.7	10	100¼	100¼	100¼	— ¼
AddM 9⅜s95	9.3	16	102⅜	100⅛	100⅛	+ ⅛
AlaP 9s2000	8.9	28	101	100½	101	—1
Alexn 5½s96	cv	2	49⅞	49⅞	49⅞	.....
Alison 8¾s79	8.8	1	98⅜	98⅜	98⅜	— ⅝
AllnGp 6s87	cv	2	70	70	70	.....
AldSu 5¾s87	cv	35	57	56½	56½	— ½
Alcoa 5¼s91	cv	159	92	89⅜	89⅜	—2⅛
Amerce 5s92	cv	4	73½	73½	73½	+ ½
A Hes 6¾s96	8.0	4	84	84	84	.....
AAirFil 6s90	8.0	16	89½	89½	89½	.....
AAirln 11s88	10.	88	104	103½	103½	— ¾
AAirl 4¼s92	cv	50	54¼	53	53	—1
ABrnd 8⅞s75	8.7	37	101¾	100½	101¾	+1¼
ABrnd 5⅞s92	7.2	5	81⅛	81⅛	81⅛	+ ⅛
ACyan 7⅜s01	7.9	4	92⅜	92⅜	92⅜	—7⅛
AExp 5¼s93f	cv	68	10	9¼	10	+ ¼
AForP 5s30	10.	13	49½	49½	49½	.....
AFoP 4.8s87	8.5	26	56	55	56	.....
Alnvt 9½s76	9.4	6	101	100⅛	100⅛	— ⅛
Alnvt 8¾s89	8.9	1	98	98	98	— ¾
AMF 4¼s81	cv	18	78	77	77	—2½
AMedcp 5s97	cv	49	46	45½	45½	.....
AMeCl 7½s78	7.8	10	96⅛	96	96	.....
AmMot 6s88	cv	17	79	78¼	79	+1⅜
ASug 5.3s93	7.7	1	68½	68½	68½	.....
ATT 8¾s2000	8.3	626	104⅜	103¾	104¼	+ ⅜
ATT 8.7s02	8.4	265	103	102¾	103	+ ⅛
ATT 7.75s77	7.8	73	99	98¼	98¼	— ⅝
ATT 7⅛s03	8.0	57	89	88½	89	+ ⅝
ATT 7s01	8.0	45	88	87½	87½	+ ⅛
ATT 6½s79	7.0	26	92⅜	92	92⅜	.....
ATT 4⅜s85	6.1	9	71⅛	71⅛	71⅛	+ ⅛
ATT 3⅞s90	6.2	1	62¼	62¼	62¼	+ ¾
ATT 3⅜s73	3.4	52	98 1-32	98	98	—1-32
ATT 2¾s75	3.0	11	91	90¼	90¼	— ¼
ATT 2¾s80	3.8	34	72⅛	71⅝	71⅝	— ⅜
ATT 2¾s82	4.1	51	67	66	66⅝	+ ⅛
ATT 2⅝s86	4.5	10	57¾	57⅛	57½	— ¼
Amfac 5¼s94	cv	97	63	62	62	—1¼
Ampx 5½s94	cv	48	44	43½	44	.....
ApcoO 5s88	cv	55	62	60¼	60¼	—1¾

Each warrant permitted the holder to buy one share of TWA stock. Tom Thomas bought a $10,000 TWA bond.

_____ a. How many warrants did he receive with the bond?

_____ b. How many shares of TWA stock could Mr. Thomas buy?

10. The tangible value of a warrant is the difference between the stock price and the exercise price. If the exercise price of a TWA is $22, and the price of the stock is $34\frac{1}{4}$,

_____ find the tangible value of the warrant.

eight

Insurance

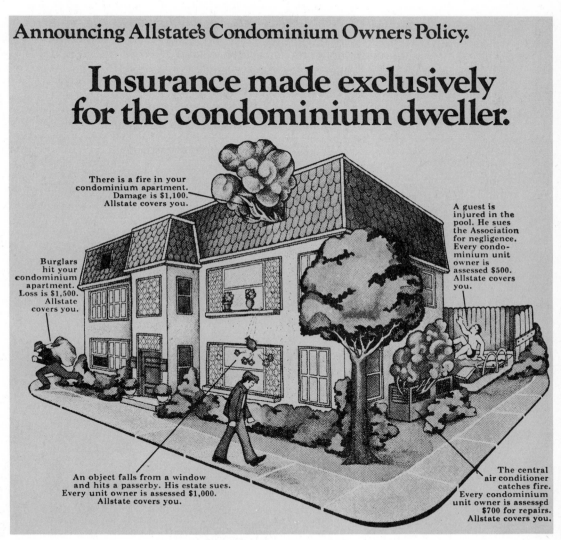

Announcing Allstate's Condominium Owners Policy.

Insurance made exclusively for the condominium dweller.

There is a fire in your condominium apartment. Damage is $1,100. Allstate covers you.

A guest is injured in the pool. He sues the Association for negligence. Every condominium unit owner is assessed $500. Allstate covers you.

Burglars hit your condominium apartment. Loss is $1,500. Allstate covers you.

An object falls from a window and hits a passerby. His estate sues. Every unit owner is assessed $1,000. Allstate covers you.

The central air conditioner catches fire. Every condominium unit owner is assessed $700 for repairs. Allstate covers you.

Courtesy of Allstate Insurance Company

8.1 FIRE INSURANCE

As you can see from the ad above, you can insure your condominium (or home) against different risks. **Fire insurance** provides protection against financial losses caused by fire, lightning, and damages resulting from attempts to extinguish a fire (water or chemical damage, damages caused by fire fighters, or other measures taken to prevent a fire from spreading).

Fire insurance requires that the insured pay, in advance, an amount of money called a **premium.** The size of the premium that the insured pays depends on several factors: the construction of the dwelling or building, its location, and the quality of fire protection available. For example, a building made of steel and cement would require a smaller premium than a frame building. Similarly, property located next to a paint store or a gasoline storage area would require a higher premium than other property located near fire hydrants and served by a large, efficient fire department.

TABLE 8–1   Annual Rate Charge (Inside City Limits)

Const.	Amounts of Insurance	Building or Contents			
		Owner Occupied In Whole or in Part		Solely Tenant Occupied	
		1–2 Families	3–4 Families	1–2 Families	3–4 Families
Masonry and Masonry Veneer	$ 500	5.39	5.49	7.54	7.64
	1,000	5.51	5.71	7.71	7.91
	1,500	5.64	5.94	7.89	8.19
	2,000	5.76	6.16	8.06	8.46
	2,500	5.89	6.39	8.24	8.74
	3,000	6.01	6.61	8.41	9.01
	4,000	6.26	7.06	8.76	9.56
	5,000	6.51	7.51	9.11	10.11
	6,000	6.76	7.96	9.46	10.66
	7,000	7.01	8.41	9.81	11.21
	8,000	7.26	8.86	10.16	11.76
	10,000	7.76	9.76	10.86	12.86
	For Each $100 Not Shown Above, Add	.025	.045	.035	.055
Frame	$ 500	10.25	10.35	14.36	14.46
	1,000	10.57	10.77	14.82	15.02
	1,500	10.90	11.20	15.28	15.58
	2,000	11.22	11.62	15.74	16.14
	2,500	11.55	12.05	16.20	16.70
	3,000	11.87	12.47	16.66	17.26
	4,000	12.52	13.32	17.58	18.38
	5,000	13.17	14.17	18.50	19.50
	6,000	13.82	15.02	19.42	20.62
	7,000	14.47	15.87	20.34	21.74
	8,000	15.12	16.72	21.26	22.86
	10,000	16.42	18.42	23.10	25.10
	For Each $100 Not Shown Above, Add	.065	.085	.092	.112

Unapproved Roof—Add $3.00 to above premiums.

Computing premiums from a table

Based on these factors, an insurance company prepared the rate schedule shown in Table 8.1* Note that there are different rates for masonry and frame buildings. If the building is inside the city limits, it will be serviced by the city fire department and, consequently, we may expect a lower rate than that charged for a similar building out-side city limits. If the owner of a one-family masonry residence in which he resides wishes to insure his property for $10,000, his annual premium would be $7.76. On the other hand, if he desires to insure the property for $10,200 his annual premium would be $7.76 + (2 × .025) = $7.81 (adding $.025 for each $100 not shown in the table).

Example 1

Mr. Henry Beltran wishes to insure his masonry residence for $15,000 fire insurance. If the residence has an unapproved roof of wooden shingles, find the annual premium.

Solution

Rate for $10,000	$ 7.76
Rate for additional $5,000: (50 × $.025)	$ 1.25
Add $3.00 for unapproved roof	$ 3.00
Total premium	$12.01

When premiums are paid in advance for more than one year, most insurance companies offer reduced premiums. These premiums are computed as follows:

Years of Coverage	Multiply annual coverage by:
2	1.85
3	2.70

Example 2

Mr. Jose Clemente wishes to buy a $25,000 fire insurance policy for his apartment building, occupied by four tenant families. If the building is a frame building with an approved roof, what is the premium for three years?

Solution

Rate for $10,000 (from Table 8–1)	$ 25.10
Rate for additional $15,000: (150 × $.112)	$ 16.80
Annual Premium	$ 41.90
	×2.70
Three-Year Premium	$113.13

*Rates vary from one state or community to another.

PROGRESS TEST 1

1. Mr. George Kosan wishes to insure his masonry apartment building occupied by two tenant families for $20,000 fire insurance. If the building has an approved roof, his annual premium will be _____.

2. His premium for two years will be _____.

Extended coverage endorsement

Most insurance policies contain an **extended coverage endorsement.** The purpose of this endorsement is to add to the list of perils which are covered by the policy. The endorsement does not increase the amount of insurance provided in the policy but extends the fire policy to include coverage caused by such perils as windstorms, hail, explosions, smoke, etc. The premium for these endorsements is usually found in a table (similar to Table 8–2 on page 367) prepared by the insurance company and is paid in addition to the premium for fire insurance. Note that again these premiums are dependent on the location (zone), the construction, and the risk the company assumes. For example, since the policy covers windstorms, premiums are more expensive on the seacoast than inland.

Example 3

Dr. William Seeker owns a masonry beach house with an approved roof in Zone 3 (inside the city limits). The building is occupied by four tenant families. Find the 3-year premium for $20,000 of fire insurance and $10,000 of extended coverage on both the building and the contents.

Solution

Rate for $10,000 of fire insurance (Table 8–1)	$12.86
Rate for additional $10,000 (100 × $.055)	$ 5.50
Rate for $10,000 of extended coverage to building (Table 8–2)	$16.80
Rate for $10,000 of extended coverage to contents	$11.20
Annual Premium	$46.36
	× 2.7
Three-Year Premium	$125.17

---

1. $10.86 + (100 × $.035) = $14.36   2. 1.85 × $14.36 = $26.57

TABLE 8–2   **Annual Extended Coverage Premiums**

| Const. | Amounts of Insurance | Seacoast Territory | | | | | | Inland Territory | |
| | | Zone 1 | | Zone 2 | | Zone 3 | | | |
		Bldg.	Conts.	Bldg.	Conts.	Bldg.	Conts.	Bldg.	Conts.
WR (Wind-Resistive)	$ 500	6.30	4.20	4.35	2.90	2.90	1.93	1.90	1.27
	1,000	7.40	4.93	5.10	3.40	3.40	2.27	2.20	1.47
	1,500	8.50	5.67	5.85	3.90	3.90	2.60	2.50	1.67
	2,000	9.60	6.40	6.60	4.40	4.40	2.93	2.80	1.87
	2,500	10.70	7.13	7.35	4.90	4.90	3.27	3.10	2.07
	3,000	11.80	7.87	8.10	5.40	5.40	3.60	3.40	2.27
	4,000	14.00	9.33	9.60	6.40	6.40	4.27	4.00	2.67
	5,000	16.20	10.80	11.10	7.40	7.40	4.93	4.60	3.07
	6,000	18.40	12.27	12.60	8.40	8.40	5.60	5.20	3.47
	7,000	20.60	13.73	14.10	9.40	9.40	6.27	5.80	3.87
	8,000	22.80	15.20	15.60	10.40	10.40	6.93	6.40	4.27
	10,000	27.20	18.13	18.60	12.40	12.40	8.27	7.60	5.07
	For Each $100, Add	.22	.147	.15	.10	.10	.067	.06	.04
SWR (Semi-Wind-Resistive)	$ 500	9.15	6.10	6.30	4.20	4.20	2.80	2.80	1.87
	1,000	10.50	7.00	7.20	4.80	4.80	3.20	3.20	2.13
	1,500	11.85	7.90	8.10	5.40	5.40	3.60	3.60	2.49
	2,000	13.20	8.80	9.00	6.00	6.00	4.00	4.00	2.67
	2,500	14.55	9.70	9.90	6.60	6.60	4.40	4.40	2.93
	3,000	15.90	10.60	10.80	7.20	7.20	4.80	4.80	3.20
	4,000	18.60	12.40	12.60	8.40	8.40	5.60	5.60	3.73
	5,000	21.30	14.20	14.40	9.60	9.60	6.40	6.40	4.27
	6,000	24.00	16.00	16.20	10.80	10.80	7.20	7.20	4.80
	7,000	26.70	17.80	18.00	12.00	12.00	8.00	8.00	5.33
	8,000	29.40	19.60	19.80	13.20	13.20	8.80	8.80	5.87
	10,000	34.80	23.20	23.40	15.60	15.60	10.40	10.40	6.93
	For Each $100, Add	.27	.18	.18	.12	.12	.08	.08	.053
M or F (Masonry or Frame)	$ 500	11.75	7.83	8.10	5.40	5.40	3.60	3.60	2.40
	1,000	13.10	8.73	9.00	6.00	6.00	4.00	4.00	2.67
	1,500	14.45	9.63	9.90	6.60	6.60	4.40	4.40	2.93
	2,000	15.80	10.53	10.80	7.20	7.20	4.80	4.80	3.20
	2,500	17.15	11.43	11.70	7.80	7.80	5.20	5.20	3.47
	3,000	18.50	12.33	12.60	8.40	8.40	5.60	5.60	3.73
	4,000	21.20	14.13	14.40	9.60	9.60	6.40	6.40	4.27
	5,000	23.90	15.93	16.20	10.80	10.80	7.20	7.20	4.80
	6,000	26.60	17.73	18.00	12.00	12.00	8.00	8.00	5.33
	7,000	29.30	19.53	19.80	13.20	13.20	8.80	8.80	5.87
	8,000	32.00	21.33	21.60	14.40	14.40	9.60	9.60	6.40
	10,000	37.40	24.93	25.20	16.80	16.80	11.20	11.20	7.47
	For Each $100, Add	.27	.18	.18	.12	.12	.08	.08	.053

PROGRESS TEST 2

1. Mr. Sam Rampello owns a one-family frame house with an approved roof in Zone 3 (inside the city limits). If Mr. Rampello lives in this house with his family, the premium for $15,000 worth of fire insurance and $12,000 of extended coverage on both the building and the contents is _____.

2. The 2-year premium for the house is _____.

EXERCISE 8.1

In Problems 1 through 5, use Table 8–1 to find the annual fire insurance premium. Assume all buildings in Problems 1 through 10 are inside city limits.

	AMOUNT OF INSURANCE	TYPE OF CONSTRUCTION	OCCUPANTS	NUMBER OF FAMILIES	ROOF
1.	$10,000	Frame	Owner	2	Approved
2.	$10,000	Masonry	Tenant	4	Not approved
3.	$15,000	Frame	Owner	1	Approved
4.	$20,000	Masonry	Tenant	4	Approved
5.	$20,000	Frame	Owner	1	Not Approved

In Problems 6 through 10, find (a) the fire insurance premium for 2 years; (b) the fire insurance premium for 3 years.

	AMOUNT OF INSURANCE	TYPE OF CONSTRUCTION	OCCUPANTS	NUMBER OF FAMILIES	ROOF
6.	$ 8,000	Masonry	Owner	1	Approved
7.	$10,000	Frame	Tenant	3	Not Approved
8.	$11,000	Masonry	Owner	2	Approved
9.	$12,000	Frame	Tenant	4	Not Approved
10.	$15,000	Masonry	Owner	1	Approved

In Problems 11 through 15, use Tables 8–1 and 8–2 to find the annual premiums. Assume all buildings are in Zone 3, inside city limits.

---

1. ($16.42 + (50 × $.065)) + (16.80 + (20 × $.12)) + (11.20 + (20 × $.08)) = $51.67
2. 1.85 × $51.67 = $95.59

	AMOUNT OF FIRE INSURANCE	AMOUNT OF EXTENDED COVERAGE (Bldg. & Conts.)	TYPE OF CONSTRUCTION	OCCUPANT	NUMBER OF FAMILIES	ROOF
11.	$10,000	$ 5,000	Masonry	Owner	1	Approved
12.	$10,000	$10,000	Frame	Tenant	3	Not Approved
13.	$12,000	$ 6,000	Masonry	Tenant	4	Approved
14.	$15,000	$10,000	Frame	Owner	1	Approved
15.	$20,000	$15,000	Masonry	Tenant	4	Not Approved

In Problems 16 through 20, find (a) the two-year premium, (b) the three-year premium for extended coverage insurance on the buildings and contents described in Problems 11 through 15.

21. Mr. Woody Garcia lives by himself in his wind-resistive frame house with an approved roof in an inland territory inside city limits. Find the 3-year premium for $20,000 of fire insurance and $5,000 of extended coverage on both the building and the contents. (Use the wind-resistive rate in Table 8.2.)

22. Repeat Problem 21, assuming the extended coverage for both the building and contents is $10,000.

23. Mr. Frank Cleaver insured the masonry building he rents to a family in Zone 3, inside city limits, for $20,000 of fire insurance. Find his 2-year premium if he also desired to have $12,000 of extended coverage on both the building and the contents. Assume the building has an approved roof.

24. Repeat Problem 23, assuming the building does not have an approved roof and the amount of extended coverage desired on the building and contents is $18,000.

25. Felicia Perez wishes to insure her masonry rooming house (with an approved roof) occupied by four families and located in Zone 1 inside city limits, for $50,000 worth of fire insurance. If she also wishes to have $30,000 worth of extended coverage to both the building and the contents, find the 2-year premium for the policy.

Got enough fire insurance?

Maybe the fire insurance on your house is giving you a sense of false security. Could be, if inflation has watered down its protection.

The question to ask: If your house burned to the ground today, would your coverage be enough to replace it?

Unless you have increased the coverage recently, the answer will be no, not at today's prices.

You don't need to carry an amount equal to the current value of house and lot, though. Only the structure burns, and not all of that. No sense insuring a lawn against fire. But how do you figure what's enough?

A clue: Take the total floor area of your house in square feet and multiply it by $20. If the resulting figure is substantially more than your coverage, talk to your insurance agent soon about updating for inflation.

Reprinted, by permission, from *Changing Times,* the Kiplinger Magazine, Copyright September, 1973.

8.2 COINSURANCE AND MULTIPLE CARRIERS

Coinsurance

Statistical evidence indicates that most fires result in small partial losses. For this reason, many owners insure their property for only a fraction of its value. In order to encourage the purchase of higher limits of coverage, insurance companies offer policies containing **coinsurance clauses.** These policies offer reduced rates for those who agree to buy insurance amounting to a specified per cent (usually 80%) of the property's value. A policy containing an 80% coinsurance clause is referred to as an 80% coinsurance policy. For example, if a building valued at $100,000 contains an 80% coinsurance clause, the insurance required on this building will be 80% of $100,000, that is, $80,000. If the owner fails to carry this amount of coverage ($80,000), the insurance company is obligated to pay only that portion of the claim which is determined by the ratio of the amount of insurance carried to the amount which the insured should carry; that is,

$$\text{Payment for loss} = \frac{\text{Amt. of Insurance Carried}}{\text{Amt. of Insurance Required}} \times \text{Amount of loss}$$

Thus, if the owner of the building mentioned above carries only $60,000 worth of insurance, the company will only pay $\frac{\$60,000}{\$80,000} = \frac{3}{4}$ of his losses. Who pays the rest? The insured does, and therefore he is called a "coinsurer". Of course, the property owner may purchase more insurance than the minimum requirement but in no case will payment for damages exceed the value of the property destroyed, regardless of the amount of insurance carried; that is, the maximum payment on a policy is always the amount of damages or the amount of the policy, whichever is smaller.

Example 1

Karen Jones owns a building valued at $50,000. Mrs. Jones carries $20,000 worth of fire insurance in a policy containing an 80% coinsurance clause.

    (a) What part of a fire loss will the company pay?

    (b) How much will the company pay on a $10,000 loss?

    (c) How much will the company pay on a $45,000 loss?

Solution

    (a) According to the coinsurance clause, 80% of the value of the property must be insured. Thus, the required insurance is 80% of $50,000 = $40,000. The amount carried by Mrs. Jones is $20,000. Hence, the company will pay $\frac{\$20,000}{\$40,000} = \frac{1}{2}$ of the amount of loss, up to $20,000.

    (b) On a $10,000 loss the company will pay $\frac{1}{2}$ of $10,000 = $5,000.

    (c) Preliminary calculations show that the company should pay $\frac{1}{2}$ of $45,000 = $22,500. However, this exceeds the value of the policy ($20,000); therefore, the company will pay only $20,000.

PROGRESS TEST 1

    1. If, in Example 1, the value of the building is $10,000 and Mrs. Jones carries $6,000 worth of insurance, the company will pay _____ of any fire loss up to $6,000.

    2. The amount the company will pay Mrs. Jones on a $1,000 loss is _____.

    3. The amount the company will pay Mrs. Jones on a $9,000 loss is _____.

    It is not unusual for the same property to be covered by more than one policy. This may happen because of several factors: the value of the property may be so high that no single company can afford to assume the entire risk; the owner of the property may decide to buy his policies from several insurance companies, thus distributing his business and creating better public relations; or he simply may have purchased coverage separately on different parts of the property

Multiple carriers

---

1. $\frac{3}{4}$ 2. $750   3. $6,000

over a period of years. In such cases, each of the companies will pay damages in the same proportion that its policy limit is of the total amount of insurance coverage. However, as with single insurers, the total amount paid by all carriers shall never exceed the value of the property destroyed.

Example 2

The Rainbow Paint Store suffered a fire loss amounting to $48,000. It carried insurance under the following policies: $25,000 with company X, $20,000 with company Y, and $15,000 with company Z. What amount will the owner receive from each of the companies? (Assume that it meets the coinsurance requirements to receive full coverage on a loss.)

Solution

The total amount of insurance carried is
$$\$25,000 + \$20,000 + \$15,000 = \$60,000.$$

Company X will pay $\dfrac{\$25,000}{\$60,000} = \dfrac{5}{12}$ of the loss, up to $25,000.

Company Y will pay $\dfrac{\$20,000}{\$60,000} = \dfrac{1}{3}$ of the loss, up to $20,000.

Company Z will pay $\dfrac{\$15,000}{\$60,000} = \dfrac{1}{4}$ of the loss, up to $15,000.

Each Company's payment is as follows:

COMPANY	PAYMENT
X	$\dfrac{5}{12}$ of $48,000 = $20,000
Y	$\dfrac{1}{3}$ of $48,000 = $16,000
Z	$\dfrac{1}{4}$ of $48,000 = $12,000

PROGRESS TEST 2

1. Crown Manufacturing Company suffered a fire loss amounting to $90,000. It carried insurance under the following policies: $125,000 with Company A; $75,000 with Company B; and $50,000 with Company C. The fractions of the loss paid by each of the companies is _____, _____, and _____, respectively.

2. The amount paid by each of the companies is _____, _____, and _____, respectively.

---

1. $\dfrac{1}{2}, \dfrac{3}{10}, \dfrac{1}{5}$ 2. $45,000, $27,000, $18,000

EXERCISE 8.2

In Problems 1 through 5, find the amount paid by the insurance company under a policy containing an 80% coinsurance clause.

	VALUE OF THE PROPERTY	INSURANCE	FIRE LOSS
1.	$30,000	$24,000	$20,000
2.	$12,000	$10,000	$11,000
3.	$25,000	$16,000	$12,000
4.	$17,500	$15,000	$18,000
5.	$15,000	$10,000	$ 7,500

In Problems 6 through 10, find the amount of insurance required by the coinsurance clause and the amount which will be paid under the stated conditions.

	VALUE OF THE PROPERTY	COINSURANCE CLAUSE	INSURANCE REQUIRED	INSURANCE CARRIED	FIRE LOSS	COMPEN- SATION
6.	$ 15,000	80%		$14,000	$ 7,500	
7.	$ 20,000	80%		$20,000	$ 6,000	
8.	$ 15,000	90%		$12,000	$ 9,000	
9.	$ 20,000	70%		$12,000	$12,000	
10.	$130,000	80%		$78,000	$24,000	

In Problems 11 through 15, find the ratio of coverage and the amount to be paid by each insurance company. (Assume that the coinsurance requirements necessary to receive full coverage are met.)

	COMPANY	AMOUNT OF POLICY	RATIO OF COVERAGE	AMOUNT OF LOSS	COMPENSATION
11.	A	$40,000		$ 60,000	
	B	$60,000			
12.	X	$24,000		$ 90,000	
	Y	$36,000			
	Z	$48,000			
13.	U	$20,000		$ 32,000	
	R	$ 8,000			
	S	$12,000			

	COMPANY	AMOUNT OF POLICY	RATIO OF COVERAGE	AMOUNT OF LOSS	COMPENSATION
14.	T	$30,000		$ 27,000	
	U	$18,000			
	V	$ 6,000			
15.	W	$26,000		$ 26,000	
	X	$18,000			
	Y	$ 8,000			
16.	A	$50,000		$160,000	
	B	$30,000			
	C	$30,000			
	D	$40,000			

17. The owner of Flower Kids Florist purchased a $70,000 fire insurance policy to cover her building valued at $100,000. If the policy contains an 80% coinsurance clause, how much money should the owner get in case of a loss amounting to (a) $32,000? (b) $80,000? (c) $96,000?

18. The owner of a $50,000 house purchased a $40,000 fire insurance policy. If the policy contains a 90% coinsurance clause, how much money should the insurance company pay in case of a loss amounting to (a) $18,000? (b) $36,000? (c) $27,000?

19. The coinsurance clause on a $75,000 building required 80% fire coverage. The building was insured for $50,000. Determine the amount to be paid if there is a loss of (a) $9,000; (b) $21,000; (c) $75,000.

20. A factory valued at $180,000 is insured for $144,000. If the policy carries a 90% coinsurance clause, find the settlement due when a fire resulted in damages amounting to (a) $54,000; (b) $108,000; (c) $144,000.

21. Phyllis Darkwood owns a building valued at $60,000. Mrs. Darkwood carries $48,000 worth of fire insurance in a policy containing an 80% coinsurance clause. Find the amount the insurance company will pay after a fire resulting in damages amounting to (a) $40,000; (b) $45,000; (c) $50,000.

22. A residence carries $36,000 of fire insurance with Company X and $24,000 with Company Y. What amount will the owner receive from each of the companies after a fire loss of (a) $15,000? (b) $40,000?

23. A warehouse is protected by the following fire policies: $30,000 with Company B, $60,000 with Company C, and $90,-000 with Company D. What is each company's share of a loss that amounted to (a) $7,500? (b) $72,000? (c) $250,000?

© 1973 United Feature Syndicate, Inc. Reprinted by permission.

8.3 SHORT-TERM AND CANCELLATION RATES

As you can see from the cartoon above, Sally is ready to buy some insurance against injury suffered while building a snowman. The insurance required will probably be a short-term policy, that is, a policy that extends for a period shorter than a year. When an insurance company sells a policy that is in effect for less than a year, the premium is computed with the aid of a short-rate table. This same table is employed to give refunds to policy holders cancelling their policies before the expiration date. Table 8–3 shows a short-rate table for 1-, 2-, and 3-year policies.

As you can see from the table, short-term policies are rather expensive. For example, a one-day fire insurance policy will cost 5% of the amount paid for a one-year policy. Thus, if the fire insurance premium on a $3,000 policy is $6.00, a one-day policy will cost 5% of $6.00, or $0.30.

Short-term policies

Example 1

Mr. J. Johnson wishes to insure his masonry residence (inside city limits) for $7,000. Assuming the residence has an approved roof, find:
  (a) the cost of a 90-day short-term policy.
  (b) the cost of a 155-day short-term policy.

Solution

  (a) The annual premium (from Table 8–1) is $7.01. The premium

TABLE 8–3 **Short Rate Table for Policies Written at Term Multiples Showing Percentage of Premium Earned**

Policy in Force	Term of Policy* 1 Yr.	Term of Policy* 2 Yrs.	Term of Policy* 3 Yrs.	Policy in Force	Term of Policy* 1 Yr.	Term of Policy* 2 Yrs.	Term of Policy* 3 Yrs.
Days	Per Cent of Premium Earned			Days	Per Cent of Premium Earned		
1	5	2.7	1.9	161–164	55	29.7	20.4
2	6	3.2	2.2	165–167	56	30.3	20.7
3–4	7	3.8	2.6	168–171	57	30.8	21.1
5–6	8	4.3	3.0	172–175	58	31.4	21.5
7–8	9	4.9	3.3	176–178	59	31.9	21.9
9–10	10	5.4	3.7	179–182	60	32.4	22.2
11–12	11	5.9	4.1	183–187	61	33.0	22.6
13–14	12	6.5	4.4	188–191	62	33.5	23.0
15–16	13	7.0	4.8	192–196	63	34.1	23.3
17–18	14	7.6	5.2	197–200	64	34.6	23.7
19–20	15	8.1	5.6	201–205	65	35.1	24.1
21–22	16	8.6	5.9	206–209	66	35.7	24.4
23–25	17	9.2	6.3	210–214	67	36.2	24.8
26–29	18	9.7	6.7	215–218	68	36.8	25.2
30–32	19	10.3	7.0	219–223	69	37.3	25.6
33–36	20	10.8	7.4	224–228	70	37.8	25.9
37–40	21	11.4	7.8	229–232	71	38.4	26.3
41–43	22	11.9	8.1	233–237	72	38.9	26.7
44–47	23	12.4	8.5	238–241	73	39.5	27.0
48–51	24	13.0	8.9	242–246	74	40.0	27.4
52–54	25	13.5	9.3	247–250	75	40.5	27.8
55–58	26	14.1	9.6	251–255	76	41.1	28.1
59–62	27	14.3	10.0	256–260	77	41.6	28.5
63–65	28	15.1	10.4	261–264	78	42.2	28.9
66–69	29	15.7	10.7	265–269	79	42.7	29.3
70–73	30	16.2	11.1	270–273	80	43.2	29.6
74–76	31	16.8	11.5	274–278	81	43.8	30.0
77–80	32	17.3	11.9	279–282	82	44.3	30.4
81–83	33	17.8	12.2	283–287	83	44.9	30.7
84–87	34	18.4	12.6	288–291	84	45.4	31.1
88–91	35	18.9	13.0	292–296	85	45.9	31.5
92–94	36	19.5	13.3	297–301	86	46.5	31.9
95–98	37	20.0	13.7	302–305	87	47.0	32.2
99–102	38	20.5	14.1	306–310	88	47.6	32.6
103–105	39	21.1	14.4	311–314	89	48.1	33.0
106–109	40	21.6	14.8	315–319	90	48.6	33.3
110–113	41	22.2	15.2	320–323	91	49.2	33.7
114–116	42	22.7	15.6	324–328	92	49.7	34.1
117–120	43	23.2	15.9	329–332	93	50.3	34.4
121–124	44	23.8	16.3	333–337	94	50.8	34.8
125–127	45	24.3	16.7	338–342	95	51.4	35.2
128–131	46	24.9	17.0	343–346	96	51.9	35.6
132–135	47	25.4	17.4	347–351	97	52.4	35.9
136–138	48	25.9	17.8	352–355	98	53.0	36.3
139–142	49	26.5	18.1	356–360	99	53.5	36.7
143–146	50	27.0	18.5	361–365	100	54.1	37.0
147–149	51	27.6	18.9				
150–153	52	28.1	19.3				
154–156	53	28.6	19.6				
157–160	54	29.2	20.0				

*2-Year Policies Written at 1.85 Annuals; 3-Year Policies at 2.7 Annuals.

for 90 days (from Table 8–3) is 35% of the annual premium. Thus, the cost of a 90-day short-term policy is

$$\frac{35}{100} \times \$7.01 = \$2.45$$

(b) The annual premium is $7.01. The premium for 155 days is 53% of the annual premium. Thus, the cost of a 155-day short-term policy is

$$\frac{53}{100} \times \$7.01 = \$3.72$$

PROGRESS TEST 1

1. Ms. Ivy Strickler owns a masonry apartment house (inside city limits) occupied by four tenant families and having an approved roof. If she desires to purchase a 180-day, $10,000 fire insurance policy, her cost will be _____.
2. If the policy were for 45 days, her cost would be

_____.

Example 2

Mr. Carter Blanche owns a masonry apartment building in Zone 2 (inside city limits). The building is occupied by four tenant families and has an approved roof. Mr. Blanche purchased a 3-year, $15,000 fire insurance policy and $5,000 of extended coverage on the building and contents. If he cancelled the policy 60 days later,
   (a) how much did the insurance company retain?
   (b) how much refund did Mr. Blanche receive?

Solution

(a) Rate for $10,000 of fire insurance	$12.86
Rate for additional $5,000: (50 × $.055)	2.75
Rate for $5,000 of extended coverage to building	16.20
Rate for $5,000 of extended coverage to contents	10.80
Annual Premium	$42.61
	× 2.7
Three-year Premium	$115.05
Per Cent of Premium Earned (Table 8–3)	10%
Total Retained by the Company	$ 11.51

(b) Since the cost of the policy is $115.05, the refund is $115.05 − $11.51 = $103.54.

---

1. 60% of $12.86 = $7.72   2. 23% of $12.86 = $2.96

```
┌─────────────────────────────────────────────────────────────┐
│                     PROGRESS TEST 2                           │
│                                                               │
│        1. If, in Example 2, Mr. Blanche cancelled the policy in │
│     160 days, the amount retained by the company would        │
│     be _____.                                        │
│        2. If, in Example 2, Mr. Blanche cancelled the policy in │
│     160 days, his refund would be _____.             │
└─────────────────────────────────────────────────────────────┘
```

EXERCISE 8.3

In Problems 1 through 5, find the premium (using Tables 8–1 and 8–3) for the specified length of time.

	AMOUNT OF INSURANCE	TYPE OF CONSTRUCTION	OCCUPANT	NUMBER OF FAMILIES	ROOF	TIME
1.	$10,000	Frame	Owner	2	Approved	30 days
2.	$10,000	Masonry	Tenant	4	Not Approved	60 days
3.	$15,000	Frame	Owner	1	Approved	90 days
4.	$20,000	Masonry	Tenant	4	Approved	60 days
5.	$20,000	Frame	Owner	1	Not Approved	160 days

In Problems 6 through 10, find the amount the insurance company retains if the given policy is cancelled after the specified time.

	AMOUNT OF INSURANCE	TYPE OF CONSTRUCTION	OCCUPANT	NUMBER OF FAMILIES	ROOF	TIME	CANCELLED AFTER
6.	$ 8,000	Masonry	Owner	1	Approved	2 years	15 days
7.	$10,000	Frame	Tenant	3	Not Approved	3 years	61 days
8.	$11,000	Masonry	Owner	2	Approved	2 years	48 days
9.	$12,000	Frame	Tenant	4	Not Approved	3 years	275 days
10.	$15,000	Masonry	Owner	1	Approved	2 years	97 days

In Problems 11 through 15, find the premiums for the specified time. Assume all buildings are in Zone 3, inside city limits.

1. $\dfrac{20}{100} \times \$115.05 = \$23.01$ 2. $\$115.05 - \$23.01 = \$92.04$

	AMOUNT OF INSURANCE	EXTENDED COVERAGE (Bldg. & (Contents)	TYPE OF CONSTRUCTION	OCCUPANT	NUMBER OF FAMILIES	ROOF	TIME
11.	$10,000	$ 5,000	Masonry	Owner	1	Approved	34 days
12.	$10,000	$10,000	Frame	Tenant	3	Not Approved	65 days
13.	$12,000	$ 6,000	Masonry	Tenant	4	Approved	145 days
14.	$15,000	$10,000	Frame	Owner	1	Approved	225 days
15.	$20,000	$15,000	Masonry	Tenant	4	Not Approved	275 days

16. Mr. Woody Garcia bought a 3-year, $20,000 fire insurance policy with $5,000 of extended coverage on both the building and the contents. If Mr. Garcia lives by himself in a wind-resistive frame house with an approved roof in an inland territory within city limits, how much money would he receive as a refund if he cancelled the policy in 90 days? (Use the wind-resistive rate in Table 8.2.)

17. Repeat Problem 16, assuming the extended coverage for both the building and the contents amounted to $10,000.

18. Mr. Frank Cleaver rents a masonry building with an approved roof to a family in Zone 3, inside city limits. He insured it for $20,000 of fire insurance and $12,000 of extended coverage on both the building and the contents. If the policy was bought for a period of three years, how much money would he receive as a refund if he cancelled the policy in 275 days?

19. Repeat Problem 18, assuming the building does not have an approved roof and the amount of extended coverage desired on the building and contents is $18,000.

20. Felicia Perez insured her masonry rooming house with an approved roof located in Zone 1, inside city limits, and occupied by four families, for $50,000 worth of fire insurance and $30,000 of extended coverage on both the building and the contents. If the policy was bought for a period of two years, how much money would she receive as a refund if she cancelled the policy in 90 days?

8.4 AUTOMOBILE INSURANCE

Most car owners carry insurance to protect themselves and their property in case of accidents or other losses. These policies are usually written for a period of one year and are divided into two basic categories:

1. **Collision and comprehensive** (damages to your car)
2. **Liability** (damage to another car or person)

We first consider collision and comprehensive insurance.

Collision insurance

Collision coverage pays your losses if your own car is damaged in a collision with other moving objects or in a single-car accident. Collision policies usually carry a **deductible clause.** Most people carry a $100 deductible policy. Under such policies, the insured agrees to pay for the first $100 worth of damages to his car and the insurance company will pay the rest. For example, if you carry a $100 deductible policy and have an accident that causes damages to your car costing $250, you pay the first $100, and the insurance company pays the remaining $150.

Comprehensive insurance

Comprehensive coverage pays for all damages to an automobile **other than collision.** Such losses as fire, theft, vandalism, hail, windstorm, and falling objects are grouped under the comprehensive coverage. Comprehensive coverage may also carry a deductible clause with provisions similar to those of the deductible clause in collision coverage.

The amount you pay for insurance depends on several factors:

1. Where you are (the territory or area in which you drive your car)

Note that new cars are classified as "1". One year old cars are "2", two year old cars are "3", etc.

2. How old your car is (Automobiles of the current year are classified as "Age Group 1"; last year's models are in "Age Group 2", etc.)
3. The price of your car when new (The model class: low priced cars have lower numbers, or letters at the beginning of the alphabet.)
4. Your age, sex, and marital status
5. Who drives the car

TABLE 8–4 Collision Premiums

Territory	Age Group	$50 Deductible Collision						$100 Deductible Collision					
		Symbol (Class and Model)						Symbol (Class and Model)					
		A-G H-I 1, 2	J-K 3	L-M 4	N-O 5	P-S 6	T-Z 7	A-G H-I 1, 2	J-K 3	L-M 4	N-O 5	P-S 6	T-Z 7
05	1	$56	$64	$75	$90	$105	$120	$35	$39	$46	$55	$64	$74
	2, 3	42	48	56	68	79	90	26	29	35	41	48	55
	4, 5	37	41	49	59	68	78	23	25	30	36	42	48
	6	31	35	41	50	58	66	19	22	25	30	35	40
06	1	39	44	52	62	73	83	29	33	39	47	55	62
	2, 3	29	33	39	47	55	62	22	25	29	35	41	47
	4, 5	25	29	34	41	47	54	19	21	25	30	35	41
	6	21	24	29	34	40	46	16	18	21	26	30	34
07	1	58	65	77	92	108	123	39	44	52	62	73	83
	2, 3	43	49	58	69	81	92	29	33	39	47	55	62
	4, 5	38	42	50	60	70	80	25	29	34	41	47	54
	6	32	36	42	51	59	68	21	24	29	34	40	46

Comprehensive Premiums

Territory	Age Group	Full Coverage Comprehensive						$50 Deductible Comprehensive					
		Symbol (Class and Model)						Symbol (Class and Model)					
		A-G H-I 1, 2	J-K 3	L-M 4	N-O 5	P-S 6	T-Z 7	A-G H-I 1, 2	J-K 3	L-M 4	N-O 5	P-S 6	T-Z 7
05	1	$13	$17	$21	$28	$37	$46	$5	$7	$9	$12	$16	$20
	2, 3	9	13	16	21	28	35	4	5	7	9	12	15
	4, 5	7	9	12	16	20	25	3	4	5	7	9	11
	6	6	8	9	13	17	21	2	3	4	6	7	9
06	1	9	12	15	20	26	33	4	6	7	9	12	15
	2, 3	7	9	11	15	20	25	3	4	5	7	9	12
	4, 5	5	7	8	11	14	18	2	3	4	5	7	8
	6	4	5	7	9	12	15	2	3	3	4	6	7
07	1	15	20	25	34	44	55	7	9	11	15	19	24
	2, 3	11	15	19	25	33	41	5	7	8	11	14	18
	4, 5	8	11	14	19	24	30	4	5	6	8	11	13
	6	7	9	11	15	20	25	3	4	5	7	9	11

6. How the car is used (pleasure, driving to and from work, business)

7. Your driving record

Table 8–4 shows the physical damage (collision and comprehensive) premiums used by a large insurance company. The table is divided into two parts, one for collision and one for comprehensive.

As you can see from the table, it is easy to compute the premium if we have the territory, age group (of the car), and model class. For example, for a V-1 car (a high priced, brand new car) driven in territory 6, the basic $50 deductible collision premium is $83; the basic $100 deductible collision premium is $62; and the basic full coverage comprehensive premium is $33.

Example 1

Find the premium for full coverage comprehensive and $50 deductible collision for a K-5 car in territory 5.

Solution

Full comprehensive premium (from Table 8–4)	$ 9
$50 deductible collision (from Table 8–4)	$41
Total premium	$50

As we mentioned before, several factors (we listed six of them) are considered in determining the amount of money you pay for collision and comprehensive insurance. Table 8–4 takes into account the first three factors mentioned in the list (where you are, how old the car is, the price of the car). Table 8–5 shows some other factors mentioned in the list that must be taken into account to determine the premium rates when there are no young drivers in the family.

Table 8–5 is used in conjunction with Table 8–4. If, for example, the operator of the car in Example 1 is a female, 35 years of age, who drives to work a distance of less than ten miles, the factor in Table 8–5 will be 1.05 and the premium will be 1.05 × $50 = $52.50.

If there is a youthful operator in the family, several other factors are taken into account. These include age, sex, marital status, whether or not the drivers have taken a driving training course, and whether the drivers are owners or principal operators of the automobile. Table 8–6 presents the factors to be used in families with a youthful operator.

TABLE 8–5 **Automobile Insurance Premium Factors (No Youthful Operator)**

AGE AND SEX		PLEASURE USE	DRIVE TO OR FROM WORK		BUSINESS USE	FARM USE
			Less than 10 Miles	*10 or More Miles*		
Only Operator in Household is a Female Age 30–64	Factor	.90	1.05	1.30	1.35	.75
Principal Operator is Age 65 or Over	Factor	.95	1.10	1.35	1.40	.80
All Other	Factor	1.00	1.15	1.40	1.45	.85

It is very important to mention that automobiles are classified according to the status of the youngest person operating the car, or the person whose classification requires the highest factor.

Important!

Example 2

"Speedy" Gonzalez is 17 and unmarried. He owns a model B automobile in age group 4. Gonzalez lives in territory 7 and drives eight miles to work. What will be the cost of $50 deductible collision and full comprehensive coverage if he has had no driver's training?

Solution

Comprehensive premium (Table 8–4)	$ 8
$50 deductible collision premium	$ 38
Base annual premium	$ 46
Youthful operator factor (unmarried male, 17, owner, drives to work, no driver's training)	×3.65
Total annual premium	$167.90

> ### PROGRESS TEST 1
>
> 1. Felicia Johnson is 30 and married. She owns a model K automobile which she uses for pleasure in territory 6. Mrs. Johnson's car is in age group 1 and she has had no driver's training. The cost of $100 deductible collision and full comprehensive coverage for her car is _____ _____.
>
> 2. If Mrs. Johnson has a 17-year-old, single daughter who has had no driver's training, the cost of $100 deductible collision and full comprehensive coverage for her car will be _____.

We now discuss the second category of automobile insurance.

Liability insurance provides financial protection for damages to another car or person. This type of insurance covers **bodily injury liability** (liability for which you become legally responsible if you injure someone else) and **property damage liability** (liability for damages to someone's property). An optional coverage is **medical**

Liability insurance

---

1. ($33 + $12) × .90 = $40.50   2. ($33 + $12) × 1.75 = $78.75. Note that the factor 1.75, the highest factor, is the one that applies.

TABLE 8–6   **Automobile Insurance Premium Factors (Youthful Operator)**

AGE			UNMARRIED FEMALE		MARRIED MALE	
			Pleasure Use or Farm Use	Drive to Work or Business Use	Pleasure Use or Farm Use	Drive to Work or Business Use
Without Driver Training	17 or Less	Factor	1.75	1.90	1.95	2.10
	18	Factor	1.60	1.75	1.85	2.00
	19	Factor	1.50	1.65	1.75	1.90
	20	Factor	1.25	1.40	1.65	1.80
With Driver Training	17 or Less	Factor	1.60	1.75	1.70	1.85
	18	Factor	1.50	1.65	1.65	1.80
	19	Factor	1.40	1.55	1.60	1.75
	20	Factor	1.20	1.35	1.55	1.70
With or Without Driver Training	21	Factor	1.15	1.30	1.50	1.65
	22	Factor	1.10	1.25	1.40	1.55
	23	Factor	1.05	1.20	1.30	1.45
	24	Factor	1.00	1.15	1.20	1.35

payment insurance, which pays the medical bills and the funeral expenses of victims of auto accidents, regardless of fault. The persons covered by this type of insurance include any persons riding in your car, as well as you and others in your family if you are injured while traveling in another car or are hit by a car.

The limit of your liability insurance (the maximum amount the company will pay) is usually described by a series of three numbers separated by a diagonal line, for example, 10/20/5. Each number represents a multiple of 1,000. The first number designates the policy's maximum payment ($10,000) for an injury to one person; the second number gives the maximum ($20,000) for all injuries in one accident; and the third number indicates the maximum payment ($5,000) for property damage.

As with collision and comprehensive, several factors determine the rates charged for liability insurance. Table 8–7 shows the basic annual premiums used by a large insurance company. This table is used in conjunction with Table 8–5 or 8–6.

For example, the basic annual premium for a 10/20/25 liability insurance policy in territory 5 is $20 + $21 = $41 ($20 for the 10/20

TABLE 8–6 Youthful Operator—*Continued*

AGE			UNMARRIED MALE			
			Not Owner or Principal Operator		Owner or Principal Operator	
			Pleasure Use or Farm Use	Drive to Work or Business Use	Pleasure Use or Farm Use	Drive to Work or Business Use
Without Driver Training	17 or Less	Factor	2.75	2.90	3.50	3.65
	18	Factor	2.55	2.70	3.30	3.45
	19	Factor	2.40	2.55	3.10	3.25
	20	Factor	2.25	2.40	2.85	3.00
With Driver Training	17 or Less	Factor	2.30	2.45	3.10	3.25
	18	Factor	2.15	2.30	2.90	3.05
	19	Factor	2.05	2.20	2.70	2.85
	20	Factor	1.95	2.10	2.55	2.70
With or Without Driver Training	21	Factor	1.90	2.05	2.50	2.65
	22	Factor	1.70	1.85	2.35	2.50
	23	Factor	1.55	1.70	2.20	2.35
	24	Factor	1.35	1.50	2.05	2.20
With or Without Driver Training	25	Factor	CLASSIFY AND RATE AS NO YOUTHFUL OPERATOR		1.90	2.05
	26	Factor			1.75	1.90
	27	Factor			1.55	1.70
	28	Factor			1.40	1.55
	29	Factor			1.25	1.40

TABLE 8–7 Liability Insurance Rates

TERRITORY	BODILY INJURY					PROPERTY DAMAGE		
	10/20	15/30	25/50	50/100	100/300	5,000	10,000	25,000
05	$20	$25	$30	$35	$40	$19	$20	$21
06	19	24	28	33	38	18	19	20
07	24	30	36	42	49	20	21	22

and $21 for the 25). However, if the operator of the car is a female, 30 years of age, who drives to work less than 10 miles (factor = 1.05, from Table 8–5), the policy will be $1.05 \times \$41 = \$43.05$.

Example 3

Mida Lariz is 24 years old and unmarried. She drives her car to work in territory 7. Find:

(a) the cost of a basic 15/30/10 liability coverage.

(b) the actual cost of her 15/30/10 liability coverage.

Solution

From Table 8–7, the basic cost of a 15/30 bodily injury policy in territory 7 is $30. The cost of $10,000 of property damage insurance in the same territory is $21. Thus, the total base premium (a) is:

Bodily injury (15/30)	$30
Property damage ($10,000)	$21
Total basic premium	$51

The factor (from Table 8–6) for a 24-year-old, unmarried female who drives to work, with or without driver's training, is 1.15. Thus, the actual cost of 15/30/10 liability coverage (b) is

Basic Coverage	$51.00
Factor (Table 8–6)	× 1.15
Actual annual cost	$58.65

PROGRESS TEST 2

1. If, in Example 3, Miss Lariz wished to have 100/300/25 coverage, her basic premium would be _____.

2. Her actual annual premium would be _____.

EXERCISE 8.4

In Problems 1 through 5, use Table 8–4 to find

(a) the premium for $50 deductible collision and full coverage comprehensive.

---

1. $49 + $22 = $71   2. $1.15 \times \$71 = \$81.65$

(b) the premium for $100 deductible collision and $50 deductible comprehensive.

1. A one-year-old car, coded K, driven in territory 5.

2. A three-year-old car, coded A, driven in territory 7.

3. A two-year-old car, coded Z, driven in territory 6.

4. A four-year-old car, coded H, driven in territory 7.

5. A two-year-old car, coded P, driven in territory 5.

In Problems 6 through 15, find the premiums for the given automobiles:

	MAKE AND MODEL	CODE	COVERAGE	DRIVERS	TERRITORY
6.	Buick Skylark	N-2	$50 Deductible Coll. and Comp.	Male, 65, pleasure use	5
7.	Cadillac DeVille	Z-4	$100 Deductible Coll. and full Comp.	Unmarried male, 17, no driver's training, farm use, not owner	6
8.	Chevrolet Camaro	I-4	$50 Deductible Coll. and Comp.	Married male, 17, driver's training, drives to work	7
9.	Dodge Dart	K-2	$100 Deductible Coll. and full Comp.	Unmarried male, 23, drives to work, owner	5
10.	Ford Maverick	B-3	$100 Deductible Coll. and full Comp.	Unmarried male, 17, owner, no driver's training, pleasure	6
11.	Ford Mustang	J-1	$50 Deductible Coll. and Comp	Unmarried male, 19, not owner, driver's training, pleasure	7
12.	Mercury Monterey	L-1	$100 Deductible Coll. and full Comp.	Unmarried male, 24, not owner, drives to work	5
13.	Lincoln Cont.	T-1	$100 Deductible Coll. and full Comp.	Unmarried male, 27, owner, drives to work 10 miles	6
14.	Oldsmobile Toronado	T-2	$50 Deductible Coll. and full Comp.	Unmarried male, 28, not owner, drives to work 10 miles	7
15.	Plymouth Belv.	J-1	$50 Deductible Coll. and Comp.	Married female, 20, pleasure use	5

In Problems 16 through 20, compute the liability premium for the given owners. (Recall that automobiles are classified according to the person who requires the highest factor.)

	COVERAGE	DRIVERS AND USE	TERRITORY
16.	10/20/5	Male, 65, pleasure use	5
17.	15/30/5	Unmarried male, 17, no driver's training, farm use, not owner	6
18.	15/30/10	Married male, 17, driver's training, drives to work	7
19.	25/50/5	Unmarried male, 23, drives to work, owner	5
20.	25/50/25	Married male, 65, son unmarried, 17, not owner, no driver's training, pleasure	6
21.	50/100/5	Unmarried male, 19, not owner, driver's training, pleasure	7
22.	50/100/10	Unmarried male, 24, not owner, drives to work	5
23.	50/100/25	Unmarried male, 28, not owner, drives to work 10 miles	6
24.	100/300/10	Male, 65, son unmarried, 19, not principal operator, no driver's training, pleasure	7
25.	100/300/25	Male, 66, daughter, unmarried, 19, drives to work, no driver's training.	5

26. Carlos Cano is 24 years old, married, and living in territory 5. He drives to work. How much must he pay for a policy containing $10,000 coverage of single bodily injuries, $20,000 for total injuries, and $5,000 for property damage?

27. Find the annual premium for Mr. Carlos Nunez, 24 years old, married, and driving to work in territory 7, if he wishes to have a 50/100/25 liability insurance policy.

28. If, in addition to the coverage given in Problem 27, Mr. Nunez is required to carry full comprehensive and $50 deductible collision insurance on his model Q new car, how much will he pay for his insurance?

8.5 LIFE INSURANCE

As you can see from the ad above, the insurance company will accept you if you are between 55 and 87 years of age. Why would anyone wish to be accepted in such a plan? The basic purpose of life insurance is to provide compensation to survivors following the death of the insured. There are two basic types of life insurance:

1. **Term insurance**
2. **Whole life insurance** (also called "straight life" or "ordinary life")

Term insurance offers protection for a specified period of time, usually one year or five years. If at the end of this time the policyholder is alive, then the policy ceases. The premiums for term insurance are less expensive than those for other types of policies, but unlike those for whole life, they go up every year or every five years. The increased premium reflects the increased probability of death as age increases.

A term policy is called **convertible** if you can convert it into a whole life policy without having a new medical examination, and **renewable** if the policy can be renewed at the end of each period simply by paying the increased premium.

Whole life premiums normally remain constant throughout the life of the policy. This type of insurance is relatively expensive because it is a form of financial investment as well as insurance protection. Each whole life insurance policy contains a table showing the **cash value** of the policyholder's investment after each year. If the insured wishes to terminate his coverage, he can elect to surrender his policy and receive this cash value.

All life insurance policies, whether term or whole life, are either **participating** or **nonparticipating**. Participating policies pay dividends

Term insurance

Definition of convertible and renewable

Whole life insurance

Participating and nonparticipating policies

to the policyholder, while nonparticipating policies do not. Of course, the premiums for policies that pay dividends are generally higher than for those that don't.

In addition to term and whole life insurance, we shall discuss two other types of policies: 20-payment life and 20-year endowment.

20-payment life policies are those in which the policyholder agrees to make premium payments for a specified number of years (usually 20). The years chosen to make these premium payments are those in which the policyholder's earnings are greatest and payments can be met without adverse economic consequences. Upon completion of premium payments, the premium ceases and the policy remains in force until death.

Endowment policies are a variation on whole life policies. As do whole life policies, endowment policies build up cash value. However, in the case of an endowment policy, the cash value builds up faster, so that it equals the entire face amount of the policy within a specified time (usually 20 years) or at a specified age (often 65). At this time, the policyholder receives the entire face amount.

Table 8–8 shows the annual premium rates for different $1,000 policies.

To read the table, we first find the age of the insured (to the nearest birthday). The amount in dollars and cents shown in the row adjacent to the age represents the annual premium for the type of insurance specified at the head of each column. For example, the annual premium for a $1,000, 10-year term policy issued to a 19-year-old male is $9.04. Similarly, the annual price for a participating ordinary life policy is $19.26.

20-payment life policies

Endowment policies

Computing life insurance rates using a table

TABLE 8–8   **Annual Premium Rates for $1,000 Policies***

AGE AT ISSUE	10-YEAR TERM	ORDINARY LIFE		20-PAYMENT LIFE		20-YEAR ENDOWMENT	
		Part.	*Nonpart.*	*Part.*	*Nonpart.*	*Part.*	*Nonpart.*
18	8.92	18.60	13.35	28.13	22.13	46.00	40.00
19	9.04	19.26	13.39	28.55	22.61	46.15	40.03
20	9.16	19.96	13.74	29.00	23.10	46.30	40.06
21	9.28	20.70	14.12	29.44	23.59	46.45	40.10
22	9.38	21.44	14.50	29.90	24.10	46.61	40.14
23	9.48	22.22	14.91	30.40	24.62	46.78	40.18
24	9.58	23.04	15.33	30.90	25.15	46.96	40.22
25	9.70	23.98	15.79	31.43	25.69	47.15	40.26
30	10.36	26.87	18.37	34.36	28.63	48.25	40.60
35	11.40	30.60	21.65	37.94	31.95	49.83	41.37
40	13.53	35.50	25.65	42.40	36.12	52.00	42.79
45	17.23	42.04	30.98	48.12	41.37	55.28	46.38
50	23.00	50.97	37.90	55.77	48.52	60.50	50.31
55	32.30	63.21	47.01	66.29	56.92	68.76	57.08
60	46.30	70.18	59.18	81.20	73.21	81.76	67.87

*This is a table for males. Because of the longer life expectancy of women, rates for females are lower.

Example 1

Find the annual premium paid by Mr. Ron Cuervo, who was 25 years old when he bought $1,000 worth of
- (a) 10-year term insurance.
- (b) nonparticipating ordinary life insurance.
- (c) participating 20-payment life.
- (d) nonparticipating 20-year endowment.

Solution

(a) We find Mr. Cuervo's age (25 years) in the first column under the heading "Age at Issue". The annual premium for a $1,000, 10-year term insurance policy is $9.70.

(b) The annual premium for a $1,000, nonparticipating ordinary life insurance policy for a man 25 years of age (see column 4) is $15.79.

(c) The annual premium for a $1,000, participating 20-payment life insurance policy for a man 25 years of age (see column 5) is $31.43.

(d) The annual premium for a $1,000, nonparticipating 20-year endowment policy for a man 25 years of age (see column 8) is $40.26.

When insurance companies are not paid in advance for their annual premiums, their rates are slightly higher. Table 8–9 shows the rates used by a certain large insurance company. (Rates vary from company to company.)

Example 2

Mr. J. Charles is 24 years old. Find the premium for a $5,000 participating ordinary life insurance policy if he decides to pay his premiums
- (a) annually.
- (b) semiannually.
- (c) quarterly.
- (d) monthly.

Solution

(a) From Table 8–8, the annual premium for $1,000 worth of participating ordinary life insurance for a man 24 years of age is $23.04. Thus, the premium for a $5,000 policy is $5 \times \$23.04 = \$115.20$.

TABLE 8–9   **Life Insurance Premium Rates and Frequency of Payment**

TYPE OF PAYMENT	PER CENT OF ANNUAL RATE
Semiannual	52
Quarterly	26.5
Monthly	8.875

(b) The semiannual premium (from Table 8–9) is 52% of the annual premium. Thus, each semiannual premium is $\frac{52}{100} \times \$115.20 = \$59.90$, and hence the total cost is \$119.80.

(c) Each quarterly premium is $\frac{26.5}{100} \times \$115.20 = \$30.53$, so the total cost is \$122.12.

(d) Each monthly premium is $\frac{8.875}{100} \times \$115.20 = \$10.22$, so the total cost is \$122.64.

PROGRESS TEST 1

1. Leonard Soniat is 30 years old. His annual premium for a \$2,000, nonparticipating 20-year endowment policy is _____.

2. His monthly premium for this policy would be _____.

3. His semiannual premium for this policy would be _____.

A major difficulty encountered by insurance buyers is the estimation of the effect that premiums, cash values, and dividends have on the cost of their policies.

Net cost method of comparing insurance policies

Insurance policies have usually been compared by their "average surrendered net cost per \$1,000" of the face amount. This method of comparison, better known as the net cost method, allows one to compute the cost of policies by using the following formulas:

For nonparticipating policies:

FORMULA 8.1
Net Cost = Total Premiums − Cash Value

For participating policies:

FORMULA 8.2
Net Cost = Total Premium − (Cash Value + Dividends)

---

1. $2 \times \$40.60 = \$81.20$ 2. $\frac{8.875}{100} \times \$81.20 = \$7.21$ 3. $\frac{52}{100} \times \$81.20 = \$42.22$

Example 3

Mr. James Reed, 35 years old, has $10,000 worth of nonparticipating ordinary life instance. The cash value of the policy at the end of 20 years is $2,500. Find the net cost per $1,000 for the 20-year period.

Solution

According to Formula 8.1, Net Cost = Total Premiums — Cash Value.

You pay:

Total premiums (10 × $21.65) × 20	$4,330.00

You receive:

Cash value at the end of 20 years	$2,500.00
Net cost for 20 years	$1,830.00
Net cost per $1,000 (divide by 10)	$ 183.00
Net cost per year per $1,000 (divide by 20)	$ 9.15

In Example 3 we obtained a positive answer. However, in many cases the answer is negative and yet insurance companies continue to sell insurance. The reason is that a most significant factor has been omitted–**interest.** Under the net cost method, a term insurance policy whose premiums start at $500 per year and decrease gradually to $100 would look as good as one whose premiums start at $100 and increase gradually to $500. Yet the second policy is a much better investment. Why? Because the money not spent on premiums in the early years could be put in a savings account in the bank and earn interest. For this reason, the life insurance industry introduced in 1970 a new method of comparing costs for life insurance policies, the so-called interest-adjusted net cost method. This method is similar to the net cost method, but interest is considered as a factor (a rate of 4% compounded annually is used for uniformity). Here is how the interest-adjusted net cost method works for 20-year policies:

Interest-adjusted net cost method of comparing insurance policies

1. The annual premium is multiplied by 30.97. (This factor corresponds to the amount of money you would have at the end of 20 years if $1 was deposited at the beginning of each year and compounded annually at the rate of 4%).

2. You subtract from the amount obtained in 1 the cash value of the policy.*

3. The amount obtained in 2 is the interest-adjusted net cost for 20 years. If you desire to find the "interest-adjusted net cost index per year per $1,000," you first divide by the number of thousands worth of insurance bought and then divide by 30.97. The resulting

---

*In the case of participating policies you also have to find the compound amount for the dividends and subtract from the quantity in 1. For simplicity, we shall restrict our discussion to nonparticipating policies.

figure represents the amou it of money you would have to deposit at the beginning of each year in an account earning 4% interest compounded annually so that at the end of 20 years you would have a sum of money equal to the net cost.

We apply this new method to the policy of Example 3.

Example 4

Find the interest-adjusted net cost and the interest-adjusted net cost index for the policy in Example 3.

Solution

You pay:

$216.50 × 30.97 (your premiums compounded)	$6,705.01

You receive:

Cash value at the end of 20 years	2,500.00
Interest-adjusted net cost for 20 years	$4,205.01
Cost per $1,000 (divide by 10)	$ 420.50
Interest-adjusted net cost index per year per $1,000 (divide by 30.97)	$ 13.58

This last amount ($13.58) represents the amount that must be invested each year in an account earning 4% interest compounded annually so that at the end of 20 years you will have accumulated the sum of money equal to the net cost of $1,000 of insurance protection for the 20-year period.

PROGRESS TEST 2

1. Mr. Michael Caballero, who is 22 years old, has $10,000 worth of nonparticipating ordinary life insurance. The cash value of his policy at the end of 20 years is $3,000. The net cost per $1,000 for the 20-year period is _____ _____.

2. The interest-adjusted net cost for 20 years is _____.

3. The interest-adjusted net cost index per year per $1,000 is _____.

1. The net cost is $((10 \times \$14.50) \times 20) - \$3,000 = -\$100$. The net cost per $1,000 is −$10.   2. $4,490.65   3. $\frac{449.07}{30.97} = \$14.50$

EXERCISE 8.5

In Problems 1 through 12, use Tables 8–8 and 8–9 to determine
  (a) the annual premium.
  (b) the semiannual premium.
  (c) the quarterly premium.
  (d) the monthly premium.

	AGE TO NEAREST BIRTHDAY	TYPE OF POLICY	AMOUNT
1.	50	10-year term	$10,000
2.	45	participating, ordinary	$15,000
3.	40	nonparticipating, ordinary	$20,000
4.	30	20-payment life, nonparticipating	$10,000
5.	24	20-year endowment, participating	$15,000
6.	22	20-payment life, nonparticipating	$20,000
7.	23	20-year endowment, nonparticipating	$25,000
8.	22	20-payment life, participating	$25,000
9.	21	nonparticipating, ordinary	$30,000
10.	20	participating, 20-payment life	$20,000
11.	19	10-year term	$15,000
12.	18	20-year endowment, nonparticipating	$50,000

In Problems 13 through 17, use Table 8–8 to find:
  (a) the net cost.
  (b) the net cost per year per $1,000.

	AGE TO NEAREST BIRTHDAY	TYPE OF POLICY	AMOUNT	DIVIDEND	CASH VALUE
13.	18	10-year term	$1,000	—	0
14.	19	20-payment life, participating	$5,000	$300	2,500
15.	20	20-year endowment, nonparticipating	$10,000	—	10,000
16.	21	20-payment life, participating	$15,000	$5,000	7,500
17.	60	20-year endowment, participating	$20,000	$7,000	20,000

In Problems 18 through 27, find (a) the interest-adjusted net cost, and
(b) the interest-adjusted net cost index per year per $1,000 for the
following $10,000 nonparticipating straight life policies.

	COMPANY	ANNUAL PREMIUM (FOR A 20-YEAR-OLD MAN)	CASH VALUE IN 20 YEARS
18.	American General Life of Delaware	$116	$2,478
19.	The Volunteer State Life Ins. Co.	$116	$2,328
20.	Kentucky Central Life Ins.	$120	$2,500
21.	American Heritage Life Ins.	$121	$2,480
22.	Monarch Life Ins.	$117	$2,180
23.	Allstate Life Ins.	$109	$2,060
24.	Occidental Life Ins.	$113	$2,120
25.	Franklin Life Ins.	$114	$2,171
26.	Continental Assurance	$118	$2,210
27.	Provident Life	$109	$1,980

SELF-TEST/CHAPTER 8

1. Mr. John Q. Public wishes to insure his masonry residence inside city limits for $10,000. If the residence has an approved roof, find

    —————— a. the annual premium.

    —————— b. the rate for $5,000 worth of additional insurance.

2. If Mr. John Q. Public of Problem 1 decides to obtain $10,000 worth of extended coverage on both the building and the contents, find

    —————— a. the annual premium, assuming the residence is in Zone 3.

    —————— b. the additional premium if Mr. Public wishes to buy $1,000 worth of additional extended coverage for both the building and the contents.

3. Ms. Jane Norman owns a building valued at $100,000. Ms. Norman carries $40,000 worth of fire insurance in a policy containing an 80% coinsurance clause. Find

    —————— a. what part of a fire loss the company will pay.

    —————— b. how much will the company pay on a $10,000 loss.

    —————— c. how much will the company pay on a $50,000 loss.

4. United Carriers suffered a fire loss amounting to $50,000. They carried insurance under three different policies as follows:

    $10,000 with Company A
    $15,000 with Company B
    $25,000 with Company C

    —————— a. How much will they collect from Company A?

    —————— b. How much will they collect from Company B?

    —————— c. How much will they collect from Company C?

5. The man of Problem 1 decides to cancel his $10,000 insurance after 10 days. Find

    —————— a. the amount the insurance company will retain.

    —————— b. his refund.

6. Mr. Kautious Smith owns a P-4 car in territory 5. Find from the table

    —————— a. the cost of basic full comprehensive coverage for his car.

_____ b.   the cost of basic \$50 deductible collision coverage for his car.

7.   Assuming Mr. Smith of Problem 6 is 65 years old, find

_____ a.   the amount of his premium if the car is used for pleasure.

_____ b.   the amount of his premium if he uses the car for business.

8.   Ms. Ivy Strickler is 30 years old and married. She drives her car to work less than 10 miles in territory 5. Find

_____ a.   the amount of basic 15/30/10 liability coverage. (See Table 8–7.)

_____ b.   the actual cost of her 15/30/10 liability coverage. (See Table 8–5.)

9.   Find the annual premium (Table 8–8) for Mr. Brian Ryan, who was 19 years old when he bought \$10,000 worth of

_____ a.   10 year term insurance.

_____ b.   nonparticipating ordinary life insurance.

10.   Mr. Joseph Rodeiro is 20 years old and wishes to buy \$10,000 worth of nonparticipating ordinary life insurance. The cash value of the policy at the end of 20 years is \$2,500. Find

_____ a.   the total premium for the 20 years. (See Table 8–8.)

_____ b.   the net cost per year per \$1,000.

part five

The Mathematics of Decision Making

nine

Probability

© 1964 United Feature Syndicate, Inc. Reprinted by permission.

9.1 SAMPLE SPACES AND PROBABILITY

We often hear such statements as "I have a good chance of getting promoted", "Probably there will be a recession next year", and "There is a 50-50 chance that the shipment will arrive today". Each of us has a sort of intuitive feeling as to what such a statement means, but it is not easy to give an exact mathematical formulation of this meaning. Probability theory will make such statements precise by giving them a numerical measure. The modern manager or businessman encounters many problems involving probability. In general, the probability of an event is the likelihood of occurrence of the event. The likelihood of occurrence of an event can be determined in one of three ways:

1. **A priori** or "before the facts" (classical) probability, that is, probability computed without collecting any empirical evidence.

2. Relative frequency (empirical) probability, for example, when we estimate the probability that a part is defective by testing the parts and determining the proportion of defective ones.

3. Subjective probability (as in the cartoon above), that is, probability based on the judgment and experience of the individual.

We shall first discuss a priori or classical probability by giving an example which shows how probabilities may be assigned to a given event.

Example 1

A fair coin is tossed. Find the probability of a head coming up.

401

Solution

At this time we are unable to solve this problem since we have not made precise the meaning of the word probability. However, our intuition tells us the following:

1. When a coin is tossed, it may turn up in either of two ways. Assuming that the coin will not stand on edge, "heads" and "tails" are the only two possible outcomes.

2. If the coin is not unbalanced (and this is what we mean by saying the coin is "fair"), the two outcomes are considered equally likely.

3. We conclude that the probability of obtaining heads when a fair coin is tossed, denoted by P(H), (read "P of H" or "the probability of H") is 1 out of 2. That is, $P(H) = \frac{1}{2}$.

Experiments and sample spaces

Activities such as tossing a coin (as in Example 1), selecting a stock at random from the stock market pages, or rolling a die are called **experiments.** The set S of all possible outcomes for an experiment is called the **sample space** for the experiment.

In Example 1, the set of all possible outcomes for the experiment is S = {H,T}. If heads come up we say that we have a **favorable outcome** or a **success.** We illustrate the use of the preceding terms in Table 9–1.

Computing probabilities

Let us now suppose that we have acquired three kinds of stocks. Each of these stocks can either go up in price (U), or go down in price (D). If each of the stocks is as likely to go up as it is to go down, can we find the probability that all three stocks will go up in price?

As before, we proceed in three steps:

1. We find the set of all possible outcomes for this experiment by drawing a tree diagram, as shown in Figure 9–1.

2. The eight outcomes are equally likely.

TABLE 9–1   **Experiments and Their Sample Spaces**

EXPERIMENT	POSSIBLE OUTCOMES	SAMPLE SPACE
A fair coin is tossed.	Heads or tails are equally likely outcomes.	{H,T}
A balanced die is rolled.	The numbers from 1 to 6 are all equally likely outcomes.	{1,2,3,4,5,6}
A stock is selected at random from among 10 stocks numbered S_1, S_2, S_3, etc.	Each of the 10 stocks is an equally likely outcome.	$\{S_1,S_2,S_3,...S_{10}\}$
A person is selected at random from a list of 25 persons.	Each of the 25 persons is equally likely to be selected.	$\{P_1,P_2,P_3,...P_{25}\}$

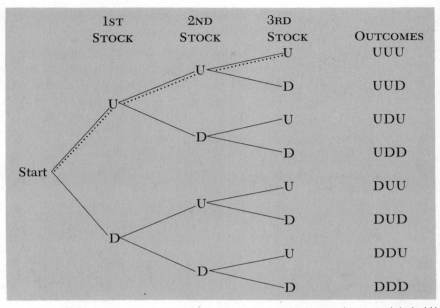

	1ST STOCK	2ND STOCK	3RD STOCK	OUTCOMES

Figure 9–1   The possibilities of the first stock going up or down are labeled U and D respectively. A similar notation is used for the second and third stocks. There are eight possible outcomes; for example, the outcome UUU, obtained by following the dotted path from left to right, means that the first, second, and third stocks went up in price.

3. We conclude that the probability that the three stocks go up in price, denoted by P(UUU), is 1 out of 8; that is, $P(UUU) = \frac{1}{8}$.

If we want to know the probability that at least two of the stocks will go up, the four outcomes UUU, UUD, UDU and DUU are "favorable", so the probability that at least two stocks go up in price is $\frac{4}{8} = \frac{1}{2}$.

In examples such as the preceding ones, in which all possible outcomes are "equally likely," the probability of any event E is given by the following definition.

DEFINITION 9.1 Suppose that an experiment has n possible outcomes, all equally likely. Suppose further that the event E occurs in m of these outcomes. Then P(E), the probability of the event E, is given by

$$P(E) = \frac{m}{n} = \frac{\text{number of favorable cases}}{\text{number of possible outcomes}}$$

We illustrate the use of Definition 9.1 in the following examples.

Example 2

A stock is selected at random from the ten most active stocks in the accompanying list. Find the probability of obtaining (a) IntTelTel stock; (b) a stock that went down in price (that is, whose change is negative).

32 THE WALL STREET JOURNAL,
Wednesday, July 11, 1973

Tuesday's Volume
15,090,000 Shares; 119,300 Warrants

Volume since Jan. 1: 1973 1972 1971
Total shares 2,005,996,502 2,257,940,409 2,218,382,797
Total warrants ... 23,733,900 30,904,500 ....

MOST ACTIVE STOCKS

	Open	High	Low	Close	Chg.	Volume
Ramada In	7½	8¼	7⅜	8¼	+ ⅞	216,600
AMF Inc	22⅝	22⅞	22⅜	22⅝	+ ⅛	201,400
Gifford Hill	13⅜	13⅜	13	13	− ⅛	180,200
EastnAirL	8⅞	9½	8⅞	9½	+ ⅝	174,400
FedNat Mtg	17⅞	18⅜	17⅞	18¼	+ ⅝	171,000
Am Cyan	23½	23⅞	23½	23⅞	+ ⅝	155,100
IntTelTel	32⅝	32⅝	32	32½	+ ¾	140,100
Phillips Pet	51¾	52	50	50¾	− ¼	124,300
Am Tel&Tel	51⅜	51⅞	51⅜	51½	+ ⅜	123,400
FstNat City	40	42	39⅞	42	+2	114,000

Average closing price of most active stocks: 27.22.

Reprinted, by permission, from *The Wall Street Journal*, July 11, 1973, p. 29.

Solution

(a) Let I be the event in which we select IntTelTel stock. Since all ten outcomes are equally likely and only one is favorable, $P(I) = \frac{1}{10}$.

(b) Let N be the event in which the stock has a negative change. Since there are two stocks with negative changes, out of ten possible outcomes, $P(N) = \frac{2}{10} = \frac{1}{5}$.

Example 3

Referring to the list of stocks given in Example 2, find the probability of selecting at random a stock whose volume exceeded 150,000 shares.

Solution

Let E be the event in which the volume of the stock exceeded 150,000 shares. Since we have six favorable outcomes out of ten possible ones, $P(E) = \frac{6}{10} = \frac{3}{5}$.

PROGRESS TEST 1

1. Referring to Figure 9–1, the probability that the three stocks will go down is _____.

2. Referring to the list in Example 2, the probability of selecting a stock whose change (Chg) was over $1 per share is _____.

3. Referring to the list in Example 2, the probability of selecting a stock whose volume was less than 100,000 shares is _____.

EXERCISE 9.1

A single stock is selected at random from the ten stocks that went up the most on the New York Stock Exchange. (See Table 9–2. Note that the stocks are numbered 1 through 10.) Find the probability of obtaining

1.   stock number 5.

2.   a stock whose net increase is greater than 2.

3.   a stock whose per cent of change is greater than 18.

4.   a stock whose sales (in hundreds) exceed 200.

5.   one of the first three or one of the last two stocks.

In Problems 6 through 10, assume that one stock is selected at random from the ten stocks that went down the most on the New York Exchange (see Table 9–2). Find the probability of obtaining

6.   a stock whose net decrease is less than 1.

7.   a stock whose sales (in hundreds) exceed 200.

8.   a stock whose number in the list is either less than 5 or odd.

9.   a stock whose last price is more than 7.

10.   a stock whose number in the list is even and whose sales in hundreds (hds) are bigger than 50.

11.   A manager has to visit five of his plants. If the plants are numbered one through five and he will select the first plant to be visited at random, find:
a. the probability that he will visit plant number one first.

---

1. $\dfrac{1}{8}$ 2. $\dfrac{1}{10}$ 3. $\dfrac{0}{10} = 0$ (We say that this event is impossible.)

TABLE 9–2

Daily Percentage Leaders On N.Y. Stock Exchange

NEW YORK—The following list shows the stocks that have gone up the most and down the most based on percent of change on the New York Stock Exchange regardless of volume for Wednesday.

Net and percentage changes are the difference between the previous closing price and yesterday's last price.

UPS

	Name	Sales(hds)	High	Low	Last	Net			Pct.
1	SCA Svc	242	9	7	8½	+	1¾	Up	25.9
2	Travlge Int	336	7¼	5¾	6⅞	+	1⅛	Up	19.6
3	Elixir Ind	34	6½	5¾	6½	+	1	Up	18.2
4	Blue Bell	258	17½	14⅞	17⅜	+	2⅝	Up	17.8
5	Bond Ind	14	5⅛	4½	5⅛	+	¾	Up	17.1
6	LehValInd	32	2¾	1½	1¾	+	¼	Up	16.7
7	Republic Cp	46	1¾	1⅝	1¾	+	¼	Up	16.7
8	Hutton EF	26	8½	7½	8⅜	+	1⅛	Up	15.5
9	Hydrometl	27	8⅜	7½	8⅜	+	1⅛	Up	15.5
10	Lynch CSys	50	7½	6⅝	7½	+	1	Up	15.4

DOWNS

	Name	Sales(hds)	High	Low	Last	Net			Pct.
1	Simm Prec	11	3¼	3⅛	3⅛	–	¼	Off	7.4
2	Overn Tran	55	20⅛	19	19	–	1½	Off	7.3
3	Penn Cent	41	1⅝	1½	1⅝	–	⅛	Off	7.1
4	UnPark Min	15	1¾	1⅝	1⅝	–	⅛	Off	7.1
5	Atlas Corp	128	2	1⅞	1⅞	–	⅛	Off	6.3
6	GtAtlPac	93	13⅝	12⅞	12⅞	–	¾	Off	5.5
7	De Soto Inc	1109	10¼	9¼	9½	–	½	Off	5.0
8	Premier Ind	10	7⅝	7½	7½	–	⅜	Off	4.8
9	Colum Pict	212	5⅜	5	5⅛	–	¼	Off	4.7
10	Nat Indust	38	2¾	2⅝	2⅝	–	⅛	Off	4.5

Reprinted, by permission, from *The Wall Street Journal*, July 12, 1973.

b. the probability that he will visit an odd numbered plant first.

12. A man has two kinds of stocks. If it is assumed that each of the stocks can go up in price (U), go down in price (D), or stay the same (S), and if all of the outcomes are equally likely,

a. draw a tree diagram to show all the possible outcomes for the two stocks.

b. find the probability that both stocks stay the same in price.

c. find the probability that exactly one stock goes up in price.

13. Three men (A, B, and C) are elected to the board of Red Tape Enterprises. If one of the men is to be the president, the second one vice-president, and the third one secretary,

a. how many different outcomes are possible? [Hint: Draw a tree diagram. One of the possible outcomes may be BCA, where (by convention) the first man (B) is the president, the second (C) is the vice-president, and the third (A) is the secretary.]

b. find the probability that A is the president, C is the vice-president, and B is the secretary.

14. The president of Diversified Enterprises is considering two possible locations for his new plant. In each of the locations he

has the choice of having an oil burning plant or a coal burning plant. If all of the outcomes are equally likely, find the probability that the second location is selected and he decides to burn oil. (Hint: Draw a tree diagram.)

15. A personnel manager has the choice of hiring male (M) or female (F) employees. If two employees are to be hired, and all the possibilities are equally likely, find the probability that
   a. two females will be hired.
   b. two males will be hired.
   c. a mixed group (of two) is hired.

16. Consolidated Motors plans on bringing out two completely new models aimed at the flower people. They are considering the names Gardenia, Rose, Violet, Wild flower, and Sandspur. If each of these names is equally likely, find the probability that one of the new models will be called the Sandspur.

17. Mary and Jane each select one integer at random from the set {1,2,3,4,5,6,7}. Find the probability that
   a. they both select the same integer.
   b. they both select integers greater than 4.
   c. the sum of the two integers selected is greater than 8.
   d. the sum of the two integers is odd.

9 Out of 10 Americans Are Lonely Because They Have Forgotten How to Have Fun

. . . Says a Leading Expert

9.2 EMPIRICAL PROBABILITY

In the headline above, a leading expert states that 9 out of 10 Americans are lonely. The expert making the statement probably has noticed that most Americans are lonely, but how did he arrive at a numerical figure such as 9 out of 10 $\left(\frac{9}{10}\right)$? His assertion is probably based on the idea of **relative frequency.** The **relative frequency** of an event equals the number of times the event occurs in a certain time period divided by the number of times it had an opportunity to occur in that period. Thus, to find the relative frequency of the event under consideration, the expert could conduct a survey, perhaps among 1,000 persons, asking the persons if they are lonely. If 900 persons

Definition of relative frequency

respond affirmatively, the relative frequency for the event L (being lonely) is $\frac{900}{1000} = \frac{9}{10}$.

The accompanying ad for *T.V. Guide* magazine claims that 96% of your ads will get in the door if you advertise in *T.V. Guide*. The claim is based on the percentage of persons who receive *T.V. Guide* at home. This percentage, or relative frequency, is 96 out of 100, or 96%.

96% guaranteed to get your ad in the door.

Reprinted, by permission, from *The Wall Street Journal*, July 12, 1973, p. 30

Intuitively, it is clear that as the number of persons surveyed increases, the relative frequency of an event becomes a more reliable measure. For example, if in the ad above, 100 readers of *T.V. Guide* were surveyed and 96 received the magazine at home, the relative frequency of this event would be found to be $\frac{96}{100} = 96\%$. Similarly, if 1000 readers were surveyed and 960 received *T.V. Guide* at home, the relative frequency would also be $\frac{960}{1000} = 96\%$. However, since there is "strength in numbers," the second estimate is certainly a more reliable measure. The ideal situation would be one in which an infinite number of readers is surveyed. Mathematicians refer to this situation as the relative frequency "in the long run" and use this idea to define empirical probability.

Definition of P(E) by using
the idea of relative frequency

DEFINITION 9.2 The probability of an event E, denoted by P(E), is the relative frequency of E in the long run.

As a result of this definition, when dealing with empirical probabilities, computations do not give the *exact* value of a probability. We are merely estimating this value by observing how often the event occurs in a finite number of repeated experiments.

Example 1

World Wide Airlines has found that over a certain period, 980 out of 1000 flights from New York to Florida arrived on time. Find

(a) the probability that the next flight from New York to Florida arrives on time.

(b) the probability that the next flight from New York to Florida does not arrive on time.

Solution

(a) The probability that the next flight will arrive on time is $\frac{980}{1000} = 98\%$.

(b) Since 980 flights were on time, 20 flights were *not* on time. Thus, the probability that the next flight will not be on time is $\frac{20}{1000} = 2\%$.

PROGRESS TEST 1

1. Nine Lives Battery Company has found out that of 2400 batteries produced, 400 were defective. The probability that a Nine Lives Battery will be defective is _____.

2. The probability that a Nine Lives Battery will not be defective is _____.

The relative frequencies for certain events can also be given by means of a table. We illustrate this idea in the following example.

Example 2

The production department of Magna-Box TV has released the data shown in Table 9–3. Find

(a) the probability that a color Magna-Box TV is defective.
(b) the probability that any Magna-Box TV is defective.
(c) the probability that a black and white Magna-Box TV is not defective.

---

1. $\frac{400}{2400} = \frac{1}{6}$ 2. $\frac{2000}{2400} = \frac{5}{6}$. Note that if the probability of obtaining a defective battery is $\frac{1}{6}$, the probability of obtaining a nondefective battery is $\frac{5}{6} = 1 - \frac{1}{6}$.

TABLE 9–3   **Television Quality**

	COLOR	BLACK AND WHITE	TOTAL
Defective	150	100	250
Nondefective	2850	900	3750
Total	3000	1000	4000

Solution

(a) From Table 9–3 we see that there are 3,000 color TV's and 150 defective ones; thus, the probability is $\frac{150}{3000} = \frac{1}{20}$.

(b) Since there are 4000 TV's and 250 are defective, the probability is $\frac{250}{4000} = \frac{1}{16}$.

(c) Since there are 1000 black and white TV's and 900 are nondefective, the probability that a black and white Magna-Box TV is not defective is $\frac{900}{1000} = \frac{9}{10}$.

PROGRESS TEST 2

1. Referring to Table 9–3, the probability that a black and white Magna-Box TV is defective is _____.

2. The probability that a Magna-Box TV is nondefective is _____.

3. The probability that a nondefective Magna-Box TV is a color TV is _____.

EXERCISE 9.2

1. Dear's Department Store has found through long experience that out of 1000 catalogs mailed to different homes, 200 purchase orders are received. Find
    (a) the probability that a person receiving a Dear's catalog will make a purchase.
    (b) the probability that a person receiving a Dear's catalog will not make a purchase.

2. The inspector for the Ready-Made Furniture Outlet has dis-

---

1. $\frac{100}{1000} = \frac{1}{10}$ 2. $\frac{3750}{4000} = \frac{15}{16}$ 3. $\frac{2850}{3750} = \frac{19}{25}$

covered 38 defective pieces of furniture among a lot composed of 700 pieces. Find the probability that a customer buying a piece of Ready-Made Furniture will get a defective piece.

3.   The manager of Denney's Department Store has found that 850 out of 1000 persons who enter the store on Mondays make at least one purchase. Find the probability that a person entering the store will buy at least one item.

The following table will be used in Problems 4 through 9.

Number of Suicides Per 100,000 Persons, Classified According to Country and Age for the Years 1966–1967

COUNTRY	AGE*			
	15–24	25–44	45–64	65 and over
United States	10	20	30	40
Canada	10	15	13	14
West Germany	20	30	50	50

*No suicides were recorded in the 1–14 age bracket.

4.   Find the probability that a person in the United States between 15 and 24 years of age will commit suicide.

5.   Find the probability that a person in the United States between 25 and 44 years of age will commit suicide.

6.   Find the probability that a person in the United States between 45 and 64 years of age will commit suicide.

7.   Find the probability that a Canadian will commit suicide.

8.   Find the probability that a West German will commit suicide.

9.   If a person is between the ages of 15 and 24 (inclusive), in which country is this person most likely to commit suicide? Explain.

The following table, showing the number of employees absent from work, will be used in Problems 10 through 15.

Employee Absences

SEX	ABSENCES (DAYS)			
	0	1–5	6–10	11 or more
Men	10	20	20	0
Women	10	10	10	20
TOTAL	20	30	30	20

10.   Find the probability that an employee will never be absent.

11. Find the probability that a woman will be absent between 1 and 5 days (inclusive).

12. Find the probability that a man will be absent between 6 and 10 days (inclusive).

13. Find the probability that a person will be absent 11 days or more.

14. Find the probability that a person will be absent between 1 and 5 days (inclusive).

15. Find the probability that a person will be absent between 6 and 10 days (inclusive).

16. An auditor has examined 290 documents belonging to a corporation. He has found 30 documents containing errors. What is the probability that the next document he examines will contain an error? What is the probability that the next document will not contain an error?

17. The record of the Countrywide Insurance Company shows that 1500 of the 1700 policy holders who bought a policy at age 30 were still alive at age 50. Find the probability that a 30-year-old person who bought a policy from Countrywide will still be alive at age 50.

18. In Problem 17, what is the probability that a person who bought a policy from Countrywide at age 30 will not be alive at age 50?

19. Weather bureau statistics reveal that in a particular community it has rained 20 times in the last 70 years on the Fourth of July. What is the probability that it will rain in this community on the next Fourth of July?

20. A stock broker has assigned (on the basis of past experience) a probability of $\frac{7}{10}$ to the event that his stock will go up in price tomorrow, and a probability of $\frac{1}{10}$ that it will stay the same. Find
    a. the probability that the stock will go down in price tomorrow.
    b. the probability that the stock will go up or down in price tomorrow.
    c. the probability that the stock will go up and down in price tomorrow.

9.3 SUBJECTIVE PROBABILITIES AND ODDS

In the cartoon above, B.C. is giving odds of 10 to 1 that the man will fall. Can we convert the odds he is willing to give into the (subjective or personal) probability that the man will fall? In this case, the ratio 10 to 1 seems to suggest that B.C. believes that there are 10 favorable possibilities for the man to fall against 1 unfavorable possibility. Assuming all outcomes are equally likely, the probability of this event (see Definition 9.1) is the number of favorable cases (10 in this case) divided by the number of possible outcomes ($10 + 1 = 11$). Thus, we find that B.C.'s subjective or personal probability that the man will fall equals $\dfrac{10}{10+1} = \dfrac{10}{11}$. This discussion can be summarized by the following definition.

> **DEFINITION 9.3** If an event has probability $p = \dfrac{f}{f+u}$, the odds in favor of the event happening are f to u.

Definition of odds

Example 1

A man is willing to give 3 to 4 odds that his stock will go up in price. What is the probability that this will be the case?

Solution

Here $f = 3$, $u = 4$, and (by Definition 9.3)

$$p = \frac{3}{3+4} = \frac{3}{7}$$

414

NINE/PROBABILITY

Example 2

The president of Razzle-Dazzle estimates that the probability that stockholders will realize a profit on their stock is $\frac{3}{4}$. What should be the odds in favor of this happening?

Solution

Here $p = \frac{3}{4} = \frac{f}{f+u}$. Thus, $f = 3$ and $f + u = 4$. But $f + u = 3 + u = 4$, so $u = 1$, and thus the odds should be 3 to 1 (or 6 to 2, or 12 to 4). This means that a betting person should be willing to win \$1 if the stockholders realize a profit but lose \$3 in the unlikely event they do not.

PROGRESS TEST 1

1. In a survey of 300 stockholders of a large company, it was found that 100 favored the continuation of a certain business practice. Based on this data, the probability that a person selected at random from the 300 stockholders will favor the continuation of this practice is _____.

2. In the problem above, the odds that a person selected at random from the 300 stockholders will favor the continuation of this practice is _____.

Subjective probability and odds

The method of subjective probabilities works out very nicely in business and in other situations in which it is difficult to ascertain all the possible outcomes with any degree of accuracy. Thus, when starting on a new business venture, a businessman may be forced to rely on "guesstimation," his own intuition and other factors such as the condition of businesses similar to his own, the demand for his products, and the available labor force. After all these aspects are carefully considered, he may make a decision to invest \$500, for example, for an expected gain of \$300. In this situation the odds are said to be 500 to 300, and consequently, his personal or subjective probability for success will be $\frac{500}{500 + 300} = \frac{5}{8}$. Conversely, if the probability of success of a new business venture is $\frac{5}{8}$, a man should be willing to invest \$500 for an expected gain of \$300.

---

1. $\frac{1}{3}$ 2. 1 to 2

PROGRESS TEST 2

1. A man is willing to invest $800 in a business that expects to realize $200 in profits. Based on this data, the probability that the business will be successful is _____.

2. The odds that will be given in favor of this event are _____.

EXERCISE 9.3

1. A man is willing to give 5 to 7 odds that his products will be better than those of his competitors. What is the probability that this will be the case?

2. The probability of launching a successful advertising campaign is $\frac{2}{3}$. What should be the odds in favor of this happening?

3. 200 defective batteries were accidentally mixed with a shipment of 800 good batteries. Find
   a. the probability of selecting at random a nondefective battery.
   b. the probability of selecting at random a defective battery.
   c. the odds for randomly selecting a nondefective battery.
   d. the odds for randomly selecting a defective battery.

4. An insurance company has determined that in 60% of the fatal accidents involving two cars, at least one of the drivers is drunk. What should the odds be for this event?

5. According to a survey of accidents conducted by a certain insurance company, the odds that a person having an automobile accident will be more than 100 miles away from home at the time are 7 to 9. What is the probability that a person will be more than 100 miles away from home when he has an accident? What is the probability that a person will not be more than 100 miles away from home when he has an accident?

6. A stockbroker is willing to bet $100 against $200 that a particular stock will go up in price. What is the probability that the stock will go up in price? What is the probability that the stock will not go up in price?

7. A man is willing to invest $200 in a business that expects to

---

1. $\frac{800}{1,000} = \frac{4}{5}$ 2. 8 to 2 (or 4 to 1)

make $400 in profits. Find the probability that this business will be successful.

8.   Find the odds in favor of the business in Problem 7 being successful.

The following table, showing the approximate number of accidental deaths by age and type, will be used in Problems 9 through 17.

Accidental Deaths by Type and Age of Victim

AGE	TYPE			
	All Types	Motor Vehicles	Falls	Others
All ages	115,000	55,000	20,000	40,000
5 to 14	9,000	4,000	200	4,800
15 to 24	25,000	16,000	400	8,600
25 to 34	15,000	8,000	400	6,600
35 and over	66,000	27,000	19,000	20,000

9.   Find the probability that if a person had an accident, it was a motor vehicle accident.

10. Find the odds in favor of the event in Problem 9.

11. Find the probability that if a person between the ages of 5 and 14 had an accident, the accident was a fall.

12. Find the odds for the event in Problem 11.

13. Find the probability that if a person between the ages of 15 and 24 had an accident, it was not a motor vehicle accident or a fall.

14. Find the odds for the event in Problem 13.

15. Find the probability that if a person between the ages of 25 and 34 had an accident, the accident was a motor vehicle accident.

16. Find the odds for the event in Problem 15.

17. If it is known that a person had a motor vehicle accident, what is the probability that this person was in the age bracket
     a. 5 to 14?
     b. 15 to 24?
     c. 25 to 34?
     d. 35 and over?
     Based on your answers, find the age bracket which is most likely to have a motor vehicle accident.

18. A businessman is willing to invest $500 in a business that expects to make $300 in profits, but not to invest $600 (expecting to make the same $300 in profits). What does this tell us

about the subjective probability that he assigns to the business's being successful?

19. The United States Bureau of the Census estimated that there are 1,565,000 single-unit, independent stores and 35,000 multiunit stores. Assume that each multiunit store has 15 stores. If a store is selected at random in the United States, find

    a. the probability that a store belonging to a multiunit is chosen.

    b. the probability that a single unit independent store is chosen.

    c. the odds in favor of selecting a store belonging to a multiunit.

    d. the odds in favor of selecting a single-unit independent store.

20. According to the *Guinness Book of World Records*, the shortest odds ever quoted on any race horse were 1 to 10,000 (for a horse named Dragon Blood in the Premio Naviglio in Milan, Italy, in June, 1967).* Based on these odds, what was the probability that Dragon Blood would win the race? (He did win!)

9.4 MATHEMATICAL EXPECTATION

In the ad above, what is the mathematical expectation of the wager for the Diners Club president? An obvious way to answer this

---

*From the *Guinness Book of World Records*, © 1974 by Sterling Publishing Co., Inc., N.Y. 10016.

question is to find out how many more establishments accept Diners Club cards than American Express. If the figure is 75,000, the answer will be $75,000.* However, let us assume that the percentage of restaurants accepting exclusively Diners Club and American Express cards are 55% and 45%, respectively. If 55% of the establishments accept Diners Club (and not American Express), the president will win $1 × 55; that is, $55 for every 100 establishments. If 45% of the establishments accept American Express (and not Diners Club), he will lose $1 × 45, that is, $45 for every 100 establishments. Thus, the Diners Club president will have a profit of $55 − $45 = $10 for every 100 establishments. His mathematical expectation per establishment will then be $\frac{\$10}{100} = \$0.10$. This discussion can be summarized in the following table:

CARD	PROBABILITY	AMOUNT	PROBABILITY × AMOUNT
Diners Club	$\frac{55}{100}$	$1	$0.55
American Express	$\frac{45}{100}$	−$1	−$0.45
Sum (profit per establishment)			$0.10

Similarly, if 100 tickets for a raffle offering a cash prize of $100 are sold, the probability of each ticket winning is $\frac{1}{100}$ and the mathematical expectation of each ticket holder is $\$100 \times \frac{1}{100} = \$1.$† If in addition, a second cash prize of $50 is offered, the mathematical expectation of each ticket increases to $\left(\$100 \times \frac{1}{100}\right) + \left(\$50 \times \frac{1}{100}\right) = \$1.50$. Note that in each of the samples above, the mathematical expectation is the sum of each of the amounts multiplied by the probability of obtaining each of these amounts.

Definition of mathematical expectation

DEFINITION 9.4 The mathematical expectation of an experiment or game is

$$E = a_1 \cdot p_1 + a_2 \cdot p_2 + a_3 \cdot p_3 + \ldots + a_k \cdot p_k$$

where $p_1, p_2, p_3, \ldots, p_k$ are, respectively, the probabilities of obtaining the amounts $a_1, a_2, a_3, \ldots, a_k$.

*This is the answer published on page 8 of the *Wall Street Journal* of July 17, 1973.
†The expectation of a game is not to be interpreted as the value that will occur in a single instance (or experiment) but the average winning (or loss) **in the long run.** Of course, when the a's of Definition 9.4 are wins, they are represented by positive numbers and when they are losses they are represented by negative numbers.

Example 1

The Nine Lives Battery Company can make 10¢ on each nondefective battery. However, if a battery is defective, the company loses 50¢. If 90% of the batteries manufactured by the Nine Lives Company are not defective, what is the mathematical expectation (expected profit) per battery?

Solution

Here $a_1 = 10¢$, $a_2 = -50¢$, $p_1 = \dfrac{90}{100}$, and $p_2 = \dfrac{10}{100}$. By Definition 9.4,

$$E = \left(10¢ \times \frac{90}{100}\right) + \left((-50¢) \times \frac{10}{100}\right) = 4¢.$$ Thus, the company can expect a profit of 4¢ per battery.

Example 2

Super-Test Petroleum estimates that it will spend $10,000 on the research for and preparation of a bid for a petroleum field which should yield $30,000 profit. Super-Test is one of five companies with an equal chance of being selected for the job. What is the mathematical expectation for this process?

Solution

Here $a_1 = \$30,000$ (the amount it can win), $a_2 = -\$10,000$ (the amount it loses if it does not get the job), $p_1 = \dfrac{1}{5}$, and $p_2 = \dfrac{4}{5}$. By Definition 9.4,

$$E = \left(\$30,000 \times \frac{1}{5}\right) + \left((-\$10,000) \times \frac{4}{5}\right) = -\$2,000.$$ Since the mathematical expectation is negative, the company is well advised not to submit a bid.

PROGRESS TEST 1

1. If the percentage of restaurants accepting Diners Club or American Express cards exclusively is 60% and 40%, respectively, the mathematical expectation (per establishment) for the wager given at the beginning of this section is _____.

2. Gadget Manufacturing makes 20¢ on each nondefective gadget. However, if a gadget is defective, the company loses 80¢. If 90% of the gadgets are not defective, the mathematical expectation per gadget is _____.

---

1. $0.20   2. 10¢

The mathematical expectation of an event or game can be used to determine the "fair price" to pay for the privilege of playing a game. For example, in the case of each of one hundred ticket holders in a raffle in which the cash prize is $100, the mathematical expectation is $100 \times \dfrac{1}{100} = \$1$. Hence, the "fair price" to pay for such a ticket will be $1, since in this case the mathematical expectation is also $1.

Example 3

A man wishes to insure a house worth $20,000 against fire. If statistics show that the chances that a house is destroyed by fire are 1 in 100, what should a fair price be for his insurance?

Solution

The mathematical expectation is $\$20{,}000 \times \dfrac{1}{100} = \$200$. Thus, a fair price to pay for this insurance is $200. Of course, the actual premium will have to be higher than this price to allow for commissions, operating expenses for the insurance company, and net income. For example, if the insurance company wishes to make $50 gross profit per customer, the price will be $200 + $50 = $250.

Even though all the problems discussed so far have presented the a's in Definition 9.4 as a cash amount, these a's can be other units. We present an example illustrating this occurrence.

Example 4

The table below shows the number of persons sitting at a table in the Good Taste Restaurant and the respective probabilities of such occurrences. Find the expected number of persons per table.

NUMBER	1	2	3	4	5
Probability	$\dfrac{15}{100}$	$\dfrac{20}{100}$	$\dfrac{30}{100}$	$\dfrac{25}{100}$	$\dfrac{10}{100}$

Solution

Here the a's are the number of persons at each of the tables, and

$$E = \left(1 \times \frac{15}{100}\right) + \left(2 \times \frac{20}{100}\right) + \left(3 \times \frac{30}{100}\right) + \left(4 \times \frac{25}{100}\right) + \left(5 \times \frac{10}{100}\right) = 2.95$$

This information can be useful in determining the number of tables that should be used, the arrangement of these tables, and the number of chairs per table. For instance, if the fire marshall has determined that the maximum seating capacity for the restaurant is 300 persons, the manager will be wise not to have more than $\frac{300}{2.95}$, or approximately 100 tables. (Why?)

PROGRESS TEST 2

1. A man wishes to insure a car worth $4,000 against theft. If statistics show that the chances of an automobile being stolen and not recovered are 1 in 100, a fair price to pay for this insurance is _____.

2. Based on the answer in Example 4, the number of chairs per table in the restaurant should be _____.

EXERCISE 9.4

1. Suppose that in the wager discussed at the beginning of this section, the percentages of restaurants accepting Diners Club and American Express cards exclusively are 55% and 45%, respectively. If the president of Diners Club offers $2 for every establishment that honors American Express in exchange for $2 for every one that honors Diners Club, what is the mathematical expectation per establishment?

2. Edison Light Bulb Company can make 20¢ on each nondefective bulb. However, if a bulb is defective, the company loses 50¢. If 90% of the bulbs manufactured by Edison are nondefective, what is the mathematical expectation per bulb?

3. If in Problem 2 the company still makes 20¢ per nondefective bulb and 90% of the bulbs are nondefective, how much can the company lose per bulb and break even? (Hint: Find the mathematical expectation of each nondefective bulb and divide by 10%.)

4. Zoom Aircraft estimates that it will spend $20,000 on the preparation of a government bid to construct the Skydive Airplane. If the expected profits on this project are estimated at $200,000 and Zoom is one of ten contractors with an equal chance of being selected for the job, what is Zoom Aircraft's mathematical expectation?

---

1. $40   2. 3

5. If in Problem 4 the profits on the project are still $200,000 and Zoom is one of the ten contractors with an equal chance of being selected for the job, how much should it be willing to spend on preparing its bid so that its mathematical expectation is 0?

6. Countrywide Insurance wishes to determine the fair price of a policy covering a $5,000 automobile. If the statistical data collected by the company indicates that the chances that the automobile will be destroyed are 1 in 50, what should the price of this policy be?

7. If in Problem 6 the company wishes to have a gross profit of $10 per policy, what should the price of the policy be?

8. The table below shows the number of persons per car entering the Dew Drive In and the probabilities of such occurrences. Find the expected number of persons per car.

NUMBER (PER CAR)	1	2	3	4	5
Probability	$\frac{1}{10}$	$\frac{3}{10}$	$\frac{3}{20}$	$\frac{7}{20}$	$\frac{2}{20}$

9. If in Problem 8 the concession stand can handle 3660 persons, and it is assumed that every person visits the concession stand, how many cars should the management admit at any given time?

10. The Crystal Clear Glass Company sells for $3 a pane of glass costing it $2. If the probability of breaking a pane of glass during installation is 0.10, what is the mathematical expectation per pane?

11. Evergreen Nursery is to bid on a landscaping job that promises to pay $2,000 in profits with probability .60. However, it can also lose $1,500 (because of lack of rain or bad weather) with probability .40. What is the mathematical expectation of bidding for the job?

12. The Gotham City Police know that the probabilities for zero, one, two, three, or four calls per patrol car on any given day are as shown in the accompanying table. Find the expected number of calls per car on any given day.

NUMBER OF CALLS	0	1	2	3	4
Probability	$\frac{1}{10}$	$\frac{1}{10}$	$\frac{1}{5}$	$\frac{3}{10}$	$\frac{3}{10}$

13. A hotel in Miami Beach has determined that the number of

guests staying there during the summer will be 2000 if it is exceptionally hot in the North, but only 1500 or 1000, respectively, if it is only hot or if it is pleasant in the North. If the probabilities of it being exceptionally hot, hot, and pleasant in the North are 30%, 40%, and 30%, respectively, what is the expected number of guests?

14. If in Problem 13 the management has determined that the profit per guest is $4, what is its expected profit?

15. A manager must decide whether to try an advertising campaign that can bring in $10,000 of additional profits, or to step up production with a possible increase of $15,000 in profits. If the probabilities of success for the advertising campaign and stepping up production are $\frac{3}{10}$ and $\frac{1}{3}$, respectively, what course of action should he take?

16. Gourmet Foods is offered a shipment of food for $10,000. It can sell this shipment for $10,000, $12,000, or $14,000 with probabilities $\frac{1}{10}$, $\frac{3}{10}$, and $\frac{3}{5}$, respectively. What is the mathematical expectation of this venture?

17. In Problem 16, what is the highest amount of money Gourmet Foods should be willing to pay for the shipment and still expect to make $1,000?

Courtesy of 7-Eleven

9.5 DECISIONS, DECISIONS, DECISIONS

The illustration above shows the cover of the December issue of a promotions booklet sent to 7-Eleven stores throughout the United States. How do these companies reach the decision of promoting some items and discontinuing others, increasing sales of some products but dropping others? Let us illustrate this idea with a fictitious example.

Decision making in the face of uncertainty

Let us assume that the manager of the products division of 7-Eleven knows that another company is about to introduce a new soft drink on the market and he is to decide if his company should do the same. Here are the four alternatives facing the manager, as well as the economic consequences for his company.

1. He recommends marketing the soft drink and it sells; the company gains $100,000.

2. He recommends marketing the soft drink and it does not sell; the company loses $50,000.

3. He recommends not marketing the soft drink and the soft drink put out by a competitor sells well; the company loses $25,000.

4. He recommends not marketing the soft drink and the soft drink put out by the competitor does not sell well; the company gains $10,000.

This information can be summarized in the following table:

OUTCOME / DECISION	Sells	Does Not Sell
Market	$100,000	-$50,000
Do not Market	-$25,000	$10,000

How can the manager make his decision using this table? We illustrate three ways in which he can do so in the next three examples.

Example 1

If the manager feels that there is a 50-50 chance that the new soft drink will sell well, find

(a) the expected gain if the company markets the new soft drink.

(b) the expected gain if the company does not market the new soft drink.

(c) the decision that the manager should make based on the answers found in parts (a) and (b).

Solution

(a) If the company markets the soft drink, the expected gain is

$$\left(\$100,000 \times \frac{1}{2}\right) + \left((-\$50,000) \times \frac{1}{2}\right) = \$25,000 \text{ (gain)}$$

(b) If the company does not market the soft drink, the expected gain is

$$\left((-\$25,000) \times \frac{1}{2}\right) + \left(\$10,000 \times \frac{1}{2}\right) = -\$7,500 \text{ (loss)}$$

(c) Since by marketing the new soft drink the company stands to make $25,000 against a loss of $7,500 if the soft drink is not marketed, the manager should recommend that the soft drink be marketed.

Example 2

If the manager is certain that his company will make a profit, what course of action should he recommend in order to maximize the company's profits?

Solution

If he is certain that the company is going to make a profit, he finds that it can gain as much as $100,000 (by marketing the product); otherwise, it can gain $10,000. For this reason the manager recommends that the soft drink be marketed.

Example 3

If the manager is certain that his company will not make a profit, what outcome should he recommend in order to minimize the company's losses?

Solution

If he is certain that the company is going to have a loss, we find that it can lose $50,000 (by marketing the soft drink); otherwise, it can lose $25,000. Thus, to minimize the company's losses, he should recommend that the soft drink not be put on the market.

From the three examples given, we can see that the manager has three different ways of reaching his decision:

1. By using mathematical expectation (This method is dependent on the correct appraisal of the probability that the new soft drink will sell.)

2. By assuming that the company will make a profit and then trying to maximize this profit (We will refer to this method as the **maximization criterion.**)

3. By assuming that the company will have a loss and then trying to minimize this loss (We will refer to this method as the **minimax criterion.**)

PROGRESS TEST 1

1. If in Example 1 the chances that the new soft drink will sell are 1 in 3, the expected gain if the company markets the soft drink is _____.

2. If in Example 1 the chances that the new soft drink will sell are 1 in 3, the expected gain if the company does not market the soft drink is _____.

3. Based on the answers to 1 and 2, the decision the manager should recommend is _____.

EXERCISE 9.5

1. The product manager of 7-Eleven has learned that another company is about to introduce a new ice cream on the market and he is to decide if his company should do the same. Here are the four alternatives:

    a. Market the ice cream and it sells; the company gains $10,000.
    b. Market the ice cream and it does not sell; the company loses $5,000.
    c. Do not market the ice cream and the ice cream put out by the competitor sells well; the company loses $2,500.
    d. Do not market the ice cream and the ice cream put out by the competitor does not sell well; the company gains $1,000.

    Make a table that summarizes this information.

2. If the manager feels that there is a 50-50 chance that the new ice cream will sell, find the expected value gain if the company markets the new ice cream.

3. If the manager feels that there is a 50-50 chance that the new ice cream will sell, find the expected gain if the company does not market the new ice cream.

4. Based on your answers to Problems 2 and 3, what decision should the manager recommend to the company?

5. Find the expected gain in Problem 2 if the manager feels that the probability that the new ice cream will sell is $\frac{1}{3}$.

6. Find the expected gain in Problem 3 if the manager feels that the probability that the new ice cream will sell is $\frac{1}{3}$.

7. If in Problem 1 the manager is certain that his company will make a profit, which alternative should he recommend in order to maximize these profits?

8. If in Problem 1 the manager is certain that his company will have a loss, which alternative should he recommend in order to minimize the loss?

9. Italian Motors is faced with the decision of building a new plant or continuing production in their present facilities. The company estimates that if the new plant is built and it can get a patent for a new emission control system, there will be a profit of $2,000,000 next year; if the new plant is built and it does not

---

1. $\left(\$100,000 \times \frac{1}{3}\right) + \left((-\$50,000) \times \frac{2}{3}\right) = 0$ 2. $\left((-\$25,000) \times \frac{1}{3}\right) + \left(\$10,000 \times \frac{2}{3}\right) =$
−$1,666.67   3. Market the soft drink.

get a patent, there will be a deficit of $250,000 next year; if the new plant is not built and it gets the patent, it will have a profit of $1,000,000 next year; and if the plant is not built and it cannot get the patent, there will be a profit of only $100,000 next year. Make a table showing all the alternatives and their economic outcomes.

10.   If in Problem 9 the probability of obtaining the patent is $\frac{1}{2}$, find the expected gain or loss if the company builds the plant.

11.   If in Problem 9 the probability of obtaining the patent is $\frac{1}{2}$, find the expected gain or loss if the company does not build the plant.

12.   If in Problem 9 the company is certain of making a profit, what alternative should it select by using the maximization criterion?

13.   If in Problem 9 the company is certain of losing money, what alternative should it select by using the minimax criterion?

14.   If in Problem 9 the odds are 2 to 3 against getting the patent, what should Italian Motors do in order to maximize its profits?

15.   Referring to Problem 9, what would you expect Italian Motors to do if it faces the prospect of going out of business unless it makes a profit of at least $1,500,000 next year?

16.   Referring to Problem 9, what would you expect Italian Motors to do if it is faced with the prospect of going out of business unless it makes a profit of at least $100,000 next year?

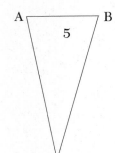

10 miles   11 miles

17.   A delivery truck is at point P (see the diagram above) and has to be refueled. The driver can get gas at station A or at station B. The operators of the stations have agreed to maintain only one of the two stations open, but he does not know which of the two stations is actually open. Construct a table showing all the alternatives and indicating the number of miles traveled. (Hint: The table can look like the one on the following page.)

	OPEN	CLOSED
A		
B		

18. Where should the driver go first if he wants to minimize the expected distance traveled and the odds are 1 to 1 that station A is open?

19. Where should the driver go first if he wants to minimize the expected distance traveled and the odds are 1 to 2 that station A is open?

20. If the driver of Problem 18 has only enough fuel to last him 10 miles, where should he go first?

21. If the driver of Problem 19 has only enough fuel to last him 15 miles, where should he go first?

Investigation of Insurance Companies' Rates Reveals...
1 OF EVERY 7 AMERICAN DENTISTS IS DISHONEST, INCOMPETENT OR BOTH

Copyright: NATIONAL ENQUIRER, Lantana, Florida

9.6 COMPOUND EVENTS

In the preceding sections, we have calculated the probability of simple events. However, there are many situations in which we must calculate the probability of **compound** events, that is, events that are combinations of simple events. For instance, the headline above suggests that the probability that a dentist is dishonest, incompetent, or both is $\frac{1}{7}$. The compound event of being dishonest, incompetent, or both can be expressed simply by using set notation. For example, if D is the event that the dentist is dishonest, and I is the event that the dentist is incompetent, then D ∪ I (read "D union I" or "D or I") is the event that the dentist is dishonest or incompetent or both.

> **DEFINITION 9.5** The union of the events A and B, denoted by A ∪ B, is the event consisting of all of the outcomes in A or in B or in both.

Thus, if C is the event that a person has a college degree and M is the event that the person is married, then C ∪ M is the event that the person has a college degree or is married or both. Similarly, the event in which C *and* M both occur, denoted by C ∩ M (read "C intersection M" or "C and M"), is the event that the person has a college degree *and* is married.

> **DEFINITION 9.6** The intersection of the events A and B, denoted by A ∩ B, is the event consisting of all of the outcomes that are both in A *and* in B.

Finally, if the event A does not occur, that fact can be denoted by A' (read "A complement" or "not A").

> **DEFINITION 9.7** The complement of an event A, denoted by A', is the event consisting of all the outcomes in the sample space in which A does not occur. That is, A' is the event that occurs if A does *not* occur.

Thus, if M is the event that the person is married, M′ is the event that the person is not married.

Example 1

If H is the event that a person has a high school education and S is the event that the person is single, express in words each of the following events:

(a) H ∪ S   (b) H ∩ S   (c) H′   (d) S′

Solution

(a) The person has a high school education or is single or both.
(b) The person has a high school education and is single.
(c) The person does not have a high school education.
(d) The person is not single.

Example 2

If R is the event that a manager will get a raise and P is the event that he will get a promotion, write in symbols each of the following events.

(a) The manager will not get a raise.
(b) The manager will get a raise and a promotion.
(c) The manager will get a raise but not a promotion.
(d) The manager will get either a raise or a promotion or both.

Solution

(a) R′   (c) R ∩ P′
(b) R ∩ P   (d) R ∪ P

PROGRESS TEST 1

1. Let M be the event that a product is introduced in the market and S be the event that the product sells. In words, M ∩ S means _____

_____.

2. In words, M ∩ S′ means _____

_____.

3. In words, M′ means _____

_____.

4. The event that the product is not introduced in the market and it does not sell can be written in symbols as

_____.

---

1. The product is introduced in the market and it sells.　2. The product is introduced in the market and it does not sell.　3. The product is not introduced in the market.　4. M′ ∩ S′.

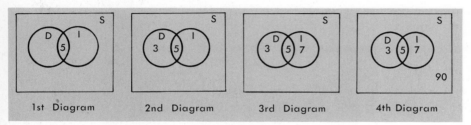

1st Diagram   2nd Diagram   3rd Diagram   4th Diagram

Figure 9-2

Let us now illustrate how the insurance companies mentioned in the headline at the beginning of this section may have reached their conclusion. Suppose, for instance, that the companies interviewed 105 persons. Of these, eight said that their dentists were dishonest, 12 said that their dentists were incompetent, and five said that their dentists were both dishonest and incompetent. Assuming that each person interviewed has a different dentist, this information can be summarized by means of a **Venn diagram** (named after John Venn, an English mathematician and logician). We first draw a rectangle to represent the sample space S, and two circles representing the dishonest dentists (D) and the incompetent ones (I). (See Figure 9.2.)

We place a 5 in the region common to the two circles of the first diagram, corresponding to the dentists reported to be both dishonest and incompetent. Since the data indicates that there are 8 dishonest dentists, we place a 3 in the region in D but outside of I as shown in the second diagram (we now have 8 dishonest dentists). Then we observe that there are 12 incompetent dentists, so we place a 7 in the region in I but not in D as shown in the third diagram. This accounts for $3 + 5 + 7 = 15$ of the dentists and thus leaves $105 - 15 = 90$ dentists who are neither dishonest nor incompetent. Hence we place a 90 outside of the two circles, as shown in the fourth diagram. We can then conclude that the probability that a dentist is dishonest or incompetent or both is $\frac{3+5+7}{105} = \frac{15}{105} = \frac{1}{7}$. Similarly, we can see that the probability that a dentist is dishonest and incompetent is $\frac{5}{105} = \frac{1}{21}$. We could have obtained a similar result by adding the number of dentists that were dishonest (8) to those that were incompetent (12) and subtracting the 5 that were counted twice, that is, the number of dishonest or incompetent dentists is $8 + 12 - 5 = 15$, and hence the probability that a dentist is dishonest or incompetent is $\frac{15}{105}$. This example illustrates the following rule.

How to find the probability of the event A or B

RULE 9.1 For any two events A and B,
$P(A \cup B) = P(A) + P(B) - P(A \cap B)$.

For example, the probability that a dentist is dishonest or incompetent is

$$P(D \cup I) = P(D) + P(I) - P(D \cap I)$$
$$= \frac{8}{105} + \frac{12}{105} - \frac{5}{105}$$
$$= \frac{15}{105}$$

Thus, the result can be obtained from the data given above without resorting to the Venn diagram.

Example 3

In a survey of 300 investors, the following data were discovered:

 120 bought stocks (S)
 150 bought bonds (B)
 70 bought both stocks and bonds (S ∩ B)

Find the probability that if an investor is selected at random from this group he will be a stock or bond buyer by using (a) Venn diagrams; (b) Rule 9.1.

Solution

(a) We first place a 70 in the region common to the two circles as shown in Figure 9–3. Since there are 120 investors buying stocks, we place a 50 in the region in S but outside B. Then we observe that there are 150 investors that bought bonds, so we enter an 80 in the region in B but outside of S. This accounts for $50 + 70 + 80 = 200$ investors and leaves $300 - 200 = 100$ outside of both circles. The probability that an investor will be a stock or bond buyer is

$$\frac{50 + 70 + 80}{300} = \frac{200}{300} = \frac{2}{3}$$

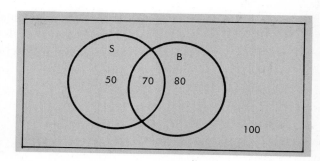

Figure 9–3

(b) By Rule 9.1,

$$P(S \cup B) = P(S) + P(B) - P(S \cap B)$$
$$= \frac{120}{300} + \frac{150}{300} - \frac{70}{300}$$
$$= \frac{200}{300} = \frac{2}{3}$$

PROGRESS TEST 2

1. Referring to Figure 9–3, the probability that an investor selected at random will have bought *only* bonds is _____.

2. Referring to Figure 9–3, the probability that an investor selected at random will have bought *only* stocks is _____.

3. Referring to Figure 9–3, the probability that an investor selected at random will have bought neither stocks nor bonds is _____.

EXERCISE 9.6

1. If P is the event that production has increased and D is the event that demand has increased, express in words each of the following events:
   (a) P ∪ D   (b) P ∩ D   (c) D′   (d) P ∩ D′

2. If P is the event that production has increased and D is the event that demand has increased, write in symbols each of the following events:
   a. Production has not increased, but demand has.
   b. Production has increased or demand has increased.
   c. Neither production nor demand has increased.
   d. Demand has increased but production has not.

3. If N is the event that a person is negligent in an accident and F is the event that the person will file a claim, express in words each of the following events:
   (a) N ∩ F   (b) N′ ∪ F   (c) N′ ∩ F   (d) N′

4. If N is the event that a person is negligent in an accident and

---

1. $\frac{80}{300} = \frac{4}{15}$ 2. $\frac{50}{300} = \frac{1}{6}$ 3. $\frac{100}{300} = \frac{1}{3}$

F is the event that the person will file a claim, write in symbols each of the following events:

 a. The person is negligent and did not file a claim.
 b. The person is not negligent or did not file a claim.
 c. The person is neither negligent nor does he file a claim.
 d. Either the person is negligent or he filed a claim.

5. Let I represent the event that interest rates go up, U be the event that unemployment increases, and D be the event that the Dow Jones average declines. With reference to the accompanying Venn diagram, the event that interest rates go up, unemployment increases, and the Dow Jones average declines corresponds to region e. (Assume that interest rates, unemployment, and the Dow Jones average either increase or decline.)

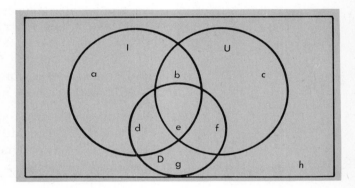

List the region or combination of regions which represent the following events:

 a. Interest rates go up, unemployment decreases, and the Dow Jones average increases.
 b. Unemployment increases and neither the Dow Jones average nor interest rates decline.
 c. The Dow Jones average declines but unemployment and interest rates do not increase.

6. Referring to Problem 5, explain in words what events are represented by the following regions:

 a. Region e
 b. Region g
 c. Region c
 d. Regions b and e together
 e. Regions a, c, and g together

7. In a survey of 200 investors, it was found that 50 owned transportation stock, 100 owned industrial stock, and 10

owned both. Draw a Venn diagram illustrating the situation and find the probability that if an investor is selected at random from this group

    a. the investor owns neither transportation nor industrial stock.

    b. the investor owns either transportation or industrial stock.

8. A company has 230 employees, of which 50 are administrators, 100 are females, and 20 are female administrators. If an employee is chosen at random, what is the probability that the employee will be

    a. male?

    b. a female that is not an administrator?

    c. a male that is not an administrator?

9. A company has 200 employees, of which 45 got a promotion, 100 got a raise, and 15 got both a raise and a promotion. If an employee is selected at random, what is the probability that this employee received

    a. a promotion *only*?

    b. a raise *only*?

    c. a raise or a promotion?

    d. neither a raise nor a promotion?

10. A company has 300 employees of which 200 are Caucasian, 150 are males, and 110 are Caucasian males. If an employee is selected at random, what is the probability that this employee is

    a. a female?

    b. a Caucasian female?

    c. a non-Caucasian male?

The following table, showing the distribution of male and female employees at Hues Paint Company according to position, will be used in Problems 11 through 15.

Employee Distribution According to Position

	SALES	CLERICAL	ADMINISTRATION
Male	60	80	20
Female	40	20	10

11. If an employee is selected at random from the 230 employees, find the probability of selecting an administrator.

12. If an employee is selected at random from the 230 employees, find the probability of selecting a salesperson.

13. If an employee is selected at random from the 230 employees, find the probability of selecting a male.

14. If an employee is selected at random from the 230 employees, find the probability of selecting a female administrator.

15. If an employee is selected at random from the 230 employees, find the probability of selecting a person that is in either the sales or clerical category.

The following table, giving the number of males and females falling into various salary classifications, will be used in Problems 16 through 20.

Salary Distribution According to Sex

SALARY	SEX		TOTAL
	Male	Female	
Low	40	200	240
Average	300	160	460
High	500	300	800
Totals	840	660	1500

16. Find the probability that a person selected at random from those surveyed has a low income.

17. Find the probability that a person selected at random from those surveyed has an average income.

18. Find the probability that a person selected at random from those surveyed has an average or a high income.

19. Find the probability that if a female is selected from those surveyed, she has a low income.

20. Find the probability that a person selected at random from those surveyed is a low-income male.

21. Of the first 50 stocks listed in the New York Stock Exchange transactions for November 5, 1973 (as reported in the *Wall Street Journal*), 26 stocks went down, 15 went up, and 9 remained unchanged. Based on this information, find the probability that a stock selected at random from this list did *not* remain unchanged.

The following table, showing the probability that there is a given number of people waiting in line at a checkout register at Dear's Department Store, will be used in Problems 22 through 25.

Number of Persons Waiting	0	1	2	3	4 or more
Probability	.10	.15	.20	.35	.20

22. Find the probability of having exactly two persons waiting.

23. Find the probability of having more than 3 persons waiting.

24. Find the probability of having more than 2 persons waiting.

25. Find the probability of having at least one person waiting.

26. The probabilities that a review board will rate an employee satisfactory, can improve, or unsatisfactory are, respectively, 0.75, 0.20, and 0.05. Find the probability that an employee is rated
   a. satisfactory or unsatisfactory.
   b. can improve or unsatisfactory.
   c. satisfactory or can improve.

27. For married couples living in a large city, the probability that the husband commutes to work is 0.72, the probability that his wife commutes is 0.63, and the probability that they both commute is 0.50. Find the probability that
   a. neither of them commutes to work.
   b. at least one of them commutes to work.

28. If $P(A) = \frac{1}{4}$, $P(B) = \frac{3}{8}$, and $P(A \cup B) = \frac{2}{8}$, find $P(A \cap B)$.

29. The probability of an event A is $\frac{1}{4}$, and the probability of another event B is $\frac{7}{8}$. If the probability that neither A nor B will occur is $\frac{2}{8}$, what is the probability that either A or B will occur?

30. If $P(A) = \frac{1}{2}$, $P(B) = \frac{5}{8}$, and $P(A' \cup B') = \frac{5}{8}$, find $P(A' \cap B')$.

THE WIZARD OF ID

9.7 CONDITIONAL PROBABILITY

As you can see from the cartoon, it frequently happens that in considering the probability of an event A, we obtain some information that may suggest a "revision" of the probability of A. For example, assume that a business has 200 employees, of which 40 are administrators (A), 20 of the employees have obtained a raise (R), and 10 of the administrators have obtained a raise (A ∩ R). If one person is selected at random from the 200 employees,

$$P(A) = \frac{40}{200} = \frac{1}{5} \text{ and } P(R) = \frac{20}{200} = \frac{1}{10}$$

But suppose that a person is selected at random and he tells you that he is an administrator. What is the probability that this person has obtained a raise? In other words, what is the probability that a person has obtained a raise, given that the person is an administrator? The expression "given that the person is an administrator" means that we must restrict our attention to the administrators. We have thus added a restrictive **condition** to the problem. Essentially, the condition that the person is an administrator requires that we use A as our sample space.

To compute P(R | A) (read "the probability of R given A"), we recall that there are 10 favorable outcomes (administrators that have obtained a raise) and 40 people in the new sample space (administrators). Hence, $P(R \mid A) = \frac{10}{40}$.

We note that

$$P(R \mid A) = \frac{\text{number of persons that have obtained a raise and are administrators}}{\text{number of persons that are administrators}} = \frac{P(R \cap A)}{P(A)}$$

This discussion suggests the next definition.

> **DEFINITION 9.8** If A and B are events in a sample space with P(B) ≠ 0, the conditional probability of A given B, denoted by P(A | B) is defined by
>
> $$P(A \mid B) = \frac{P(A \cap B)}{P(B)}$$

Example 1

The purchasing director of Hurts Rent-A-Car wishes to buy a Chrysler automobile. In the absence of any other information, he decides to select one at random from the accompanying list. What is the probability he will select a Monaco 4-door, given that he chooses a car whose latest price rise has been less than $100.

Here are some examples of Chrysler's price increases These are suggested retail prices, including suggested dealer preparation charges, if any, but excluding shipping charges, local taxes and optional equipment. (Some 1974 prices include items that were optional in 1973.) Car buyers are often able to obtain sizable discounts from these "sticker" prices.

	1973 price	Old 1974 price	New 1974 price	Latest rise	Latest %rise
Duster 6 cyl	$2,376	$2,511	$2,661	$150	6.0
Satellite 8 cyl	2,867	2,880	3,038	158	5.5
Regent 2-seat wgn	3,621	3,634	3,811	177	4.9
Fury I 8 cyl	3,575	3,620	3,692	72	2.0
Newport 2-door	4,254	4,254	4,326	72	1.7
Imperial 2-door	6,829	7,062	7,262	200	2.8
Dart 8 cyl	2,651	2,786	2,936	150	5.4
Charger 8 cyl hdtp	3,171	3,178	3,286	108	3.4
Monaco 4-door	3,729	3,774	3,846	72	1.9
Monaco Brougham 3-seat wgn	4,859	5,126	5,126	unch	unch

Reprinted, by permission, from *The Wall Street Journal*, December 17, 1973, p. 4

Solution

(Method 1) Let M be the event in which a Monaco 4-door is selected and L be the event in which the latest price rise has been less than $100. By Definition 9.6,

$$P(M \mid L) = \frac{P(M \cap L)}{P(L)} = \frac{1/10}{4/10} = \frac{1}{4}$$

(Method 2) Since he chooses a car whose latest price rise has been less than $100, the man has four choices and only one of them (the Monaco 4-door) is favorable; thus the probability is $\frac{1}{4}$.

Example 2

The table below shows the results of a survey conducted after Mr. Jones was fired from his job.

	MANAGERS (M)	WORKERS (W)	TOTAL
Support Employer (E)	45	15	60
Support Mr. Jones (J)	10	90	100
Totals	55	105	160

One of these 160 persons is to be selected at random to be on the board of review for the case. Find the probability that the person

(a) will support the employer, given that the person is a manager.

(b) will support Mr. Jones, given that the person is a worker.

Solution

(a) (Method 1) $P(E \mid M) = \dfrac{P(E \cap M)}{P(M)} = \dfrac{45/160}{55/160} = \dfrac{45}{55} = \dfrac{9}{11}$

(Method 2) Since 45 of the 55 managers support the employer, the probability that a person selected at random will support the employer, given that the person is a manager, is $\dfrac{45}{55} = \dfrac{9}{11}$.

(b) (Method 1) $P(J \mid W) = \dfrac{P(J \cap W)}{P(W)} = \dfrac{90/160}{105/160} = \dfrac{90}{105} = \dfrac{6}{7}$

(Method 2) Since 90 out of 105 workers support Mr. Jones, the probability that a person selected at random will support Mr. Jones, given that the person is a worker, is $\dfrac{90}{105} = \dfrac{6}{7}$.

PROGRESS TEST 1

1. Referring to Example 1, the probability that the man selects a Dart 8-cylinder, given that he chooses a car whose latest price rise has been between $100 and $175, is _____.

2. Referring to Example 2, the probability that the person is a worker, given that the person supports the employer, is _____.

3. Referring to Example 2, the probability that the person is a manager, given that the person supports Mr. Jones, is _____.

1. $\dfrac{1}{4}$ 2. $\dfrac{15}{60} = \dfrac{1}{4}$ 3. $\dfrac{10}{100} = \dfrac{1}{10}$

TABLE 9-4   Results of Advertising Survey

	BOUGHT THE PRODUCT (B)	DID NOT BUY THE PRODUCT (B')	TOTALS
Saw the ad (S)	10	30	40
Did not see the ad (S')	15	45	60
Totals	25	75	100

An important concept in probability, especially for managers and other persons in decision making capacities, is the idea of **independent** events. For example, the manager of a store decided to run an ad on the local television station. He then conducted a survey of 100 persons. The data for the survey is shown in Table 9–4.

From the table we see that $P(B \mid S) = \frac{10}{40} = \frac{1}{4}$ and $P(B) = \frac{25}{100} = \frac{1}{4}$; that is, $P(B \mid S) = P(B)$. This shows that the probability of event B (the event that the person buys the product) is the same regardless of whether the customer has seen the ad (S) or not. When this is the case, we say that event B is independent of event S and perhaps for this reason the manager would be wise to discontinue the ad.

From this discussion, we have seen that when B and S are independent, then $P(B \mid S) = P(B)$. In general, when A and B are independent, $P(A \mid B) = P(A)$, and by substituting $P(A)$ for $P(A \mid B)$ in Definition 9.6 and multiplying both sides by $P(B)$ we obtain the following rule.

How to find if two events are independent

RULE 9.2 When A and B are independent, $P(A \cap B) = P(A) \cdot P(B)$.

Example 3

An insurance company is trying to determine the relationship between accidents and marital status. The accompanying table gives the data for accidents in Cycle City, north and south of Main Street, in 1975.

	HAD AN ACCIDENT (A)	DID NOT HAVE AN ACCIDENT (A')
Single (S)	50	1950
Married (M)	25	975

(a) Are A and S independent?
(b) Are A' and M independent?

Solution

(a) By Rule 9.2, we have to check if $P(A \cap S) = P(A) \cdot P(S)$.
$P(A \cap S) = \dfrac{50}{3000}$, $P(A) = \dfrac{75}{3000}$, and $P(S) = \dfrac{2000}{3000}$ Since $P(A \cap S) =$
$P(A) \cdot P(S) = \dfrac{75}{3000} \cdot \dfrac{2000}{3000} = \dfrac{50}{3000}$, A and S are independent.

(b) Similarly, $P(A' \cap M) = P(A') \cdot P(M) = \dfrac{975}{3000}$, so A' and M are

also independent.

PROGRESS TEST 2

1. Referring to Example 2, $P(W \cap J) = $_____.
2. $P(W) = $_____.
3. $P(J) = $_____.
4. Based on your answers to 1, 2, and 3 above, are W
and J independent? _____ Why? _____.

EXERCISE 9.7

1. If D is the event that a stock has paid high dividends and G is
    the event that the stock is a good investment, state in words
    what probabilities are represented by the following:

    (a) $P(G \mid D)$ (b) $P(D' \mid G)$ (c) $P(D \mid G')$ (d) $P(G' \mid D')$

2. If I is the event that an executive is working for I.B.M., C is the
    event that he was once a computer programmer, and S is the
    event that he graduated from college summa cum laude, ex-
    press each of the following probabilities in symbolic form:
    a. The probability that an executive with I.B.M. who was
       once a computer programmer graduated from college
       summa cum laude
    b. The probability that an executive with I.B.M. who did
       not graduate from college summa cum laude was once a
       computer programmer
    c. The probability that an executive with I.B.M. graduated
       from college summa cum laude but was never a com-
       puter programmer
    d. The probability that an executive with I.B.M. who was

---

1. $\dfrac{90}{160} = \dfrac{9}{16}$ 2. $\dfrac{105}{160} = \dfrac{21}{32}$ 3. $\dfrac{100}{160} = \dfrac{5}{8}$ 4. No. $P(W \cap J) \neq P(W) \cdot P(J)$

never a computer programmer graduated from college summa cum laude

New York to San Antonio		
From LaGuardia		
Leave		Arrive
8:45 a.m.	Direct	12:49 p.m.
2:00 p.m.	Direct	5:49 p.m.
4:45 p.m.	Direct	8:19 p.m.
From Newark		
Leave		Arrive
6:40 a.m.		12:49 p.m.
9:40 a.m.		1:49 p.m.
1:15 p.m.		4:49 p.m.
5:15 p.m. (Ex. Sat.)		9:04 p.m.
From Kennedy		
Leave		Arrive
8:00 a.m.		12:49 p.m.
10:25 a.m.	Direct	3:49 p.m.
2:10 p.m.	Direct	6:49 p.m.
4:15 p.m.	Direct	8:29 p.m.
7:00 p.m.	Direct	10:49 p.m.
9:50 p.m. (Ex. Sat.)	Direct	2:24 a.m.

Reprinted, by permission, from *The Wall Street Journal,* July 17, 1973.

3. An executive wishes to fly from New York to San Antonio. Assuming that he instructs his secretary to pick his flight at random from the accompanying schedule, find
   a. the probability that he will be on the 4:15 p.m. flight.
   b. the probability that he will be on the 4:15 p.m. flight, given that he wishes to leave from Kennedy Airport.

4. For the executive in Problem 3, find
   a. the probability that he is scheduled to arrive in San Antonio at 12:49 p.m.
   b. the probability that he is scheduled to arrive in San Antonio at 12:49 p.m., given that he left from Kennedy Airport.

5. For the executive in Problem 3, find
   a. the probability that the executive will fly direct.
   b. the probability that the executive will fly direct, given that he is to leave from La Guardia Airport.
   c. the probability that the executive will fly direct, given that he is to leave from Newark.
   d. the probability that the executive took a direct flight, given that he arrived at 12:49 p.m.

6. Let D be the event in which the executive flies direct and K be the event in which the executive leaves from Kennedy Airport. Referring to the schedule given in Problem 3, are D and K independent?

7. A company is to interview 100 applicants for a job. The distribution according to the marital status and number of years of college is given in the accompanying table.

	MARRIED (M)	NOT MARRIED (M′)
At least two years of college (T)	20	10
Less than two years of college (L)	40	30

Find the following probabilities:
(a) P(M)   (b) P(T ∩ M)   (c) P(T|M)

8. Referring to Problem 7, find the following probabilities:
(a) P(M′)   (b) P(T ∩ M′)   (c) P(T|M′)

9. Using your answers to Problems 7 and 8, verify the following:

(a) $P(T|M) = \dfrac{P(T \cap M)}{P(M)}$ (b) $P(T|M') = \dfrac{P(T \cap M')}{P(M')}$

10. An executive estimates that the probability that she will get a raise is $\dfrac{2}{10}$, the probability that she will get a promotion is $\dfrac{4}{10}$, and the probability that she will get both is $\dfrac{1}{10}$. Find

a. the probability that the executive will get a raise, given that she is going to get a promotion.
b. the probability that the executive will get a promotion, given that she is going to get a raise.
c. the probability that the executive will not get a promotion, given that she is not going to get a raise.
(Hint: Draw the Venn diagram and fill in the probabilities associated with the different regions.)

11. The personnel director of Gadget Manufacturing has compiled the accompanying table showing the percentage of men and women employees who were absent the indicated number of days.

Employee Absences According to Sex and Frequency

SEX	ABSENCES				
	0 Days	1 Day	2 Days	3 or More Days	Total
Male	10%	20%	20%	0	50%
Female	10%	10%	10%	20%	50%

Find the probability that a given employee missed
(a) 1 day, given that the employee is a woman.
(b) 2 days, given that the employee is a man.

12. The Merrilee Brokerage House studied two groups of industries (computers and petroleum) and rated them as low risks or high risks as indicated in the accompanying table.

High and Low Risk Investments

	Low Risk (L)	High Risk (H)
Computers (C)	5	10
Petroleum(P)	20	15

If a person selected a stock at random from the two groups, find the probability that the person selected a computer stock, given that the person selected a low risk stock.

13.   Referring to Problem 12, find the probability that the person selected a petroleum stock, given that the person selected a high risk stock.

14.   Referring to the table in Problem 12, are C and L independent?

15.   An efficiency expert has determined that the probability that an employee will arrive on time to work is 0.64 and the probability that the employee will arrive on time and leave on time is 0.08.
   a. What is the conditional probability that an employee who arrived on time will also leave on time?
   b. If it is also known that the probability that an employee will leave on time is 0.44, what is the conditional probability that an employee who left on time had also arrived on time?

16.   Which of the following events would you suppose are independent and which are dependent?
   a. Increasing production and increasing profits
   b. Increasing production and decreasing demand
   c. Increasing production and the manager's name being George

17.   A company has two plants whose respective productions can be regarded as being independent. If the probabilities of increasing production in each of these plants are $\frac{1}{5}$ and $\frac{3}{7}$, respectively, find the probability that
   a. both plants will increase production.
   b. neither plant will increase production.

18.   A radio repair shop has estimated that the probability that a radio sent to their shop has a bad tube is $\frac{1}{4}$, the probability that the radio has a bad rectifier is $\frac{1}{8}$, and the probability that it has a bad condenser is $\frac{2}{3}$. If it is assumed that tubes, rectifiers, and condensers work independently, find the probability that

    a. the tubes, the condenser, and the rectifier are bad in a radio sent to the shop.

    b. none of the three parts (tubes, condenser, and rectifier) is bad in a radio sent to the shop.

19.   A company has estimated that the probabilities of success for three products introduced in the market are $\frac{1}{4}$, $\frac{2}{3}$, and $\frac{1}{2}$, respectively. Assuming independence, find the probability that

    a. the three products are all successful.

    b. none of the products is successful.

20.   The Apollo module has five components: the main engine, the propulsion system, the command service module, the lunar excursion module, and the lunar excursion module engine. If each of the systems is considered to be independent of the others and the probability that each of the systems performs satisfactorily is 0.90, what is the probability that the Apollo module will perform satisfactorily?

SELF-TEST/CHAPTER 9

1.   A stock is selected at random from the ten stocks that went up
      the most on the New York Stock Exchange. Find the prob-
      ability of selecting

_____ a.   a stock whose sales (in hundreds) are less than 75.

_____ b.   a stock whose net is between 2 and 4.

_____ c.   a stock whose net is higher than 3 and whose
                   per cent (PCT) increase is higher than 15.

Daily Percentage Leaders On N.Y. Stock Exchange

NEW YORK—The following list shows the stocks that
have gone up the most and down the most based on percent of change on the New York Stock Exchange regardless of volume for Tuesday.
     Net and percentage changes are the difference be-
tween the previous closing price and yesterday's last
price.

UPS

Name	Sales(hds)	High	Low	Last	Net		Pct.
1 Parker Pen	58	20¼	17½	20¼	+ 3⅜	Up	20.0
2 vjReadg 2pf	119	3⅝	2⅞	3½	+ ½	Up	16.7
3 Cook Unit	255	7½	6⅜	7¼	+ 1	Up	16.0
4 MSL Ind	53	24⅝	24½	24⅝	+ 3⅜	Up	15.9
5 Alexandrs	144	5⅛	4½	5	+ ⅝	Up	14.3
6 Handy Har	206	24⅞	21½	24	+ 3	Up	14.3
7 Nthgate Ex	259	6¼	5⅝	6¼	+ ¾	Up	13.6
8 Relian pf B	1	39	39	39	+ 4½	Up	13.0
9 Int Indst pf	38	2¼	2	2¼	+ ¼	Up	12.5
10 vjReadg 1pf	12	3⅜	2⅞	3⅜	+ ⅜	Up	12.5

DOWNS

Name	Sales(hds)	High	Low	Last	Net		Pct.
1 Rite Aid	934	14	11¼	11⅝	− 4	Off	25.6
2 Hardees	173	8⅛	6⅛	6¼	− 1½	Off	19.4
3 Lynch CSys	103	8	7	7	− 1¼	Off	15.2
4 Whittakr	161	2⅝	2¼	2¼	− ⅜	Off	14.3
5 Mobil Home	242	5⅞	5½	5½	− ⅞	Off	13.7
6 Morse EIP	57	7¾	6⅞	6⅞	− 1	Off	12.7
7 CLC Am	26	4⅞	4⅜	4⅜	− ⅝	Off	12.5
8 Kings DStr	200	6⅛	5¼	5⅜	− ¾	Off	12.2
9 Ward Foods	55	7¼	6½	6½	− ⅞	Off	11.9
10 Nat Airlines	65	14¼	13⅛	13⅛	− 1¾	Off	11.8

Reprinted, by permission, from *The Wall Street Journal*,
January 9, 1974, p. 33.

2.   A man can buy stocks in the New York Stock Exchange or
      in the American Stock Exchange. If he wishes to buy Trans-
      portation or Industrial Stocks and each of these stocks can go
      up or down in price,

_____ a.   make a tree diagram to show all the possibilities.

_____ b.   Find the probability that the man selects a
                   Transportation Stock from the New York Ex-
                   change and the price of the stock goes up.

3.   There are 50 applicants for a job. Their experience and marital status are given in the table below.

Martial Status of Job Applicants

	MARRIED	SINGLE
At least 2 years experience	10	8
Less than 2 years experience	20	12

_____ a.   Find the probability that if an applicant is chosen at random for the job, the applicant is married and has at least two years experience.

_____ b.   Find the probability that if an applicant is chosen at random for the job, the applicant is single.

4.   Referring to Problem 3, find the probability that

_____ a.   the applicant is married, if it is known that the applicant has at least two years experience.

_____ b.   the applicant has at least two years experience, if it is known that the applicant is married.

5.   Referring to Problem 3, let M be the event that the person is married, S be the event that the person is single, A be the event that the person has at least two years experience, and L be the event that the person has less than two years experience.

_____ a.   Are A and S independent? Show why or why not.

_____ b.   Are M and L independent? Show why or why not.

6.   An investor feels that the odds that his stock will go up in price are 2 to 3, and the odds that they will go down in price are 1 to 3.

_____ a.   Find the probability that his stock will go up in price.

_____ b.   Find the probability that the stock will go down in price.

7.   The probability that Corporal Motors stock will go up in price is $\frac{1}{7}$, the probability that it will go down in price is $\frac{4}{7}$, and the probability that the price will stay the same is $\frac{2}{7}$.

_____ a.   Find the odds in favor of Corporal Motors stock going up.

_____ b. Find the odds in favor of Corporal Motors stock going down or staying the same.

8. A small company is about to introduce a new product on the market. The president of the company feels that if the new product is put on the market and it sells, the company will make $2000; however, if the new product is put on the market and it does not sell, the company will lose $1000. If he recommends that the new product not be put on the market and a competitor introduces a similar product which sells, the company will lose $4000; finally, if the president recommends that the new product not be put on the market and the one introduced by his competitor does not sell, his company will gain $500.

_____ a. Find the expected gain of introducing the new product on the market, if the president feels that the odds that the product will sell are 3 to 1.

_____ b. If the president is convinced that his company is going to make money, what should he recommend?

_____ c. If the president is convinced that his company is going to lose money, what should he recommend?

9. In a survey of 100 investors it was found that 50 owned Transportation stock, 40 owned Industrial stock, and 20 owned both.

_____ a. How many investors owned Transportation or Industrial stock?

_____ b. Find the probability that if an investor is selected at random, this investor owns Industrial stock only.

10. The probabilities for zero, one, two, three, or four fires in Wood City are given below.

Fires	0	1	2	3	4
Probability	$\frac{2}{10}$	$\frac{1}{10}$	$\frac{1}{5}$	$\frac{1}{10}$	$\frac{3}{10}$

_____ a. Find the expected number of fires in this city.

_____ b. If each fire costs $500, find the expected costs for the fires.

ten

Statistics

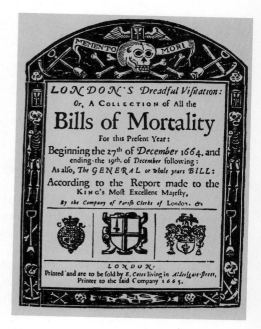

Reprinted, by permission, from Mario F. Triola, *Mathematics and the Modern World,* Cummings Publishing Company, Inc., 1973, p. 198

10.1 FREQUENCY DISTRIBUTIONS

The word *statistics* brings to the minds of most people an image of a mass of numerical data. To a statistician, statistics means the analysis of this data and the deduction of logical conclusions from it. It is in this sense that the science of statistics is one of the most important branches of applied mathematics.

It is said that statistical analysis began with the studies of an English shopkeeper, John Graunt (1620–1674), who tried to analyze the causes of death in London for approximately the first half of the seventeenth century. In 1662 Graunt published a remarkable book, *Natural and Political Observation Upon The Bills of Mortality* (see illustration).

After this humble beginning many mathematicians, among them such famous ones as Laplace (1749–1827) and Gauss (1777–1855), made important contributions to the basic ideas of statistics.

Today, statistics is used throughout industry in the manufacture of goods, in the study of wages and work conditions, in insurance and investments, and in many other ways. No one can leaf through a newspaper or a news magazine without seeing evidence of the impact of statistics on our daily lives. We are constantly exhorted to buy this and not to buy that, to read this magazine, to see that movie, to eat certain foods, and not to smoke cigarettes, all on the basis of statistical evidence that seems to show the desirability of following this advice.

Let us look at a statistics problem that should interest a manager and his team of 25 salesmen. Below you can find the number of sales made by each of the 25 salesmen.

6	5	4	0	9
2	0	8	8	1
10	6	8	5	5
8	7	9	10	9
6	5	8	4	7

This listing shows at once that there are some good salesmen and some poor ones; but, since sales are not arranged in any particular order, it is difficult to conclude anything else from the list.

Definition of frequency distribution

A **frequency distribution** is often a suitable way of organizing a list of numbers to show what patterns may be present. We proceed in three steps.

1. The number of sales from 0 through 10 is listed in order in a column (see Table 10–1).

2. Going through the original list in the order in which it is given, we make a mark on the appropriate line of the table for each salesman.

3. In a third column we can list how many times each number occurs. This number is the **frequency** of the sales.

It is now easier to see that the most frequent number of sales was eight. This number of sales was made by $\frac{5}{25} = \frac{1}{5} = 20\%$ of the salesmen. Ten of the salesmen, or 40%, made eight or more sales. Only six, or 24%, made less than five sales.

TABLE 10–1   Frequency Distribution of Sales

NUMBER OF SALES	TALLY MARKS	FREQUENCY
0	II	2
1	I	1
2	I	1
3		0
4	II	2
5	IIII	4
6	III	3
7	II	2
8	JHT	5
9	III	3
10	II	2
		$\overline{25}$ (TOTAL)

TABLE 10–2   **Frequency Distribution of Sales by Intervals of 2**

NUMBER OF SALES	FREQUENCY
0–2	4
3–4	2
5–6	7
7–8	7
9–10	5

If there are very many items in a set of numerical data, then it is usually necessary to shorten the frequency distribution by grouping the data into intervals. For instance, in the preceding distribution we can group the number of sales in intervals of two to obtain the listing in Table 10–2.

Of course, some of the detailed information in the first table has been lost in the second table, but for some purposes a condensed table may furnish all the information that is required.

It is also possible to present the information contained in Table 10–1 by means of a **bar graph.** If there is no space between bars, the graph is called a **histogram.** In the histogram of Figure 10–1, the units

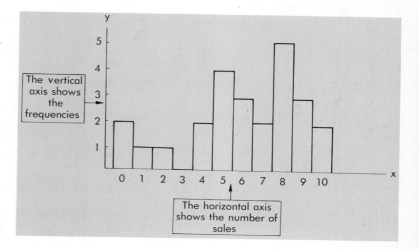

Figure 10–1

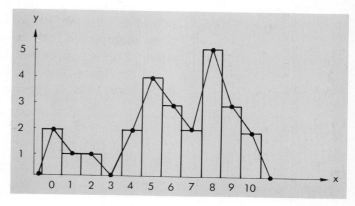

Figure 10–2

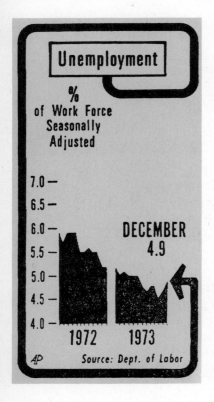

Figure 10–3   Reprinted, by permission, from *The Tampa Tribune,*
January 5, 1974, p. 1

of the vertical line (called y-axis) represent the frequencies, while
those on the horizontal line (called the x-axis) indicate the number of
sales made.

From this histogram we can construct a **frequency polygon** (or
line graph) by connecting the midpoints of the tops of each bar, as
shown in Figure 10–2.

PROGRESS TEST 1

1. In the frequency polygon in Figure 10–3, the horizontal axis represents the 12 months of the year for a 2-year
period and the vertical axis represents the per cent of persons unemployed. The per cent of unemployed persons in
June, 1972, is approximately _____.

2. In Figure 10–3, the per cent of unemployed persons
in January, 1973, is approximately _____.

---

1. 5.5   2. 5.1

EXERCISE 10.1

1. Thirty employees were asked to count the number of overtime hours they had worked during the preceding week. The following figures represent the results.

1	5	4	7	10	8	2	3	9	6
6	12	8	14	3	4	8	7	2	1
0	3	5	8	10	12	0	15	1	4

    a. Make a frequency distribution of the number of overtime hours worked. Label the three columns NUMBER OF HOURS, TALLY MARKS, and FREQUENCY.
    b. What is the most frequent number of overtime hours worked per employee?
    c. How many worked more than ten hours of overtime?
    d. How many worked five hours or less of overtime?
    e. What per cent of employees worked more than seven hours of overtime?

2. Prepare a histogram for the data obtained in Problem 1a.

3. Here are 25 common stocks listed on the New York Stock Exchange and their closing prices in dollars per share on August 17, 1973.

1. American Airlines	$9\frac{3}{4}$	13. Gulf Oil	$22\frac{1}{4}$
2. American Motors	$7\frac{1}{8}$	14. Inland Steel	$27\frac{3}{8}$
3. American Telephone		15. Kaiser Aluminum	$19\frac{4}{4}$
& Telegraph	$47\frac{1}{4}$	16. McDonalds	62
4. Burlington Industries	$27\frac{5}{8}$	17. PanAmerican Airlines	$6\frac{1}{4}$
5. Canadian Pacific	$16\frac{5}{8}$	18. Phillips Petroleum	$54\frac{7}{8}$
6. Chrysler Motors	$23\frac{3}{4}$	19. Reynolds Metal	15
7. Delta Airlines	$45\frac{3}{8}$	20. Sears	96
8. Eastern Airlines	$8\frac{3}{8}$	21. Sun Oil	$46\frac{1}{2}$
9. Ford Motor Company	$53\frac{7}{8}$	22. Texaco	30
10. General Dynamics	$18\frac{3}{4}$	23. Transamerica	$11\frac{5}{8}$
11. General Motors	$62\frac{1}{2}$	24. United Airlines	$16\frac{3}{8}$
12. Greyhound	$14\frac{3}{8}$	25. U. S. Steel	$27\frac{7}{8}$

a. Make a frequency distribution of these stock prices grouped in intervals of $10. The first line of your table should look like this:

PRICE	TALLY MARKS	FREQUENCY
0–10	IIII	4

b. What is the most frequent price interval for these stocks?

c. How many of the stocks sold for more than $50 per share?

d. What per cent of these stocks sold for prices between $21 and $31 per share?

e. What per cent of these stocks sold for less than $31 per share?

4. Prepare a histogram for the data obtained in Problem 3a.

5. Prepare a frequency polygon for the data in Problem 3a.

6. The following table gives the 1972 state sales tax rate (not including local tax rates) for thirty-nine states.

1972 State Sales Tax Rates for Thirty-Nine States

STATE	RATE (%)	STATE	RATE (%)	STATE	RATE (%)
Alabama	4	Maine	5	Ohio	4
Arkansas	3	Maryland	4	Oklahoma	2
California	4	Massachusetts	3	Pennsylvania	6
Colorado	3	Michigan	4	Rhode Island	5
Florida	4	Minnesota	3	South Carolina	4
Georgia	3	Mississippi	5	South Dakota	4
Idaho	3	Missouri	3	Texas	4
Illinois	4	Nevada	3	Utah	4
Indiana	2	New Jersey	5	Vermont	3
Iowa	3	New Mexico	4	Virginia	3
Kansas	3	New York	4	West Virginia	3
Kentucky	5	North Carolina	3	Wisconsin	4
Louisiana	3	North Dakota	4	Wyoming	3

a. Make a frequency distribution for these rates.
b. Make a histogram for these data.
c. Now make a frequency polygon for the data.

7. Here is the stock of shoes in the Easy Walker shoe store.

SIZE	NUMBER OF PAIRS
7	5
$7\frac{1}{2}$	6
8	10

$8\frac{1}{2}$	8
9	6
$9\frac{1}{2}$	5
10	4

a. Prepare a histogram for this data.

b. Prepare a frequency polygon from the histogram in 7a.

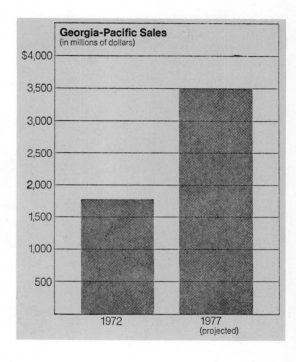

Courtesy of Georgia-Pacific

8.   The accompanying graph gives the amount of sales of Georgia-Pacific for the years 1972 and 1977 (projected).

   a. How many millions did it sell in 1972?

   b. How many millions is it projecting to sell in 1977?

   c. The sales (in millions) from 1972 to 1977 are as shown.

YEAR	SALES (IN MILLIONS)
1972	1,750
1973	2,000
1974	2,500
1975	2,750
1976	3,000
1977	3,500

Prepare a histogram for this data.

9.   Prepare a frequency polygon from the histogram of Problem 8c.

10.   The accompanying table gives the amount of savings (in thousands of dollars) held by the employees of Walt's Auto Supply.

Amount (in thousands of dollars)	1	2	3	4	5	6
Frequency	3	4	6	5	4	3

a. Prepare a histogram for this data.
b. Prepare a frequency polygon from the historgam in 10a.

Dow Jones Averages

	Open	High	Low	Close	Chg.
30 Industrials	851.01	859.16	841.41	855.32	+4.46
20 Transportation	196.73	199.94	194.60	198.20	+2.01
15 Utilities	89.65	91.45	89.02	91.23	+1.81
65 Stocks	272.84	276.39	269.99	274.93	+2.42

Reprinted, by permission, from *The Wall Street Journal*, December 24, 1973

10.2 MEASURES OF CENTRAL TENDENCY

As you can see in the table above, one of the important ideas in statistics is that of an **average.** Let us see how this idea can be used.

Johnny and Jimmy were discussing their number of sales in the last nine days. Their records of sales looked like this:

DAY	1	2	3	4	5	6	7	8	9	TOTAL
Johnny	10	7	10	7	7	10	9	10	2	72
Jimmy	10	7	10	7	7	7	10	7	7	72

Which do you think is the better salesman? As you can see, Johnny's **average** number of sales is $\frac{72}{9} = 8$, and Jimmy's **average** is also $\frac{72}{9} = 8$. Johnny thinks that averages do not tell the whole story so he tries something else. First, he makes a frequency distribution of the two sets of numbers:

SALES	FREQUENCY	
	Johnny	Jimmy
2	1	0
7	3	6
8	0	0
9	1	0
10	4	3

Upon inspecting this list, Johnny said, "I did better than you did, Jimmy, because I made ten sales more often than any other number and you made seven more often than any other number." Would you agree with Johnny?

The average number that we first gave (8) is called the **mean.** It is the one that most of us think of as the average.

> **DEFINITION 10.1** The mean of a set of numbers is the sum of the numbers divided by the number of numbers in the set. The mean is usually denoted by the symbol $\bar{x}$ (read "bar x").

Definition of mean

Johnny used a different kind of measure that is really not an average at all. The measure he used is called the **mode.**

> **DEFINITION 10.2** The mode of a set of numbers is that number of the set that occurs most often.

Definition of mode

If no number in the set occurs more than once, then there is no mode. However, if several numbers all occur an equal number of times and more than all the rest, then all of these several numbers are modes. Thus, it is possible for a set of numbers to have more than one mode.

The mean and the mode are useful because they give an indication of a sort of center of the set. For this reason they are called measures of **central tendency.**

Example 1

The prices (in dollars) of five popular stocks on the New York Stock Exchange are recorded below.

$$74 \qquad 76 \qquad 76 \qquad 77 \qquad 82$$

Find (a) the mean (average) price; (b) the mode of the prices.

Solution

(a) The mean is $x = \dfrac{74 + 76 + 76 + 77 + 82}{5} = 77$.

(b) The mode is the most frequently occurring number, 76.

There is a third commonly used measure of central tendency, called the **median.**

Definition of median

> **DEFINITION 10.3** The median of a set of numbers is the middle number when the numbers are arranged in order of magnitude. If there is no middle number, then the median is the mean of the two middle numbers.

Let us list Johnny's and Jimmy's sales in order of magnitude:

Johnny: 2   7   7   7   ⑨   10   10   10   10

Jimmy: 7   7   7   7   ⑦   7   10   10   10

The median is circled in each case.

Now let us look at the three measures that we have found for the number of sales.

MEASURE	JOHNNY	JIMMY
Mean	8	8
Mode	10	7
Median	9	7

The mode and the median in this case give a truer picture of the original sales, and we have to admit now that Johnny is a better salesman than Jimmy.

PROGRESS TEST 1

1. The percentage interest rates on conventional loans quoted by five lending institutions are $8\frac{1}{2}$, $7\frac{1}{4}$, $8\frac{1}{4}$, 9, and 7. The mean of these rates is _____.

2. The median of the percentage interest rates in question 1 is _____.

3. The mode (if it exists) of the percentage interest rates in question 1 is _____.

---

1. 8   2. $8\frac{1}{4}$ 3. nonexistent, i.e., there is none

The ideas in this section can be applied in many ways. For example, have you ever been in line at the counter of a supermarket or department store for so long that you were tempted to walk out? There is a mathematical theory called queuing (pronounced cue-ing) that studies the ways in which lines at supermarkets, department stores, etc. can be reduced to a minimum. Here is an example that shows how the manager can estimate the average number of people waiting at a particular counter.

Applications to queuing theory

Suppose in a 5-minute interval the following customers arrive. (Arrival time is assumed to be at the beginning of each minute.)

Time	Customers
1	A,B
2	C,D
3	
4	E,F
5	

If it is known that each customer takes one minute to be served, we can construct the following diagram showing the line during each minute.

In the first minute A and B arrived. During the second minute B moved to the head of the line (A was gone, since it took one minute to serve him) and C and D arrived, etc.

Example 2

From the preceding diagram find
(a) the average (mean) number of people in line.
(b) The mode of the number of people in line.

Solution

(a) The average is $\dfrac{2 + 3 + 2 + 3 + 2}{5} = 2.4$

(b) The mode is 2 (the number of people most often encountered in line).

PROGRESS TEST 2

1. If in Example 2 the number of persons in line during the first five minutes is 2, 4, 3, 3, 3, the mean number of people in line is _____.

2. The mode of the number of people in line is _____.

EXERCISE 10.2

1. Find the mean and the median for each of the three sets of numbers:

   (a) $\{1, 5, 9, 13, 17\}$ (b) $\{1, 3, 9, 27, 81\}$ (c) $\{1, 4, 9, 16, 25\}$

   For which of these sets are the mean and the median the same? Which measure is the same for all three sets? Which (if any) of the sets has a mode?

2. Show that the median of the set of numbers $\{1, 2, 4, 8, 16, 32\}$ is 6. How does this compare with the mean?

3. Out of 10 possible points, a class of 20 students made the following test scores: 0, 0, 0, 2, 4, 5, 5, 6, 6, 6, 7, 8, 8, 8, 8, 9, 9, 9, 10, 10. Find the mean, the median, and the mode. Which of these three measures do you think is the least representative of the set of scores?

4. Find the mean and the median of the following set of numbers: $\{0, 3, 26, 43, 45, 60, 72, 75, 79, 82, 83\}$

5. Use the situation of Example 2 and suppose that the list of arrivals is as follows:

Time	Customers
1	A
2	B
3	C,D,E
4	F
5	

   a. Draw a diagram showing the line during each minute.
   b. Find the mean of the number of people in line during each of the first five minutes.
   c. Find the mode of the number of people in line.

---

1. 3   2. 3

6.   Here are the temperatures at one-hour intervals from 1 p.m. to 5 p.m. on August 19 in Hot Valley, U.S.A.

1	90
2	93
3	93
4	94
5	100

   a. Find the mean temperature from 1 p.m. to 5 p.m.
   b. Find the mode of the temperatures from 1 p.m. to 5 p.m.

7.   Here are the temperatures at one hour intervals from 1 p.m. on August 20, 1973, to 9 a.m. on August 21, 1973, in Denver, Colorado:

1 p.m.	90	8 p.m.	81	3 a.m.	66
2 p.m.	91	9 p.m.	79	4 a.m.	65
3 p.m.	92	10 p.m.	76	5 a.m.	66
4 p.m.	92	11 p.m.	74	6 a.m.	64
5 p.m.	91	12 m	71	7 a.m.	64
6 p.m.	89	1 a.m.	71	8 a.m.	71
7 p.m.	86	2 a.m.	69	9 a.m.	75

   a. What was the mean temperature? The median temperature?
   b. What was the mean temperature from 1 p.m. to 9 p.m.? The median temperature?
   c. What was the mean temperature from midnight to 9 a.m.? The median temperature?

8.   An elevator is designed to carry a maximum load of 1,600 pounds. Is the elevator overloaded if it is carrying
   a. ten persons whose average (mean) weight is 150?
   b. eight children whose average (mean) weight is 50 pounds and five adults whose average (mean) weight is 150 pounds?

9.   A truck fleet consisting of five trucks has found that the miles per gallon on each of their five trucks is as follows:

        12   13   11   10   9

   Find (a) the mean (average) miles per gallon for the trucks; (b) the median miles per gallon for the trucks.

10.   On the same day five appliance stores sampled posted the following prices (in dollars) for a Junetag Washing Machine:

        270   280   275   285   265

Find (a) the average (mean) of the prices; (b) the median of the prices; (c) the mode of the prices.

11. The grade point averages for five seniors at P.U. University are 3.2, 2.4, 3.8, 3.6, 2.0. Find (a) the mean (average) of the scores; (b) the median of the scores; (c) the mode of the scores.

Amer. Stock Exchange Bonds

Total Volume $1,290,000

SALES SINCE JANUARY 1

1974	1973	1972
$4,572,000	$11,422,000	$24,228,000

	Mon	Fri	Thurs	Wed
Issues traded	75	72	69	54
Advances	46	43	46	24
Declines	16	11	6	11
Unchanged	13	18	17	19
New Highs, 1973-74	0	1	1	0
New Lows, 1973-74	1	1	3	2

Reprinted, by permission, from *The Wall Street Journal*, January 8, 1974, p. 23

12. Referring to the accompanying statistics, find
   a. the mean (average) number of bonds traded from Wednesday through Monday.
   b. the mean (average) number of advances from Wednesday through Monday.
   c. the mean (average) number of declines from Wednesday through Monday.

13. The prices (in dollars) of five stocks listed on the American Stock Exchange are as follows:

$$38 \quad 40 \quad 44 \quad 36 \quad 42$$

Find (a) the mean (average) price; (b) the median price; (c) the mode of the prices.

14. The mean score on a test taken by 20 students is 75. What is the sum of the 20 test scores?

15. A mathematics professor lost a test paper belonging to one of his students. He remembered that the mean score for the class of 20 was 81, and he found that the sum of the other 19 scores was 1560. What was the grade on the paper he lost?

16. If in Problem 15 the mean was 82, and the sum of the 19 other scores was still 1560, what was the grade on the lost paper?

17. The mean salary for the 20 workers in Company A is $90 per week, while in Company B the mean salary for its 30 workers is $80 per week. If the two companies merge, what is the mean salary for the 50 employees of the new company?

18.   A student has a mean score of 88 on five tests taken. What score must he obtain on his next test to have a mean (average) score of 80 on all six tests?

19.   In some instances it is desirable to assign different weights to individual measurements in a set of data. For example, if a professor wishes to give three hour exams during the term and one two-hour final exam, the final exam score should be counted twice as much as each hour exam score. This can be done by treating the final exam score as two scores. If a student had grades of 60, 70, and 80 on his three hour exams and a grade of 75 on his final exam, his average (weighted) should be

$$\frac{60 + 70 + 80 + 75 + 75}{5} = 72$$

This calculation could also have been written as

$$\frac{60 + 70 + 80 + 2(75)}{5} = 72$$

Using this idea, find the average (weighted) of a student obtaining grades of 75, 78, 76 in his three hour exams and a final exam grade of 68.

20.   Using the ideas of Problem 19, find the average cost per share for an investor buying 50 shares of Fly-Hi Airlines at $60 a share, 60 shares at $50 a share, and 40 shares at $75 a share.

Schools Seek 15-20% Reduction In Fuel Use

Reprinted, by permission, from *The Tampa Tribune*, December 28, 1973, p. 2B

10.3 MEASURES OF DISPERSION

Most of the time we want to know more about a set of numbers than we can learn from a measure of central tendency. For instance, the two sets of numbers {3, 5, 7} and {0, 5, 10} both have the same mean and the same median, 5, but the two sets of numbers are quite different. Clearly, some information about how the numbers vary will be useful in describing the set.

A number that describes how the numbers of a set are spread out or "dispersed" is called a **measure of dispersion**. A very simple example of such a measure is the **range**. For example, the range of fuel savings in the headline above is 5%.

Definition of range

> **DEFINITION 10.4**   The range of a set of numbers is the difference between the greatest and the least of the numbers in the set.

The two sets {3, 5, 7} and {0, 5, 10} have ranges, $7 - 3 = 4$ and $10 - 0 = 10$, respectively. Since the range is determined by only two numbers of the set, you can see that it gives us very little information about the other numbers of the set. The range actually gives us only a general notion of the "spread" of the given data.

Another measure of dispersion is called the **standard deviation**. It is the most commonly used of these measures and the only additional one that we shall consider. The easiest way to define the standard deviation is by means of a formula.

Definition of standard deviation

> **DEFINITION 10.5**   Let a set of n numbers be denoted by $x_1, x_2, x_3, \ldots, x_n$ and let the mean of these numbers be denoted by $\overline{x}$. Then the standard deviation, σ (lower case Greek letter sigma) is given by

$$\sigma = \sqrt{\frac{(x_1 - \overline{x})^2 + (x_2 - \overline{x})^2 + (x_3 - \overline{x})^2 + \ldots + (x_n - \overline{x})^2}{n}}$$

To find the standard deviation, we must find
  1. the mean, $\overline{x}$, of the set of numbers;
  2. the difference (deviation) between each number of the set and the mean;
  3. the squares of these deviations;
  4. the mean of the squares;
  5. the square root of this last mean. This is the number σ.

Example 1

The number of years of schooling of five employees was found to be 7, 9, 10, 11, and 13. Find the standard deviation σ for this set of years.

Solution

We follow the preceding five steps, making the table shown below.

TABLE 10-3 **Standard Deviation in Number of Years of Schooling of Five Employees**

YEARS OF SCHOOL x	$\bar{x}$	DIFFERENCE FROM MEAN $x - \bar{x}$	SQUARE OF DIFFERENCE $(x - \bar{x})^2$
7	10	-3	9
9	10	-1	1
10	10	0	0
11	10	1	1
13	10	3	9

50 (Sum of Years of School)

20 (Sum of Squares)

$\bar{x} = \frac{50}{5} = 10$ (Means of Years of School)

$\frac{20}{5} = 4$ (Mean of Squares)

$\sqrt{4} = 2 = \sigma$

1. The mean of the five numbers is

$$\bar{x} = \frac{7 + 9 + 10 + 11 + 13}{5} = \frac{50}{5} = 10$$

This number is placed on each line of Column 2.
   2. The difference (deviation) between each number and the mean is given in Column 3.
   3. We square the numbers in Column 3 to obtain the numbers in Column 4.
   4. The mean of the numbers in Column 4 is

$$\frac{9 + 1 + 0 + 1 + 9}{5} = \frac{20}{5} = 4$$

   5. The standard deviation is the square root of the number found in Step 4. Thus, $\sigma = \sqrt{4} = 2.$*

The number σ, though it seems complicated to compute, is a most useful number to know. In many practical applications, about 70% of the data is within one standard deviation of the mean. That is, 70% of the numbers lie between $\bar{x} - \sigma$ and $\bar{x} + \sigma$. Also, about 95% of the data is within two standard deviations of the mean; that is, 95% of the numbers lie between $\bar{x} - 2\sigma$ and $\bar{x} + 2\sigma$.

For example, if we are told that for a set of 1000 numbers, the mean is 200 and the standard deviation is 25, then we know that about 700 of the numbers lie between 175 and 225 and that all but about 50 of the numbers lie between 150 and 250. Thus, even with no further information, the number σ gives a fair idea of how the data is dispersed about the mean.

---

*Recall that $\sqrt{a}$ equals a number b so that $b^2 = a$, thus $\sqrt{4} = 2$ because $2^2 = 4$ and $\sqrt{9} = 3$ because $3^2 = 9$.

Let us return to Johnny and Jimmy and the argument about their sales. We calculate the standard deviation for each of them.

JOHNNY				JIMMY			
x	$\bar{x}$	$x - \bar{x}$	$(x - \bar{x})^2$	x	$\bar{x}$	$x - \bar{x}$	$(x - \bar{x})^2$
2	8	−6	36	7	8	−1	1
7	8	−1	1	7	8	−1	1
7	8	−1	1	7	8	−1	1
7	8	−1	1	7	8	−1	1
9	8	1	1	7	8	−1	1
10	8	2	4	7	8	−1	1
10	8	2	4	10	8	2	4
10	8	2	4	10	8	2	4
10	8	2	4	10	8	2	4
72			56	72			18

$\bar{x} = \dfrac{72}{9} = 8$ $\dfrac{56}{9} \approx 6.2$ $\bar{x} = \dfrac{72}{9} = 8$ $\dfrac{18}{9} = 2$

$\sigma = \sqrt{6.2} \approx 2.5$ $\sigma = \sqrt{2} = 1.4$

(The square roots can be found by use of Table 3 in the Appendix.)

We see now that the only one of Johnny's number of sales that lies more than one standard deviation away from his mean is 2. On the other hand, Jimmy's four 10s all lie more than one standard deviation away from his mean. Again, we have an indication that Johnny is a somewhat better salesman than Jimmy.

PROGESS TEST 1

1. The mean of the numbers {4, 6, 7, 7} is _____.
2. The difference from the mean, respectively, of each of the numbers in 1 is _____.
3. The standard deviation of the numbers given in 1 is _____.

EXERCISE 10.3

In Problems 1 through 10, (a) state the range, and (b) find the standard deviation.

1.   3, 5, 8, 13, 21   3.   5, 10, 15, 20, 25

2.   1, 4, 9, 16, 25   4.   6, 9, 12, 15, 18

---

1. 6   2. −2, 0, 1, 1   3. $\sqrt{1.5} \approx 1.2$

5. 5, 6, 7, 8, 9   8.   2, 0, 4, 6, 8, 10, 8, 2

6. 4, 6, 8, 10, 12   9.   −3, −2, −1, 0, 1, 2, 3

7. 5, 9, 1, 3, 8, 7, 2   10. −6, −4, −2, 0, 2, 4, 6

11.   Out of 10 possible points, a class of 21 business math students made the following test scores: 0, 0, 1, 2, 4, 5, 5, 5, 6, 6, 6, 7, 8, 8, 8, 8, 9, 9, 9, 10, 10
   a. What is the mode?
   b. What is the median?
   c. What is the mean?
   d. Calculate the standard deviation.
   e. What per cent of the scores lie within one standard deviation of the mean?
   f. What per cent of the scores lie within two standard deviations of the mean?

12.   Suppose the four students that scored lowest on the test in Problem 11 dropped the course. Answer the same questions as in Problem 11 for the remaining students.

13.   The prices of a certain stock (in dollars per share) in the last ten consecutive business days are as follows: 103, 110, 113, 102, 105, 110, 111, 110, 110, 106
   a. What is the mode of the prices?
   b. What is the median of the prices?
   c. What is the mean score of the prices?
   d. Calculate the standard deviation of the prices.
   e. Which of the prices are more than one standard deviation from the mean score? On what per cent of the days does this occur?

14.   Answer the questions in Problem 13 for the highest eight prices given.

15.   Suppose the standard deviation of a set of numbers is zero. What does this tell you about the numbers?

16.   Two classes, each with 100 students, took an examination with a maximum possible score of 100. In the first class the mean score was 75 and the standard deviation was 5. In the second class, the mean score was 70 and the standard deviation was 15. Which of the two classes do you think had more scores of 90 or better? Why?

17.   A stock was quoted at the following prices (in dollars) during the past week:

$$7 \quad 10 \quad 12 \quad 16 \quad 15$$

Find the mean and the standard deviation of the prices.

18.   The following numbers represent the number of years worked by five employees at Walt's Auto Supply:

$$7 \quad 9 \quad 10 \quad 11 \quad 13$$

Find the mean and the standard deviation of the number of years.

19.   The weekly gross earnings of tour managers (in dollars) are

$$290 \quad 310 \quad 320 \quad 280$$

Find the mean and the standard deviation of these earnings.

20.   A person in an assembly line took

$$11 \quad 12 \quad 13 \quad 15 \quad 20 \quad 20 \quad 21$$

minutes to do a certain job. Find the mean and the standard deviation of these times.

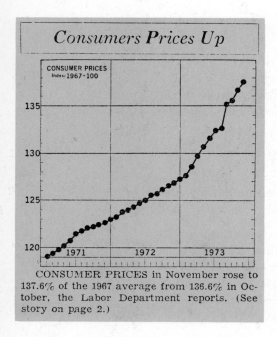

Consumers Prices Up

CONSUMER PRICES
Index: 1967 = 100

135

130

125

120

1971   1972   1973

CONSUMER PRICES in November rose to 137.6% of the 1967 average from 136.6% in October, the Labor Department reports. (See story on page 2.)

Reprinted, by permission, from *The Wall Street Journal*, December 24, 1973, p. 1

10.4   STATISTICAL GRAPHS

A graph of a set of data can often provide information at a glance that might be difficult to glean from a table of numbers. No table of numbers would make the visual impact created by the graph at the

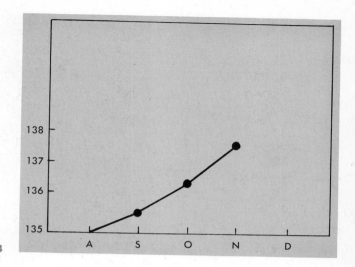

Figure 10-4

beginning of this section. In this graph the equal intervals in the horizontal scale represent the months, and the numbers in the vertical scale represent the price index. Thus, to check if Consumers Prices rose to 137.6 in November of 1973, we locate November (eleventh month) of 1973 on the horizontal scale and read the value of the index, (137.6), the last dot in the graph on the vertical scale.

It is almost always possible to alter the appearance of a graph to make things seem better than they are. For instance, the graph in Figure 10-4 is a portion of the graph given at the beginning of this section but with a compressed vertical scale. Obviously, things look better on this graph! Can you see why an economist might feel it politically advantageous to publish one of these graphs rather than the other?

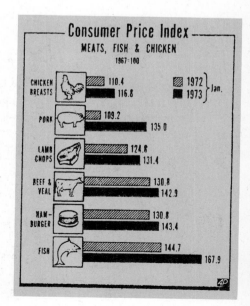

Figure 10-5

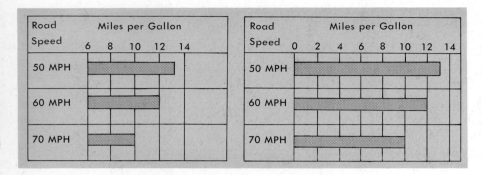

Road Speed	Miles per Gallon				
	6	8	10	12	14
50 MPH					
60 MPH					
70 MPH					

Road Speed	Miles per Gallon							
	0	2	4	6	8	10	12	14
50 MPH								
60 MPH								
70 MPH								

Figure 10–6

Newspapers and magazines often publish **bar graphs** of the type shown in Figure 10–5. These graphs again have the advantage of displaying the data in a form that is easy to understand. It would be very difficult for most people to obtain the same information from a table of numbers. As in the case of line graphs, bar graphs may also be made to distort the truth. For example, consider the two graphs in Figure 10–6. The left-hand graph does not have the bars starting at zero, so it gives a somewhat exaggerated picture of the proportion of gasoline saved at lower speeds, even though the numerical data displayed is the same for both graphs. The right-hand graph gives a correct picture of the proportion of gasoline saved. Why do you think the first bar graph rather than the second would be published?

Graphs like those in Figure 10–7 are called circle graphs or pie charts. Such graphs are a very popular means of displaying data. They are also susceptible of being drawn so as to make things look better

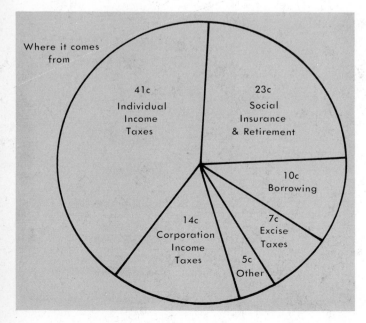

Where it comes from

41c Individual Income Taxes

23c Social Insurance & Retirement

10c Borrowing

14c Corporation Income Taxes

7c Excise Taxes

5c Other

Figure 10–7

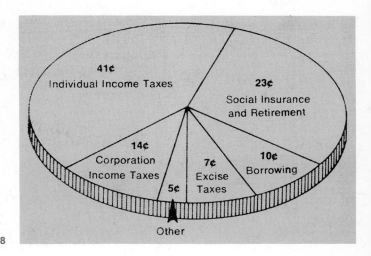

41¢
Individual Income Taxes

23¢
Social Insurance
and Retirement

14¢
Corporation
Income Taxes

7¢
Excise
Taxes

5¢

10¢
Borrowing

Other

Figure 10–8

than they are. For instance, compare the graph in Figure 10–7 with the version of these data that was published by the Internal Revenue Service in 1972 (Figure 10–8). Doesn't the visual impression of Figure 10–8 make you feel that individual income taxes are not quite so large a chunk of the Federal Income as Figure 10–7 indicates?

Circle graphs are quite easy to draw if you know how to use a simple compass and a protractor. For the graph in Figure 10–7, which shows the source of the typical dollar of federal money, the entry 23¢ represents 23% of the dollar. Since the entire circle corresponds to 360°, you would use 23% of 360° or 82.8° ≈ 83° to represent the 23¢ that comes from social insurance and retirement. A similar computation will give the proper angle for each of the other slices. This is the most accurate and honest way to present data on a circle graph.

PROGRESS TEST 1

1. Referring to Figure 10–7, the slice that represents the 41¢ corresponding to individual income taxes would use _____ degrees.

2. Referring to Figure 10–7, the slice that represents the 10¢ corresponding to borrowing would use _____ degrees.

1. 147.6° ≈ 148°   2. 36°

EXERCISE 10.4

1. The approximate average earnings per farm in the United
    States from 1963 through 1972 are as follows:

YEAR	EARNINGS
1963	$3,500
1964	3,800
1965	4,000
1966	5,000
1967	4,300
1968	4,600
1969	5,600
1970	5,700
1971	5,300
1972	6,300

    Make a bar graph to show these data.

2. In January, 1972, United States companies had the following
    investments in Mideast oil and gas:

Crude oil and natural gas production facilities	$3,385 million
Pipelines, refineries, and other plants	$1,995 million
Marketing facilities and other related investments	$1,035 million

    Make a bar graph to show these data.

3. The U.S. Department of Labor updated to Autumn, 1972, its
    theoretical budgets for a retired couple. The high budget for
    such a couple is apportioned approximately as follows:

Food	22%	Medical Care	6%
Housing	35%	Other Family Costs	7%
Transportation	11%	Miscellaneous	7%
Clothing	6%	Income Taxes	3%
Personal Care	3%		

    Make a circle graph to show this budget.

4. The pie chart in Figure 10–9 appeared side by side with the
    one in Figure 10–8. Make a circle graph to present the same
    data. Compare the impression made by your circle graph with
    the pie chart in Figure 10–9.

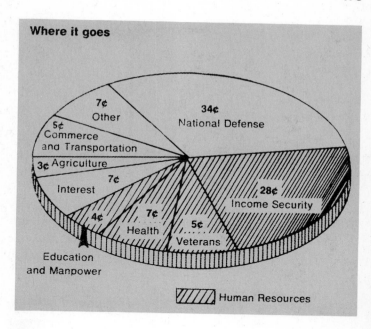

Figure 10–9

5. According to an ad for a color television, the top six brands of television sets were voted as best by the following percentages of about 2700 people:

Brand:	1	2	3	4	5	6
Percentage:	50.1	21.1	8.8	8.5	5.8	5.7

   a. Make a circle graph to illustrate the above data.
   b. Make a bar graph for the same data.
   c. Which of these do you think makes the stronger impression? Why?

6. A survey made by the University of Michigan's Institute for Social Research showed that most women really enjoy keeping house. The survey found that about 67% of the women that responded had an unqualified liking for housework while only 4 per cent had an unqualified dislike for housework. Make a bar graph to illustrate these data.

7. The Mighty Midget Canning Company wants to impress the public with the growth of Mighty Midget business, which they claim has doubed over the previous year. They publish the pictorial graph in Figure 10–10.
   a. Can you see anything wrong with this? (Hint: Your mind compares the volumes pictured here. The volume of a cylinder is r²h. What happens if you double the radius r and the height h?)
   b. Draw a bar graph that correctly represents the situation.

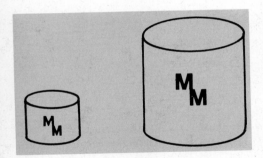

Figure 10–10

8.   The U. B. Wary Company wants to give its stockholders a very strong impression of the rapid rate at which earnings have grown and prints the bar graph in Figure 10–11 in its annual report. Redraw this graph to give a more honest impression.

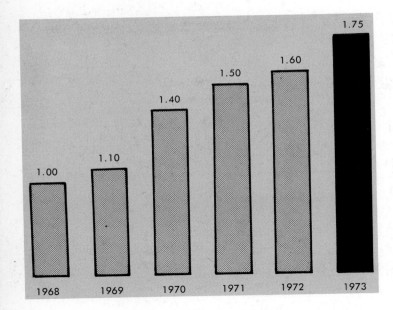

Figure 10–11

SELF-TEST/CHAPTER 10

1. The salaries of eight workers in a small firm were as follows: $21,000, $19,000, $18,000, $17,500, $16,000, $14, 465, $14, 465, $12,810.

    _____ a.   Find the mean of the salaries.
    _____ b.   Find the median of the salaries.
    _____ c.   Find the mode of the salaries.

2. The following table shows the number of minutes a certain employee was late for work in the past six weeks:

7	15	10	2	5
6	10	12	3	14
9	14	11	3	7
7	13	12	2	5
3	13	11	0	3
6	12	1	8	4

    _____ a.   Make a frequency distribution for this data and find the number of times the employee was more than ten minutes late.
    _____ b.   What percentage of the time was the employee more than ten minutes late?

3. Make a histogram for the data of Problem 2 in the space below.

4. The number of hours worked by an employee during the last five days is as follows: 7, 9, 10, 11, 13.

    _____ a.   Find the range for the set of hours.

_____ b.   Find the mean number of hours worked by the
              employee.
_____ c.   Find the standard deviation for the hours.

5.   The mean score on a test taken by 30 students is 75; find
_____ a.   the sum of the 30 test scores.
_____ b.   the grade on a paper that was lost by the pro-
              fessor, if the sum of the other 29 papers was
              2,180.

6.   The graph below shows the increase in the size of a fleet meas-
      ured in deadweight tons from December 31, 1968, to Decem-
      ber 31, 1976 (projected). Find
_____ a.   the number of deadweight tons (in millions)
              added between Dec. 31, 1972, and Dec. 31, 1973.
_____ b.   the period of time in which the greatest number
              of deadweight tons (in millions) was added.
_____ a.   the approximate number of deadweight tons (in
              millions) added during the period of time men-
              tioned in part b.

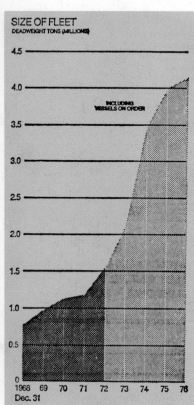

Reprinted, by permission, from *The Wall Street Journal,* April 3, 1973, p. 31.

7. The budget of a retired couple is as follows:

Food	20%
Housing	35%
Transportation	10%
Clothing	5%
Medical	15%
Miscellaneous	15%

Make a circle graph to show this budget.

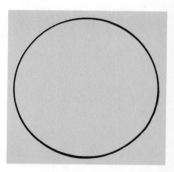

8. If in Problem 7 it is known that the total income of the couple is $10,000, make a bar graph to show the amount (in dollars) spent for each of the items.

9. The following table shows the arrival time of several customers to a supermarket checkout counter. (Arrival time is assumed to be at the beginning of each minute.) If it is known that each customer takes one minute to be served, construct a diagram showing the line during each of the five minutes.

Time	Customers
1	A,B
2	C,D,E
3	F
4	
5	G

1   2   3   4   5

10.   Referring to Problem 9, find

_____   a.   the mean number of people in line.
_____   b.   the mode of the number of people in line.
_____   c.   the median number of people in line.

The Metric System

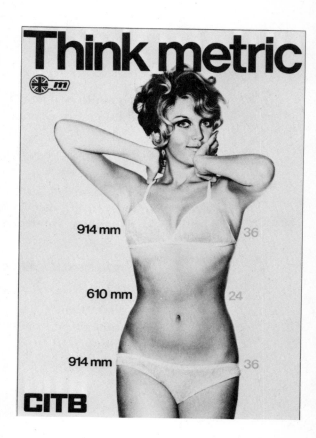

Think metric

914 mm   36

610 mm   24

914 mm   36

CITB

Reprinted by permission of the Construction Industry Training Board, London, England.

In Chapter 2, we saw that a rational number can always be written as a decimal. We now review quickly the four fundamental operations with terminating decimals.

To add 0.43 and 0.31, we can change these decimals to fractions and add. Thus,

$$0.43 + 0.31 = \frac{43}{100} + \frac{31}{100} = \frac{74}{100} = 0.74$$

This procedure suggests that the addition of decimals can be carried out by writing the addends in the form with the decimal points of the two numbers placed in a vertical column.

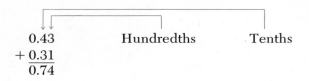

$$0.43$$
$$+\ \underline{0.31}$$
$$0.74$$

Subtraction is done in a similar manner. For example, $0.43 - 0.31$ can be carried out by writing

$$0.43$$
$$-\ \underline{0.31}$$
$$0.12$$

To multiply decimals, we can employ a procedure similar to that for addition. For example, to multiply 0.5×0.9, we write

$$0.5 \times 0.9 = \frac{5}{10} \times \frac{9}{10} = \frac{45}{100} = 0.45$$

This problem suggests that to multiply decimals, we multiply the numbers in the usual way; the product will have as many decimal places as there are decimal places in the two factors together.

Example 1

(a) Add 0.91 and 0.84.
(b) Subtract 0.84 from 0.91.
(c) Multiply 0.91 by 0.84.

Solution

(a) 0.91 (b) 0.91
      $+\ \underline{0.84}$ $-\ \underline{0.84}$
        1.75 0.07

(c) 0.84 (2 decimal places)
      $\times\ \underline{0.91}$ (2 decimal places)
          84
        $\underline{756}$
      0.7644 ($2 + 2 = 4$ decimal places)

To divide a decimal by another decimal, we can change the decimals to fractions and divide these fractions, using the rules given in Chapter 2. Thus,

$$0.48 \div 3 = \frac{48}{100} \div 3 = \frac{48}{100} \times \frac{1}{3} = \frac{16}{100} = 0.16$$

This problem could also be written as:

$$
\begin{array}{r}
0.16 \\
3\overline{)0.48} \\
\underline{3} \\
18 \\
\underline{18} \\
0
\end{array}
$$

divisor   quotient dividend

Notice that we carried out the division in the usual way, being careful to place the decimal point in the quotient directly above the decimal point in the dividend.

When dividing decimals, it is usually easier to change the divisor to a whole number. For example, to divide 24.28 by 1.2 we proceed as follows:

$$\frac{24.28}{1.2} = \frac{24.28 \times 10}{1.2 \times 10} \qquad \text{(Multiplying the numerator and denominator by 10)}$$

$$= \frac{242.8}{12}$$

We then proceed in the usual way and write

$$
\begin{array}{r}
20.2 \\
12\overline{)242.8} \\
\underline{24} \\
02\;8 \\
\underline{2\;4} \\
4
\end{array}
$$

Example 2

Divide 8.5 by 0.012.

Solution

$$\frac{8.5}{0.012} = \frac{8.5 \times 1{,}000}{0.012 \times 1{,}000} = \frac{8500}{12}$$

and

$$
\begin{array}{r}
708 \\
12\overline{)8500} \\
\underline{84} \\
100 \\
\underline{96} \\
4
\end{array}
$$

The fundamental operations with decimals can be used to convert measurements from the English to the metric system and vice versa. The metric system is a decimal system in which each unit of measure is exactly ten times as large as the unit just smaller. In this system any unit may be changed to the next higher unit by moving the decimal point one place to the left and any unit may be reduced to the next lower unit by moving the decimal point one place to the right. In the metric system, the three principal units of measure are the following:

1. The meter (the unit of linear measure)
2. The liter (the unit of capacity measure)
3. The gram (the unit of weight or mass measure)

Table 1 shows the linear, liquid, and mass measures in the metric system as well as the English and the metric equivalents.

TABLE 1 **Metric Equivalents**

LENGTH	VOLUME	MASS
1 meter = 10 decimeters = 100 centimeters = 1000 millimeters = 0.1 dekameter = 0.01 hectometer = 0.001 kilometer	1 liter = 10 deciliters = 100 centiliters = 1000 milliliters = 0.1 dekaliter = 0.01 hectoliter = 0.001 kiloliter	1 gram = 10 decigrams = 100 centigrams = 1000 milligrams = 0.1 dekagram = 0.01 hectogram = 0.001 kilogram
English Units and Approximate Equivalents		
12 inches = 1 foot 3 feet = 1 yard 5280 feet = 1 mile 320 rods = 1 mile	1 inch = 2.54 centimeters 1 yard = 0.914 meter 1 mile = 1.6 kilometers 1 pound = 0.45 kilogram 1 quart = 0.95 liter	1 centimeter = 0.4 inch 1 meter = 1.1 yards 1 kilometer = 0.62 mile 1 kilogram = 2.2 pounds 1 liter = 1.05 quarts

Example 3

How many centimeters are there in 325 meters?

Solution

From the table, 1 meter = 100 centimeters; thus,
$$325 \text{ meters} = 325 \times 100 \text{ centimeters}$$
$$= 32{,}500 \text{ centimeters.}$$

Example 4

How many meters are there in 3.2 kilometers?

Solution

From the table, 1 meter = 0.001 kilometers; thus,
$$1 \text{ kilometer} = 1{,}000 \text{ meters.}$$
$$3.2 \text{ kilometers} = 3{,}200 \text{ meters.}$$

Example 5

The speed limit on a highway is 60 miles per hour. How many kilometers per hour is this?

Solution

1 mile = 1.6 kilometers.
60 miles = 60 × 1.6 kilometers
          = 96 kilometers.
Thus, 60 miles per hour is equivalent to 96 kilometers per hour.

Example 6

The top speed of a European car is 200 kilometers per hour. How many miles per hour is this?

Solution

1 kilometer = 0.62 miles.
200 kilometers = 200 × 0.62 miles
               = 124 miles.
Thus, 200 kilometers per hour is equivalent to 124 miles per hour.

Example 7

A housewife bought 3 quarts of milk. How many liters of milk is this?

Solution

1 quart = 0.95 liter.
3 quarts = 3 × 0.95 liters
         = 2.85 liters.

Example 8

The largest car ever built was the Bugatti "Royale", type 41, with an 8-cylinder engine of 12.7 liter capacity. How many quarts is this?

Solution

1 liter = 1.05 quarts.
12.7 liters = 12.7 × 1.05 quarts
            ≃ 13.34 quarts.*

---

*The symbol ≃ means "is approximately equal to."

In most cases, a table of common conversion factors, such as in Table 2, suffice for everyday usage.

TABLE 2   **Common Conversion Factors**

	IF YOU WANT TO CONVERT	TO	MULTIPLY BY:
Linear Measure	inches	millimeters	25
	feet	centimeters	30
	yards	meters	0.9
	miles	kilometers	1.6
	millimeters	inches	0.04
	centimeters	inches	0.4
	meters	yards	1.1
	kilometers	miles	0.62
Capacity Measure	ounces	milliliters	30
	pints	liters	0.47
	quarts	liters	0.95
	gallons	liters	3.8
	milliliters	ounces	0.034
	liters	pints	2.1
	liters	quarts	1.05
	liters	gallons	0.26
Weight or Mass	ounces	grams	28
	pounds	kilograms	0.45
	grams	ounces	0.035
	kilogram	pounds	2.2

Example 9
Convert:

(a) 10 inches to millimeters
(b) 50 ounces to milliliters
(c)   5 pounds to kilograms

Solution

(a) From the first line in Table 2, we can see that to convert inches to millimeters we multiply by 25. Thus,

$$10 \text{ inches} = 10 \times 25 = 250 \text{ millimeters}$$

(b) To convert ounces to milliliters, we multiply by 30. Thus,

$$50 \text{ ounces} = 50 \times 30 = 1,500 \text{ milliliters}$$

(c) To convert pounds to kilograms, we multiply by 0.45. Thus,

$$5 \text{ pounds} = 5 \times 0.45 = 2.25 \text{ kilograms}$$

EXERCISE 1

In Problems 1 through 15, perform the indicated operations.

1.	$0.8 + 0.9$	2.	$0.13 + 0.19$	3.	$0.312 + 0.98$
4.	$0.123 + 1.318$	5.	$0.43 - 0.19$	6.	$0.97 - 0.49$
7.	$1.189 - 0.029$	8.	$3.423 - 0.8987$	9.	$10.08 - 0.0003$
10.	0.23×3.165	11.	2.3×3.412	12.	0.0015×123.8
13.	$499.20 \div 3.2$	14.	$481.65 \div 25.35$	15.	$0.0084 \div 0.12$

In Problems 16 through 24, change to meters. (Use Table 1.)

16.	32 kilometers	17.	3,230 centimeters	18.	1,000 millimeters
19.	54 kilometers	20.	4,800 centimeters	21.	3,200 millimeters
22.	30 miles	23.	50 miles	24.	2,300 feet

In Problems 25 through 30, change to miles. (Use Table 1.)

25.	250 kilometers	26.	398 kilometers	27.	3,200 meters
28.	2,800 meters	29.	3,500 meters	30.	6,200 meters

In Problems 31 through 33, change to liters. (Use Table 1.)

31.	5 quarts	32.	7 quarts	33.	19 quarts

In Problems 34 through 36, change to quarts. (Use Table 1.)

34.	10 liters	35.	15 liters	36.	9.7 liters

In Problems 37 through 39, change to pounds. (Use Table 1.)

37.	9 kilograms	38.	17.8 kilograms	39.	10.7 kilograms

In Problems 40 through 42, change to kilograms. (Use Table 2.)

40.	25 pounds	41.	43 pounds	42.	154.7 pounds

43. Convert: (use Table 2.)
   a. 20 inches to millimeters
   b. 10 feet to centimeters
   c. 15 yards to meters
   d. 5 miles to kilometers

44. Convert: (Use Table 2.)
   a. 50 millimeters to inches
   b. 40 centimeters to inches
   c. 5 meters to yards
   d. 9 kilometers to miles

45.   Convert: (use Table 2.)
       a. 25 ounces to milliliters   b. 3 pints to liters
       c. 10 quarts to liters   d. 9 gallons to liters

46.   Convert: (Use Table 2.)
       a. 800 milliliters to ounces   b. 5 liters to pints
       c. 20 liters to quarts   d. 100 liters to gallons

47.   Convert: (Use Table 2.)
       a. 50 ounces to grams   b. 100 pounds to kilograms
       c. 300 grams to ounces   d. 50 kilograms to pounds

Hand Calculators

In the late 1950s the cost of a desk calculator was more than $1,000. These calculators could perform fantastic computations and, consequently, the saving in time and labor made them well worth the money, but the price put them out of reach of the average person.

Improved technology permitted drastic reductions in both price and size, and by the early 1970s battery operated, hand-held models costing less than $100 were available. The picture at the beginning of this section shows a typical calculator that appeared on the market in 1974.

The keyboard is essentially the same for all models, but there are some minor variations that deserve attention.

One important difference is the sequence of operations (button pushing) for addition and subtraction. There are two different methods for addition (and subtraction) and for convenience we call them methods A and B.

Method A (Arithmetic Logic). In this method the number is entered first, and this is followed by pressing the + or − key for the desired operation.

Method B (Algebraic logic). The + or − key is operated *before* entering the number to be added or subtracted.

The calculator shown in Figure 1 is designed for method A. Because these models are more widely used, we illustrate their use in the following examples.

Example 1

Compute 1858 + 1953.

	OPERATION	NUMBER ON PANEL DISPLAY
Solution	Press "on"	EEEEE
	Press C	0
	Press 1,8,5,8	1858
	Press +=	1858
	Press 1,9,5,3	1953
	Press +=	3811

The answer is 3,811.

Example 2

Compute 6349 − 1242.

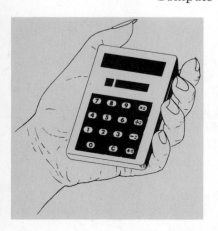

	OPERATION	NUMBER ON PANEL DISPLAY
Solution	Press "on"	EEEEE
	Press C	0
	Press 6,3,4,9	6349
	Press +=	6349
	Press 1,2,4,2	1242
	Press −=	5107

The answer is 5,107.

Example 3

Compute $1{,}308 \times 19$.

Solution

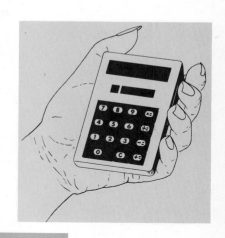

OPERATION	NUMBER ON PANEL DISPLAY
Press "on"	EEEEE
Press C	0
Press 1,3,0,8	1308
Press +=	1308
Press 1,9	19
Press ×=	24852

The answer is 24,852.

Example 4

Divide 56,088 by 123.

Solution

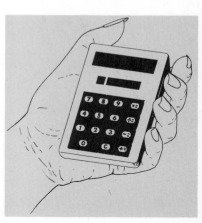

OPERATION	NUMBER ON PANEL DISPLAY
Press "on"	EEEEE
Press C	0
Press 5,6,0,8,8	56088
Press +=	56088
Press 1,2,3	123
Press ÷=	456

The answer is 456.

Note that in this case there is no remainder. In case you were dividing 56,100 by 123, similar steps would be taken and the answer would come to 456. This is because the calculator shown has no **floating decimal.** For a few more dollars, one can purchase a more sophisticated machine with a floating decimal, that is, a machine in which the decimal point appears where it belongs when computations are performed.

Since each calculator is accompanied by instructions which will give complete details on the proper operational methods, we will not discuss any others here. When approaching a new calculator, the reader is well advised to begin by working a few simple problems where the answer is already known, such as:

$$2 + 3 = 5 \qquad 2 \times 3 = 6 \qquad 11 - 9 = 2$$

$$5 \times 7 = 35 \qquad \frac{72}{8} = 9 \qquad \frac{81}{3} = 27$$

In this manner, the user will check the method of operation and, at the same time, test for possible defects.

The student desiring more practice with calculators can go back to Chapters 1 and 2 and redo the problems in those chapters using the calculator.

Tables

COMPOUND INTEREST

See accompanying tables on following pages.

TABLE A–1

COMPOUND AMOUNT

When principal is 1

$$s = (1 + i)^n$$

n	$1\frac{1}{4}\%$	$1\frac{3}{8}\%$	$1\frac{1}{2}\%$	$1\frac{5}{8}\%$	n
1	1.0125 0000	1.0137 5000	1.0150 0000	1.0162 5000	1
2	1.0251 5625	1.0276 8906	1.0302 2500	1.0327 6406	2
3	1.0379 7070	1.0418 1979	1.0456 7838	1.0495 4648	3
4	1.0509 4534	1.0561 4481	1.0613 6355	1.0666 0161	4
5	1.0640 8215	1.0706 6680	1.0772 8400	1.0839 3388	5
6	1.0773 8318	1.0853 8847	1.0934 4326	1.1015 4781	6
7	1.0908 5047	1.1003 1256	1.1098 4491	1.1194 4796	7
8	1.1044 8610	1.1154 4186	1.1264 9259	1.1376 3899	8
9	1.1182 9218	1.1307 7918	1.1433 8998	1.1561 2563	9
10	1.1322 7083	1.1463 2740	1.1605 4083	1.1749 1267	10
11	1.1464 2422	1.1620 8940	1.1779 4894	1.1940 0500	11
12	1.1607 5452	1.1780 6813	1.1956 1817	1.2134 0758	12
13	1.1752 6395	1.1942 6656	1.2135 5244	1.2331 2545	13
14	1.1899 5475	1.2106 8773	1.2317 5573	1.2531 6374	14
15	1.2048 2918	1.2273 3469	1.2502 3207	1.2735 2765	15
16	1.2198 8955	1.2442 1054	1.2689 8555	1.2942 2248	16
17	1.2351 3817	1.2613 1843	1.2880 2033	1.3152 5359	17
18	1.2505 7739	1.2786 6156	1.3073 4064	1.3366 2646	18
19	1.2662 0961	1.2962 4316	1.3269 5075	1.3583 4664	19
20	1.2820 3723	1.3140 6650	1.3468 5501	1.3804 1977	20
21	1.2980 6270	1.3321 3492	1.3670 5783	1.4028 5160	21
22	1.3142 8848	1.3504 5177	1.3875 6370	1.4256 4793	22
23	1.3307 1709	1.3690 2048	1.4083 7715	1.4488 1471	23
24	1.3473 5105	1.3878 4451	1.4295 0281	1.4723 5795	24
25	1.3641 9294	1.4069 2738	1.4509 4535	1.4962 8377	25
26	1.3812 4535	1.4262 7263	1.4727 0953	1.5205 9838	26
27	1.3985 1092	1.4458 8388	1.4948 0018	1.5453 0810	27
28	1.4159 9230	1.4657 6478	1.5172 2218	1.5704 1936	28
29	1.4336 9221	1.4859 1905	1.5399 8051	1.5959 3868	29
30	1.4516 1336	1.5063 5043	1.5630 8022	1.6218 7268	30
31	1.4697 5853	1.5270 6275	1.5865 2642	1.6482 2811	31
32	1.4881 3051	1.5480 5986	1.6103 2432	1.6750 1182	32
33	1.5067 3214	1.5693 4569	1.6344 7918	1.7022 3076	33
34	1.5255 6629	1.5909 2419	1.6589 9637	1.7298 9201	34
35	1.5446 3587	1.6127 9940	1.6838 8132	1.7580 0275	35
36	1.5639 4382	1.6349 7539	1.7091 3954	1.7865 7030	36
37	1.5834 9312	1.6574 5630	1.7347 7663	1.8156 0207	37
38	1.6032 8678	1.6802 4633	1.7607 9828	1.8451 0560	38
39	1.6233 2787	1.7033 4971	1.7872 1025	1.8750 8857	39
40	1.6436 1946	1.7267 7077	1.8140 1841	1.9055 5875	40
41	1.6641 6471	1.7505 1387	1.8412 2868	1.9365 2408	41
42	1.6849 6677	1.7745 8343	1.8688 4712	1.9679 9260	42
43	1.7060 2885	1.7989 8396	1.8968 7982	1.9999 7248	43
44	1.7273 5421	1.8237 1999	1.9253 3302	2.0324 7203	44
45	1.7489 4614	1.8487 9614	1.9542 1301	2.0654 9970	45
46	1.7708 0797	1.8742 1708	1.9835 2621	2.0990 6407	46
47	1.7929 4306	1.8999 8757	2.0132 7910	2.1331 7387	47
48	1.8153 5485	1.9261 1240	2.0434 7829	2.1678 3794	48
49	1.8380 4679	1.9525 9644	2.0741 3046	2.2030 6531	49
50	1.8610 2237	1.9794 4464	2.1052 4242	2.2388 6512	50

Reprinted, by permission, from Stephen P. Shao, ed., *Mathematics for Management and Finance,* 2nd ed., South-Western Publishing Co., 1969, Appendix pp. 33–44. Adapted from Charles H. Gushee, *Financial Compound Interest and Annuity Tables,* Financial Publishing Company, Boston, 1958, and James W. Glover, *Compound Interest and Insurance Tables,* Wahr's University Bookstore, Ann Arbor, 1957.

COMPOUND AMOUNT
When principal is 1

$$s = (1 + i)^n$$

n	$1\frac{1}{4}\%$	$1\frac{3}{8}\%$	$1\frac{1}{2}\%$	$1\frac{5}{8}\%$	n
51	1.8842 8515	2.0066 6201	2.1368 2106	2.2752 4668	51
52	1.9078 3872	2.0342 5361	2.1688 7337	2.3122 1944	52
53	1.9316 8670	2.0622 2460	2.2014 0647	2.3497 9300	53
54	1.9558 3279	2.0905 8019	2.2344 2757	2.3879 7714	54
55	1.9802 8070	2.1193 2566	2.2679 4398	2.4267 8177	55
56	2.0050 3420	2.1484 6639	2.3019 6314	2.4662 1697	56
57	2.0300 9713	2.1780 0780	2.3364 9259	2.5062 9300	57
58	2.0554 7335	2.2079 5541	2.3715 3998	2.5470 2026	58
59	2.0811 6676	2.2383 1480	2.4071 1308	2.5884 0934	59
60	2.1071 8135	2.2690 9163	2.4432 1978	2.6304 7099	60
61	2.1335 2111	2.3002 9164	2.4798 6807	2.6732 1614	61
62	2.1601 9013	2.3319 2065	2.5170 6609	2.7166 5590	62
63	2.1871 9250	2.3639 8456	2.5548 2208	2.7608 0156	63
64	2.2145 3241	2.3964 8934	2.5931 4442	2.8056 6459	64
65	2.2422 1407	2.4294 4107	2.6320 4158	2.8512 5664	65
66	2.2702 4174	2.4628 4589	2.6715 2221	2.8975 8956	66
67	2.2986 1976	2.4967 1002	2.7115 9504	2.9446 7539	67
68	2.3273 5251	2.5310 3978	2.7522 6896	2.9925 2636	68
69	2.3564 4442	2.5658 4158	2.7935 5300	3.0411 5492	69
70	2.3858 9997	2.6011 2190	2.8354 5629	3.0905 7368	70
71	2.4157 2372	2.6368 8732	2.8779 8814	3.1407 9551	71
72	2.4459 2027	2.6731 4453	2.9211 5796	3.1918 3343	72
73	2.4764 9427	2.7099 0026	2.9649 7533	3.2437 0073	73
74	2.5074 5045	2.7471 6139	3.0094 4996	3.2964 1086	74
75	2.5387 9358	2.7849 3486	3.0545 9171	3.3499 7754	75
76	2.5705 2850	2.8232 2771	3.1004 1059	3.4044 1467	76
77	2.6026 6011	2.8620 4710	3.1469 1674	3.4597 3641	77
78	2.6351 9336	2.9014 0024	3.1941 2050	3.5159 5713	78
79	2.6681 3327	2.9412 9450	3.2420 3230	3.5730 9143	79
80	2.7014 8494	2.9817 3730	3.2906 6279	3.6311 5417	80
81	2.7352 5350	3.0227 3618	3.3400 2273	3.6901 6042	81
82	2.7694 4417	3.0642 9881	3.3901 2307	3.7501 2553	82
83	2.8040 6222	3.1064 3291	3.4409 7492	3.8110 6507	83
84	2.8391 1300	3.1491 4637	3.4925 8954	3.8729 9488	84
85	2.8746 0191	3.1924 4713	3.5449 7838	3.9359 3104	85
86	2.9105 3444	3.2363 4328	3.5981 5306	3.9998 8992	86
87	2.9469 1612	3.2808 4300	3.6521 2535	4.0648 8813	87
88	2.9837 5257	3.3259 5459	3.7069 0723	4.1309 4257	88
89	3.0210 4948	3.3716 8646	3.7625 1084	4.1980 7038	89
90	3.0588 1260	3.4180 4715	3.8189 4851	4.2662 8903	90
91	3.0970 4775	3.4650 4530	3.8762 3273	4.3356 1622	91
92	3.1357 6085	3.5126 8967	3.9343 7622	4.4060 6999	92
93	3.1749 5786	3.5609 8916	3.9933 9187	4.4776 6863	93
94	3.2146 4483	3.6099 5276	4.0532 9275	4.5504 3074	94
95	3.2548 2789	3.6595 8961	4.1140 9214	4.6243 7524	95
96	3.2955 1324	3.7099 0897	4.1758 0352	4.6995 2134	96
97	3.3367 0716	3.7609 2021	4.2384 4057	4.7758 8856	97
98	3.3784 1600	3.8126 3287	4.3020 1718	4.8534 9675	98
99	3.4206 4620	3.8650 5657	4.3665 4744	4.9323 6607	99
100	3.4634 0427	3.9182 0110	4.4320 4565	5.0125 1702	100

Reprinted, by permission, from Shao

COMPOUND AMOUNT
When principal is 1
$$s = (1 + i)^n$$

n	$1\frac{3}{4}\%$	$1\frac{7}{8}\%$	2%	$2\frac{1}{4}\%$	n
1	1.0175 0000	1.0187 5000	1.0200 0000	1.0225 0000	1
2	1.0353 0625	1.0378 5156	1.0404 0000	1.0455 0625	2
3	1.0534 2411	1.0573 1128	1.0612 0800	1.0690 3014	3
4	1.0718 5903	1.0771 3587	1.0824 3216	1.0930 8332	4
5	1.0906 1656	1.0973 3216	1.1040 8080	1.1176 7769	5
6	1.1097 0235	1.1179 0714	1.1261 6242	1.1428 2544	6
7	1.1291 2215	1.1388 6790	1.1486 8567	1.1685 3901	7
8	1.1488 8178	1.1602 2167	1.1716 5938	1.1948 3114	8
9	1.1689 8721	1.1819 7583	1.1950 9257	1.2217 1484	9
10	1.1894 4449	1.2041 3788	1.2189 9442	1.2492 0343	10
11	1.2102 5977	1.2267 1546	1.2433 7431	1.2773 1050	11
12	1.2314 3931	1.2497 1638	1.2682 4179	1.3060 4999	12
13	1.2529 8950	1.2731 4856	1.2936 0663	1.3354 3611	13
14	1.2749 1682	1.2970 2009	1.3194 7876	1.3654 8343	14
15	1.2972 2786	1.3213 3922	1.3458 6834	1.3962 0680	15
16	1.3199 2935	1.3461 1433	1.3727 8571	1.4276 2146	16
17	1.3430 2811	1.3713 5398	1.4002 4142	1.4597 4294	17
18	1.3665 3111	1.3970 6686	1.4282 4625	1.4925 8716	18
19	1.3904 4540	1.4232 6187	1.4568 1117	1.5261 7037	19
20	1.4147 7820	1.4499 4803	1.4859 4740	1.5605 0920	20
21	1.4395 3681	1.4771 3455	1.5156 6634	1.5956 2066	21
22	1.4647 2871	1.5048 3082	1.5459 7967	1.6315 2212	22
23	1.4903 6146	1.5330 4640	1.5768 9926	1.6682 3137	23
24	1.5164 4279	1.5617 9102	1.6084 3725	1.7057 6658	24
25	1.5429 8054	1.5910 7460	1.6406 0599	1.7441 4632	25
26	1.5699 8269	1.6209 0725	1.6734 1811	1.7833 8962	26
27	1.5974 5739	1.6512 9926	1.7068 8648	1.8235 1588	27
28	1.6254 1290	1.6822 6112	1.7410 2421	1.8645 4499	28
29	1.6538 5762	1.7138 0352	1.7758 4469	1.9064 9725	29
30	1.6828 0013	1.7459 3734	1.8113 6158	1.9493 9344	30
31	1.7122 4913	1.7786 7366	1.8475 8882	1.9932 5479	31
32	1.7422 1349	1.8120 2379	1.8845 4059	2.0381 0303	32
33	1.7727 0223	1.8459 9924	1.9222 3140	2.0839 6034	33
34	1.8037 2452	1.8806 1172	1.9606 7603	2.1308 4945	34
35	1.8352 8970	1.9158 7319	1.9998 8955	2.1787 9356	35
36	1.8674 0727	1.9517 9582	2.0398 8734	2.2278 1642	36
37	1.9000 8689	1.9883 9199	2.0806 8509	2.2779 4229	37
38	1.9333 3841	2.0256 7434	2.1222 9879	2.3291 9599	38
39	1.9671 7184	2.0636 5573	2.1647 4477	2.3816 0290	39
40	2.0015 9734	2.1023 4928	2.2080 3966	2.4351 8897	40
41	2.0366 2530	2.1417 6833	2.2522 0046	2.4899 8072	41
42	2.0722 6624	2.1819 2648	2.2972 4447	2.5460 0528	42
43	2.1085 3090	2.2228 3760	2.3431 8936	2.6032 9040	43
44	2.1454 3019	2.2645 1581	2.3900 5314	2.6618 6444	44
45	2.1829 7522	2.3069 7548	2.4378 5421	2.7217 5639	45
46	2.2211 7728	2.3502 3127	2.4866 1129	2.7829 9590	46
47	2.2600 4789	2.3942 9811	2.5363 4352	2.8456 1331	47
48	2.2995 9872	2.4391 9120	2.5870 7039	2.9096 3961	48
49	2.3398 4170	2.4849 2603	2.6388 1179	2.9751 0650	49
50	2.3807 8893	2.5315 1839	2.6915 8803	3.0420 4640	50

Reprinted, by permission, from Shao

COMPOUND AMOUNT
When principal is 1
$$s = (1 + i)^n$$

n	$1\frac{3}{4}\%$	$1\frac{7}{8}\%$	2%	$2\frac{1}{4}\%$	n
51	2.4224 5274	2.5789 8436	2.7454 1979	3.1104 9244	51
52	2.4648 4566	2.6273 4032	2.8003 2819	3.1804 7852	52
53	2.5079 8046	2.6766 0295	2.8563 3475	3.2520 3929	53
54	2.5518 7012	2.7267 8926	2.9134 6144	3.3252 1017	54
55	2.5965 2785	2.7779 1656	2.9717 3067	3.4000 2740	55
56	2.6419 6708	2.8300 0249	3.0311 6529	3.4765 2802	56
57	2.6882 0151	2.8830 6504	3.0917 8859	3.5547 4990	57
58	2.7352 4503	2.9371 2251	3.1536 2436	3.6347 3177	58
59	2.7831 1182	2.9921 9355	3.2166 9685	3.7165 1324	59
60	2.8318 1628	3.0482 9718	3.2810 3079	3.8001 3479	60
61	2.8813 7306	3.1054 5276	3.3466 5140	3.8856 3782	61
62	2.9317 9709	3.1636 8000	3.4135 8443	3.9730 6467	62
63	2.9831 0354	3.2229 9900	3.4818 5612	4.0624 5862	63
64	3.0353 0785	3.2834 3023	3.5514 9324	4.1538 6394	64
65	3.0884 2574	3.3449 9454	3.6225 2311	4.2473 2588	65
66	3.1424 7319	3.4077 1319	3.6949 7357	4.3428 9071	66
67	3.1974 6647	3.4716 0781	3.7688 7304	4.4406 0576	67
68	3.2534 2213	3.5367 0046	3.8442 5050	4.5405 1939	68
69	3.3103 5702	3.6030 1359	3.9211 3551	4.6426 8107	69
70	3.3682 8827	3.6705 7010	3.9995 5822	4.7471 4140	70
71	3.4272 3331	3.7393 9329	4.0795 4939	4.8539 5208	71
72	3.4872 0990	3.8095 0691	4.1611 4038	4.9631 6600	72
73	3.5482 3607	3.8809 3517	4.2443 6318	5.0748 3723	73
74	3.6103 3020	3.9537 0270	4.3292 5045	5.1890 2107	74
75	3.6735 1098	4.0278 3463	4.4158 3546	5.3057 7405	75
76	3.7377 9742	4.1033 5653	4.5041 5216	5.4251 5396	76
77	3.8032 0888	4.1802 9446	4.5942 3521	5.5472 1993	77
78	3.8697 6503	4.2586 7498	4.6861 1991	5.6720 3237	78
79	3.9374 8592	4.3385 2514	4.7798 4231	5.7996 5310	79
80	4.0063 9192	4.4198 7248	4.8754 3916	5.9301 4530	80
81	4.0765 0378	4.5027 4509	4.9729 4794	6.0635 7357	81
82	4.1478 4260	4.5871 7156	5.0724 0690	6.2000 0397	82
83	4.2204 2984	4.6731 8103	5.1738 5504	6.3395 0406	83
84	4.2942 8737	4.7608 0317	5.2773 3214	6.4821 4290	84
85	4.3694 3740	4.8500 6823	5.3828 7878	6.6279 9112	85
86	4.4459 0255	4.9410 0701	5.4905 3636	6.7771 2092	86
87	4.5237 0584	5.0336 5089	5.6003 4708	6.9296 0614	87
88	4.6028 7070	5.1280 3185	5.7123 5402	7.0855 2228	88
89	4.6834 2093	5.2241 8245	5.8266 0110	7.2449 4653	89
90	4.7653 8080	5.3221 3587	5.9431 3313	7.4079 5782	90
91	4.8487 7496	5.4219 2591	6.0619 9579	7.5746 3688	91
92	4.9336 2853	5.5235 8703	6.1832 3570	7.7450 6621	92
93	5.0199 6703	5.6271 5428	6.3069 0042	7.9193 3020	93
94	5.1078 1645	5.7326 6343	6.4330 3843	8.0975 1512	94
95	5.1972 0324	5.8401 5086	6.5616 9920	8.2797 0921	95
96	5.2881 5429	5.9496 5369	6.6929 3318	8.4660 0267	96
97	5.3806 9699	6.0612 0970	6.8267 9184	8.6564 8773	97
98	5.4748 5919	6.1748 5738	6.9633 2768	8.8512 5871	98
99	5.5706 6923	6.2906 3596	7.1025 9423	9.0504 1203	99
100	5.6681 5594	6.4085 8538	7.2446 4612	9.2540 4630	100

Reprinted, by permission, from Shao

COMPOUND AMOUNT
When principal is 1

$$s = (1 + i)^n$$

n	$2\frac{1}{2}\%$	$2\frac{3}{4}\%$	3%	$3\frac{1}{4}\%$	n
1	1.0250 0000	1.0275 0000	1.0300 0000	1.0325 0000	1
2	1.0506 2500	1.0557 5625	1.0609 0000	1.0660 5625	2
3	1.0768 9063	1.0847 8955	1.0927 2700	1.1007 0308	3
4	1.1038 1289	1.1146 2126	1.1255 0881	1.1364 7593	4
5	1.1314 0821	1.1452 7334	1.1592 7407	1.1734 1140	5
6	1.1596 9342	1.1767 6836	1.1940 5230	1.2115 4727	6
7	1.1886 8575	1.2091 2949	1.2298 7387	1.2509 2255	7
8	1.2184 0290	1.2423 8055	1.2667 7008	1.2915 7754	8
9	1.2488 6297	1.2765 4602	1.3047 7318	1.3335 5381	9
10	1.2800 8454	1.3116 5103	1.3439 1638	1.3768 9430	10
11	1.3120 8666	1.3477 2144	1.3842 3387	1.4216 4337	11
12	1.3448 8882	1.3847 8378	1.4257 6089	1.4678 4678	12
13	1.3785 1104	1.4228 6533	1.4685 3371	1.5155 5180	13
14	1.4129 7382	1.4619 9413	1.5125 8972	1.5648 0723	14
15	1.4482 9817	1.5021 9896	1.5579 6742	1.6156 6347	15
16	1.4845 0562	1.5435 0944	1.6047 0644	1.6681 7253	16
17	1.5216 1826	1.5859 5595	1.6528 4763	1.7223 8814	17
18	1.5596 5872	1.6295 6973	1.7024 3306	1.7783 6575	18
19	1.5986 5019	1.6743 8290	1.7535 0605	1.8361 6264	19
20	1.6386 1644	1.7204 2843	1.8061 1123	1.8958 3792	20
21	1.6795 8185	1.7677 4021	1.8602 9457	1.9574 5266	21
22	1.7215 7140	1.8163 5307	1.9161 0341	2.0210 6987	22
23	1.7646 1068	1.8663 0278	1.9735 8651	2.0867 5464	23
24	1.8087 2595	1.9176 2610	2.0327 9411	2.1545 7416	24
25	1.8539 4410	1.9703 6082	2.0937 7793	2.2245 9782	25
26	1.9002 9270	2.0245 4575	2.1565 9127	2.2968 9725	26
27	1.9478 0002	2.0802 2075	2.2212 8901	2.3715 4641	27
28	1.9964 9502	2.1374 2682	2.2879 2768	2.4486 2167	28
29	2.0464 0739	2.1962 0606	2.3565 6551	2.5282 0188	29
30	2.0975 6758	2.2566 0173	2.4272 6247	2.6103 6844	30
31	2.1500 0677	2.3186 5828	2.5000 8035	2.6952 0541	31
32	2.2037 5694	2.3824 2138	2.5750 8276	2.7827 9959	32
33	2.2588 5086	2.4479 3797	2.6523 3524	2.8732 4058	33
34	2.3153 2213	2.5152 5626	2.7319 0530	2.9666 2089	34
35	2.3732 0519	2.5844 2581	2.8138 6245	3.0630 3607	35
36	2.4325 3532	2.6554 9752	2.8982 7833	3.1625 8475	36
37	2.4933 4870	2.7285 2370	2.9852 2668	3.2653 6875	37
38	2.5556 8242	2.8035 5810	3.0747 8348	3.3714 9323	38
39	2.6195 7448	2.8806 5595	3.1670 2698	3.4810 6676	39
40	2.6850 6384	2.9598 7399	3.2620 3779	3.5942 0143	40
41	2.7521 9043	3.0412 7052	3.3598 9893	3.7110 1298	41
42	2.8209 9520	3.1249 0546	3.4606 9589	3.8316 2090	42
43	2.8915 2008	3.2108 4036	3.5645 1677	3.9561 4858	43
44	2.9638 0808	3.2991 3847	3.6714 5227	4.0847 2341	44
45	3.0379 0328	3.3898 6478	3.7815 9584	4.2174 7692	45
46	3.1138 5086	3.4830 8606	3.8950 4372	4.3545 4492	46
47	3.1916 9713	3.5788 7093	4.0118 9503	4.4960 6763	47
48	3.2714 8956	3.6772 8988	4.1322 5188	4.6421 8983	48
49	3.3532 7680	3.7784 1535	4.2562 1944	4.7930 6100	49
50	3.4371 0872	3.8823 2177	4.3839 0602	4.9488 3548	50

Reprinted, by permission, from Shao

COMPOUND AMOUNT
When principal is 1
$$s = (1 + i)^n$$

n	$2\frac{1}{2}\%$	$2\frac{3}{4}\%$	3%	$3\frac{1}{4}\%$	n
51	3.5230 3644	3.9890 8562	4.5154 2320	5.1096 7263	51
52	3.6111 1235	4.0987 8547	4.6508 8590	5.2757 3700	52
53	3.7013 9016	4.2115 0208	4.7904 1247	5.4471 9845	53
54	3.7939 2491	4.3273 1838	4.9341 2485	5.6242 3240	54
55	3.8887 7303	4.4463 1964	5.0821 4859	5.8070 1995	55
56	3.9859 9236	4.5685 9343	5.2346 1305	5.9957 4810	56
57	4.0856 4217	4.6942 2975	5.3916 5144	6.1906 0991	57
58	4.1877 8322	4.8233 2107	5.5534 0098	6.3918 0473	58
59	4.2924 7780	4.9559 6239	5.7200 0301	6.5995 3839	59
60	4.3997 8975	5.0922 5136	5.8916 0310	6.8140 2339	60
61	4.5097 8449	5.2322 8827	6.0683 5120	7.0354 7915	61
62	4.6225 2910	5.3761 7620	6.2504 0173	7.2641 3222	62
63	4.7380 9233	5.5240 2105	6.4379 1379	7.5002 1651	63
64	4.8565 4464	5.6759 3162	6.6310 5120	7.7439 7355	64
65	4.9779 5826	5.8320 1974	6.8299 8273	7.9956 5269	65
66	5.1024 0721	5.9924 0029	7.0348 8222	8.2555 1140	66
67	5.2299 6739	6.1571 9130	7.2459 2868	8.5238 1552	67
68	5.3607 1658	6.3265 1406	7.4633 0654	8.8008 3953	68
69	5.4947 3449	6.5004 9319	7.6872 0574	9.0868 6681	69
70	5.6321 0286	6.6792 5676	7.9178 2191	9.3821 8999	70
71	5.7729 0543	6.8629 3632	8.1553 5657	9.6871 1116	71
72	5.9172 2806	7.0516 6706	8.4000 1727	10.0019 4227	72
73	6.0651 5876	7.2455 8791	8.6520 1778	10.3270 0540	73
74	6.2167 8773	7.4448 4158	8.9115 7832	10.6626 3307	74
75	6.3722 0743	7.6495 7472	9.1789 2567	11.0091 6865	75
76	6.5315 1261	7.8599 3802	9.4542 9344	11.3669 6663	76
77	6.6948 0043	8.0760 8632	9.7379 2224	11.7363 9304	77
78	6.8621 7044	8.2981 7869	10.0300 5991	12.1178 2582	78
79	7.0337 2470	8.5263 7861	10.3309 6171	12.5116 5516	79
80	7.2095 6782	8.7608 5402	10.6408 9056	12.9182 8395	80
81	7.3898 0701	9.0017 7751	10.9601 1727	13.3381 2818	81
82	7.5745 5219	9.2493 2639	11.2889 2079	13.7716 1734	82
83	7.7639 1599	9.5036 8286	11.6275 8842	14.2191 9491	83
84	7.9580 1389	9.7650 3414	11.9764 1607	14.6813 1874	84
85	8.1569 6424	10.0335 7258	12.3357 0855	15.1584 6160	85
86	8.3608 8834	10.3094 9583	12.7057 7981	15.6511 1160	86
87	8.5699 1055	10.5930 0696	13.0869 5320	16.1597 7273	87
88	8.7841 5832	10.8843 1465	13.4795 6180	16.6849 6534	88
89	9.0037 6228	11.1836 3331	13.8839 4865	17.2272 2672	89
90	9.2288 5633	11.4911 8322	14.3004 6711	17.7871 1159	90
91	9.4595 7774	11.8071 9076	14.7294 8112	18.3651 9271	91
92	9.6960 6718	12.1318 8851	15.1713 6556	18.9620 6147	92
93	9.9384 6886	12.4655 1544	15.6265 0652	19.5783 2847	93
94	10.1869 3058	12.8083 1711	16.0953 0172	20.2146 2415	94
95	10.4416 0385	13.1605 4584	16.5781 6077	20.8715 9943	95
96	10.7026 4395	13.5224 6085	17.0755 0559	21.5499 2641	96
97	10.9702 1004	13.8943 2852	17.5877 7076	22.2502 9902	97
98	11.2444 6530	14.2764 2255	18.1154 0388	22.9734 3374	98
99	11.5255 7693	14.6690 2417	18.6588 6600	23.7200 7034	99
100	11.8137 1635	15.0724 2234	19.2186 3198	24.4909 7262	100

Reprinted, by permission, from Shao

COMPOUND AMOUNT
When principal is 1

$$s = (1 + i)^n$$

n	$3\frac{1}{2}\%$	$3\frac{3}{4}\%$	4%	$4\frac{1}{2}\%$	n
1	1.0350 0000	1.0375 0000	1.0400 0000	1.0450 0000	1
2	1.0712 2500	1.0764 0625	1.0816 0000	1.0920 2500	2
3	1.1087 1788	1.1167 7148	1.1248 6400	1.1411 6613	3
4	1.1475 2300	1.1586 5042	1.1698 5856	1.1925 1860	4
5	1.1876 8631	1.2020 9981	1.2166 5290	1.2461 8194	5
6	1.2292 5533	1.2471 7855	1.2653 1902	1.3022 6012	6
7	1.2722 7926	1.2939 4774	1.3159 3178	1.3608 6183	7
8	1.3168 0904	1.3424 7078	1.3685 6905	1.4221 0061	8
9	1.3628 9735	1.3928 1344	1.4233 1181	1.4860 9514	9
10	1.4105 9876	1.4450 4394	1.4802 4428	1.5529 6942	10
11	1.4599 6972	1.4992 3309	1.5394 5406	1.6228 5305	11
12	1.5110 6866	1.5554 5433	1.6010 3222	1.6958 8143	12
13	1.5639 5606	1.6137 8387	1.6650 7351	1.7721 9610	13
14	1.6186 9452	1.6743 0076	1.7316 7645	1.8519 4492	14
15	1.6753 4883	1.7370 8704	1.8009 4351	1.9352 8244	15
16	1.7339 8604	1.8022 2781	1.8729 8125	2.0223 7015	16
17	1.7946 7555	1.8698 1135	1.9479 0050	2.1133 7681	17
18	1.8574 8920	1.9399 2928	2.0258 1652	2.2084 7877	18
19	1.9225 0132	2.0126 7662	2.1068 4918	2.3078 6031	19
20	1.9897 8886	2.0881 5200	2.1911 2314	2.4117 1402	20
21	2.0594 3147	2.1664 5770	2.2787 6807	2.5202 4116	21
22	2.1315 1158	2.2476 9986	2.3699 1879	2.6336 5201	22
23	2.2061 1448	2.3319 8860	2.4647 1554	2.7521 6635	23
24	2.2833 2849	2.4194 3818	2.5633 0416	2.8760 1383	24
25	2.3632 4498	2.5101 6711	2.6658 3633	3.0054 3446	25
26	2.4459 5856	2.6042 9838	2.7724 6978	3.1406 7901	26
27	2.5315 6711	2.7019 5956	2.8833 6858	3.2820 0956	27
28	2.6201 7196	2.8032 8305	2.9987 0332	3.4296 9999	28
29	2.7118 7798	2.9084 0616	3.1186 5145	3.5840 3649	29
30	2.8067 9370	3.0174 7139	3.2433 9751	3.7453 1813	30
31	2.9050 3148	3.1306 2657	3.3731 3341	3.9138 5745	31
32	3.0067 0759	3.2480 2507	3.5080 5875	4.0899 8104	32
33	3.1119 4235	3.3698 2601	3.6483 8110	4.2740 3018	33
34	3.2208 6033	3.4961 9448	3.7943 1634	4.4663 6154	34
35	3.3335 9045	3.6273 0178	3.9460 8899	4.6673 4781	35
36	3.4502 6611	3.7633 2559	4.1039 3255	4.8773 7846	36
37	3.5710 2543	3.9044 5030	4.2680 8986	5.0968 6049	37
38	3.6960 1132	4.0508 6719	4.4388 1345	5.3262 1921	38
39	3.8253 7171	4.2027 7471	4.6163 6599	5.5658 9908	39
40	3.9592 5972	4.3603 7876	4.8010 2063	5.8163 6454	40
41	4.0978 3381	4.5238 9296	4.9930 6145	6.0781 0094	41
42	4.2412 5799	4.6935 3895	5.1927 8391	6.3516 1548	42
43	4.3897 0202	4.8695 4666	5.4004 9527	6.6374 3818	43
44	4.5433 4160	5.0521 5466	5.6165 1508	6.9361 2290	44
45	4.7023 5855	5.2416 1046	5.8411 7568	7.2482 4843	45
46	4.8669 4110	5.4381 7085	6.0748 2271	7.5744 1961	46
47	5.0372 8404	5.6421 0226	6.3178 1562	7.9152 6849	47
48	5.2135 8898	5.8536 8109	6.5705 2824	8.2714 5557	48
49	5.3960 6459	6.0731 9413	6.8333 4937	8.6436 7107	49
50	5.5849 2686	6.3009 3891	7.1066 8335	9.0326 3627	50

Reprinted, by permission, from Shao

COMPOUND AMOUNT
When principal is 1

$$s = (1 + i)^n$$

n	$3\frac{1}{2}\%$	$3\frac{3}{4}\%$	4%	$4\frac{1}{2}\%$	n
51	5.7803 9930	6.5372 2412	7.3909 5068	9.4391 0490	51
52	5.9827 1327	6.7823 7003	7.6865 8871	9.8638 6463	52
53	6.1921 0824	7.0367 0890	7.9940 5226	10.3077 3853	53
54	6.4088 3202	7.3005 8549	8.3138 1435	10.7715 8677	54
55	6.6331 4114	7.5743 5744	8.6463 6692	11.2563 0817	55
56	6.8653 0108	7.8583 9585	8.9922 2160	11.7628 4204	56
57	7.1055 8662	8.1530 8569	9.3519 1046	12.2921 6993	57
58	7.3542 8215	8.4588 2640	9.7259 8688	12.8453 1758	58
59	7.6116 8203	8.7760 3239	10.1150 2635	13.4233 5687	59
60	7.8780 9090	9.1051 3361	10.5196 2741	14.0274 0793	60
61	8.1538 2408	9.4465 7612	10.9404 1250	14.6586 4129	61
62	8.4392 0793	9.8008 2272	11.3780 2900	15.3182 8014	62
63	8.7345 8020	10.1683 5358	11.8331 5016	16.0076 0275	63
64	9.0402 9051	10.5496 6684	12.3064 7617	16.7279 4487	64
65	9.3567 0068	10.9452 7934	12.7987 3522	17.4807 0239	65
66	9.6841 8520	11.3557 2732	13.3106 8463	18.2673 3400	66
67	10.0231 3168	11.7815 6709	13.8431 1201	19.0893 6403	67
68	10.3739 4129	12.2233 7586	14.3968 3649	19.9483 8541	68
69	10.7370 2924	12.6817 5245	14.9727 0995	20.8460 6276	69
70	11.1128 2526	13.1573 1817	15.5716 1835	21.7841 3558	70
71	11.5017 7414	13.6507 1760	16.1944 8308	22.7644 2168	71
72	11.9043 3624	14.1626 1951	16.8422 6241	23.7888 2066	72
73	12.3209 8801	14.6937 1774	17.5159 5290	24.8593 1759	73
74	12.7522 2259	15.2447 3216	18.2165 9102	25.9779 8688	74
75	13.1985 5038	15.8164 0961	18.9452 5466	27.1469 9629	75
76	13.6604 9964	16.4095 2497	19.7030 6485	28.3686 1112	76
77	14.1386 1713	17.0248 8216	20.4911 8744	29.6451 9862	77
78	14.6334 6873	17.6633 1524	21.3108 3494	30.9792 3256	78
79	15.1456 4014	18.3256 8956	22.1632 6834	32.3732 9802	79
80	15.6757 3754	19.0129 0292	23.0497 9907	33.8300 9643	80
81	16.2243 8835	19.7258 8678	23.9717 9103	35.3524 5077	81
82	16.7922 4195	20.4656 0754	24.9306 6267	36.9433 1106	82
83	17.3799 7041	21.2330 6782	25.9278 8918	38.6057 6006	83
84	17.9882 6938	22.0293 0786	26.9650 0475	40.3430 1926	84
85	18.6178 5881	22.8554 0691	28.0436 0494	42.1584 5513	85
86	19.2694 8387	23.7124 8467	29.1653 4914	44.0555 8561	86
87	19.9439 1580	24.6017 0284	30.3319 6310	46.0380 8696	87
88	20.6419 5285	25.5242 6670	31.5452 4163	48.1098 0087	88
89	21.3644 2120	26.4814 2670	32.8070 5129	50.2747 4191	89
90	22.1121 7595	27.4744 8020	34.1193 3334	52.5371 0530	90
91	22.8861 0210	28.5047 7321	35.4841 0668	54.9012 7504	91
92	23.6871 1568	29.5737 0220	36.9034 7094	57.3718 3241	92
93	24.5161 6473	30.6827 1603	38.3796 0978	59.9535 6487	93
94	25.3742 3049	31.8333 1789	39.9147 9417	62.6514 7529	94
95	26.2623 2856	33.0270 6731	41.5113 8594	65.4707 9168	95
96	27.1815 1006	34.2655 8233	43.1718 4138	68.4169 7730	96
97	28.1328 6291	35.5505 4167	44.8987 1503	71.4957 4128	97
98	29.1175 1311	36.8836 8698	46.6946 6363	74.7130 4964	98
99	30.1366 2607	38.2668 2524	48.5624 5018	78.0751 3687	99
100	31.1914 0798	39.7018 3119	50.5049 4818	81.5885 1803	100

Reprinted, by permission, from Shao

COMPOUND AMOUNT
When principal is 1

$$s = (1 + i)^n$$

n	5%	$5\frac{1}{2}\%$	6%	$6\frac{1}{2}\%$	n
1	1.0500 0000	1.0550 0000	1.0600 0000	1.0650 0000	1
2	1.1025 0000	1.1130 2500	1.1236 0000	1.1342 2500	2
3	1.1576 2500	1.1742 4138	1.1910 1600	1.2079 4963	3
4	1.2155 0625	1.2388 2465	1.2624 7696	1.2864 6635	4
5	1.2762 8156	1.3069 6001	1.3382 2558	1.3700 8666	5
6	1.3400 9564	1.3788 4281	1.4185 1911	1.4591 4230	6
7	1.4071 0042	1.4546 7916	1.5036 3026	1.5539 8655	7
8	1.4774 5544	1.5346 8652	1.5938 4807	1.6549 9567	8
9	1.5513 2822	1.6190 9427	1.6894 7896	1.7625 7039	9
10	1.6288 9463	1.7081 4446	1.7908 4770	1.8771 3747	10
11	1.7103 3936	1.8020 9240	1.8982 9856	1.9991 5140	11
12	1.7958 5633	1.9012 0749	2.0121 9647	2.1290 9624	12
13	1.8856 4914	2.0057 7390	2.1329 2826	2.2674 8750	13
14	1.9799 3160	2.1160 9146	2.2609 0396	2.4148 7418	14
15	2.0789 2818	2.2324 7649	2.3965 5819	2.5718 4101	15
16	2.1828 7459	2.3552 6270	2.5403 5168	2.7390 1067	16
17	2.2920 1832	2.4848 0215	2.6927 7279	2.9170 4637	17
18	2.4066 1923	2.6214 6627	2.8543 3915	3.1066 5438	18
19	2.5269 5020	2.7656 4691	3.0255 9950	3.3085 8691	19
20	2.6532 9771	2.9177 5749	3.2071 3547	3.5236 4506	20
21	2.7859 6259	3.0782 3415	3.3995 6360	3.7526 8199	21
22	2.9252 6072	3.2475 3703	3.6035 3742	3.9966 0632	22
23	3.0715 2376	3.4261 5157	3.8197 4966	4.2563 8573	23
24	3.2250 9994	3.6145 8990	4.0489 3464	4.5330 5081	24
25	3.3863 5494	3.8133 9235	4.2918 7072	4.8276 9911	25
26	3.5556 7269	4.0231 2893	4.5493 8296	5.1414 9955	26
27	3.7334 5632	4.2444 0102	4.8223 4594	5.4756 9702	27
28	3.9201 2914	4.4778 4307	5.1116 8670	5.8316 1733	28
29	4.1161 3560	4.7241 2444	5.4183 8790	6.2106 7245	29
30	4.3219 4238	4.9839 5129	5.7434 9117	6.6143 6616	30
31	4.5380 3949	5.2580 6861	6.0881 0064	7.0442 9996	31
32	4.7649 4147	5.5472 6238	6.4533 8668	7.5021 7946	32
33	5.0031 8854	5.8523 6181	6.8405 8988	7.9898 2113	33
34	5.2533 4797	6.1742 4171	7.2510 2528	8.5091 5950	34
35	5.5160 1537	6.5138 2501	7.6860 8679	9.0622 5487	35
36	5.7918 1614	6.8720 8538	8.1472 5200	9.6513 0143	36
37	6.0814 0694	7.2500 5008	8.6360 8712	10.2786 3603	37
38	6.3854 7729	7.6488 0283	9.1542 5235	10.9467 4737	38
39	6.7047 5115	8.0694 8699	9.7035 0749	11.6582 8595	39
40	7.0399 8871	8.5133 0877	10.2857 1794	12.4160 7453	40
41	7.3919 8815	8.9815 4076	10.9028 6101	13.2231 1938	41
42	7.7615 8756	9.4755 2550	11.5570 3267	14.0826 2214	42
43	8.1496 6693	9.9966 7940	12.2504 5463	14.9979 9258	43
44	8.5571 5028	10.5464 9677	12.9854 8191	15.9728 6209	44
45	8.9850 0779	11.1265 5409	13.7646 1083	17.0110 9813	45
46	9.4342 5818	11.7385 1456	14.5904 8748	18.1168 1951	46
47	9.9059 7109	12.3841 3287	15.4659 1673	19.2944 1278	47
48	10.4012 6965	13.0652 6017	16.3938 7173	20.5485 4961	48
49	10.9213 3313	13.7838 4948	17.3775 0403	21.8842 0533	49
50	11.4673 9979	14.5419 6120	18.4201 5428	23.3066 7868	50

Reprinted, by permission, from Shao

COMPOUND AMOUNT
When principal is 1

$$s = (1 + i)^n$$

n	5%	5½%	6%	6½%	n
51	12.0407 6978	15.3417 6907	19.5253 6353	24.8216 1279	51
52	12.6428 0826	16.1855 6637	20.6968 8534	26.4350 1762	52
53	13.2749 4868	17.0757 7252	21.9386 9846	28.1532 9377	53
54	13.9386 9611	18.0149 4001	23.2550 2037	29.9832 5786	54
55	14.6356 3092	19.0057 6171	24.6503 2159	31.9321 6963	55
56	15.3674 1246	20.0510 7860	26.1293 4089	34.0077 6065	56
57	16.1357 8309	21.1538 8793	27.6971 0134	36.2182 6509	57
58	16.9425 7224	22.3173 5176	29.3589 2742	38.5724 5233	58
59	17.7897 0085	23.5448 0611	31.1204 6307	41.0796 6173	59
60	18.6791 8589	24.8397 7045	32.9876 9085	43.7498 3974	60
61	19.6131 4519	26.2059 5782	34.9669 5230	46.5935 7932	61
62	20.5938 0245	27.6472 8550	37.0649 6944	49.6221 6198	62
63	21.6234 9257	29.1678 8620	39.2888 6761	52.8476 0251	63
64	22.7046 6720	30.7721 1994	41.6461 9967	56.2826 9667	64
65	23.8399 0056	32.4645 8654	44.1449 7165	59.9410 7195	65
66	25.0318 9559	34.2501 3880	46.7936 6994	63.8372 4163	66
67	26.2834 9037	36.1338 9643	49.6012 9014	67.9866 6234	67
68	27.5976 6488	38.1212 6074	52.5773 6755	72.4057 9539	68
69	28.9775 4813	40.2179 3008	55.7320 0960	77.1121 7209	69
70	30.4264 2554	42.4299 1623	59.0759 3018	82.1244 6327	70
71	31.9477 4681	44.7635 6163	62.6204 8599	87.4625 5339	71
72	33.5451 3415	47.2255 5751	66.3777 1515	93.1476 1936	72
73	35.2223 9086	49.8229 6318	70.3603 7806	99.2022 1461	73
74	36.9835 1040	52.5632 2615	74.5820 0074	105.6503 5856	74
75	38.8326 8592	55.4542 0359	79.0569 2079	112.5176 3187	75
76	40.7743 2022	58.5041 8479	83.8003 3603	119.8312 7794	76
77	42.8130 3623	61.7219 1495	88.8283 5620	127.6203 1101	77
78	44.9536 8804	65.1166 2027	94.1580 5757	135.9156 3122	78
79	47.2013 7244	68.6980 3439	99.8075 4102	144.7501 4725	79
80	49.5614 4107	72.4764 2628	105.7959 9348	154.1589 0683	80
81	52.0395 1312	76.4626 2973	112.1437 5309	164.1792 3577	81
82	54.6414 8878	80.6680 7436	118.8723 7828	174.8508 8609	82
83	57.3735 6322	85.1048 1845	126.0047 2097	186.2161 9369	83
84	60.2422 4138	89.7855 8347	133.5650 0423	198.3202 4628	84
85	63.2543 5344	94.7237 9056	141.5789 0449	211.2110 6229	85
86	66.4170 7112	99.9335 9904	150.0736 3875	224.9397 8134	86
87	69.7379 2467	105.4299 4698	159.0780 5708	239.5608 6712	87
88	73.2248 2091	111.2285 9407	168.6227 4050	255.1323 2349	88
89	76.8860 6195	117.3461 6674	178.7401 0493	271.7159 2451	89
90	80.7303 6505	123.8002 0591	189.4645 1123	289.3774 5961	90
91	84.7668 8330	130.6092 1724	200.8323 8190	308.1869 9448	91
92	89.0052 2747	137.7927 2419	212.8823 2482	328.2191 4912	92
93	93.4554 8884	145.3713 2402	225.6552 6431	349.5533 9382	93
94	98.1282 6328	153.3667 4684	239.1945 8017	372.2743 6441	94
95	103.0346 7645	161.8019 1791	253.5462 5498	396.4721 9810	95
96	108.1864 1027	170.7010 2340	268.7590 3028	422.2428 9098	96
97	113.5957 3078	180.0895 7969	284.8845 7209	449.6886 7889	97
98	119.2755 1732	189.9945 0657	301.9776 4642	478.9184 4302	98
99	125.2392 9319	200.4442 0443	320.0963 0520	510.0481 4181	99
100	131.5012 5785	211.4686 3567	339.3020 8351	543.2012 7103	100

Reprinted, by permission, from Shao

COMPOUND AMOUNT
When principal is 1

$$s = (1 + i)^n$$

n	7%	$7\frac{1}{2}\%$	8%	$8\frac{1}{2}\%$	n
1	1.0700 0000	1.0750 0000	1.0800 0000	1.0850 0000	1
2	1.1449 0000	1.1556 2500	1.1664 0000	1.1772 2500	2
3	1.2250 4300	1.2422 9688	1.2597 1200	1.2772 8913	3
4	1.3107 9601	1.3354 6914	1.3604 8896	1.3858 5870	4
5	1.4025 5173	1.4356 2933	1.4693 2808	1.5036 5669	5
6	1.5007 3035	1.5433 0153	1.5868 7432	1.6314 6751	6
7	1.6057 8148	1.6590 4914	1.7138 2427	1.7701 4225	7
8	1.7181 8618	1.7834 7783	1.8509 3021	1.9206 0434	8
9	1.8384 5921	1.9172 3866	1.9990 0463	2.0838 5571	9
10	1.9671 5136	2.0610 3156	2.1589 2500	2.2609 8344	10
11	2.1048 5195	2.2156 0893	2.3316 3900	2.4531 6703	11
12	2.2521 9159	2.3817 7960	2.5181 7012	2.6616 8623	12
13	2.4098 4500	2.5604 1307	2.7196 2373	2.8879 2956	13
14	2.5785 3415	2.7524 4405	2.9371 9362	3.1334 0357	14
15	2.7590 3154	2.9588 7735	3.1721 6911	3.3997 4288	15
16	2.9521 6375	3.1807 9315	3.4259 4264	3.6887 2102	16
17	3.1588 1521	3.4193 5264	3.7000 1805	4.0022 6231	17
18	3.3799 3228	3.6758 0409	3.9960 1950	4.3424 5461	18
19	3.6165 2754	3.9514 8940	4.3157 0106	4.7115 6325	19
20	3.8696 8446	4.2478 5110	4.6609 5714	5.1120 4612	20
21	4.1405 6237	4.5664 3993	5.0338 3372	5.5465 7005	21
22	4.4304 0174	4.9089 2293	5.4365 4041	6.0180 2850	22
23	4.7405 2986	5.2770 9215	5.8714 6365	6.5295 6092	23
24	5.0723 6695	5.6728 7406	6.3411 8074	7.0845 7360	24
25	5.4274 3264	6.0983 3961	6.8484 7520	7.6867 6236	25
26	5.8073 5292	6.5557 1508	7.3963 5321	8.3401 3716	26
27	6.2138 6763	7.0473 9371	7.9880 6147	9.0490 4881	27
28	6.6488 3836	7.5759 4824	8.6271 0639	9.8182 1796	28
29	7.1142 5705	8.1441 4436	9.3172 7490	10.6527 6649	29
30	7.6122 5504	8.7549 5519	10.0626 5689	11.5582 5164	30
31	8.1451 1290	9.4115 7683	10.8676 6944	12.5407 0303	31
32	8.7152 7080	10.1174 4509	11.7370 8300	13.6066 6279	32
33	9.3253 3975	10.8762 5347	12.6760 4964	14.7632 2913	33
34	9.9781 1354	11.6919 7248	13.6901 3361	16.0181 0360	34
35	10.6765 8148	12.5688 7042	14.7853 4429	17.3796 4241	35
36	11.4239 4219	13.5115 3570	15.9681 7184	18.8569 1201	36
37	12.2236 1814	14.5249 0088	17.2456 2558	20.4597 4953	37
38	13.0792 7141	15.6142 6844	18.6252 7563	22.1988 2824	38
39	13.9948 2041	16.7853 3858	20.1152 9768	24.0857 2865	39
40	14.9744 5784	18.0442 3897	21.7245 2150	26.1330 1558	40
41	16.0226 6989	19.3975 5689	23.4624 8322	28.3543 2190	41
42	17.1442 5678	20.8523 7366	25.3394 8187	30.7644 3927	42
43	18.3443 5475	22.4163 0168	27.3666 4042	33.3794 1660	43
44	19.6284 5959	24.0975 2431	29.5559 7166	36.2166 6702	44
45	21.0024 5176	25.9048 3863	31.9204 4939	39.2950 8371	45
46	22.4726 2338	27.8477 0153	34.4740 8534	42.6351 6583	46
47	24.0457 0702	29.9362 7915	37.2320 1217	46.2591 5492	47
48	25.7289 0651	32.1815 0008	40.2105 7314	50.1911 8309	48
49	27.5299 2997	34.5951 1259	43.4274 1899	54.4574 3365	49
50	29.4570 2506	37.1897 4603	46.9016 1251	59.0863 1551	50

Reprinted, by permission, from Shao

COMPOUND AMOUNT
When principal is 1

$$s = (1 + i)^n$$

n	7%	$7\frac{1}{2}\%$	8%	$8\frac{1}{2}\%$	n
51	31.5190 1682	39.9789 7698	50.6537 4151	64.1086 5233	51
52	33.7253 4799	42.9774 0026	54.7060 4084	69.5578 8778	52
53	36.0861 2235	46.2007 0528	59.0825 2410	75.4703 0824	53
54	38.6121 5092	49.6657 5817	63.8091 2603	81.8852 8444	54
55	41.3150 0148	53.3906 9004	68.9138 5611	88.8455 3362	55
56	44.2070 5159	57.3949 9179	74.4269 6460	96.3974 0398	56
57	47.3015 4520	61.6996 1617	80.3811 2177	104.5911 8332	57
58	50.6126 5336	66.3270 8739	86.8116 1151	113.4814 3390	58
59	54.1555 3910	71.3016 1894	93.7565 4043	123.1273 5578	59
60	57.9464 2683	76.6492 4036	101.2570 6367	133.5931 8102	60
61	62.0026 7671	82.3979 3339	109.3576 2876	144.9486 0141	61
62	66.3428 6408	88.5777 7839	118.1062 3906	157.2692 3253	62
63	70.9868 6457	95.2211 1177	127.5547 3819	170.6371 1729	63
64	75.9559 4509	102.3626 9515	137.7591 1724	185.1412 7226	64
65	81.2728 6124	110.0398 9729	148.7798 4662	200.8782 8041	65
66	86.9619 6153	118.2928 8959	160.6822 3435	217.9529 3424	66
67	93.0492 9884	127.1648 5631	173.5368 1310	236.4789 3365	67
68	99.5627 4976	136.7022 2053	187.4197 5815	256.5796 4301	68
69	106.5321 4224	146.9548 8707	202.4133 3880	278.3889 1267	69
70	113.9893 9220	157.9756 0360	218.6064 0590	302.0519 7024	70
71	121.9686 4965	169.8247 4137	236.0949 1837	327.7263 8771	71
72	130.5064 5513	182.5615 9697	254.9825 1184	355.5831 3067	72
73	139.6419 0699	196.2537 1675	275.3811 1279	385.8076 9678	73
74	149.4168 4048	210.9727 4550	297.4116 0181	418.6013 5100	74
75	159.8760 1931	226.7957 0141	321.2045 2996	454.1824 6584	75
76	171.0673 4066	243.8053 7902	346.9008 9236	492.7879 7543	76
77	183.0420 5451	262.0907 8245	374.6529 6374	534.6749 5335	77
78	195.8549 9832	281.7475 9113	404.6252 0084	580.1223 2438	78
79	209.5648 4820	302.8786 6046	436.9952 1691	629.4327 2195	79
80	224.2343 8758	325.5945 6000	471.9548 3426	682.9345 0332	80
81	239.9307 9471	350.0141 5200	509.7112 2101	740.9839 3610	81
82	256.7259 5034	376.2652 1340	550.4881 1869	803.9675 7067	82
83	274.6967 6686	404.4851 0440	594.5271 6818	872.3048 1418	83
84	293.9255 4054	434.8214 8723	642.0893 4164	946.4507 2338	84
85	314.5003 2838	467.4330 9878	693.4564 8897	1026.8990 3487	85
86	336.5153 5137	502.4905 8119	748.9330 0808	1114.1854 5283	86
87	360.0714 2596	540.1773 7477	808.8476 4873	1208.8912 1633	87
88	385.2764 2578	580.6906 7788	873.5554 6063	1311.6469 6971	88
89	412.2457 7558	624.2424 7872	943.4398 9748	1423.1369 6214	89
90	441.1029 7988	671.0606 6463	1018.9150 8928	1544.1036 0392	90
91	471.9801 8847	721.3902 1447	1100.4282 9642	1675.3524 1025	91
92	505.0188 0166	775.4944 8056	1188.4625 6013	1817.7573 6512	92
93	540.3701 1778	833.6565 6660	1283.5395 6494	1972.2667 4116	93
94	578.1960 2602	896.1808 0910	1386.2227 3014	2139.9094 1416	94
95	618.6697 4784	963.3943 6978	1497.1205 4855	2321.8017 1436	95
96	661.9766 3019	1035.6489 4751	1616.8901 9244	2519.1548 6008	96
97	708.3149 9430	1113.3226 1858	1746.2414 0783	2733.2830 2319	97
98	757.8970 4390	1196.8218 1497	1885.9407 2046	2965.6120 8016	98
99	810.9498 3698	1286.5834 5109	2036.8159 7809	3217.6891 0698	99
100	867.7163 2557	1383.0772 0993	2199.7612 5634	3491.1926 8107	100

Reprinted, by permission, from Shao

PRESENT VALUE

TABLE A–2

PRESENT VALUE
When Compound Amount Is 1

$$p = (1 + i)^{-n} \quad [OR, \; v^n = (1 + i)^{-n}]$$

n	$1\frac{1}{4}\%$	$1\frac{3}{8}\%$	$1\frac{1}{2}\%$	$1\frac{5}{8}\%$	n
1	0.9876 5432	0.9864 3650	0.9852 2167	0.9840 0984	1
2	0.9754 6106	0.9730 5696	0.9706 6175	0.9682 7537	2
3	0.9634 1833	0.9598 5890	0.9563 1699	0.9527 9249	3
4	0.9515 2428	0.9468 3986	0.9421 8423	0.9375 5718	4
5	0.9397 7706	0.9339 9739	0.9282 6033	0.9225 6549	5
6	0.9281 7488	0.9213 2912	0.9145 4219	0.9078 1352	6
7	0.9167 1593	0.9088 3267	0.9010 2679	0.8932 9744	7
8	0.9053 9845	0.8965 0571	0.8877 1112	0.8790 1347	8
9	0.8942 2069	0.8843 4596	0.8745 9224	0.8649 5791	9
10	0.8831 8093	0.8723 5113	0.8616 6723	0.8511 2709	10
11	0.8722 7746	0.8605 1899	0.8489 3323	0.8375 1743	11
12	0.8615 0860	0.8488 4734	0.8363 8742	0.8241 2539	12
13	0.8508 7269	0.8373 3400	0.8240 2702	0.8109 4750	13
14	0.8403 6809	0.8259 7682	0.8118 4928	0.7979 8032	14
15	0.8299 9318	0.8147 7368	0.7998 5150	0.7852 2048	15
16	0.8197 4635	0.8037 2250	0.7880 3104	0.7726 6468	16
17	0.8096 2602	0.7928 2120	0.7763 8526	0.7603 0965	17
18	0.7996 3064	0.7820 6777	0.7649 1159	0.7481 5218	18
19	0.7897 5866	0.7714 6020	0.7536 0747	0.7361 8911	19
20	0.7800 0855	0.7609 9649	0.7424 7042	0.7244 1732	20
21	0.7703 7881	0.7506 7472	0.7314 9795	0.7128 3378	21
22	0.7608 6796	0.7404 9294	0.7206 8763	0.7014 3545	22
23	0.7514 7453	0.7304 4926	0.7100 3708	0.6902 1938	23
24	0.7421 9707	0.7205 4181	0.6995 4392	0.6791 8267	24
25	0.7330 3414	0.7107 6874	0.6892 0583	0.6683 2243	25
26	0.7239 8434	0.7011 2823	0.6790 2052	0.6576 3584	26
27	0.7150 4626	0.6916 1847	0.6689 8574	0.6471 2014	27
28	0.7062 1853	0.6822 3771	0.6590 9925	0.6367 7259	28
29	0.6974 9978	0.6729 8417	0.6493 5887	0.6265 9049	29
30	0.6888 8867	0.6638 5615	0.6397 6243	0.6165 7121	30
31	0.6803 8387	0.6548 5194	0.6303 0781	0.6067 1214	31
32	0.6719 8407	0.6459 6985	0.6209 9292	0.5970 1071	32
33	0.6636 8797	0.6372 0824	0.6118 1568	0.5874 6442	33
34	0.6554 9429	0.6285 6546	0.6027 7407	0.5780 7077	34
35	0.6474 0177	0.6200 3991	0.5938 6608	0.5688 2732	35
36	0.6394 0916	0.6116 3000	0.5850 8974	0.5597 3168	36
37	0.6315 1522	0.6033 3416	0.5764 4309	0.5507 8148	37
38	0.6237 1873	0.5951 5083	0.5679 2423	0.5419 7440	38
39	0.6160 1850	0.5870 7850	0.5595 3126	0.5333 0814	39
40	0.6084 1334	0.5791 1566	0.5512 6232	0.5247 8046	40
41	0.6009 0206	0.5712 6083	0.5431 1559	0.5163 8914	41
42	0.5934 8352	0.5635 1253	0.5350 8925	0.5081 3199	42
43	0.5861 5656	0.5558 6933	0.5271 8153	0.5000 0688	43
44	0.5789 2006	0.5483 2979	0.5193 9067	0.4920 1169	44
45	0.5717 7290	0.5408 9252	0.5117 1494	0.4841 4434	45
46	0.5647 1397	0.5335 5612	0.5041 5265	0.4764 0280	46
47	0.5577 4219	0.5263 1923	0.4967 0212	0.4687 8504	47
48	0.5508 5649	0.5191 8050	0.4893 6170	0.4612 8909	48
49	0.5440 5579	0.5121 3860	0.4821 2975	0.4539 1301	49
50	0.5373 3905	0.5051 9220	0.4750 0468	0.4466 5487	50

Reprinted, by permission, from Stephen P. Shao, ed., *Mathematics for Management and Finance,* 2nd ed., South-Western Publishing Co., 1969, Appendix pp. 56–67. Adapted from Charles H. Gushee, *Financial Compound Interest and Annuity Tables,* Financial Publishing Company, Boston, 1958, and James W. Glover, *Compound Interest and Insurance Tables,* Wahr's University Bookstore, Ann Arbor, 1957.

PRESENT VALUE
When Compound Amount Is 1
$$p = (1 + i)^{-n} \quad [OR, \; v^n = (1 + i)^{-n}]$$

n	$1\frac{1}{4}\%$	$1\frac{3}{8}\%$	$1\frac{1}{2}\%$	$1\frac{5}{8}\%$	n
51	0.5307 0524	0.4983 4003	0.4679 8491	0.4395 1278	51
52	0.5241 5332	0.4915 8079	0.4610 6887	0.4324 8490	52
53	0.5176 8229	0.4849 1323	0.4542 5505	0.4255 6940	53
54	0.5112 9115	0.4783 3611	0.4475 4192	0.4187 6448	54
55	0.5049 7892	0.4718 4820	0.4409 2800	0.4120 6837	55
56	0.4987 4461	0.4654 4829	0.4344 1182	0.4054 7933	56
57	0.4925 8727	0.4591 3518	0.4279 9194	0.3989 9565	57
58	0.4865 0594	0.4529 0770	0.4216 6694	0.3926 1564	58
59	0.4804 9970	0.4467 6468	0.4154 3541	0.3863 3766	59
60	0.4745 6760	0.4407 0499	0.4092 9597	0.3801 6006	60
61	0.4687 0874	0.4347 2749	0.4032 4726	0.3740 8124	61
62	0.4629 2222	0.4288 3106	0.3972 8794	0.3680 9962	62
63	0.4572 0713	0.4230 1461	0.3914 1669	0.3622 1365	63
64	0.4515 6259	0.4172 7705	0.3856 3221	0.3564 2179	64
65	0.4459 8775	0.4116 1731	0.3799 3321	0.3507 2255	65
66	0.4404 8173	0.4060 3434	0.3743 1843	0.3451 1444	66
67	0.4350 4368	0.4005 2709	0.3687 8663	0.3395 9601	67
68	0.4296 7277	0.3950 9454	0.3633 3658	0.3341 6581	68
69	0.4243 6817	0.3897 3568	0.3579 6708	0.3288 2245	69
70	0.4191 2905	0.3844 4949	0.3526 7692	0.3235 6452	70
71	0.4139 5462	0.3792 3501	0.3474 6495	0.3183 9067	71
72	0.4088 4407	0.3740 9126	0.3423 3000	0.3132 9956	72
73	0.4037 9661	0.3690 1727	0.3372 7093	0.3082 8985	73
74	0.3988 1147	0.3640 1210	0.3322 8663	0.3033 6024	74
75	0.3938 8787	0.3590 7483	0.3273 7599	0.2985 0946	75
76	0.3890 2506	0.3542 0451	0.3225 3793	0.2937 3625	76
77	0.3842 2228	0.3494 0026	0.3177 7136	0.2890 3936	77
78	0.3794 7880	0.3446 6117	0.3130 7523	0.2844 1757	78
79	0.3747 9387	0.3399 8636	0.3084 4850	0.2798 6969	79
80	0.3701 6679	0.3353 7495	0.3038 9015	0.2753 9453	80
81	0.3655 9683	0.3308 2609	0.2993 9916	0.2709 9093	81
82	0.3610 8329	0.3263 3893	0.2949 7454	0.2666 5774	82
83	0.3566 2547	0.3219 1263	0.2906 1531	0.2623 9384	83
84	0.3522 2268	0.3175 4637	0.2863 2050	0.2581 9812	84
85	0.3478 7426	0.3132 3933	0.2820 8917	0.2540 6949	85
86	0.3435 7951	0.3089 9071	0.2779 2036	0.2500 0688	86
87	0.3393 3779	0.3047 9971	0.2738 1316	0.2460 0923	87
88	0.3351 4843	0.3006 6556	0.2697 6666	0.2420 7550	88
89	0.3310 1080	0.2965 8748	0.2657 7997	0.2382 0468	89
90	0.3269 2425	0.2925 6472	0.2618 5218	0.2343 9575	90
91	0.3228 8814	0.2885 9652	0.2579 8245	0.2306 4772	91
92	0.3189 0187	0.2846 8214	0.2541 6990	0.2269 5963	92
93	0.3149 6481	0.2808 2085	0.2504 1369	0.2233 3051	93
94	0.3110 7636	0.2770 1194	0.2467 1300	0.2197 5942	94
95	0.3072 3591	0.2732 5468	0.2430 6699	0.2162 4543	95
96	0.3034 4287	0.2695 4839	0.2394 7487	0.2127 8763	96
97	0.2996 9666	0.2658 9237	0.2359 3583	0.2093 8512	97
98	0.2959 9670	0.2622 8594	0.2324 4909	0.2060 3702	98
99	0.2923 4242	0.2587 2843	0.2290 1389	0.2027 4245	99
100	0.2887 3326	0.2552 1916	0.2256 2944	0.1995 0057	100

Reprinted, by permission, from Shao

PRESENT VALUE
When Compound Amount Is 1

$$p = (1 + i)^{-n} \quad [OR, v^n = (1 + i)^{-n}]$$

n	$1\frac{3}{4}\%$	$1\frac{7}{8}\%$	2%	$2\frac{1}{4}\%$	n
1	0.9828 0098	0.9815 9509	0.9803 9216	0.9779 9511	1
2	0.9658 9777	0.9635 2892	0.9611 6878	0.9564 7444	2
3	0.9492 8528	0.9457 9526	0.9423 2233	0.9354 2732	3
4	0.9329 5851	0.9283 8799	0.9238 4543	0.9148 4335	4
5	0.9169 1254	0.9113 0109	0.9057 3081	0.8947 1232	5
6	0.9011 4254	0.8945 2868	0.8879 7138	0.8750 2427	6
7	0.8856 4378	0.8780 6496	0.8705 6018	0.8557 6946	7
8	0.8704 1157	0.8619 0426	0.8534 9037	0.8369 3835	8
9	0.8554 4135	0.8460 4099	0.8367 5527	0.8185 2161	9
10	0.8407 2860	0.8304 6968	0.8203 4830	0.8005 1013	10
11	0.8262 6889	0.8151 8496	0.8042 6304	0.7828 9499	11
12	0.8120 5788	0.8001 8156	0.7884 9318	0.7656 6748	12
13	0.7980 9128	0.7854 5429	0.7730 3253	0.7488 1905	13
14	0.7843 6490	0.7709 9808	0.7578 7502	0.7323 4137	14
15	0.7708 7459	0.7568 0793	0.7430 1473	0.7162 2628	15
16	0.7576 1631	0.7428 7895	0.7284 4581	0.7004 6580	16
17	0.7445 8605	0.7292 0633	0.7141 6256	0.6850 5212	17
18	0.7317 7990	0.7157 8536	0.7001 5938	0.6699 7763	18
19	0.7191 9401	0.7026 1139	0.6864 3076	0.6552 3484	19
20	0.7068 2458	0.6896 7989	0.6729 7133	0.6408 1647	20
21	0.6946 6789	0.6769 8640	0.6597 7582	0.6267 1538	21
22	0.6827 2028	0.6645 2653	0.6468 3904	0.6129 2457	22
23	0.6709 7817	0.6522 9598	0.6341 5592	0.5994 3724	23
24	0.6594 3800	0.6402 9053	0.6217 2149	0.5862 4668	24
25	0.6480 9632	0.6285 0604	0.6095 3087	0.5733 4639	25
26	0.6369 4970	0.6169 3845	0.5975 7928	0.5607 2997	26
27	0.6259 9479	0.6055 8375	0.5858 6204	0.5483 9117	27
28	0.6152 2829	0.5944 3804	0.5743 7455	0.5363 2388	28
29	0.6046 4697	0.5834 9746	0.5631 1231	0.5245 2213	29
30	0.5942 4764	0.5727 5824	0.5520 7089	0.5129 8008	30
31	0.5840 2716	0.5622 1668	0.5412 4597	0.5016 9201	31
32	0.5739 8247	0.5518 6913	0.5306 3330	0.4906 5233	32
33	0.5641 1053	0.5417 1203	0.5202 2873	0.4798 5558	33
34	0.5544 0839	0.5317 4187	0.5100 2817	0.4692 9641	34
35	0.5448 7311	0.5219 5521	0.5000 2761	0.4589 6960	35
36	0.5355 0183	0.5123 4867	0.4902 2315	0.4488 7002	36
37	0.5262 9172	0.5029 1894	0.4806 1093	0.4389 9268	37
38	0.5172 4002	0.4936 6277	0.4711 8719	0.4293 3270	38
39	0.5083 4400	0.4845 7695	0.4619 4822	0.4198 8528	39
40	0.4996 0098	0.4756 5836	0.4528 9042	0.4106 4575	40
41	0.4910 0834	0.4669 0391	0.4440 1021	0.4016 0954	41
42	0.4825 6348	0.4583 1058	0.4353 0413	0.3927 7216	42
43	0.4742 6386	0.4498 7542	0.4267 6875	0.3841 2925	43
44	0.4661 0699	0.4415 9550	0.4184 0074	0.3756 7653	44
45	0.4580 9040	0.4334 6798	0.4101 9680	0.3674 0981	45
46	0.4502 1170	0.4254 9004	0.4021 5373	0.3593 2500	46
47	0.4424 6850	0.4176 5894	0.3942 6836	0.3514 1809	47
48	0.4348 5848	0.4099 7196	0.3865 3761	0.3436 8518	48
49	0.4273 7934	0.4024 2647	0.3789 5844	0.3361 2242	49
50	0.4200 2883	0.3950 1984	0.3715 2788	0.3287 2608	50

Reprinted, by permission, from Shao

PRESENT VALUE
When Compound Amount Is 1

$$p = (1 + i)^{-n} \quad [OR, v^n = (1 + i)^{-n}]$$

n	$1\frac{3}{4}\%$	$1\frac{7}{8}\%$	2%	$2\frac{1}{4}\%$	n
51	0.4128 0475	0.3877 4954	0.3642 4302	0.3214 9250	51
52	0.4057 0492	0.3806 1305	0.3571 0100	0.3144 1810	52
53	0.3987 2719	0.3736 0790	0.3500 9902	0.3074 9936	53
54	0.3918 6947	0.3667 3168	0.3432 3433	0.3007 3287	54
55	0.3851 2970	0.3599 8202	0.3365 0425	0.2941 1528	55
56	0.3785 0585	0.3533 5658	0.3299 0613	0.2876 4330	56
57	0.3719 9592	0.3468 5308	0.3234 3738	0.2813 1374	57
58	0.3655 9796	0.3404 6928	0.3170 9547	0.2751 2347	58
59	0.3593 1003	0.3342 0298	0.3108 7791	0.2690 6940	59
60	0.3531 3025	0.3280 5200	0.3047 8227	0.2631 4856	60
61	0.3470 5676	0.3220 1424	0.2988 0614	0.2573 5801	61
62	0.3410 8772	0.3160 8759	0.2929 4720	0.2516 9487	62
63	0.3352 2135	0.3102 7003	0.2872 0314	0.2461 5635	63
64	0.3294 5587	0.3045 5954	0.2815 7170	0.2407 3971	64
65	0.3237 8956	0.2989 5415	0.2760 5069	0.2354 4226	65
66	0.3182 2069	0.2934 5193	0.2706 3793	0.2302 6138	66
67	0.3127 4761	0.2880 5097	0.2653 3130	0.2251 9450	67
68	0.3073 6866	0.2827 4942	0.2601 2873	0.2202 3912	68
69	0.3020 8222	0.2775 4544	0.2550 2817	0.2153 9278	69
70	0.2968 8670	0.2724 3724	0.2500 2761	0.2106 5309	70
71	0.2917 8054	0.2674 2306	0.2451 2511	0.2060 1769	71
72	0.2867 6221	0.2625 0116	0.2403 1874	0.2014 8429	72
73	0.2818 3018	0.2576 6985	0.2356 0660	0.1970 5065	73
74	0.2769 8298	0.2529 2746	0.2309 8687	0.1927 1458	74
75	0.2722 1914	0.2482 7236	0.2264 5771	0.1884 7391	75
76	0.2675 3724	0.2437 0293	0.2220 1737	0.1843 2657	76
77	0.2629 3586	0.2392 1760	0.2176 6408	0.1802 7048	77
78	0.2584 1362	0.2348 1482	0.2133 9616	0.1763 0365	78
79	0.2539 6916	0.2304 9308	0.2092 1192	0.1724 2411	79
80	0.2496 0114	0.2262 5087	0.2051 0973	0.1686 2993	80
81	0.2453 0825	0.2220 8674	0.2010 8797	0.1649 1925	81
82	0.2410 8919	0.2179 9926	0.1971 4507	0.1612 9022	82
83	0.2369 4269	0.2139 8700	0.1932 7948	0.1577 4105	83
84	0.2328 6751	0.2100 4859	0.1894 8968	0.1542 6997	84
85	0.2288 6242	0.2061 8267	0.1857 7420	0.1508 7528	85
86	0.2249 2621	0.2023 8789	0.1821 3157	0.1475 5528	86
87	0.2210 5770	0.1986 6296	0.1785 6036	0.1443 0835	87
88	0.2172 5572	0.1950 0659	0.1750 5918	0.1411 3286	88
89	0.2135 1914	0.1914 1751	0.1716 2665	0.1380 2724	89
90	0.2098 4682	0.1878 9449	0.1682 6142	0.1349 8997	90
91	0.2062 3766	0.1844 3631	0.1649 6217	0.1320 1953	91
92	0.2026 9057	0.1810 4178	0.1617 2762	0.1291 1445	92
93	0.1992 0450	0.1777 0972	0.1585 5649	0.1262 7331	93
94	0.1957 7837	0.1744 3899	0.1554 4754	0.1234 9468	94
95	0.1924 1118	0.1712 2845	0.1523 9955	0.1207 7719	95
96	0.1891 0190	0.1680 7701	0.1494 1132	0.1181 1950	96
97	0.1858 4953	0.1649 8357	0.1464 8169	0.1155 2029	97
98	0.1826 5310	0.1619 4706	0.1436 0950	0.1129 7828	98
99	0.1795 1165	0.1589 6644	0.1407 9363	0.1104 9221	99
100	0.1764 2422	0.1560 4068	0.1380 3297	0.1080 6084	100

Reprinted, by permission, from Shao

PRESENT VALUE
When Compound Amount Is 1

$$p = (1 + i)^{-n} \quad [OR, v^n = (1 + i)^{-n}]$$

n	$2\frac{1}{2}\%$	$2\frac{3}{4}\%$	3%	$3\frac{1}{4}\%$	n
1	0.9756 0976	0.9732 3601	0.9708 7379	0.9685 2300	1
2	0.9518 1440	0.9471 8833	0.9425 9591	0.9380 3681	2
3	0.9285 9941	0.9218 3779	0.9151 4166	0.9085 1022	3
4	0.9059 5064	0.8971 6573	0.8884 8705	0.8799 1305	4
5	0.8838 5429	0.8731 5400	0.8626 0878	0.8522 1603	5
6	0.8622 9687	0.8497 8491	0.8374 8426	0.8253 9083	6
7	0.8412 6524	0.8270 4128	0.8130 9151	0.7994 1000	7
8	0.8207 4657	0.8049 0635	0.7894 0923	0.7742 4698	8
9	0.8007 2836	0.7833 6385	0.7664 1673	0.7498 7601	9
10	0.7811 9840	0.7623 9791	0.7440 9391	0.7262 7216	10
11	0.7621 4478	0.7419 9310	0.7224 2128	0.7034 1129	11
12	0.7435 5589	0.7221 3440	0.7013 7988	0.6812 7002	12
13	0.7254 2038	0.7028 0720	0.6809 5134	0.6598 2568	13
14	0.7077 2720	0.6839 9728	0.6611 1781	0.6390 5635	14
15	0.6904 6556	0.6656 9078	0.6418 6195	0.6189 4078	15
16	0.6736 2493	0.6478 7424	0.6231 6694	0.5994 5838	16
17	0.6571 9506	0.6305 3454	0.6050 1645	0.5805 8923	17
18	0.6411 6591	0.6136 5892	0.5873 9461	0.5623 1402	18
19	0.6255 2772	0.5972 3496	0.5702 8603	0.5446 1407	19
20	0.6102 7094	0.5812 5057	0.5536 7575	0.5274 7125	20
21	0.5953 8629	0.5656 9398	0.5375 4928	0.5108 6804	21
22	0.5808 6467	0.5505 5375	0.5218 9250	0.4947 8745	22
23	0.5666 9724	0.5358 1874	0.5066 9175	0.4792 1302	23
24	0.5528 7535	0.5214 7809	0.4919 3374	0.4641 2884	24
25	0.5393 9059	0.5075 2126	0.4776 0557	0.4495 1945	25
26	0.5262 3472	0.4939 3796	0.4636 9473	0.4353 6993	26
27	0.5133 9973	0.4807 1821	0.4501 8906	0.4216 6579	27
28	0.5008 7778	0.4678 5227	0.4370 7675	0.4083 9302	28
29	0.4886 6125	0.4553 3068	0.4243 4636	0.3955 3803	29
30	0.4767 4269	0.4431 4421	0.4119 8676	0.3830 8768	30
31	0.4651 1481	0.4312 8391	0.3999 8715	0.3710 2923	31
32	0.4537 7055	0.4197 4103	0.3883 3703	0.3593 5035	32
33	0.4427 0298	0.4085 0708	0.3770 2625	0.3480 3908	33
34	0.4319 0534	0.3975 7380	0.3660 4490	0.3370 8385	34
35	0.4213 7107	0.3869 3314	0.3553 8340	0.3264 7346	35
36	0.4110 9372	0.3765 7727	0.3450 3243	0.3161 9706	36
37	0.4010 6705	0.3664 9856	0.3349 8294	0.3062 4413	37
38	0.3912 8492	0.3566 8959	0.3252 2615	0.2966 0448	38
39	0.3817 4139	0.3471 4316	0.3157 5355	0.2872 6826	39
40	0.3724 3062	0.3378 5222	0.3065 5684	0.2782 2592	40
41	0.3633 4695	0.3288 0995	0.2976 2800	0.2694 6820	41
42	0.3544 8483	0.3200 0968	0.2889 5922	0.2609 8615	42
43	0.3458 3886	0.3114 4495	0.2805 4294	0.2527 7109	43
44	0.3374 0376	0.3031 0944	0.2723 7178	0.2448 1462	44
45	0.3291 7440	0.2949 9702	0.2644 3862	0.2371 0859	45
46	0.3211 4576	0.2871 0172	0.2567 3653	0.2296 4512	46
47	0.3133 1294	0.2794 1773	0.2492 5876	0.2224 1658	47
48	0.3056 7116	0.2719 3940	0.2419 9880	0.2154 1558	48
49	0.2982 1576	0.2646 6122	0.2349 5029	0.2086 3494	49
50	0.2909 4221	0.2575 7783	0.2281 0708	0.2020 6774	50

Reprinted, by permission, from Shao

PRESENT VALUE
When Compound Amount Is 1

$$p = (1 + i)^{-n} \quad [OR, v^n = (1 + i)^{-n}]$$

n	$2\frac{1}{2}\%$	$2\frac{3}{4}\%$	3 %	$3\frac{1}{4}\%$	n
51	0.2838 4606	0.2506 8402	0.2214 6318	0.1957 0725	51
52	0.2769 2298	0.2439 7471	0.2150 1280	0.1895 4698	52
53	0.2701 6876	0.2374 4497	0.2087 5029	0.1835 8061	53
54	0.2635 7928	0.2310 9000	0.2026 7019	0.1778 0204	54
55	0.2571 5052	0.2249 0511	0.1967 6717	0.1722 0537	55
56	0.2508 7855	0.2188 8575	0.1910 3609	0.1667 8486	56
57	0.2447 5956	0.2130 2749	0.1854 7193	0.1615 3497	57
58	0.2387 8982	0.2073 2603	0.1800 6984	0.1564 5034	58
59	0.2329 6568	0.2017 7716	0.1748 2508	0.1515 2575	59
60	0.2272 8359	0.1963 7679	0.1697 3309	0.1467 5617	60
61	0.2217 4009	0.1911 2097	0.1647 8941	0.1421 3673	61
62	0.2163 3179	0.1860 0581	0.1599 8972	0.1376 6269	62
63	0.2110 5541	0.1810 2755	0.1553 2982	0.1333 2948	63
64	0.2059 0771	0.1761 8253	0.1508 0565	0.1291 3267	64
65	0.2008 8557	0.1714 6718	0.1464 1325	0.1250 6796	65
66	0.1959 8593	0.1668 7804	0.1421 4879	0.1211 3120	66
67	0.1912 0578	0.1624 1172	0.1380 0853	0.1173 1835	67
68	0.1865 4223	0.1580 6493	0.1339 8887	0.1136 2552	68
69	0.1819 9242	0.1538 3448	0.1300 8628	0.1100 4893	69
70	0.1775 5358	0.1497 1726	0.1262 9736	0.1065 8492	70
71	0.1732 2300	0.1457 1023	0.1226 1880	0.1032 2995	71
72	0.1689 9805	0.1418 1044	0.1190 4737	0.0999 8058	72
73	0.1648 7615	0.1380 1503	0.1155 7998	0.0968 3349	73
74	0.1608 5478	0.1343 2119	0.1122 1357	0.0937 8546	74
75	0.1569 3149	0.1307 2622	0.1089 4521	0.0908 3338	75
76	0.1531 0389	0.1272 2747	0.1057 7205	0.0879 7422	76
77	0.1493 6965	0.1238 2235	0.1026 9131	0.0852 0505	77
78	0.1457 2649	0.1205 0837	0.0997 0030	0.0825 2305	78
79	0.1421 7218	0.1172 8309	0.0967 9641	0.0799 2548	79
80	0.1387 0457	0.1141 4412	0.0939 7710	0.0774 0966	80
81	0.1353 2153	0.1110 8917	0.0912 3990	0.0749 7304	81
82	0.1320 2101	0.1081 1598	0.0885 8243	0.0726 1311	82
83	0.1288 0098	0.1052 2237	0.0860 0236	0.0703 2747	83
84	0.1256 5949	0.1024 0620	0.0834 9743	0.0681 1377	84
85	0.1225 9463	0.0996 6540	0.0810 6547	0.0659 6976	85
86	0.1196 0452	0.0969 9795	0.0787 0434	0.0638 9323	86
87	0.1166 8733	0.0944 0190	0.0764 1198	0.0618 8206	87
88	0.1138 4130	0.0918 7533	0.0741 8639	0.0599 3420	88
89	0.1110 6468	0.0894 1638	0.0720 2562	0.0580 4765	89
90	0.1083 5579	0.0870 2324	0.0699 2779	0.0562 2048	90
91	0.1057 1296	0.0846 9415	0.0678 9105	0.0544 5083	91
92	0.1031 3460	0.0824 2740	0.0659 1364	0.0527 3688	92
93	0.1006 1912	0.0802 2131	0.0639 9383	0.0510 7688	93
94	0.0981 6500	0.0780 7427	0.0621 2993	0.0494 6914	94
95	0.0957 7073	0.0759 8469	0.0603 2032	0.0479 1200	95
96	0.0934 3486	0.0739 5104	0.0585 6342	0.0464 0387	96
97	0.0911 5596	0.0719 7181	0.0568 5769	0.0449 4322	97
98	0.0889 3264	0.0700 4556	0.0552 0164	0.0435 2854	98
99	0.0867 6355	0.0681 7086	0.0535 9382	0.0421 5839	99
100	0.0846 4737	0.0663 4634	0.0520 3284	0.0408 3137	100

Reprinted, by permission, from Shao

PRESENT VALUE
When Compound Amount Is 1

$$p = (1 + i)^{-n} \quad [OR,\ v^n = (1 + i)^{-n}]$$

n	$3\frac{1}{2}\%$	$3\frac{3}{4}\%$	4%	$4\frac{1}{2}\%$	n
1	0.9661 8357	0.9638 5542	0.9615 3846	0.9569 3780	1
2	0.9335 1070	0.9290 1727	0.9245 5621	0.9157 2995	2
3	0.9019 4271	0.8954 3834	0.8889 9636	0.8762 9660	3
4	0.8714 4223	0.8630 7310	0.8548 0419	0.8385 6134	4
5	0.8419 7317	0.8318 7768	0.8219 2711	0.8024 5105	5
6	0.8135 0064	0.8018 0981	0.7903 1453	0.7678 9574	6
7	0.7859 9096	0.7728 2874	0.7599 1781	0.7348 2846	7
8	0.7594 1156	0.7448 9517	0.7306 9020	0.7031 8513	8
9	0.7337 3097	0.7179 7125	0.7025 8674	0.6729 0443	9
10	0.7089 1881	0.6920 2048	0.6755 6417	0.6439 2768	10
11	0.6849 4571	0.6670 0769	0.6495 8093	0.6161 9874	11
12	0.6617 8330	0.6428 9898	0.6245 9705	0.5896 6386	12
13	0.6394 0415	0.6196 6167	0.6005 7409	0.5642 7164	13
14	0.6177 8179	0.5972 6426	0.5774 7508	0.5399 7286	14
15	0.5968 9062	0.5756 7639	0.5552 6450	0.5167 2044	15
16	0.5767 0591	0.5548 6881	0.5339 0818	0.4944 6932	16
17	0.5572 0378	0.5348 1331	0.5133 7325	0.4731 7639	17
18	0.5383 6114	0.5154 8271	0.4936 2812	0.4528 0037	18
19	0.5201 5569	0.4968 5080	0.4746 4242	0.4333 0179	19
20	0.5025 6588	0.4788 9234	0.4563 8695	0.4146 4286	20
21	0.4855 7090	0.4615 8298	0.4388 3360	0.3967 8743	21
22	0.4691 5063	0.4448 9926	0.4219 5539	0.3797 0089	22
23	0.4532 8563	0.4288 1856	0.4057 2633	0.3633 5013	23
24	0.4379 5713	0.4133 1910	0.3901 2147	0.3477 0347	24
25	0.4231 4699	0.3983 7985	0.3751 1680	0.3327 3060	25
26	0.4088 3767	0.3839 8058	0.3606 8923	0.3184 0248	26
27	0.3950 1224	0.3701 0176	0.3468 1657	0.3046 9137	27
28	0.3816 5434	0.3567 2459	0.3334 7747	0.2915 7069	28
29	0.3687 4816	0.3438 3093	0.3206 5141	0.2790 1502	29
30	0.3562 7841	0.3314 0331	0.3083 1867	0.2670 0002	30
31	0.3442 3035	0.3194 2487	0.2964 6026	0.2555 0241	31
32	0.3325 8971	0.3078 7940	0.2850 5794	0.2444 9991	32
33	0.3213 4271	0.2967 5123	0.2740 9417	0.2339 7121	33
34	0.3104 7605	0.2860 2528	0.2635 5209	0.2238 9589	34
35	0.2999 7686	0.2756 8702	0.2534 1547	0.2142 5444	35
36	0.2898 3272	0.2657 2242	0.2436 6872	0.2050 2817	36
37	0.2800 3161	0.2561 1800	0.2342 9685	0.1961 9921	37
38	0.2705 6194	0.2468 6072	0.2252 8543	0.1877 5044	38
39	0.2614 1250	0.2379 3805	0.2166 2061	0.1796 6549	39
40	0.2525 7247	0.2293 3788	0.2082 8904	0.1719 2870	40
41	0.2440 3137	0.2210 4855	0.2002 7793	0.1645 2507	41
42	0.2357 7910	0.2130 5885	0.1925 7493	0.1574 4026	42
43	0.2278 0590	0.2053 5793	0.1851 6820	0.1506 6054	43
44	0.2201 0231	0.1979 3535	0.1780 4635	0.1441 7276	44
45	0.2126 5924	0.1907 8106	0.1711 9841	0.1379 6437	45
46	0.2054 6787	0.1838 8536	0.1646 1386	0.1320 2332	46
47	0.1985 1968	0.1772 3890	0.1582 8256	0.1263 3810	47
48	0.1918 0645	0.1708 3268	0.1521 9476	0.1208 9771	48
49	0.1853 2024	0.1646 5800	0.1463 4112	0.1156 9158	49
50	0.1790 5337	0.1587 0651	0.1407 1262	0.1107 0965	50

Reprinted, by permission, from Shao

PRESENT VALUE
When Compound Amount Is 1

$$p = (1 + i)^{-n} \quad [OR, \ v^n = (1 + i)^{-n}]$$

n	$3\frac{1}{2}\%$	$3\frac{3}{4}\%$	4 %	$4\frac{1}{2}\%$	n
51	0.1729 9843	0.1529 7013	0.1353 0059	0.1059 4225	51
52	0.1671 4824	0.1474 4109	0.1300 9672	0.1013 8014	52
53	0.1614 9589	0.1421 1189	0.1250 9300	0.0970 1449	53
54	0.1560 3467	0.1369 7532	0.1202 8173	0.0928 3683	54
55	0.1507 5814	0.1320 2440	0.1156 5551	0.0888 3907	55
56	0.1456 6004	0.1272 5243	0.1112 0722	0.0850 1347	56
57	0.1407 3433	0.1226 5295	0.1069 3002	0.0813 5260	57
58	0.1359 7520	0.1182 1971	0.1028 1733	0.0778 4938	58
59	0.1313 7701	0.1139 4671	0.0988 6282	0.0744 9701	59
60	0.1269 3431	0.1098 2815	0.0950 6040	0.0712 8901	60
61	0.1226 4184	0.1058 5846	0.0914 0423	0.0682 1915	61
62	0.1184 9453	0.1020 3225	0.0878 8868	0.0652 8148	62
63	0.1144 8747	0.0983 4434	0.0845 0835	0.0624 7032	63
64	0.1106 1591	0.0947 8972	0.0812 5803	0.0597 8021	64
65	0.1068 7528	0.0913 6359	0.0781 3272	0.0572 0594	65
66	0.1032 6114	0.0880 6129	0.0751 2762	0.0547 4253	66
67	0.0997 6922	0.0848 7835	0.0722 3809	0.0523 8519	67
68	0.0963 9538	0.0818 1046	0.0694 5970	0.0501 2937	68
69	0.0931 3563	0.0788 5346	0.0667 8818	0.0479 7069	69
70	0.0899 8612	0.0760 0333	0.0642 1940	0.0459 0497	70
71	0.0869 4311	0.0732 5622	0.0617 4942	0.0439 2820	71
72	0.0840 0300	0.0706 0841	0.0593 7445	0.0420 3655	72
73	0.0811 6232	0.0680 5630	0.0570 9081	0.0402 2637	73
74	0.0784 1770	0.0655 9643	0.0548 9501	0.0384 9413	74
75	0.0757 6590	0.0632 2547	0.0527 8367	0.0368 3649	75
76	0.0732 0376	0.0609 4022	0.0507 5353	0.0352 5023	76
77	0.0707 2828	0.0587 3756	0.0488 0147	0.0337 3228	77
78	0.0683 3650	0.0566 1451	0.0469 2449	0.0322 7969	78
79	0.0660 2560	0.0545 6821	0.0451 1970	0.0308 8965	79
80	0.0637 9285	0.0525 9586	0.0433 8433	0.0295 5948	80
81	0.0616 3561	0.0506 9481	0.0417 1570	0.0282 8658	81
82	0.0595 5131	0.0488 6246	0.0401 1125	0.0270 6850	82
83	0.0575 3750	0.0470 9635	0.0385 6851	0.0259 0287	83
84	0.0555 9178	0.0453 9407	0.0370 8510	0.0247 8744	84
85	0.0537 1187	0.0437 5332	0.0356 5875	0.0237 2003	85
86	0.0518 9553	0.0421 7188	0.0342 8726	0.0226 9860	86
87	0.0501 4060	0.0406 4759	0.0329 6852	0.0217 2115	87
88	0.0484 4503	0.0391 7840	0.0317 0050	0.0207 8579	88
89	0.0468 0679	0.0377 6232	0.0304 8125	0.0198 9070	89
90	0.0452 2395	0.0363 9741	0.0293 0890	0.0190 3417	90
91	0.0436 9464	0.0350 8184	0.0281 8163	0.0182 1451	91
92	0.0422 1704	0.0338 1383	0.0270 9772	0.0174 3016	92
93	0.0407 8941	0.0325 9164	0.0260 5550	0.0166 7958	93
94	0.0394 1006	0.0314 1363	0.0250 5337	0.0159 6132	94
95	0.0380 7735	0.0302 7820	0.0240 8978	0.0152 7399	95
96	0.0367 8971	0.0291 8380	0.0231 6325	0.0146 1626	96
97	0.0355 4562	0.0281 2897	0.0222 7235	0.0139 8685	97
98	0.0343 4359	0.0271 1226	0.0214 1572	0.0133 8454	98
99	0.0331 8221	0.0261 3230	0.0205 9204	0.0128 0817	99
100	0.0320 6011	0.0251 8776	0.0198 0004	0.0122 5663	100

Reprinted, by permission, from Shao

PRESENT VALUE
When Compound Amount Is 1
$$p = (1 + i)^{-n} \quad [OR, v^n = (1 + i)^{-n}]$$

n	5 %	$5\frac{1}{2}\%$	6 %	$6\frac{1}{2}\%$	n
1	0.9523 8095	0.9478 6730	0.9433 9623	0.9389 6714	1
2	0.9070 2948	0.8984 5242	0.8899 9644	0.8816 5928	2
3	0.8638 3760	0.8516 1366	0.8396 1928	0.8278 4909	3
4	0.8227 0247	0.8072 1674	0.7920 9366	0.7773 2309	4
5	0.7835 2617	0.7651 3435	0.7472 5817	0.7298 8084	5
6	0.7462 1540	0.7252 4583	0.7049 6054	0.6853 3412	6
7	0.7106 8133	0.6874 3681	0.6650 5711	0.6435 0621	7
8	0.6768 3936	0.6515 9887	0.6274 1237	0.6042 3119	8
9	0.6446 0892	0.6176 2926	0.5918 9846	0.5673 5323	9
10	0.6139 1325	0.5854 3058	0.5583 9478	0.5327 2604	10
11	0.5846 7929	0.5549 1050	0.5267 8753	0.5002 1224	11
12	0.5568 3742	0.5259 8152	0.4969 6936	0.4696 8285	12
13	0.5303 2135	0.4985 6068	0.4688 3902	0.4410 1676	13
14	0.5050 6795	0.4725 6937	0.4423 0096	0.4141 0025	14
15	0.4810 1710	0.4479 3305	0.4172 6506	0.3888 2652	15
16	0.4581 1152	0.4245 8109	0.3936 4628	0.3650 9533	16
17	0.4362 9669	0.4024 4653	0.3713 6442	0.3428 1251	17
18	0.4155 2065	0.3814 6590	0.3503 4379	0.3218 8969	18
19	0.3957 3396	0.3615 7906	0.3305 1301	0.3022 4384	19
20	0.3768 8948	0.3427 2896	0.3118 0473	0.2837 9703	20
21	0.3589 4236	0.3248 6158	0.2941 5540	0.2664 7608	21
22	0.3418 4987	0.3079 2566	0.2775 0510	0.2502 1228	22
23	0.3255 7131	0.2918 7267	0.2617 9726	0.2349 4111	23
24	0.3100 6791	0.2766 5656	0.2469 7855	0.2206 0198	24
25	0.2953 0277	0.2622 3370	0.2329 9863	0.2071 3801	25
26	0.2812 4074	0.2485 6275	0.2198 1003	0.1944 9579	26
27	0.2678 4832	0.2356 0450	0.2073 6795	0.1826 2515	27
28	0.2550 9364	0.2233 2181	0.1956 3014	0.1714 7902	28
29	0.2429 4632	0.2116 7944	0.1845 5674	0.1610 1316	29
30	0.2313 7745	0.2006 4402	0.1741 1013	0.1511 8607	30
31	0.2203 5947	0.1901 8390	0.1642 5484	0.1419 5875	31
32	0.2098 6617	0.1802 6910	0.1549 5740	0.1332 9460	32
33	0.1998 7254	0.1708 7119	0.1461 8622	0.1251 5925	33
34	0.1903 5480	0.1619 6321	0.1379 1153	0.1175 2042	34
35	0.1812 9029	0.1535 1963	0.1301 0522	0.1103 4781	35
36	0.1726 5741	0.1455 1624	0.1227 4077	0.1036 1297	36
37	0.1644 3563	0.1379 3008	0.1157 9318	0.0972 8917	37
38	0.1566 0536	0.1307 3941	0.1092 3885	0.0913 5134	38
39	0.1491 4797	0.1239 2362	0.1030 5552	0.0857 7590	39
40	0.1420 4568	0.1174 6314	0.0972 2219	0.0805 4075	40
41	0.1352 8160	0.1113 3947	0.0917 1904	0.0756 2512	41
42	0.1288 3962	0.1055 3504	0.0865 2740	0.0710 0950	42
43	0.1227 0440	0.1000 3322	0.0816 2962	0.0666 7559	43
44	0.1168 6133	0.0948 1822	0.0770 0908	0.0626 0619	44
45	0.1112 9651	0.0898 7509	0.0726 5007	0.0587 8515	45
46	0.1059 9668	0.0851 8965	0.0685 3781	0.0551 9733	46
47	0.1009 4921	0.0807 4849	0.0646 5831	0.0518 2848	47
48	0.0961 4211	0.0765 3885	0.0609 9840	0.0486 6524	48
49	0.0915 6391	0.0725 4867	0.0575 4566	0.0456 9506	49
50	0.0872 0373	0.0687 6652	0.0542 8836	0.0429 0616	50

Reprinted, by permission, from Shao

PRESENT VALUE
When Compound Amount Is 1

$$p = (1 + i)^{-n} \quad [OR, v^n = (1 + i)^{-n}]$$

n	5 %	$5\frac{1}{2}$ %	6 %	$6\frac{1}{2}$ %	n
51	0.0830 5117	0.0651 8153	0.0512 1544	0.0402 8747	51
52	0.0790 9635	0.0617 8344	0.0483 1645	0.0378 2861	52
53	0.0753 2986	0.0585 6250	0.0455 8156	0.0355 1982	53
54	0.0717 4272	0.0555 0948	0.0430 0147	0.0333 5195	54
55	0.0683 2640	0.0526 1562	0.0405 6742	0.0313 1638	55
56	0.0650 7276	0.0498 7263	0.0382 7115	0.0294 0505	56
57	0.0619 7406	0.0472 7263	0.0361 0486	0.0276 1038	57
58	0.0590 2291	0.0448 0818	0.0340 6119	0.0259 2524	58
59	0.0562 1230	0.0424 7221	0.0321 3320	0.0243 4295	59
60	0.0535 3552	0.0402 5802	0.0303 1434	0.0228 5723	60
61	0.0509 8621	0.0381 5926.	0.0285 9843	0.0214 6218	61
62	0.0485 5830	0.0361 6992	0.0269 7965	0.0201 5229	62
63	0.0462 4600	0.0342 8428	0.0354 5250	0.0189 2233	63
64	0.0440 4381	0.0324 9695	0.0240 1179	0.0177 6745	64
65	0.0419 4648	0.0308 0279	0.0226 5264	0.0166 8305	65
66	0.0399 4903	0.0291 9696	0.0213 7041	0.0156 6484	66
67	0.0380 4670	0.0276 7485	0.0201 6077	0.0147 0877	67
68	0.0362 3495	0.0262 3208	0.0190 1959	0.0138 1105	68
69	0.0345 0948	0.0248 6453	0.0179 4301	0.0129 6812	69
70	0.0328 6617	0.0235 6828	0.0169 2737	0.0121 7664	70
71	0.0313 0111	0.0223 3960	0.0159 6921	0.0114 3346	71
72	0.0298 1058	0.0211 7498	0.0150 6530	0.0107 3565	72
73	0.0283 9103	0.0200 7107	0.0142 1254	0.0100 8042	73
74	0.0270 3908	0.0190 2471	0.0134 0806	0.0094 6518	74
75	0.0257 5150	0.0180 3290	0.0126 4911	0.0088 8750	75
76	0.0245 2524	0.0170 9279	0.0119 3313	0.0083 4507	76
77	0.0233 5737	0.0162 0170	0.0112 5767	0.0078 3574	77
78	0.0222 4512	0.0153 5706	0.0106 2044	0.0073 5751	78
79	0.0211 8582	0.0145 5646	0.0100 1928	0.0069 0846	79
80	0.0201 7698	0.0137 9759	0.0094 5215	0.0064 8681	80
81	0.0192 1617	0.0130 7828	0.0089 1713	0.0060 9090	81
82	0.0183 0111	0.0123 9648	0.0084 1238	0.0057 1916	82
83	0.0174 2963	0.0117 5022	0.0079 3621	0.0053 7010	83
84	0.0165 9965	0.0111 3765	0.0074 8699	0.0050 4235	84
85	0.0158 0919	0.0105 5701	0.0070 6320	0.0047 3460	85
86	0.0150 5637	0.0100 0664	0.0066 6340	0.0044 4563	86
87	0.0143 3940	0.0094 8497	0.0062 8622	0.0041 7430	87
88	0.0136 5657	0.0089 9049	0.0059 3040	0.0039 1953	88
89	0.0130 0626	0.0085 2180	0.0055 9472	0.0036 8031	89
90	0.0123 8691	0.0080 7753	0.0052 7803	0.0034 5569	90
91	0.0117 9706	0.0076 5643	0.0049 7928	0.0032 4478	91
92	0.0112 3530	0.0072 5728	0.0046 9743	0.0030 4674	92
93	0.0107 0028	0.0068 7894	0.0044 3154	0.0028 6079	93
94	0.0101 9074	0.0065 2032	0.0041 8070	0.0026 8619	94
95	0.0097 0547	0.0061 8040	0.0039 4405	0.0025 2224	95
96	0.0092 4331	0.0058 5820	0.0037 2081	0.0023 6831	96
97	0.0088 0315	0.0055 5279	0.0035 1019	0.0022 2376	97
98	0.0083 8395	0.0052 6331	0.0033 1150	0.0020 8804	98
99	0.0079 8471	0.0049 8892	0.0031 2406	0.0019 6060	99
100	0.0076 0449	0.0047 2883	0.0029 4723	0.0018 4094	100

Reprinted, by permission, from Shao

PRESENT VALUE
When Compound Amount Is 1

$$p = (1 + i)^{-n} \quad [OR, \ v^n = (1 + i)^{-n}]$$

n	7 %	$7\frac{1}{2}$ %	8 %	$8\frac{1}{2}$ %	n
1	0.9345 7944	0.9302 3256	0.9259 2593	0.9216 5899	1
2	0.8734 3873	0.8653 3261	0.8573 3882	0.8494 5529	2
3	0.8162 9788	0.8049 6057	0.7938 3224	0.7829 0810	3
4	0.7628 9521	0.7488 0053	0.7350 2985	0.7215 7428	4
5	0.7129 8618	0.6965 5863	0.6805 8320	0.6650 4542	5
6	0.6663 4222	0.6479 6152	0.6301 6963	0.6129 4509	6
7	0.6227 4974	0.6027 5490	0.5834 9040	0.5649 2635	7
8	0.5820 0910	0.5607 0223	0.5402 6888	0.5206 6945	8
9	0.5439 3374	0.5215 8347	0.5002 4897	0.4798 7968	9
10	0.5083 4929	0.4851 9393	0.4631 9349	0.4422 8542	10
11	0.4750 9280	0.4513 4319	0.4288 8286	0.4076 3633	11
12	0.4440 1196	0.4198 5413	0.3971 1376	0.3757 0168	12
13	0.4149 6445	0.3905 6198	0.3676 9792	0.3462 6883	13
14	0.3878 1724	0.3633 1347	0.3404 6104	0.3191 4178	14
15	0.3624 4602	0.3379 6602	0.3152 4170	0.2941 3989	15
16	0.3387 3460	0.3143 8699	0.2918 9047	0.2710 9667	16
17	0.3165 7439	0.2924 5302	0.2702 6895	0.2498 5869	17
18	0.2958 6392	0.2720 4932	0.2502 4903	0.2302 8450	18
19	0.2765 0833	0.2530 6913	0.2317 1206	0.2122 4378	19
20	0.2584 1900	0.2354 1315	0.2145 4821	0.1956 1639	20
21	0.2415 1309	0.2189 8897	0.1986 5575	0.1802 9160	21
22	0.2257 1317	0.2037 1067	0.1839 4051	0.1661 6738	22
23	0.2109 4688	0.1894 9830	0.1703 1528	0.1531 4965	23
24	0.1971 4662	0.1762 7749	0.1576 9934	0.1411 5176	24
25	0.1842 4918	0.1639 7906	0.1460 1790	0.1300 9378	25
26	0.1721 9549	0.1525 3866	0.1352 0176	0.1199 0210	26
27	0.1609 3037	0.1418 9643	0.1251 8682	0.1105 0885	27
28	0.1504 0221	0.1319 9668	0.1159 1372	0.1018 5148	28
29	0.1405 6282	0.1227 8761	0.1073 2752	0.0938 7233	29
30	0.1313 6712	0.1142 2103	0.0993 7733	0.0865 1828	30
31	0.1227 7301	0.1062 5212	0.0920 1605	0.0797 4035	31
32	0.1147 4113	0.0988 3918	0.0852 0005	0.0734 9341	32
33	0.1072 3470	0.0919 4343	0.0788 8893	0.0677 3586	33
34	0.1002 1934	0.0855 2877	0.0730 4531	0.0624 2936	34
35	0.0936 6294	0.0795 6164	0.0676 3454	0.0575 3858	35
36	0.0875 3546	0.0740 1083	0.0626 2458	0.0530 3095	36
37	0.0818 0884	0.0688 4729	0.0579 8572	0.0488 7645	37
38	0.0764 5686	0.0640 4399	0.0536 9048	0.0450 4742	38
39	0.0714 5501	0.0595 7580	0.0497 1341	0.0415 1836	39
40	0.0667 8038	0.0554 1935	0.0460 3093	0.0382 6577	40
41	0.0624 1157	0.0515 5288	0.0426 2123	0.0352 6799	41
42	0.0583 2857	0.0479 5617	0.0394 6411	0.0325 0506	42
43	0.0545 1268	0.0446 1039	0.0365 4084	0.0299 5858	43
44	0.0509 4643	0.0414 9804	0.0338 3411	0.0276 1160	44
45	0.0476 1349	0.0386 0283	0.0313 2788	0.0254 4848	45
46	0.0444 9859	0.0359 0961	0.0290 0730	0.0234 5482	46
47	0.0415 8746	0.0334 0428	0.0268 5861	0.0216 1734	47
48	0.0388 6679	0.0310 7375	0.0248 6908	0.0199 2382	48
49	0.0363 2410	0.0289 0582	0.0230 2693	0.0183 6297	49
50	0.0339 4776	0.0268 8913	0.0213 2123	0.0169 2439	50

Reprinted, by permission, from Shao

PRESENT VALUE
When Compound Amount Is 1

$$p = (1 + i)^{-n} \quad [OR, v^n = (1 + i)^{-n}]$$

n	7 %	$7\frac{1}{2}$ %	8 %	$8\frac{1}{2}$ %	n
51	0.0317 2688	0.0250 1315	0.0197 4188	0.0155 9852	51
52	0.0296 5129	0.0232 6804	0.0182 7952	0.0143 7651	52
53	0.0277 1148	0.0216 4469	0.0169 2548	0.0132 5024	53
54	0.0258 9858	0.0201 3460	0.0156 7174	0.0122 1221	54
55	0.0242 0428	0.0187 2986	0.0145 1087	0.0112 5549	55
56	0.0226 2083	0.0174 2312	0.0134 3599	0.0103 7372	56
57	0.0211 4096	0.0162 0756	0.0124 4073	0.0095 6104	57
58	0.0197 5791	0.0150 7680	0.0115 1920	0.0088 1201	58
59	0.0184 6533	0.0140 2493	0.0106 6592	0.0081 2167	59
60	0.0172 5732	0.0130 4644	0.0098 7585	0.0074 8541	60
61	0.0161 2834	0.0121 3623	0.0091 4431	0.0068 9900	61
62	0.0150 7321	0.0112 8951	0.0084 6695	0.0063 5852	62
63	0.0140 8711	0.0105 0187	0.0078 3977	0.0058 6039	63
64	0.0131 6553	0.0097 6918	0.0072 5905	0.0054 0128	64
65	0.0123 0423	0.0090 8761	0.0067 2134	0.0049 7814	65
66	0.0114 9928	0.0084 5359	0.0062 2346	0.0045 8815	66
67	0.0107 4699	0.0078 6381	0.0057 6247	0.0042 2871	67
68	0.0100 4392	0.0073 1517	0.0053 3562	0.0038 9743	68
69	0.0093 8684	0.0068 0481	0.0049 4039	0.0035 9210	69
70	0.0087 7275	0.0063 3006	0.0045 7443	0.0033 1069	70
71	0.0081 9883	0.0058 8842	0.0042 3558	0.0030 5133	71
72	0.0076 6246	0.0054 7760	0.0039 2184	0.0028 1228	72
73	0.0071 6117	0.0050 9544	0.0036 3133	0.0025 9196	73
74	0.0066 9269	0.0047 3995	0.0033 6234	0.0023 8891	74
75	0.0062 5485	0.0044 0925	0.0031 1328	0.0022 0176	75
76	0.0058 4565	0.0041 0163	0.0028 8267	0.0020 2927	76
77	0.0054 6323	0.0038 1547	0.0026 6914	0.0018 7030	77
78	0.0051 0582	0.0035 4928	0.0024 7142	0.0017 2377	78
79	0.0047 7179	0.0033 0165	0.0022 8835	0.0015 8873	79
80	0.0044 5962	0.0030 7130	0.0021 1885	0.0014 6427	80
81	0.0041 6787	0.0028 5703	0.0019 6190	0.0013 4956	81
82	0.0038 9520	0.0026 5770	0.0018 1657	0.0012 4383	82
83	0.0036 4038	0.0024 7228	0.0016 8201	0.0011 4639	83
84	0.0034 0222	0.0022 9979	0.0015 5742	0.0010 5658	84
85	0.0031 7965	0.0021 3934	0.0014 4205	0.0009 7381	85
86	0.0029 7163	0.0019 9009	0.0013 3523	0.0008 9752	86
87	0.0027 7723	0.0018 5124	0.0012 3633	0.0008 2720	87
88	0.0025 9554	0.0017 2209	0.0011 4475	0.0007 6240	88
89	0.0024 2574	0.0016 0194	0.0010 5995	0.0007 0267	89
90	0.0022 6704	0.0014 9018	0.0009 8144	0.0006 4762	90
91	0.0021 1873	0.0013 8621	0.0009 0874	0.0005 9689	91
92	0.0019 8012	0.0012 8950	0.0008 4142	0.0005 5013	92
93	0.0018 5058	0.0011 9953	0.0007 7910	0.0005 0703	93
94	0.0017 2952	0.0011 1585	0.0007 2138	0.0004 6731	94
95	0.0016 1637	0.0010 3800	0.0006 6795	0.0004 3070	95
96	0.0015 1063	0.0009 6558	0.0006 1847	0.0003 9696	96
97	0.0014 1180	0.0008 9821	0.0005 7266	0.0003 6586	97
98	0.0013 1944	0.0008 3555	0.0005 3024	0.0003 3720	98
99	0.0012 3312	0.0007 7725	0.0004 9096	0.0003 1078	99
100	0.0011 5245	0.0007 2303	0.0004 5459	0.0002 8644	100

Reprinted, by permission, from Shao

SQUARE ROOTS

TABLE A-3   Squares and Square Roots

N	N²	√N	√10N	N	N²	√N	√10N
1	1	1.00 000	3.16 228	51	2 601	7.14 143	22.58 32
2	4	1.41 421	4.47 214	52	2 704	7.21 110	22.80 35
3	9	1.73 205	5.47 723	53	2 809	7.28 011	23.02 17
4	16	2.00 000	6.32 456	54	2 916	7.34 847	23.23 79
5	25	2.23 607	7.07 107	55	3 025	7.41 620	23.45 21
6	36	2.44 949	7.74 597	56	3 136	7.48 331	23.66 43
7	49	2.64 575	8.36 660	57	3 249	7.54 983	23.87 47
8	64	2.82 843	8.94 427	58	3 364	7.61 577	24.08 32
9	81	3.00 000	9.48 683	59	3 481	7.68 115	24.28 99
10	100	3.16 228	10.00 00	60	3 600	7.74 597	24.49 49
11	121	3.31 662	10.48 81	61	3 721	7.81 025	24.69 82
12	144	3.46 410	10.95 45	62	3 844	7.87 401	24.89 98
13	169	3.60 555	11.40 18	63	3 969	7.93 725	25.09 98
14	196	3.74 166	11.83 22	64	4 096	8.00 000	25.29 82
15	225	3.87 298	12.24 74	65	4 225	8.06 226	25.49 51
16	256	4.00 000	12.64 91	66	4 356	8.12 404	25.69 05
17	289	4.12 311	13.03 84	67	4 489	8.18 535	25.88 44
18	324	4.24 264	13.41 64	68	4 624	8.24 621	26.07 68
19	361	4.35 890	13.78 40	69	4 761	8.30 662	26.26 79
20	400	4.47 214	14.14 21	70	4 900	8.36 660	26.45 75
21	441	4.58 258	14.49 14	71	5 041	8.42 615	26.64 58
22	484	4.69 042	14.83 24	72	5 184	8.48 528	26.83 28
23	529	4.79 583	15.16 58	73	5 329	8.54 400	27.01 85
24	576	4.89 898	15.49 19	74	5 476	8.60 233	27.20 29
25	625	5.00 000	15.81 14	75	5 625	8.66 025	27.38 61
26	676	5.09 902	16.12 45	76	5 776	8.71 780	27.56 81
27	729	5.19 615	16.43 17	77	5 929	8.77 496	27.74 89
28	784	5.29 150	16.73 32	78	6 084	8.83 176	27.92 85
29	841	5.38 516	17.02 94	79	6 241	8.88 819	28.10 69
30	900	5.47 723	17.32 05	80	6 400	8.94 427	28.28 43
31	961	5.56 776	17.60 68	81	6 561	9.00 000	28.46 05
32	1 024	5.65 685	17.88 85	82	6 724	9.05 539	28.63 56
33	1 089	5.74 456	18.16 59	83	6 889	9.11 043	28.80 97
34	1 156	5.83 095	18.43 91	84	7 056	9.16 515	28.98 28
35	1 225	5.91 608	18.70 83	85	7 225	9.21 954	29.15 48
36	1 296	6.00 000	18.97 37	86	7 396	9.27 362	29.32 58
37	1 369	6.08 276	19.23 54	87	7 569	9.32 738	29.49 58
38	1 444	6.16 441	19.49 36	88	7 744	9.38 083	29.66 48
39	1 521	6.24 500	19.74 84	89	7 921	9.43 398	29.83 29
40	1 600	6.32 456	20.00 00	90	8 100	9.48 683	30.00 00
41	1 681	6.40 312	20.24 85	91	8 281	9.53 939	30.16 62
42	1 764	6.48 074	20.49 39	92	8 464	9.59 166	30.33 15
43	1 849	6.55 744	20.73 64	93	8 649	9.64 365	30.49 59
44	1 936	6.63 325	20.97 62	94	8 836	9.69 536	30.65 94
45	2 025	6.70 820	21.21 32	95	9 025	9.74 679	30.82 21
46	2 116	6.78 233	21.44 76	96	9 216	9.79 796	30.98 39
47	2 209	6.85 565	21.67 95	97	9 409	9.84 886	31.14 48
48	2 304	6.92 820	21.90 89	98	9 604	9.89 949	31.30 50
49	2 401	7.00 000	22.13 59	99	9 801	9.94 987	31.46 43
50	2 500	7.07 107	22.36 07	100	10 000	10.00 000	31.62 28
N	N²	√N	√10N	N	N²	√N	√10N

Answers: Exercises and Self-Tests

EXERCISE 1.1 (page 6)

1. a. no   b. yes   c. yes   d. no   e. yes

3. a. the set of the three officers on the Howard Hues Co. board of directors
   b. {Mr. Black, Mr. Brown, Mr. White}

5. a. {Marathn Oil, McDonald, Ill Power}
   b. ϕ
   c. {Marathn Oil, McDonald, Ill Power, Texasgulf, Am T&T wt, Am Tel & Tel, FedNat Mfg, NatCashR, Phillips Pet, IntTelTel}
   d. {Marathn Oil, McDonald, Ill Power, Texasgulf, Am T&T wt, Am Tel & Tel}

7. a. {3,4}   b. {a,e,i,o,u}   c. {T,A,L,H,S,E}

9. {6, 7}

EXERCISE 1.2 (page 14)

1. 17
3. 14
5. 77
7. 552
9. 4312
11. 194
13. 210
15. 97
17. 2312
19. 2765
21. a, c
23. 151
25. 140
27. 990
29. a. 2   c. 8
    b. 2   d. 3

31. a.

53	354
37	198
90	552

b.

	checking number
37 →	1
53 →	8
90 →	0

	checking number
354 →	3
198 →	0
552 →	3

35. $6040
37. $5225
39. a. $21,160
    b. $2,656
41. 2407
43. $2562
45. $9447 million
47. 44
49. a. 14, 810
    b. 2, 425
51. Thursday, 26
53. a. 115   b. 206   c. 234
55. a. $1054   b. $952

EXERCISE 1.3 (page 28)

1. a. 14   b. 6   c. 196   d. 239   e. 88

3. a.

	checking number
18	9
+ 14	5
32	5

b.

	checking number
39	3
+ 6	6
45	0

c.

	checking number
349	7
+ 196	7
545	5

d.

	3
435	3
+ 239	5
674	8

e.

	4
877	4
+ 88	7
965	2

5. $4.00

7. $6.00

9. dress $26.00;   coat $22.00;   shoes $7.00

11. $30.00

13. $(58 + 3) - (17 + 3) = 41$

15. $(432 + 8) - (392 + 8) = 40$

17. $(573 + 11) - (289 + 11) = 284$

19. $(453 + 13) - (187 + 13) = 266$

21. $7033

23. $9802

25. $1200

27. $234,884

29. $679

31. $201 profit

33.
$34,842,808	total operating income
− 29,418,960	total operating expenses
5,423,848	INCOME BEFORE TAXES
− 770,354	applicable income taxes and minority interest
4,653,494	INCOME BEFORE SECURITIES GAINS OR LOSSES

35. $2,094,982

37.
1970 − 126,252,000
1971 − 127,929,000
1972 − 127,135,000
1973 − 125,866,000

EXERCISE 1.4 (page 39)

1.   a. 15,390   b. 30,114   c. 24,531   d. 36,822

3.   a.

	checking number	b.		checking number	c.		checking number
342	0		478	1		629	8
× 45	× 0		× 63	× 0		× 39	× 3
15,390	0		30,114	0		24,531	6

   d.

969	6
× 38	× 2
36,822	3

5.   a. 18   b. 6   c. 2   d. 49

7.   a. 378   b. 399   c. 448   d. 264   e. 39
   f. 1,530

9.   a. $8(50 - 1) = 8(50) - 8(1) = 392$
   b. $5(40 - 2) = 5(40) - 5(2) = 190$
   c. $7(100 - 1) = 7(100) - 7(1) = 693$
   d. $4(50 - 2) = 4(50) - 4(2) = 192$

11.   a. 10,850   b. 11,546   c. 4,884   d. 15,351

13.   a. 12,555   b. 12,684   c. 6,754   d. 108,960

15. $4,320,000

17. $252

19. $256

21. $10,074

23. $3,029

25.   a. $13.50   b. $11.00   c. $9.18

EXERCISE 1.5 (page 48)

1.   a. 3 r54   b. 2 r110   c. 24 r176   d. 930

3.

a.	134	b.	234	c.	345	d.	10
	× 3		× 2		× 24		× 930
	402		468		8280		9300
	+ 54		+ 110		+ 176		
	456		578		8456		

5. $4.00

7.   gidget—$7.00; gadget—$9.00

9.   64

11. $7.00

13.   a. $16.50   b. $22.00   c. $24.75   d. $27.75

15.   a. 14   b. 6   c. 50   d. 280

17.   a. 1586   b. 793   c. 393

19.   1,850,000

EXERCISE 1.6 (page 56)

1.   a. −18   b. 14   c. −9   d. 8   e. −4

3.   a. −3   b. 3   c. −8   d. −10

5.   a. 5   b. −1   c. −1   d. −7

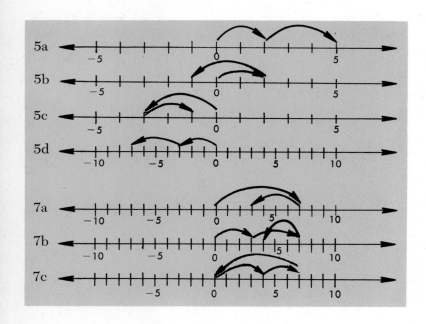

7.   a. 3   b. 4   c. 0

9.   a. −1   b. 2   c. 7   d. 11

11.   a. 12   b. 3   c. −1   d. 7

13.   15,156,000 bushels

15.   a. 30¢   b. 22¢   c. 17¢   d. 8¢   e. 36¢
       f. 35¢

17. $174 million total income

19. $215

EXERCISE 1.7 (page 62)

1.   a. 32   b. −56   c. −45   d. 27

3.   a. 12   b. 32

5.   a. 108   b. −113   c. −108   d. 113

7.

Olds Supr.	$1188
Chevy Imp.	$1128
Buick	$1572
Cadillac	$1908
Pontiac	$1464
Eldorado	$2592

9. $56,600

11. $2.00

13.   −1

15. $31,000

17. $1,767

19. $6,000 gross profit

SELF-TEST/CHAPTER 1 (page 65)

1.   a. {a,b,c}   b. {1,2,3,4}   c. {B,U,S,I,N,E}

2.   c

3.   a

4.   a. 3   b. 4   c. 2

5.   a. 15,312   b. 4,075

6.   a. $2.70   b. $6.00   c. $2.52

7.

	TOTAL HOURS	TOTAL WAGES
Rex, T	35	$ 87.50
Jones, J	37	$114.70
Phillips, P	33	$ 92.40

8.   a. −16   b. 7   c. 40

9.   a. 3   b. 27   c. 116

10.   a. −2

       b. 5

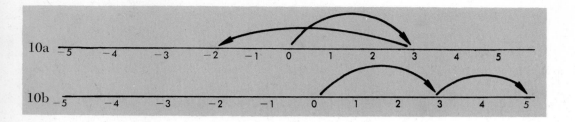

11. a. 360   b. −507   c. 115

12. 72

13. a. $13,684   b. $2,261   c. $15,945

14. c

15. a. $26   b. $169   c. $106

EXERCISE 2.1 (page 72)

1. a. proper   b. proper   c. improper
    d. mixed   e. proper   f. mixed

3. Pitney Bow   mixed
    WellsFar Co   mixed
    IntTelTel   mixed
    Chrysler   mixed
    CoastSt Gas   improper
    Autom Data   improper
    Phillips Pet   improper
    Mor Nor   mixed
    Am Tel&Tel   mixed
    Winnebago   improper

5. Pitney Bow: $\dfrac{47}{4}$;   Wells Far Co: $\dfrac{165}{8}$

7. (c) $\dfrac{52}{88}$

9. a. $\dfrac{5}{9}$ b. $\dfrac{4}{5}$ c. $\dfrac{3}{7}$ d. $\dfrac{4}{35}$

11. a. true   b. true   c. false   d. true
     e. true   f. false

13. a. 12   b. 96   c. −36   d. −20

15. Pitney Bow $\dfrac{16}{16}$

     WellsFar Co $\dfrac{-4}{16}$

IntTelTel	$\frac{18}{16}$
Chrysler	$\frac{20}{16}$
CoastSt Gas	——
Autom Data	$\frac{-14}{16}$
Phillips Pet	$\frac{44}{16}$
Mor Nor	$\frac{-2}{16}$
Am Tel&Tel	$\frac{14}{16}$
Winnebago	$\frac{24}{16}$

EXERCISE 2.2 (page 80)

1. a. $\frac{3}{4}$ b. $\frac{9}{10}$ c. $\frac{3}{4}$ d. $\frac{2}{3}$ e. 0

3. a. $2^2\times3^4$ b. $2^2\times3^2\times5$ c. $2^4\times3\times5^2$
    d. $2^2\times3^2\times7$ e. $2\times3\times5^2\times7^2$

5. a. 1   b. 5   c. 9

7. a. 21   b. 75   c. 270

9. a. 75   b. 54   c. 270

11. a. 30   b. 60   c. 72

13. a. 1   b. 3   c. 6

15. a. $\frac{9}{10}$ b. $\frac{19}{60}$ c. $\frac{13}{72}$

EXERCISE 2.3 (page 88)

1. a. $\frac{5}{8}$ b. $\frac{7}{17}$ c. $\frac{25}{47}$

3. a. $\frac{1}{2}$ b. $\frac{2}{7}$ c. $\frac{2}{19}$

5. a. $\frac{17}{12}$ b. $\frac{45}{56}$ c. $\frac{92}{65}$

7. a. $\frac{4}{3}$ b. $\frac{3}{2}$ c. $\frac{101}{72}$

9. LCM is 80: $\frac{7}{80}$

11. LCM is 84: $\dfrac{5}{84}$

13. a. $\dfrac{31}{24}$ b. $\dfrac{23}{56}$

15. a. $9\dfrac{5}{8}$ b. $18\dfrac{79}{84}$ c. $22\dfrac{11}{24}$

17. a. $2\dfrac{7}{40}$ b. $2\dfrac{19}{56}$

19. $31\dfrac{3}{4}$

21. $2\dfrac{3}{7}$ lb.

23. $62\dfrac{13}{30}$

25. $42\dfrac{31}{60}$

27. $\dfrac{13}{24}$

29. $20\dfrac{11}{24}$

31. $1\dfrac{17}{32}$

33. $\dfrac{5}{16}$

EXERCISE 2.4 (page 97)

1. a. $\dfrac{3}{10}$ b. $\dfrac{3}{5}$ c. $\dfrac{7}{10}$

3. a. 1   b. $21\dfrac{7}{18}$ c. $61\dfrac{3}{5}$

5. a. $1\dfrac{1}{6}$ b. $1\dfrac{1}{6}$ c. 4

7. a. 1   b. $\dfrac{3}{5}$ c. $119\dfrac{7}{10}$

9. a. $\$42\dfrac{1}{2}$ b. $\$38\dfrac{1}{2}$ c. $\$91\dfrac{7}{8}$

11. a. $\$5\dfrac{1}{12}$ b. $\$1\dfrac{5}{12}$ c. $\$4\dfrac{1}{2}$

13. a. 1 cup   b. $2\dfrac{1}{2}$ cups   c. $3\dfrac{1}{8}$ cups

15.   a. $2\dfrac{2}{3}$ b. $5   c. $6\dfrac{1}{3}$

17. $378\dfrac{3}{4}$

19.   Bob $2250
        Carol $1500
        Ted $750
        Alice $3000

21.   400

23. $2\dfrac{1}{2}$ hours

EXERCISE 2.5 (page 107)

1.   a.   .7   b.   .17   c.   .0378   d.   .030

3.   a. $(4 \times 10^1) + (2 \times 10^0)$ b. $(3 \times 10^2) + (8 \times 10^1) + (7 \times 10^0)$
    c. $(4 \times 10^3) + (7 \times 10^1) + (3 \times 10^0)$ d. $(4 \times 10^4) + (3 \times 10^2)$ $+ (8 \times 10^0)$

5.   a.   387   b.   8722   c.   4703   d.   402,103

7.   a.   .37   b.   .393   c.   .0021   d.   8.93

9.   a.   terminating   b.   nonterminating   c.   nonterminating   d.   terminating   e.   terminating

11.   a.   .375   b. $.66\dfrac{2}{3}$ c. $.14\dfrac{2}{7}$ d.   .2
    e.   1.5

13.   a. $\dfrac{33}{100}$ b. $3\dfrac{7}{25}$ c. $221\dfrac{187}{500}$

15.   a. $.33\dfrac{1}{3}$ b.   .20   c. $.42\dfrac{6}{7}$ d. $.44\dfrac{4}{9}$

17.   a. $\dfrac{1}{12}$ b. $\dfrac{3}{13}$ c. $\dfrac{3}{10}$ d. $\dfrac{1}{8}$

19.

	open	high	low	close
Gulf Oil	21.75	21.875	21.5	21.875
Gen Motors	48.125	48.75	48.125	48.75
Nat Can	7.875	7.875	7.375	7.5

21.   AdmExp $14\dfrac{16}{25}$

      Advance $13\dfrac{23}{50}$

      aAmGnBd $24\dfrac{83}{100}$

$$\text{AmGenCv} \qquad 20\frac{69}{100}$$

$$\text{Am-SoAf} \qquad 65\frac{21}{50}$$

23. AdmExp   12.625
     Advance   14.75
     aAmGvBd   27.375
     AmGenCv   19.875
     Am-SoA   62.875

EXERCISE 2.6 (page 116)

1.	15.12	3.	59.425	5.	11.478
7.	0.0262	9.	68.49	11.	49.36
13.	28.646	15.	67.062		

17. a. $.75   b. $.75   c. $.42   d. $1.62
     e. $1.26   f. $.52   g. $.52

19. Adjusted Balance = $578.87

21. Adjusted Balance = $722.70

EXERCISE 2.7 (page 124)

1. a. 379.6   b. 21.36   c. .1506   d. .083
    e. .4386   f. 75.0708

3. a. $19.08   b. $41.22   c. $18.07

5. a. $6.45   b. $6.23   c. $3.87

7. $33.00

9. a. $5808.24   b. $6374.40   c. $6972.84

11. a. $1.80   b. $2.16

13. a. $73.20   b. $73.88   c. $78.84   d. $79.88

15. a. $85.24   b. $89.76   c. $95.92   d. $100.76

17. Hammers $ 6.00
    Screwdrivers   6.00
    Hand Saws   16.00
    Total   28.00

19. a. .72   b. 74.81   c. 2343.33

21. a. $8912.25   b. $9113.61   c. $7623.45
    d. $4725.09

23.   a. $101.98   b. $102.34   c. $93.04
       d. $100.12   e. $100.86

25.   a. $5.40   b. $7.71   c. $3.38

SELF-TEST/CHAPTER 2 (page 130)

1. $\dfrac{7}{2}; \dfrac{447}{8}; \dfrac{15}{4}$

2.   a.   12   b.   180

3.   a. $\dfrac{19}{90}$ b. $9\dfrac{1}{6}$ c.   11   d.   12

4.   a. $\dfrac{3}{8}$ b. $20\dfrac{1}{4}$

5.   a. $\$32\dfrac{1}{8}$ b. $\$18\dfrac{5}{8}$

6.   a.   21.595   b.   2.69584   c.   1.16

7.

Bank Balance	$ 840.50	Checkbook Balance	$1062.17
Add: Outstanding Deposit	$ 310.49		
Total	$1150.99		
Less: Outstanding Checks	$ 91.32	Less: Bank Charges	$ 2.50
Adjusted Balance	$1059.67	Adjusted Balance	$1059.67

8.   a. $\dfrac{39}{125}$ b. $\dfrac{163}{200}$ c. $\dfrac{1}{3}$

9.   a.   .09   b.   .625   c. $.42\dfrac{6}{7}$

10.   a.   1.618   b. $8912.25   c.   8.054

EXERCISE 3.1 (page 139)

1.   a. $\dfrac{3}{5}$ b. $\dfrac{8}{7}$ c. $\dfrac{4}{9}$ d. $\dfrac{55}{25}$ or $\dfrac{11}{5}$

3. $\dfrac{4}{5}$

5. $\dfrac{7}{106}$

7. $\dfrac{16}{1}$

9.   30¢

11. $1500, $1200

13. $14.40

15.   Bob $18,000
        Al $12,000

17.   Xerox Corp   42
        Polaroid Corp   46

19.   .007

EXERCISE 3.2 (page 144)

1.   130

3.   135

5.   .09

7.   .13

9. $\dfrac{15}{4}$

EXERCISE 3.3 (page 150)

1.	6	11.	28	21.	69 miles
3.	21	13.	21	23.	2000
5.	36	15.	4800	25.	1067
7.	36	17.	2500	27.	$427.50
9.	6	19.	139	29.	$356.25

EXERCISE 3.4 (page 157)

1.	$\dfrac{11}{50}$	11.	80%	21.	2130%
3.	$1\dfrac{1}{2}$	13.	$71\dfrac{3}{7}\%$	23.	33%
5.	$\dfrac{7}{200}$	15.	$42\dfrac{6}{7}\%$	25.	120%
7.	$\dfrac{1}{500}$	17.	22%	27.	2025%
9.	25%	19.	370%	29.	a. 522
					b. 312
					c. 10.50

31. a. 50%

  b. $33\frac{1}{3}\%$

  c. 20%

33. a. 240
  b. 300
  c. 100

35. $2325

37. $23\frac{1}{3}\%$

39. $14,705.88

41. 23%

43. a. 20%
  b. $3200

45. 160 inches

47. 385

49. a. 8664
  b. 25,992

EXERCISE 3.5 (page 165)

1. $44

3. $28.09

5. $44.00

7. $28.00

9. $425.50

11. $16.22

13. a. $12.60   b. $48.60

15. markup = 25% of the cost = $12.50
  selling price = $50 + $12.50 = $62.50

17. $200 each

19. $12,960

21. a. $30   b. 25%   c. 33%

23. a. $4   b. 16%   c. 19%

25. a. $84.60   b. 33%   c. 49%

27. 9.1%

29. 53.8%

EXERCISE 3.6 (page 169)

1. a. $24   b. 20%

3. a. $.74   b. 11%

5. a. $.84   b. 10%

7. a. $1.11   b. 10%

9. a. $.82   b. 25%

11. a. $.33   b. 17%

13. #5—cookie jar
     #6—mug tree and mug set
     #7—revolving spice rack

15. Yes; all markdowns range from 10% to 25% (to the nearest per cent).

17. a. total markdown = 10% of $20,000 = $2000   b. $18,000

19. a. $4,000   b. 14% (to the nearest per cent)

SELF-TEST/CHAPTER 3 (page 172)

1. a. 5:1
    b. 25 secretaries
        5 supervisors

2. Executives get 800
    Managers get 600
    Employees get 600

3. Al gets $10,000
    Bob gets $20,000

4. $10,000/$2,000 = 5

5. a. 32
    b. 1
    c. 6
    d. 64

6. a. 40
    b. 4.9

7. a. $33\frac{1}{3}$
    b. 450

8. $48.00

9. $200.00

10. $50

11. a. $20.00
     b. 11.11%
     c. 10%

12. a. 25%
     b. 13%

13.   a. $10.00
      b.   10%

14.   a. $5,000.00
      b. $50,000.00

EXERCISE 4.1 (page 178)

1.   discount = $175; net price = $525

3.   discount = $224.33; net price = $448.67

5.   net price = $37.40; rate = 25.20%

7.   net price = $4856.40; rate = 14.50%

9.   net price = $1116; rate = 55%

11.   a. $13   b. $7   c. $650

13.   net price = 427,500; profit = $47,500

15.   single discount = 55%; net price = 45% of list price
      dishwasher $89.10
      washer $80.55
      range $71.10
      17 cu. in. refrigerator $129.60
      freezer $80.10
      19 cu. in. refrigerator $156.60

17.   25%

19. $31\frac{3}{5}\%$

21.   70%

23.   list price = $800

25. $.16 change

EXERCISE 4.2 (page 184)

1.   a. $ .58   b. $28.42

3.   a. $1.82   b. $43.68

5.   a. $ .81   b. $39.69

7.   a. $ .60   b. $29.20

9.   a. $ .00   b. $83.00

11.   a. $ .82   b. $39.98

13.   a. $ .61   b. $19.83

15. $235.69

17.   cash discount = $9.20; amount due = $450.80

19. $201.52

21. $385.43

23.   a. $180.19   b.   February 8 (the amount due then is
                                  $185.50)

25.   a. $181.96   b.   February 8

EXERCISE 4.3 (page 191)

1.   a. $141   b. $248   c. $266.50

3. $383.88

5. $568

7. $9,657.50

9. $267

11. $98.25

13.   Bell: $47.25; Lariz: $60.30; Tryon: $42.30

15.   Prime Cost = $145; Gross Cost = $179.85

17.   Gross Proceeds = $542.50; Charges = $45.73. Coswell Riper
       received $496.77.

19.   Gross Cost = $6,556.40

EXERCISE 4.4 (page 201)

1. $370,710 per year

3. $751,000

5. $355.290.06

7.   Annual Depreciation $= \dfrac{\$4600 - \$1000}{5} = \$720.$

End of Year	Annual Depreciation	Accumulated Depreciation	Book Value
0	–	–	$4600
1	$720	$ 720	$3880
2	$720	$1440	$3160
3	$720	$2160	$2440
4	$720	$2880	$1720
5	$720	$3600	$1000

9.   Sum of the years' digits $= \dfrac{5 \times 6}{2} = 15$.

END OF YEAR	ANNUAL DEPRECIATION	ACCUMULATED DEPRECIATION	BOOK VALUE
0	—	—	$4600
1	$\dfrac{5}{15}$ of $3600 = $1200	$1200	$3400
2	$\dfrac{4}{15}$ of $3600 = $ 960	$2160	$2440
3	$\dfrac{3}{15}$ of $3600 = $ 720	$2880	$1720
4	$\dfrac{2}{15}$ of $3600 = $ 480	$3360	$1240
5	$\dfrac{1}{15}$ of $3600 = $ 240	$3600	$1000

11. $800

13. $1200

15.   Annual straight line depreciation = $32.00.
Monthly straight line depreciation = $2.67.

17.   Annual straight line depreciation = $1000.
Accumulated depreciation at the end of 5 years = $5000.00.
Book value at the end of 5 years = $2500.00.
$2500 − $175 = $2325 difference.

19. $867

21.   1st year $1,824; 2nd year $2,208; 3rd year $1,728; 4th year $2,304; 5th year $1,536.

23. $843.75.

25.

END OF YEAR	ANNUAL DEPRECIATION	ACCUMULATED DEPRECIATION	BOOK VALUE
0	—	—	$4000
1	$\dfrac{1}{2}$ of $4000 = $2000	$2000	$2000
2	$\dfrac{1}{2}$ of $2000 = $1000	$3000	$1000
3	$\dfrac{1}{2}$ of $1000 = $ 500	$3500	$ 500
4	$400	$3900	$ 100

Note that the depreciation figured by use of the declining balance rate would not have placed the salvage value at $100 by the end of year 4. Thus, the remaining depreciation, $400, must be deducted during year 4.

27. $3,300

29. $800.

31.   Sum of the years' digits $= \dfrac{4 \times 5}{2} = 10.$

END OF YEAR	ANNUAL DEPRECIATION	ACCUMULATED DEPRECIATION	BOOK VALUE
0	—	—	$3400
1	$\dfrac{4}{10}$ of $3000 = $1200	$1200	$2200
2	$\dfrac{3}{10}$ of $3000 = $ 900	$2100	$1300
3	$\dfrac{2}{10}$ of $3000 = $ 600	$2700	$ 700
4	$\dfrac{1}{10}$ of $3000 = $ 300	$3000	$ 400

EXERCISE 4.5 (page 207)

1.   a. $840   b. $1,300

3.   a. $840   b. $1,628.57

5. $2,457.60

7. $10,000 cost   Ordinary straight line de-
      −2,000 first year allowance   preciation = $6000 ÷ 6 =
      $ 8,000 $1000
      −2,000 salvage value
      $ 6,000 remaining value

END OF YEAR	ANNUAL DEPRECIATION	ACCUMULATED DEPRECIATION	BOOK VALUE
0	—	—	$10,000
1	$1000 + $2000 = $3000	$3000	$ 7,000
2	$1000	$4000	$ 6,000
3	$1000	$5000	$ 5,000
4	$1000	$6000	$ 4,000
5	$1000	$7000	$ 3,000
6	$1000	$8000	$ 2,000

9. $8,000 cost   Sum of years' digits = 28
    −1,600 first year allowance
    $6,400
    − 800 salvage value
    $5,600 remaining value

END OF YEAR	ANNUAL DEPRECIATION	ACCUMULATED DEPRECIATION	BOOK VALUE
0	—	—	$8000
1	$1600 + $\frac{7}{28}$ of $5600 = $1600 + $1400 = $3000	$3000	$5000
2	$\frac{6}{28}$ of $5600 = $1200	$4200	$3800
3	$\frac{5}{28}$ of $5600 = $1000	$5200	$2800
4	$\frac{4}{28}$ of $5600 = $ 800	$6000	$2000
5	$\frac{3}{28}$ of $5600 = $ 600	$6600	$1400
6	$\frac{2}{28}$ of $5600 = $ 400	$7000	$1000
7	$\frac{1}{28}$ of $5600 = $ 200	$7200	$ 800

EXERCISE 4.6 (page 213)

1. $6,400

3.

Net Sales	$30,000
Cost of Goods Sold	23,800
Gross Profit	$ 6,200
Operating Expenses	2,500
Net Income	$ 3,700

BRIMSTONE TIRE COMPANY
Income Statement
For Month Ended December 31, 19___

			PER CENTS
Income:			
Sales...		$51,000	102
Less sales returns and allowances...............		1,000	2
Net sales..		$50,000	100
Less cost of goods sold:			
Inventory, December 1, 19___......................	$ 5,000		10
Purchases...	30,000		60
Goods available for sale..........................	$35,000		70
Less inventory, December 31, 19___...............	5,500		11
Cost of goods sold................................		$29,500	59
Gross profit on sales..............................		$20,500	41
Operating expenses:			
Selling expenses..................................	$12,500		25
Delivery expenses.................................	2,000		4
Office expenses....................................	3,000		6
Miscellaneous expenses............................	1,000		2
Total operating expenses......................		$18,500	37
Net income...		$ 2,000	4

5.

7.

Comparative Income Statement
For Years Ended December 31, 1977 and 1976

	1977	1976	INCREASE OR DECREASE* DURING 1977	
			Amount	Per Cent
Sales..	$112,000	$111,000	$ 1,000	.9
Less sales returns and allowances................	2,000	11,000	9,000	81.8
Net sales.....................................	110,000	100,000	10,000	10
Less cost of goods sold:				
Merchandise inventory, January 1.................	$ 60,000	$ 50,000	$10,000	20
Purchases....................................	50,000	40,000	10,000	25
Goods available for sale.........................	$110,000	$ 90,000	$20,000	22.2
Less inventory, December 31......................	33,600	32,000	1,600	5
Cost of goods sold...........................	76,400	58,000	18,400	31.7
Gross profit...................................	$ 33,600	$ 42,000	$ 8,400*	20*
Operating expenses:				
Selling expenses..............................	$ 12,000	$ 10,000	$ 2,000	20
General expenses..............................	12,000	8,000	4,000	50
Total operating expenses......................	$ 24,000	$ 18,000	$ 6,000	33.3
Net income...................................	$ 9,600	$ 24,000	$14,400*	60*

HOWARD HUES PAINT COMPANY Comparative Balance Sheet June 30, 1977 and 1976				
			INCREASE OR DECREASE*	
	1977	1976	*Amount*	*Per Cents*
ASSETS				
Current assets...	$ 32,000	$ 30,000	$ 2,000	6.7
Investments..	57,000	50,000	7,000	14
Fixed assets (net)..	65,000	60,000	5,000	8.3
Total assets..	$154,000	$140,000	$14,000	10
LIABILITIES				
Current liabilities..	$ 42,000	$ 35,000	$ 7,000	20
Long-term liabilities...	45,000	50,000	5,000	10
Total liabilities...	$ 87,000	$ 85,000	$ 2,000	2.4
STOCKHOLDERS' EQUITY				
Preferred stock (6%, $100 par).........................	$ 20,000	$ 12,000	$ 8,000	66.7
Common stock ($10 par)..................................	40,000	32,000	8,000	25
Retained earnings..	7,000	11,000	4,000	36.4
Total stockholders' equity.................................	$ 67,000	$ 55,000	$12,000	21.8
Total liabilities & stockholders' equity................	$154,000	$140,000	$14,000	10

9.

EXERCISE 4.7 (page 222)

1.   a. 1¢   b. 3¢   c. 1¢   d. 12¢

3.   a. 2¢   b. 4¢   c. 2¢   d. 21¢

5.   a. 103% of sales = $3296
      sales = $3296/1.03 = $3200
   b. sales tax = $3296 − $3200 = $96.

7.   a. $9.90   b. $2.45   c. $ .75

9.   a. $21   b. $30   c. $65

11. $2.00

13. $6.00

15.   a. $176.40   b. $116.55

17. $10.50

19.   a. $337.50   b. $155.25   c. $51.75

SELF-TEST/CHAPTER 4 (page 225)

1.   a. $375   b. $2125

2.   a. 23.5%   b. $1175   c. $3825

3.   a. $388   b. $388

4.   a. $392   b. $380

5.   a. $85   b. $1045

6.   a. $616   b. $104.30   c. $720.30

7.   a. $2000   b. $1166.67   c. $2666.67

8.   a. $3142.86   b. $2500.00   c. $3733.33

9.   a.

HOWARD HUES PAINT			
Income Statement			
For Month Ended December 31, 19__			
			PER CENTS
Income:			
Sales..		$91,800	102
Less sales returns and allowances..............		1,800	2
Net sales..		$90,000	100
Less cost of goods sold:			
Inventory, December 1, 19___........................	$ 9,000		10
Purchases.....................................	40,500		45
Goods available for sale.....................	$49,500		55
Less inventory, December 31, 19___..............	10,800		12
Cost of goods sold........................		$38,700	43
Gross profit on sales............................		$51,300	57
Operating expenses:			
Selling expenses..............................	$18,000		20
Delivery expenses............................	14,400		16
Office expenses.............................	4,500		5
Miscellaneous expenses.....................	7,200		8
Total operating expenses....................		$44,100	49
Net income...		$ 7,200	8

b.

			Comparative Income Statement For Years Ended December 31, 1977 and 1976		INCREASE OR DECREASE* DURING 1977	
	1977	**1976**			*Amount*	*Per Cent*
Sales...	$224,000	$222,000			$ 2,000	.9
Less sales returns and allowances.................	4,000	22,000			18,000*	81.8*
Net sales...	220,000	200,000			20,000	10
Less cost of goods sold:						
Merchandise inventory, January 1.................	$120,000	$100,000			$20,000	20
Purchases..	100,000	80,000			20,000	25
Goods available for sale.............................	$220,000	$180,000			$40,000	22.2
Less inventory, December 31.......................	67,200	64,000			3,200	5
Cost of goods sold................................	152,800	116,000			36,800	31.7
Gross profit...	$ 67,200	$ 84,000			$16,800*	20*
Operating expenses:						
Selling expenses......................................	$ 24,000	$ 20,000			$ 4,000	20
General expenses.....................................	24,000	16,000			8,000	50
Total operating expenses.......................	$ 48,000	$ 36,000			$12,000	33.3
Net income...	$ 19,200	$ 48,000			$28,800*	60*

10.　a. $1,200　　　b. $24,000　　　c. $192

EXERCISE 5.1 (page 234)

1.	$84	9.	$50
3.	$6.50	11.	$264
5.	$60	13.	$642
7.	$100	15.	$936

17.　Interest = $133.33; Amount of home purchased = $6.67

19.　Interest = $100; Principal = $28.50

21.　$1654.67

23.　$65.63

25.　Interest = $5152; Monthly check = $107.33

27.　Interest = $12,880; Monthly check = $268.33

29.　Interest = $28,000; Monthly check = $583.33

EXERCISE 5.2 (page 242)

1. Exact Interest = $16.20; Ordinary Interest = $16.43
3. 162 days
5. a. $73   b. $72.39   c. $71.80   d. $71.20
7. Ordinary Interest = $71.88; Exact Interest = $70.89
9. Interest due = $80; amount paid = $4,080
11. $523.18
13. $1,666.67
15. $10.14

EXERCISE 5.3 (page 247)

1.	$3.60	11.	$1.34	21.	$3.25
3.	$4.56	13.	$8.80	23.	$36.78
5.	$9.00	15.	$1.77	25.	$54.54
7.	$3.52	17.	$10.00	27.	$1558.50
9.	$24.23	19.	$ .97	29.	$82,587.50

EXERCISE 5.4 (page 253)

1. P = $120; S = $120.80
3. P = $4,500; S = $4,725
5. P = $358.78
7. P = $3,000
9. r = 7%
11. I = 24.68, r = 8%
13. t = 1 year and 6 months
15. $1,200
17. $37,920
19. 6%
21. 7%
23. 36%
25. 8 months

27.   45 days

29.   1 year and 36 days

EXERCISE 5.5 (page 258)

1.	a. $208.66	b. $208.71
3.	a. $2,188	b. $2,192.89
5.	a. $1,075	b. $1,075.91
7.	a. $520.27	b. $520.51
9.	a. $5,178.50	b. $5,181.30
11.	a. $431	b. $431.41

EXERCISE 5.6 (page 263)

1.   Discount = $15; Proceeds = $985

3.   Discount = $240; Proceeds = $1,260

5.   Discount = $3.56; Proceeds = $376.44

7. $588

9. $2,174.33

11. $4,069.25

13. $519.40

15. $303.55

17. $330.90

19. $523.42

21. $756.17

23. $801.24

25. $468,750,000

EXERCISE 5.7 (page 267)

1. $400

3. $300

5. $1,104.97

7. $520.83

9. $1,030.93

11. $894.01

13. $480.77 at simple interest; $480 at bank discount

15.   a. $454.55   b. $470

17.   9.88%

19.   3.85%

21.   10.13%

23.   4.17%

25.   3.85%

SELF-TEST/CHAPTER 5 (page 269)

1.   a. $400   b. $10,400

2.   a. $1971   b. $1944

3.   a. $8.64   b. $12.96

4.   a. $800   b. $900

5.   a. $450   b. $4.50

6.   a. $416.50   b. $416.63

7.   a. $56.60   b. $943.40

8.   a. $2,061.86   b. $61.86

9.   5.06%

10.   4.94%

EXERCISE 6.1 (page 277)

1.   a. 7%   b. 10   c. $1.97

3.   a. 4%   b. 12   c. $1.60

5.   a. $3\frac{1}{2}\%$ b. 20   c. $596.94

7.   a. 4%   b. 10   c. $1480.24

9.   a. $3\frac{1}{2}\%$ b. 9   c. $1362.90

11. $5126.57

13. $8100.62

15. $ .01 (see problems 11 and 12)

17.   Compound amount = $1,282.04; Compound interest = $282.04

19. $203.99

21. $1,567.22

23. $ .02

EXERCISE 6.2 (page 283)

1.   6.09%

3.   8.16%

5.   10.25%

7.   5.09%

9.   7.19%

11.   10% compounded semiannually

13. $ .30

15. $8\frac{1}{2}$% semiannually is better.

EXERCISE 6.3 (page 287)

1. $ .93

3. $ .66

5. $150.77

7. $456.39

9. $780.01

11. $2966.82

13. $862.30

15.   She saves $16.20 by buying the land for $4,700.

17.   Buy the lot in one year.

19.   a. $1,126.49   b. $961.45

EXERCISE 6.4 (page 301)

1. $8.00

3. $35.00

5. $66.65

7.   11.25%

9.   11.75%

11. $433.76

13.   12%

15.   No

17. $19.71

19.   12.08

21.   Finance charge = $324.50; Monthly payment = $117.69

23.   Finance charge = $464.36; Monthly payment = $85.12

25.   The $2,600 car

EXERCISE 6.5 (page 307)

1.   a. $106.08   b. $6.08   c. 11%

3.   a. $1161.72   b. $161.72   c. 10%

5.   a. $2259.60   b. $259.60   c. 12%

7.   a. $4359.60   b. $859.60   c. 9%

9.   a. $4125.24   b. $625.24   c. 11%

11.   a. $289.30   b. $1320   c. 25%

13.   a. $179.58   b. $1693.20   c. 11%

15.   a. $471.82   b. $2472   c. 21.25%

17.   11.22%

19.   10.49%

EXERCISE 6.6 (page 313)

1. $141.35

3. $185.01

5. $557.48

7.   a. $1.28   b. $236.28   c. $11.81

9.   a. $5.16   b. $409.16   c. $20.46

11.   a. $1.21   b. $135.15   c. $10.00

13.   a. $ .84   b. $92.73   c. $10.00

15.   a. $ .52   b. $122.81   c. $10.00

17.   a. $2.85   b. 18%

19. $1.35

EXERCISE 6.7 (page 318)

1.   a. $2.00   b. $98

3.   a. $8.40   b. $261.60

5.   a. $4.18   b. $45.82

SELF-TEST/CHAPTER 6 (page 319)

1.   a. $693.71   b. $2,693.71

2.   a. 8.24%   b. First

3.   a. $1,351.13   b. $1,351.13

4.   a. $3,600   b. $600

5.   12.25%

6.   a. $587.10   b. $99.64

7.   a. $289.31   b. $122.26   c. $167.04

8.   a. $4.50   b. $354.50

9.   a. $30   b. $120

10.   a. $8,101.74   b. $98.26

EXERCISE 7.1 (page 328)

1. $100

3. $708.90

5. $86.40

7. $10,062.50

9. $10,150

11. $7.53

13.   Preferred, $2.50; common, $ .63

15.   Preferred, $6; common, $1.40

17.   Preferred, $6; common, $1.75

19.   Preferred, $9; common, $5.10

EXERCISE 7.2 (page 334)

1. $123.45

3. $415.96

5. $87.69

7.   Commission = $63.28; Proceeds = $2,031.72

9.   Commission = $103.33; Proceeds = $5,482.30

11.   a. $ .04   b. $5.00

13.   a. $ .18   b. $8.75

15.   a. $ .05   b. $3.44

17. $2,155.35

19. $5,477.05

EXERCISE 7.3 (page 339)

1.   4.7%

3.   6.1%

5.   2.8%

7.   5%

9.   7.3%

11.   1.9%

13.   3.5%

15.   2.5%

17.   a. $913.85   b. $963.85   c. 62.8%

19.   a. $1816.68   b. $2416.68   c. 59.3%

EXERCISE 7.4 (page 345)

1. $1005

3. $640

5. $5875

7. $817.50

9. $738.19

11.   a. $5,275   b. $112.50   c. $12.50   d. $5,400

13.   a. $11,750   b. $100   c. $25   d. $11,875

15.   a. $10,050   b. $194.40   c. $25   d. $10,269.40

17.   a. $8,000   b. $50   c. $ .16

19.   a. $14,600   b. $100   c. $ .30

EXERCISE 7.5 (page 350)

1.   a. $80   b. $1,000   c. 8%

3.   a. $85.00   b. $1,050   c. 8.1%

5.   a. $60   b. $870   c. 6.9%

7.   a. $58.75   b. $310   c. 19%

9.   a. $67.50   b. $920   c. 7.3%

11.   4.8%

13.   2.9%

15.   5.7%

17.   5.6%

19.   6.5%

EXERCISE 7.6 (page 359)

1.   190 shares; 444 warrants

3. $10,070; 17,649

5. $8811.25 loss

SELF-TEST/CHAPTER 7 (page 360)

1.   a. $600   b. $2750

2.   a. $5   b. $7.50

3.   a. $10   b. 0

4.   a. $200.86   b. $46.75   c. $247.61

5.   a. $10¢   b. $21.10

6.   a. 3.5%   b. 43.48%

7. $487.50   b. $9.17

8.   a. 10%   b. 5.71%

9.   a. 100   b. 100

10. $12.25

EXERCISE 8.1 (page 368)

1. $16.42

3. $19.67

5. $25.92

7.   a. $51.99   b. $75.87

9.   a. $56.13   b. $81.92

11. $25.76

13. $33.96

15. $59.36

17.   a. $51.80   b. $75.60

19.   a. $51.80   b. $75.60

21. $82.59

23. $85.77

25. $333.17

EXERCISE 8.2 (page 373)

1. $20,000

3. $9,600

5. $6,250

7. $6,000

9. $10,285.71

11.   A pays $24,000, and B pays $36,000.

13.   U pays $16,000, R pays $6,400, and S pays $9,600.

15.   W pays $13,000, X pays $9,000, and Y pays $4,000.

17.   a. $28,000   b. $70,000   c. $70,000

19.   a. $7,500   b. $17,500   c. $50,000

21.   a. $40,000   b. $45,000   c. $48,000

23.   a. B pays $1,250, C pays $2,500, and D pays $3,750.

      b. B pays $12,000, C pays $24,000, and D pays $36,000.

      c. B pays $41,666.67 C pays $83,333.33, and D pays $125,000.

EXERCISE 8.3 (page 378)

1. $3.12

3. $6.88

5. $14.00

7. $7.59

9. $24.58

11. $5.15

13. $16.98

15. $48.08

17. $83.39

19. $115.97

EXERCISE 8.4 (page 387)

1.	a. $81	b. $46	15.	$71.00	
3.	a. $87	b. $59	17.	$115.50	
5.	a. $107	b. $60	19.	$115.15	
7.	$162.25		21.	$127.10	
9.	$98.70		23.	$74.20	
11.	$151.70		25.	$100.65	
13.	$133.00		27.	$86.40	

EXERCISE 8.5 (page 395)

1.	a. $230	b. $119.60	c. $60.95	d. $20.41
3.	a. $513.00	b. $266.76	c. $135.95	d. $45.53
5.	a. $704.40	b. $366.29	c. $186.67	d. $62.52
7.	a. $1,004.50	b. $522.34	c. $266.19	d. $89.15
9.	a. $423.60	b. $220.27	c. $112.25	d. $37.59
11.	a. $135.60	b. $70.51	c. $35.93	d. $12.03
13.	a. $89.20	b. $8.92		
15.	a. −$1988	b. −$9.94		
17.	a. $5704	b. $14.26		
19.	a. $1264.52	b. $4.08		
21.	a. 1267.37	b. $4.09		
23.	a. $1315.73	b. $4.25		
25.	a. $1359.58	b. $4.39		
27.	a. $1395.73	b. $4.51		

SELF-TEST/CHAPTER 8 (page 397)

1.   a. $7.76   b. $1.25
2.   a. $28.00   b. $2.00
3.   a. ½ of the loss up to $40,000   b. $5,000   c. $25,000
4.   a. $10,000   b. $15,000   c. $25,000
5.   a. $ .78   b. $6.98
6.   a. $20   b. $68
7.   a. $83.60   b. $123.20
8.   a. $45   b. $47.25
9.   a. $90.40   b. $133.90
10.   a. $2,748   b. $1.24

EXERCISE 9.1 (page 405)

1. $\dfrac{1}{10}$

3. $\dfrac{3}{10}$

5. $\dfrac{1}{2}$

7. $\dfrac{1}{5}$

9. $\dfrac{2}{5}$

11.   a. $\dfrac{1}{5}$ b. $\dfrac{3}{5}$

13.   a. 6   b. $\dfrac{1}{6}$

15.   a. $\dfrac{1}{4}$ b. $\dfrac{1}{4}$ c. $\dfrac{1}{2}$

17.   a. $\dfrac{1}{7}$ b. $\dfrac{9}{49}$ c. $\dfrac{3}{7}$ d. $\dfrac{24}{49}$

EXERCISE 9.2 (page 410)

1.   a. $\dfrac{1}{5}$ b. $\dfrac{4}{5}$ 5. $\dfrac{1}{5,000}$

3. $\dfrac{17}{20}$ 7. $\dfrac{13}{25,000}$

9. West Germany

11. $\frac{1}{5}$

13. $\frac{1}{5}$

15. $\frac{3}{10}$

17. $\frac{15}{17}$

19. $\frac{2}{7}$

EXERCISE 9.3 (page 415)

1. $\frac{5}{12}$

3. a. $\frac{4}{5}$ b. $\frac{1}{5}$ c. 4 to 1   d. 1 to 4

5. $\frac{7}{16}; \frac{9}{16}$

7. $\frac{1}{3}$

9. $\frac{11}{23}$

11. $\frac{1}{45}$

13. $\frac{43}{125}$

15. $\frac{8}{15}$

17. a. $\frac{4}{55}$ b. $\frac{16}{55}$ c. $\frac{8}{55}$ d. $\frac{27}{55}$

19. a. $\frac{105}{418}$ b. $\frac{313}{418}$ c. 105 to 313   d. 313 to 105

EXERCISE 9.4 (page 421)

1. 20¢

3. $1.80

5. $22,222.22

7. $110

9. 1200

11. $600

13. 1500

15. Step up production

17. $12,000

EXERCISE 9.5 (page 427)

1.

OUTCOME DECISION	SELLS	DOES NOT SELL
Market	$10,000	−$5,000
Do not market	−$2,500	$1,000

3. −$750

5. 0

7. Market the product

9.

OUTCOME DECISION	PATENT	NO PATENT
Build	$2,000,000	−$250,000
Do not build	$1,000,000	$100,000

11. $550,000

13. Build

15. Build

17.

	OPEN	CLOSED
A	10	15
B	11	16

19. Go to B

21. A

EXERCISE 9.6 (page 434)

1. a. Production has increased or demand has increased or both.
   b. Production has increased and demand has increased.
   c. Demand has not increased.
   d. Production has increased but demand has not increased.

3.   a. The person is negligent and will file a claim.
      b. The person is not negligent or will file a claim or both.
      c. The person is not negligent and will file a claim.
      d. The person is not negligent.

5.   a. a   b. b   c. g

7.   a. $\frac{3}{10}$ b. $\frac{7}{10}$

9.   a. $\frac{3}{20}$ b. $\frac{17}{40}$ c. $\frac{13}{20}$ d. $\frac{7}{20}$

11. $\frac{3}{23}$

13. $\frac{16}{23}$

15. $\frac{20}{23}$

17. $\frac{23}{75}$

19. $\frac{10}{33}$

21. $\frac{41}{50}$

23. $\frac{1}{5}$

25. $\frac{9}{10}$

27.   a. $\frac{3}{20}$ b. $\frac{17}{20}$

29. $\frac{3}{4}$

EXERCISE 9.7 (page 443)

1.   a. The probability that a stock is a good investment given that it has paid high dividends.
      b. The probability that a stock has not paid high dividends given that it is a good investment.
      c. The probability that a stock has paid high dividends given that it is not a good investment.
      d. The probability that a stock is not a good investment given that it has not paid high dividends.

3.   a. $\frac{1}{13}$ b. $\frac{1}{6}$

5.   a. $\dfrac{8}{13}$ b. 1   c. 0   d. $\dfrac{1}{3}$

7.   a. $\dfrac{3}{5}$ b. $\dfrac{1}{5}$ c. $\dfrac{1}{3}$

9.   a. $\dfrac{1}{3}=\dfrac{\frac{20}{100}}{\frac{60}{100}}$ b. $\dfrac{1}{4}=\dfrac{\frac{10}{100}}{\frac{40}{100}}$

11. a. $\dfrac{1}{5}$ b. $\dfrac{2}{5}$

13. $\dfrac{3}{5}$

15. a. $\dfrac{1}{8}$ b. $\dfrac{2}{11}$

17. a. $\dfrac{3}{35}$ b. $\dfrac{16}{35}$

19. a. $\dfrac{1}{12}$ b. $\dfrac{1}{8}$

SELF-TEST/CHAPTER 9 (page 448)

1.   a. $\dfrac{1}{2}$ b. $\dfrac{3}{10}$ c. $\dfrac{1}{5}$

2.   a.   b. $\dfrac{1}{8}$

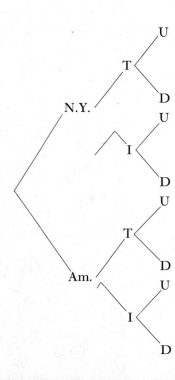

3.   a. $\dfrac{1}{5}$ b. $\dfrac{2}{5}$

4.   a. $\dfrac{5}{9}$ b. $\dfrac{1}{3}$

5.   a. Not independent   b. Not independent

6.   a. $\dfrac{2}{5}$ b. $\dfrac{1}{4}$

7.   a. 1 to 6   b. 6 to 1

8.   a. $1250   b. Market the product
       c. Market the product

9.   a. 70   b. $\dfrac{1}{5}$

10.   a. 2 fires   b. $1000

EXERCISE 10.1 (page 455)

1.   a.

Number of Hours	Tally Marks	Frequency
0	II	2
1	III	3
2	II	2
3	III	3
4	III	3
5	II	2
6	II	2
7	II	2
8	IIII	4
9	I	1
10	II	2
11		0
12	II	2
13		0
14	I	1
15	I	1

    b. 8   c. 4   d. 15   e. 36.67

3.   a.

Price	Tally Marks	Frequency
0–10	IIII	4
11–20	IIIIII	7
21–30	THtl	6
31–40		0
41–50	III	3
51–60	II	2
61–70	II	2

71–80		0
81–90		0
91–100	I	1

b. \$11–\$20   c. 5   d. 24%   e. 68%

5.

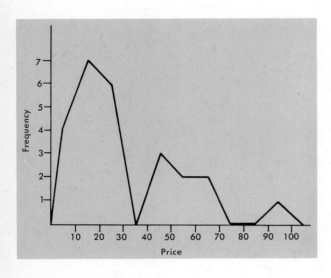

7.   a. The histogram is shown with the solid lines.
       b. The frequency polygon is shown with the broken lines.

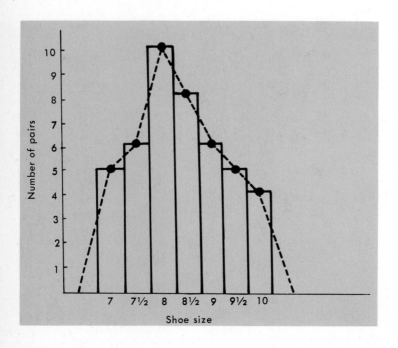

9.

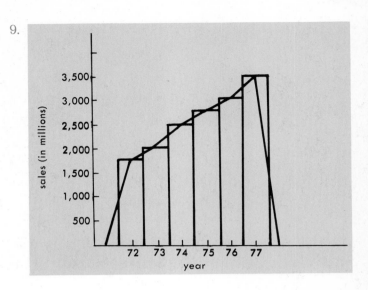

EXERCISE 10.2 (page 462)

1.   a. 9; 9   b. 24.2; 9   c. 11; 9   The median is the
      same for all three sets.   None of the sets has a mode.

3.   Mean = 6; median = 6.5; mode = 8.   The mode is least
      representative.

5.

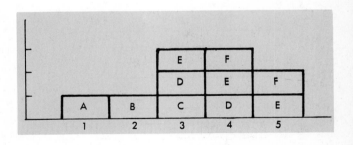

      b. 2   c. 1 or 3

7.   a. mean = 77.3; median = 75   b. mean = 87.9; median = 90
      c. mean = 68.2; median = 67.5

9.   a. 11   b. 11

11.   a. 3.0   b. 3.2   c. none

13.   a. 40   b. 40   c. none

15.   60

17. $84 per week

19.   73

EXERCISE 10.3 (page 468)

1.   a. 18   b. $\sqrt{41.6}$
3.   a. 20   b. $\sqrt{50}$
5.   a. 4   b. $\sqrt{2}$
7.   a. 8   b. $\sqrt{8.29}$
9.   a. 6   b. 2
11. a. 8   b. 6   c. 6   d. $\sqrt{9.33}$ e. 71.4%
     f. 100%
13. a. 110   b. 110   c. 108   d. $\sqrt{12.4}$
     e. 102, 103, 113; 30%
15. They may all be zero or they may all be the same.
17. $12.00; $\sqrt{10.80}$
19. $300; $\sqrt{250}$

EXERCISE 10.4 (page 474)

1.

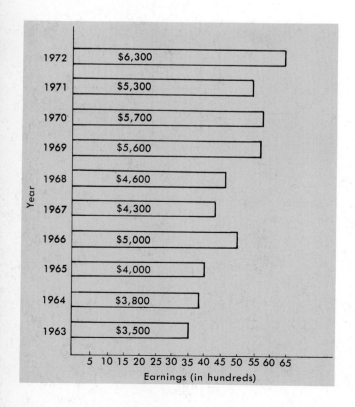

3.

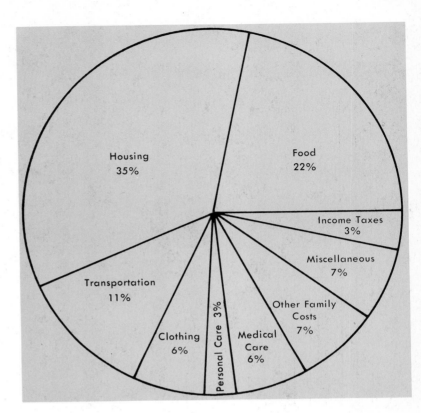

5.   a.

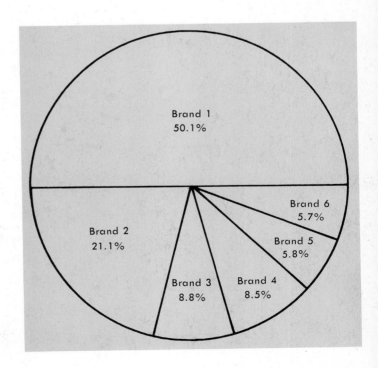

b.

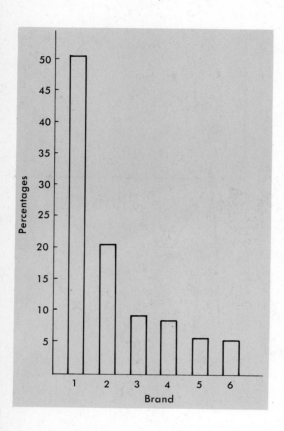

7. a. If you double both the radius r and the height h, the volume
        is increased by a factor of 8.
    b.

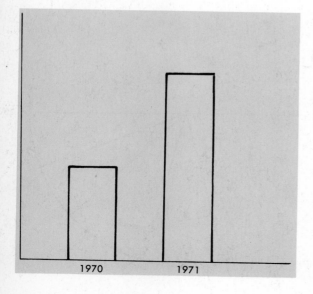

SELF-TEST/CHAPTER 10 (page 477)

1. a. $16,655 b. $16,750 c. $14,465

2. a.

SCORE	TALLY	FREQUENCY
0	I	1
1	I	1
2	II	2
3	IIII	4
4	I	1
5	II	2
6	II	2
7	III	3
8	I	1
9	I	1
10	II	2
11	II	2
12	III	3
13	II	2
14	II	2
15	I	1

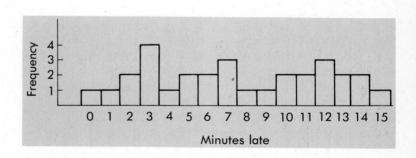

b. $33\frac{1}{3}\%$

3.

4. a. 6   b. 10   c. 2

5. a. 2,250   b. 70

6. a. $\frac{1}{2}$ million   b. Dec. 31, 1973, to Dec. 31, 1974

c. 1.5 million

7.

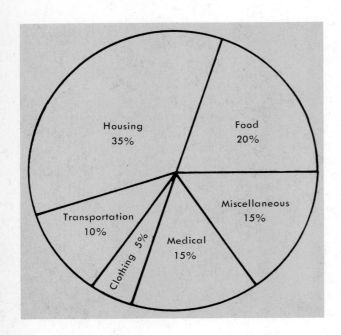

8.

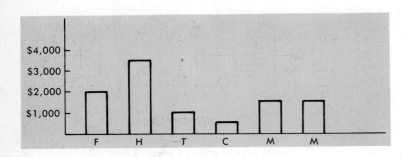

9.

10.   a. 3.2   b. 4 and 3   c. 3

APPENDIX 1

1. 1.7
3. 1.292
5. 0.24
7. 1.16
9. 10.0797
11. 7.8476
13. 156
15. 0.07
17. 32.30 meters
19. 54,000 meters
21. 3.2 meters
23. 80,000 meters
25. 155 miles
27. 1.984 miles
29. 2.17 miles
31. 4.75 liters
33. 18.05 liters
35. 15.75 quarts
37. 19.80 pounds
39. 23.54 pounds
41. 19.35 kilograms
43. a. 500 millimeters   b. 300 centimeters   c. 13.50 meters
    d. 8 kilometers
45. a. 750 milliliters   b. 1.41 liters   c. 9.5 liters
    d. 34.20 liters
47. a. 1400 grams   b. 45 kilograms   c. 10.5 ounces
    d. 110 pounds

INDEX